NATURE KNOWLEDGE AND GOD

AN INTRODUCTION TO THOMISTIC PHILOSOPHY

BROTHER BENIGNUS, F.S.C., Ph.D.
MANHATTAN COLLEGE, NEW YORK CITY

THE BRUCE PUBLISHING COMPANY
MILWAUKEE

Nihil obstat: RT. REV. MSGR. JOHN M. A. FEARNS, S.T.D., Censor librorum
Imprimatur: ✠ FRANCIS CARDINAL SPELLMAN, Archbishop of New York
July 28, 1947

To My Father and Mother

NOTE ON THE CITATIONS OF
ST. THOMAS' WORKS

A brief note about the manner of citing St. Thomas is in order, although the real task of directing the students to the intelligent use of the writings of the Angelic Doctor belongs to the teacher. The following are some sample abbreviations used in the present text, and their meanings:

S. Theol., I, 49, 1, c, reads *Summa Theologica,* Part One, question 49, article 1, body of the article.

S. Theol., I, 7, 2, ad 3, reads *Summa Theologica,* Part One, question 7, article 2, answer to the third objection.

S. Theol., I–II, 6, 2, ad 3, reads *Summa Theologica,* First Part of the Second Part, question 6, article 2, answer to the third objection.

Con. Gen., II, 2, reads *Summa Contra Gentiles,* Book Two, chapter 2.

In I Sent., d. 8, q. 5, 2, c, reads Commentary on the Second Book of the *Sentences,* distinction 8, question 5, article 2, body of the article.

De Ver., XXII, 2, reads Disputed Question, *De Veritate,* question XXII, article 2.

De Pot., IV, 1, c, reads Disputed Question, *De Potentia,* question IV, article 1, body of the article. Other Disputed Questions cited are *De Malo, De Spiritualibus Creaturis,* and *De Anima.* The last is given as *Q. D. De Anima* in order to distinguish it from the Commentary on Aristotle's *De Anima,* which is cited as follows: *In III De Anima,* 7, nos. 687–688, which reads Commentary on the Third Book of the *De Anima,* lecture 7, paragraphs 687–688.

The student must also note the differences in citations of a work of Aristotle and of a commentary of St. Thomas upon it. Thus, *Meta.,* V, 7, means Aristotle's *Metaphysics,* Book V, chapter 7; whereas *In V Meta.,* 7, means St. Thomas' *Commentary on Aristotle's Metaphysics,* Book V, lecture 7.

PREFACE

Several years of unavailing search for a textbook of Thomistic philosophy which would present that philosophy as a coherent whole and in a manner suitable for the college student of today led to the writing of the present book. Experience both as a student and as a teacher of philosophy taught the author that the study of a series of books departmentalizing philosophy into cosmology, psychology, epistemology, ontology, and so forth, fails to produce any single, integral picture of the universe in which we live. St. Thomas Aquinas certainly had such a picture, and the study of his philosophy should give this picture to the student. To give the picture is the primary purpose of the present book.

In order to accomplish this purpose in at least a partial way, the author has tried to utilize a few simple principles of method. The first of these is to be concerned at all times with some concrete being, as St. Thomas was at all parts of the Summa, instead of dealing with some abstraction lifted out of its actual concrete setting. The second is a principle of pedagogical order: it is to develop the subject matter in such a way that the new is always prepared for by the old, and to avoid, as far as possible, the anticipated employment of principles not yet explicitly studied. The third is to introduce as early as possible the explanation and demonstration of those few basic principles which find continual application in St. Thomas' construction of his worldview. A good number of these principles are contained in Chapter IV, which in some respects is the key chapter of the entire text. In order to keep the student constantly orientated and to impress upon him the remarkable unity and integrity of the Angelic Doctor's thought, a further device has been used; namely, the explicit pointing out of the repeated application of the same basic principles and the explicit indication of the relations of each newly studied part of St. Thomas' philosophy to the previously studied parts. With what success these efforts have met is a matter for the reader's judgment.

A glance at the table of contents will tell the reader the scope and the limitations of the book. An effort has been made to cover the entire speculative philosophy of the Angelic Doctor, but his moral teachings have not been touched upon at all; and those parts of his doctrine — the greatest parts — which are explanations of the revealed truths of the Catholic religion have not been included.

After the writings of St. Thomas and Aristotle, the author acknowledges his greatest debt to the works of many contemporary Thomists, notably, E. Gilson (whose *Philosophy of St. Thomas Aquinas* the author used as a textbook for several years at Manhattan College), A. D. Sertillanges, R. Garrigou-Lagrange, G. H. Joyce, and J. Maritain. The persons who greatly helped him in the preparation of the book are many, and the author wishes here to express his deep gratitude to them all. A few he feels obliged to single out for more special thanks: Brothers Anthony John and Bernard of Mary and Mr. James V. Mullaney, for valuable critical comments and suggestions; Brother Augustine Philip, for proofreading the entire book in galleys; and Mrs. Theresa A. Devine, for her patient, intelligent, and devoted work through many tedious typings of successive revisions, and for her invaluable aid in all the myriad details involved in seeing the book through to the printing presses. Last, I should mention those to whom I owe most; namely, the hundreds of students who have studied the text in multigraph form under my direction at Manhattan College during the past five years, and whose comments and questions have been a very large factor in giving to the book whatever value it may possess.

BROTHER BENIGNUS, F.S.C.

Manhattan College
New York City
September 3, 1947

CONTENTS

PART THREE   KNOWLEDGE AND BEING

PART. FOUR   GOD AND CREATURES

NATURE, KNOWLEDGE, AND GOD

PART ONE

INTRODUCTORY

CHAPTER I

PHILOSOPHY AND PHILOSOPHIES

I. THE DEFINITION OF PHILOSOPHY

1. Throughout its history, philosophy has undergone a development which, without essentially changing its original significance, has progressively narrowed that significance by more clearly distinguishing philosophy from other types of knowledge. At first the boundary line between philosophy and other departments of human knowledge was not clearly defined, and by philosophy was meant every striving after knowledge. Philosophy and science originated as one thing when certain men of ancient Greece began to seek a rational explanation or account of the world in which they found themselves. This effort to search out the nature of the world without appeal to myth and poetic symbolism established science and philosophy as something distinct from poetry and mythology, but left science and philosophy still confused with each other and with religion.

Plato took a long step nearer a more precise conception of philosophy when he defined the philosopher as one who apprehends the essence or reality of things, in distinction from their sensible appearances, or phenomena. Even prior to Plato (427–347 B.C.) this distinction between the reality of things and their appearances had been made; and, in a sense somewhat different from that in which Plato meant it, it may still be maintained today that that is precisely what distinguishes the philosopher from the scientist: the former deals with essences, that is, the inward natures of things, the latter with appearances or phenomena.

Aristotle (384–322 B.C.), a former pupil of Plato, wrote, "All men consider philosophy as concerned with first causes and principles." Though he did not himself succeed in clearly distinguishing philosophy from the special sciences, Aristotle gave in the above sentence the true principle of distinction: philosophy is concerned with *first* causes and principles, the special sciences with *secondary* causes and principles. *St. Thomas Aquinas* adopted this distinction, writing, "Wisdom [i.e., philosophy] is the science which studies first and universal causes; wisdom considers the first causes of all causes." The main tradition of philosophy has retained this conception of philosophy as the science of first causes.

It was not until the Middle Ages that philosophy was clearly distinguished from religion. The Christian philosophers had something which the ancient Greeks had never had, namely, a revealed religion. Possessing it, and seeking also to possess philosophy, they found themselves faced with the problem of distinguishing the one from the other and of determining the precise relations that exist between them. True religious faith rests on divine Revelation; philosophy is purely human knowledge, its only sources being man's sense experience and rational thought. The relations between philosophy and religion we shall treat in detail in a later chapter; here we merely wish to bring out another character of philosophy — it is *human* wisdom as opposed to divinely revealed wisdom.

2. Science of First Causes. Philosophy, we have said, seeks the *first causes* of things. Philosophy begins with experience and proceeds by way of reasoning. The facts that we experience in our life cry aloud for explanation, and the rational quest for their ultimate explanation is the pursuit of philosophy. Philosophy, like the other sciences, is not a mere collection of facts, but an ordered, systematic explanation of facts. It differs from the other sciences in that it gives the ultimate explanation, whereas they give explanations which are not ultimate and which, in fact, leave the most fundamental and important questions unanswered.

Physics, for example, formulates the laws of motion, stating how the velocity and direction of any movement are determined, but it neither asks nor answers the question, "Why is there motion in the universe?" Chemistry analyzes material substances into their ultimate chemical constituents, and formulates the laws governing the combinations of the various elements, but it neither seeks nor finds the primary nature of matter itself nor the reason for the existence of the material world. Biology sets forth the likenesses and the differences of living things and the laws that govern the genesis, the functioning, the growth, the decay of living beings, but it does not explain the origin, the principle, or the purpose of life itself. Experimental psychology describes the behavior of men and its physiopsychic antecedents, but it cannot discover the essence or nature of a man, the principle that makes a man what he is, nor the reason for which men exist. All the natural sciences taken together cannot tell us why we live or why the world exists. It is the function of philosophy to answer all these fundamental questions which the experimental sciences leave unanswered.

All-Inclusiveness of Philosophy. Besides seeking first causes, philosophy differs from every other science in taking as its field everything that exists; indeed, everything that can exist. Physics studies material beings inasmuch as these possess mass, energy, and motion; chemistry studies them inasmuch as they have definite elementary constitutions. Botany studies the plant kingdom, zoology the animal kingdom; astronomy studies the heavenly bodies, geology the inorganic bodies that make up the earth. Only philosophy studies all beings.

Material Object and Formal Object. This universality of philosophy's object does not imply that philosophy is the sum of all the other sciences. A science is constituted in its nature and distinguished from other sciences not only by what it studies, but also and principally by the point of view from which, and the aspect under which, it studies it. For example, human anatomy and physiology both study the human body in all the details of its multitudinous parts, but they are different sciences because anatomy is concerned with the structure of the various parts and their structural relations, while physiology is concerned with their functions and functional relations. Similarly, philosophy differs from the sum of the other sciences because they are concerned with phenomena and secondary causes, whereas philosophy is concerned with essences and primary causes. The subject matter, or the mere "what" a science studies is called its *material object.* The material object of philosophy is all being. The aspect under which the science studies its subject matter is called its *formal object.* The formal object of philosophy is first causes and first principles.

3. **Chief Problems of Philosophy.** Though we say that philosophy is the study of all things, we do not mean that every bit of information about everything is of interest to philosophy. To begin with, philosophy studies things only from the point of view of their ultimate causes. Furthermore, the actual history of philosophy has singled out certain very definite questions as those which philosophy is primarily interested in answering. The most fundamental are concerned with the

nature of reality itself: What is real and what is unreal? Is there an ultimate unity at the basis of all reality? Is the multiplicity that experience finds at the surface of reality a real multiplicity or only an appearance of multiplicity? Is there more than one kind of reality? Is reality ultimately spiritual or ultimately material? Other questions less fundamental than these and more obvious arise before them and lead to them: *What is the constitution of the physical world?* What is its origin, if it had an origin? Is there any purpose in its existence? Is it governed in its laws by any purposive design? Other questions bear more precisely upon *man himself:* What is his fundamental nature? What is his place in the universe? Is he more than, or no more than, a part of the material universe? What is his origin? What is his destiny? Are there any absolute laws of his conduct? What is the source of moral obligation, of right and wrong in action? All these questions lead inevitably to the supreme question: *Is there a God?* They lead to it because they cannot be adequately answered until that question is first answered; and because on the answer to that depends the ultimate character of the answers given to all the others. In addition to all these questions there arises another one of a quite different nature. The asking and answering of all the above presuppose the ability of man to think about reality and to know reality. But even this the philosopher cannot take for granted, and hence he asks: *What is knowledge?* Does knowledge actually attain to the real? Does the mind in knowledge transcend itself and its own acts and grasp being independent of itself? How far can human knowledge be trusted?

4. The Value of Philosophy. Have we any right to philosophize? Has man with his limited intellect any justification for probing into the mystery of being itself, for seeking the ultimate? W. E. Hocking, in his *Types of Philosophy,* Chapter I, raises and very satisfactorily answers this question. He insists that philosophy is not presumptuous, that men are not wrong in seeking by the exercise of their own powers to fathom the depths of reality, to solve the riddle of the universe. Our ability to think is precisely what distinguishes us as human beings, and our insistent tendency to probe into the unexplained and to seek for an ultimate explanation of all our experience is not a vice, but an expression of what is highest in our nature. Our conviction that the right use of our reason will bring us ever nearer the ultimate truth, and not away from it, is perfectly valid. Philosophy is not human impudence in the face of the infinite, but, on the contrary, it is the highest purely human expression of man's nature. Its study forces us to exert our powers on the level that is most truly human, on the level where the rationality of man most completely overcomes the disadvantages of his animality, and most clearly manifests that he is made according to God's own "image and likeness."

II. CONFLICTING DOCTRINES

If philosophy is what we have said it is in the above paragraphs, then it should be one integral body of knowledge that seeks, and, as far as possible, finds the first causes of all the elements of human experience. Consequently, it is somewhat confusing to the student of philosophy to discover that there is not one philosophy but many. These several philosophies are not different in the way in which the several sciences are different, that is to say, by being concerned with different subject matters and answering different questions, but they are different by giving different answers to the same questions on the same subject matter. Thus, to the question, "What is the ultimate nature of reality?" there is a philosophy that answers, "Matter," a second which says, "Spirit," another that says, "Both matter and spirit," and still another that replies, "Neither matter nor spirit, but a neutral stuff." In other words, the different philosophies have arisen not out of a division of labor but out of differences of opinion. The broad fundamental agreement that has been reached by scientists about scientific matters has not yet been attained by philosophers about philosophical matters. Certain fundamental oppositions have given rise to several different types of philosophical systems or beliefs.

Each of the great rival philosophical doctrines has some truth in it, or at least is based upon a truth. Disagreement among the great philosophers has generally arisen from the tendency of each one to overemphasize the particular truth into which he has an especially clear insight, and to deny, as a contradiction of that truth and therefore as a falsity, another truth which in fact is the complement of his truth, and without which the latter becomes a falsity. One of the most striking characteristics of St. Thomas as a philosopher was his steadfast refusal to sacrifice one truth to another, to falsify half the truth by making it the whole truth. A mark of the validity of Thomistic philosophy is the broad hospitality which it exhibits toward the positive truths of rival philosophies; it embraces within itself all the affirmations of all the great philosophers, rejecting only their negations.

The following account of the various philosophical doctrines is most summary and of necessity superficial. Its purpose is to do no more than supply a context or backdrop for the exposition of Thomism which is to follow. It would be unfortunate if any student were to think that this brief account gives him any real understanding of the systems of philosophy mentioned or of the thought of the philosophers named. It is intended only to give the student a very general idea of the problems which have seemed important to philosophers through the ages and the chief conflicting views advanced about these problems.

III. MONISM AND PLURALISM

Two of the great contradictory types of philosophy arise out of the question whether reality is one or multiple. Certainly the world seems to be made up of a vast multitude of different things. But one of the facts most commonly experienced as our knowledge grows is that we discover more and more unity in what at first seemed a hopeless multiplicity. As a very simple illustration we can take motion. As soon as we are able to use our eyes, we see all sorts of movements all around us — slow movements and fast movements, up movements and down movements, regular movements and irregular movements. Later, when we study physics, we find that all these movements take place according to the same few simple laws of motion. These laws of motion are a unity binding together all the billions of apparently independent movements that occur in the world. Some philosophers have been so impressed by the fact that the more our knowledge of things increases and deepens the more we discover unities underlying superficial multiplicities that they have reached the conclusion that all multiplicity is *merely* superficial and that, *at bottom,* reality is a perfect unity. This philosophical doctrine, that reality is ultimately one, or, in other words, that only one being exists, is called *monism.* A system of philosophy built upon this doctrine is called monistic or absolutistic. The contradictory doctrine, namely, that there exist not only one being but several beings, or in other words, that the multiplicity we see in the world is not merely apparent but is real, is called pluralism, and a philosophy built upon it is called pluralistic.

1. **Monism.** Among the great monistic philosophies were those of

Parmenides and Plotinus in ancient times and of Spinoza and Hegel in modern times. A word about one of these will suffice to illustrate monism. Benedict Spinoza, a Portuguese Jew who lived in Holland in the seventeenth century, taught that there is but one reality — Substance, which is infinite and is everything. We know this Substance under two of its infinite attributes — *extension* (which means the attribute of taking up room or being spread out, like space itself or some object in space) and *thought*. In its attribute of thought it is *God;* in its attribute of extension it is *Nature*. God and Nature, therefore, are identical, because Substance is one with itself and Substance is both God and Nature. The multitude of finite things, persons, and events (including, of course, ourselves) which we seem to experience in the world are not really distinct things, persons, or events at all, but are simply "finite modes" of Nature or of God — finite modes which somehow exist in infinite, self-identical Substance without in any way dividing or multiplying it. According to Spinoza, therefore, God and Nature are the same thing, and God (or Nature) is the sole existing being. The separate individuality of things and persons is an illusion — you and I only appear to ourselves to exist as distinct persons, but we do not really so exist.

2. **Pluralism.** Many of the great philosophers of ancient times and modern times, for example, Plato, Aristotle, St. Thomas Aquinas, Descartes, Leibniz, Locke, Berkeley, Kant, agree with the common sense of ordinary men, and reject monism in favor of pluralism. There are so many different systems of pluralistic philosophy that it would serve no purpose to give an account of any of them here. They all agree in affirming the reality of multiplicity and distinctness, that is to say, they all maintain that the universe is not one being but a plurality of beings.

A word of caution seems to be necessary before leaving the subject of monism and pluralism. For a philosopher to hold that there is *now* actually a plurality of beings as experience testifies, it is not at all necessary that he hold that there *always was* a plurality of beings. The questions of the actual status of the real world and of the origin of the real world are clearly different questions, though they have, unfortunately, often been confused by philosophers themselves. There is nothing at all inconsistent in maintaining that there are now a plurality of beings, which, however, have all come from one original Being which is the sole cause of all the universe. This, as a matter of fact, is

the doctrine taught by St. Thomas Aquinas and all Catholic philosophers, as well as by many non-Catholic and non-Christian philosophers.

IV. MATERIALISM, IDEALISM, DUALISM

The distinction between two kinds of reality, material and spiritual,
is commonplace for nearly all of us, even though we may have rather
confused ideas about it. We would say, for example, that stones, soil,
water, trees, air, and such like things that take up space and that we
can see or feel or hear, or at least whose effects we can see, feel, or in
some way sense, are material; while beings like God, the angels, and
ghosts are immaterial or spiritual. We would say that a color, a shape,
a noise, a smell, a weight, or a volume is a material quality; while faith,
charity, honesty, loyalty are spiritual qualities. We would say that our
bodies are material and our souls spiritual; that bodily actions, like
walking or eating, are material; and mental actions, like thinking or
making a decision, are spiritual. Some things might make us hesitate
as to where to place them (e.g., you might object to calling loyalty
spiritual since dogs seem to be capable of loyalty); some, we might
have to say, seem to be both material and spiritual, as talking or studying. But in general we have a pretty fair idea of the distinction between
the material and the spiritual. Some philosophers deny that any such
thing as immaterial or spiritual being exists and hold that all reality
is material. This doctrine is called *materialism*. Others swing to the
extreme from this and teach that mental or spiritual being is the only
being that is ultimately real and that matter has no existence outside
minds. This is the doctrine of *spiritualism,* or, as it is more frequently
called, *idealism*. Still others hold that both material being and spiritual
being really exist and really are distinct and different from each other.
This doctrine is known as *dualism*.

1. Materialism. Materialism maintains that matter is the only reality; and hence that willing and thinking and all mental operations
are nothing more than functions of highly developed material organisms; that there is no world of spiritual beings outside the material
world of nature; that there is in man no spiritual soul, and that if
man has a "soul" at all it is nothing else than the complex organization
of the matter in his body. In general, materialists are atheists, as you
would expect, that is to say, they deny the existence of God. They are
also sensists, maintaining that all knowledge is merely sensation and
that there is no such thing as nonsensuous intellectual thought. Ma-

terialists are usually determinists, holding that every event that occurs in the world is necessarily and solely determined by the laws of physics that govern matter and its movements and that there is no conscious aim or purpose operating in nature; that this physical determinism extends to all man's actions, so that there is no such thing as free will. Finally, believing that a man is merely his body, they believe that physical death is the final and complete end of him.

The outstanding materialistic system of philosophy of ancient times was Atomism, founded by Leucippus and Democritus in the fifth century B.C. and classically expounded in *De Rerum Natura* by Lucretius in the first century A.D. Only two modern philosophers of any stature have been thoroughgoing materialists. They are *Thomas Hobbes* (1588–1679) and *Karl Marx,* the nineteenth-century founder of Communism.

2. **Idealism or Spiritualism.** Idealism is not so simple a doctrine as materialism, and many philosophical systems called idealism by their authors have been in serious disagreement with one another. Idealists agree (or almost agree) on one fundamental doctrine, and then break up into many camps in regard to the philosophical systems they build upon that doctrine. This basic doctrine is that reality is fundamentally and ultimately of the nature of idea or mind, and that whatever is not idea or mind, like rivers, trees, stones — material things — is dependent upon mind. This fundamental principle of idealism we may call the idealistic postulate, or the doctrine of the primacy of the spiritual (whence the name *spiritualism* as the alternate of idealism). Idealists believe that, as between those kinds of things that we call material, like stones, soil, hydrogen, atoms, and those that we call mental or spiritual, like souls, minds, ideas, ideals, the latter are more fundamental, more primary, and more real. Some idealists go so far as to hold that these latter alone are real.

Even idealists who do not go so far as the last mentioned, do, nevertheless, make idea and not *thing* or *stuff* primary in reality. Some have expressed their belief in words like the following: All reality is of the nature of idea; there is nothing that is through and through non-idea, no "matter" that is merely matter, out of all relation to mind. Nothing merely *is;* whatever is also is some meaning or *significance,* and hence is idea. Often themselves accused of subjectivism (i.e., that they make things merely the subject's ideas), some idealists retort that it is the denial of their doctrine that leads to subjectivism. For if material things merely exist, without meaning or value in their very essence, then they have meaning or value *only to the subject* that gets to know them; if nature is not itself idea, then the idea of it that each of us has is only his own subjective, private idea. Therefore, they argue, idealism is the only road of escape from subjectivism.

The mere fact that we have experience at all is, to some idealists, sufficient proof of their doctrine. If things were not, of their very essence, knowables or ideas, then mind could not exist. For if the nature of mind is to know (and no one denies that it is), then it must be that the nature of things is to be knowable; mind could not exist in a world of unknowables. The fact that nature is intelligible and does conform to rational laws shows clearly which we must accept as fundamental — mind or matter. That nature *is* intelligible means simply that matter is dominated by, and dependent upon, mind. Not matter, therefore, but mind is the ultimate reality.

There is nothing in this basic doctrine of idealism that is not perfectly acceptable to Thomists. Indeed, if the above were all that is to be understood by the term *idealism,* the supreme expression of idealism would be the philosophical system of St. Thomas Aquinas. But nearly all modern idealists, when erecting a philosophical system upon this fundamental postulate of the primacy of the spiritual, build into their systems one or more of certain doctrines which we may call idealistic aberrations. These are unwarranted deductions from the idealistic postulate.

The first of these unwarranted deductions may be called *mentalism.* It consists in the belief, held more or less explicitly by many idealists, that things and ideas are the same thing. From the belief that nature is dependent upon mind, too many idealists slip easily into the belief that nature is nothing but the mind's ideas. From the truth that all reality is knowable in its very essence, they deduce too readily that the essence of things consists in their relation to knowing minds.

This easy deduction springs from a postulate introduced into modern philosophy by René Descartes,[1] and confused by many idealists with the idealistic postulate. Descartes held it to be self-evident that what we know directly and immediately are our own ideas. According to this doctrine, when I am looking at a tree on the campus, what I am seeing directly and immediately is not the external tree, but the idea or image of the tree in my mind. Idealists do their own philosophy a

[1] Chapter XIV contains an account and criticism of Descartes's philosophy.

great disservice when they call this doctrine the "idealistic postulate," for they are making it impossible for idealism to escape subjectivism. Descartes's postulate should be called, as it often is, "the subjectivist postulate" because it means that the immediate object of knowledge is something *within* the knowing subject, namely, his own idea. The only philosophy that can be built with complete consistency upon this subjectivistic postulate is a phenomenalism like David Hume's.

Closely connected with this first aberration of idealism is a second one, namely, that nature is "appearance" as opposed to "reality." Nature, as here used, means the world of material or sensible things: the world of change and movement, of shapes, sounds, and colors, of oxygen, hydrogen, and carbon, of men, beasts, and little fishes — in a word, the world of common sense, of science, and of history. Science, always advancing, teaches us more and more about this world; but there always is a residue that refuses to be reduced to any set or system of ideas, for of its nature every new advance of science uncovers new problems. Starting with Plato, idealists down the ages have shown a tendency to regard this world of sense and change as a little less than real, as an appearance or shadow *behind which* reality lies. Their argument, put bluntly, goes like this: Reality is intelligible; nature is not fully intelligible; *ergo,* nature is not fully real. If by "not fully real" they mean, "not independently existing," Thomists could agree with them. But they seem to mean, "merely the appearance of something else." The root of this second aberration seems again to be the subjectivistic postulate; for if the immediate objects of my perceptions are my own ideas, it seems much more likely that these objects are "appearances" of reality than that they are reality itself.

Another "idealistic heresy" that has arisen from too easy deduction from the basic principle of idealism is the belief that matter or nature is a necessary product or emanation of mind. The truth that *nature must have come from mind* is changed into the very different belief that *mind must produce nature.* From this belief it is another easy step (which not all idealists take) to a doctrine of pure immanentism and necessitarianism: The Supreme Mind is *in* nature, indistinct from nature except in appearance. And so we get various types of spiritual or idealistic monism. This doctrine ties in with the "appearance-reality" doctrine, and mind becomes the Absolute, with nature its appearance. Other minds (viz., *our* minds) find their place in this system as finite or partial expressions of Absolute Mind. Thus, individual personality is swallowed up in Infinity, and a host of unsolvable problems about error, evil, and freedom, to say nothing of common sense, arise. Most often these, too, are swallowed up in Infinity, or, at any rate, are swallowed.

3. Dualism: Thomistic and Cartesian. Dualistic philosophers maintain that there are two types of being, material and spiritual, which are of essentially different natures. Most dualists believe that besides and superior to the material world of nature there is another world of immaterial substances or persons, that is, spirits; they believe that bodies, whether living or non-living, and all the qualities and operations of bodies, in a word, all that is in any way perceptible by the senses, are material. They believe that thinking and willing are spiritual operations and that the agents that think and will are spiritual beings. They believe that man is a composite being whose body is material and whose soul is immaterial. Finally they believe that spirit and all that relates to spirit is more primary, more valuable, and more lasting than matter and what relates to matter, and that the good man prizes the things of the spirit above the things of matter. Plato, Aristotle, St. Thomas Aquinas and nearly all Catholic philosophers, Descartes, Locke, Kant were all dualists in this sense of the term.[2] The dualistic system that we shall study throughout this course is called, more specifically, hylemorphism or the theory of matter and form. It was originated by Aristotle and developed by St. Thomas and the Scholastics. It is often referred to as Thomistic or Scholastic dualism, and is very different from other systems of dualistic philosophy, especially Cartesian dualism.

Exaggerated dualism was brought into modern philosophy by Descartes. This doctrine considers both matter and mind as real, as utterly different from each other and as independent of each other. So different and so mutually independent are the two, that any kind of real relation or interaction between them is inconceivable. This doctrine spawned innumerable false problems concerning the nature of man and the nature of knowledge. It has put modern philosophy through three centuries of agonized wrestling with a monster of its own creation, the notorious body-mind problem. Some of its more famous children and grandchildren are subjectivistic idealism, phenomenalism, pantheism, a variety of "double-aspect" and "parallelistic" theories, crude material-

---

[2] The term *dualism* has another usage in connection with the problem of the origin of the world. See Chapter XXIV on creation.

istic mechanism, behaviorism, absolute spiritualism, and, the children of its despair, pragmatism, positivism, and naturalism. A few of these are worth a word of explanation.

V. FOUR SKEPTICAL PHILOSOPHIES

Some of the philosophical views which developed out of the subjectivism of modern thought are completely or partly skeptical; that is, they are denials that we can hope to know reality at all; the best we can hope for is knowledge of our own reactions to reality, whatever that may be. Phenomenalism. Kantian criticism, positivism, and pragmatism are philosophies of this sort.

1. **Phenomenalism.** Phenomenalism, which we have already mentioned as being the position to which "the subjectivistic postulate" of Descartes really leads, was taught in its most extreme form by the Scottish philosopher, David Hume. Hume, holding as axiomatic this postulate, that the only direct objects of our knowledge are our own ideas, drew the inevitable conclusion that all we can ever know is the flux of experience, the succession of mental states that constitute our conscious life. We cannot know any "external reality" that causes these states, nor can we know any substantial mind or self that possesses and abides permanently through these successive states; we know only the series of impressions, experiences, or phenomena.

2. **Kant's Critical Philosophy.** Immanuel Kant tried to save philosophy from the dire consequences of Hume's phenomenalism. He failed because he, too, never questioned either the subjectivistic postulate or the exaggerated dualism of Descartes. In a system which he called transcendental criticism, Kant sharply distinguished phenomena, or things-as-they-appear-to-us, from noumena, or things-as-they-are-in-themselves. The latter were the "realities" banished by Hume. They might just as well have remained banished, because according to Kant we can never know noumena. We can never know anything as it is in itself; we can only know phenomena, things-as-they-appear-to-us. Practical reason, or faith, gives us certitude in the noumenal order, but this certitude is not knowledge.[3]

3. **Positivism.** One result of this teaching was that many philosophers and scientists accepted Kant's systematic phenomenalism, according to which science, or any knowledge attainable by pure reason,

[3] In Chapters XV and XVI the philosophies of Hume and Kant are studied and criticized.

is concerned with phenomena alone, while they rejected the non-phenomenalistic side of his doctrine. One thing Kant had made clear to them: reason is competent to deal only with phenomena, that is to say, with material, sensible things. You may call them things or phenomena — there is no need of quarreling about words — but whichever you call them you mean the stuff that physics, chemistry, biology, astronomy, and all the natural sciences deal with. About these you can be sure; about "noumena" you cannot; so why worry about noumena? Therefore, real knowledge, the kind you are sure about, is the kind of knowledge that the natural sciences give. Hence there arose the doctrine of positivism, namely, that the only true systematic knowledge is knowledge that is concerned with the sort of things that the natural sciences deal with and that attains its results by means of the methods which those sciences use.

4. Pragmatism. It was inevitable that the confusion of modern thought about knowledge and truth should lead someone to question the very notions of knowledge and truth which modern philosophers held. Charles Sanders Pierce, William James, and John Dewey, in America, and F. C. S. Schiller in England, believed that the root of the trouble lay in a false notion of truth itself. Truth was traditionally held to be some sort of correspondence between what you are thinking and a real state of affairs outside your mind — if your thought represented that state of affairs as it really was, your thought was said to be true; if it did not, it was said to be false. Against this conception of truth the men mentioned above advanced a new notion of truth in a doctrine that received the name *pragmatism*. In their belief, a thought is true, not because it agrees with some extramental reality, but because it works out right when it is applied to some specific situation; it is false, not because it misrepresents reality, but because, when it is used, it does not work out right. Truth, therefore, consists in the usefulness of an idea in practice: a proposition is not true or false in itself as an inactive thought in the mind; it is verified or falsified, that is, made true or false, by proving usable or non-usable in action.

VI. NATURALISM

Out of the maelstrom of conflicting opinions in modern thought there has arisen in our day a new philosophical system or attitude which claims the allegiance of great numbers of contemporary philosophers, especially in America. This philosophical attitude, called

Naturalism, is the greatest single enemy of Thomistic philosophy today, and, as naturalists are coming to recognize, Thomism is its most redoubtable foe.

Professional philosophers, especially in very recent years, have been cold toward crude materialism. But in the case of many of them it has been the word they have disliked rather than the doctrine. Indeed, our day might be called the age of bashful materialism. Many philosophers of the present day who would formerly have been called materialists prefer to call themselves naturalists.

Naturalism in philosophy might be expressed in the following propositions: Whatever things exist and whatever laws operate in the whole realm of reality are beings and laws that belong to and are part of nature. Nature is self-sufficient, and outside nature there is nothing. All reality can be studied and accounted for by a method like the method of the natural sciences. Mental and moral processes are part of nature and are subject matter for study by the natural sciences. There is no mind or spirit apart from nature. The only explanations that are admissible in the study of reality are "natural" explanations; "supernatural" explanations are barred. An example of a "supernatural" explanation would be to account for man's power of rational thought by attributing this power to a non-material principle in man called the soul. If by soul you mean anything more than the body's natural organization, then man has no soul, for such a soul would be "outside nature" or "supernatural." Soul, mind, spirit, call it what you will, is simply a stage of organization reached in the evolution of nature.

Why do contemporary naturalists object to being called materialists? In the first place, there is a certain odium attached to the name materialist, as to the names atheist, infidel, cynic. Second, it has long been pointed out that materialism is the most dogmatic of all beliefs, and there is nothing that so hurts the contemporary intellectual as to be considered dogmatic. Then, again, materialism is associated in the popular mind with a sort of anti-humanism — we think of the materialist as pulling man down to the level of the brute. The contemporary naturalist is not anti-humanist at all; indeed, he often refers to himself as a humanist, by which he means, among other things, that he believes that there is nothing at all superior to man. Finally, contemporary advances in physics have wrought such a change in our conceptions of the nature of matter that the old-fashioned materialism today looks a little childish: the "stuff" that the nineteenth-century materialists dogmatically asserted to be everything does not today seem to be even anything. Solid atoms have given way before almost ethereal electrons and protons, and matter itself seems in grave danger of dissolving into energy, radiation, or whatnot. "Materialists" are as dated as Aristotelians.

Despite all these very good reasons to the contrary, it still seems to the impartial observer that the philosophical naturalist ought to be a bit more frank and confess that he really is a materialist. He does believe the propositions that constitute the essence of materialism: that all beings are made of whatever the physical world is made of; that all laws are the laws of the physical world, operating on one or another of nature's levels of development; that human nature and human values are products of subhuman nature; that mind is a function of the organization of physical elements; that there is no such thing as spiritual being which is independent of physical nature; that nature is the ultimate reality. The fact that the most recent physics does not allow us to believe that matter is what the old materialists thought it to be is quite irrelevant; as long as a man believes that the physical universe is the whole of reality, he is a materialist regardless of what his conception of matter is. Finally, the modern naturalist exhibits all the dogmatism that is characteristic of materialists. The older materialists at least thought that they had discovered a fact, a truth, and it was to that supposed truth that they swore allegiance. The newer naturalist has not even a supposed truth for his dogma; he has sworn eternal loyalty to his way of doing things; he is honor bound never to admit the possibility that there is any other way to get to know anything than the way in which he gets to know the things he wants to know. He believes in the One, Holy, Universal, Scientific Method.

Naturalism bases itself upon an act of blind faith, namely, full and firm assent to the proposition that everything is explicable in terms of a single method of research. Those things that now seem incapable of explanation within the terms of this method will, the naturalist's faith assures him, be so explained at some future date when human science has reached a further point of progress.

VII. "PHILOSOPHIA PERENNIS"

This multiplicity of conflicting philosophical beliefs raises the question: Is there one true philosophy? Or are all systems equally true? Or equally false? Must man abandon hope of attaining truth on these all-important matters; or, worse, is there no truth to be attained? The answer is that there *is* one true philosophy. To each of the questions with which philosophers deal there is an answer that agrees with the facts. For example, to the question, "Is reality solely material?" either the answer "yes" is true, or "no" is true; and so on for the other questions. The sum total of all the correct answers constitutes true philosophy.

What is this true philosophy? There can be only one test: the true philosophy must (1) not contradict human experience in any detail, (2) give a satisfactory explanation of man's experience. Any philosophy that does not fulfill these conditions must be rejected as false.

We maintain that there is a *philosophia perennis* which fulfills these two conditions and which has carried down through the ages, amidst all the conflict of false philosophies, the positive truths that human reason has attained. We do not maintain that this *philosophia perennis* is complete, that is, that it has yet, or ever will, attain the whole truth; we do not maintain that it can ever rest on its accomplishments, for it must ever face new problems and ever seek to refine its acquired principles; we do not deny that much truth is to be found in other philosophies. What we claim is that there does exist, open for the study of all, a clear body of demonstrated philosophical truths, that these constitute "philosophy" itself taken historically, and that they constantly approach to "philosophy itself" absolutely speaking. We further maintain that the supreme expression thus far of this perennial philosophy is Thomism.

CHAPTER II

FROM THALES TO PLATO

I. THE MILESIANS

In the two and one-half millenia that have elapsed since philosophy came to birth in the Greek colony of Ionia, the framework and general direction of philosophical thinking have undergone few developments which have departed very radically from the patterns laid down by the Greeks themselves in their first three centuries of speculations. If we follow the course of Greek philosophy through its first 250 years of life — from birth to maturity — we shall get a very good picture of what philosophy is trying to do and what its primary problems are. We shall also get an excellent introduction to Thomistic philosophy, since that, to a very great extent, is the product and the heir of the wisdom of the Greeks.

Greek philosophy did not have its beginning in Greece proper but on the Aegean coast of Asia Minor. The first three philosophers, Thales, Anaximander, and Anaximenes, were associated with the town of Miletus in Ionia; hence they are called the Milesians or Earlier Ionians in histories of philosophy. Their problem was cosmological: they sought to know what stuff this universe around us is made of, and how it is constructed. The solutions which they advanced for this problem are of little importance; what is important is that they raised the question and sought to give it a rational answer.

1. **Thales.** Thales, who was living in 585 B.C., is considered the first philosopher of our western civilization because, so far as history has recorded, he was the first Greek who tried to work out a rational account of the world, ignoring the mythological and poetical accounts in which Greek literature and religion abounded. By asking himself what the world is made of and by seeking to discover the answer by

rational inquiry, he initiated the philosophical and scientific era of Greek life and he set both philosophy and science upon the paths that have ever since been recognized as their rightful paths.

Thales taught, according to Aristotle, that everything is made of water, which is the original and primary substance. The earth is a disk floating upon water. Aristotle also attributes to him the doctrine that everything has a soul or god in it. Why Thales fixed upon water as the primary substance we do not know. Perhaps because, as Aristotle conjectured, he observed that the nutriment of all things is moist, that the seeds whence things are generated are moist, that water is necessary for the life and growth of everything.

2. **Anaximander.** Unlike Thales, who wrote nothing, his immediate successor, Anaximander, was the author of a work, "On Nature," of which only this obscure fragment remains: "The beginning of that which is, is the Boundless; but whence that which is arises, thither must it again return of necessity; for the things give satisfaction and reparation to one another for their injustice, as is appointed according to the ordering of time." Thales had picked out as the primary substance one of the substances which we see around us; Anaximander, on the other hand, names no visible substance as primary but seems to mean that all the special substances with their special natures have come from some one general, infinite or indefinite substance without any special nature of its own. From this Boundless the special things arise by a process of "separating out" — first warm and cold separating out, then the moist, then earth, air, and fire. The earth is a cylinder, swinging free, equidistant from the boundaries of the universe, and at rest. Around it are first air, then the "circle of fire." Through apertures in the air we see fragments of the fire, which are the stars.

3. **Anaximenes.** The third of the Milesians, Anaximenes, held that air is prior to water and is the first principle of all bodies. All the materials in the world, he taught, are formed from air by a two-way process of condensation and rarefaction. Air is infinite in extent, and holds the universe together, giving it unity. "As our soul, which is air, holds us together, so breath and air encompass the universe." The necessity of air for life, and the belief that the world is a living organism, may have led him to choose air as the fundamental substance.

The originality of Anaximenes lies in his attempt to explain *how* the primary principle becomes all things. By condensation air becomes successively wind, clouds, rain, earth, rocks; and by rarefaction it becomes fire. The process is carried on by the eternal motion of air, which is a living power, a god.

II. THE PYTHAGOREANS

1. The Pythagorean Order. *Pythagoras,* an Ionian by birth, settled in middle life in Crotona, a Greek city in southern Italy. Here he founded a society which was at once religious, philosophical, and political. He died in 496 B.C. The fundamental doctrine of the Pythagoreans was that of reincarnation or transmigration of souls; that is, the belief that after death the soul takes up another life upon earth in another body, either human or otherwise. These reincarnations are punishments for sin, because life on earth is really death and the body is the soul's tomb. To escape from the cycle or wheel of reincarnations and to attain true life, the soul must be purified, freed from the trammels of the body, and so made fit to take up its abode in the regions of the blessed, to dwell there eternally with the gods. The purpose of the Pythagorean order was to furnish its members with a way to freedom from the everlasting wheel of reincarnations by means of certain secrets and practices imparted to the initiate. The practices were moral, ascetic, hygienic, and intellectual; there were laws and rules of conduct, special practices, bodily exercises, medicine, and music; but the highest purification of all was the intellectual purification of the soul through the pursuit of science, knowledge, or wisdom.

2. Pythagorean Philosophy: Numbers and the Unlimited. Seeking to answer the same question as the Milesians, the Pythagoreans advanced a doctrine which strikes us today as very strange indeed: they taught that natural substances are made of numbers. From numbers all things proceed and to numbers they return. Numbers are the patterns imitated by things, but they are internal patterns, constituting the things. This doctrine becomes a little less incomprehensible when we know something of the Pythagorean conception of numbers. Numbers, for them, were not abstractions but rather geometrical figures. Nor were they abstract geometrical figures. They seem to have been conceived as concrete physical shapes cut out of the infinite stuff which the Pythagoreans called the Unlimited. This Unlimited, they identified both with empty space and with air. The two Pythagorean teachings, namely, that numbers are the principles of all things, and that the world is formed by the imposition of Limit upon the Unlimited, would seem to be related somewhat in this way: number brings things into being by imposing the Limit on the Unlimited. Thus, unity or one is a point, that is, the first unit or Limit in the Unlimited; any two points mark off a line in the Unlimited; three points marking off three lines constitute a plane; four planes are needed to determine a solid. Everything is made of points, lines, surfaces, solids. Hence, all things come from the Unlimited and the Limit; and numbers are the principles of all things.

III. HERACLEITUS

The Milesians and the Pythagoreans had all accepted the fact of *change* in the world as something self-evident. They had also assumed that there is some one primary stuff that undergoes change and so becomes the various substances of nature. The next two important philosophers, Heracleitus and Parmenides, instead of taking change and permanent substance for granted, made these two very notions the subject of their inquiry. They arrived at diametrically opposite conclusions about them.

Heracleitus was a native of Ephesus in Asia Minor, and lived in the early part of the fifth century B.C. He was not a scientist and even despised scientists, saying that much learning fails to give wisdom. True wisdom consists, not in knowing many curious things, but in knowing one thing. That thing is the word, the Logos, and Heracleitus has come to teach it.

1. **The Primordial Fire.** Heracleitus is best known for two doctrines, the doctrine of the Fire and that of the Flux. Fire, he taught, is the universal principle that constitutes all things. From it all things come and to it they return. "There is exchange of all things against fire and of fire against all things, as there is exchange of goods against gold and gold against goods." The process goes on perpetually, the opposite movements balancing one another so that the quantity of matter, fire, remains the same. But in each cycle fire gains, getting back more than it gives, and therefore, "as it advances fire will judge and convict all things" in a final conflagration. But then the cycle will begin again and a new world will be produced, only to return again to fire, and so on eternally.

2. **The Conflict of Opposites, and the Flux.** The whole universe is at every moment dependent upon the conflict of contraries. "War is the father of all things, the ruler of all." Because of conflict or strife between contraries, one contrary is constantly passing over into the

other; the burning materials become fire, fire rises in vapors, these become clouds; and so the conflict goes on. Stop it, and the universe would cease. It is the condition of all change. Because the contraries tend constantly to substitute themselves for one another, each encroaching upon the others' domain, the whole of reality is in a state of unceasing movement. "Everything flows," nothing remains the same; you cannot step twice in the same river. You do not remain the same yourself for successive periods of time, but change constantly as new thoughts replace old, as waking gives way to sleeping. This is the famous doctrine of the flux, more inseparably linked than any other with the name of Heracleitus.

3. **Universal Law and God.** In the constant flux and the passing into one another of opposites there is not only war and discord, but also harmony. All change, the entire universe, is governed by law, by one divine law, which "dominates everything as much as it pleases, is sufficient in everything, and surpasses everything." This law is immanent in all things; it is itself the contraries; it is the conflict and the harmony between them; it is the substance of all things, the fire that goes throughout the world; it is God. God is the true ruler of everything, the harmony which rules the contraries; He is "day and night, winter and summer, war and peace, satiety and hunger"; He is "the invisible Harmony, superior to the visible harmony."

4. **The Soul.** Heracleitus recognized the importance of the soul. The soul is an emanation of the universal fire. Everything is full of souls, and soul is the most real thing of all. The soul must be kept dry. "It is death to souls to become water" as is shown by the pitiable plight of the drunkard, whose soul is wet. The soul is fully alive only when awake. Moisture brings sleep, and eventually death. But just as sleeping is followed by waking, and night by day, so too will death be followed by life. For the soul will not perish; it will live on as part of the everlasting fire.

5. **The One Wisdom.** But the most important thing to know, the Word that Heracleitus would teach men if they were not too dull to listen and comprehend, is the great truth that in the pure fire, the eternal wisdom, God, all the opposition and discord of the contraries disappear. God is "beyond good and evil." Good and evil are only passing forms of one reality that transcends them both. The general run of men, no matter how learned, never see this unity, but only the discord. Wisdom consists in finding the general formula or *Logos* of

change and conflict. Individual life is really death; true life and good life consists in setting oneself, in this life if one can, in the universal stream. "Wisdom is to say true things and to act according to nature, listening to its voice." Passion is the expression of the individual's effort to raise himself above the natural or divine order and to forget his dependence. True religion must be the merging of one's thought in the divine thought of the fire that goes about in the world. The image worshiping and blood sacrifices of the vulgar religions are tommyrot.

IV. PARMENIDES

Parmenides the Eleatic[1] flourished about 475 B.C. and wrote after Heracleitus and apparently in intentional opposition to him. He was a citizen of Elea, a town in southern Italy, the laws of which city he wrote. He is one of the most important of the early Greek philosophers, for it was out of the problem posed by his teaching that the doctrines of the greatest of the Greek philosophers, Plato and Aristotle, grew.

1. Truth and Opinion. The prelude to Parmenides' poem, "On Nature," represents him as borne on a chariot and attended by Sunmaidens to the Gate of Night and Day, which is locked and barred. The Sunmaidens persuade Dike (Justice) to unlock it, and Parmenides is taken through, out of the realm of Night into that of Day, and to the palace of a goddess who instructs him in the two ways, the Way of Truth and the deceptive Way of Opinion. We may interpret this to mean that Parmenides has been converted from error (Night) to truth (Day), and now sets out in his poem the truth which he has found and the error from which he has been released. The poem is in two parts, "On Truth" and "On Opinion." The Way of Truth is the real philosophy of Parmenides himself, and the Way of Opinion is a system which he rejects, and which was probably both Ionian and Pythagorean in character.

2. Absolute Monism. Parmenides taught a doctrine of pure monism; namely, that only one being exists, that plurality and change are impossible, and that their apparent existence is an illusion of the senses. His argument is very interesting. The fundamental and undeniable truth, he wrote, is that *being is* and *not-being is not*. The greatest error is to confuse being and not-being; and that is exactly what every phi-

---

[1] The three other members of the Eleatic School, Xenophanes, Zeno, and Melissus. we have not space to consider.

losopher does who admits the reality of change and multiplicity. Reason shows conclusively that there can be but one being, and that this being is unchanging:

a) Being is; hence, if anything is being, it is one with being; and if it is different from being, it is not-being, and is not. Therefore, a plurality of beings is impossible, and being is one.

b) Change means a coming-to-be of being. But being cannot come to be from being, for in that case it already is before it comes to be, which is absurd. Nor can it come from anything else, for anything else than being is not-being, and nothing can come from not-being since not-being is not. Therefore, all becoming is impossible, and being is unchanging.

Thus, one unchanging being is all that exists. The one being is identical with thought, according to Parmenides. "Thinking and being are the same thing." This is the primary principle of pure idealism.

It would be difficult to exaggerate the importance of Parmenides in the development of Greek thought, indeed in the development of all Western philosophy. To refute his denial of the possibility of becoming and change was no child's play; the concepts necessary for a valid criticism of his thought were not yet evolved, and we may say that new instruments of thought had to be invented to escape from the dilemma into which he had thrown philosophers. These new instruments fell into two main systems, that of the Atomists and that of the Socratic-Platonic-Aristotelian school. Before we study these, however, two more primitive attempts to solve the paradox of Parmenides must be examined.

V. EMPEDOCLES

The philosophy of Parmenides was bound to be followed by attempts to break away from the uncomfortable position in which he had placed thought. Some way of reintroducing motion into the picture of reality had to be found. Empedocles of Agrigentum (about 495 to 435 B.C.) accepted one of the fundamental theses of Parmenides, viz., that there is no absolute beginning or passing away of being, but at the same time refused to deny what experience shows us, viz., that particular things are constantly coming into and passing out of existence. The apparent generations of things, he taught therefore, are simply new combinations or mixtures of ungenerated, eternal elements or roots, and the apparent passing away of beings is only the separation of these roots. These eternal roots, whose different combinations produce all that exists, are the famous "four elements," earth, air, fire, and water.

1. **The Four Elements.** These four elements are eternal, changeless in form, indestructible, and existing in equal amounts. Two or more of them combine in various ways to produce the various types of being found in the universe. Nothing really comes into being or passes out of being. "There are only mingling, and then exchange between the things which have been mingled. Generation is but a name, accredited by men." The combinations are governed by a law of affinity. From all bodies effluences are continually given off and are flowing to the pores of other bodies; where there is affinity, or a proportion between the effluences of one and the pores of another, mixture takes place; otherwise, like oil and water, they cannot mix.

2. **Love and Hate.** All motion and change are caused by two forces, Love and Hate, the former inside the elements and causing them to unite, the latter outside them and causing them to separate. Each of these forces constantly strives to get the upper hand, and there results a series of cosmic cycles. When Love has complete domination, the world is one perfect sphere, which is a god, for in it all is in perfect unity and all hate is excluded from it. But this state does not last. Hate, or Discord, at the outermost extremes of the sphere, starts to penetrate it, separating the elements more and more until the unity is almost completely destroyed. Almost, but not quite; for Love remains at the center, and once Discord is exhausted in its surge, Love recommences the work of union, until the sphere is formed again.

VI. ANAXAGORAS

Anaxagoras, an Ionian, came to reside in Athens around the middle of the fifth century B.C., bringing to that city the philosophy of the Milesians, whose tradition had somehow lived. Accused of impiety, probably for political reasons, he fled from Athens in 432.

1. **The Seeds.** Anaxagoras starts from the primary tenet of the Eleatics, the denial of becoming. Nothing is really generated and nothing ever passes out of being. Instead of speaking of coming to be and ceasing to be we should speak of commingling and decomposition. "Nothing is born nor destroyed, but there is mixture and separation of things which exist." According to Anaxagoras, bone, for example, as well as every other kind of thing, is a real substance,

essentially different from all others, and indecomposable. When one thing is produced from another, it simply means that it already actually existed in that other. The production or generation of a substance is merely its separation out from a mixture in which the distinct parts could not be seen. The elements that make up the mixture are "seeds." These seeds are infinite in number, each contains all qualities, not merely potentially, but actually; each is infinitely divisible, and each part into which it is divided is like every other part, and like the seed itself. Nothing can come into being from anything else; Empedocles' belief that certain elements can unite to produce, say, hair, is absurd, for how could hair ever come from what is not hair? If hair comes from the food that we eat, then that food must really contain hair, just as it must contain blood, flesh, and bones. It does contain all these and everything, because the seeds which make it up are precisely the same as all other seeds and contain, each of them, and each part of each, all qualities, fire and air, earth and water, flesh and blood, hot and cold, and so on for the practically infinite number of individual substances found in the world.

2. The Mixture and the Nous. From all eternity the seeds existed in the infinite mixture, in which all the qualities were so equally distributed that the whole mass was to all appearances homogeneous. But when motion entered the mixture, individual things began to separate out, to be distinguished. This distinction is simply a question of proportion and distribution of the qualities. The motion which causes the separation out of the mixture of individual things does not originate from the seeds themselves; they are eternally inert. It comes from a reality external to and superior to the mixture. This reality is Reason, Intelligence, or Mind — the *Nous*. It is simple, self-existent, and the source of all the order and movement of the world. It produces in the mixture a circular movement, a whirlpool, which extends itself little by little around its center, reaching out till it traverses infinite space. The mechanical action of this whirlpool causes the separation of the various elements out from the mixed in a series of contraries; warm, dry, light, rare, and vapor on the one hand, and cold, moist, dark, dense, and mist on the other. From these contraries the world is formed.

3. Knowledge. The Nous, the universal mind, is participated in by all living beings. In man, sense perception is a function of mind, but is inferior to reason. It does not take place, as Empedocles said,

through likes, but, on the contrary, through unlikes. It is in the pupil of the eye, which is itself dark, that the luminous image is produced; and it is to the warm hand that an object feels cold, while to the cold hand it will feel warm. The senses report correctly as far as they go, but they are much too inadequate to give true knowledge. Only reason, a higher function of mind, gives real knowledge. Since the chief function of the mind or Nous is that of separating the various elements out of the mixture, and since human knowledge is nothing but the activity of the Nous participated in by the individual man, knowledge is essentially a process of separating, distinguishing, or discerning.

4. Monotheism, Dualism, and Teleology. To some extent Anaxagoras was a precursor of *monotheism.* Whereas Empedocles attributed divinity to many things, including the roots or elements, Anaxagoras denied it to all things except the Nous. To him, only this eternal, simple, infinite source of all motion, order, life, and knowledge, this all-dominant Mind which knows and distinguishes all things, is God. This doctrine of an immaterial mind distinct from matter and ruling over it is the first important step toward the great systems of dualism of Plato, Aristotle, and St. Thomas Aquinas, and the teleological view of nature taken by these philosophers. *Teleology* is the doctrine that the processes of nature are directed toward predetermined ends, or, in other words, that there is purpose or design in nature.

VII. DEMOCRITUS

1. Materialism. This step toward a philosophy that makes room for mind and purpose in the movements of nature was not followed up by the next group of philosophers who sought an explanation of the being-change problem. *Atomism,* founded by Leucippus, but best represented by his great disciple, Democritus, is a completely materialistic and mechanistic system, which seeks to reduce everything in the world to particles of matter and their movements.

The theory of Leucippus and Democritus is very obviously an attempt to rescue philosophical thought from the apparent *cul-de-sac* into which the Eleatic philosophers had led it. Parmenides had taught that being is and not-being is not, and had concluded that being is one and unchanging. His disciple, Melissus, had said that if beings were multiple, all would have to be precisely what the One is. He had stated this as an obviously untenable absurdity, but it seems to have been the very concept that Leucippus seized upon as the foundation of his system. He and Democritus were convinced as firmly as were the Eleatics of the impossibility of absolute beginning or destruction, but they were convinced also of what experience shows us on every hand — the reality of change and multiplicity. Their problem was to find a way of reconciling these two certainties.

Their solution was to parcel the Being or the One of Parmenides into an infinite multiplicity of beings, namely, the atoms. Each of these atoms is, like the Eleatic One, eternal, unchanging, and imperishable; they are the whole of being, and therefore there is neither absolute beginning nor absolute destruction of being. But not-being also exists; it is, as truly as Being is. It is the Void, and the atoms are in it and separated from one another by it, and moving eternally in it. These three things, then, are the elements of the Atomist philosophy — the atoms, the void, and the eternal movement of the atoms in the void. By means of them Leucippus and Democritus attempt to account for the whole world of experience.

2. Atomism. According to Democritus everything is composed of atoms. Atoms are extremely small particles of matter or solid extension. They have *no qualities* — no color, taste, hardness, or softness; they merely have, or are, volume, shape, and weight, and even the largest of them is too small to be seen. There are an infinite number of them. Each one is perfectly solid, containing no void. They never undergo any change except local motion, and they have eternally been moving.

3. Mechanism. The atomist's account of the formation of the world and everything in it is completely mechanistic: it seeks to explain everything by means of two principles alone — particles of matter and the movement of these particles. The atoms, which are being (or the full), exist in the void (non-being or empty space). They fall eternally through the void. As they fall, the larger ones, being heavier, fall faster, catch up on the smaller, lighter ones, and bump them. This bumping knocks the smaller atoms out of the straight line of falling, and then anything can happen, and does. Once a few of the atoms depart from the straight line of flight, they are bound to bump still others until the bumping becomes universal. This causes the falling motion to be changed into a great number of whirling motions, or eddies. In these whirlpools the atoms, which are all of different shapes, hook on to one another, and come apart again, and form new combinations, and all this goes on eternally and produces our universe with its stars and suns and planets and the earth with all the living and non-living things upon it.

No presiding mind governs the motion and combinations of the atoms. They move simply by natural necessity; being in empty space they fall through it—as you would if you were in empty space—and all their different combinations are the necessary result of their movement. This doctrine is the wellspring of all western philosophical materialism.

4. **Psychology of Democritus:** The psychological teaching of Democritus is an immediate application of his physical theory to the problem of knowledge. Sensation is explained by a mechanical theory of "images." Objects give off or exude images or copies of themselves. These images enter into those sense organs which are fitted to receive them, and set the soul, which is itself composed of atoms, in motion, thus giving rise to perception. Perception, therefore, according to Democritus, is simply the impact of atoms from without upon the atoms of the soul; the sense organs are merely "passages" through which these outer atoms reach the soul. The qualities, for example, color and taste, that we distinguish in perception are due to the differences in roughness and smoothness in the shape of the atoms. They do not belong to the atoms at all, but only to the perception; that is, they are in the subject, not in the object.

Errors in perception arise from the fact that the effluences or images do not arrive at the sense organ in the same condition in which they left the external object. In passing from the object to the organ the image becomes distorted by impact with the atoms of the intervening air. Consequently, the greater the distance the less distinctly we see and hear. Sense knowledge, therefore, is not very trustworthy. By it we know nothing with certainty. It depends on the disposition of the body and its sense organs. Hence different men receive different impressions from the same thing. Nor is thought much better off. For thought, according to Democritus, is simply an internal movement in the soul of these same images. It can be no more faithful than the images that make it up.

This would be very close to sheer skepticism if Democritus stopped here. But he does not. Besides sense knowledge we have another and higher knowledge. The atoms outside us, Democritus held, can affect the soul directly without the intervention of any sense organs.

This is possible because the atoms of the soul permeate the body everywhere and can therefore have immediate contact with external objects, or with finer images which copy the atomic structure of these objects. Thus the soul can know things as they really are.

It is clear that this "trueborn knowledge" of Democritus is not different in nature from sense knowledge. Like it, it is a matter of mechanical impact of atoms upon atoms, the atoms of the known object setting those of the soul in motion. It is also clear that this knowledge, like sense knowledge, is something quite subjective — movements of the soul atoms.

5. The Soul. The soul itself, as is made evident in the above paragraphs, is material. It is composed of atoms, but they are the finest, roundest, smoothest, and most nimble atoms, the same atoms that make up fire. The soul is, therefore, a fiery substance which floats in the air until pressed by the weight of the air into a body. This is shown by the fact that respiration maintains life and ceases at death. The soul is the noblest part of man; he who loves the goods of the soul loves what is most divine; he who loves the goods of the body, the tent of the soul, loves what is merely human.

VIII. THE SOPHISTS

1. The atomists mark the end of what has often been called the scientific or cosmological period of Greek philosophy. During this period attention had been almost exclusively directed to the nature of the physical universe and the problems of being and becoming as these presented themselves in the material cosmos. In the period which followed, physical problems receded to the background and man himself stepped forward as the chief object of interest.

Democracy, as practiced in the Greek cities of the middle of the fifth century B.C., gave every free man both a chance and a motive for becoming a politician. In the strife of clashing ambitions the most important weapon was the tongue. The young men of the Greek city-states needed masters to teach them the arts of oratory, argumentation, and rhetoric, and the science and arts of the day. The men who undertook to be these masters were the Sophists. The Sophists sold what their customers wanted; and the customers wanted, not real knowledge and wisdom, but the tools of success. Hence, there was little depth to the teachings of the Sophists. The net product of whatever teaching they did about truth was pragmatism and relativism in the case of *Protagoras,* and nihilism in the case of *Gorgias.*

2. **Protagoras,** the greatest of the Sophists, lived from about 480 to 410 B.C., much of this time being spent in Athens. He adopted the materialistic account of knowledge given by Democritus — knowledge is the motion in the soul caused by the shock of material replicas of external things striking the soul through the sense organs — and drew the logical consequences of this doctrine. "Man" he wrote, "is the measure of all things, of the being of those that are, and of the not-being of those that are not." This is a completely relativistic account of knowledge, which takes all objectivity away from truth, making it entirely dependent upon the individual man and his changing sense impressions. It equates knowledge with sense perception and makes the latter wholly subjective. A thing may taste sweet to me and bitter to you; what it is in itself neither you nor I can ever know, because all knowledge is merely sensation and we can never know anything except as our senses present it to us. The quality, that is, the object of the sensation, exists only in the sensation; things in themselves are not hot or cold, sweet or bitter, moist or dry. When a thing affects one of our senses, its motion, meeting the reacting motion of the sense organ, gives rise to the perceptual image. This image is all that can ever be known, and it tells, not what the object is, but only *how it appears to the perceiver at the precise moment of perception.* Truth, therefore, for anyone, is simply his own sensations: knowledge is merely perceiving what appears, and no one can perceive anything other than what appears to him; hence, whatever appears to anyone is true. Man, that is, the individual perceiving man, is the measure of all things, the standard of all truth.

It is clear that this doctrine makes truth entirely relative: there is nothing that is objectively true, that is, true in itself and for everyone whether everyone knows it or not; but on the contrary something is true only relatively to a particular person at a particular moment. The doctrine is also skeptical: what appears false to one person may at the same time appear true to another; but whatever appears true to anyone is true, and whatever appears false is false; hence, the same thing is at once true and false. Indeed, everything that anyone thinks is true; because when he thinks it, it appears to him, and appearance is all the truth there is. Finally, the doctrine of Protagoras is pragmatic, for it identifies the true with the better, the more expedient, the more useful opinion; if honey tastes bitter to me, my opinion is "false," that is, it is not so good as the opinion of a man to whom honey tastes sweet. The true and the false mean merely the useful and the useless, the desirable and the undesirable.

3. Gorgias carried skepticism to even greater lengths than had Protagoras. In a book which he entitled *On Nature or the Non-Existent*, he defends three propositions: (1) that nothing exists; (2) that if anything did exist, it would be unknowable anyway; (3) that if anyone did know something he could not, in any case, communicate this knowledge to anyone else. Gorgias was the complete nihilist, the perfect skeptic.

Sensism does, in fact, give the conclusions that Gorgias inferred from it. If I know only immediate appearances, I do not know any *thing* which appears or any self to which it appears; in a word, I do not know *being*. And certainly I could never communicate knowledge: if I exist and someone else also exists, my sensations would be mine and his would be his, and no identification of them would ever be possible.

Skepticism in regard to knowledge could go no further. But skepticism can go beyond theory of knowledge, and it did go beyond in later Sophists. Nihilism in morals follows from sensism just as surely as does nihilism in epistemology. A true morality must be founded upon what is universal in man, that is, upon reason. Deny reason, and in ethics as in knowledge the individual man is the measure of all things. The ethical value of law is destroyed, for no law can be just if there is no objective and universal standard of justice. If everything is true, then everything is right; if nothing is true, then nothing is right. Right and wrong become what the individual makes them. Justice is the right of the stronger, or, in a democracy, of the majority. Might, in a word, is right; the individual is the measure, and the "right" measure is, surely, whatever one prevails.

IX. SOCRATES

Socrates, one of the most interesting figures of world history, was born about 470 B.C. He lived all his life in Athens, leaving that city only once or twice when necessity compelled. He was a firm believer in the immortality of the soul and in the life to come. His refusal to stop publicly teaching his views about the moral and political corruption in Athens led him to disfavor with successive Athenian governments and finally to his condemnation to death on trumped-up charges of atheism, introducing new gods, and corrupting the youth of the city.

1. **Teleology.** Socrates was acquainted with the teachings of the natural philosophers and was especially impressed by the doctrine of the all-governing Mind taught by Anaxagoras. But none of these philosophers satisfied him, because they all gave mechanical causes for the natures of things, and what he was seeking was a *reason* why things should be as they are. To suppose that mechanical causes explain things seemed to him to be as childish as to "explain" the fact that "Socrates is sitting on a porch in Athens" by describing the disposition of his limbs. Mechanical causes only describe a fact; they do not explain it. Something is explained, according to Socrates, only when it is shown *to be what it is because it is good for it to be so*. Socrates was the complete teleologist.

2. **Definition and Induction.** Aristotle wrote that two things may fairly be attributed to Socrates, namely, the demonstration that knowledge is based on universal concepts, and induction. What Aristotle referred to is clearly apparent in any of Plato's Socratic dialogues. Socrates would ask someone, say a famous general noted for his courage, what courage is. The general would reply by offering some example of courage: "Courage is never turning one's back to the enemy." Socrates, then, by questions and suggestions, would show that this example does not adequately express what courage is, for many different examples can be given; and that it is not correct anyway, because sometimes it is good warcraft to turn one's back to the enemy. He would then draw out from those present further instances and, by analyzing them, seek to lead his interlocutors to the knowledge of what constitutes courage in itself. He was, therefore, working his way inductively toward a definition or concept of courage.

3. **Intellectualism.** By constantly applying this method and impressing it upon the minds of his followers, Socrates was formulating a new theory of knowledge. He was showing that the true object of knowledge is not the particular instance of a thing, nor the sense perception, but the nature or essence of the thing as expressed in its definition. We have seen that many of the philosophers before Socrates had hinted at or expressly taught the difference between sense knowledge and reason, but none had clearly formulated the distinction by showing what the true object of reason is. This is what Socrates did, and the importance of his accomplishment cannot be overestimated.

Its immediate effect was to furnish a weapon to combat the attacks of Sophism upon the objectivity and universality of truth. The Sophists, by making knowledge consist simply in sense perception, had made it relative to each individual, for one man cannot communicate his sensations to another. They are private to him. But reason is not private. It is common to all men, and the same in all men, and its content can be communicated by one man to another. Reason gives an objective standard valid for all men; sensation gives only a subjective standard valid for each man. Concepts are acts of the reason or intelligence of man, not of his senses. When a satisfactory concept of something, for example, justice, is formulated and expressed in a definition, that is, when the essence of a thing is made known, this concept is equally valid for everyone and can be understood by everyone. Individual, subjective standards are overruled. The Sophist can no longer say with any show of plausibility that the individual man is the measure of all things, that truth is what is useful in a given circumstance, that justice is the strength of the stronger. Thus Socrates saved knowledge and morality from the abyss of skepticism, and at the same time gave a new turn to philosophy by more clearly formulating its true object, which is knowledge of the essence of things.

4. **Socrates' Teaching on Virtue.** Perhaps the most famous of all the Socratic teachings is the identification of virtue with knowledge. All evil-doing, he held, is ignorance or the result of ignorance. No man can know a thing to be evil and deliberately do it. Therefore, when a man does evil, it is because he lacks knowledge. What knowledge does he lack? Obviously, he lacks knowledge of what is good for himself. He does not know the good of man. The knowledge, then, that Socrates makes identical with virtue is the knowledge of what is good for man.

X. PLATO

1. Plato, considered by many scholars as the greatest genius who ever graced our planet, was born in Athens in 427 B.C. He was, for eight years before the death of Socrates (399 B.C.), a friend and to some extent a pupil of the latter. To him Socrates was "the wisest and the best" of men and the pattern of the true philosopher. Some years after Socrates had been condemned to death and had drunk the hemlock, Plato, about 387 B.C., founded the *Academy,* which might be called Europe's first university. This academy continued until A.D. 529, when

it was suppressed by the Emperor Justinian. It had long since become, ironically, the home of skepticism. Plato's writings were in the form of dialogues or conversations, Socrates being the central figure in most of them. The influence of Plato upon philosophical thought is immeasurable. One prominent philosopher has called the history of philosophy a series of footnotes to Plato.

The ruling principle of Plato's entire philosophy is his *Doctrine of Ideas*. According to this doctrine, real being is not to be found in the particular sensible objects that make up what we call Nature, but in the universal essences which are the objects, not of sense, but of the conceptions of the intellect. Particular beautiful persons or things, for example, are not real beauty; only the universal essence or Idea Beauty is. Particular sensible things only *imitate* reality in so far as they imitate the Ideas; particular trees are only imitations of the one, eternal, universal Tree, or the Idea Tree.

2. **Plato's Concept of Philosophy.** Socrates had established for all time that true knowledge is rational knowledge, that the elements of knowledge are not sensations but concepts. Parmenides had made it clear, through all his vagaries, that the only possible object of true knowledge is being. The philosophy of Plato is, to a large extent, the expansion of these two intuitions. Since the concept or definition is the true principle of knowledge, and since being or reality is the true object of knowledge, then that which the concept represents or defines must be the only true reality. That which a concept represents Plato calls the Idea or Form. Ideas, then, are reality. Philosophy, since it is the science of true being, is therefore the science of the Ideas. This knowledge of the Ideas, the essential part of philosophy, is called *dialectic*. Dialectic is not, however, the whole of philosophy. Having gained the world of Ideas, the philosopher must return to the sensible world and teach men what he has learned. This task involves explaining the true nature of the sensible world, which men mistakenly take for reality. The account of the true nature of the world of phenomena is called *physics*, and is the second part of philosophy. It consists in "opinion" rather than knowledge. Above all, the truth which the philosopher has contemplated in the world of Ideas must be made the rule of men's conduct. Hence, *ethics*, or the application of the science of the Ideas to the actions of men, forms the third part of Plato's philosophy. And since men live in society, that is, in the state, a major part of ethics will be the study of the ideal state.

The philosopher's knowledge of true reality imposes a grave obligation upon him. The men of his city have not true knowledge but live by opinion, which they think is knowledge. Consequently the city is overrun by scandals and evils of every sort. Therefore, it is the duty of the philosopher to show men how properly to govern the city, even if this means that he must himself become the head of the city and the maker of its laws. "Until philosophers are kings, or the kings and princes of this world have the spirit and power of philosophy, and political greatness and wisdom meet in one, and those common natures who pursue either to the exclusion of the other are compelled to stand aside, cities will never have rest from their evils — no, nor the human race, as I believe — and then only will this our State have a possibility of life and behold the light of day."

3. The Doctrine of Ideas. Knowledge consists, not in the perceptions of sense, but in the conceptions of the intellect. Therefore, since to know is to know reality, it follows that that which is represented in the concept is the only true reality. This must be real, because if it were not, our knowledge would have no object, science would be impossible, and skepticism would be inevitable. But concepts represent, not the particular, changing, imperfect objects of sense perception, but rather universal, permanent, perfect essences, forms, or Ideas. They are also, unlike sense phenomena, incorporeal or immaterial. The senses present us with a multitude of things of a certain nature, but do not grasp the nature itself. Reason, or intellect, on the contrary, apprehends the nature, and also sees that none of the individuals is the nature itself. No sensible tree is all that is meant by tree, no man all that is meant by man, no just act justice itself. But the object of the concept is the universal tree, the universal man, the universal justice: it is *what is meant by tree, man, justice.*

Plato is drawing attention here to the distinction between the *particular* and the *universal.* A little reflection shows us that our knowledge is concerned with two distinct sets of objects. One set is made up of individual things, the other of classes of things. Although the objects which make up the world we live and move in are particular things, these things are also assignable to, or members of, universal classes. What we perceive with our senses is not the classes but the individuals; what our intellect grasps is the class nature. I *see* thousands of individual men, and I *know* that each one belongs to the species man, but I do not see the species. Intellect grasps the universal by means of concepts; sense grasps only the particular by means of sensation. Now, the very essence of Plato's doctrine of Ideas is that the universals are the true realities and the particulars are only half-real imitations of these true realities.

Plato's Idea (*eidos, idea*) is not, as the English usage would suggest, something in our mind; it is primarily objective, real in itself. It is an objective universal essence existing apart from the phenomena of the sense world and apart from our conceptual representation of it. Ideas are prior to human minds and exist whether men know them or not. The world of Ideas and the world of sense are separate; the world of Ideas is the prototype and exemplar of the world of sense, and the latter is the copy or ectype of the former. The Ideas are causes, and are the only true causes; they cause things both to be and to be known. They are subsistent, immutable, eternal, perfect, and one. The Idea of beauty, for example, is "beauty only, absolute, separate, simple, and everlasting." They are outside space and time, that is, they are immaterial.

Our concepts represent the Ideas: to every concept there corresponds an Idea which is its cause; and the laws of thought which rule the world of concepts mirror the laws of being which rule the world of Ideas. The Ideas form an ordered series from the highest genera down to individuals, and it is the task of science to reconstruct this series in our thought. In the system which the Ideas form — e.g., color presiding over blue, red, white, etc.; virtue over prudence, justice, etc.; quality over color, taste, shape, etc. — the superior Idea is the *cause* of its inferiors (i.e., color is the cause of red, green, etc.; virtue the cause of prudence, justice, etc.); and there is one highest Idea that presides over all the others — the Idea of the Good — and this is the cause of all the other Ideas and of all things.

4. The Idea of the Good. Like the sun in the sensible world, the Good gives life, being, and nature to every Idea, causing the other Ideas both to be and to be known. It is the *end* of all the other Ideas. As the Good is the end of the other Ideas, each Idea is the end, ground, reason, or final cause of those which fall under it; and the Ideas are the ground or reason of sensible phenomena. Men exist for the sake of the ideal Man, earthly states for the sake of the ideal State, just acts for the sake of Justice, and everything for the sake of the Good: as Socrates had put it, the reason why things are as they are must be because it is good for them to be so. Plato's philosophy is thoroughly teleological: everything is explained by its end rather than by its beginning; but a reason, not by mechanical causes — Socrates sits in Athens because he has a reason for so doing; because it is good to do so, not because of the position of his limbs.

5. **The Visible World.** The physics of Plato deals with the imitations of the Ideas, that is to say, with the phenomenal world of sense. Physics is not limited, however, to corporeal objects, for in the phenomenal world there are incorporeal *souls,* and physics treats also of these.

The world of phenomena, that is, this visible world in which we live, is characterized by change, multiplicity, and imperfection; it is quite the contrary of the world of Ideas. It is a realm of half reality, a mixture of being and not-being. There is some contact between it and the world of Ideas, because phenomena partake of or imitate the Ideas. The concrete, particular good, for example, a good man, a good act, participates in the absolute Good; a horse or a fire participates in horse-in-itself or fire-in-itself. There is some shred or appearance of permanence, unity, and reality in the sense world, and this appearance is due to the sense world's imitation of the Ideas; but precisely because the Ideas are the principles of unity, permanence, and reality, they cannot account for the multiplicity, change, and unreality of phenomena. Plato therefore assumes another principle, opposite to the Ideas, in order to account for these characteristics. This principle he variously calls space, mass, the receptacle, the unlimited, not-being, the great and the small. It corresponds roughly to what Aristotle will later call matter (*hyle*). It is that in which all things appear, grow, and decay; it is a principle of limitation, essentially a negation. It exists but is not real; it is known by a kind of spurious reason. It is without nature, quality, feature, or form; it would seem almost to be nothing at all; and, indeed, Plato calls it not-being.

6. **"Creation" of the World.** The creation of the world is set forth in the *Timaeus* in the form of a myth. Plato uses myths with great frequency in the dialogues. The myth-form often indicates that the matter being explained is a matter of opinion or belief rather than knowledge. The study of the phenomenal world is such a matter since its object is not the Ideas, with which alone true science is concerned. According to the myth of the *Timaeus* this is how the world was generated: God, the Demiurgos, the Creator, finds the receptacle (space, matter) in a state of formless chaos, lacking all perfection, all

intelligibility, all beauty. Because he is good and there is no envy in him, he wishes to make this chaos into an ordered cosmos, to make it good, as much like himself as possible. This is the meaning behind the myth of the *Timaeus* — that the world is a beautiful work of art; its beauty of structure and movement is not the result of a chance concurrence of mechanical causes, but is due to an intelligence which aims at the general good and has arranged everything according to a premeditated plan. The plan was, of course, taken from the higher world, the World of Ideas, which the Demiurgos contemplates. That is to say, God created the world by fashioning the original chaos after the pattern of the Ideas.

7. The World-Soul. First God created the World-Soul. This mediates between the Ideas and matter and is the proximate cause of all life, order, and motion in the universe, as well as of all knowledge. The universe is, therefore, a living organism, and its soul is the most perfect and intelligent of all souls. The World-Soul and all souls are self-moving beings and cause all the movement in everything else.

8. The Human Soul. The soul of man is similar to the World-Soul, created by God himself out of the same materials, though less pure, from which he made the latter. It is a self-moving principle, the moving cause of the body. It has affinity to both the world of Ideas and the world of sense, but belongs properly to neither. Man's soul existed before it was joined to the body, and its present existence in the body, which is its prison, is a punishment.

9. Theory of Reminiscence. This doctrine of the pre-existence of the soul is set-forth by Plato as an explanation of our knowledge, and is intimately related to his famous *theory of reminiscence*. All learning seems to be a recollection of what the soul already knows; hence, the soul must have had this knowledge in a former life, a life in which it was not united to the body. Otherwise how could we ever attain knowledge of the Ideas? Such knowledge could not possibly come to us from the senses, since the senses reach only phenomena and not the Ideas. Sense objects *suggest* the Ideas; but nothing can be suggested unless it is already known. A picture of a friend suggests the friend to me, that is, reminds me of him; but a picture of someone whom I do not know suggests no one to me. It is, however, undeniable that sense objects remind us of the Ideas — a beautiful thing brings the Idea of Beauty to my mind — and therefore it is also undeniable that the knowledge of the Ideas must be already within us. As Socrates shows in the case of *Meno's* slave boy, we do not *give* a child knowledge when we teach him something, let us say, mathematics; we simply lead him to look into his mind and see what he already knows but has forgotten.

Why, then, does not the soul know all the Ideas without learning? Plato's answer, given in a myth, is that this life is a punishment of the soul for evil done in its previous state, and that in descending from the World of Ideas to the sensible world it suffered an obscuration of its knowledge, a forgetting. It must be reminded, and reminding is the function of education.

10. **Metempsychosis.** Plato seems to have believed, or half believed, in reincarnation or metempsychosis, which he presents in myths. We choose our own reincarnations; the gods are free of all blame in the matter. In a word, by the character of our life now we determine the character of our future life — that is what Plato was driving at.

11. **The Immortality of the Soul.** Plato is the first philosopher to attempt to prove the immortality of the soul. He advances several arguments. The soul is simple, akin to the Ideas, since it can know them; hence like them it is indestructible. It is capable of going counter to the body, as is clearly shown in moral struggle against bodily passion. Therefore it cannot be dependent upon the body, that is, it cannot be its "harmony" as the Pythagoreans held. Consequently, the perishing of the body will not entail the perishing of the soul. Finally, an idea cannot pass into its opposite. Life belongs to the very idea of the soul; soul is the principle of life; death in the principle of life is a contradiction, an impossibility.

12. **The Refutation of Sensism.** In developing his conception of knowledge, Plato examines and refutes the doctrine of the Sophists — that perception is knowledge. The belief that perception is knowledge can be shown to be false in many ways. (1) Perception gives contradictory impressions to different perceivers or to the same perceiver at different times; that is to say, men frequently differ as to the appearance of the same thing. Therefore, perception cannot be knowledge, for to know the truth means to be able to choose correctly between contradictory impressions. (2) The theory renders demonstration and teaching impossible. For demonstration and teaching presuppose an object of knowledge common to the demonstrator and the one to whom he is demonstrating, and to the teacher and the one taught. But each man's perceptions are his own alone. (3) Animals have sense

perception, and, therefore, if perception were knowledge, a pig as much as a man would be "the measure of all things." (4) The theory that perception is knowledge is self-refuting. According to it, whatever appears true to me, is true; but it appears true to me that this doctrine is false. (This argument is not a mere trick with words. What Plato means is that a theory which provides grounds for its own refutation is internally inconsistent and self-destructive, and therefore worthless. Sensism is such a theory.) (5) The theory in question destroys the objectivity of truth, making the distinction between truth and error meaningless. In that case there is no knowledge at all. The result is skepticism.

Of course, some men are willing to accept skepticism and the argument that perceptionism leads to it will fail to impress them. Plato, therefore, goes on to show directly that perception cannot be knowledge. (6) Even in the simplest proposition, for example, "This desk is wood," there is something more than direct perception. To attribute a predicate to a subject I must compare two present percepts and compare my present perceptions with my past perceptions. To do this I must first classify the percepts under concepts. All these acts are impossible to sense, since sensation is always an isolated, present impression unrelated to any other. In knowledge, therefore, I exercise a power that is above the senses. This higher power is evidenced further by the fact that different sensations suggest the same idea to me, for example, this orange both looks round and feels round. The roundness is not the look, because in that case feeling could never suggest it; nor is it the feel, for the opposite reason. Yet I know from either seeing it or feeling it or both that it is round. Clearly there is in knowledge a higher power which sense serves and which judges sense.

What, then, is knowledge? It is, as Socrates showed, comprehension by means of a concept or definition which is fixed and permanent and the same for all minds. It belongs to reason and not to sense. It gives the objective essence of a thing, not a private appearance. Its object is nothing of this phenomenal world, but the eternal Idea. True knowledge is the rational comprehension of the Ideas.

CHAPTER III

ARISTOTLE AND THOMISM

I. ARISTOTLE

1. Aristotle was born in 384 B.C., in the town of Stagira (whence the name often given to him in literature, "The Stagirite") on the northern coast of the Aegean Sea. In 367, his seventeenth year, he entered the Academy and was associated with it for the next twenty years until the death of Plato. The master influence of his life was Plato's philosophy. Though fundamental differences developed between the thought of the two, no page of Aristotle's writings is without the impress of Platonism. After Plato's death Aristotle left the Academy, and in 335 he set up his own school in Athens. This school became known as the Lycaeum. He died in 322 B.C.

The Lycaeum soon overshadowed the Academy. For the twelve years from its foundation until Aristotle's death its scientific output was enormous. Aristotle's own work, unparalleled for its extent and variety, was practically an encyclopedia of all the knowledge of the time as well as the embodiment of the most influential system of philosophy that the world has ever seen. One of the most competent Aristotelian scholars of our own day summarizes the work of Aristotle thus: "Aristotle fixed the main outlines of the classification of the sciences in the form which they still retain, and carried most of the sciences to a further point than they had hitherto reached; in some of them, such as logic, he may fairly claim to have had no predecessor, and for centuries no worthy successor."[1] It may be said of biology, as of logic, that Aristotle founded it as a science; and to this day not a few biologists regard him as being without a peer in that science. "As a biologist Aristotle has had his detractors, but for me, as for others, he is the greatest biologist that ever lived."[2] In philosophy, too, Aristotle

---

[1] W. D. Ross, *Aristotle*, p. 6.
[2] H. B. Adlemann, *The Scientific Monthly*, June, 1944, Vol. LVIII, No. 6, p. 416.

has had his detractors, and far more severe and unfair than in biology; but the verdict of the ages is that he is the greatest philosopher that ever lived. St. Thomas always wrote of him as "The Philosopher," and the name is justified.

2. **The Nature of Philosophy.** Aristotle connects as directly with Plato as Plato does with Socrates. He presupposes throughout his philosophy the general point of view which characterized the Socratico-Platonic theory of Ideas. His task is to work out on the same general lines a more perfect system of knowledge. Much has been made in history of his opposition to Plato, but in fact his agreement with his great predecessor and master is greater than his divergence, though the divergence occurs in regard to matters that are fundamental.

For Aristotle, as for Plato, the object of philosophy can only be being itself. Being is understood only when its causes are known, and consequently, philosophy treats of the highest and most ultimate causes of things. To discover what kinds of causes things have and then to determine in each case what these causes are — that is the whole of philosophy. For Aristotle, as for Plato, knowledge in the full sense is concerned with what is universal and necessary; of the particular, the changing, and the contingent, there can only be opinion. But opinion and knowledge have not quite the same meaning for him as they had for Plato: we have opinion, according to Aristotle, when we believe that a thing is so but might be otherwise; we have knowledge when we know that a thing is so and why it must be so and cannot be otherwise. We cannot, therefore, have both knowledge and opinion about the same thing at the same time. Aristotle is as much the foe of sensism as were Socrates and Plato: knowledge cannot consist in sense perception, for that tells us only of particulars and not of universals, only of the contingent and not of the necessary, only of facts and not of their reasons. He is the more redoubtable foe than they, because he does not lightly brush sensation aside but gives it its own full value as the beginning of knowledge; and this is what sensism cannot abide — a true evaluation of sensation. If sensation is given no value, a man may be excused for revolting and giving it the whole value of knowledge; if it is properly located with respect to knowledge, there is no excuse for confusing it with knowledge. Aristotle leaves the nominalists and the positivists with no excuse for their sensism.

3. **Experience and Knowledge.** The difference between Plato and Aristotle about the value of experiences of the world of sense leads

them to conceptions of philosophy that are not quite the same. Experience for Plato was in no way or degree knowledge, but was at best an incentive or reminder to rise to knowledge. For Aristotle, experience is a condition and a beginning of knowledge; it is out of experience that we abstract essences and form ideas. For Plato the pure Ideas are the one essential object of philosophy, and the Ideas abide apart from the sensible world; the mind, stirred to thought by sense experience, must *rise up and away from* the sensible object to the Ideas in order to attain knowledge. For Aristotle, universal essences are likewise the object of philosophy, but these essences (forms or ideas) reside in the sensible world; the mind, stirred to thought by sense experience, must probe more deeply *into* the sensible object and find therein the intelligible essence which is the object of true knowledge. Knowledge, therefore, for Aristotle is not reminiscence, but is the rational flowering of what, germinally, is perception; knowledge grows out of perception instead of simply happening on the occasion of perception. This would seem to be the fundamental difference between Platonism and Aristotelianism, the difference whence all the other differences spring.

4. **The Visible World.** The most important difference that springs out of this fundamental one concerns the status of the sensible world. Plato does not regard the physical world as truly real. The change and imperfection that characterize it are marks of its unreality. The Ideas are reality; and though the phenomenal world imitates the Ideas, the latter exist apart from it and not in it. Aristotle could never accept this evaluation of nature. Corporeal, sensible things are what we know first and best; if our knowledge of these is not true knowledge, then we can have no true knowledge of any reality. This world may be imperfect and unstable, but such as it is, it is real; and it is our world. There may be higher, better worlds, but we can know them only through the world that our senses present to us. To know is to attain to true ideas, but these ideas are in things; the separate World of Ideas is an illusion. Forming the true conception of a thing consists in disengaging the universal unchanging form of the thing from the particular changing matter in which it is embodied, not in turning away from the thing to some disembodied Form which would be nothing like the thing in question and which cannot exist anyway. For Plato, sensible things had a semblance of reality because they imitated Ideas or Essences; for Aristotle, they are realities because they embody forms or essences.

5. Materialism, Idealism, and Hylemorphism. This doctrine of Aristotle — that sensible substances are the real embodiments of forms, natures, or ideas in matter — is called hylemorphism (from *hyle,* matter, and *morphe,* form). Its basic meaning is that every natural thing is a composite of a potential, determinable, and passive principle called matter, and an actual, determining, and active principle called form; and that the form, which is a definite nature but needs a subject in which to exist, communicates its nature to the matter, which is a potential subject lacking any determinate nature of its own; so that the union of the two constitutes one real and actual thing of a definite kind.

Aristotle's hylemorphism may be regarded as a middle way between the materialism of Democritus and the idealism of Plato. According to Democritus all the myriad beings of the world are merely fortuitous aggregates of material elements, the atoms. No plan or idea directs the formation of substances; atoms simply bunch together accidentally, and different bunches are different substances. Democritus completely suppressed the intelligible or immaterial in his account of nature. Plato, in his doctrine of Ideas, tried to take account of the material and immaterial, the changing phenomena and the permanent essences. The Ideas are reality, and phenomena are mere imitations of Ideas and hence mere imitations of reality. This doctrine does apparently account for some very obvious facts of experience. Natures or essences remain ever the same, while the things possessing the natures constantly change. *Humanity,* for example, is eternal and immutable, while *men* are born and die. Again, a nature or essence is one, while the things possessing it are a multitude: there is only one humanity, but millions of men. These facts of permanence amid change and unity amid multiplicity are accounted for if, as the doctrine of Ideas maintains, phenomena are merely imitations of the Idea; men merely imitations of the one humanity. Plato's theory, however, had one very grievous defect. It stripped this actual world we live in of reality, and it placed reality in an ideal world in which we do not live. It was, in brief, an idealistic system of the appearance-reality type, and the inspiration of nearly all such later systems.

Aristotle rejected both materialism and idealism for a type of dualism. In his view, both the material element and the intelligible element are real, and both are *in* nature. He affirmed the immaterial principle denied by Democritus, and then rescued it from the ideal world of Plato, restoring it to this world of experience. Democritus tried to explain nature without ideas, Plato tried to explain it by ideas outside it, Aristotle explains it by ideas within it. The relation of hylemorphism to the theory of Ideas may be briefly expressed thus: for Plato sensible objects *imitate* ideas; for Aristotle they *embody* ideas; the form is the idea embodied; the matter is the stuff in which it is embodied; and the substance is the concrete embodiment of the idea.

6. The Nature of Man. Their differences about knowledge, about sensible things, and about ideas, lead Plato and Aristotle to different conceptions of man. Both distinguish body and soul in man. But Plato tends, at least, to identify the soul with the man and to regard the body as an accidental and regrettable piece of baggage. Man belongs primarily in the World of Ideas, and the body would certainly be an impertinent intruder there. Man's having a body does not seem, in Plato's philosophy, to be proper to his essential nature, but rather a characteristic of his present unfortunate state. For Aristotle, on the other hand, man is very clearly a composite substance, a single individual composed of matter and form, that is, of body and soul. Without either he would not be man. A soul for Aristotle is essentially the animating principle of a body — its substantial form; for Plato a soul is essentially a complete spiritual being. Only by myths can he explain how souls ever got mixed up with bodies to begin with.

There is no need to carry our present account of Aristotle's philosophy beyond these few indications of its relation to Platonism, because in the chapters to follow we shall constantly be concerned either with Aristotelianism or with the most brilliant and faithful Christian interpretation of Aristotelianism, namely, Thomism.

II. ST. THOMAS AQUINAS

1. St. Thomas Aquinas was born in A.D. 1225 at Rocca Sicca, Italy. He became a Dominican priest, and taught theology in several of the leading universities in Europe, notably the University of Paris. He died in 1274. Along with St. Augustine, Aristotle, Plato, and a handful of others, he stands as one of the intellectual giants of history. The influence of his thought outside Catholic circles is greater today than in any previous age, and this influence gives promise of growing steadily in the years to come.

During the sixteen centuries between the life of Aristotle and that of St. Thomas Aquinas the face of man's world changed as it never had before and never can again. It was not the lapse of the sixteen centuries that wrought the change; it was an event, the central event of human history. About three centuries after the wisest of pagan philosophers died, Eternal Wisdom Itself, the Word of God, became man in the womb of the Immaculate Virgin. Nothing in the life of man could ever be the same again. Slowly but surely pagan civilization and the pagan conception of the world gave way before Christianity and the Christian world-view. The Church founded by Christ grew steadily, and in the thirteenth century — St. Thomas' century — it attained a new high level of organizational and intellectual maturity. In the whole western world its influence upon the ways and thoughts of men was all-pervasive and unchallenged. And no man of the thirteenth century was more passionately attached to this Church or more thoroughly formed according to its mind than Thomas Aquinas. The influence of his Catholic faith was strong and deep upon every word he ever wrote. He was, par excellence, the Christian Philosopher.

2. **Christian Philosophy.** Those contemporary Scholastics who still maintain that there is not and cannot be any such thing as a Christian philosophy must read an Aquinas of their own mind's creating. St. Thomas did not suffer from intellectual schizophrenia, nor was he a devotee of make-believe; he did not do his thinking on Mondays, Wednesdays, and Fridays and his believing on Tuesdays, Thursdays, and Saturdays. He knew what proving is and he knew what supernatural faith is, and he never confused the two; but from the outset of his proving he knew what he wanted to prove, because he knew what he believed. No service is done to him or to Catholic thought by pretending that the case was otherwise. To maintain that a great and saintly Christian could formulate, sincerely, a philosophy not influenced in its most inward parts by his religious faith is to voice a psychological ·anomaly. To maintain that he *ought to* form his philosophy in freedom from this influence is to imply a doubt either of the truth of Christian doctrine or of the coherence of truth. The Bible and the teachings of the Catholic Church are not items in St. Thomas' philosophy, but they are — by far — the most important influences that entered into its formation. St. Thomas once said that he lived only to teach about God, and we need have no more doubt than he himself had about what God he meant. Christian philosophy is not philosophy using Christian dogmas as starting points or principles of demonstration —

such a thing would not be philosophy. Christian philosophy is purely rational philosophy guided and illumined by Christian faith, and Thomism is a distinctly Christian philosophy.[3]

More perfectly, perhaps, than any other of the world's great thinkers did St. Thomas bring to realization the ideal that the present should lose nothing of the past. The pre-Socratic philosophers, Socrates, Plato, Aristotle, the Stoics, the Neoplatonists—the great pagan thinkers—contributed grist for St. Thomas' mill. So did the Church Fathers, Tertullian, Origen, the Basils, Chrysostom, Jerome, Hilary, Augustine, John Damascene; so did Boethius, Pseudo-Dionysius, Anselm, Peter Lombard, and the other great theologians. Moses Maimonides, the great medieval Jewish theologian, Avicebron, the Jewish philosopher, Avicenna and Averroes, the great Arabian Aristotelians, made further very important contributions. The story ends only with St. Thomas' own contemporaries, whose work he used generously, whether to approve, improve, correct, or reject. It is a story which we have not space to tell. Welded out of all these elements, by the flame of a great genius, came a new philosophy, still basically Aristotelian in its fundamental principles, but owing very much also to St. Augustine. A mark of the true originality of this Aristotelian-Augustinian philosophy is the fact that the two most incessant conflicts of St. Thomas' philosophical life were waged against, respectively, contemporary Aristotelians and Augustinians. In many of the battles of this conflict St. Thomas was a better Aristotelian than the Aristotelians and a better Augustinian than the Augustinians, yet he never fought for Aristotle or Augustine but always for truth.

III. ARISTOTELIANISM AND THOMISM

1. **The Thomistic Revolution.** The philosophy of St. Thomas Aquinas is Aristotelian, but it is Aristotelianism seen under the brilliant and steady light of divine Revelation. The chief parts of Aristotle's philosophy, his physics, metaphysics, and psychology, had been largely obscured and forgotten during the first twelve centuries of the growth of Christian thought. Platonism was far better known to the Church fathers and theologians, and those who sought a philosophical groundwork on which to rear the structure of theology sought it generally in Platonism. This was above all true of the greatest of the

---

[3] The relations between reason and faith and the conception of Christian philosophy will be explained at more length in Chapter XX.

fathers, St. Augustine. From the fifth to the thirteenth century, St. Augustine's theology held supreme and undisputed authority, and its philosophical moorings were Platonic. In St. Augustine's hands, Plato's World of Ideas had become the divine Exemplars; his theory of reminiscence had become the Augustinian doctrine of innate ideas and divine illumination; his vagueness and ambiguity about the nature of man had carried over into Augustine's doctrine of the soul; Augustine and Augustinians were not entirely free from Platonic contempt for matter and the sensible world. A new and very important characteristic marked Augustinianism in addition to all the above: philosophy was not granted an area of its own and principles of its own distinct from those of theology. The only true philosophy was Christian theology.

The Thomistic revolution in Christian thought consisted in, among other things, mooring theological speculation upon a new metaphysical foundation, Aristotelianism in place of Platonism. This entailed replacing Platonic innatism and illumination by the Aristotelian doctrine of the abstraction of ideas from the data of sense perception; St. Thomas denied that we have any innate ideas. It entailed also the doctrine that man's rational soul is the substantial form of his body and is essentially united to the body because it *needs* the body. It entailed insistence upon the reality of this sensible world and, further, insistence that all our knowledge, no matter what heavenly heights it may attain, is anchored in and depends upon our sense perception of corporeal things; that, indeed, if we cannot be sure of them we cannot be sure of anything. Finally, and most history-making of all, the Thomistic revolution entailed insistence upon the fact that philosophy, though the handmaiden of theology, is a true science in its own right, with its own inviolable area of investigation and its own self-sufficient principles. This Thomistic doctrine of philosophy is human thought's Charter of Liberty, and, though it is a charter often abused, it is unlikely that theology will ever seriously endeavor to abrogate it. St. Thomas has frequently, of late, been called "the first modern philosopher"; we may call him that without making him responsible for any of the aberrations of modern philosophy: none of them arose because human thought had too much freedom; they all arose either because some philosophers thought too carelessly or because their thought was enslaved by deep-seated prejudices.

St. Thomas was an Aristotelian in his philosophy, but it would be very erroneous to suppose either that he found Aristotle's philosophy ready at hand when he began his own philosophical work or that he slavishly followed Aristotle in everything which the latter had taught. On the contrary, Aquinas, living sixteen centuries after Aristotle, had to rediscover the real Aristotelian philosophy, digging it out from underneath the barnacles of additions and perversions with which it had become encrusted through the intervening ages; and he also had to correct many errors which Aristotle himself had made.

2. **The Neoplatonized Aristotle.** The Western Latin world of the thirteenth century received the writings of Aristotle in a very round-about way. For the first twelve centuries of the Christian era Aristotle's writings, with the exception of those on logic, were not available to the Latin philosophers of Europe. When Christian doctrine sought a philosophical and scientific context, it adopted, as we have seen, the philosophy of Plato in its Augustinian guise. But during these same centuries the study of Aristotle had continued in non-Latin eastern Christendom, in the monasteries of Syria. In the seventh and eighth centuries several Syrian translations of Aristotle's writings appeared. During the Moslem conquests, Arabian scholars came into contact with Aristotle through the conquered Syrians, and by the end of the ninth century all Aristotle's work had been translated into Arabic. Finally, in the late twelfth and the thirteenth centuries the Latin scholars of western Europe were introduced to Aristotle through his Arabian commentators, and translations were now made of his writings from Arabic into Latin.

The Arabian versions of Aristotelianism were shot through and through with Platonism and especially with that form of Platonism developed by *Plotinus,* the last of the great Greek pagan philosophers. Plotinus lived in the third century A.D. He and his followers are known in history as the *Neoplatonists.* One of their purposes was the reconciliation of Plato and Aristotle. These two masters, they said, were not in fact opposed to each other, but rather they viewed reality at different levels: Aristotle on the level of sensible things and Plato on the level of intelligible being, or the Ideas. Taken together, their doctrines embrace all reality. In his highest speculations, for example when he treats of God, of the Intelligences which move the heavenly spheres, and of the active intellect, Aristotle, say the Neoplatonists, reaches the Platonic level of thought and his conclusions agree with those of Plato.

3. **Neoplatonism.** Although Plotinus maintained that his own philosophy contained nothing new and was only a unified statement of

Platonic and Aristotelian philosophy, he really advanced a highly original system of thought based upon Platonism and making generous use of Aristotelian terminology. This system is built around three realities or hypostases, namely, the One, the Nous, and the Soul, and a non-reality, namely, Matter. The fundamental principle of the system would seem to be that everything which contains within itself any multiplicity or diversity has its origin and its explanation in a higher unity. The highest unity of all, and the source of all being, is unity itself, that is, the One. This notion of the One, Plotinus got from Plato's conception of the Idea of the Good, which the latter had said is above all being and is the source of all being.

Everything that is, proceeds from the One by way of emanation, a sort of overflowing of the superabundance of the One by which it produces being. This emanation in no way affects the One itself, which preserves its own perfect unity. That which proceeds directly from the One is the Nous; the Nous is Intelligence, or the World of Ideas. It is the Intelligibles or Being, and it is Contemplation. It is a world of intelligible beings, each of which, in thinking itself, thinks all the others, so that all form one unique Intelligence. The Nous of Plotinus is Plato's World of Ideas regarded as self-knowing. It has a less perfect unity than the One, because in its unity there is distinction of the intelligible and intelligence, even though these are the same reality.

As the Nous proceeds eternally from the One, so the World-Soul proceeds eternally from the Nous. The World-Soul, as it were, faces two ways: it contemplates the Nous whence it emanates; and it animates, orders, and directs the world of sense. The other element that makes up the world of sense is Matter. Matter is non-being; it is the product of the final dissipation of the stream of being which emanates from the One. It is related to being as darkness is to light. As darkness is what remains at the extremity of the light's emanation, so matter is what remains at the extremity of the emanation of being; as the rays of light dwindle finally off into darkness, so the stream of being dwindles finally off into matter. Sensible things, or nature, are the reflections of being (i.e., the Ideas) thrown back from the screen of non-being or matter.

Matter, being the opposite and negation of the One or the Good, is evil; it is not merely bad, but is Evil itself. Evil, however, since it is matter, is a mere negation. Man is a composite of matter and the soul.

Man's soul is immaterial, produced from the World-Soul, and is united to the body as a punishment for its tendency toward things of sense. It is immortal, but it may be reincarnated if it is not free from all attraction to matter. Escape from matter is escape from evil. Consequently, happiness can be attained only by the soul's withdrawal from all preoccupation with the body and sensible things.

To attain salvation, therefore, the soul must turn its attention away from the body and bodily desires and contemplate itself. In contemplating itself, it will be drawn on to the contemplation of the higher unity which is its own source, namely, the World-Soul. From this it will be raised to contemplation of the Nous, whence the World-Soul emanated. Finally, it will be raised to ecstatic union with the ineffable One. This last union is not one of knowledge, for in knowledge there is distinction, while in the One there is only perfect unity; in the ecstatic union the soul transcends knowledge and becomes one with the One.

Such was the philosophy which Plotinus claimed to be Aristotelianism restated on a higher level of thought. How a good deal of it was taken to be authentic Aristotelianism by the medieval Arabian philosophers is an interesting story.

4. Aristotle and the Arabians. In the sixth century there appeared a treatise called *Theologia Aristotelis,* which, it was claimed, was an original work of Aristotle just rediscovered. In a preface, "Aristotle" writes that this work is the crown of all his philosophy. The same preface restates the Aristotelian doctrine of the four causes[4] in such a way as to identify these causes with the four hypostases of Plotinus: the final cause is the One or God, the formal cause is the Nous or the Ideas, the efficient cause is the Soul, and the material cause is nature or matter; and then "Aristotle" goes on to state that the purpose of the work is to show how these causes are generated from God. In truth, the *Theologia Aristotelis* was actually made up of excerpts from the *Enneads* of Plotinus, but it was translated in the ninth century into Arabic as an authentic work of Aristotle.

Along with the above work, another Neoplatonic book was accepted as Aristotle's own writing. This was the famous *De Causis,* which is really a translation of the *Elements of Theology* of Proclus, the greatest disciple of Plotinus, and which is concerned with the nature and properties of the One, the Nous, and the Soul. With these two works

---

[4] See Chapter IV.

as guides, the Arabian interpretation of Aristotle was inevitably strongly Neoplatonistic. An example will make this clear. An early Arabian philosopher, Al Farabi, wrote a work called the *Harmony of Plato and Aristotle*. Wherever he came upon apparent disharmony, he cleared it away by recourse to the doctrine of the *Theologia Aristotelis*. Thus, for example, this book gave him authority for showing that Aristotle did not deny the World of Ideas even though he states in the *Physics* that the only substances are individuals.

In this way the Arabian interpretation of Aristotle was dominated by two books which were really the work of the two greatest Neoplatonists. Especially lending themselves to such interpretation, and thus becoming the heart of Arabian Aristotelianism, were Book V of Aristotle's *Metaphysics,* Book VIII of the *Physics*, where the Stagirite gives the doctrine of the intelligences which move the heavenly spheres, and Book III of the *De Anima*, where he treats of thought and propounds his famous and puzzling doctrine of the agent intellect.[5]

5. St. Thomas and the Real Aristotelianism. In the thirteenth century the Aristotelian systems of two great Arabian philosophers, Avicenna and Averroes, became very widely known among the philosophers of western Europe. These systems were taken, most generally, as being pure Aristotelianism. In many respects they were opposed to Catholic faith. The philosophy of Averroes, for example, denied the creation of the world by God, the doctrine of divine providence, the freedom of the human will, the immortality of the soul, and taught that there is but one rational soul for all men. Some Catholic philosophers followed the Averroistic system and sought to escape the charge of heresy by proclaiming the doctrine of the double truth, namely, that what was true philosophically might be false theologically; a doctrine, by the way, which they derived from Averroes himself. Others, the greater number, simply rejected Aristotelianism because of its obvious errors and its heretical doctrines, and clung to Augustinian Platonism. St. Thomas followed neither course. He perceived three facts: first, that the Arabian versions of the Aristotelianism were not in truth the philosophy of Aristotle; second, that although Aristotle had made some serious errors himself, these could be corrected; and finally, that the real Aristotelianism, stripped of its errors, was the truest system of natural knowledge which the world had ever seen, and would be,

---

[5] The above account of the neoplatonizing of Aristotle is taken from Bréhier. *La Philosophie du Moyen Age* (Paris: Albin Michel, 1937), pp. 83–87.

therefore, a far better servant of Catholic doctrine than Platonism, which was fundamentally wrong in its attitude toward nature and knowledge. He set himself, therefore, the tremendous task of rediscovering the real Aristotle, of pruning the Aristotelian philosophy of its errors while preserving its truth, and of pressing this truth into the service of Catholic theology.

IV. SCHOLASTIC PHILOSOPHY

Thomistic philosophy is one system of Scholastic philosophy. The philosophy taught in the universities (i.e., the "schools") during the Middle Ages came to be known as *Scholastic philosophy*. Later on, when modern philosophy broke away from the great stream of traditional philosophy, those who continued to teach the doctrines of the great medievals were known as Scholastics. The term Scholastic philosophy is almost equivalent to Catholic philosophy, since it is the philosophy taught, by papal rescript, in Catholic colleges and seminaries. However, in every age there have been first-rate Catholic thinkers who have not adhered to Scholasticism. (There is, of course, no question of their adherence to Catholic doctrine; to believe in revealed truths you do not have to believe in any philosopher's explanation of their metaphysical foundations or implications.) The greatest masters of Scholasticism besides St. Thomas were St. Bonaventure, the great champion of Augustinianism, and Duns Scotus, who embodied in his philosophy both Augustinian and Aristotelian elements. The former was a contemporary of St. Thomas and the latter half a century his junior; both were Franciscans. A few centuries later a Jesuit, Francisco Suarez, added still another system to these great Scholastic philosophies. In our own day Scholasticism, and especially Thomism, has many outstanding representatives, and their number constantly grows. The present great revival of Thomistic thought is very largely due to, besides purely philosophical reasons, the encyclical[6] of Pope Leo XIII on Scholastic and especially Thomistic theology and philosophy, and to the great work, both organizational and philosophical, of Cardinal Mercier of the University of Louvain. The rebirth of wide interest in St. Thomas has led also to a reawakening of interest in the other great ancient Scholastics, so that during the past three or four decades, research into the writings and the significance of St. Bonaventure,

[6] *Aeterni Patris,* August 4, 1879.

Duns Scotus, and other medieval thinkers has increased immeasurably over all that was done for centuries preceding.

Hardly a field of human interest has been left untouched by the Scholastic revival. Metaphysics, epistemology, psychology, were perhaps the first fields where this new-old force made itself felt; but from these it spread out to the criticism of the arts, the philosophy of law, and to all areas where philosophy is pertinent. At present, the politico-social-economic sphere is perhaps receiving the fullest impact of Thomistic thought, with the problem of the nature of knowledge in the natural sciences and its relation to philosophy coming next. This latter problem offers to Thomists and to philosophers generally their greatest challenge today; it would appear that the progress of philosophy depends upon its solution. A satisfactory solution would be itself a major step forward in human thought, and would open the way to many other roads that seem to be impassable as long as the problem is not solved.[7]

V. THE DIVISIONS OF PHILOSOPHY

1. Aristotle — and St. Thomas followed him in this — divided science into three main kinds: speculative, practical, and productive. Speculative science has as its primary end or aim knowledge itself; practical science is directed to action; and productive science to the making or production of things for man's use or enjoyment, for example, statues, houses, poems, plays. He then distinguishes three speculative sciences: physics, which studies sensible things inasmuch as they are movable; mathematics, which studies them inasmuch as they possess quantity; and metaphysics, called first philosophy or theology by Aristotle, which studies non-sensible or immaterial being. Of the many practical sciences, Aristotle considered one supreme, namely, politics (or statecraft). The productive sciences are several, including all the arts and crafts, but we are not interested in them from the point of view of philosophy.

Natural science and philosophy were not clearly distinguished in Aristotle's day, and consequently his division as he gave it would include under mathematics both the various mathematical sciences and the philosophy of mathematics, and under physics both the various natural sciences and what we call today the philosophy of nature.

---

[7] The problem of science and philosophy will arise frequently throughout the present text, and is studied explicitly in Chapters VII and XIX.

Accordingly, in order to use his division of science as a division of philosophy we have to make certain changes in it, omitting all those sciences that are sciences in the modern sense of that term, and retaining only those divisions of knowledge that are concerned with first causes.

Aristotle's third division, productive science, is omitted altogether from a division of philosophy, and we have two chief branches: theoretical (or speculative) philosophy and practical philosophy. Theoretical philosophy aims at knowledge of reality for the sake of knowledge itself; practical philosophy seeks the knowledge for the sake of directing human action. Hence, the ultimate goal of speculative philosophy is Truth, or the True; while the ultimate goal of practical philosophy is the Good. Theoretical philosophy has three parts: the philosophy of nature, the philosophy of mathematics, and metaphysics or first philosophy. Practical philosophy is one science, ethics, and politics is a part of ethics.

2. Theoretical Philosophy. The object of theoretical philosophy is the *being* of things. It is the object that distinguishes theoretical philosophy from the various special sciences, which study selected properties, operations, and relations of things. The first two parts of theoretical philosophy, the philosophy of nature and the philosophy of mathematics, study the being of sensible things in so far as they are sensible. Hence, these two parts of philosophy study the being of material things or bodies. These two branches of philosophy are distinguished from each other by their respective *formal* objects. Body, or material substance, may be considered dynamically or statically; that is, as a moving, dynamic part of the physical universe, or as simply possessing the primary characters of body — quantity, extension, and number. The philosophy of nature considers body in the first way, and has as its formal object corporeal being in so far as it is mobile or dynamic; hence it studies the nature of mobile being. The philosophy of mathematics considers body in the second way, and has as its formal object corporeal being in so far as it is quantified; hence it studies the nature of quantity, extension, and number.

Metaphysics or first philosophy is distinguished from both the former parts of philosophy because its object is not the being of sensible things, but being as such or immaterial being. The expression "immaterial being" may be taken in two senses. It can mean: (1) Being that can exist indifferently either in matter or separate from

matter. Examples of such being are being-as-such, substance and accident, potential being and actual being, contingent and necessary
being, unity, truth, goodness, beauty, causality, knowledge; (2) Being
that is necessarily separate from matter, and which we call spiritual
being.

Metaphysics studies immaterial being in both these senses. In its
study of being-as-such, the primary divisions of being-as-such (viz.,
substance and accident, potentiality and actuality, contingency and
necessity, cause and effect), and the transcendental attributes of being
(viz., unity, truth, goodness, and beauty), it is called general metaphysics or ontology. In its study of spiritual being and knowledge, it
is called special metaphysics, and has two divisions: natural theology,
or the rational study of God; and epistemology, or the critical study
of knowledge.

3. **Practical Philosophy.** Practical philosophy, the part of philosophy
that aims at action, is called ethics. Ethics has as its ultimate object
the Good; and its function is to establish the principles of right human
action, that is to say, the principles that direct human conduct so that
man will attain the good proper to him as a man. Hence, ethics

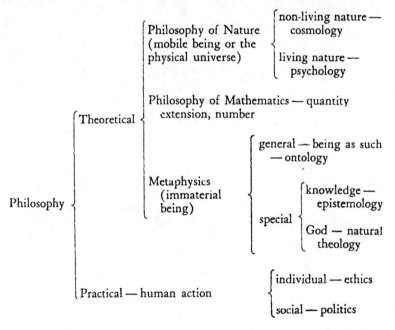

studies the final end of man, the means that he has for attaining this end, and the principles that must govern his use of these means so that he will in fact attain this end.

Adopting this Aristotelian scheme of the philosophical sciences, and modifying it somewhat in order to adapt it to more modern terminology, we may represent the divisions of philosophy in the outline on page 59.

PART TWO

NATURE AND MAN

CHAPTER IV

THE PRINCIPLES OF NATURE

I. THE PHILOSOPHY OF NATURE

1. **Definition.** Philosophy begins in wonder, as Aristotle wrote, and we first wonder about the things that are closest at hand. Hence it is that the philosophy of nature is historically as well as logically the first part of philosophy; for it was with the inquiry into the nature of the physical world that philosophy had its birth. The first philosophers sought, as we have seen, to know of what stuff the world is made.

The term *nature* has many different meanings, but the philosopher of nature takes the word in its two most general senses: (1) the principle or root within a thing of its activity or movement; (2) the total universe of material (i.e., sensible) things. These two meanings of nature determine the object of the philosophy of nature. The *material object* is the totality of beings that man sensibly experiences; the *formal object* is the first principle of movement in sensible beings, or, in other words, the essence of mobile being.

Sensible being, as used above, means being that man can perceive by his senses, that is to say, that he can see, hear, feel, measure, etc. It is contrasted with non-sensible being, which means being that cannot be perceived by the senses, that cannot be seen, heard, felt, measured, etc. Bodies, physical forces and energies, weights, colors, temperatures, shapes, odors, flavors, etc., are sensible beings. Ideas, decisions, virtues, ideals, souls, angels, God, etc., are non-sensible beings. Roughly, the term sensible is equivalent to material, and the term non-sensible to immaterial.

Mobile or changeable being means being capable of movement. Movement involves materiality, and consequently it may be said generally that sensible or material being is mobile, while immaterial or non-sensible being is immobile. To avoid misconception on this

63

point, two words of caution are necessary. First, immobile does not mean inactive; indeed, mobility and activity in beings vary in inverse ratio. Second, an immaterial being though in itself immobile, may be accidentally movable in virtue of its relation to a material being. Man's soul, for example, is immobile *per se* but mobile *per accidens* because of its relation to man's body. Hence its study falls in part under the philosophy of nature.

The philosophy of nature may now be defined as the study of the first principles of sensible being considered as mobile. It has, therefore, two primary objects of study, motion or change and the being that moves or changes. Since it is most obviously the physical or corporeal substances of nature that move or change, two of the primary problems of the philosophy of nature are: What is the essence of change (or motion)? What is the essence of corporeal substance? After these primary problems come a host of others, some of great importance to man.

2. Scope. The bodies that make up nature present themselves to man's experience as divided into two distinct classes: non-living bodies and living bodies. Animate nature offers itself to man's experience quite as directly as inanimate nature, and consequently a new set of problems present themselves for the philosopher's inquiry: What is life? What is the principle of life in a living being?

Living bodies themselves present clear distinctions to experience: life manifests itself on three different levels. There are living bodies which do not possess the power of sensation, living bodies that do possess this power, and living bodies, namely, men, that possess in addition to life and sensation, another power, thought. Wherefore, the philosopher of nature finds a new set of questions: Are these apparent differences among living bodies truly essential differences? Must we postulate distinct life-principles in order to account for these three levels of life? The peculiarity of thought or reason possessed by man raises especially difficult and important problems: Is the principle of thought in man the same as man's life-principle? Can the thought-principle be properly considered part of material nature at all, or must it be classed among spiritual beings? If it is spiritual, how can the spiritual and the material be united in one being? In seeking to answer these questions the philosopher of nature has reached the upper limits of his inquiry and is knocking at the gates of metaphysics.

The study of motion, too, gives rise to many more questions. Some of these occupy the very border line between the philosophy of nature and metaphysics. Is the motion of nature self-sufficient and self-explanatory, or is nature itself moved from outside? If every motion in nature is motion toward some end, does it follow that nature as a whole moves toward an end? Is purpose a principle of nature? If it is, is it within nature or from outside? Everything in nature changes; does nature itself change? Do natures evolve or develop into new natures? Natural motion is according to law: then is everything in nature necessary? Is there any place in nature for contingency (i.e., non-necessity)? Is freedom possible within nature?

The purpose of the present chapter is to give an over-all view of the primary principles of nature as these are demonstrated in the Aristotelian-Thomistic philosophy of nature. Subsequent chapters will give fuller treatment to the various principles touched upon here.

II. MATTER, FORM, AND PRIVATION

1. Aristotle prefaces his inquiry into Nature by a criticism of the doctrines of his predecessors. He recognizes and preserves whatever of the truth they had attained, and carefully points out their error where he thinks that they have departed from the truth.[1] The same critique is repeated more fully at the beginning of the *Metaphysics* (I, 2–10).

What the philosopher of nature must seek first is the first principle or principles of nature:

> When the objects of an inquiry, in any department, have principles, conditions, or elements, it is through acquaintance with these that knowledge, that is to say scientific knowledge, is attained. For we do not think that we know a thing until we are acquainted with its primary conditions or first principles, and have carried our analysis as far as its simplest elements. Plainly therefore in the science of Nature, as in other branches of study, our first task will be to try to determine what relates to its principles.[2]

2. **The Contraries.** All the previous philosophers had agreed in making *contraries* first principles: e.g., the hot and the cold, the rare and the dense, the full and the void, the straight and the round. Now none of these named may actually be first principles, but the

[1] Aristotle, *Phys.*, I, 2–4.
[2] *Ibid.*, I, 1.

idea that some contraries are first principles is a valid one. "For first principles must not be derived from one another nor from anything else, while everything has to be derived from them. But these conditions are fulfilled by the primary contraries, which are not derived from anything else because they are primary, nor from each other because they are contraries."[3]

We can reason to this same conclusion in another way. That from which a thing is generated must lack the nature of the thing generated, for otherwise that thing would already have existed and would not in fact be generated. A thing, therefore, is generated out of its opposite or contrary: water, to *become* hot, must first have been not-hot; that which *becomes* a tree or a house must first not have been a tree or a house. Consequently, *every* generation involves contraries, and therefore some contraries must be first principles.[4]

3. The Substratum. Contraries make two first principles to begin with, but there must be more than two. For contraries cannot act upon each other, but only upon some third thing; for example, hot does not make cold hot, but it makes *something* cold hot. Furthermore, contraries are never substances, since a substance has no opposite, but rather attributes or predicates of substances. Now a substance cannot be derived from a predicate, but is presupposed to the predicate; wherefore, substance cannot be derived from the contraries. Nor could the contraries themselves exist unless they were in a substance, since attributes depend on a substance; for example, neither hot nor cold can exist in itself, but only *in something* which is hot or cold. But both substances and contraries do exist and are generated; and therefore we must assume besides the primary contraries some primary substance which is their substratum and like them a first principle.[5]

Hence, Aristotle goes on to say, we find that in all cases of becoming or change "there must always be an underlying substance, namely that which becomes, and that this, though always one numerically, in form at least is not one."[6] "Plainly then, if there are conditions and principles which constitute natural objects and from which they primarily are or have come to be — have come to be, I mean, what each is said to be in its essential nature, not what each is in respect of a concomitant attribute — plainly, I say, everything

---

[3] *Ibid.*, I, 5.
[4] *Ibid.*, I, 5.
[5] *Ibid.*, I, 6.
[6] *Ibid.*, I, 7, 190a. 14–15.

comes to be from both subject and form."[7] Therefore, the number of the first principles of natural objects which are subject to generation are three, for "it is clear that there must be a substratum for the contraries, and that the contraries must be two."[8] The contraries, however, need not be two in the sense of two distinct positive forms, for one contrary will serve to effect the change by its successive absence and presence.[9]

4. Matter, Form, and Privation. At various places in this argument Aristotle gives to the substratum or substance the name matter, to the contrary regarded as present in the matter the name form, and to the absence of this form from the matter the name privation. We may now briefly restate his argument, using these expressions which he himself adopts as technical terms. There are three primary principles of natural substances: viz., *matter* (the substratum), *form* (the contraries), *privation* (the lack of some form in the matter). In every change some matter lacking a certain form acquires that form. For example, water (matter) which is not hot (privation) becomes hot (form); or elements (matter) which are not a tree (privation) are combined in nature to become a tree (form). Throughout the change the matter persists, having first one form and then another. Wherefore, Aristotle defines matter as "the primary substratum of each thing, from which it comes to be without qualification, and which persists in the result."[10] The form, on the other hand, does not persist but in every change a form is replaced by its contrary, or to say the same thing from a different point of view, replaces its contrary.

This analysis of change solves the difficulties of the earlier philosophers and does away with the paradox of Parmenides. That philosopher had maintained that being cannot come to be either from being or from not-being, and that therefore change or coming-to-be is impossible. Aristotle has now shown that nothing comes to be *simply* from being or *simply* from non-being. Rather it comes from something which is at once relative being and relative not-being, namely, a substratum with a privation. This substratum is being inasmuch as it is something; and it is non-being inasmuch as it is not the being that comes from it, since it lacks the form of that being. In a word, a thing comes to be from that which is it *in potentiality* but not *in actuality*.[11]

[7] *Ibid.*, 190b, 16–20.
[8] *Ibid.*, 191a, 4–8.
[9] *Loc. cit.*

[10] *Ibid.*, 1, 9, 192a, 30–31.
[11] *Ibid.*, 1, 8.

III. / POTENTIALITY AND ACTUALITY[12]

1. The last sentence above introduces us to one of the central doctrines of Aristotle's physics and metaphysics: the division of being into actual being and potential being.

Parmenides started from two abstract concepts, being and not-being, and concluded, against all experience, that change is impossible. Aristotle starts from the *fact* of change as given in experience and works out the implications of that fact. Changes occur, and in every change something comes to be from something else, or becomes something else: there is the fact. Its first implication is that before the change, the being from which the change started not only was what it was, but was also able to become something else. Every being, therefore, that is capable of changing *is* something and at the same time *has the capacity* for being something else. What a thing *is,* Aristotle calls *actuality;* its capacity to become something else, he calls *potentiality.* Actual being is that which is; potential being is that which can be.

2. **Reality of Potency and Act.** This division of being is of primary importance. Whatever is in any way subject to change is a compound of potentiality and actuality; such a thing is actual since it exists, and it is in some respect potential since it can change. Everything that comes within our experience, that is to say every natural object, is subject to change; wherefore, every natural object is a mixture of potency and act. If there is any being that is *pure actuality,* that being will not be in nature but will transcend nature; such a being will not be material, because matter is the very substratum and first subject of change and hence is the very root of potentiality. Indeed, if we can prove that there does exist a being which is pure actuality, we shall have to call that being God. But we must leave that discussion for another place.

Potentiality (or *potency*) is real; it is not merely another name for not-being — Aristotle is not simply juggling words. You cannot get blood out of a stone and you cannot make a silk purse out of a sow's ear, because there is no blood in a stone and no silk in a sow's ear either actually or potentially. An acorn can become an oak tree because it is an oak tree potentially; it cannot become an elm because it simply is not an elm, either actually or potentially. Neither a blind man nor

---

[12] *Ibid.,* I, 9; *Meta.,* V, 7; *Meta.,* IX.

a normal man *actually* sees in the dark, but the normal man *potentially* sees, and that is something very real.

IV. SUBSTANCE AND ACCIDENT

1. Intimated throughout the above arguments, and connected closely with his theory of hylemorphism explained below, is Aristotle's doctrine of substance and accident. That which possesses being fully and completely — that which exists *in itself,* as water, or a tree, or a man — is called *substance.* It is clear that such existence is not the only type of existence. Water may be hot or cold, a tree may be green or brown, a man may be sick or healthy, but coldness, greenness, health, are not things existing in themselves. Without doubt they possess being, but they possess it *in something else.* It is of their nature to inhere in another, to be a quality, a determination of the being of something else. Such determinations Aristotle calls *accidents.* A substance may be briefly defined as a being that exists in itself or that has separate existence. An accident may be defined as a being that has no separate existence but which exists by inhering in another. In ordinary speech, things and persons are substances; while quantities, qualities, relations, appearances, actions, conditions, etc., are accidents.

2. **Substantial and Accidental Change.** In a further analysis of change, Aristotle distinguishes between substantial change (generation and corruption, i.e., coming into being and passing out of being) and various types of accidental change (qualitative change, increase and decrease, movement). In a substantial change the substratum that undergoes the change acquires a new nature, becomes a different kind of thing. Food that we eat, for example, loses its nature and becomes part of our body tissue; water submitted to electrolysis turns from water into hydrogen and oxygen. In an accidental change, the substratum remains itself throughout the change and merely acquires new accidental modifications. For example, water that is boiled remains water though it passes from a liquid to a vaporous state.

V. HYLEMORPHISM

Aristotle's quest for the first principles of nature is carried further in Book II of the *Physics,* and here he enunciates two more of his primary teachings, the doctrine of hylemorphism and the doctrine of the four causes.

Hylemorphism is the theory of matter (*hyle*) and form (*morphe*). It states that every natural substance, that is, every complete material substance, is a composite of two essential intrinsic principles, one a principle of potentiality, viz., primary matter, and the other a principle of actuality, viz., substantial form. This doctrine, first formulated by Aristotle, remains today one of the major theories of the constitution of natural bodies, and nearly all Scholastic philosophers maintain that it is the only adequate theory.

The primary proof of hylemorphism is based upon the fact of substantial change, and is simply the amplification of Aristotle's previous analysis of change. The negative principle, privation, is dropped out of the picture and the two positive principles, the substratum or matter, and the form, are more precisely defined. They are now presented as the *intrinsic* principles of change, and the account of change is completed by the introduction of two *extrinsic* principles, the agent or efficient cause and the end or final cause. Thus the doctrine of hylemorphism and that of the four causes are so closely related as to be in fact two sides of the same theory of nature.

VI. THE FOUR CAUSES: MATERIAL, FORMAL, EFFICIENT, AND FINAL

1. Aristotle's doctrine of cause in nature recapitulates his teaching on all the topics studied above — potentiality and actuality, substance and accident, hylemorphism and motion. What the philosopher of nature is seeking is knowledge or understanding of nature. There are, Aristotle finds, four primary kinds of causes, and no natural thing or event is understood unless all the four causes bringing it about are known. He enumerates and describes these four kinds of causes in many places, for example, in *Physics*, II, 3, and II, 7; in *Metaphysics*, I, 3, and II, 2.

These four types of principle have received the names *material, formal, efficient,* and *final* cause. A thing, in order to be produced, needs first of all something out of which it is produced, something which is made into it, as wood is made into a desk. This cause is the material cause, or the matter. The matter alone, however, cannot become the thing unless it receives a certain form, nature, or pattern. The wood must receive a certain shape and structure in order to become a desk. The structure or pattern is the formal cause, or the form. Wood does not of itself take the shape of a desk; something or someone must act so as to impart the proper shape to it. This third cause which moves the matter to receive the form of the thing to be produced is the efficient cause; for example, the desk maker is the efficient cause of a desk. Finally, even given the matter, the form and the efficient cause, this particular effect will not be produced rather than some other, indeed the efficient cause will not even begin to act at all, unless there is some end or goal aimed at in the process, something "for the sake of which" the whole process takes place. In our example the desk considered as a good-to-be-attained is the end, and it is this end which determines the activity of the three prior causes. The end or good-to-be-attained is the final cause (from *finis,* end).

2. **Intrinsic and Extrinsic Causes.** The efficient and final causes are extrinsic and the material and formal causes intrinsic to the effect produced. An extrinsic cause is one that produces an effect but is not an element or constituent part of the effect when it has been produced. Intrinsic causes produce the effect and also enter into it as constituent parts. A sculptor is an extrinsic cause of a statue; marble is an intrinsic cause. The form of the statue pre-existing in the artist's intellect and will as the end to be attained by his work is an extrinsic cause; the same form realized in the marble is an intrinsic cause.[13]

3. **Analytic Deduction of the Four Causes.** In commenting on Aristotle's fourfold division of causality, St. Thomas shows that the four kinds of causes can be analytically deduced from the nature of any production of being, without recourse to illustrations taken from art:

> There must of necessity be four causes: because when a cause exists, upon which the being of another thing follows, the being of that which has the cause may be considered in two ways. First, absolutely; and in this way the cause of being is a form by which something is a being-in-act. Second, insofar as an actual being comes to be from a potential being; and because whatever is in potency is reduced to act by something that is being-in-act, it follows of necessity that there are two other causes, namely the matter and the agent that reduces the matter from potency to act. But the action of an agent tends to something determinate, just as it proceeds from some determinate principle, for every agent does what is in conformity with its nature. That to which the action of the agent tends is called the final cause. Thus there are necessarily four causes.[14]

[13] *Meta.,* XII, 4.
[14] *In II Phys.,* lect. 10.

In the above selection St. Thomas is answering the question, what conditions are requisite for something to come to be? He finds four necessary conditions. (1) What comes into being must be something of a determinate nature, and hence must have a *form* determining that nature. (2) What comes into being must come from something which was it potentially. This is *matter*. (3) For the matter to pass from potentially being the product to actually being it, it must be moved by an agent in act. This is the *efficient cause*. (4) This efficient cause, in moving the matter to actuality, must tend in its action toward something determinate befitting its own determinate nature. That to which it tends is the *final* cause. Wherefore, in every production of being these four causes must be present.

4. The Ways of Causing. Cause, "that which contributes positively to the production of anything," is obviously an analogical and not a univocal concept, that is to say, it is applied to each of the four types of cause in senses which are not precisely the same. Each cause, the material, formal, efficient, and final, exerts a positive influence in bringing the effect to pass, but each exerts a different influence.

The explanation in sections 5 to 9 below will be easily understood if the following illustration is kept in mind: In a United States mint a disk of silver is struck on one side by a die which gives it a certain figure or impression, let us say, the head of George Washington, and on the other side by another die which stamps it with the impression of the American eagle, and so it becomes a twenty-five cent piece, or a quarter. The effect is the finished quarter. The material cause is the silver: it contributes to the production of the effect by undergoing a change in which it receives the impressions. The formal cause is the impressions: these produce the effect by being received in the silver and communicating a new character to it. The efficient cause is the two dies: they produce the effect by communicating the impressions to the silver, or, in other words, by inducing the form in the matter. The final cause, which starts the whole operation going, is the quarter to be produced: it produces the finished quarter by being the goal toward which the whole process was aimed. Now let us analyze in technical terms precisely what the causal influence of each of the four kinds of cause is.

5. Material Causality. The material cause contributes to the production of the effect by assuming a new form induced in it by the action of the efficient cause. The causality of the material cause is exerted, therefore, not through any action of the matter but through its "passion," which is the reverse side of the action of the efficient cause. The latter as agent moves the former as patient to the actuality of the effect. The one movement is the action in the efficient cause and passion in the material cause.[15] The matter is truly a cause of the effect since the movement which eventuates in the effect is quite as impossible without a patient moved as it is without an agent moving, and because the agent could not actualize the form of the effect in the matter unless the matter itself possessed, and contributed to the process, the requisite potentiality for receiving that form. Matter, therefore, is an actual cause by suffering or undergoing a change at the hands of an efficient cause. It causes, but not by acting, since it is by essence passive. "Action is the act of what is active and passion is the act of what is passive," wrote St. Thomas,[16] and, "matter does not become a cause in act except inasmuch as it is altered and changed."[17]

6. **Formal Causality.** The formal cause contributes to the production of the effect by communicating its own determination intrinsically to the matter, forming it actually into the effect which of itself the matter is only potentially; thus it causes the effect by forming actually in the matter and with the matter what the matter of itself is only potentially, namely, the effect. The causality of the form is neither action nor passion but specification or determination; the formal cause is, as Aristotle calls it, a formula. It does not *do* anything any more than the precise formula of a chef's recipe, or the relations between notes in a harmony do anything, if by *doing* is meant acting. But by virtue of its union with the matter, the effect is produced and exists.

7. **Efficient Causality.** The efficient cause, the principle of movement in some other thing, contributes to the production of the effect by acting upon the matter and moving it from potential possession of the form to actual possession of it. Its causality is exerted in action, and the formal effect of this action is the induction in the matter of a form which the agent itself possesses in some way; or, more precisely, the induction of that form which determines the agent in its character of efficient cause. The matter possesses this form potentially, but in order to possess it actually it must be moved by an agent which does

[15] Aristotle, *Phys.*, III, 3; St. Thomas, *In III Phys.*, lect. 5.
[16] *In III Phys.*, lect. 5.
[17] *Con. Gen.*, I, 17.

possess it actually. In any movement the agent is the mover in precisely that respect in which the patient is moved; the motion is at once the actuality of agent and of patient — the action of the agent and the passion of the patient. Prior to the motion, the agent has the power to act and the patient the potentiality for being acted upon. The motion is the single actuality of these two potencies.[18] Therefore, in every movement the mover is moving the patient in precisely the same respect in which the patient is being moved; obviously what the agent *does* must be what the patient *gets done to it*.

This means that the form that is being brought to actuality in the patient (i.e., the matter) is the same form by which the agent (i.e., the efficient cause) is acting upon the patient. This form is said to be "educed from the potency of the matter." This does not conflict with the statement that it is induced in the matter by the action of the efficient cause communicating its own form. The form is not a concrete something that is transferred from agent to patient. It is, in the agent, a specificative principle determining its nature, power, and operation. It is communicated to the patient inasmuch as the action of the agent on the patient produces a determinate effect conforming to the form of the agent. This effect, the new form of the patient, could not be produced in the patient unless the latter had the potentiality for assuming that new form. Hence, it is quite true to say that "the form is educed from the potency of the matter."

8. Final Causality. The final cause exerts its influence as a good attracting the efficient cause to perform an operation for the sake of realizing this good. It must not be thought of as an efficient cause which acts upon a subject. It causes, not by existing and acting, but by being intended or desired.[19] It is an end-to-be-attained, not an end-attained; the end-attained is an effect; the end as cause is the end-intended. For example, the presidency desired is the final cause of the candidate's activities up to election day; the presidency attained is the effect of those activities. Scholastics call the end-attained the *finis in executione;* it comes last and is an effect. They call the end-desired the *finis in intentione;* it comes first and is a cause.

Final causality is very easy to understand in reference to conscious agents like ourselves. We conceive of something as good, it attracts us, we desire to attain it, and we then begin to act in ways suitable for

[18] Aristotle, *Phys.*, III, 3; St. Thomas, *In III Phys.*, lect. 5
[19] *De Ver.*, XXII, 2.

attaining it. Such causality is the stuff of our daily lives. A student goes to college to win a degree, a nation trains and arms men for the purpose of conquering an enemy, a missionary leaves his home and native land in order to bring the word of God to pagans. The student, the nation, the missionary are efficient causes of the effects which they produce; the degree, the victory, the spreading of the Gospel are the final causes.

But if final causality operates by attracting the agent to attain it as a good, how can it be maintained that it operates in nature, that is, in the field of non-conscious agents? It can hardly be said that an acorn *desires* to become a mighty oak. Mechanists deny that final causality plays any part in natural processes, and they label as anthropomorphism the belief that it does. Scholastic philosophers and teleologists in general maintain that final causes do operate in nature, because (1) their operation is quite evident, and (2) we cannot explain the effects that occur in nature without attributing them to final causes. They do not maintain that natural agents, such as inanimate bodies and plants, have any knowledge of the ends toward which their actions are directed or any conscious desire for those ends, but they do maintain that these agents do nevertheless tend toward these ends by their natures. "All things in their own manners are inclined by appetite toward the good, but each in a different manner. For certain ones are inclined toward the good solely by natural disposition without knowledge, such as plants and inanimate bodies; and such an inclination to the good is called natural appetite."[20]

At this point we are not trying to *prove* final causality in nature, but simply to explain what is meant by it. But enough proof must be indicated to make clear why we hold that it does in fact operate in natural processes. The regular, orderly, and beneficial character of the activities of physical agents inescapably implies in them natures which tend to their own development and so operate as to attain goods which perfect them. This can be readily seen in the growth of any seed into a mature plant, in the development of any egg into an adult animal, in the instinctive acts by which animals provide, as if with conscious foresight, for their own lives and those of their progeny, in the photosynthetic process by which green plants manufacture their food and maintain their growth, in the special processes in both plants and animals by which injuries to the organism are repaired, in the subordina-

[20] *S. Theol.*, I, q. 49, a. 1.

tion of the separate parts of any organism to the life of the whole. Natural agents regularly act *as if* they apprehended the goods of their own natures and consciously tended toward them. *How* they do so, lacking consciousness, or at any rate intellect, we may not be able to say. But that there are goods suitable to their natures and that they do in fact regularly act so as to attain these goods cannot be denied. The next chapter will present formal proofs of the reality of final cause in nature.

9. Primacy of Final Cause. Among the four causes the final cause has the primacy — it is the cause of causes. It becomes a cause by influencing the efficient cause and thus initiating the action of the latter; and, as we have already seen, it is the action of the efficient cause that makes the material and formal causes actual causes.

> The efficient cause and the end are reciprocal because the agent is the beginning of the movement and the end its termination. So, too, are the matter and the form; for the form gives being and the matter receives it. Therefore, the agent is the cause of the end, but the end is also the cause of the agent. The agent is the cause of the end in regard to being, for the agent by moving brings it about that the end exists. But the end is the cause of the agent not in regard to being but in regard to the reason of causality. For the efficient cause is a cause insofar as it acts; but it does not act except thanks to an end. Wherefore, the agent has its causality from the end. . . .[21] It should be understood that although the end is last among things in being, it is always prior in causality; whence it is called the *cause of causes*, because it is the cause of causality in all the causes. For it is the cause of the causality of the agent, as shown above; and the agent is the cause of the causality of the matter and the form.[22]

10. Exemplary Cause. An exemplar is an ideal to be imitated, as, for example, Christ is our Exemplar. The being after which an effect is to be patterned, and the idea of the effect in the mind of the agent prior to its actual production, are often called exemplary causes. Thus the original of a portrait is the exemplary cause of the portrait; and the idea of the house in the mind of the builder is the exemplary cause of the house. Exemplary causality is not a fifth genus, but is variously reducible to formal, efficient, and final causality according as the exemplar is viewed (1) as the form considered apart from the matter, (2) as a form equipping the agent to act, or (3) as the representation of the end to be attained.

[21] *In V Meta.,* lect. 2, No. 775.
[22] *Ibid.,* lect. 3, No. 782. Cf. *De Principiis Naturae.*

VII. MOTION

1. "Nature," wrote Aristotle, "has been defined as a principle of motion and change, and it is the subject of our inquiry. We must therefore see that we understand the meaning of 'motion'; for if it were unknown, the meaning of 'nature' too would be unknown."[23] The question of the nature of motion or change is one of the most important questions in Thomistic philosophy. It is from the mobility or changeableness of nature that St. Thomas reasons to the contingency, or non-self-existence, of nature, and thence to the existence of God, the cause of nature, distinct from nature. It is characteristic of monism and naturalism, the two types of philosophy most opposed, at opposite extremes to Thomism, that they lack any real analysis of the nature of motion, the former denying its reality and the latter accepting it as an ultimate, unexplainable, brute fact.

When Aristotle and St. Thomas write of motion, they do not limit the meaning of the term to local motion, that is, motion through space from here to there; they intend by the term all real change from one terminus to another. Thus, not only would the movement of a baseball from pitcher to catcher be motion, but so also would the production of an oak from an acorn, the changing of water from hot to cold, the expansion of a column of mercury because of a rise in temperature, the building of a house, the learning of a scientific principle by a student. Local movement is only one of four kinds of motion: besides it there are substantial change (i.e., coming to be and passing away, or generation and corruption), qualitative change, and quantitative change.

2. **The Definition of Motion.** Aristotle[24] starts his analysis of motion by distinguishing three modes of being: (1) what exists in a state of actuality or fulfillment only, (2) what exists as potential, (3) what exists both as potential and as actual. He then points out that motion is not one of the genera or categories of being, but is something relative to each of the categories. For example, motion is not a quality, like hot and cold; but is relative to hot and cold, since it is the passage of something from hot to cold or vice versa. Next he gives a definition of motion, namely, the actuality of what exists potentially, in so far as it exists potentially, is motion.[25] For example,

[23] *Phys.*, III, 1.
[24] *Ibid.*
[25] *Ibid.*, 201a, 10.

the process of being built is the actuality of a house's potentiality to be built; the purely potential house is not a motion, for it is in potency only; the finished house is not a motion, for it is in actuality only; the *being built* of a house is a motion, for it is precisely the actuality of the house's potentiality for being built. "It is the fulfillment of what is potential when it is already fully real and operates not as *itself* but as *movable,* that is motion."[26] Thus, wood is combustible; its burning is motion because it is the fulfillment or actuality of this combustibility; the potentiality (combustibility) is fully real when the wood is burning. Before it burns, the wood has this potentiality, but the potentiality is not fully realized; the process of burning is its full realization, and is a motion; that is, it is the actuality of the potential as such. The burning is not the actuality of the wood as itself, but as combustible. Hence, it fits Aristotle's definition of motion: "[Motion] is the actuality of what is potential when it is already fully real and operates not as *itself* but as *movable . . .*"

3. Whatever Is in Motion Is Moved by Something Else. From this analysis of the nature of motion it follows that whatever is in motion is moved by something else. Aristotle presents arguments for this principle in *Physics,* VII, 1, and VIII, 4. The argument to be given now is based upon his, but does not follow it directly.

a) **Nothing Can Move Itself.** Movement is an incomplete actuality. It is the actuality or fulfillment of the potential as such: for example, the burning of wood is the actuality of the wood's combustibility; the process of being built is the actuality of the house as buildable; the motion of a body from one place to another is the actuality of the body's mobility in respect to place. No movement is a complete potentiality, for a complete potentiality is rest, that is, it is the point from which the motion starts: the combustibility of the wood is not motion, nor is the buildableness of a house, nor the mobility of a body. Nor is any movement complete actuality, for complete actuality is also rest, that is, it is the point at which the motion (if there has been a motion) has terminated: the ashes, the finished house, the body arrived at the new place — none of these is a motion. Every movement is an incomplete actuality, because the movement exists only so long as the potency of which it is the act is still being actualized; before the potency is at all actualized there is no motion, and when it is completely actualized, the motion has ceased.

[26] *Ibid.,* 201a, 28.

The traditional Scholastic argument for the principle *quidquid movetur ab alio movetur* runs as follows: Whatever is in motion, that is, whatever is in any way changing, is at each moment of its movement gaining a new actuality; the motion is the continuing actualization of the potential. Every motion, therefore, involves the actualizing of some potency. Consequently, everything that is in motion is in potency in some respect, and anything that moves something is in act in precisely that respect in which what it moves is in potency. Nothing, therefore, can move itself; because in order to do so it would have to be in act and in potency in the same respect at the same time — which is self-contradictory. Therefore, whatever is in motion is moved by something else.

b) **Nothing Can Be by Essence in Motion.** This argument overlooks the possibility that there is something which is of itself, by virtue of its nature, in motion. Its motion is uncaused in that it has no efficient cause; it is in motion without moving itself and without being moved by something else. Yet its motion has a sufficient reason, namely, the nature or essence of the thing. It is, in respect to motion, its own actuality; it is self-moving in the sense in which God is self-existing. We might point out, as plausible examples of such a thing, electrons. Electrons, so far as physical science can discover, are always in motion and have no cause for their motion. If electrons really are such self-moving beings, their movement can very easily be conceived as sufficiently accounting for all the movements of nature, since all natural changes are ultimately reducible to the movements of electrons.

The conception of something in motion by essence does not, however, stand up under examination. A thing in motion is not in act in the respect in which it is in motion. It is becoming actual in a respect in which it was potential, but in so far as it has become actual it is not now in motion. Nor is a thing purely in potency in a respect in which it is in motion. Its potency in that respect is now fully actualized as potency; it was mere capacity to be act, but now it is actually becoming act. The question whether a thing can be by essence in motion amounts, therefore, to the question whether anything can of itself possess a potency fully realized as potency — a potency becoming act. In one way, it would seem that this question should be answered affirmatively and universally — it seems to express what is precisely the case of material or mobile being; natural substance is perpetually in motion; existence in time is existence maintained only by continual becoming:

every material substance as such is in motion. This is not, however, the Aristotelian-Thomistic view. That view holds that material substance is essentially *mobile*, but not essentially in motion — a material thing might be at rest. The essential mobility of natural substances is a consequence of their essential passivity, that is, their passive potentiality, which in turn is a consequence of their matter. But if mobility arises from passivity, then motion requires a cause. The crux of the problem is, therefore, whether the Aristotelian conception of motion is universally valid.

Appeal to our experience of movement turns out to be inconclusive. St. Thomas could say in his day that we know by induction that no body is in motion except it be moved by another,[27] but his induction was limited to the bodies of common sensible experience and did not take into account molecular, atomic, and subatomic movements. Today we would be inclined to say that so far as "experience"[28] goes, subatomic particles seem to be naturally in motion without any cause of their motion; it is assumed that electrons in the orbits of atoms are in motion always, and nobody asks why. We might say the same thing about the heavenly bodies. Yet, we obviously do not know that these movements, whether subatomic or sidereal, are uncaused; we just do not know of any cause. On the other hand, we do know that these movements are subject to determination by extrinsic causes; every outside influence or force alters the direction or velocity of the movement. So induction really fails to settle the problem, though the amenability of motion to external causes seems to establish a presumption that motion is itself caused.

Therefore, it seems that the problem can be solved only by determining whether any other conception of motion than Aristotle's is tenable. The answer seems to be in the negative. Any other conception must deny that motion is the continuing actualization of potentiality. If it does this, it will end by making motion some sort of being instead of a process that a being undergoes. Then it will have ruled process out of nature, leaving only being. Process is a real phase of nature, but it is denied if it is viewed as anything but the actualization of the potential. It is easy enough to say that Scholastics are all tied up in their Aristotelian terminology and categories, but it is not so easy to

---

[27] S. Theol., I, 3, 1, c.

[28] Our knowledge of subatomic particles and of atoms is, in truth, very far from being experience. Many physicists regard electrons as convenient fictions.

supply alternate terminology and categories without getting out of step with nature. In the present connection, the Aristotelian terminology has at least the virtue of affording a definition of motion which is intelligible. What other intelligible definitions of motion or process are there? Whatever ones there may be, if they make of motion a *thing* or a *state* of some sort, they are most certainly false, because they deny the very existence of motion. To answer Parmenides it is necessary to show how beings move; it is futile to try to substitute motion for being.

The issue, whether the Aristotelian definition of motion is valid, seems to hinge upon the question whether process and efficient causation are real or illusory. Real becoming and causation cannot be admitted without the admission also of the reality of potentiality. Nothing can affect anything else unless there are both real activity and real passivity in nature. The Aristotelian analysis of causation, the high point of which is the identification in a single *motus* of the *passio* of the patient and the *actio* of the agent, seems to be the only analysis ever advanced which renders causation intelligible. But this account of causation is identical with Aristotle's account of the nature of motion, expressed differently because approached from a different angle. Motion (the *motus* in causation) is the actuality of the potency or mobility in the thing in motion. It is something real, or else there is no becoming or process in nature. The question is, *whence* is this *motus?*

Something may belong to a being, St. Thomas says, in one of three ways: (1) as its essence or part of its essence; (2) as following from its essential constituent principles; (3) as caused in it by an extrinsic cause. Can motion be the essence or part of the essence of something? We may answer no. That which belongs to a thing as essential must be in the thing in complete actuality, if the thing exists at all. But something in a being in complete actuality is not in process. Where no potency is becoming actual, there is no process. Can motion follow from the essential constituents of anything? Again we can answer no. Something may be *mobile* because of its essential principles, for example, because of matter, but it cannot be actually in motion by virtue of an essential principle. What follows from the essence of a thing must be as stable as the essence. It is just this principle which leads a thinker like Spinoza to deny real change. Everything in a system like his is either essence itself or a necessary consequent of essence; and therefore nothing can ever change. All absolutists at least approach this position. No matter how they strive to fit becoming into their universe, it is not real becoming; everything that is, is from eternity, and becoming is merely appearance. Real change cannot follow from the essential principles of anything because the whole function of essential principles is to make a thing what it is, not something else. An essential principle — matter, for example — may make a thing mobile or passive, and that thing will be subject to change as long as it retains this principle; but the principle, which makes it what it is, will never make it change; something else will have to do that. Therefore, motion can belong to a thing only in the third way named by St. Thomas; namely, in virtue of the action of a cause. This cause, as we have seen, cannot be the moved thing itself. Consequently, whatever is in motion is moved by another.

CHAPTER V

THE PRINCIPLE OF FINALITY

I. MECHANISM VS. TELEOLOGY

1. Nothing is more characteristic of Aristotelian-Thomistic philosophy than the doctrine that *final causes, as well as material and efficient causes, regularly operate in nature.* By a *final cause* in nature is meant a preordained end or goal toward which a natural operation or process tends. To say that final causes operate in nature is to say, for example, that man's stomach and intestines are constructed in the way in which they are, and operate the way they do, in order that man may digest and assimilate food, and that, therefore, digestion and assimilation are *true causes* of the structure and activity of the stomach and intestines. To deny final causality in nature is to deny (to use the same example) that the stomach and intestines are intended for, or meant for, digestion and assimilation, and to say, on the contrary, that digestion and assimilation are pure effects of the structure and action of these organs, and in no way the cause of their being the way they are or acting the way they do.

Down through the ages philosophers have been split into opposing camps on the question of the reality of final causes in nature. Those who hold that there is end, purpose, design, or finality in natural processes, for example, in the growth of plants and animals, are called *teleologists,* and their doctrine is called teleology (*telos* is Greek for "end"; "end" in Latin is *finis,* hence *final* cause). Those who hold that all natural processes are the results solely of mechanical causes and do not tend toward preordained goals or ends are called mechanists. Mechanists admit only material and efficient causes, rejecting both formal and final causes. The form or pattern into which the matter-particles fall is to them in no sense a cause, but entirely an effect, of the movements and interactions of the particles, and no end or purpose directs these movements.

In the play, "You Can't Take It With You," the playwriting mother of the happy-go-lucky household wrote plays because a typewriter had been delivered, through some error, to the house. Having a typewriter, she wrote plays. What could be more natural? She also used a kitten, a live one, as a paperweight while she typed. These things were humorous in the play. But mechanists believe that they faithfully represent nature. Birds fly because they happen to find themselves with wings, just as Mamma wrote plays because she happened to find herself with a typewriter. And wings are no more "meant for" flying than a kitten is "meant for" keeping papers from blowing away. It just happens that wings can be used for flying and that a kitten can be used as a paperweight. In the mechanist's view of the world, nothing is meant for, or intended for, anything. Certain concatenations of events occur, and the result is some new event; but the prior events were not in any way pointed toward or designed for the production of the subsequent event. The teleologist, on the contrary, believes that in nature the thousand and one physical causes that lead up to the production of some normal, natural result, say the growth of a tree, or better still, the adornment of the earth's surface with trees, were all intended for and directed toward the production of that very result; and that consequently this result itself is not a mere accidental outcome of the series of causes leading up to it, but is itself a cause of all those events; viz., the final cause, the goal. In a word, all these prior events occur *in order that* there may be trees.

2. **Mechanical and Final Cause Are Reciprocal.**[1] What makes the mechanists' view plausible is that the mechanical or physical causes that produce a tree, or wings on a bird, or eyes in a man, or a digestive and reproductive system in animals, are unquestionably real causes, and the trees, wings, eyes, digestive and reproductive systems are indeed their effects. How, then, can these latter be called causes of the former? The teleologist, who, of course, does not deny that birds fly because they have wings, or that men see because they have eyes, answers, with Aristotle, that the mechanists are wrong in making this fact *the whole story.* Two things can be mutually causes of each other as long as they are causes in different ways. If I keep healthy by taking an hour's walk every day, the walking is the cause of my health; but so is my health the cause of my walking, since it is the health aimed at that leads me to do the walking. The walking is the physical or mechanical

[1] Aristotle, *Phys.*, II. 7–9.

cause of the health, and the health is the final cause of the walking. In like manner, wings are the physical cause of flying, while flying is the final cause of wings; that is, the end for which wings are designed. We would see nothing funny about using a kitten, which obviously is not designed for such a purpose, as a paperweight, unless we had experience in nature of many things that obviously are designed for certain purposes; there is, for example, nothing funny about using water for drinking, or the mouth for drinking it.

II. THE PRINCIPLE OF FINALITY

St. Thomas Aquinas carried teleology to its furthest possible application. The reality of final cause is not, for him, merely a truth about natural substances, known by induction from natural operations; it is, on the contrary, an absolutely universal truth: Whatever acts, acts for an end and a good. He expresses it in a universal principle which Thomists call the principle of finality: *Every agent acts for an end.* He states and proves this principle in the *Summa Theologica,* I–II, q. 1, art. 2, and in the *Summa Contra Gentiles,* Book III, Chapter 2. The following two proofs, borrowed here from a contemporary Thomist, are based upon those of St. Thomas.

1. The Proof From Sufficient Reason. To say that natural beings possess immanent finality is to say merely that they have within themselves a tendency, direction, or ordination toward definite operations rather than others. That they have such a tendency is clearly evident from the fact that each type of being does in fact behave in a definite way, that is, it performs regularly the same operations under the same circumstances. Dogs regularly act like dogs, and birds like birds. Oxygen can be depended upon to do certain things regularly under certain circumstances. Bodies falling in space follow regularly the same law of acceleration. Acorns falling in fertile ground, and given half a chance, regularly become oak trees, and oak trees regularly produce acorns. Every agent in nature, in a word, regularly produces one effect rather than another. Consequently, everything in nature has an immanent tendency or ordination to produce a particular effect. It is directed toward this effect as its end. If the effect regularly produced is not actually tended toward, that is to say, if it is not the final cause of the agent's operation, then there is no sufficient reason why it is regularly produced rather than some other effect.

To deny the principle of finality is to deny that everything that occurs has a sufficient reason for its occurrence, for it is to deny that things tend naturally to produce the effects which they regularly do produce. It is to deny, for example, that seeing is the natural end of eyes or hearing of ears; to deny, even, that eyes have any more tendency to see than they have to hear. It is to make sight a mere accidental effect of eyes, as the destruction of a village is an accidental effect of a flood; it is to say that the conjunction of eyes, light, and colored objects is a mere coincidence, like meeting an old friend in Times Square, and not a coincidence once, but every time we see. If it be admitted that natural agents do naturally tend to certain effects, then they act for an end. And if every agent in nature actually does produce one effect rather than another (in other words, if different things do in fact act differently) then "every agent acts for an end." St. Thomas states the case very pithily: "Every agent acts for an end, otherwise one thing would not follow from the action of the agent more than another, unless it were by chance." But what occurs by chance does not occur regularly.[2]

2. **The Proof From Potency and Act.** The nature of potentiality and actuality considered in reference to an agent makes it evident that the agent must act for an end. Every natural agent operates according to its active potency; that is, its operation is always the actuality of some power for acting which it possesses. This power is a potency in the agent, and it is a potency for a certain determinate actuality, since potency has no meaning except in relation to a corresponding actuality. Wherefore, *to have the power to act is to tend to a certain effect, and to actualize this power in operation is to act for an end.* Consequently, the very conception of an agent with a determinate nature endowed with determinate powers involves the proposition that the agent acts for an end. Therefore the principle of finality is as certain as the fact that in nature there are agents or efficient causes and that they have determinate natures. If, in other words, natural substances, whether inorganic or organic, have different proper operations corresponding to their different natures — if oxygen behaves regularly like oxygen and not like chlorine; if birds regularly build nests and beavers, dams; if men regularly see with their eyes, hear with their ears, and think with their intellects — then every agent acts for an end.[3]

---

[2] *S. Theol.*, I, 44, 4. Cf. Garrigou-Lagrange, *God — His Existence and Nature* (St. Louis: Herder, 1934), Vol. I, pp. 200–201.

[3] Aristotle, *Phys.*, II, 8; St. Thomas, *Con. Gen.*, II, 2, next to last paragraph.

III. FINALITY VS. CHANCE AND NECESSITY

1. Chance. Those who deny final causes must explain the regularity of natural phenomena in either of two ways: as the result of chance, or as the result of necessity. Chance cannot stand up at all as an explanation. In the first place, chance and regularity are mutually repugnant, so repugnant, in fact, that when what we have considered a chance event begins to recur regularly we very quickly cease regarding it as the result of chance — if seven turns up too often we examine the dice. Second, chance presupposes necessity, intention, or both. If I run into an old friend in Times Square, that is a chance encounter. But he was there intentionally, and so was I, though we did not intend to meet. If an army loses a campaign because a flood wipes out its supplies, that is chance or accident. But the army was there according to plan and the flood was caused by natural meteorological causes. Chance cannot, by its very nature, ever be the ultimate explanation of anything; it is itself always explainable by causes in which there is no chance.[4]

2. Indeed, as St. Thomas points out, the very fact that we recognize some events as due to chance, the fact that we have the concept of chance at all, is clear proof that natural operations are intended for definite ends.

> To the first objection it is to be said that those things are called "under the sun" which undergo generation and corruption by the movement [i.e., energy] of the sun. In all these things chance is found; not however in such a way that everything in them occurs by chance, but because in some of them something due to chance can be found. And this very fact that something due to chance is discovered in these things demonstrates that they are subject to the government of some-thing. For unless corruptible things of this kind were governed by some superior being, they would not intend anything, especially those which have no knowledge; and consequently there would not be found in them anything outside their intention, which is what constitutes the nature of chance.[5]

The exception proves the rule because it is recognizable as an exception.

3. Necessity. Nor can necessity stand up as the sole explanation of the regularity of natural processes and operations. To put forth necessity as the *sole* cause of natural events is to maintain that whatever happens, happens because it has to happen — nothing else can possibly

[4] Cf. Aristotle, *Ibid.*, II, 5–6.
[5] *S. Theol.*, I, 103, 5 ad 1.

happen. The eye sees because it must see — that is the way it is constructed. Birds fly because they must fly. Hydrogen and oxygen unite to become water because under given conditions they cannot do anything else. Electrons, protons, neutrons, build up into the atoms of the ninety-two elements because physical law necessitates their doing so. The human organism was evolved from nature because the laws of nature could produce no other product, given the antecedent conditions. The substances of nature are what they are for the same reason that the angles of every plane triangle total 180 degrees; they could not be otherwise.[6]

There is a certain attractiveness, the attractiveness of apparent simplicity, about this doctrine; but there is not the slightest reason in the world for thinking that it is true. Those who hold it confuse hypothetical necessity with absolute necessity. It is necessary that a freely falling body fall with an acceleration of 32 feet per second per second, that light travel with a velocity of 186,000 miles per second, and that sodium and chlorine combine in a ratio of one to one in salt, *given the physical laws that do as a matter of fact operate in the world.* But why do those laws operate, and not others? Are they the only possible laws? The "necessity" of the laws of nature does not explain nature; these laws themselves are the nature to be explained. There is no reason in the world for believing that they are the only laws possible. Many men of science in the nineteenth century believed that little hard particles of matter called atoms exist because they have to exist, move according to Newton's three laws of motion because these laws are the only possible laws, attract one another according to Newton's law of gravitation because it is absolutely necessary that bodies should so attract each other, and by moving and so attracting each other build up our whole world and us, because nothing else can happen and this has to happen. Today no scientist believes that these things happen at all, to say nothing of their happening necessarily.

No matter to what extent mechanists may reduce natural operations to the rule of necessity — that is, to physical law — they come in the end face to face with stark contingency. Given matter, the nature which it actually has and its original distribution, and probably many other things, the present universe — let us admit — *must* have evolved. But you are given an awful lot when you are given matter, its nature, and its distribution! Starting with them, you can construct a universe

[6] Cf. Aristotle, *Phys.,* II, 8–9.

in terms of the necessary laws of the movement of such matter so distributed; but this necessity comes into the picture only after the matter is presupposed. The necessity, therefore, is the product of a sheer contingency and consequently is itself contingent through and through: it is, but it might not have been.

The necessity of physical laws is, in the view of the teleologist, hypothetical, that is to say, it presupposes a prior condition. And what it presupposes is finality. *Natural laws could have been otherwise; they are what they are so that the world may be the world it is.* If there are to be certain substances in the world with certain properties and operations, then there must be certain elements obeying certain laws of affinity and valence; if these elements are to obey these laws, they must have a certain atomic structure and, hence, there must be protons, neutrons, and electrons; if living organisms are to exist, they must have certain special structures to supply the needs of individual life and the life of the species; if the organisms are such as to need oxygen for life, there must be oxygen; if all living things need the radiant energy of the sun, the sun must exist; if men are to see, they must have eyes, and there must be light. "And God said, 'Let there be light.'" Both the necessity of natural laws and the contingencies upon which they depend are intelligible in the light of an intention which is prior to both of them, and are unintelligible without this prior intention.

IV. INTRINSIC FINALITY

The two proofs of the principle of finality given in section II above are supplemented by appeal to the innumerable evidences afforded by natural processes of the real operation in them of final causes. These evidences fall into two classes: first, evidences of *intrinsic* finality, or the means-to-end character of the operations of living agents and of the operations of the parts of a living organism in relation to the organism as a whole; second, evidences of *extrinsic* finality, or the means-to-end character of the different substances in nature in relation to one another, especially in the relation of the lower orders of natural substances to the higher. "Means-to-end" and "lower and higher" are not intended here as question-begging terms but merely as useful descriptive terms; whether the peculiar and perhaps unique set of circumstances that obtains in the inorganic realm on and around the earth exists *in order to* support biological life is the point at issue, but to describe it as actually serving as a means to that end is merely to state a fact.

1. Development of an Organism. Every living being, no matter how complex, arose from a single cell. Each human body with its many different tissues and organs started its life history as a single fertilized ovum, the zygote. This first cell divided into two, these two into four, and so on. There are several billion cells in the mature human body, but the continuity of production from that first cell has never been broken. All the food that we have eaten had to become part of the existing cells before these divided to become new cells. By this simple process of *feeding, dividing, growing,* the original cell gave rise to our body with all its highly specialized parts. Skin, fat, muscle, bone, hair, nerve, blood, lymph, all very different in cellular structure, some not even themselves alive, some rather *in* the organism than part of it — all came ultimately from that one first cell. The many organs of the body — of structural delicacy that human art would find hard to duplicate, and of functional co-ordination that human art never can approach — all came into being by the simple process of one cell turning into two and these two into four, and so on. It is as if you could make a great airplane by getting one tiny piece of steel and watering it.

Hans Driesch,[7] famous German biologist and philosopher, allowed a sea urchin's egg to divide once, twice, three times, till eight cells were formed. Then he cut four of them away to see what the four left would do. They went right ahead dividing into eight, sixteen, and so on, and formed a sea urchin, complete in all its parts and operations, but smaller than normal. It is as if you watered your piece of steel until it had become eight pieces of steel, and you cut away four, and the four remaining pieces went right ahead and turned into a half-size airplane.

The movement and work, the commands given and carried out, the materials brought up to the workers, the order of procedure from one section of the belt line to the next, the hundred thousand different operations that are done in an airplane factory are intelligible only in view of the finished plane. All these things make sense because they are all directed toward an end or goal. Likewise, the billions of operations, the millions of different special processes, the constant bringing

[7] *The Science and Philosophy of the Organism* (London: A. and C. Black, 1929), pp. 38-43; "The Breakdown of Materialism," in *The Great Design,* ed., F. Mason (New York: Macmillan, 1935), pp. 283-303.

up and absorbing of food materials, the manufacture of these materials into living protoplasm in cells, the growth and division of these cells — all this is intelligible only in view of the finished organism, only if this product of cell activity is regarded as the true end or goal of the cell activity. *Surely it is not an argument or a conclusion but a simple statement of fact to say that the processes of development in an organism operate as means to an end; and therefore that final causes regularly operate in nature.*

2. **Vital Processes in an Organism.** The food which you eat is digested mainly in your stomach and small intestine. Digestion consists of a series of chemical processes which involve tens of thousands of separate organs, most of them glands and muscles. The digested food in the small intestine (chiefly) is absorbed into the blood stream. Like digestion, this absorption process is made up of a great number of chemical reactions, the compounds formed by the digestion processes now combining again with the compounds in the blood plasma. These new compounds are carried in the blood stream to all parts of the body where they serve as food for each of the individual cells, which, by the processes called metabolism, absorb them, grow, divide, and thus produce new cells, and so carry on the whole life of the organism by carrying on their own cell lives.

Metabolism, i.e., cell nutrition, growth, and reproduction, cannot be carried on without the presence of oxygen in addition to the substances of the food stream and the cells. The oxygen is carried also in the blood stream, not, however, in the plasma but in the red blood corpuscles. In the lungs these red blood cells cast off carbon dioxide and absorb oxygen; the oxygen-absorbing agent is the hemoglobin in the cells. All the blood channels of the body, viz., the veins and arteries with their capillaries, start out from and return to the great pumping station called the heart. The veins carry the "used up" blood, the blood that has already fed the body cells and is "out of oxygen," back to the heart. The heart sac called the right atrium receives this venous blood, contracts, and forces the blood into the right ventricle; this contracts, the blood closing the valves back to the atrium and forcing its way through the only available opening, the valves of the pulmonary artery. This artery divides into two and carries the blood to the lungs where it passes through innumerable capillaries around the air sacs of the lungs. Through the permeable membranes of these sacs carbon dioxide passes from the venous blood into the air and oxygen from the air into the blood. The capillaries unite to form the two pulmonary veins, through which the blood, with its new supply of oxygen, passes from the lungs into the left atrium of the heart. This contracts and forces the blood into the left ventricle. From here the blood is pumped into the aorta, the great trunk artery, and through its branch arteries and capillaries to all parts of the body, where, as we have seen, its substances are assimilated by the separate cells. The capillaries unite to form veins and so the blood is returned to the right atrium of the heart, completing the circuit. *It certainly seems that these three great systems, the digestive, circulatory, and respiratory, and all their separate organs, are working together toward a common end or aim.*

And that is not the whole story. Another great system of organs, the nervous system, has its finger in every operation of digestion, circulation, and respiration. Nerves from the autonomic (or "involuntary") nervous network reach from the centers or ganglia of the network to every muscle and gland of the whole digestive system from the mouth to the intestines, furnishing the nerve impulses which set the muscles rhythmically contracting to mix the food and push it along on its way and set the glands secreting the chemical substances that combine with the food substances, forming soluble and assimilable compounds. Other nerves go to the heart muscles, causing them to relax and contract, allowing the blood to pour into the heart and then pumping it from the right ventricle to the lungs and from the left ventricle to the body in general. Similarly, breathing, which fills the lungs with oxygen-laden air and expels the carbon-dioxide-filled breath, is activated and regulated by nerves of the autonomic system, which cause the rib and diaphragm muscles to contract and relax rhythmically so that air is constantly drawn in to fill the cavity created by the expansion of the ribs and relaxation of the diaphragm, and forced out again when these contract. *The autonomic nervous system certainly seems to be meant for or intended for or to tend toward a definite end, the regular and co-ordinated functioning of the vital organs of the body.*

If one organ of an organism, say the eyes or the wings of a bird, is selected for study, the real operation of the final cause or end in producing it becomes, if possible, even more evident. A million complicated, precisely measured, timed, and co-ordinated cellular operations go into the formation of the eye or of a bird's wings. In the case of the eye, at any rate, some of the processes begin and progress for some time without any apparent connection with each other and yet combine in the end to form the one complex and delicately adjusted product: the eyeball with its many essential parts develops from cells in the skin-part of the embryonic face, while the retina with its nerve connections begins from cells in the brain, and these independent processes grow together in the formation of the eye. Yet the eyes and the wings, both products of a million prior events, and both in themselves very complex structures, perform operations that are perfectly one and simple — seeing and flying. Whence comes this perfect unity of effect arising from unimaginably multitudinous causes? Surely from a real principle of unity operative throughout the whole processs of development.

> Those who reject final causation contend that these constituent parts, acting separately and independently, result in a combined effect; but such an explanation is philosophically impossible. There must, of necessity, be in them a veritable principle of unity: otherwise they could not be the seat of a single activity. A plurality of causes acting independently may be imagined to unite by chance to produce a composite result. But only in virtue of an objective principle of unity can diverse agents energize as a single cause productive of a perfection which is not complex but simple. What, then, is this principle of unity? The only answer is that it is a principle consisting in a relation to the end to be realized. Only in virtue of such relatedness could the manifold elements of the organ issue in an activity which is one: the office of the relation being to determine the separate agents to the production of this end. In other words the agents are determined in view of their final causes.[8]

3. Death in Life. Let us close our discussion of intrinsic finality in organisms with one very remarkable case in point, namely, the subordination in nature of death itself to life, or, to express it differently, death as a means to fuller life. A very interesting and provocative treatment of the subject is presented by Orville T. Bailey:

> Death enters here and there into growth as gold thread is woven through a tapestry to accent the pattern. Here death becomes indispensable to life; without death of this kind, the process of normal growth as we know it would be impossible.[9]

This weaving of death into the very life process takes three general forms. Bailey describes actual processes of each of the three groups. The first group is exemplified by the growth of the skin, nails, and

[8] G. H. Joyce, *Principles of Natural Theology* (New York: Longmans, 1923), pp. 124–125.
[9] "Death in Life," *The Scientific Monthly*, February, 1944, Vol. LVIII, No. 2, p. 117.

hair; the second group, by the production of the red blood cells; the third group, by the formation of certain bones. The case of the skin will clarify all the other cases sufficiently for our purposes.

> The pattern [of human skin] is composed of cells which carry out the function of the skin important to the body as a whole and of the cells which support and maintain the cells of the first group. The inner portion of the skin . . . is composed of connective tissue cells, fibers produced by them, and blood vessels. This is a portion of the tissue pattern which is concerned with support and nutrition of the cells which form the outer layers. The layer is sharply separated from the layer of covering cells. Growth is confined to that region in which the two layers come into contact. The cells nearer the surface die; they are not in contact with a tissue to furnish support and nutrition. They die, however, in a special way, or, rather, in the process of dying they are transformed into keratin, a firm, horny substance which forms the outer layer of the skin. This material keeps the tissue fluid in and foreign materials out. There are very few bacteria which can enter the skin so long as the keratin layer is unbroken. Keratin, which is built from the dead bodies of cells, is essential for the maintenance of the body as a whole. It is, therefore, an instance of the participation of death in life.[10]

After a description in more detail of the process of skin growth, Dr. Bailey has the following very interesting and suggestive paragraph:

> One of the strangest aspects of this situation is the relation of the amount of keratin produced with the requirements for it. When much is lost, much is produced. When little is rubbed off, then just that much is formed. In certain places and under special circumstances, the width of the keratin layer is increased. If some special region of the body is subjected to long continued rubbing as, for instance, in a region irritated by an orthopedic brace, there is an increase in the amount of keratin on the skin below; this returns to normal when the source of irritation has been removed. On the palms and soles, there is a much wider layer of keratin than elsewhere on the body surface. These regions are the ones most subject to the endless little injuries which are a part of our daily experience. Yet that is not the whole story, because the keratin layer on the palms and soles, even before birth, is thicker than that of the skin elsewhere. The production of keratin depends upon cellular death. If growth is to be regarded as the attainment and maintenance of a series of patterns, then death is here a necessary part of growth.[11]

All through his article, Dr. Bailey speaks of growth as "the attainment and maintenance of a series of patterns." Surely this is equivalent to saying that growth is a process directed toward definite ends.

[10] *Ibid.*, 117.
[11] *Ibid.*, 118.

Death is not an essential or inevitable companion of biological life. The simplest organisms, for example, bacteria, do not naturally die; they subdivide into living offspring. Where death first appears upon nature's scene as a normal thing, it is found to be subordinated to the more perfect life of advanced organisms.[12] Death finally overtakes these organisms themselves; but before dying they have lived and, normally, have left living progeny. It is very difficult to see how anyone can reflect upon this phenomenon of the living organism regularly utilizing the death of certain of its parts for the growth and maintenance of its own whole life without being convinced that the parts and normal part-processes of organisms are certainly preordained to the perfection of the organism as a whole; or, in other words, that these processes are acting for a true end. If the end or final cause is denied, the regularity of these phenomena in the multitudes of species in which they occur and their obviously beneficial and indispensable character remain quite unintelligible.

V. EXTRINSIC FINALITY

Obviously animals could not live except for the vegetative realm upon which they feed, the water which they drink, the oxygen which they draw from the air or the water. If lungs are meant for breathing air, then obviously air is meant to be breathed; is it therefore meant *for* being breathed? Many philosophers and scientists say that we have no real grounds for believing that it is; rather, in our narrow human way, we find it good for us to breathe and therefore we conclude that it exists for us to breathe it. There is plenty of evidence, however, that air is meant for being breathed, or to put the picture on a larger canvas, that the inorganic substances of the earth and its immediate environment are definitely preordained for the support of life. We call this extrinsic finality.

1. **Life the End of Inorganic Nature.** On the earth and in its immediate environment, the same chemical species, that is to say, the elements and their compounds, constantly recur in nature. The physical particles of matter — electrons, protons, neutrons, etc. — which build up into atoms and molecules, build up into the same unvarying patterns and constantly produce the same natural substances. The same elements always show the same affinity for certain other elements, always combine with these in the same relations of volume and weight

[12] *Ibid.*, pp. 125–128.

and, under the same conditions, produce the same compounds. The compounds so produced are always decomposable into the same constituent elements. Each of the elements and each of the compounds has always its same distinctive set of properties and modes of behavior. The geological evolutions that have occurred through the long ages of the past, taken together with the earth's relation to the other heavenly bodies, especially the sun, have produced the physical conditions requisite for the support of living things. The slightest departure of the elements from their regular properties and ways of behaving would have made this impossible, and the slightest departure now would disrupt it instantaneously. If, for example, hydrogen and oxygen were to cease combining to form water, or if carbon were to oxidize rapidly at normal earth temperatures, or if normal earth temperatures were to fall below 0 deg. C. or to rise above 100 deg. C., life on earth would cease. If the laws of gravitation did not hold the earth in its orbit around the sun or did not hold the earth's atmosphere close to its surface, the conditions for life could not exist more than momentarily.

Professor Lawrence J. Henderson, famous biochemist of Harvard University, studying the physicochemical conditions for life and the possibility of their occurring accidentally or by sheer physical necessity, concluded that their actual occurrence in the earth and its atmosphere is "almost infinitely improbable as the result of contingency, can only be regarded, is in truth only fully intelligible even if mechanically explained, as a preparation for the evolutionary process." We are, he says, "obliged to regard the collocation of properties as in some intelligible sense a preparation for the process of planetary evolution."[13] Preparation presupposes the end prepared for. What Henderson wrote is equivalent to saying that the physical and chemical conditions which obtain on the earth are directed toward the evolution of biological life. There are many ways of saying this, but they all mean that on the earth the inorganic realm is related to the living realm as means to an end.

2. Evolution and Finality. Many evolutionists have sought to put forward evolution itself as a substitute for finality in nature. The substitution does not go. If we grant evolution as a fact, we have to grant a great many important facts prior to it: the existence of natural substances with the properties and conditions necessary to support life,

[13] Quoted by W. R. Thompson in *The Thomist*, January, 1943, Vol. V, p. 230.

the existence of an urge to live and to develop in living things, a definite direction in that urge toward greater fullness of life, the ability to adapt to changed conditions without abandoning the general direction of the urge to live more fully. Evolution would only bring us around the circuit and back to finality again. Evolution is not a cause that does something; it is a process that is gone through. If the developmental character of individual biological life is matched by development in the whole realm of biological life, then the whole problem of final causality occurs all over again under this new aspect. And just as the particular mechanisms of development in an individual organism are unintelligible if the mature organism as their goal is left out of account, so also the particular mechanisms of development in the general order of living things are unintelligible if the organic patterns attained through these mechanisms are not regarded as their goals. Natural selection may account for specific survivals and specific developments in the contest for life; but it presupposes the contest, the urge to survive and the capacity for development. No Darwinian can so much as explain what is meant by natural selection without assuming finality in nature to give his explanation sense. A struggle for existence in which the fit survive presupposes a definite determination in all the strugglers toward survival as an end; "few are chosen" makes no sense without "many are called."

3. "The Fitness of the Environment." Evolutionists speak of fitness of the organism *for* the environment as a prime factor in the survival and development of living species. They apparently take for granted an environment in which life can fit. Professor Henderson, cited above, points out that the fitness *of* the environment *for* life is quite as important and certainly a prior factor. He entitled a book in which he examined the whole subject *The Fitness of the Environment*.[14] We have seen that he concluded that even if all the mechanical causes by which the earth-environment became fit to support life are known, they still remain unintelligible except as a preparation for life. Here intrinsic and extrinsic finality join hands, and we can say that neither the mechanical causes of an environment fit for life nor the mechanical causes of living things fit to take advantage of this environment are intelligible unless the living things themselves be regarded as the goal or end of both sets of mechanical causes. To put it in Aristotelian

[14] L. J. Henderson, *The Fitness of the Environment* (New York: Macmillan, 1913); *The Order of Nature* (Cambridge, Mass.: Harvard University Press, 1925).

terminology, the final cause is the cause of causes because without it the other causes would not operate. A paragraph from the same article of W. R. Thompson which we have already cited will make this point clear.

> As Dr. Julian Huxley truly and profoundly puts it, evolutionary progress is measured by its upper levels. Since the upper level is something perfectly specific and definite, the number of ways in which it can be attained is not limitless. Human beings can survive only within certain environmental limits. They cannot survive even within these limits unless bodily mechanisms are of a certain definite type. These mechanisms could not be what they are were it not for the properties of the organic compounds built up by the organisms. These, in turn, would not form were not the inorganic elements predetermined to their formation. We cannot live without oxygen; we cannot take in oxygen without our red blood corpuscles; the ability of the corpuscles to take up oxygen depends on the presence of hemoglobin; the properties of hemoglobin depend strictly on the properties of iron; iron exists because the elements of the subatomic world are predetermined to its formation. The argument could be developed through innumerable channels. The upper levels of nature exist only because the lower levels are predetermined to their production. The upper levels, such as the human organism, require for their emergence and maintenance an infinite multitude of delicate adjustments and co-ordinations, which are possible only because the elements of the universe are predetermined to that end. Predetermination is another name for finality. We can thus say that the final cause or object to which the universe is predetermined is man, or as Dr. Huxley puts it, conceptual thought: and that this predetermination is fundamental, or *ab origine*.[15]

VI. TELEOLOGY DOES NOT DENY MECHANICAL CAUSATION

Mechanical causation and final causation are not alternatives or rivals; they are reciprocal or mutually complementary. The Aristotelian-Thomistic philosophy of nature views every natural thing or event as the effect of material, formal, efficient, and final causes working together, each doing a different kind of work. A separate, unbroken chain of each kind of cause leads up to the production or emergence of each effect. Each chain must be complete in its own order, or else the effect will not be produced; a link missing in one of the chains can never be made up for by a link from one of the other chains: the most perfect blueprint will never beget a house without the brick and mortar; the best of intentions accomplish nothing without efficient

[15] *Op. cit.*, pp. 235–236.

action — and *vice versa!* It is the *vice versa* that teleologists are forced to insist upon.

Many scientists oppose any teleological and hylemorphic concepts because they believe that such concepts have, in the past, hindered the progress of science by being regarded as scientific explanations and thus closing the road to the sort of explanations now considered as scientific. The charge goes back at least as far as Francis Bacon. To what extent it was justified is at present irrelevant, since the modern conception of scientific explanation is now well established. But scientists can, and some of them do, fall into the opposite error when they insist upon the scientific explanations as the only ones; they are closing the road to other equally valid modes of explanation. The two questions, for example, "How do living organisms come into being?" and "Why do living organisms exist?" are not interchangeable; they are plainly different questions demanding different answers. To insist upon the answer to either one of them for both is to hinder the progress of human knowledge.

VII. IMMANENT AND TRANSCENDENT FINALITY

1. Philosophers who agree that finality operates in nature may yet disagree fundamentally about the significance of this finality. Many contemporary philosophers of various evolutionary schools of thought recognize only immanent finality in nature and deny transcendent finality; that is, they maintain that nature and natural beings tend by some *immanent* power, urge, force, or *élan* to certain ends or to a certain end, but that no external or *transcendent* cause, for example God, directs or moves them to these ends. They deny that we can validly argue from the teleology of nature to an Intelligence which moves and directs nature.

All philosophers who admit teleology and yet deny any transcendent directing cause of natural processes and development commit themselves to the proposition that the total cause, efficient and final as well as material and formal, of the dynamics of nature is to be found within nature itself. This is true of three popular theories, viz., emergent evolution, creative evolution, and what we may call, for want of a better name, naturalistic evolution. But certain serious difficulties — difficulties which amount to impossibilities — are involved in the above proposition, and consequently in every theory which implies that proposition.

Any theory of nature which admits immanent finality alone while denying any transcendent finality and agency, must of necessity place the whole final causality and agency of the process of nature within time, for process and time are inseparable. Such a theory rules out creation, in the Christian sense of the term, and consequently rules out any beginning of the process and any eternal or timeless cause of the process. It postulates, therefore, an infinite time already consumed in the process. Now a universe in process for an infinite time and having no extrinsic cause is, according to many scientists, a physical impossibility; for it is a closed energy system which functions indefinitely. An energy system must have either a beginning and an ending of its functioning or an extrinsic source of its energy. Such theories as those under discussion exclude both from the energy system which we call nature.

Second, a theory which posits immanent finality in nature and yet denies an external cause of nature postulates a moving agency in nature which is wholly within the process of nature. Such an agency undergoes the processes which it produces. It is mover and moved in the same motion; it passes continuously from potency to act without being moved by any agency in act; it is a self-actualizing potency. Such a being is, as we have seen in Chapter IV, impossible. That it should move at all is impossible; and that it should move regularly toward determinate ends is doubly impossible. The end of any regular operation must be a cause of that operation, as we have seen; but nothing which has no existence of any sort can be a cause. The ends at which a self-actuating potency would arrive, if such a potency were possible, would have no being at all before their realization at the end of the process, and consequently could not be causes. Emergent evolution and similar theories posit finality without final causes, since the agency which they posit in order to explain the end-attaining process is wholly within the process.

Third, such theories as we have been discussing end up, in the final analysis, by leaving nature completely unexplained. They make matter, its processes, and the finalistic character of these processes ultimate unexplainables. These realities, in such a view, are simply there; either they are sheer necessities, self-existent and self-sufficient, or they are sheer contingencies, existing when they might just as likely not have existed and being what they are when they might as likely have been something else. The true meaning of a philosophy which accepts such a situation is that explanation of the given is no function of philosophy. This proposition — that explanation of the given is no function of philosophy — while it sounds to a Scholastic like a *reductio ad absurdum,* is in very truth the essence of naturalism; for the basic principle of naturalism is that natural processes are to be "explained" only by natural processes. A naturalist, for example, who discovers and admits finality in nature, say in evolution, can "explain" it by saying that matter (if he wishes to use that term) is of its nature in process, that the process follows definite laws, and has a tendency to attain higher levels of organization and function. He cannot, without ceasing to be a naturalist, add one thing more to his "explanation" of evolution.

2. St. Thomas' View. St. Thomas was not satisfied with purely immanent finality as an explanation of nature's behavior. Natural processes tend to ends, and ends are true causes. A true cause must have some kind of real being in order to exert any kind of real influence in bringing an effect to pass. In the case of agents possessed of knowledge, the end or final cause of their actions truly exists as a part of the agent's own equipment, that is, as a thing-desired, constituting a motive for action. But the generality of natural agents have no knowledge of the ends toward which they tend; the end as such is no actual part of their equipment as agents — it does not exist in them. Yet it must actually exist in some way, since it actually operates in producing the effect. Consequently, St. Thomas argues, the unknowing agents in nature, not being able to direct themselves to their ends, yet regularly tending to these ends, must be directed to them by an external or transcendent agent in whom the end or final cause has actual being. This transcendent agent is God, who moves and directs all natural things to the ends preordained by Himself, moving each according to its own nature and according to the natural tendency to its end which He has created in it.[16]

---

[16] See Chapter XXV, "God in Nature."

CHAPTER VI

HYLEMORPHISM

I. THE PROBLEM OF THIS CHAPTER

1. Nature is made up of a great multitude of material substances which undergo change, acting upon and being acted upon by one another. Superficially, at any rate, these substances are of two great classes, the non-living and the living. Each of these two great classes has many subdivisions; each living substance is either plant or animal, and there are a great many different "species" of plants and animals; each inorganic substance is either one of the 92 elements or some compound of two or more of these elements. Each element, each compound, each plant, and each animal is a different "species" of material substance. There are, in a word, many species of material substance.

A species, however, is only a class, a universal. The actual substances of nature are individuals. Real existence belongs, for example, not to the class "tree," but to this, that, and a billion trees; each tree is one individual substance of the species tree. Similarly, not the species dog or man is ultimately real, but individual men and dogs. Finally, not the species oxygen, hydrogen, sodium chloride, but individual quantities of oxygen, hydrogen, and sodium chloride are real material substances. Of such individuals — inorganic and organic — is nature made up.

We call such individuals material substances, corporeal substances, or natural substances. Our task in the present chapter is to determine the essential principles or elements in every corporeal substance — the ultimate intrinsic principles that make it a corporeal substance, a substance of a determinate species, and the individual substance which it is. Obviously such a task is a fundamental one for the philosopher of nature.

2. Essential Principles and Physical Parts. One view of the problem is that it is not a problem for the philosopher at all, because the scientist answers it: the physicist and chemist describe the ultimate nature of matter and inorganic substances, and the biologist the ultimate nature of living substances. This view is not accepted by contemporary Thomists. It is based upon a confusion of the essential principles of natural substances with their physical parts and a confusion of the function and aim of philosophy with the function and aim of natural science.

We are not seeking in this chapter for physical or chemical ultimates. We accept the expert authority of the chemist and physicist when they tell us about the molecular and atomic structure of natural substances, and we accept whatever they say about electrons, protons, neutrons, photons, quanta, and the like. But after we have accepted all these, our original problem remains unsolved; we still have to find the essential constituents of material substances. As this chapter proceeds, it should become clearer to the student how the philosophical quest differs from that of the natural sciences, and the next chapter should entirely clear away any confusion of the two points of view. For the present we may simply ignore the confusion and turn our attention to the rival philosophical theories.

3. The Rival Theories: Merism and Hylemorphism. There are fundamentally only two contradictory theories as to the essence of natural substances. *Mechanism* or *merism* claims that the substances of nature are all made out of the same ultimate physical components differently aggregated or lumped together, and that no nature-giving principle transcending the separate components exists or plays any part in the constitution of natural things. A tree and a chunk of granite, for example, are both aggregates of simple physical particles, and nothing else. Hylemorphism claims that in addition to the matter or stuff in natural substances there is also a nature-giving principle which determines the matter to be this or that kind of substance, for example, a tree or granite. There are many different particular theories under these two general types, but the decisive difference by which they can be grouped is the affirmation or denial of a unifying principle of nature in substances in addition to the material components. All doctrines of atomism and dynamism are, broadly speaking, meristic, and all theories of organism and holism, hylemorphic. *Hylosystemism,* a new theory proposed by some Scholastic philosophers, is, as we shall see, meristic in character. In this chapter we shall study, first hylemorphism, then three meristic theories, viz., mechanistic atomism, dynamic atomism, and dynamism. Hylosystemism we shall examine in Chapter VII.

II. HYLEMORPHISM

1. **Its Place in Thomistic Philosophy.** Hylemorphism is far more than a theory of the essential nature of matter. It is no exaggeration to say that it is the most all-pervasive principle of Thomistic philosophy; there is hardly a problem which St. Thomas touches that he does not solve in terms of matter and form. He by no means limits his application of the matter-form thesis to the material universe. God is infinite form, the Form of forms; the form of any creature is its reflection of the divine Form. Whatever exists, has or is form: whatever lacks form does not exist. Good, Truth, Beauty are form; and evil, falsity, ugliness are deformity or privation of form. Angels are pure forms subsisting independently of matter in complete concreteness. The human soul is a pure form which can subsist independently of matter, but which cannot fulfill its capacities, exercise its faculties, nor attain its end without union with matter. The forms of all beings below man need matter in which to exist. They actualize or dominate the matter in which they exist to a greater or lesser degree according as they are more or less perfect forms. The reason why matter exists is in order that certain forms may attain concrete actuality; or as St. Thomas so often expressed it, "Matter exists for the sake of form." Beings capable of knowing are distinguished from beings incapable of knowing because they are able to possess the forms of other things as well as their own. The difference between spiritual beings and material things is simply and solely that the forms of the former are capable of existing without matter and consequently are not bound and limited by material laws, while the forms of the latter cannot exist apart from matter and therefore are bound and limited by material laws. What makes man such a mysterious being is that his form is both independent of and dependent upon matter: he is both free of and bound by material laws.[1]

2. **As a Theory of the Essence of Body.** But hylemorphism is, to

[1] *In I Phys.*, No. 81; *In I Sent.*, 35, 1, 1, c; *S. Theol.*, I, 14, 1, c; *ibid.*, 75, 2, c; *ibid.*, 76, 1, c; *Con. Gen.*, II, 91; *ibid.*, III, 68 and 97; *De Spirit. Creat.*, I, 12.

begin with, a theory of the essential constitution of corporeal substance and it is only as such that we are concerned with it in the present chapter. Aristotle advanced it in opposition to other theories such as those of Empedocles, Anaxagoras, and Democritus. All these doctrines, regardless of how they differed otherwise, had one assumption in common; namely, that the ultimate elements out of which the various bodies of the world were generated are themselves actual and determinate substances — the four elements in the case of Empedocles, the seeds in the case of Anaxagoras, and the atoms in the case of Democritus. This assumption is precisely what Aristotle denied. The first principles of material substance are not, he insisted, themselves actual substances. The first actual complete substances are the four elements, earth, air, fire, and water; *but these are not first principles.* Each is itself a composite of primary matter and certain elementary forms. This matter and these forms are *first principles.*

Today we count ninety-two elements instead of four, but the meaning of hylemorphism remains the same. None of the ninety-two elements is an ultimate, irreducible principle; but all are composites of the same primary matter and different substantial forms. Hylemorphism is not a rival to any scientific theory of the chemical or physical constitution of matter. If physical theory says that all matter is composed of electrons, hylemorphism will not deny this. But it will say that if an electron is itself an actual particle of matter, then it is composite and is constituted essentially by primary matter united to some form. If modern physics says that matter is not the solid, chunky stuff that former ages believed it to be, but that it is energy, hylemorphism will not disagree; but it will say that if material substance is energy, then energy in its various species is a composite of primary matter and some substantial form.

In the concrete, the meaning of the hylemorphic theory of corporeal substances is that *every* individual actual substance of whatever kind is essentially composite of a determinable and a determining principle. None of the so-called elements of chemistry or the ultimate particles of physics are *essentially* elementary or ultimate. Oxygen is not an "element" from the philosophical point of view; it is a composite of two elements, viz., a determinable potential element, primary matter, and a determining actual element, the form of oxygen; hydrogen has the same determinable potential element in common with oxygen, viz., primary matter, and a different determining actual element, viz., the form of hydrogen. Hence, *primary matter is common to all material substances:* whatever is material is made out of this same ultimate potential stuff. *But each different kind of substance contains this matter under a different actual form.*

3. Substantial Form and Accidental Form; Primary and Secondary Matter. It was, as we have seen in Chapter IV, from his analysis of change that Aristotle derived his doctrine of hylemorphism. He explained change as the acquisition by some matter of a new form. We also noted the distinction between substantial change and accidental change. Now, since every change is the acquisition by some matter of a form which it had not possessed, then the difference between substantial and accidental change must be rooted in some differences found in matter and form themselves. When a change is merely an accidental change, as when water freezes, the new form acquired as a result of the change is an *accidental form;* that is, it is a form that does not determine the nature of the substance that undergoes the change, but determines only some accidental quality or quantity, etc., of that substance. In the case of substantial change, for example, of water into hydrogen and oxygen, the new forms acquired are *substantial forms* — forms that determine the nature of the substance.[2]

Not only are the forms involved in substantial and accidental change different, but so are the matters or substrata. When water freezes, the substratum that persists throughout the change is water. When water is decomposed into hydrogen and oxygen, water does not persist throughout the change, nor does hydrogen or oxygen. What does persist is matter itself, which is neither water nor hydrogen nor oxygen nor any other definite substance. A definite substance, like water, that undergoes accidental changes is called *secondary matter.* The substratum of a substantial change, the matter that persists when a substance loses its nature to take on a new nature, is called *primary matter.* Secondary matter is matter which possesses substantial form; primary matter is matter lacking substantial form. A substantial form unites with, or is received by, primary matter, making it a specific substance, that is, some kind of secondary matter. An accidental form is received by secondary matter, that is, by a determinate substance, which it further determines to some mode of accidental being, e.g., hot, cold, red, healthy, sick.

4. What Primary Matter Is. Primary matter does not mean atoms

_____

[2] *S. Theol.,* I, 76, 4, c; *ibid.,* 6, c.

or protons or electrons or any definite actual thing. Primary matter, matter properly so called, is characterless, natureless, indefinitely mutable; it is mere capacity to become something or be made into something, but is not in itself anything actual. In a word, it is formless. It is that out of which all sensible objects are made; and since it is capable of becoming any material object, while in itself it is actually nothing, it is *pure potentiality*. Since it is in itself only a potentiality of being something, it never actually exists by itself, but only under some substantial form which it has received. Pure potentiality cannot exist as such, for then it would be actual and not purely potential.[3]

5. **Relation of Matter and Form.** Primary matter and substantial form cannot be physically separated. A given form can be separated from a given quantity of matter, but the matter simultaneously takes on a new form, and the old form ceases to possess actual existence in that matter. Primary matter can never exist apart from substantial form; and those forms that unite with matter, with the exception of the human soul, can never exist apart from matter. All natural substances are mixtures of actuality and potentiality; they are actually something and potentially other things; they have one form and can lose it to receive another. Primary matter has no form but can receive any form; it is actually nothing, but it is potentially anything. In itself it is entirely indeterminate, possesses no positive character, has no nature proper to it, has no essence, no idea. It can neither exist nor be known in itself. It does exist, but only in union with substantial forms which actualize it; it is known, but only through substantial forms which determine it. Substantial form is determining, definitive. It determines primary matter to substantial being, to a definite species of being; it gives it a nature. Substantial form is essence or idea. It *informs* primary matter, making it something intelligible, making it definite and definable.[4]

6. **The Unicity of Substantial Form.** According to St. Thomas and the Thomists generally, one substance can have only one substantial form. This is called the doctrine of the unicity of substantial form, and is opposed to the doctrine of the plurality of substantial forms taught by many philosophers of the Augustinian school. St. Thomas advanced a very simple argument to prove his doctrine. "One thing," he wrote, "has but one substantial being. But substantial form gives

---

[3] *S. Theol.,* I, 7, 2, ad 3; 77, 1, ad 2.
[4] *De Pot.,* IV, 1, c; *In I Phys.,* 14; *Q.D. de Anima,* XII, ad 12.

substantial being. Therefore, of one thing there is but one substantial form."⁵ Put in different words, this doctrine means that in
any one substance, no matter how complex it may be, there is only
one substantial nature, and all the parts of the substance are made
what they are by that one substantial nature. In water, for example,
there is only the substantial form of water, not those of oxygen and
hydrogen. In the human organism there is just one substantial form,
the rational soul, and this informs every part of the body, giving to
each part its structure and function and making the whole a complete, unified, integral organism. The various chemical elements and
compounds which, according to chemists, make up the different tissues
of the human body, are not, according to Thomists, actually present
as distinct substances in the body. If they were, the human person
would not be one substance but an aggregate of many substances.
The substantial forms of these elements and compounds do not
exist within the body; but the soul, uniting with primary matter and
conferring actuality and determinateness upon it, molds it to the end
of the organism as such, and confers upon the different parts the
properties needed for the right functioning of those parts. Hence,
*only the accidental forms of the elements and compounds are present
in the body, and all the matter throughout the whole body is united
with one substantial form, the human soul.*⁶

7. The Higher Form Contains the Lower Forms Virtually. According to the Thomistic view, the parts of a substance are potencies of the
matter made actual by the form; and a given substantial form can be
received by and can actualize only matter that is prepared, or has a
proximate potency, for it. In hylemorphic language, two elementary
atoms with affinity for each other are apt, that is to say, have a proximate potentiality, for the form of a certain compound; the compound
is the actuality of these potencies under the determination of the
form. Since the form is received into suitable or prepared matter, it
should not be surprising that this prepared matter, that is, the
atoms, should be found in the new compound. Finally, although the
atoms are found there is no reason for supposing that they retain the
substantial natures which they had before the combination. These
natures made the atoms actually the two elements they were, and
potentially the compound they were to become; the actualizing of

---

⁵ *S. Theol.,* I, 76, 4, *Sed contra.*
⁶ *S. Theol.,* I, 76, 4, c; *ibid.,* 6, c; 7, c; *Con. Gen.,* IV, 81; *De Mixtione Elementorum.*

this potency in the new form is simultaneously the lapsing of the old forms into potentiality. The elements have not gone completely; they remain potentially in the compound. There are varying degrees of potentiality, and they have a very high degree, just as the Republican or Democratic nominee for president has a high degree of potentiality for that office, as compared with John Doe, also potentially president. This high potency is the reason for their reappearance as elements when the compound decomposes.

The doctrine of unicity of substantial form does not mean that the parts of a compound substance or of an organism are accidents. They are substantial, not accidental; but they are *parts,* not complete substances. They are all determined, in their separate qualities, by the one substantial form of the substance of which they are parts. These various parts have certain properties which are similar to those of certain substances, for example, oxygen, hydrogen, nitrogen, carbon, or some compound of these and other elements. These elementary and compound substances are not in the organism as substances; because the latter is *one* substance, not several. Nor are they in it as accidents; because they are not, and cannot be, accidents. They are not in it at all. But the properties which characterize these elements and compounds are in the various parts of the organism as the accidents of these parts. The parts have these accidents because the organism, that is, the substance, cannot exist without these accidents (powers and properties) in its parts. But the powers and properties are accidental forms, not of the elements or compounds whose properties they exactly resemble, but of the one substantial form of the organism. Thus, this higher form contains the substantial forms of the lower substances *virtually,* but not actually; and the higher substance contains the lower substances virtually without containing them as actually distinct substances.

More probable, however, seems the opinion of the Commentator [Averroes] . . . who . . . says that the forms of the elements neither remain in the compound nor are entirely corrupted, but that out of them is made one intermediate form, according as they are augmented or diminished. But since it is not proper to speak of a substantial form as suffering augmentation or diminution, it seems that his statement ought to be understood in the following way: that the forms of the elements are not augmented or diminished as actual substantial forms [*secundum se*], but inasmuch as they remain virtually in the elementary qualities, as if in their own instruments; so that it may be said that the forms do not remain as actual substantial forms, but only as being present virtually in their qualities, from which one intermediate quality is made.[7]

What contains something virtually possesses its accidents, that is, its properties and powers, without actually being it. Thus, a police sergeant has the powers of a patrolman, and a lieutenant the powers of a sergeant and of a patrolman; water has in itself the properties of hydrogen and oxygen; and the human body has, in its various parts, the properties of many chemical substances. That which contains something else virtually is not *actually* what it contains, not because it is not all that the latter is, but because it is all that and more. Consequently, when the final actuality which makes it what it is ceases to determine it, it lapses into what it virtually was. Water, on being decomposed, becomes hydrogen and oxygen. The human body, deprived of the soul, its substantial form, lapses into the chemical elements and compounds whose accidental forms and powers its various parts had. For a very brief time the dead body seems to be a unity, but actually it is but a heap of chemicals. Corruption sets in at once, because it has lost the principle of unity and action by which, during life, it resisted the very same external agencies against which it is now helpless.

At first sight this doctrine, denying the substantial presence of chemical elements and compounds in an organism and of elements in a compound, appears audacious and presumptuous, but its paradoxical character begins to disappear as soon as we reflect that never in an organism do the "chemical substances" act precisely as they do out of an organism. Always there is something extra, "something new has been added," some direction of their activities toward the purposes of the organism as a whole. That is why no purely chemical description of an organism is ever adequate; it is always another case of Hamlet without the Prince of Denmark; it explains all about the organism except its organization. The same observation is true below the organic level. Physical analysis discovers the hydrogen atom and oxygen atom still intact in the water molecule; it would seem then a very simple step to the conclusion that hydrogen and oxygen still persist as substances in water. But Thomists say that such a conclusion is not justified, because it takes no account of the very obvious fact that the atoms of hydrogen and oxygen do not act

[7] St. Thomas, *In Boet. de Trin.*, IV, 3, ad 6.

while in the water molecule in the same way in which they do in their respective hydrogen and oxygen molecules.

The fact that physicists find the elementary atoms still intact in the compound molecule is no objection to the Thomistic theory. It is seen as an objection only by those who assume that the hylemorphic constitution of a substance implies homogeneity, that is, sameness of structure and properties, throughout the substance. Of course, it implies no such thing, as is obvious from the fact that Aristotle and St. Thomas considered organisms to be hylemorphic in constitution and certainly did not think that an organism is homogeneous throughout its parts.

8. **Generation Is From Suitable Matter.** That the compound should bear the marks of its origin from particular elements and show a relationship to these elements in its properties, that it should even retain some of the properties of the elements that have gone into its making, gives no evidence, in the Thomistic view, that it is not a distinct new substance. Generation is not from any matter, but from *materia apta,* as St. Thomas called it. Matter in changing from a lower to a higher form need not cease to exhibit certain traits manifested under the lower form. These same traits may now be determined in it by the higher form if they serve the ends of that higher form, as some of them certainly will do, since the matter would not have received the higher form in the first place unless something in the nature which it possessed made it suitable for the higher form. Like many other phenomena put forth as objections against the Thomistic thesis, this one is in fact something that should be expected if that thesis is true.[8]

9. **Hylemorphic Theory of Corporeal Substance Summarized.** We may now summarize all the above, recapitulating the hylemorphic doctrine of the essence of corporeal substance. Every material or corporeal substance, that is to say every complete natural body, is essentially a single individual thing compounded of two intrinsic essential principles, primary matter and substantial form. In a material substance primary matter is potential, passive, determinable. It is the root of passivity and receptivity. In virtue of it, the body can be acted upon, moved, divided, changed, corrupted. The substantial form

[8] *S. Theol.,* I, 76, 4, ad 4; *ibid.,* 8, c; *Con. Gen.,* IV, 81; *De Mixt. Elem.* Since the above was written, an article has appeared treating the Thomistic doctrine of the unity of substantial form, from the same point of view, but with more scientific authority: W. R. Thompson, F.R.S., "The Unity of the Organism," *The Modern Schoolman,* Vol. XXIV, No. 3 (March, 1947), pp. 125–157.

is actualizing, determining, and active. In virtue of it, the body maintains its own identity, possesses its own properties, acts, causes changes in other bodies, makes itself known. In virtue of the form, the body is of a certain nature, belongs to a certain species; in virtue of the matter it is an individual embodiment of this nature, an individual member of this species. All bodies of the same species have the same substantial form in different parcels of matter; bodies of different species have different forms as well as different matters./Matter and form are the intrinsic causes of the substance: matter, by receiving the form and embodying it in concrete being; form, by actualizing the matter and determining it to a specific nature. Form is the principle of nature or species, and matter is the principle of individuation.[9]

III. MERISM

1. Merism is a term which some Scholastic writers have used recently to designate the philosophical theories which have traditionally been known as mechanism. The term merism is derived from the Greek word *meros* meaning particle, and is a suitable name for all theories of corporeal substance which hold that the various substances of nature are aggregates of similar physical particles and nothing more. It is a better term for this purpose than mechanism, because the latter more primarily designates anti-teleological philosophies of nature. However, such philosophies have generally been meristic as well as mechanistic. We may distinguish three types of meristic doctrines. (1) Classical atomism or mechanism, which we have already studied in its original formulation by Leucippus and Democritus, and which was widespread in the seventeenth, eighteenth, and nineteenth centuries. Descartes, Gassendi, and Hobbes all taught some variation of this theory in the seventeenth century. (2) Dynamic atomism, which succeeded classical atomism among many modern scientists and philosophers. (3) Dynamism, which is usually considered as diametrically opposed to atomism, but which is, nevertheless, meristic in character.

2. **Classical or mechanistic atomism** attempts to account for all nature by two factors alone, homogeneous material masses and their movements in space. According to this theory, every material substance

[9] *S. Theol.*, I, 3, 2, ad 3; *De Ver.*, II, 6, ad 1, *In Boet. de Trin.*, IV, 2, c. Matter as the principle of individuation is explained in the last section of the present chapter.

—living as well as non-living—is composed of solid, indivisible, unchangeable, extended particles, which are irreducible ultimates, unanalyzable into any more fundamental principles. These particles are qualityless and inert. They are in motion, and communicate motion to one another by shock when they bump. Their ceaseless movement causes them to combine in various patterns. Corporeal substances of all kinds—inorganic and organic—are merely different aggregations of the matter-particles; that is, each kind of substance is a different particle-pattern with a different motion-pattern in the particles. The different properties of different substances arise from the differences in aggregation and pattern among the particles.

3. **Dynamic Atomism** differs from classical mechanism only by attributing to each particle intrinsic forces or energies; that is to say, the particles are not inert but are centers of force, for example of gravitational, magnetic, and electrical force.

4. **Dynamism.** The older atomism denied the reality of force or energy, recognizing only extended material particles as real; dynamic atomism asserted the reality of forces as well as of extended particles; the next theory, *dynamism,* denies the reality of extended particles and recognizes only forces as real. According to dynamists, the ultimate constituent elements of all material substances are *simple, unextended force-points.* Matter, in other words, does not consist in chunks of solid volume but in unit-points of activity or force. These force-particles, combining in a way pretty much similar to the way in which the atomists thought the atoms combine, give rise to all the different substances with their different properties.

A Jesuit scientist and mathematician, *R. J. Boscovich* (1711–1787), maintained a theory of dynamism. The first elements of matter are points absolutely indivisible and without any extension. These elementary points are homogeneous and by their different relations and activities give rise to all the material substances of experience. The essence of these points is a force, or a determination to decrease or increase the distance which separates them from one another. When the force-points are infinitesimally close, the force is repulsive; as the distance between them increases, the repulsive character of the force decreases, and when a certain distance is reached the force becomes attractive in character. This reversibility of force accounts, on the one hand, for the stability of bodies whereby they are held together, and, on the other, for their (apparent) extension whereby they do not merge or coalesce into a single point. Leibniz and Kant, among modern philosophers, also taught theories of dynamism.

More recently, within the Scholastic fold, Father *Dominick Palmieri*, S.J. (1829–1909), adopted a theory somewhat similar to that of Father Boscovich. The ultimate constituents of material substance are simple, indivisible, unextended, substantial elements. He recognized in them three essential properties: virtual extension, force of resistance, and force of constriction. The extension of sensible bodies he attributed to the "virtual" extension of the elementary forces. By virtual extension he understood the power of a simple unextended body to exist in and exert its activity in the whole of and each part of an extended space, without itself being spread out part by part through that space. For the concept of space-possession by space-filling, he simply substituted the concept of space-possession by total action throughout the space.

Against the proponents of hylemorphism, Palmieri held that the unity of compound bodies can be reconciled with the persistence in them of unchanged ultimate constituents. Corporeal substances are distinguished from one another by their distinctive properties. Now while it is true that the properties of a composite body do not belong to its constituent elements in isolation, there is no reason to believe that the union of these elements cannot produce these new powers — powers distinctive of the composite body. Therefore, from the union of the simple unextended elements a new *nature* is produced, nature being the first principle within a being of its operations and properties. This last point really makes Palmieri's doctrine hylemorphic.

IV. THE PROOF OF HYLEMORPHISM

Many proofs of hylemorphism have been offered by Scholastic philosophers, but we shall be content here with giving the oldest and most traditional of all the arguments, the proof from substantial change. This argument is essentially Aristotle's demonstration that the first principles of generation are matter, form, and privation.[10] We shall first present the proof in its simple form, then in the setting of the whole physical universe as we have studied that universe in Chapter V. Our argument will proceed, not merely from individual generations of isolated substances, but from the omnipresent and unceasing processes of transformation which, together with the beings which undergo these processes, constitute nature.

[10] Cf. Chapter IV, Section II.

1. **The Argument in Brief.** *a*) Substantial change is the transformation of a substance, or substances, into a new substance of a different nature; as, for example, the transformation of hydrogen and oxygen into water or vice versa. Substantial change is contrasted with accidental change, in which a substance is altered or modified in some aspect of its being but remains the same substance; as, for example, the alteration of water from a liquid to a solid or vaporous state.

b) Every substantial change involves an original substance and a new substance produced out of it. Therefore, there must be: (1) something substantial common to the two substances and carried over through the change, since otherwise the new substance would not be in fact produced out of the old one; (2) something substantial different in each of the two, since otherwise they would not in fact be different substances.

c) That which is common and carried over must not of itself possess what is peculiar to either of the substances, since at one time it has and at another time it lacks the peculiar nature of each. To become first the one and then the other, it must not of itself have any determinate substantial nature, but must, on the contrary, have the capacity to receive any such nature. It must, in a word, be in itself indeterminate and potential. This indeterminate and potential substratum — the essential potency in every natural substance making it changeable — is *primary matter.*

d) The two termini of the change, that is, the substance present before and the one present after the change, are both determinate, actual substances with specific natures. Hence, they cannot be merely the indeterminate substratum of change, but must have in them some other substantial principle. Each must contain a substantial principle which makes it the actual substance that it is by determining the primary matter to a specific determinate nature. This second principle is determining and actual. It is the substantial form.

e) Wherefore, we conclude, every natural changeable substance is a composite of two essential, intrinsic, constitutive principles, one determinable, the other determining, namely, primary matter and substantial form.[11]

2. **The Argument in Larger Setting.** Many recent Scholastic philoso-

---

[11] The above form of the argument follows very closely that of the late John F. McCormick, S.J., in *Scholastic Metaphysics.* I (Chicago: Loyola University Press, 1928), pp. 188–189.

phers are dissatisfied with this argument, whose validity depends entirely upon the actual occurrence of substantial changes. They call upon the findings of chemistry and physics for evidence that none of the changes in inorganic nature are really substantial changes, but are explainable in terms of rearrangements of elementary physical particles. Other Scholastics defend the argument, calling upon chemistry and physics for evidence of the reality of substantial change. In plain fact, there is no point in seeking in chemistry and physics any decision as to whether a change is substantial or accidental. Since the concepts of substance and accident, as Scholastic philosophers understand them, play no part in chemical and physical science, these sciences can hardly be expected to furnish a criterion of substantial change. Our evaluation of the traditional argument must, therefore, be determined by quite other considerations. We must evaluate the proof in the light of what we have already discovered about nature.

In Chapter V we explained and demonstrated both intrinsic and extrinsic finality in nature; that is to say, we demonstrated that natural agents act for ends, that natural substances possess determinate natures with distinctive properties and operations, that the same elements and compounds constantly recur in nature, and taken together with the physical conditions prevailing in the earth-environment, serve to support living organisms, that these organisms both in their development and vital operations, are organized for definite ends, namely, the life and well-being of the individual and of the species. All that adds up to this: that the physical world is an ordered cosmos or universe and not a mere aggregate of mutually indifferent things; that nature, in a word, is marked by finality and order. This fact is very relevant to the question of the essence of corporeal substance. For the corporeal substances of nature — the elements, the compounds, and the organisms — are the unit-parts in the order or design of nature; it is through their being what they are that this order is established and maintained. They are therefore not indifferent to this order but essential to it; the order is in truth the order of these elements, compounds, and organisms. It arises from their natures and is, in very fact, the relations and interactions resultant from their properties and operations. These substances *are*, collectively, the physical world, and the laws of the physical world are nothing else than the regular modes of their actions and interactions.

The corporeal substances which make up the physical world are endowed with immanent finality, that is to say, they are of their very natures directed toward definite ends. This finality is apparent whether the various substances are considered individually or in relation to one another and to the whole material universe. We must, consequently, posit in every corporeal substance an intrinsic principle which determines the substantial nature and the specific properties of the substance; we must, in other words, recognize that the distinctive properties and operations of every corporeal substance belong to the substance itself, arising out of its nature and not being merely thrust upon it by extrinsic causes. The only alternative is to deny that these substances possess any unifying immanent principle which endows them with their nature, properties, and operations and determines them to their natural end.

All *meristic* theories, which reduce corporeal substances to mere aggregates of similar particles and admit no unifying substantial principle which organizes these particles, dissociate the peculiar properties of each substance from the substance itself, since the particles are of themselves indifferent to the various properties of elementary and compound bodies, having now one set, now another. These systems, therefore, fail to account for the invariable recurrence of the same elements and compounds, for their unchanging possession of the same properties, and for their co-operation in producing the order of the universe. In a word, they fail to account for the immanent finality of material substances.

The doctrine of *hylemorphism,* on the other hand, offers the only possible explanation of the immanent finality of nature, namely, an intrinsic, essential, nature-determining principle in each substance — a principle which organizes the matter into a substance of a definite nature and endows it with a specific set of properties. This unifying principle must be admitted in every substance, because diverse parts, e.g., atoms or force-points, or protons and electrons, cannot by themselves form a true unity; of themselves they are a plurality, and if they are subordinated to a unity they must be so subordinated by a principle which organizes them into one substance with a single nature. Furthermore, by the fact that in various combinations they manifest different substantial natures with their different sets of properties they show that *in themselves* they are indifferent to any particular substantial nature. Consequently, if they are to become now one and now another specific substance, they must be specifically determined by a substantial principle distinct from themselves — a unifying and organizing principle. This principle is the substantial form.

Since the elements in a compound lose the specific properties which they possess in a free state and take on a new set, and since each of these sets of properties must be attributed to an intrinsic, substantial, organizing principle, then the elements in entering a compound must pass from one substantial state to another, and hence must lose one substantial form and take on another. And since the compound is truly produced out of something in the elements and not created out of nothing, some determinable, passive principle must be transformed from one substance into another. In itself, this principle must have no substantial form, but must be capable of receiving now one now another, and must therefore be related to actual substances as a potentiality. Therefore, there must be in every corporeal substance a passive principle which is in itself no substance in actuality but every material substance in potentiality. This is primary matter.

Consequently, the only theory that satisfactorily accounts for the observable phenomena of the physical universe is hylemorphism, the theory that every corporeal substance is a composite of two essential intrinsic principles, one a passive, determinable principle of potentiality, viz., primary matter, and the other an active, determining principle of actuality, viz., substantial form.

3. **The Refutation of Merism.** The proof of hylemorphism is the proof that natural substances are not mere aggregates of physical particles, but that the matter of each substance embodies a real principle of substantial unity which actualizes, organizes, and determines that matter to a specific nature. All mechanistic and dynamistic theories deny the existence of any such principle, and, consequently, the demonstration of hylemorphism is at the same time the refutation of these theories, and of all meristic theories. This positive proof of hylemorphism is the *only* philosophical refutation of merism.

4. **Some Poor Arguments Against Merism.** Many Scholastic cosmologists give several further reasons for rejecting mechanism and dynamism, but it seems to the present writer that most of these reasons are scientific rather than philosophical in character, that they are far from certain in their scientific foundations, and that they quite miss the point at issue. Mechanism and dynamism, except for their denial of any principle of substantial unity in natural bodies, have no relation to hylemorphism and no philosophical significance at all.

Stripped of this primary denial, they become scientific hypotheses of the physical constitution of bodies or of matter, using the latter term as physicists use it; that is to say, they are concerned with *the ultimate physical particles* of which bodies are composed, and *not with their primary essential constituents;* therefore, judgment as to their truth or falsity is in the province of the physicist, not of the philosopher of nature. The verdict of physics is important in its own right, but is irrelevant to the issue of hylemorphism *versus* merism. *Physical mechanism, whether atomic or dynamistic, is not incompatible with hylemorphism.*

The same thing is true of dynamism. Some hylemorphists argue against dynamism on the ground that it denies the real extension of bodies by making them aggregates of unextended particles, since no number of unextended units can ever add up to an extended total. This argument against dynamism is based upon a common misunderstanding of hylemorphism. Dynamism, considered as a *physical* theory having nothing to say for or against substantial form, does not deny the real extension of bodies in any way that is philosophically significant. Substantially a body must be considered as continuously extended, even though its physical parts are discrete, as long as it is a substantial unit from terminus to terminus. Thus, there is no question that hylemorphism considers an organism as a *continuous substantial unit,* despite the fact that the organism is *physically discontinuous,* being composed of separate molecules. Hylemorphism insists upon the substantial unity of bodies, but says nothing whatsoever of the continuous physical extension of the bodies or their parts; that is to say, hylemorphism does *not* posit continuous physical extension in substances in the sense that the body or any part of it must "fill up" the space which it occupies in the way in which we imagine water to fill a pail.

A similar comment may be made about another argument advanced in many textbooks. Dynamism, it is said, involves action at a distance, since in that theory the parts of a substance, not being extended, could not be in contact and yet would be acting upon one another. But action at a distance is philosophically untenable. Hence, dynamism must be rejected. Here again the argument misses the point. As long as it retains its denial of substantial form, dynamism involves action at a distance; but considered as a purely physical theory it does not imply action at a distance in any way that is philosophically significant. The physical particles of a substance might be spatially separated when considered simply as individual particles; but considered as parts of the same substance, actualized and organized by the one substantial form, they cannot be said, in any meaningful sense, to be interacting "at a distance." Dynamism is false because it denies substantial form, not because it posits unextended ultimate physical components in matter.

The evident implication of these last paragraphs is that the only element in mechanism, dynamism, and similar theories, that makes them rivals to hylemorphism is their denial of hylemorphism. If the hylemorphist regards these theories as physical hypotheses, there is no reason why he should not expect one or other of them to be verifiable on the physical level. As a matter of fact, Father Palmieri's theory is strikingly similar to the view that many physicists take today in respect to electrons. They regard the latter, not as bulks filling a space or moving through the space, but as units of force or energy *acting throughout a space*. Why could not substantial forms actualize the pure potentiality of primary matter into such ultimate physical parts of substances? The thesis so often given in Scholastic manuals in connection with hylemorphism, namely, that bodies and their ultimate parts have continuous physical extension, is in fact no part of hylemorphism, and would seem to be far less certain than hylemorphism.

V. INDIVIDUATION

1. **The Problem.** We have been concerned, thus far in the present chapter, with the *essence* of material substances. The essence or nature of any material substance is its matter and form. But a material substance is not identical with its essence. Thus, Socrates is a man, but he is not human nature. The definition of man, which expresses the quiddity or essence of man, is predicable of every man, not only of Socrates. Socrates, on the other hand, cannot be predicated of anything but himself. Human nature is what Aristotle called a *second substance*. It is universal, or communicable to many. Socrates is a *first substance*. He is individual and incommunicable. Second substance means an essence or nature. First substance means an individual thing having an essence or nature. Our problem in the present section is to discover what that principle is by virtue of which a multitude of first substances which have the same essence are distinct individuals. In other words, what is the principle of individuation in corporeal substances?

In order to understand St. Thomas' theory of individuation in material substances, it is necessary to have clearly in mind the problem which he was trying to solve and the conditions which were part of the problem. Material substances possess natures which are not themselves individual, since each of these natures is found in many different substances and is one in all of them. If any such nature had within itself the principle of its own individuation and incommunicability, it would be capable of existing by itself in concrete individuality as the subject of its own existence, and it would not need a subject *in which* to exist. It would, in a word, be both a nature and a first substance, as are simple essences or "separated forms," that is, the angels. But, by the same token, it would be incapable of any multiplicity of existences; its individuality would be identical with its nature, for it is itself the nature. The individualization of a simple essence is its act of existence. Once it exercises that act, it exists as an individual substance, a *suppositum*. It cannot repeat the act; it cannot now come into existence, for it exists. Hence, an essence which is itself a subject of existence can exist only as one individual. Now this most certainly is not the mode of being of corporeal essences. These are not simple forms, but exist in combination with matter; they are not incommunicable individuals, but exist in a multitude of instances; they are not themselves ultimate subjects of existence, but exist in subjects. Consequently it cannot be that they have within themselves the principle of their own individuation.

> Forms which can be received in matter are individuated by matter, which cannot be in another as in a subject since it is the first underlying subject; although form of itself, unless something else prevents it, can be received by many. But that form which cannot be received in matter, but is self-subsisting, is individuated precisely because it cannot be received in a subject. . . . [12]

The essence of any corporeal substance is, as stated above, its matter and form. Thus, all the trees in a forest have the same essence or nature because they are all composites of matter and the same one form. The common form which they all possess cannot, certainly, account for their individual distinctness or otherness, because this form is the principle of their oneness or sameness, and is, considered in itself, uni-

[12] *S. Theol.*, I, 3, 2, ad 3 (*Basic Writings of St. Thomas Aquinas*, ed. Anton C. Pegis, New York: Random House, Inc., 1945, Vol. I, p. 28. Copyright 1945, by Random House, Inc. Reprinted by permission of Random House, Inc.). Cf. *ibid.*, 3, 3, c.

versal, since it is obviously communicable to many. Consequently, the principle of their individual otherness must be sought in their matter. Matter, however, is also common to all of them: they are not individually different by virtue of matter considered in itself, since they all contain it. Indeed, matter is part of their very essence, and, as we have seen, that essence is *not* individual or incommunicable. Yet this is certain: matter must in some way be the principle of individuation for trees, for it is undeniable that the reason why there may be a multiplicity of trees is the fact that there can be multiple portions of matter to embody the same nature, tree. Hence, we must seek for something about matter which makes it individualize forms in distinct and incommunicable substances.

2. The Principle of Individuation: Matter Marked by Quantity. The matter which is in the essence of a natural substance is merely matter in general, not this or that individual matter — in man's essence are flesh and bones, but not *this* flesh and *these* bones. Matter in the essence is not marked off or determined by certain dimensions or individual accidents. The matter which is proper to the individual, on the other hand, is individual matter marked off from all other matter by certain dimensions; for example, this flesh and these bones. Dimensions are determinations of quantity. It is, therefore, the accident of quantity that makes matter divisible into separate parts or portions having certain dimensions; and it is this divisibility of matter which makes it possible that one same form should unite with distinct portions of matter to constitute a plurality of individuals having the same nature. Thus, matter marked off by quantity (*materia quantitate signata*) is the principle of individuation in material substances.

This may be made clearer if we consider that the individuation of material substances involves three problems: (1) By what principle does the essence of a material substance acquire the character of incommunicability whereby it is an individual? (2) By what principle does it receive the numerability by which a multiplicity of individuals of this essence are possible? (3) By what principle does it become an ultimate subject of existence and predication? The answer to the first and second questions is quantitative dimensions, and the answer to the third is matter. The answer to all three is matter determined by quantitative dimensions.

(1) A material thing is incommunicable and individual, not by virtue of its form, which is found in others as well as in it, nor by virtue

of matter taken simply, which is also found in others, but by virtue of certain spatial and temporal boundaries which set it off from everything else. Hence, in answer to the first question, quantitative dimensions are the principle of incommunicability in a material substance. (2) A material nature can be repeated or multiplied in several individuals because it can be received in a subject which is divided into a plurality of portions which differ only numerically, being mere repetitions of one another. But it is the spatial and temporal dimensions of matter which divide it into parcels which duplicate one another and differ only numerically, so that all are capable of receiving the same nature. Hence the answer to the second question is, again, quantitative dimensions. (3) The third question requires an additional consideration. Quantity and its dimensions are accidents, but an ultimate subject of existence cannot be in the genus accident, because accidents exist only by inhering in substance. Hence an ultimate subject of existence must be substantial as well as incommunicable. Matter is in the genus substance; it is substance in potentiality, or potency for being *per se*. It is not predicable of anything, but forms are predicable of it. Hence, in answer to the third question, the substantiality required of an ultimate subject of existence is, in corporeal substances, to be found in their matter. Therefore, finally, matter determined by quantitative dimensions is the substantial subject which receives the substantial form, particularizing it as an incommunicable first substance or individual, and allowing, by its own divisibility, the multiplication of individuals possessing this same form. Matter marked by quantity is the principle of individuation in corporeal substances.[13]

3. **Difficulties and Answers.** St. Thomas' doctrine of individuation in corporeal substances has often been called in question by other Scholastic philosophers.[14] There seem to be two chief reasons for this. One reason is that St. Thomas taught emphatically and unmistakably that matter has no proper nature, no activity, no determinate character, but is pure potentiality. Now, how can something so described be called a *principle*? By "the principle of individuation" we ought to mean that which determines a being to be an individual. But matter is never determining; it is always determinable. It is not the root of a single

---

[13] For this whole section so far, cf.: *De Pot.*, IX, 1; *In X Meta.*, 3; *De Ente*, II; *In Boet. de Trin.*, IV, 2; *S. Theol.*, I, 3, 2, ad 3; *ibid.*, 3, 3, c; *ibid.*, 75, 4. See also Sertillanges, *S. Thomas d'Aquin* (Paris: Felix Alcan, 1912), Vol. I, pp. 79–90.

[14] For a recent criticism see H. Meyer, *The Philosophy of St. Thomas Aquinas* (St. Louis: Herder, 1945), pp. 72–80.

positive character in a composite, for every definite intelligible determination is due to form; and matter only *receives* determinations.
Hence, it would seem, St. Thomas contradicts his own conception of
matter when he states that it is the principle of individuation in individual material substances. The other reason is related to this one. Individuality is the final substantial perfection of every substance; indeed,
a thing's individuality is nothing less than itself. Surely this crowning
determination of a nature — its ultimate condition for real existence —
cannot be conferred on it by matter. Especially is this so in the case of
man. A man, as we shall see in a later chapter, is a composite of matter and form, and his form is his soul. A man's individuality is his
personality itself. Are we to attribute this to the matter in him? Are
different men different persons merely by virtue of their bodily differences? Is not a man's soul the root of his personality?

If these difficulties were in fact involved in St. Thomas' doctrine of
individuation, he would indeed be in a most precarious position. But
they are not. The Angelic Doctor never regarded matter as an *active*
principle of anything, and he did not regard it as the source or root
of individuality. He never spoke of matter as any sort of principle
except a *material principle,* and for him a material principle is always
receptive, never active. As for individuality, the ultimate substantial
perfection, the positive root of it is unquestionably the substantial form,
which in man is his spiritual soul. Yet St. Thomas is quite right and
quite accurate in calling matter the principle of individuation. Let us
try to understand how this can be so.

4. **The Individual and Individual Differences.** To say that matter
is the principle of individuation is not equivalent to saying that it is
the active determinant of the individual, or the root of substantial
individuality. Actualization by some substantial form is always necessary for matter to be a principle in any respect. Quantity, which is the
necessary condition in matter, fitting it to be the principle of individuation, does not exist except in matter which is actually united with
substantial form. Quantity is itself an accidental form, and all accidental forms are subsequent to and dependent upon substantial form.[15]
This same thing is true of all those qualities or dispositions in matter
which are the basis of the individual differences of different substances.
None of them can be considered as existing in the matter in actuality

[15] *In I Sent.,* d. 8, q. 5, 2, c; *In II Sent.,* d. 30, q. 2, 1, c; *S. Theol.,* I, 76, 6, c;
De Nat. Mat.

prior to the determination of the substantial form. They exist in the matter "in incomplete actuality." This means that in the determinate concrete substance out of which a new substance is made or generated, there exist actual quantitative and qualitative accidents which are pre-dispositions in the matter for the reception of the new form. You can't make a silk purse out of a sow's ear, and you cannot produce a given substance out of *any* prior substance but only out of one predisposed by certain actual qualities — that is to say, out of suitable matter. When the new substance is generated, it will possess some determinations like those of the old substance. The active determining principle of these determinations will be the substantial form of the thing generated. Since in different productions of substances of the same kind the substantial form will be received by different quantities of matter differently disposed or prepared, and since the substantial form can actualize only the potentialities waiting for actualization, the substances which emerge from distinct processes of generation will possess distinct individual characteristics. Thus, both the actual being of the substance, which, strictly speaking, is its individuality, and the distinct individual characteristics which it possesses, have as their active root and principle the substantial form, to which, as St. Thomas always held, every positive character of the individual is due.

The dependency of accidental form upon substantial form is as true of quantity, which makes matter the principle of individuation, as it is of any accidental form. Matter has an essential potency for quantity, but this potency is posterior to matter's potency for substantial form. The first principles of actual quantity are the substantial forms which unite with matter — those forms which St. Thomas frequently calls material forms or natural forms, and which are contrasted with separated forms. It is these natural forms which determine the natures of the substances which result from their union with matter; and these substances are always bodies, that is to say they are characterized by spatial dimensions. Matter exists in order to *receive* the quantitative determinations required in this kind of substance; but the active determining principle of quantity is substantial form. For corporeal substance is quantitative by essence; and the positive intrinsic determinant of essence is substantial form. In other words, matter exists because certain forms of being require extended bodies in order actually to exist.[16]

[16] *De Ente*, II; *Q.D. de Anima*, 9, c.

From these considerations it is clear that in calling quantified matter the principle of individuation St. Thomas did not imply that matter is an active principle, or that it possesses any determinations in itself apart from substantial form, or that it confers upon a substance some positive individual characteristics, or, especially, that it constitutes the individuality of the concrete substance. *Individuality* must not be confused with *individuation*. Individuality is a positive perfection; it is, as we have said, nothing less than the concrete reality of the substance and it is conferred upon matter by form and by an efficient cause. Individuation is merely a name used to indicate that natural forms, although universal and one when considered in themselves, are, in the order of being, actually realized only in particular and multiple embodiments. Only individuals are real existents, and these forms are individual only when determining quantified matter. And since it is the attribute of quantity, which they confer upon the matter, which makes the matter divisible and gives it dimensions marking off distinct portions, and making possible an *otherness* different from the specific otherness of forms, thus allowing the forms to be repeatedly induced in different portions of matter, matter is rightly called the principle of individuation. Since these distinct parts or portions of matter are differently disposed for actualization by a given form, the same form, received into different matters, will determine them to individually different embodiments of itself. Thus, when St. Thomas attributes to the matter of a substance its peculiar individual accidents,[17] he means, not that the individual is determined to the accidental mode by the matter, but rather that the conditions imposed by the prior dispositions of the matter constitute a limit on the determining efficacy of the form and thus produce the individual differences of substances; the same principle actualizing different potencies produces different results. Thus, men with better disposed bodies have higher intelligence,[18] yet certainly intelligence is attributable to the soul as its principle and not to the body.

[17] *S. Theol.*, I, 54, 3, ad 2.
[18] *S. Theol.*, I, 85, 7, c.

CHAPTER VII

HYLOSYSTEMISM VS. HYLEMORPHISM

I. THE PHYSICAL STRUCTURE OF MATTER

1. Many Scholastic cosmologists of recent years have been pre-occupied, when treating of the doctrine of hylemorphism, with the problem of reconciling that doctrine with contemporary scientific concepts of the nature and structure of matter. Some of them, as noted in the previous chapter, have gone so far as to reject hylemorphism as a theory of the essential constitution of inorganic substances and to replace it with a new theory, hylosystemism. This new theory is based upon, and bases its arguments against hylemorphism upon the findings of modern physics, especially on contemporary scientific views about the atomic structure of matter. In this chapter we shall examine this new theory, not because of any intrinsic importance in the theory, but because such an examination will afford us an occasion to present a defense of hylemorphism against the objections derived from modern science. In order to do this we must do two other things first: (*a*) summarize the physical facts and theories which the hylosystemists consider relevant; (*b*) explain certain principles concerning the relation of the philosophy of nature to the data of the natural sciences.

2. **The Contemporary Scientific View of Matter.** *a*) *Elements and Compounds.* In the view of modern chemistry every material substance is either a simple substance, called an element, or a composite substance called a compound. An element is a form of matter which cannot be decomposed chemically into any simpler forms. Hydrogen, oxygen, carbon, chlorine, and the like, are elements. A compound is a form of matter which can be decomposed chemically into simpler forms, that is, into two or more elements. Water is decomposable into hydrogen and oxygen, common salt into sodium and chlorine.

b) *Molecules and Atoms.* To the senses of sight and touch, material substances appear to be continuously extended. That is to say, when you look at or feel, for example, a bar of iron, it looks and feels as if from one end to the other there is an unbroken stretch of iron; it does not look or feel as if it were made up of separate particles of iron in the way in which, for example, a pile of sand is made up of separate particles of sand. Nevertheless the chemist teaches us that every substance is composed of distinct tiny quantities which do not form a continuous single quantity but are in fact separated from one another. These tiny quantities are the smallest amounts of the substance which can exist. Each one of them has the nature and properties of the whole substance; they are the chemical units of which all natural bodies, whether elementary or compound, are composed. They are called molecules.

Molecules are themselves made up of still smaller units called atoms. (The atoms of modern chemistry have only the vaguest sort of relation to the atoms of Leucippus and Democritus.) A molecule of hydrogen, for example, is composed of two hydrogen atoms; a molecule of oxygen, of two oxygen atoms. The molecules of the compounds consist of two or more different elementary atoms — a molecule of water is made up of two atoms of hydrogen and one of oxygen (H_2O); a molecule of sulphuric acid is composed of two atoms of hydrogen, one of sulphur, and four of oxygen (H_2SO_4). Chemical combination, therefore, is the uniting of atoms of different elements to form a molecule of a single compound; chemical decomposition is the breaking down of a compound molecule into its constituent elementary atoms.

c) *Electrons, Protons, Neutrons, etc.* For a good part of the nineteenth century, chemists thought of atoms as simple, indivisible, homogeneous particles, very much like the atoms of Democritus. Such a view is not held today. Contemporary physics and chemistry look upon atoms as having, not a simple, but a complex structure. The atom is far from solid: it consists of a central nucleus and surrounding shells (or rings or orbits); and the "empty" space between the nucleus and shells far exceeds the space filled by the particles which make up the nucleus and revolve in the orbits. The atom has frequently been compared to the solar system; the nucleus being compared to the sun, the shells to the planetary orbits, and the particles of the shells to the planets. The analogy is useful, but must not be pressed too hard; it is impossible to describe an atom today in any language except that of electricity.

The nucleus of an atom is positively charged. It consists of *protons*, which are particles of matter carrying a positive electrical charge, or of protons and neutrons, which are particles of the same mass as protons but electrically neutral. A neutron may, perhaps, be a proton and an electron bound together and neutralizing each other's charge. The mass of the atom is determined by the number of protons and neutrons in its nucleus.

The shells or orbits of the atom consist of *electrons* whirling at tremendous speeds around the nucleus. An electron is negatively charged; it has a mass of only about $1/1845$ of that of the proton. The chemical and physical properties (other than mass) of the elements are functions of the orbital electrons. The negative charge on an electron equals in magnitude the positive charge on a proton; and the number of electrons in the shells of an atom equals the number of protons in its nucleus, making the atom itself electrically neutral. Besides protons, neutrons, and electrons, physicists also speak of other ultimate particles of matter, e.g., positrons and mesotrons.

Just as matter has been analyzed into discontinuous and heterogeneous physical particles, so, too, has modern physics discovered "particles" or units of energy and light. According to the quantum theory, which has revolutionized physics, energy is not expended in continuous outpouring, like water from a spring, but in individual, discrete packets, like bullets from a machine gun. These ultimate packets of energy are called *quanta* (singular, *quantum*). Light, too, is emitted in individual quantities called *photons*. Photons seem to possess the properties of both waves and particles — properties presumed to be incompatible. To complicate matters further, energy-units like photons, and matter-units like positrons and electrons seem to be transmutable into each other, so that matter seems to become energy and energy to become matter.

3. All these data, and others like them, have often been put forward as conflicting with, and, in fact, destroying utterly the hylemorphic theory of the essential constitution of material substances. On the other hand, some Scholastic philosophers have sought to show in these data evidence for hylemorphism. Others, again, have tried to alter or "doctor up" hylemorphism in order to make it compatible with these physical facts. Finally, some have concluded that we must abandon hylemorphism. In the present writer's opinion all these views are erroneous and are based upon two misunderstandings: (1) a misunder-

standing of the relations of physical science and the philosophy of nature, and (2) a misunderstanding of St. Thomas' doctrine of hylemorphism.

II. SOME RELATIONS OF SCIENCE AND PHILOSOPHY[1]

1. Essential Principles and Ultimate Physical Parts. By the essence or the essential constituents of a corporeal substance is meant the first principle or principles within a corporeal substance that make it a corporeal substance, a substance of a determinate nature or species, and the particular substance that it is. By the first essential principles of corporeal substance we do not mean the ultimate physical parts of the material substance. The latter are the first physical or empirical actualities in the substance, but they may themselves be composed of essential, metaphysical, or meta-empirical principles or they may be united with, actualized by, and organized by a metaphysical principle to constitute the substance. The first essential principles of anything composite are the ultimate components whose union constitutes the composite one thing, though compound. The quest for these first essential principles is a task for the philosopher of nature. The discovery of the first physical parts of matter is a task for the physicist; and the philosopher of nature cannot assume that they are the essential principles which he is seeking.

The philosopher must not assume that the ultimate essential principles of bodies are the same things as their ultimate physical components because he knows that one and the same quest can never discover both sets of principles even if, in the end, these turned out to be the same things. The search for physical components and the search for essential constituents follow different methods and aim at different results. The first quest is carried out in the order of phenomena, that is to say, sensible objects, events, and relations; the second quest is carried out in the order of essences, that is to say, intelligible beings and real causes. The self-imposed conditions of scientific method, which always makes final appeal to observational or experimental verification, make it impossible that scientific research should ever discover anything in the realm of essences; and the quest of the philosopher for the pure intelligible underlying the sensible can never lead directly to discovery in the realm of phenomena. If a physicist should ever deter-

---

[1] Chapter XIX will be entirely devoted to the relations of natural science and philosophy.

mine the essential constituents of material substances, it would be because he had for the time being disregarded the rules of his own game and had been playing philosopher. But whatever he should discover under such conditions would not be part of physical science and should not be presented as such. A philosopher, by the same token, might discover the ultimate physical components of material bodies, but he could do so only by using the methods of physical research, and he would not be, for his discovery, one whit the wiser as a philosopher.

2. **The Philosopher Must Know Scientific Facts.** This does not imply that the philosopher of nature can ignore the work of the natural scientist. Far from it; he should be as well acquainted as possible with the established findings of the physical sciences, and his own philosophical conclusions must be compatible with these findings. He could not, for example, maintain a theory about the first essential principles of material substance which would make it appear impossible for matter to have the first physical parts which science demonstrates beyond doubt it actually has. Theory cannot stand against fact. Because essences are the underlying causes of phenomena, philosophical theories, which are about essences, have implications in the realm of phenomena. When these implications are in contradiction with any established fact in the phenomenal order, it is the theory that must give way before the fact.

3. **Philosophical Theory Does Not Give Scientific Explanation.** But while the philosophical theory must not contradict the scientific fact, it does not have to provide a scientific explanation of the fact. A philosophical theory about the essential constitution of material substance is not meant to be a scientific account of material phenomena. Furthermore, a philosophical theory of the nature of material substance does not have to be based upon and derived from the scientific account of matter. What philosophy seeks to do is to give an intelligible and true explanation of human experience in terms of first principles and essences, and it may well be that such an explanation can be given without having recourse to the data advanced by science. Science also seeks to give an intelligible account of human experience, in terms, however, not of first principles, but of physical causes in the order of observable phenomena. The two accounts must be mutually compatible, but it is not at all self-evident that either one of them cannot be given quite independently of the other. As a matter of fact, the Scholastic theory of the essential nature of material substance is not derived from

the data of science; it is derived from common sensible experience which has been subjected to critical examination. Science and the philosophy of nature go far beyond common experience, but both must start with it and both must look back to it; it is the norm, and neither a scientific conclusion nor a philosophical conclusion can contradict it and remain tenable.

4. Philosophy Need Not Consider Scientific Explanations. If the philosopher of nature makes use of scientifically demonstrated facts, he is *not* obliged to consider the scientific explanation of these facts, except in so far as such consideration may be necessary to establish the facts as facts. If they are truly facts, and are fruitful for philosophical inference, their physical, chemical, or biological explanations and antecedents are irrelevant so far as the philosopher is concerned. To illustrate with a case pertaining to the problem of the present chapter: if we use the scientifically established facts that in nature certain elements constantly recur, that these elements by combining with one another form all other natural bodies, that each element has a constant affinity for certain other elements, that every element and every compound invariably possesses certain specific properties and manifests certain invariable modes of behavior; and we find that these facts are fertile for inferences about the first principles of corporeal substance, we do not have to consider any physical or chemical explanation of the facts themselves; we do not, for example, have to examine any theory, even a certainly established one, about atomic structures as the physical basis and explanation of these facts. All that we need to know from science about the facts is that they are facts.

5. Philosophical and Scientific Explanation Each Complete in Its Own Order. It is necessary to emphasize this last point, because it does not seem to be well understood by either scientists or philosophers. Sometimes, for instance, it is advanced against the doctrine of hylemorphism that the atomic structures of the elements account for all their properties and for the laws by which they combine to form compounds, and that therefore there is no need for the doctrine of hylemorphism. More annnoying even than this argument itself, is the effort of some Scholastic philosophers to refute it by denying the fact on which the invalid inference is based. None but a very muddle-minded Scholastic flatters himself that scientists have any scientific need of his philosophical doctrine of the essence of corporeal substance. If it is a philosophical error to suppose that science can disclose the meaning of nature, it is another to suppose either that the scientific account cannot be complete in its own order of causes, or can be completed in this order by any possible philosophical account. A complete physical, chemical, or biological account of any natural phenomenon would leave nothing whatsoever unexplained of what the physicist, chemist, or biologist had set out to explain. The scientific account of a natural fact explains its sensible or phenomenal antecedents in a selected and abstracted realm, for example, the physical, the chemical, or the biological realm. None of these antecedents touches upon the significance or first causes of the fact, and these alone are what philosophy is interested in. Consequently, the philosopher of nature who has taken from science a philosophically fertile fact does not need to consider the scientific explanation of that fact.

6. **Hylemorphism and Physical Mechanism.** To be very specific: only the grossest and most sensistic misinterpretation of hylemorphism could lead anyone to suppose that in the physical account of some natural phenomenon, say the formation of a compound from two elements, the description of the material and mechanical causes would give an incomplete picture needing to be completed by a description of the work of the formal cause. Scholastic philosophers, for example, who attempt a scientific refutation of mechanism as a *philosophical* rival of hylemorphism are as wide of the mark as mechanists who attempt to refute hylemorphism by a scientific demonstration of the universality of the operation of mechanical laws and causes in nature. The truth of hylemorphism is quite irrelevant to the adequacy or inadequacy of mechanism in the realm of physics, chemistry, or even biology; and the adequacy or inadequacy of mechanism in these realms is quite irrelevant to the truth or falsity of hylemorphism. The substantial form of an organism actualizes the material-mechanical causes of the evolution of the organism, but the latter remain mechanical causes and if they are defective as mechanical causes the organism will be defective; the substantial form will not make up the difference. Science may give reason to believe that rigid mechanism does not prevail even in the domain of physics, to say nothing of biology, but hylemorphism gives no reason for such a belief.

III. HYLOSYSTEMISM

1. Some contemporary Scholastic philosophers, convinced that hylemorphism as a theory of the essential constitution of elements and

compounds is incompatible with modern scientific findings about the constitution of inorganic matter, propose in its place a doctrine which has received the name hylosystemism. The name arises from the fact that the theory holds material bodies to be *essentially systems* of matter-particles (hylons). This new doctrine is explained and compared to hylemorphism by Father Celestine Bittle.[2] In the following account all page references are to that book. All italics are Bittle's, except in one case which is noted.

According to this theory, a natural body is "an *atomary*[3] *energy system,* in the sense that the atom of an element and the molecule of a compound are composed of subatomic particles (protons, electrons, etc.) united into a dynamic system working as a functional unit" (p. 322). The *essential* parts of a compound molecule are individual elementary atoms, and those of an atom are the nuclear protons, neutrons, electrons, and positrons, the planetary electrons, and energy particles, i.e., quanta and photons (p. 323). These essential parts are themselves complete material substances. The constitution of the body which they form is not, therefore, hylemorphic, but hylomeric (from *hyle,* matter, and *meros,* particles); i.e., the body is a system of corporeal substances (p. 324). Such a constitution is demanded by the data of the empirical sciences (p. 327). Some of those data given by Bittle, and his accompanying arguments, follow.

2. Arguments Against Hylemorphism. Neither the elements nor the compounds are indefinitely divisible, but in each case division must stop at certain minimal parts, namely, atoms in the case of the elements, and molecules in the case of the compounds. Furthermore, the minimal parts of each element and each compound have their distinctive mass and weight, differing from those of the other elements and compounds. Hylosystemism, regarding molecules and atoms respectively as the essential parts of compounds and elements, accounts for these facts; hylemorphism, giving no other parts than primary matter and substantial form, does not. On the contrary, hylemorphism supposes homogeneity throughout the corporeal substance and merely "assumes" that bodies have minimal parts (pp. 327–328).

In substantial change protons, neutrons, and electrons retain their

[2] Celestine N. Bittle, O.F.M.Cap., *From Aether to Cosmos* (Milwaukee: The Bruce Publishing Co., 1941), Chap. XIV.

[3] "Atomary" in this definition has nothing to do with physical atoms. The expression goes back to the root of the word and means "indivisible." An atomary energy system means one which is unitary and indivisible as a system.

identity; when an atom breaks down wholly or in part, these particles have an existence of their own outside the atom; in chemical displacements groups of atoms, called radicals, act as units as if they were single atoms. All these facts are contrary to the hylemorphic theory, according to which nothing remains through substantial change except primary matter and nothing is present in a compound except primary matter and a single form (p. 331). All these facts are easily accounted for by hylosystemism.

In a substantial change more changes than the substantial form; there is *"change of system, matter, and energy*. Hylomorphism, of course, also maintains that accidental forms change with the substance. This change of accidents, however, is not an integral part of the substantial change; within the substance itself nothing changes but the substantial form" (p. 331). The fact that the change of system, matter, and energy is what brings about the transformation of one type of body into another presupposes a hylomeric, not a hylemorphic constitution (pp. 331–332).

Bodies change without being acted upon by extraneous causes, as in the case of the radioactive elements. "If hylomorphism were correct, such a phenomenon would be impossible" (p. 332). Furthermore, "hylomorphists link the fact of bodily change with the axiomatic principle of movement in general: 'Whatever is changed, is changed by another' . . ." (pp. 333–334).

A radioactive element in a compound continues its radioactivity; for example, radium in radium chloride and in radium sulphate continues to decompose into radon. "It is a cardinal principle of hylomorphism, that in a chemical compound there is nothing but primary matter and a single form; the elements lose their identity and are only virtually, not actually, present. . . . It is only on the supposition that radium and chlorine *retain* their identity in the compound that one can understand how radium can be transmuted into radon, while it is part of the compound. And this is impossible if the constitution of radium chloride is hylomorphic" (p. 333). It is easily explained if this constitution is hylomeric.

The protons, neutrons, and electrons in an atom are spatially separated from one another, each existing separately within the larger whole. Each should have, therefore, a distinct substantial form, but hylomorphism admits only one substantial form in the atom. How can "this single form traverse the intervening gaps of space? Since it cannot exist outside matter, and there being no matter (in the accepted sense) between the nucleus and the orbital electrons, there seems to be no possibility for one form to inform all the parts of the atom at once. In that case, however, it fails in its essential function" (p. 335).

3. **Hylosystemism Is Meristic.** The theory of hylosystemism is unquestionably meristic in character. It is in fact one species of dynamic atomism. In company with classical mechanism, dynamic atomism, and dynamism, it embodies the fundamental principle of all meristic systems, namely, the explanation of the whole solely in terms of the parts; or, to state the same principle negatively, the denial of any unifying substantial principle in material substances. Its proponents desire to limit its application to inorganic substances, but, as we shall see, such limitation is unfounded and inconsistent.

IV. EXAMINATION OF HYLOSYSTEMISM

1. **Hylosystemism Is Based Upon a Misunderstanding of Hylemorphism.** That hylosystemism rests its case upon a grave misunderstanding of hylemorphism is very clearly evidenced by the facts which it alleges as incompatible with hylemorphism and by the arguments which it advances against that theory.

a) *Heterogeneity and Doctrine of Virtual Presence.* The proton-electron constitution of atoms, the atomic constitution of molecules, the molecular constitution of gross bodies — in brief, the discontinuity and internal heterogeneity of material substance — all these are facts which, according to the hylosystemists, contradict the doctrine of the hylemorphic constitution of corporeal substance. If this alleged contradiction were real, it is clear that no responsible philosopher could, for a moment, retain belief in hylemorphism. Yet many, practically all Thomists, do. This apparent anomaly should lead the hylosystemists to re-examine their own conception of hylemorphism. If they did, they would not make the statement that hylemorphism supposes homogeneity throughout the corporeal substance (p. 327). Aristotle, St. Thomas, and their followers regard organisms as hylemorphic in constitution: do they therefore believe that the human body is homogeneous throughout its parts?

The heterogeneity of the parts of a compound body is allowed for in hylemorphic theory by the Thomistic doctrine of the virtual presence of the lower forms in the higher explained in the last chapter. This doctrine is applicable both to organisms and to the inorganic compounds. Indeed it is in reference to the latter that St. Thomas explains the doctrine in *De Mixtione Elementorum*.[4] St. Thomas may have believed that chemical compounds are homogeneous throughout, but he certainly did not believe that their hylemorphic constitution requires this homogeneity. *If he had believed this, he could never have insisted upon the unicity of substantial form in living organisms.* He may have made a scientific error, natural enough under the circumstances of his time, but this error in no way affects his philosophical doctrine of hylemorphism.

b) Substantial Change Is Change of System. Father Bittle, giving the hylosystemists' argument against hylemorphism, writes that in a substantial change, more changes than the form; there is *"change of system, matter, and energy.* Hylomorphism, of course, also maintains that accidental forms change with the substance. *This change of accidents, however, is not an integral part of the substantial change;*[5] within the substance itself nothing changes but the substantial form." The last clause is unintelligible to the present writer,[6] but the preceding one says something quite definite and quite false. In Thomistic theory, the accidental changes are the necessary and immediate condition of the substantial change. The latter takes place when the accidents of the subject have become so modified that its matter is no longer adapted to support the substantial form which, until then, informed the matter of the subject. "Every substantial form," wrote St. Thomas,[7] "requires a proper disposition in the matter, without which it cannot exist; wherefore, qualitative change is the road to generation and corruption."

c) Radioactivity. Radioactivity is, according to hylosystemists, incompatible with hylemorphism. "If hylomorphism were correct, such a phenomenon would be impossible" (pp. 332–333). In truth, radioactivity is in no way opposed to hylemorphism. The hylemorphist considers the radioactivity of certain elements just as he considers all the activities of substances: they proceed directly from some accidental form or power of the substance, and ultimately from the first intrinsic principle of every actuality of the substance, its substantial form. If

---

[4] Mandonnet edition, *Opuscula Omnia*, Vol. I, pp. 19–21. Cf. references in Chapter VI.

[5] These italics are mine.

[6] It is unintelligible because, in hylemorphic theory, substantial change is the total corruption of one substance and the generation of another.

[7] *De Mixt. Elem.*, p. 19.

radioactivity contradicts the principle that whatever is changed is changed by another (pp. 332–333), then there is a real problem; but it is concerned with that principle, not with hylemorphism. What Scholastic philosophers believe about the extrinsic causes of change is part of their doctrine of efficient causality, not part of hylemorphism. On the other hand, hylosystemists make a rather large and easy assumption when they state that radioactivity is motion without any efficient cause. Radioactive elements do not exist in splendid isolation, but are part of a world in which everything seems to interact with everything else. Indeed, the fact that some substances which ordinarily are not radioactive can be made temporarily so by being subjected to certain energy bombardments, would seem to establish the presumption that some natural energy is acting upon radioactive elements causing their radiations. Cosmic-ray energy does, as a matter of fact, influence radioactivity; and this fact had to be taken into serious consideration in the manufacture of the atomic bomb.[8]

Radioactive elements in compounds retain their property of radioactivity. Radium in radium chloride continues to be transmuted into radon. "It is only on the supposition that radium and chlorine *retain their identity in the compound* that one can understand how radium can be transmuted into radon, while it is part of the compound. And this is impossible, if the constitution of radium chloride is hylomorphic" (p. 333). The truth, of course, is that the fact adduced does not warrant the conclusion that radium and chlorine retain their identity in the compound, and is in no way incompatible with hylemorphism. According to the Thomistic theory, the substantial form informs the whole matter, determining each part of it to the properties suitable for the substance in question, just as the substantial form of an organism determines the tissue and structure of every organ. The properties that belong to both the element and the compound are now rooted in the one substantial form of the compound, which contains virtually, that is to say, by their powers, the substantial forms of the elements. The higher form confers on the matter whatever was formerly conferred by the lower forms and is now required in the new substance. That something of the old is required in the new is to be expected in view of the fact that the new substance is produced from suitable secondary matter; you can't make a silk purse out of a sow's

[8] H. D. Smyth, *Atomic Energy for Military Purposes* (Princeton, N. J.: Princeton University Press, 1945), p. 211.

ear, or radium chloride out of anything but radium and chlorine.

d) *Discontinuity of Parts, and Formal Cause.* The discontinuity of bodies is offered as an argument against hylemorphism and for hylosystemism. An atom consists of protons, neutrons, electrons, and so forth, which are separated from one another, each possessing a separate existence of its own within the larger whole. Hylemorphism maintains that the atom has only a single substantial form. "How," asks Father Bittle (p. 335), "can this single form traverse the intervening gaps of space? Since it cannot exist outside matter, and there being no matter (in the accepted sense) between the nucleus and the orbital electrons, there seems to be no possibility for the one form to inform all the parts of the atom at once. In that case, however, it fails in its essential function." Father Bittle mentions three answers given by some hylemorphists to this difficulty. All three are inept and two are abandonments of hylemorphism. The fact of the matter is that the difficulty advanced is a false one, and efforts to solve it in the terms in which it is stated are bound to falsify hylemorphism.

To allege the spatial separation of the material particles in a body as an argument against hylemorphism, is to represent the substantial form as some sort of material fluid, gas, or whatnot, that spreads out through the matter, permeating it. This is absurd in view of the fact that the primary supposition of hylemorphism is that form is not matter — not the matter with which it is united, not some other matter that mixes with the latter or binds it together. The substantial form is the immaterial element, the idea, that is embodied in the matter and determines it to a specific substantial nature. The misconception already pointed out, namely, that hylemorphism posits continuous extension in bodies, is also at the base of this argument.

The true hylemorphic account of an atom attributes to the substantial form *all* the actuality and determination of the atom. The protons, neutrons, and electrons are protons, neutrons, and electrons *because* the primary matter is determined by a substantial form to these particular actualities; the movements, positions, energies, and mutual interactions of these particles are all actualized and determined by the substantial form. The substantial form, unlike the "hylomeric system," does not insinuate itself into or among or around the subatomic particles, trying to take credit for what the physical properties and forces of these particles accomplish on the physical level; on the contrary, it determines the potency of the matter to the actuality of these particles with all their properties and forces; in a word, it makes atoms out of prime matter by informing, actualizing, and determining the pure potency that is prime matter. The hylemorphist is not afraid that the physical particles and forces will put the substantial form out of its job by doing its function; for the substantial form is the formal cause of these particles and forces, with all their special spatial and energy relations; and if its determining action were to cease, so would the particles and forces. The physical structure of an atom is not a datum with which the substantial form has to be reconciled; *the substantial form is responsible for that structure.*

2. Hylosystemism Is Based on a Misconception of the Respective Functions of Scientific and Philosophical Explanation. Not one of the facts adduced by hylosystemists as contradicting hylemorphism does, in truth, contradict it. What they do contradict is a doctrine mistakenly believed to be hylemorphism. This error about the nature of hylemorphism arises from a prior error about its function. The difference between physics and philosophy of nature is lost sight of, and a philosophical theory of the essence of corporeal substance is called upon to furnish a physical explanation of physical phenomena. Then, primary matter and substantial form are treated as sensible, and an imaginative construction of physical phenomena is attempted with these "sensibles" as building blocks. The attempt is, of course, a dismal failure, and so hylemorphism is rejected. In its place is substituted hylosystemism, which regards a natural body as "an *atomary energy system,* in the sense that the atom of an element and the molecule of a compound are composed of subatomic particles (protons, electrons, etc.) united into a *dynamic system* working as a functional unit" (p. 322). Here a truly imaginative construction in terms of *sensibilia* is attained. Unfortunately, however, something is missing, namely, an account of the essence of corporeal substance in terms of *intelligibilia,* that is, in terms of first principles in the order of essences and real causes. The hylosystemist has not risen above the level of phenomena.

Hylosystemism is a scientifico-philosophical hybrid, and is marked with the sterility of its kind. It seeks to fulfill a function that only a physical theory can fulfill; namely, to describe the ultimate physical components of matter and the physical relations that obtain among these components in physical bodies. And while it is busy repeating the dicta of the physicist, it forgets the proper task of the philosopher of nature. While it is saying that elementary atoms are constituted by a system of protons, neutrons, electrons, quanta, photons, and all the rest, it neglects to answer the question why material particles, whatever they may be, regularly build up into the elements out of which the present cosmos is fashioned, why the particles are such as regularly to become these elements. It does not explain anything, either on the physical level or the philosophical level; it merely repeats the physicist's explanations and pronounces them philosophical. Hylosystemism, in a word, is based upon failure to understand the respective functions of natural science and philosophy of nature. Starting from physical facts, hylosystemism works downward to physical analysis instead of upward to ontological analysis; it explains a body by dividing it into its parts, instead of by determining the principles that make it the body it is with the parts it has.

3. **Hylosystemism Involves the Denial of Immanent Finality in Nature.** An examination of hylosystemism in its own right, without any reference to hylemorphism, reveals its inadequacy on at least two counts. In the first place, hylosystemism, by locating the essential principles of bodies *solely in the particles that physically constitute them,* denies to the bodies themselves any immanent principle of finality. It thus becomes liable to all the philosophical criticisms that are directed against mechanism and dynamism. Hylosystemists limit their theory to inorganic bodies, but they have no valid grounds for doing so. To be consistent they should extend it to the whole natural order and deny the reality of any substantial principle of unity and organization in living bodies. To deny the need for positing a substantial principle of unification forming the material particles in elements and compounds into a single specific substance is equivalent to denying the operation of immanent final causality throughout the entire material universe. For when substantial form is denied in inorganic substances, both elements and compounds and all their activities are explained as aggregations of protons, neutrons, electrons, and whatever other ultimate physical particles physicists distinguish. These particles, however, have not in themselves any of the particular distinctive properties of the elements and compounds; these properties arise only when the particles are bound together in an atom or a molecule. The properties, therefore, in this view, must be regarded as external resultants of the particle-patterns of the atom and molecule,

If this be admitted, then it seems impossible to defend the thesis that there must be a principle of life and organization in living organisms. If particle-patterns can generate·specific sets of properties and modes of activity which in no way belong to the particles as such, there is no clear reason for denying that they can generate the properties and functions peculiar to organisms.

The reason why Scholastics reject theories of the organism which recognize only material causes is the evident teleological character of the functioning of an organism. The parts, down to the least cell, are dominated by the whole; the whole is not merely the resultant of the parts, but is also a cause of the parts being what they are. A human brain is composed of billions of cells and is physically identical with the matter composing those cells, but the matter in the cells is what it is because it has evolved within a developing human organism. Wherefore, Scholastics maintain, in addition to the material causes of the organism, there must be recognized a principle of the whole, that is to say, a substantial form.

If that argument is valid, there seems to be no reason why it does not hold in regard to the elements and the compounds. The ultimate physical particles of matter show at least as much determination to build up into the elements and their compounds as do the nutriments absorbed by an organism to grow into the organism. If no intrinsic teleological principle is required to account for this determination on the part of the matter-particles, then none is required to account for it on the part of the material causes of an organism. Furthermore, the means-end relationship that is apparent *between* the inorganic and organic kingdoms corroborates this view; the world cannot be half finalistic and half mechanistic.

4. Hylosystemism Has No Scientific Foundation. Finally, in the interests of truth, it must be pointed out that the much appealed to scientific basis of hylosystemism simply does not exist. Hylosystemism is a theory of the essence of natural bodies; it is worthless if it is not applicable to at least all inorganic bodies. Its scientific basis is the findings of physical science about the bodies and energies that exist upon the earth and in the surface or crust of the stars. These bodies are composed of protons, electrons, neutrons, photons, etc. If it can be supposed that these particles are in no sense irreducible ultimate components of all material bodies, but are instead merely the ultimate parts of natural bodies which exist *under certain special conditions,* then the whole scientific basis of hylosystemism is dissolved into thin air. But this very supposition can be and is made by some physicists, and not without very good evidence. These physicists believe that in the interior of stars, under tremendous pressures and temperatures, protons and electrons annihilate or neutralize each other and produce the photons that constitute cosmic rays; matter, in other words, is transformed into radiant energy. The reverse of this process also seems to occur, radiant energy being transformed into matter in the formation of positrons and electrons from photons.[9] Furthermore, both these processes are now produced by human technology on a fairly large scale. In the atom bomb, one process accompanying the fission of the atom nucleus is the transformation of quantities of matter into quantities of energy; and by means of the betatron built by the General Electric Company energy is transformed into particles of matter and vice versa.[10] In view of facts like these, no theory of the *essence* of material substance can be based upon atomic or molecular structures.

5. **Hylemorphism Is Independent of Scientific Fashions.** Hylemorphism in contrast to hylosystemism has nothing to fear from present or future findings of physical science, because it does not rest its case upon the special conclusions of science, and it does not try to give scientifico-philosophical explanations of natural phenomena. It is based upon the data of common experience corroborated by scientific explanation and viewed in the light of intelligible principles. It is based upon the immanent finality evident in nature, and upon the two facts that matter undergoes substantial transformations and that we find in the world multitudes of bodies possessing the same nature; it is, indeed, hardly more than a differently worded statement of these facts since all it says, in essence, is that matter is a potency for a variety of substantial forms.

St. Thomas did not believe the primary matter or substantial forms were ever created as separate entities. They could not be, because they are not entities; they are not beings, but principles of being. What he thought to be the term of the creative act were the elements — that is, certain actual physical bodies.[11] That these elements combine in natural processes to give rise to compound substances proves that they

[9] Cf. Jauncey, *Modern Physics* (New York: Van Nostrand, 1942), pp. 476, 480, 491–493.

[10] John J. O'Neil, *New York Herald-Tribune*, October 21, 1945, pp. 1, 31, 33.

[11] *De Pot.*, IV, 1 and 2; *S. Theol.*, I, 66, 1.

are bipolar in essence; that they are compounded of two essential principles. Without different proper principles in each, no combination of them could give rise to a new nature; without a principle common to all of them, there would be nothing in them to pass from one nature to another. Without a common passive principle, none would be amenable to the action of another; without an active principle, one could not act upon another; and without different proper active principles, the action of one would not differ from the action of another; except with both principles there could not be a changing, dynamic, many-natured world.[12] Precisely what the ultimate physical components are does not appear to have much bearing on the problem.

The physical science of Aristotle's time may hold that the ultimate physical components of all bodies are the four elements, earth, air, fire, and water; the science of a later date may name ninety-two elements; a still more modern science may speak of atoms and molecules, then of protons, neutrons, electrons, and photons, and finally of some basic energy or matter which is the matrix even of protons, electrons, neutrons, and photons. In any case, science will never speak of primary matter and substantial form, because these are not empirical but meta-empirical. Yet science is not disagreeing with hylemorphism, and is even giving some evidence of its truth. For regardless of what the ultimate physical condition of matter is, it is of necessity bipolar in constitution. In the ultimate physical elements there is a common and a proper part; material transformations would be impossible without these two parts. Without the common part there could be no theater of transformations, and without the proper part no change of actors and action. There must be something in which natural processes take place, and something which each process newly attains. The common part, the theater of action, is in itself indefinite, indeterminate, potential, passive; the proper part, the action, is definite, determinate, actual, active. The common part is primary matter, and the proper part is substantial form.

[12] *De Pot.*, III, 7, c; *Con. Gen.*, III, 69: *Item, apparet per inductionem* (near middle) and *non est etiam verum* (near end).

CHAPTER VIII

LIFE AND SOUL

I. THE NATURE OF LIFE

Bodies or natural substances present themselves to man's experience as being of two kinds, living and non-living; and living bodies themselves are of three kinds, namely, plants, animals, and men. These facts of common experience give rise to many questions of interest to the philosopher of nature. What is life? Are living bodies essentially different from non-living bodies? What is the principle of life in a living body? Are the three kinds of living bodies essentially different from one another? What is the nature of vital activity? Do we need to posit a soul in order to account for life and vital activity in organisms? In the present chapter we shall present the Thomistic answers to these questions, and we shall note and evaluate the answers offered by other schools of thought, especially mechanism and vitalism.

1. Living Bodies Are Self-Moving. The "nature" of anything is, as Aristotle says, the principle of movement and rest within it. This is true of living things as well as non-living things. It follows that the fundamental or essential difference between living and non-living substances is to be found in the kind of motion which they possess by virtue of their respective natures. The motion proper to living things is self-motion. A living thing is one which by nature is able to move itself.[1]

2. Living Bodies Are Organic. We saw in Chapter IV that nothing can move itself totally — the whole moving the whole. In order to do so it would have to be agent and patient, actual and potential, in the same process, which is clearly impossible. Therefore, that which is mover in something cannot be identical with that which is moved in

---

[1] Aristotle, *Phys.*, VIII, 254b; St. Thomas, *S. Theol.*, I, 18, 1 and 2; I–II, 3, 2, ad 1; *In II De Anima*, I

the one motion. Hence, if something in any way moves itself, it can do so only by being mover and moved in different respects: one part of it moves another part. Consequently, a living body, since it possesses the power of self-motion, must be made up of separate parts; that is, it must be *organic*. This fact is so obvious that living bodies have received the name *organisms*.[2]

3. Self-Movement Means Immanent Activity. Self-movement means the performance by an agent of an operation which remains in the agent itself; it is *immanent activity* as opposed to transeunt activity, which passes out to a patient distinct from the agent. A few passages from the *Summa Theologica* state very clearly St. Thomas' conception of life and its essential nature, namely, self-movement or immanent activity.

> By vital operations are meant those whose principles are within the operator, and in virtue of which the operator produces such operations of itself.[3]
>
> We can gather to what things life belongs, and to what it does not, from such things as manifestly possess life. Now life manifestly belongs to animals. . . . We must, therefore, distinguish living from lifeless things by comparing them to that by reason of which animals are said to live: and this it is in which life is manifested first and remains last. We say then that an animal begins to live when it begins to move of itself: and as long as such movement appears in it, so long is it considered to be alive. When it no longer has any movement of itself, but is moved only by another power, then its life is said to fail, and the animal to be dead. Whereby it is clear that those beings are properly called living that move themselves by some kind of movement. . . . Accordingly, all things are said to be alive that determine themselves to movement or to operation of any kind; whereas those things that cannot by their nature do so cannot be called living, unless by some likeness.[4]
>
> As is stated in Metaph. IX [VIII, 8, 1050a, 22], action is twofold. Actions of one kind pass out to external matter, as to heat or to cut, while actions of the other kind remain in the agent, as to understand, to sense, and to will. The difference between them is this, that the former action is the perfection, not of the agent that moves, but of the thing moved; whereas the latter action is the perfection of the agent. Hence, because movement is an act of the thing in movement, the latter action, in so far as it is the act of the operator, is called its movement,

---

[2] St. Thomas, *Con. Gen.*, I, 13.

[3] *S. Theol.*, I, 18, 2, ad 2 (*Basic Writings of St. Thomas Aquinas*, Ed. Anton C. Pegis [New York: Random House, 1945], Vol. I, p. 190).

[4] *Ibid.*, I, 18, 1, c (Pegis, *op. cit.*, Vol. I, p. 187).

on the basis of the similitude that as movement is an act of the thing moved, so an action of this kind is the act of the agent. And although movement is an act of the imperfect, that is, of what is in potentiality, this kind of action is an act of the perfect, that is to say, of what is in act, as is stated in De Anima [III, 7, 431a, 6].[5]

4. Life Is Not an Operation, But Is the Living Thing's Being. Self-movement is the activity by which a living thing is known and named, but the term life does not signify properly the operation but rather the very being or substance of the living thing.

> The name [life] is given from a certain external appearance, namely, self-movement, yet not precisely to signify this, but rather a substance to which self-movement, or the application of itself to any kind of operation, belongs naturally. *To live,* accordingly, is nothing else than for a substance with such a nature *to be:* and *life* signifies this very fact, but abstractly, as *running* abstractly signifies *to run.* Hence *living* is not an accidental, but a substantial predicate. . . . [6]

5. Grades of Life. Since to live is to have the power of immanent activity, it follows that the grade of perfection of life depends upon the degree to which the movements of the living agent are determined by the agent itself from within. Using this standard of comparison, St. Thomas distinguishes three grades of life: the vegetative, the sensitive, and the intellective. Thus, plants, which have only the first grade of life, move themselves in growth by assimilating substances from the world around them and transforming these substances into their own substance. It is the plant's own nature which is the executor of this movement; for the plant grows by imposing its own form or plan of organization upon the nutriments which it absorbs. This form of the plant, however, is given to the plant itself from without and is strictly determined to one operation as a principle of movement. An animal performs immanent operations of a higher degree, since not only is its own nature the executor of its movement, but in addition the forms which are the principles of its various movements are forms which it possesses within itself, having received them through sense. Thus a dog moves itself to procure a bone by virtue of already possessing the form of the bone through sense apprehension. Animals cannot, on the other hand, propose to themselves, or determine for themselves, the ends of their own operations; they are moved by natural instinct to those sensible goods which they apprehend. Man,

[5] *Ibid.,* I, 18, 3, ad 1 (Pegis, *op. cit.,* Vol. I, p. 192).
[6] *Ibid.,* I, 83, 2, c (Pegis, *op. cit.,* Vol. I, p. 189).

therefore, is superior to them, for by virtue of his power of reason he can himself propose the end of his own operation, and he can choose by what means he will act to attain this end. He is not, like the animal, necessarily determined to the good whose form his sense has apprehended; on the contrary, he himself determines to which of various apprehended goods he will move himself.[7]

The immanent activities of all three grades of life differ radically from the operations of inorganic bodies. The latter act upon other bodies and produce changes in them, and are similarly acted upon by other bodies, and undergo changes at their hands. The operations of non-living bodies are *transeunt* (transient); the agent and patient are distinct, and the action of the agent passes over from it to produce its effect in the patient. The terminus of the act is something outside the agent. In vital operations the effect of the operation is produced in the agent itself. The terminus of the operation is a perfection of the agent itself: it grows, it moves from here to there, it perceives, it thinks, all of which operations have as effect a new actuality in the agent itself.

Vital self-movement or immanent activity does not overthrow the general principle that whatever is in motion is moved by another. In the first place, as we have seen, in the self-movement of an organism one part of the organism moves another. In the second place, while the vital movement is self-determining, the beginning of this self-determining movement is always a prior movement from outside. Thus, a plant in growth is self-determining, but in order to grow, the plant must be moved by the sun, the air, etc.; an animal moves himself to a desired object, but first his sense must be moved by the object; a man determines to what end and by what means he will move himself, but first his intellect and will must be moved by an intelligible good.

II. ORGANISMS ARE HYLEMORPHIC IN CONSTITUTION

As soon as we raise the question, what is the first principle of life in a living body? we realize that we have already answered it in Chapters VI and VII. Living bodies as well as inorganic bodies are corporeal substances, and, therefore, unless we are willing to cast away all the conclusions which we have reached up to this point, we have no choice but to say that every living corporeal individual is a composite of two complementary principles, primary matter and sub-

[7] *Ibid.*, I, 18, 3, c.

stantial form; and that, as in every composite substance, the substantial form is the root principle of the nature and activities of the individual; hence the principle of life in every living body is its substantial form. An amoeba and a man is each a compound of a certain quantity of matter and a certain substantial form; the amoeba is a living individual of one species and the man a living individual of another; the principle of all the amoeba's vital activities is its substantial form; the principle of all a man's vital activities is his substantial form. The matter that goes to make up an amoeba is, in itself, potentially an amoeba and is made an actual amoeba by the form; the matter that goes to make up a man is, in itself, potentially a man and is made actually a man by the form. The properties which matter exhibits in an amoeba are determined in the matter by the form of the amoeba; the properties that matter exhibits in a man are determined by the man's form.

In a word, the Aristotelian-Thomistic conception of a living body, i.e., an organism, is not a special theory, but merely an application of hylemorphism to living nature. We have proved that corporeal substances are composites of matter and form, and we illustrated that by saying that hydrogen and oxygen, sodium and chlorine, water, salt, and radium chloride, are composites of matter and form. Now, when we come to consider living corporeal substances, we are not going to take back anything we have said; these, too, are hylemorphic composites. As a matter of fact, the argument that establishes the hylemorphic constitution of living bodies is the same as that which establishes hylemorphism as a general theory of nature; the only difference is that since it is concerned with a special application of the theory it selects special data as evidence.

III. THE SOUL

1. **The Name "Soul."** We say that living things have souls and that non-living beings do not have. What do we mean? In one sense, we mean nothing at all; we are merely wording a tautology, saying, that is, that living beings are alive and non-living beings are not. By "soul" we mean the first immanent principle of vital operations in a living body. But the first immanent principle of all the operations in any natural individual is its substantial form. Hence, by the soul of a living thing we mean its substantial form. Soul, therefore, is simply a name which, following Aristotle, we use to designate a sub-

stantial form which confers upon the matter which it actualizes and determines the ability to perform what we call vital operations.

2. Kinds of Soul. In his *Treatise on the Soul* (*De Anima*), Aristotle distinguishes the kinds of souls according to the kinds of vital operations which living beings perform. All living beings, of no matter what kind, nourish themselves with food from their environ, grow, and reproduce individuals of the same kind as themselves. These three activities, therefore, may be taken as the minimal characters of life; and so we say that living creatures are distinguished from non-living ones by their capacity for nutrition, growth, and reproduction. We also say that the most fundamental type of soul is the soul which gives these three powers and nothing more. Aristotle called this fundamental soul the nutritive soul, a far better term than "vegetative" soul, which later replaced it.

All living creatures eat, grow, and reproduce their kind, but some do only that, while others do that and something else besides. Some, that is to say, perceive or sense. Animals and men do; plants do not. Wherefore, the substantial forms of animals are different from those of plants, since they give an added perfection to the matter. This second grade of soul Aristotle called the sensitive soul. Among animals some have the power of locomotion and some have not; some again seem to have imagination and some do not; but we do not need to distinguish a special soul for locomotion and imagination, since these two powers arise from perception and desire, both of which are powers of the sensitive soul.

But there is a third operation that cannot be traced to the sensitive soul. Among animals, some, namely men, think, while the others do not. Thought is essentially different from perception and imagination, and so cannot be called a power of the sensitive soul. Wherefore, there is a third grade of soul, the rational soul; and this is, in man, the principle of thought. Thought and sense are both cognition, and wherever there is cognition there is appetite or desire. Hence, there are two kinds of desire, sensitive desire and rational desire. The latter we call will. The rational soul, therefore, may be defined as the first principle in man of thought and will.

3. Definition of Soul. The last sentence brings to notice a point deserving of mention. Aristotle gives two definitions of soul. The first we may call the essential definition and the second the functional definition. The two taken together make very clear how thoroughly his doctrine of soul is subordinated to his doctrine of hylemorphism. The soul, he says first, "is the first grade of actuality of a natural body having life potentially in it." The soul, consequently, is the substantial form, since the substantial form is the first actuality of matter, making it something, while accidental forms are second actualities, giving the material substance this or that non-substantial determination, for example, warm or cold. A couple of pages later he writes, "soul is the source of these phenomena and is characterized by them, namely, by the powers of self-nutrition, sensation, thinking, and movement." The soul is again presented as substantial form, since substantial form is the first source or root in anything of those powers which it possesses.[8]

4. **The Unity of Soul.** An animal perceives *and* nourishes itself; a man thinks *and* perceives *and* nourishes himself. Has an animal, therefore, a sensitive soul *and* a nutritive soul, and has a man a rational soul *and* a sensitive soul *and* a nutritive soul? Aristotle and St. Thomas held that one living being has but one soul. The soul is the substantial form of the living substance; one substance has but one substantial form; hence, one living substance has but one soul. The animal's sensitive soul is the principle of both perception and nutrition; man's rational soul is the principle of thought, perception, and nutrition; the one soul in any organism is the vital principle of every living part of the organism, of every single cell in a multicellular organism. If this were not so, an organism would not be a single substance but merely a collection of a great many independent substances.

> So, therefore, we say that in this man there is no other substantial form than the rational soul, and that through this the man not only is a man, but an animal, a living thing, a body, a substance and a being. . . . For the form is the likeness of the agent in the matter. Now, in respect to active and operative powers it is found that the higher a power is, the more things it comprehends, not compositely but in unity; as, for example, the sensus communis by one power extends itself to all sensibles, which the special senses apprehend by diverse powers. Now it belongs to the more perfect agent to induce the more perfect form; whence the more perfect form does by one [actuality] all that the inferior forms do by diverse [actualities], and still more. For instance, if the form of an inanimate body makes matter to be and to be a body, and if the form of a plant makes it both this and further to live, then the sensitive soul makes it this and also to be sentient, and the rational soul makes it this and above this to be rational. . . . So,

[8] Aristotle, *De Anima*, II, 1, 412b; 2, 413b.

therefore, the intellective soul contains the sensitive virtually, because it has this and yet more; but not in such a way that there are two souls [in the man].[9]

IV. GENERAL ARGUMENT OF THE CHAPTER

1. Unity and Purposiveness of the Organism. We have answered all the questions proposed in the first paragraph of the present chapter. Have we proved our answers? Without a doubt we have — for anyone who understands and accepts our demonstration of hylemorphism in Chapter VI and VII. But not everyone does, and so our work in this chapter is just beginning instead of being finished. There are philosophers and scientists, as well as ordinary people, who reject the notion of soul altogether, and there are others who hold doctrines of the nature of soul very different from the doctrine above explained. We cannot ignore them or their arguments. Hence, we must try to demonstrate the truth of our conception of soul, at the same time answering the objections advanced against it. The demonstration will be, in essence, the same as our demonstration of hylemorphism in general, but will start from data offered by the study of living things.

There is no need of adding many illustrations to those given in Chapter V to show that natural processes in living things give evidence of unity of design, nature, and substance. Your own body is as good an illustration as any. You stay alive by eating and drinking. Most of the food you find is not ready to enter at once into the chemical processes that maintain your body. To get it ready, nature has given you a movable lower jaw with strong muscles, and a row of hard, sharp teeth to cut and grind the food to a swallowable condition while the salivary glands are pouring into your mouth a softening fluid containing an enzyme, ptyalin, which breaks starch molecules into smaller and soluble maltose molecules, thus getting the food ready for your stomach.

The work of the body upon the food continues in the stomach. About 35,000,000 glands secrete gastric juices into the stomach. Various chemical compounds in these juices act upon the food, while the continual muscular contractions of the stomach make it an ideal mixing bowl, so that the juices get to all parts of the food. The most important part of the digestive process takes place in the small in-

[9] St. Thomas, *De Spirit. Creat.*, Art. III, c.

testines. The process is carried out chiefly by the peristaltic movements of the intestine and by the chemical action of three secretions, the pancreatic fluid, and succus entericus, and the bile.

All processes from beginning to end occur in such a way that your body is maintained in life and grows. From the stomach some of the materials required for the building up of new cell tissue pass into the blood stream, and from the small intestine by far the largest part of them. This is the process called absorption. It leads to cell metabolism, a distinctive character of living bodies. Metabolism has two phases: anabolism, meaning all those processes by which living cells make food substances from the blood into living protoplasm and various products stored up for special functions; and catabolism, the breaking-down processes by which cells change into simpler substances by the splitting of complex molecules into simpler ones, and by hydrolysis and oxidation. The whole life, indeed the very identity of the body, is maintained by this constant metabolic process. It involves the co-operative activity of practically every part of the body: digestive organs, specialized cells in each organ, the respiratory apparatus, the heart and circulatory system, the materials supplied by the food, the over-all activating and co-ordinating accomplished by the nervous system. And it, in turn, keeps all these parts in being, for they are all composed of living cells which must metabolize or die, which must be continually fed, repaired, or replaced. The impression that these vital processes give of the whole organism acting as a unit and for a definite purpose is overwhelming. And the actions themselves, namely, nutrition and growth, are acts which are never performed by a non-living body.

2. **The Uniqueness of Life.** Metabolism occurs only in living things. So do growth and reproduction, which are simply phases of the whole metabolic process given special names. These operations are distinctive criteria of life, and nothing remotely resembling them occurs in non-living matter. Metabolism is found in every living thing, but it is different in each one. The protoplasm of each species of animal is distinctive of that species, and yet many different kinds of animals feed on the same kinds of food; there is no such thing as discovering the particular chemical formula of metabolism; in each case it is a particular process or series of processes, but in each case it is different. Nor can we speak accurately of the chemical formula of protoplasm; not only is protoplasm different in different living things, but it is

constantly changing in each living thing and each living cell — that is, it is metabolizing. When it is dead, it is found to have distinctive chemical ingredients, but that hardly explains its life before it dies.

3. **The Origin of Life?** Science has not yet been able to give any account at all of the origin of life. Yet there is no doubt that *life has originated,* that is to say, it is known definitely that it cannot have always existed on this earth. It is not so long ago, as geologists measure time, when conditions on our planet were such as to preclude the possibility of any life in any way like the life that we observe now. It was far too hot, and there was no water. Yet life exists on the earth now. Many scientists, disliking to accept divine creation as the direct and only cause of life, assume that, as the planet cooled and water formed, and new chemical combinations previously impossible began to occur, together with great electrical disturbances in the sky, some carbon compounds were somehow jolted into the peculiar unstable chemical balance that continually falls apart and rights itself, and which we call metabolism. It might be presumptuous to say that this is impossible, but it may be said that there is no evidence for it. It is either a pure assumption, which most scientists recognize it as, or else it is a dogmatic postulate necessary as a foundation for a particular theory of materialistic evolution. There is no evidence for it, but there is one rather strong piece of evidence against it: it does not occur now. No principle of biological science is more firmly established than the dictum *omne vivum ex vivo,* every cell from a cell, every living thing from an egg and the egg from a living thing. If matter once came alive, why does it not do so now? The conditions now are most favorable. Matter is capable of coming alive, and constantly is doing so in being made into living cells; but this takes place only *in* already living cells. Why this is so, we may not be able to say, but the fact that it is so is surely not without significance.

4. Books have been filled with data like the above, data all of which show with an almost irresistible force of self-evidence the uniqueness and purposiveness of life, and the presence in living bodies of a true vital principle distinct from the material elements of these bodies. We say "almost" irresistible because in every age there have been many who have successfully resisted the evidence, and have refused to admit the uniqueness or the purposiveness of life or the reality of a vital principle. If we examine why they remain unconvinced before the evidence, it will help us to see the problem clearly, and its answer.

V. MECHANISM, VITALISM, AND HYLEMORPHISM

1. In the Gifford Lectures[10] of 1937–1938, Sir Charles Sherrington, world-famed British physiologist, who stands at the very top of his science, examines the question whether the study of living things leads the mind to a religious attitude toward the universe, and to what sort of religious attitude. Through chapter after chapter, the great physiologist passes in review one form of life after another, one phase of vital action after another. Always he faces the question: Is a vital principle, i.e., a soul, in some way distinct from the physical parts of this living body, necessary to account for its vital operations? Always he presents, in the strongest and fairest way possible, the evidence that such a principle must be recognized; his book is a veritable mine of "evidences for teleology in nature." But always he concludes that there is no need to posit such a principle: the parts of the organism together with its "surround" adequately account, when adequately known, for everything vital about the organism. Why does he so conclude? In every case, *because every vital operation of the organism is completely describable in terms of chemical reagents in the organism and in its surround.* Life is chemistry; and chemistry, he notes once or twice, is physics. Living bodies, no matter how simple or how complex, whether amoeba or man, are systems of molecules reacting with surrounding molecules, and all their vital operations — feeding, growing, moving, reproducing, repairing themselves, and finally, dying — are chemical processes. Living things do what they do because of the molecules they are; and these molecules do what they do because of the atoms they are; and the atoms, because of the electrons and protons they are. The parts account for the whole.

In another excellent book, *The Great Design,*[11] a score of scientists, all of them eminent, and some of them as eminent in their fields as Sherrington in his, each takes his own science, and from the data which it affords, in many cases the precise data presented by Sir Charles, reaches the conclusion that the parts do not account for the whole; that every natural whole, whether living or non-living, is directed or governed by something distinct from its parts and their surround; that chemistry does not explain life; that, indeed, physics and chemistry and biology and all their offspring do not together go any distance at all toward explaining either life or the world it lives in.

[10] C. S. Sherrington, *Man on His Nature* (New York: Macmillan, 1941).
[11] Edited by Frances Mason (New York: Macmillan, 1935).

2. The Account of the Parts Is Not the Explanation of the Whole.
What is the source of this contrariety of conclusions drawn from the
same evidence? It is to be found in a fundamental difference of point
of view with which the scientists in question approached what they
were to study. Sherrington was looking for a *cause which would account completely for the effect by explaining precisely what happened
and how it happened in every single moment and every single part
of the effect's existence.* He found it, and since it left nothing whatever of the effect unexplained in the way in which he wanted it explained, he saw no reason for positing any further cause. Now, the
others, of course, found Sherrington's cause too, but it was not what
they were looking for. It did not answer the question which they
had asked. *Since it left the question unanswered, although it was itself
complete, they knew that it could never answer the question.* Do not
say that it is not complete, that science itself is not complete, and that,
therefore, they may be wrong. The kinds of causes sought and found
by Sherrington and by mechanists down through the ages, may not
now or at any moment be completely known, but they can be easily
imagined as complete, and the scientists who wrote *The Great Design*
so imagined them, and still said that these causes did not and never
would answer the question which they wanted answered. One of
them, A. S. Eve, puts the case very clearly:[12]

> That living creatures are constructed of matter, no one will for
> a moment dispute; that there are, in life, transferences of energy which
> fully obey the laws of physics and chemistry no one will deny, but to
> insist that these laws or theories, as we know them now, or even as
> they may develop, impose a necessary limitation to our conception of
> life, or to regard them even remotely as causation, is a step quite un-
> warrantable. What then do we need to add? There is nothing to suggest!
> But because no answer is at present forthcoming we cannot assume that
> an answer is forever impossible. No doubt one important factor is the
> organization as a whole, which is not merely a sum of its parts.

What is it, then, that Eve and his collaborators want answered
which Sherrington's analysis leaves unanswered? It may be called,
from one point of view, the "wholeness" of the living thing. Vital
activity in a cell or in a man is carried on, at any moment, by a part of
the cell or by a part of the man; but the sort of activity it is, that is
to say, what it accomplishes, is intelligible only in view of the whole

[12] A. S. Eve, *The Great Design*, ed., Frances Mason, p. 82. By permission of the
Macmillan Company, publishers.

cell or the whole man. The whole seems to act in and to be implied in every part; the whole can be analyzed into the parts, but the parts can be understood only in view of the whole. The lungs of man replenish the blood's oxygen supply, but this act is meaningless unless seen in reference to the whole human organism. This implication of the whole in its parts is most strikingly evident in the development of an organism. The whole process, from the single fertilized egg from which it starts, through the unceasing cell divisions, the evolution of specialized types of cells, the formation of wondrously varied tissues, up to the final building of the whole eating, walking, breathing, blood-circulating, feeling, seeing organism is meaningless unless the observer keeps that finished organism in view during the whole process. Identical kinds of cells from the skin tissue form the eyeball with its transparent cornea, the colored iris with its opening, the pupil, the adjustable shutter, the flexible, transparent, crystalline lens, cells from the brain form the retina, with its millions of sensitive rods and cones, and the nerve fibers of the optic nerve; and the two unrelated processes culminate by merging in the right place at the right time; and this happens independently for each eye: and it all happens while the human embryo is wrapped in the utter darkness of its mother's womb. What does it mean, how can reason grasp it, if the whole seeing child or man is excluded from consideration? *Mechanism, denying end in nature, excludes the finished organism from every study of its development.*

3. **The Failure of Positivism.** Mechanists, and positivists generally, are philosophers who distrust thinking. They believe only in seeing and measuring. Their answer to the above argument is that the influence or causality of the whole on the parts is only inferred, but cannot be seen or measured, while the activity of the parts producing the whole can be seen and measured. They limit human knowledge to what can be dealt with by certain methods called, generically, the scientific method. Aside from pure dogmatism arising from a faith in materialism, their one reason for equating all knowledge with scientific method is the obvious and continuing success of scientific method in dealing with the problems to which it can be and has been applied. They cannot, apparently, see what seems so evident to the non-positivist, namely, that the vaunted success of the positivistic method is a fiction if science is supposed to produce *understanding* of the natures which it studies. Life is a good example of the method's failure;

the only explanation that renders the genesis of an organism intelligible cannot be admitted by a positivist.

Biologists ought to be able to discern the error of positivism, for it negates the very thing which they study. What account does it give of life? An organism is its cells and their behavior. The cell is its molecules and their behavior. The molecules are atoms and their behavior. The atoms are electrons and protons and their behavior. The environment is also electrons and protons, and some very important photons. Biology is physics. What has become of the organism? What is left of life? The biologist deals with forms of life, and he has to use the forms which nature furnishes; above all he has to respect scrupulously the conditions of life which nature supplies; if he ignores them, he finds himself studying forms of death. Of necessity, he stays closer to nature than does the physicist. He cannot so easily fall prey to the delusion that he can divide without destroying: an organ out of an organism is very patently a different thing from that organ in the organism; an atom out of a molecule is less evidently a different thing from the atom in the molecule. When an organism has been reduced in fact to energy-particles, it has been destroyed utterly; when it has been reduced in thought to energy-particles, it has been forgotten.

4. Vitalism vs. Hylemorphism. Some biologists have tried to answer the question of what life is by the hypothesis of a special life force — "vital force" or "biotic energy" — in an organism. Those who affirmed such a force were called *vitalists,* and those who denied it, *mechanists.*[13] Thomists (if philosophers must be drawn into this controversy) find themselves on the side of the biological mechanists. No vital force additional to the physical and chemical forces is to be expected in a hylemorphic organism. The hylemorphist's vital principle is the soul, that is to say, the substantial form. A substantial form actualizes and determines the matter with which it is united. It does not work alongside the matter, but through the matter. It forms the organism by conferring a certain nature and certain powers upon the matter. Consequently, the operations of the organism will all be exercised and manifested in and through the matter. Therefore, no non-material vital force will be found causing the vital operations of the organism; but all the discoverable and measurable causes of these operations will be matter and material forces. These will, if completely known, add

---

[13] This is the fourth sense in which we have met this remarkable word!

up to the vital process, without leaving any margin or difference which some "vital force" might be expected to fill in. The soul itself will not be a vital force additional to the physical forces of the material elements; it is the determining principle which confers all these forces and powers on the material elements.

The hylemorphist's "soul" is, therefore, very different from the vitalist's "vital force." If in a living individual the parts add up to the whole and yet the whole is more than the parts, what more is it? It cannot be something added to the parts; it cannot be some added vital force or energy that turns all the chemical matter into biological matter. All the force or energy is already counted in, in the parts, and it is futile to look for more; it would be looking for another part besides all the parts. *The vital principle which we are seeking must make the parts more than they are without it, while at the same time adding nothing separate to them.* It must make them into the actual whole. The parts without this principle are potentially the whole; with it they are actually the whole. The vital principle that we are seeking, therefore, is related to the matter of the organism as actuality to potentiality. It is the soul of the organism, defined by Aristotle as the first actuality of a body which possesses life potentially. It is the substantial form of the organism; the immanent essential principle which determines the matter to a specific nature and determines in it the properties due that nature. Parts and whole, matter and form, body and soul, are distinct in each case, but distinct only as a potency and its actuality.

5. Biological Mechanism and Hylemorphism. One aim of natural science in studying living things is to gain more and more knowledge of the part-aspects of living wholes; to drive always toward a complete explanation of the whole in terms of its parts, and their relations. For example, living bodies are composed of chemical elements in certain compounds, and vital operations are, in one real aspect, chemical processes: hence, complete description of every vital process in terms of chemical reagents is the legitimate goal of biochemistry; and the biochemist must assume as a methodological postulate that such complete description is theoretically possible, and that therefore there is no limit to biochemical progress short of the complete explanation of living processes in chemical terms. Any philosophical theory that would require the biochemist to think otherwise would be dubious from any point of view, and definitely false from the hylemorphic point of view: as soon as you begin to think that something happens in nature without mechanical, i.e., material-efficient, causes, you cease thinking in terms of hylemorphism. If you believe that substantial forms have determined all matter on this earth into the ninety-two elements, you cannot also believe that (barring miracles) any event in nature can skip chemistry; you cannot believe that material organisms are born, feed, grow, and reproduce in independence of chemical law. For any philosopher to say that the principle of life in a living thing is its soul, and that, *therefore*, its life cannot be explained in bio-physico-chemical terms, is for him to deny the legitimacy of the scientific study of living beings. For a scientist to say that life is explainable in bio-physico-chemical terms and, *therefore*, there is no such thing as soul, is for him to deny the legitimacy of the philosophical study of living things. The latter error is made by philosophical mechanists; the former by philosophers who hope to prove the reality of the soul by destroying the mechanist's evidence instead of by showing the invalidity of the conclusion which he draws from it.

6. **Philosophical Mechanism vs. Hylemorphism.** To get back to our argument: Why must we posit a soul in every living thing? We have seen that a living organism reveals itself to inspection as something more than its physical parts; indeed we have seen the "whole" acting as a cause of the very being of the parts before it actually existed as their sum. It is, therefore, something more than its parts; some principle is in it which cannot be reduced to its matter. And this principle is what gives it life, and what determines its essence. Because of this principle a living thing is essentially different from the non-living. Sherrington denies this on the grounds that all vital operations are chemical in nature. What does he mean? He does not deny that the chemical processes of living things cannot be found in non-living; it is by them that he distinguishes the two orders. Inorganic chemical processes tend to stable equilibrium and, reaching it, cease. Life, from the chemical point of view, is destroyed by stable equilibrium; that is death. What life does chemically is a constant making and unmaking of equilibrium; it is called metabolism. Metabolism is a chemical process, and it obeys all the laws that rule chemical processes in inorganic nature. Is that a reason for denying any essential difference between the living and the non-living? Must the laws of chemistry and physics not operate in living beings if we are to acknowledge their essential difference from non-living? What conceivable scientific or philosophical principle would call for what conclusion?

7. **Life and Chemistry.** Life cannot negate chemistry, if living things are made of matter; but it can elevate matter and direct it in its processes. This is what it does, and that is why we say that there is more in a cell than chemicals. Matter in living bodies does new chemical things by means of doing the old chemical things: as soon as we start to analyze the new chemical things, we find ourselves viewing the old. If we then get so engrossed in the old as to forget what we started with, we shall be mechanists. If we remember the new, even as we analyze it into the old, we shall be convinced that it is more than its parts, and we shall not be mechanists. The new chemical phenomena are analyzable into the old, but not reducible to them.

If we wish to view the life-problem from the point of view of chemical evidence, we shall find sufficient reason for affirming an essential distinction between the living and the non-living. This evidence is that chemical processes of a characteristic kind occur in and distinguish living things. These processes are analyzable into the simpler processes which occur in non-living things, but these simpler processes never occur in the non-living combined in the distinctive patterns in which they occur in the living. That is chemical evidence, and it is good evidence if we have already established an independent criterion by which we distinguish the living from the non-living. That independent criterion is the fact that the kinds of being which we call living perform certain activities of a type never performed by non-living beings. These activities are what we call immanent action. They are, as a minimum, nutrition, growth, self-repair, and reproduction. These activities, as a prior standard of distinction, enable us to compare the two orders of things as to their chemical processes.

VI. PROCESS AND ACTION

1. **Vital Actions Involve Vital Processes, But Action Is Not Process.** A distinction which is very relevant to the differences between the physicochemical and the philosophical study of living things is the distinction made by Aristotle and St. Thomas between motion and action, or process and operation. Motion or process is the act of the potential as such, the act of that which is incomplete and imperfect; it is a being-acted-upon rather than an acting. Operation or action, on the other hand, is the act of that which is already actual or complete; it is an acting and not a being-acted-upon. The philosopher, viewing vital operations, views them as the actions of a living being and seeks

within that being a principle adequate to account for this type of action. The physicist or chemist views vital phenomena as processes or motions, and seeks the antecedent processes from which they arise. The truth is that the philosopher and the scientist are viewing actually different things. For an organism to nourish itself and grow by assimilating food is an action, and it is this action — proper to living things — in which the philosopher is interested. It is, however, an action which of necessity involves certain processes in the food substances assimilated and in the organs which are instrumental in assimilation. These processes are what the scientist is interested in. They can be expressed in chemical formulas, for they are chemical reactions. But they are *not* the operation of self-nourishment and growth; they are processes or movements which are effected as the organism exercises that operation. They do not explain that operation, and they are not its causes; indeed they are rather its effects.

All action in the realm of material things involves motion, and therefore involves both an agent and a patient. Vital action is immanent, that is to say, its effect is produced in the agent. Yet, if it is the vital action of a material thing, it necessarily needs a patient; and consequently the organism is at once agent and patient under different aspects. That is what is meant by self-movement. The physicochemical analysis of vital processes is concerned with the organism and its surround as patients or things moved. The philosophical analysis is concerned with the organism as agent. Nutrition, growth, reproduction, locomotion are actions performed by the organism; they are its operation, its actualities — they are second actualities of a first actuality, or acts of the perfect. Being actions done through material instrumentalities — the organs, tissues, cells, etc. — and in a material surround, they involve processes in material patients. As we have seen in Chapter IV, every motion is at once the act of the agent and of the patient — action in the agent and passion in the patient. This identification of the two actualities involved in causation is the only philosophical or scientific theory ever advanced to explain how real causation is possible. When it is applied to self-movement, its necessary consequence is that the action and passion are going to be found in the same being. That fact is what gives occasion for the mechanistic error.

2. **The Mechanistic Error and an Opposite Error.** The mechanist examines, analyzes, and formulates in physicochemical laws the processes which are the act of the organism as patient or moved-thing in

the self-movement, and overlooks the organism as agent in the same movement. When a dog walks he is active, he is an agent in operation; but the physiology of walking is not an analysis of this operation; it is an analysis of what the organism gets done to itself by itself as the dog walks. The physiological processes are not what essentially distinguish the organism from non-living bodies; its power to perform the vital operation is. Hence, the physicochemical descriptions of the physiology of walking and of self-nourishment are not explanations or even descriptions of the acts of walking and self-nourishment. Each of those acts is a simple, single operation of the dog as a dog. The physiological processes are an extremely multiple and complex series of physicochemical movements in a vast multitude of causally related cells. They do not make the dog walk or nourish himself; he makes them occur by walking and nourishing himself. To mistake them for the vital actions is the error of mechanism. The opposite error is to deny the completeness and self-containedness of the processes as a series of causally related changes adding up to the total change. The error is committed by those who maintain that the physicochemical description of vital processes must always leave these processes incompletely described, and who seek gaps in the description — gaps which they then try to fill in with some non-physical causation. They also forget that vital activity is immanent and that the organism is patient as well as agent. They confuse action and process as badly as does the mechanist; and they disregard the law of causality as thoroughly as he does. He implies that there are effects without causes; they seem to want causes without effects.

The second error described above is inexcusable for any follower of Aristotle and St. Thomas. The doctrine of the four causes and hylemorphism logically implies the completenesss of mechanical causation on its own level in any natural process. Incompleteness of such causation in the production of any natural effect would mean that a formal cause had produced a material effect without a material cause in which to operate, and that a final cause had produced a physical effect without the mediation of the physical action of an efficient cause. Such an occurrence would have scandalized Aristotle and St. Thomas.

3. **Science and Philosophy of Organism Both Possible.** If we bear in mind this real distinction of action and motion, operation and process, we shall be able to understand how two distinct studies of the living organism can both be legitimate and how they complement

rather than contradict each other. The scientist seeks to formulate in the most basic and most general laws possible the processes which are manifested in the vital operations of all kinds of organisms; the philosopher seeks to determine the nature of the principle within every kind of organism which makes it capable of performing vital operations. Because these operations are distinctive marks of living bodies, the philosopher concludes that living bodies are essentially different from non-living bodies and possess an immanent first principle of life and of vital powers, to which first principle he gives the name soul. Then, because the first immanent principle of the nature, powers, and operations of any material substance is its substantial form, he identifies the soul of an organism with its substantial form, and defines the soul as the first actuality of an organic body which is potentially alive. The soul is to the organic body as form is to matter, as actuality is to potentiality.

VII. PROOF OF THE SOUL

1. But is the soul real? Are a potency and its act really distinct? Yes. Soul and body, act and potency, are really distinct, and distinct in precisely the way in which they must be if an organism is to be comprehended at all. There is no special "living matter" that live things are made out of; every bit of matter in every living cell was once matter outside any living cell. But no bit of matter can be thought of for a moment existing outside a living cell *as it exists in one*. At every instant non-living matter is being made alive by being taken into living cells; it was, then, potentially alive, and in the cell it becomes actually alive. Nothing has been added, but a potency has become an act — and what a difference there is! That is real distinction enough. The soul is very real: without it matter does not live; with it matter, without having anything added, lives. To ask for a greater distinction is to wish to analyze the simple act of life into parts; or to wish to separate the living thing and its life.

2. We are now in a position to give a summary of our whole argument:

a) All the living things that we can examine are material, that is, are composed physically of matter. They should, therefore, exhibit in all their corporeal activity strict adherence to the laws of chemical and physical behavior. They do.

b) But without ever breaching chemical or physical law they characteristically behave in ways in which no non-living being behaves.

They metabolize, grow, reproduce. They do these things "by chemis-try," but they alone do them.

c) The matter in them is all ordinary matter, not special "living matter"; it comes alive only when it becomes part of one of them. In all cases known to man, the living thing makes the matter alive, and not vice versa.

d) When a living thing is analyzed as far as it may be, the parts into which it is analyzed are non-living: if the analysis is physical, they are really non-living; if it is conceptual, they are conceived as non-living. From this fact mechanists conclude that there is nothing in living things except non-living matter. From it the Thomist concludes that there is something in living things besides matter. He reasons thus:

(1) Since matter becomes living in a living thing, it is in itself potentially living. To become living is to have this potency actualized. Since there is a real difference between being alive and not being alive, between potency and act, there is a real difference between a living being and its matter; the living thing is more than its matter.

(2) What it is more is not something material, for there is no ma-terial factor known in organisms that is not found also in non-living matter, and yet everything material in the organism is accounted for. Mechanists have shown this by their painstaking analysis of living organisms and protoplasm.

(3) What is in the living thing besides its matter is a principle of its life.

e) What there is in a living thing besides its matter is not something additional to the matter; it is simply a new actuality of the matter, the actuality of its potentiality for life. Since the vital actualizing principle is not something separate from the matter, the mechanist cannot find it, because he looks for something additional to the matter by analyzing the living thing instead of contemplating its life: he cannot see the tree for the wood.

f) This vital principle we call the soul, and, following Aristotle, define it as the first actuality of the potentially living body and the root of its vital operations.

g) The offense of this, to the mechanists, lies in giving the soul priority to the matter, the living whole priority to its parts. Yet we must give it such priority:

(1) The subordination of parts to whole in a single cell or in a complex organism strikes with all "the force of a self-evident truth." This last expression is borrowed from Sherrington.[14] He quotes an observer who wrote, after watching a moving picture, taken by microscope, of a cell mass in the process of making bone: "Team work by cell masses. Chalky spicules of bone-in-the-making shot across the screen, as if laborers were raising scaffold-poles. The scene suggested purposive behavior by individual cells, and still more by colonies of cells arranged as tissues and organs." Sherrington himself adds, "That impression of concerted endeavour comes, it is no exaggeration to say, with the force of a self-evident truth."

(2) The development of an organism proceeds as if directed by something distinct from and having power over the parts, and exerting this power to make the parts make the whole. The whole and parts appear to inspection as reciprocal causes, with the whole having priority since the action of the parts is unintelligible except in relation to that of the whole and since the effect worked toward is the good of the whole; the whole appears as end, the parts as means.

h) The causal influence of the whole on the parts in generation cannot be denied; yet the whole does not exist as such until the developmental process is completed. But it is absurd to speak of the causal action of something which in no way exists. Hence, we must discover a way in which the whole exists before it is materially constituted in the completeness of the parts.

i) Hylemorphism offers us such a way. The form is not a being, nor is the matter; the concrete substance is the only being. Form and matter are *principles of being*. The matter is determinable, the form determining. At any stage in the development of the individual, the individual is itself a being, and hence can act as a cause. It does so in interaction with its surround. But in doing so it is "causing itself," that is, it is making its parts and making them make it. Acted upon by the surround, it can make itself, because at any moment it really is a being, and really is determinable, having matter, and really is determining, having form; as a material being it is moved by the surround; as form it determines the matter of the surround into its own parts, and these

14 *Man on His Nature*, p. 120.

parts into itself. This seems to be the only way in which an organism could possibly make itself, and that organisms do in fact make themselves is an undeniable datum of experience.

j) The form, or soul, must, therefore, be recognized in the living thing. As far as its matter and its surround are concerned, the thing could be or become anything or nothing. It is the form or soul that makes it what it is, makes it become what it becomes.

k) We must therefore conclude that every living individual in the corporeal world is an essential composite of primary matter and substantial form, the form being called the soul and conferring life, or vital activity, upon the matter.

CHAPTER IX

MAN THE INDIVIDUAL

I. MAN IS A HYLEMORPHIC COMPOSITE

Much that there is to be said about man we have already said in preceding chapters, especially Chapter VIII. A man is a corporeal substance and therefore a hylemorphic composite, that is to say, an individual compounded of two essential intrinsic principles, primary matter and substantial form. He is a living organism and therefore his substantial form is one of those to which we give the name soul; hence a man is a composite of body and soul. His soul, like any soul, is "the first actuality of a body potentially possessing life"; it is also the first root and principle in him of all his vital operations, viz., nutrition, growth, reproduction, perception, desire, imagination, movement, thought, and will. As his substantial form, it is the determining principle that makes the matter in him what it is, a human organism. Finally, since every substance has but one substantial form, so has a man; and therefore his rational soul is the only substantial form of his body. He has no nutritive or sensitive soul; nutritive and sensitive powers are conferred on his body by his one rational soul.

A man, therefore, is an individual substance possessed of a hierarchy of powers. Of that hierarchy of powers, one, the highest, stands out as peculiar to man, as, in fact, defining him. That power is thought or reason; therefore we call man a rational animal. It is this power that makes man the mystery that he is; without it he would be merely a high type of animal. That, it is true, would be mystery enough; but there would be no one to note the mystery, animals being little introspective. So it is his thinking that makes man a mystery to himself and makes men able to disagree with one another, as to what they all are, some being able even, by thinking, to deny that they think.

II. SOME MODERN THEORIES OF HUMAN NATURE

Theories as to man's nature may be broadly classified as materialistic, spiritualistic, and dualistic. Dualistic theories may be further classified as moderate (Aristotelian) or extreme (Cartesian). St. Thomas' theory is one of moderate dualism.

1. Materialism. The materialistic theories refuse to recognize any reality of a spiritual nature in man. The old-fashioned materialists deny the existence of a soul altogether, regarding life and mind as material phenomena fully explicable in terms of the bodily parts of man, as being in fact matter in motion, just as everything else is. The mental and the material are not in any way different. The latest, but probably not the last, theory of this type was behaviorism. Behaviorists went so far as to deny the fact of consciousness and pictured man after the fashion of a slot machine: you push in a stimulus and out pops a response. That kind of materialism is out of vogue just at present. The more up-to-date "naturalist" distinguishes between mind and matter, and regards crude materialism with a sort of indulgent disapproval: the material and the mental are so obviously distinguishable. The mental (or soul, if you insist) is neither the body nor a part of it; it is an activity of the body. Santayana compares body and spirit to a candle and its flame. The seat of the mind is the brain, particularly the cerebrum. Mind is the conscious activity of the organism, and is the latest product of the evolution of matter. Soul in its true sense does not fit into the picture at all. This, of course, is materialism, whatever it may be called.

St. Thomas deals briefly with materialism in question 75, article 2, of the First Part of the *Summa Theologica*. He points out that while a body may be a principle of life or of vital action, as the heart is a a principle of life in an animal and the eye a principle of sight, no body can be the first principle of life in a living being. A body which is a principle of life is so, not *as body,* but as *such a body.* If a body *as body* were a principle of life, every body would be living, because every body is body. Now a body is *such a body* because of its actuality or act, and it is this actuality which is the first principle of life in a body which is alive or is a principle of life. This first actuality of a living body is what we call its soul.

The answer of materialists to this argument is that it proves merely that a body is not the first principle of life in a living thing, but it does not prove that the special organization of the parts of the whole body is not the first principle of its life or that living bodies are distinguished from non-living ones by anything more than the organization of their parts; the act of the body, in a word, is merely its organization. We answered that argument in Chapter VIII when we showed that the soul, or the principle of organization in a living body, has priority to the parts of the body and their vital organization. The parts are organized toward the whole-life of the organism, according to the *idea* or *immanent plan* of the living being. The organization is not a mere resultant of the parts acting independently, but is attained through a law of the whole organism. The law is prior in reality and function to the parts which it organizes. The whole is in some way in the parts from the start of the organism's development, for it rules the parts during that development. The organization is not the mere resultant of the parts, nor is it the cause of the whole; on the contrary, it is caused by the idea, plan, law, or form of the whole. A human body does not become a man because of the way its parts fall together; on the contrary, its parts fall together as they do because the form of man is present in them determining their organization into a living man. This determining form is the soul. The parts make up the whole physically; but the soul makes the parts what they are, and makes them make up the whole, by being in them from the start and determining the plan which their development brings to physical realization. It is their formal cause.

We may add, when it is a question of the human soul, the argument of Plato which we noted in Chapter II. The soul cannot be merely the "harmony" or organization of the body, because a mere resultant of a number of elements can never have tendencies and movements opposed to the tendencies and movements of those elements; it is merely their summary. Yet nothing is a more obvious feature of human life than the frequent opposition between tendencies of the body and the tendency of the soul.[1]

2. Cartesian Dualism. Soul does not find much place in contemporary theories of human nature because almost all discussion of man in modern philosophy has centered around the body-mind problem. Descartes defined mind and matter in such a way as to make any sort of unification or relation between them seem impossible. Mind, he wrote, is thinking substance, and matter is extended substance. Exten-

[1] *Con. Gen.*, II, 63–64.

sion can never be predicated of thought, nor thought of extension. A man seems to be a substance which is at once extended and thinking; but that is impossible. We must say that man's body is one substance and his mind another. Descartes tended to look upon the mind alone as the man. The body is an extended machine which operates by pushes and pulls, like any other machine. The mind is a pure spirit that thinks. Thinking, for Descartes, includes every conscious affection of mind: thought, will, desire, pleasure and pain, sensation, emotion, etc. These two utterly unlike substances certainly seem in man to interact with each other. But in fact they cannot. Each has its own inviolable nature and laws, and any influence from the other would violate these laws. How can mind, which is not energy, move body without violating the law of the conservation of energy? How can body, which is extension, affect mind? Extension can only push, and mind cannot be pushed. Descartes worked out a meeting place of the two in the pineal gland,[2] through which pass all the "animal spirits" which are the pulleys that move the body. The mind sits in that gland, and somehow, without actually adding any motion to the animal spirits, affects the direction which they will take as they move on through the bodily organs, and thus it influences the movements of the body. Through the same mechanism these movements in turn influence the mind. This strange theory emphasizes what difficulties may arise when such an obvious fact as the substantial unity of the human being is denied or weakened. What is for our present purposes most noteworthy about Descartes' account of man is how completely soul has been left out of the picture. The body, a machine, does not need a soul. The mind, a pure spirit, is in no sense a soul. The body-soul explanation of man has become the body-mind problem about man.

3. **The Monads of Leibniz.** Modern philosophers, in all their efforts to solve the body-mind problem, seemed to be under the shadow of Descartes' exaggerated dualism. Gottfried Leibniz (1646-1716) taught a kind of spiritualistic dynamism about nature in general, and his doctrine of body and soul is part of his general theory of nature. Any sub-

[2] The pineal gland is a small body situated in the center of the head underneath the brain. Descartes believed it to be a part of the brain. He chose it as the seat of the soul because it is single, while all the "other" parts of the brain are paired — left and right; and the simple soul obviously needs a single dwelling place. The "animal spirits" were thought to be a subtile fluid which flows through the nerves, and all the animal spirits were believed to flow through the pineal body since it is the only single or unpaired part of the brain. Thus it furnished the soul with a very strategic position in the body.

stance, he maintained, must be a unitary individual, because a substance is primarily a being capable of acting. But nothing that is extended can be a true unit, because it is indefinitely divisible. Hence, the constituent principles of substance must be unextended. They are purely units of internal activity; they have no parts, no shape, no possibility of division; they have only activity. These ultimate elements Leibniz called monads.

The activity of the monads is not a material force, but a psychic energy. Leibniz does not explain matter; he denies it. Monadic activity is twofold: perception and appetition. By the former the monad "represents" within itself the entire universe; by appetition it passes from one representation to another. In the higher monads the power of representation is conscious and is endowed with memory and reflection. Such monads are souls and spirits. God is the Infinite Monad, representing all reality perfectly in Himself. A man's soul is a single monad which mirrors or represents perfectly the activities of the collection or system of monads which constitute his body.

Monads never act upon one another. Their activity is purely internal. The apparent influence of one upon the other is due to the fact that each represents the whole universe, so that the internal activity of all is represented in the internal activity of each one although there is no interaction among them. This parallelism of activity is given to the monads by God, who in creating them endowed them with *"pre-established harmony."*

For Leibniz, therefore, there is no interaction between body and mind because there is no interaction between any substances. The soul of man is a high-grade monad, which is self-conscious and "represents" with some degree of clarity all other monads in the world, including those of its body, without ever affecting or being affected by any of them. Its activity and development correspond to the activities and development of the man's body-monads, but the body-monads and the soul-monad do not act upon each other. The correspondence of their successive moments is due to a divinely pre-established harmony.

4. **Spinoza's Parallelism.** In *Spinoza's* philosophy[3] the mind is the *idea corporis,* the idea of the body. It should be recalled that in this philosophy men are not individual beings at all, but only finite modes of the one being, Substance. Body and mind in a man are related to each other in a way similar to the relation between Nature and God in Substance. Nature and God are in reality identical, the former being

---

[3] See Chapter I, Section III, No. 1, and Chapter XXIV, Section I, Nos. 5–7.

Substance conceived under its attribute of extension, the latter Substance conceived under its attribute of thought. God is the idea of Nature. Body and mind in man are identical and opposite in a similar way. The body is a complex of finite modes of extension, and to each of these modes there corresponds a finite mode of thought, that is to say, the idea of the mode of extension. The complexus of all these ideas is the soul or mind. Thus the soul is the idea of the body; that is, the series of states that make up conscious life is the series of the ideas of the physical events that make up the life of the body.

5. **Double-Aspect Theory.** Many later philosophers, while not accepting Spinoza's absolute monism, followed him more or less closely in his account of body and mind. Thus there arose two very famous and very silly doctrines: the *double-aspect* theory and *psychophysical parallelism.* The former regards body and mind as two different aspects of one single underlying reality and process. There is something, and it undergoes certain affections and performs certain actions: that is all there really is; but one aspect of this thing and its operations is the body and its movements; another aspect is the mind and its ideas. This doctrine, if it means anything at all, can only mean, for example, that nerve impulses course through the cerebral cortex (body aspect) and know what they are doing (mind aspect), the knowledge being in fact the same as the doing. Its absurdity is apparent from the fact that what is done is not, by any stretch of the imagination, what is known. Neural impulses indeed travel from place to place in my brain, but what I know is something very different; it is, for example, the double-aspect theory of the relation of body and mind.

6. **Psychophysical Parallelism.** Psychophysical parallelism is little, if any, more intelligible than the double-aspect theory. Mind and body are two separate and independent chains of events. All the events in the mind-chain are mental, and every mental event has a mental cause or antecedent, and no physical cause. Every event in the body-chain is physical, has a physical cause, and can have no mental cause. Mind can never affect body, and vice versa. The two chains never cross but run along parallel to each other, with each event in one corresponding to an event in the other. Thus, if a rock falls upon my toe (physical event), I concurrently feel a pain referred to my toe (psychic event); if I turn my eyes from the interior of my room toward the street outside (physical event), the conscious content of my visual field changes (psychic event). There is no causal connection between these concomitant alter-

ations in body and mind; they are simply parallel. Critical comment upon such a belief seems unnecessary; nevertheless this doctrine is a logical development of Descartes' original sundering of the one thing, man, into two things, a body and a mind.

7. The Spiritualism of Berkeley. Two other developments were pure spiritualism and pure phenomenalism. Berkeley developed the former doctrine by settling the body-mind problem as simply as did the materialists. Whereas they said there is no mind, he said there is no body. Man is a spirit and has ideas. The material world, including a man's own body, is nothing except his ideas; matter is simply the ideas of mind. Its being consists in being perceived; its *esse* is *percipi*. Altogether, there exist an infinite spirit (God), finite spirits (men), and their ideas. Some of his ideas man gets from God, and these are the real world, or nature. Others he makes up himself, and these are imaginary. You can eat a real loaf of bread, and you cannot eat an imaginary loaf; but the real one is, nevertheless, an idea; and in fact eating it is an idea. Since there are only minds and their ideas, there is no body-mind problem.

8. The Phenomenalism of Hume. All that we know directly is our own ideas: everybody from Descartes on seemed to agree about that. Well, then, asked David Hume, can we *ever* know anything more? Can we ever break through the circle of our ideas to some substantial reality underlying them? Hume believed that we cannot, except by an act of natural belief. Wherefore, not only must we abandon our belief that we perceive any material substances or can demonstrate their existence, but we must also stop talking as though we directly know or can demonstrate our own spiritual substance, that is, our soul or permanent ego. We know only the flux of impressions and ideas that constitute our incessantly changing conscious states; we know no mind that has these states nor any body that has this mind. Body and mind are now both gone, and all that is left is appearances or phenomena. J. S. Mill, William James, and some others developed theories somewhat similar to this one.

III. THE SOUL AND THE UNITY OF A MAN

1. "Soul" Missing From Modern Philosophy. Many other attempts to describe or define the nature of man and his mind have been proposed by modern and contemporary philosophers. No purpose would be served by giving an account of all of them. From the Thomistic point of view, most of them have one outstanding character in common: *they ignore the very notion of soul.* Some of the philosophers reject the soul; others think that they are talking about it when they talk about mind. If they were, they would not have any body-mind problem. There is no meaning to questions about how the body and soul interact or how their affections and operations correspond; for soul and body are not distinct substances somehow bound together; they are opposite and complementary principles of one complete substance. There is no interaction or correspondence of action where there is only one thing acting.

2. **The Whole Man Is the Agent in All His Acts.** Once the concept of soul as substantial form is understood, the problem of the relations of the bodily and the mental in man's behavior disappears. His soul does not feel injuries to his body; he feels injuries to himself. His soul does not command his body to walk; he wills to walk and walks. The willing and walking are not the same act under different aspects (double-aspect theory), nor different acts in separate and unrelated series (psychophysical parallelism), nor the willing the idea of the walking (Spinoza), nor both of them simply ideas (Berkeley and Hume), nor is one an act of the mind and the other an act of the body; the willing and walking are different acts, one mental and the other physical, of the same agent, the man. The two acts form parts of one series, the series of acts of that one agent. The willing is the cause of the walking in the sense that the agent walks because he wills to. Strictly speaking, the agent, the man, is the cause of both acts. All his affections and actions form one series, each leading to the next in causal sequence; but some are bodily and some are mental. That mental ones should lead to bodily ones and vice versa is not at all strange if the agent is himself a single substance with a hierarchy of powers, some bodily and some mental.

A man, like oxygen or a tree or an amoeba, is a hylemorphic composite — that was proved in the last chapter. A man is made of matter, and that matter is a man because it is determined in actuality by a certain specific substantial form which we call the human soul. As a hylemorphic composite, a man is as solidly a single substance as is a tree or a dog. Conceived separately by the intellect, the matter in him is potentially the man, and the soul is the first actuality of this matter, making it the man. Matter and form complement each other to constitute one perfectly individual substance. In all this a man is like any of the living things discussed in the last chapter; indeed that chapter was concerned as much with man as with any other living organism. We should not expect physics and chemistry to fail in their application to the human organism any more than in respect to any other organism. If chemistry did not work in man, medicine could never have become a science; instead of physicians we would still have medicine men. But if chemistry cannot give a satisfactory explanation of the humblest plant or animal, certainly it cannot give one of man. Man has a soul, since he is a living corporeal substance. So much we learned in the last chapter.

3. The Soul Is the First Principle of All the Acts. As we saw above, a man's soul does not do some things and his body others; for instance, his soul think and his body walk. The man thinks and the man walks. But body and soul play far from equal parts in a man's actions. In all a man's acts, the soul is the first immanent principle of operation; it is the "dynamo" as much in walking as in thinking. It is the first active source of all a man's being and operation. It is even the first intrinsic principle of as purely a physical thing as falling. For it is the man's substantial form, and substantial form makes prime matter a body with actual quantity and mass. That is one implication of St. Thomas' doctrine of the unicity of substantial form in a substance.

4. Principle, Subject, and Agent. St. Thomas explains[4] how the powers and the operations of man are to be attributed to the soul as their *principle,* and either to the soul or to the composite as their *subject* depending on what kind of power is in question. By the subject of an operation or a power is meant that being or part of a being which is able to perform the operation and does perform it. Now, no vital operation is performed by the body alone, because without the soul the body has no life; but some of man's operations, namely, thinking and willing, are performed without the use of any corporeal organ, and therefore the powers of these operations are in the soul; and the soul, therefore, is said to be their subject. Other powers and operations, however, namely, the nutritive and sensitive and all those which need a bodily organ, have as their subject, not the soul, but the composite of body and soul. Yet even these powers and operations are attributed to the soul as to their principle, "because it is by the soul that the composite has the power to perform such opera-

---

[4] *S. Theol.*, I, 77, 5. c.

tions."[5] Finally, not the soul nor the body, but the man himself is the *agent* in all his operations, even in those whose subject is the soul alone; for it is not the soul which thinks and wills but the man who thinks and wills by his intellectual power, which resides in his soul as in its subject, just as it is the man who sees by the power which resides in his eye.[6] "Action belongs to the composite, as does being. Now the composite has being substantially through the substantial form which in man is his soul, and it operates by the power which results from the substantial form."[7]

5. Powers Are the Immediate Principles of Operations.[8] The soul, therefore, is the first principle of the operations of the living thing. It is not, however, the immediate principle of operation. Each operation is the act of some power, as, for example, seeing is the act of the power of sight and thinking is the act of the intellectual power. The operations cannot be the act of the soul itself, because the soul is by essence an act, not a potency; it is the act which makes the body a living thing. If operations were the immediate acts of the soul, as the soul is the act of the body, then every living thing would of necessity always perform all its operations, since the soul is by its essence always in act. Hence, operations are immediately the acts of powers in the soul and not of the substance of the soul. These powers are accidental forms in the soul, or in the composite if they are powers which use a corporeal organ. These accidental forms are the immediate principles of the operations of the being, but that they are such principles is due to the substantial form, i.e., the soul, just as their being is due to the substantial form.[9]

6. How the Soul Moves the Body. The manner in which the soul moves the body perplexed Descartes and his followers because they regarded the soul as being merely the mind and as being something primarily distinct from the body. St. Thomas' explanation of how the soul moves the body was, in its polemical aspects, directed against the Platonists, but it is equally valid against Cartesianism. It is implied in much of what we have already studied in the last chapter and in this one, especially in the paragraphs immediately above.

In a certain sense the expression "how the soul moves the body" is

<hr/>

[5] *Ibid.*, I, 77, 5, ad 1.
[6] *De Ver.*, II, 6, ad 3.
[7] *S. Theol.*, I, 77, 1, ad 3.
[8] Throughout the following paragraph *operation* means action; and *act*, actuality.
[9] *S. Theol.*, I, 77, 1, c; ad 3; ad 4.

inaccurate. For it is living bodies with which we are concerned, and a living body is, by definition, one which moves itself. In other words, it is the living organism, body and soul, which moves itself, and not the soul which moves the body. The soul, to be sure, is the first immanent principle of the movement, as it is of all the actions of the living body; but the composite of body and soul is the agent in the movement, as it is in all its operations. Furthermore, though the soul is the first principle of movement in the body, it is not by its essence the immediate principle, as we have just seen; the immediate principle is some power of which the soul is the determining source and which it communicates to the body. For the soul is the substantial form, that is to say, the formal cause of the living individual; and the function of a form as such is not action but specification;[10] the soul, as form, does not do something to the body, but it determines and actualizes matter, making it a living body of a certain nature and communicating to it, with this nature, the powers which are due to a body of such nature. Primary among these powers is that of self-movement or immanent activity.[11] Consequently, to say that the soul moves the body is really to say that the living body which includes the soul as its substantial form, moves itself by the powers which the soul confers upon it in informing and actualizing it.[12]

This account of the soul's movement of the body does away with certain difficulties felt by modern philosophers. If the mind, as an external agent, moved the body, it would seem that the law of the conservation of energy would be defied; for the mind, an immaterial being, could not be brought under this law and would yet be initiating an increase of energy in the physical world. That was the problem which Descartes tried to solve by means of the theory that the mind "directed" the movements of the animal spirits without adding to or subtracting from the sum of their motion. Any such theory is obviously a failure; it does not save the physical law. It is, however, no more futile than the double-aspect and parallelistic theories which attempt to solve the problem by saving the physical law at the price of the denial of either the distinction between or the union of body and mind. The difficulty which gave rise to such theories does not appear in the Thomistic system. It is not a question of how *this thing*, the

[10] See Chapter IV, Section VI, especially No. 6.
[11] *De Ver.*, II, 14, c.
[12] *Ibid.*, XXII, 3.

soul, moves *that other thing,* the body, but of how the animated body moves itself according to its different parts. Each movement in any cell or organ of the body, or the local movement of the whole body, obeys the laws of chemistry and physics; but all the movements are determined from within and carry out an immanent plan. They are all integrated by the one soul under a higher law than physics, a law that makes use of physical and chemical law for its own ends — the law of the living organism, the law of its nature, given to it by its soul.[13]

IV. MAN'S INTELLECTUAL SOUL IS HIS
ONE SUBSTANTIAL FORM

1. **Arguments Against This View.** There were in St. Thomas' day many philosophers who were loath to admit that man's intellectual soul was the one substantial form of his body.[14] Because it is intellectual, it is a spiritual substance; and how, they asked, can a spiritual substance be the act of a body? They quoted St. Thomas' Philosopher against St. Thomas: Aristotle said that the intellect is separate from matter; therefore it is not the act of any body. Furthermore, the intellect receives the forms of things immaterially and universally, and this power is what makes it intellect. But if it were the act of a body it would receive the forms of things materially and individually, as every body does. Again, it is clear that the operation of the intellect is not the action of any body. Therefore, the intellectual power is not the power of any body, because a power and its operation necessarily have the same subject. Consequently, the essence whence this power arises, namely, the substance of the intellect, is not the form of any body. Furthermore, a form is not a being, but a principle of being. The intellect is a subsisting being, and therefore cannot be the form of the body. Finally, since form is the act of matter, it is by essence united with matter. But the intellectual soul, being incorruptible, exists separate from matter after the dissolution of the body. Therefore, it cannot be the form of the body.

2. **St. Thomas' Arguments for This View.** St. Thomas answers that it is man's intellectual soul which gives him his proper operations, namely, thought and will, and which distinguish him from brute animals, constituting him in his own species. But that which gives any-

---

[13] Cf. Sertillanges, *S. Thomas d'Aquin.*. II, pp. 89–95.
[14] *S. Theol.,* I, 76, 1, Objs. 1, 3, 4, 5, 6. Cf. *Con. Gen.,* II, 56; *De Spirit. Creat.,* Art. II, Objs.; *Q. D. De Anima,* Art. I, Objs.

thing its own proper species and operations is its substantial form; consequently, man's intellectual principle is his substantial form.

> . . . that whereby primarily anything acts is a form of the thing. . . . The reason for this is that nothing acts except in so far as it is in act; and so a thing acts by that whereby it is in act. Now it is clear that the first thing by which the body lives is the soul. And as life appears through various operations in different degrees of living things, that whereby we primarily perform each of these vital actions is the soul. For the soul is the primary principle of our nourishment, sensation and local movement; and likewise of our understanding. Therefore this principle by which primarily we understand, whether it be called the intellect or the intellectual soul, is the form of the body.[15]

To this direct argument the Angelic Doctor adds other arguments based upon the fact that every act of understanding is the act of an individual man. What relationship between the man and his intellect can account for this fact, if the intellect is not the substantial form of the man? (1) Some say that the intellect is the whole man. That, if true, would explain why the act of understanding is attributed to the individual man. But this is not true. Our intellectual and sensory life form, not two, but one stream of consciousness; it is the same man, in each case, who perceives, feels, and thinks. Now, feeling and perception require acts of the body; and consequently the intellect alone cannot be the whole man; the body is undoubtedly part of the man. (2) Perhaps, then, the intellect is in some way united to the body to make up the man, but is not the substantial form of the body; it might be, for example, the mover of the body. This will not do either. For if the intellectual principle is not the form of the man, it is outside his essence altogether, since obviously it is not his matter, and form and matter make up the essence. But if a man's intellect is outside his essence, *he* will not understand when *it* understands, for understanding, like every immanent action, remains in the agent; and if the agent, that is, the intellect, is outside the essence of the man, its action will not enter into him. (3) Furthermore, if the intellectual principle is merely the mover of the body, its action cannot be attributed to the man whom it moves, except as to an instrument, just as a man's act of writing can be attributed to his pen only as his instrument. But the man is a corporeal substance, and the intellect, as the opponents them-

---

[15] *Ibid.*, I, 76, 1, c (*Basic Writings of St. Thomas Aquinas*, ed. Anton C. Pegis [New York: Random House, 1945], Vol. I, p. 696). Cf. *Con. Gen.*, II, 59, 68; *De Spirit. Creat.*, Art. II, c; *Q. D. De Anima*, I, c; *ibid.*, II c.

selves point out, does not use any corporeal instrument. The truth of the matter is that the only theory of the nature of the intellectual soul that will justify us in attributing the act of understanding to the man himself is that it is the substantial form of the man, that is to say, the first actuality of his body. The power of intellect belongs to the whole man because it is a power whose first principle is his substantial form.

3. Yet the Soul Has an Immaterial Power. There is nothing astonishing about the idea of a form which is the act of a body and yet has an immaterial power. The more perfect a form is, the more it rises in its power above matter; and man's form is the highest of all forms in nature:

> But we must observe that the nobler a form is, the more it rises above corporeal matter, the less it is subject to matter, and the more it excels matter by its power and operation. Hence we find that the form of a compound has an operation not caused by its elemental qualities. And the higher we advance in the nobility of forms, the more we find that the power of the form excels the elementary matter; as the vegetative soul excels the form of the metal; and the sensitive soul excels the vegetative soul. Now the human soul is the highest and noblest of forms. Therefore, in its power it excels corporeal matter by the fact that it has an operation and power in which corporeal matter has no share whatsoever. This power is called the intellect.[16]

4. Answers to the Objections Above. It is clear now how we are to answer the arguments given above by those who deny that the intellective principle is the substantial form of the body. Intellect is a power of the soul, which is the substantial form of the body, and it is a power which does not use any bodily organ for its operation. Hence, as Aristotle says, it is separate from matter. But the soul of which it is a power is not separate from matter, but is the first act of the body, making it alive and conferring upon it all the powers of the composite. This answers the first objection. The second is answered similarly. Man, the composite of body and soul, is able to understand things immaterially and universally because his substantial form or soul has the immaterial power of intellect. The soul's possession of this power is sufficient to enable the man to understand immaterially without the necessity of the soul being separate from matter in itself and in all its powers. The third argument has already been answered in the above. The human soul, the most perfect of forms, is not immersed in or entirely embraced by matter. Its proper perfection consists pre-

[16] S. Theol., I, 76, 1, c (Pegis, op cit., Vol. 1, p. 698). Cf. other places last cited.

cisely in its transcendence of matter to such a degree that it has a power and an operation in which matter has no part, although by its essence it is the form of the body.[17]

The last two objections require answers somewhat different from the above. The human soul is a form, but it is the most perfect of natural forms, having as the objection says, being in itself. But it is this very being which, as form, it communicates to the matter; so that the being of the whole composite is also the being of the soul. Therefore, it subsists after the dissolution of the body, while the less perfect forms recede into the potency of matter when the body which they inform is corrupted. Since the soul is the form of the body, it is true that it is of its very essence to be united to the body; and, although it does subsist after it is separated from the body, it remains always essentially inclined to union with the body and does not live its full proper natural life while apart from the body.[18]

5. Man's Rational Soul Is His Only Substantial Form. Since man's intellectual principle is his substantial form, it is his only substantial form and his only soul. This follows from St. Thomas' doctrine of the unicity of substantial form in a substance and the virtual presence of lower forms in higher, a doctrine which we have already had occasion to study more than once. If a man had more than one substantial form or more than one soul, he would not be a being at all, but a group of beings: a body, a plant, an animal, and a man. What would unite these into one? Not the body, certainly; for the body does not give unity to the form, but receives unity from it. Furthermore, there is no need at all to attribute separate forms to man to make him living, sentient, and rational. The higher form contains virtually whatever belongs to the lower forms. The rational soul, by its higher power, confers on the matter with which it unites whatever is conferred on other bodies by the lower forms separately; it makes the matter a body; makes it a living, sentient being; and makes this being a rational man.[19] If there were a substantial form in man besides and prior to his intellectual soul, the latter would only be an accidental form, for it could not give substantial being to the man since he would already have it from the prior form.

[17] *Ibid.*, I, 76, 1, ad 1: ad 3; ad 4.
[18] *Ibid.*, I, 76, 1, ad 5; ad 6. Cf. for all the above arguments and others: *Con. Gen.*, II, 69, 70; *De Spirit. Creat.*, II, answers to Obj.; *Q. D. De Anima*, I, answers to Obj.
[19] *S. Theol.*, I, 76, 3, c.

Whence we must conclude that there is no other substantial form in man besides the intellectual soul; and that just as the soul contains virtually the sensitive and nutritive souls, so does it contain virtually all inferior forms, and does alone whatever the imperfect forms do in other things. The same is to be said of the sensitive soul in brute animals, and of the nutritive soul in plants, and universally of all the more perfect forms in relation to the imperfect.[20]

6. The Whole Soul Is in Each Part of the Body. Since one substance has but one substantial form, it follows that that form determines and perfects not only the whole body with which it is united, but each part of the body. Without the soul, the hand or eye of a man is no more a real hand or eye than the dead body is a real man; the soul makes the whole organism a man, and it makes each part of the organism a part of the man. No part has its proper nature or operation without the soul. Therefore, the soul, or substantial form, is in every part of the body.

But is the whole soul in each part of the body? A thing may be whole in three ways: (1) according to quantity, as an extended thing is whole when it has all its parts; (2) according to species or essence, as a thing is whole when it has all that is due to its nature; (3) according to power, as a thing is whole when it is capable of exerting all its powers in operation. The first kind of wholeness does not pertain to the human soul at all, since the latter is simple, indivisible, and without quantity. The second kind, wholeness of essence, does properly belong to the soul; and the soul is whole in each part of the body and in the whole body according to essence, since, being simple and indivisible, it possesses its whole perfection of nature wherever it is. The third, wholeness of power, also belongs properly to forms or souls. In relation to the whole body, which is its proper and proportionate matter, the soul is whole with wholeness of power. But, since it does not exert all its powers through each part, but one through one part and another through another part, as sight through the eye and hearing through the ear, it is not whole with a wholeness of power in each part but only in the whole organism as such. This same thing is true of any soul, because a soul is the form of a living body and a living body must be organic, that is, it must have a variety of parts making up the whole so that one part can move another. The soul determines this

[20] *Ibid.*, I, 76, 4, c (Pegis, *op. cit.*, Vol. I, p. 708). Cf. *Con. Gen.*, II, 58, 71; *De Spirit. Creat.*, III, c; *Q. D. De Anima*, XI.

variety of parts for the sake of the whole, and exercises different powers in the different parts, and its whole power only in the whole.[21]

V. THE MULTIPLICITY AND INDIVIDUALITY OF SOULS

1. **The Doctrine of Universal Mind or Absolute Reason,** which had
some vogue among idealistic philosophers of the Hegelian school in
modern times, also had its proponents in the time of St. Thomas. This
theory regards thought, intellect, or reason as some thing-in-itself,
superior to all individual minds and the cause of conscious thought in
them: thus, I do not really think nor do you; but Thought thinks in
me and the same Thought thinks in you. Catholic philosophers have
always rejected theories such as this because, for one thing, they tend
to the denial of human individuality, freedom, and personal immortality. Intellect is a man's token of immortality, and if his intellect is
not his own, neither is his immortality; it is the base and root of his
free will, and if his thoughts are thought in him by an intellect which
transcends him, then his will-acts are willed in him but not by him;
finally, it is by intellect that a man knows himself as himself, and if
this intellect is nothing of his own his self-hood is an illusion.

The vogue which the doctrine of the unity of intellect had in the
time of St. Thomas was due to the way in which the Arabian philosophers, Avicenna, Averroes, and others, had interpreted Aristotle's teaching on active and passive reason.[22] His obscurity gave occasion for
many divergent interpretations, and certainly gave ample excuse for
the view that he regarded intellect, or at least active intellect, as a
substance distinct from any individual mind, but acting in all human
minds, giving them knowledge. Such a doctrine fitted in very nicely
with the Neoplatonic doctrine of the emanation of intelligence and
soul, which the Arabians confused with Aristotle's philosophy.[23] St.
Thomas interpreted the Stagirite quite differently and rejected the
doctrine of the unity of intellect.[24]

2. **Arguments Against Unity of Intellect.** The intellect is a power of
the man's soul, and the man's soul is his substantial form. The form
of an individual is his principle of being, and it is as impossible for
several individuals to have one form as it is for them to have one

---

[21] *S. Theol.*, I, 76, 8. Cf. *Con. Gen.*, II, 72; *De Spirit. Creat.*, IV; *Q. D. De Anima*, X.

[22] This teaching will be briefly explained in the next chapter.

[23] See Chapter III above, Section III, Nos. 2–5.

[24] *De Unitate Intellectus Contra Averroistas*; *S. Theol.*, I, 76, 2; *Con. Gen.*, II,
73–78; *De Spirit. Creat.*, IX–X; *Q. D. De Anima*, III and V.

being. Since each man has his own form, he has his own intellect. Furthermore, every being derives its proper operation from that principle from which it derives its species, namely, its substantial form. If the intellect is not a part or a power of a man's soul, it does not derive from his form and consequently it is not proper to his species. Therefore, if the intellect is a separate substance outside individual human souls, reason is not man's proper or specific operation, and man is not in a different species from brute animals. In the third place, if it is one intellect which thinks in you and in me, then your act of understanding something and my act are not really distinct acts. Even if we are considered as different instruments of the same intellect, this one intellect would be the principal agent and there would be only one understander. But in truth, there would also be only one act of understanding, because, as we have seen, the intellect does not use any instrument in its operation. Now all these things are quite contrary to our everyday experience.[25]

3. **Each Man Has His Own Intellect.** Each man, according to the Angelic Doctor, has his own intellect. The intellect, as we have seen, is a power of the human soul, and that soul is the substantial form of the body. Like any form which unites with matter to constitute a composite substance, the soul is individuated by the matter with which it unites. Matter, which has an essential potency to quantity, is never actualized except as marked by quantity. Since it is has quantity, it is divisible. And since it is divisible, different parts of matter can be actuated by different forms or by the same form. Embodied in the matter, the form is not the mere abstract universal which represents the species, but is a concrete, physical principle determining an individual substance. The same specific form, therefore, is multiplied numerically as often as a different quantity of matter embodies it. This is as true of man's intellectual soul as it is of any form uniting with matter. Consequently, not some universal intellect exists, but my individual intellect in my soul and yours in your soul.

4. **Human Souls Are Individually Different.** One man's soul is not the same as another's. The men are individually different and so are their souls. All human souls are specifically or essentially the same; but to say that is only to say that all men are specifically or essentially the same. So are all oak trees. But one oak tree is individually different from another; and since form is the actuality of matter in the

25 Cf. citations in last footnote.

concrete substance, the form of one oak tree is, in actual physical being, different from that of another. The form cannot be realized in the matter without being particularized by the matter. The form or idea in our intellect by which we know and define the natures of individuals is the same for all individuals of the same species; but the form in our mind is only an idea, a form *abstracted from* the matter, a purely logical being. The forms of material substances have physical being only in the substances, only embodied in matter; and so embodied they are of necessity individuated or particularized.

According to St. Thomas, quantified matter is the principle of individuation. The reason why there can be a multiplicity of particular physical oak trees instead of one ideal oak tree is that there are many particular quantities of matter which are potentially oak trees, that is, capable of becoming oak trees. Each actual oak is a particular embodiment of the one form of being, namely, oak tree. Similarly, because there is much matter that can become human organisms, there can be many men instead of one ideal man. Each actual man is a particular embodiment of the one form of being, man. And any two men will differ both as to matter, the potency, and form, the actuality of this potency.

The souls of different men are as different from one another as the men are. Substantial forms unite with primary matter, but in the concrete generation of any substance the new substance is produced from a previous substance, that is, from prepared or suitable matter, as we have noted in a previous chapter. All suitable matters are not equally suitable; all have not precisely the same potencies. In each generation of a substance, the new form will actualize the matter in strict accordance with the potency which the matter offers for actualization. In the case of an oak tree, for example, the precise potency of the matter that is becoming the tree will itself be antecedently determined by differences of soil, rainfall, sunlight, temperature, and a thousand accidental causes and conditions. The form or nature oak will itself introduce no differences, but one oak will be different actually from another because of the different potencies of the matter. The case is similar with men. Heredity is an important factor introducing differences of potentiality into the matter which is to become the man. The souls of different men, being actualities of different matters, will differ as the potentialities of the matters differ. You can't make a silk purse out of a sow's ear, nor a Newton out of a Kallikak. God creates each human soul, but He creates each for a particular body prepared for it; and the bodies are very different.[26]

5. What Remains to Be Said. All that we have said of man up to this point is true, but all the most important things about him remain to be said. When a man is understood as a single, individual substance composed of matter and form, that is, of body and soul, the problem concerning his mental-physical mode of activity disappears; but the mystery of his nature is only deepened. For in Thomistic philosophy a man is conceived as an individual substance that is at once material and spiritual. His soul is the form of his body, but it is itself a spiritual substance. Man holds a middle place in the universe of substances, and is continuous with every being below him and with every being above him. Below him are multitudes of material things ranging from the highest animals down through the animal and plant kingdoms into the inorganic realm of compounds and elements, to dwindle off, finally into the utter imperfection of pure potentiality which is primary matter. Stretching away above him is a hierarchy of pure spirits rising from a spiritual being but little higher than himself up through increasingly more perfect ones to the absolute perfection, the pure actuality that is God. Standing athwart the threshold of matter and spirit, a man is himself at once matter and spirit; nothing material is alien to him, nor anything spiritual. Up to this point we have stressed man's solidity with nature; in the next chapter we must see how he is also a citizen of the kingdom of the spiritual.

[26] *S. Theol.*, I, 85, 7, c; *ibid.*, ad 3; *In Boet. de Trin..* IV, 4, ad 5.

CHAPTER X

MAN'S SPIRITUAL SOUL

I. THE ARGUMENT IN BRIEF

The Thomistic account of human nature is hard to believe, but is the only account that is demonstrable. It is hard to believe because it presents the human soul as being at the same time the form or actuality of a material organism and a spiritual substance in its own right. It is the only demonstrable account because it is the only one that takes full cognizance of the whole of human behavior and explains this behavior as rooted in a nature really capable of being its source. St. Thomas' doctrine of human nature may be briefly stated thus: a man is a single, composite substance constituted by the union of a body and a soul: this soul is the substantial form or first actuality of the body, and is in itself an immaterial substance, a spirit, intrinsically independent of the body in its being.

The proof that man's soul is a spiritual substance is based upon man's distinctive operations and powers, and upon the principle that a cause cannot produce effects transcending its own nature. This principle is pithily expressed in the Scholastic axiom, *operatio sequitur esse.*

Man's intellectual cognitions, his predominant and distinctly human interests and aspirations, and his freedom of will transcend the powers of any principle which is material or essentially dependent upon matter. But a cause cannot produce effects transcending its own nature. Therefore, the first principle of man's operations, his rational soul, is neither itself material nor is it essentially dependent upon matter. But if the soul were merely the organization of the body, or some activity of the body or of some part of the body, it would be essentially dependent upon matter. Hence, the soul of man is a spiritual substance possessing its being in essential independence of the body. The remainder of the chapter will develop this argument.

II. ARISTOTLE AND THE INTELLECT

1. Thought has always been recognized as an action which at least seems immaterial. Plato and, much later, Descartes made of it so purely an act of spirit that they came to regard man himself as being merely his mind. Aristotle could not take this view: man is too obviously his body as well as his mind. The question for Aristotle was not whether the mind or the body is the man, but whether the mind is anything apart from the body.

> A further problem [he wrote] presented by the affections of the soul is this: are they all affections of the complex of body and soul, or is there any one among them peculiar to the soul by itself? To determine this is indispensable but difficult. . . . Thinking seems the most probable exception; but if this too proves to be a form of imagination or to be impossible without imagination, it too requires a body as a condition of its exercise. If there is any way of acting or being acted upon proper to the soul, soul will be capable of separate existence; if there is none, its separate existence is impossible.[1]

In what immediately follow this, the Stagirite seems to conclude that there is no operation of the soul that is not dependent upon the body. But further on, treating explicitly of thought, he takes a different view.

> Thus that in the soul which is called mind (by mind I mean that whereby the soul thinks and judges) is, before it thinks, not actually any real thing. For this reason it cannot reasonably be regarded as blended with the body: if so, it would acquire some quality, for example, warmth or cold, or even have an organ, like the sensitive faculty; as it is, it has none.[2]

2. **Passive and Active Intellect.** Mind, Aristotle goes on to say, thinks essences separate from the matter in which they are embodied in nature; for example, straightness and crookedness separate from any straight or crooked stick. Sense cannot do this. Therefore "in so far as the realities it knows are capable of being separated from their matter, so it is also with the powers of mind." Furthermore, what is in matter (that is, form or essence) is not thinkable until it is disengaged from matter and made one with mind.[3] Wherefore, Aristotle concludes, there must be within the soul two powers of mind, or two

[1] Aristotle, *De Anima*, I, 1, 403a.
[2] *Ibid.*, III, 4, 429a.
[3] *Ibid.*, 429b–430a.

minds: one which *makes* intelligible things (by separating them from matter) and one which *becomes* them (by receiving their form). These two minds are the famous active and *passive* reason of the medieval Aristotelians, or the active and possible intellect of St. Thomas. It is not easy to say just what Aristotle meant by them. The latter, possible intellect, is the one which he has been describing in the passages cited above: it is a mere potentiality until it becomes what it thinks; still, it is "separable from the body." If it were not, it could not become all intelligible things since it would never be itself free from matter. The former, active intellect, is a positive immaterial agent. Just as light makes potential colors actual colors in the realm of sense, so, in the realm of intellect, this mind makes potentially intelligible objects actually intelligible. Aristotle describes it in a passage whose obscurity has puzzled commentators for two thousand years, but in which one thing anyway is abundantly clear: this mind is immaterial and fully independent of matter.

> Mind, in this sense of it, is separable, impassive, unmixed, since it is in its essential nature activity (for always the active is superior to the passive factor, the originating force to the matter which it forms).
> Actual knowledge is identical with its object: in the individual, potential knowledge is in time prior to actual knowledge, but in the universe as a whole it is not prior even in time. Mind is not at one time knowing and at another time not. When mind is set free from its present conditions it appears as just what it is and nothing more: this alone is immortal and eternal (we do not, however, remember its former activity because, while mind in this sense is impassible, mind as passive is destructible), and without it nothing thinks.[4]

3. The Mystery of Human Mind. We need not enter the age-old controversy about the nature of this "active reason" in order to see clearly where the source of Aristotle's obscurity lies. On the one hand, it is clear to him that human mind operates through the body, particularly through the senses; it is a power of man's soul or form. On the other hand, it is equally clear that thought is ultimately predicable only of an immaterial agent, an intellect which is pure, unmixed intellect, unalloyed with and unaffected by matter, immutable and eternal. Can the form of man's body be this? Honest thinker that he was, Aristotle, unable to solve the dilemma, presents its two horns and leaves it at that. Man thinks; therefore in his soul operates immaterial pure mind, which is eternal and imperishable: but man's

[4] *Ibid.*, 430a, 17–25.

mind is embodied in matter; therefore his mind perishes. Has man then two minds? Aristotle seems to see no other answer. The difficulty is felt by anyone who seriously studies mind. Sherrington[5] states it very forcibly: science deals with matter or energy in all its forms and transformations, and nothing is more certain than that mind is none of these transformations. When they are all accounted for and, none missing, mind is not among them; yet mind is found in nature and is found yoked to energy.

III. THE IMMATERIALITY AND SUBSISTENCE OF THE SOUL

1. St. Thomas' Argument. From the fact that the soul of man can know all material things, St. Thomas argues that it is itself immaterial and subsistent. By calling the soul subsistent, he means that it exists in itself as a substance (though a specifically incomplete one), and not merely by inhering in the body as an accidental form, or as a substantial form which is dependent upon and inseparable from its matter. By calling it incorporeal and subsistent, he means that it is a spiritual substance. His argument may be summarized as follows: only what subsists in itself can operate by itself; but the soul does operate by itself when it understands corporeal substances; therefore the soul is subsistent. The crux of the argument is the assertion that the soul could not understand all corporeal substances unless, in its act of understanding, it were itself free from corporeality and free from dependence on any corporeal instrument. The Angelic Doctor supports this assertion by claiming that if there were any matter in the soul or in an instrument used by the soul in understanding, this matter, having a determinate nature of its own, would prevent the soul from understanding the natures of other corporeal things; it would affect the intellect's efforts to understand diverse natures as colored glasses affect the eye's efforts to see diverse colors. Here is his argument in full:

> It must necessarily be allowed that the principle of intellectual operation, which we call the soul of man, is a principle both incorporeal and subsistent. For it is clear that by means of the intellect man can know all corporeal things. Now whatever knows certain things cannot have any of them in its own nature, because that which is in itself

[5] *Man on His Nature*, Chapters VII–XI. Sherrington is not referring particularly to *human* mind or to thought.

naturally would impede the knowledge of anything else. Thus we observe that a sick man's tongue, being unbalanced by a feverish and bitter humor, is insensible to anything sweet, and everything seems bitter to it. Therefore, if the intellectual principle contained within itself the nature of any body, it would be unable to know all bodies. Now every body has its own determinate nature. Therefore it is impossible for the intellectual principle to be a body. It is also impossible for it to understand by means of a bodily organ, since the determinate nature of that organ would likewise impede knowledge of all bodies; as when a certain determinate color is not only in the pupil of the eye, but also in a glass vase, the liquid in the vase seems to be of that same color.

Therefore the intellectual principle, which we call the mind or intellect, has essentially an operation in which the body does not share. Now only that which subsists in itself can have an operation in itself. For nothing can operate but what is actual, and so a thing operates according as it is; for which reason we do not say that heat imparts heat, but that what is hot gives heat. We must conclude, therefore, that the human soul, which is called intellect or mind, is something incorporeal and subsistent.[6]

It is true, as one opponent of St. Thomas pointed out, that the intellectual soul does use the body in its operations; for it is the senses, which are powers residing in corporeal organs, that supply the intellect with the phantasms or images from which it abstracts the natures of corporeal things. But this fact does not damage the above argument. For the phantasm is not used by the intellect as an organ of knowledge, but as an object; and therefore it is as true in regard to the phantasms as in regard to corporeal things, that the intellect could not know them all unless it were itself free from any of the corporeal natures it knows in them. The fact that understanding is in some manner dependent on the body does not mean that the soul is not subsistent; for if we could argue that way, we would have to say that animals are not subsistent since their sensations depend upon sensible, external bodies.[7]

Animals, of course, are subsistent, but their souls are not. The knowledge enjoyed by animals does not go beyond sensation and the attendant sensory operations, and all these operations are accompanied by movements in the bodily sense organs. Their souls have no operation in which the body does not play a part; all their oper-

[6] S. Theol., I, 75, 2, c (Basic Writings of St. Thomas Aquinas, ed. Anton C. Pegis [New York: Random House, 1945], Vol. I, p. 685).

[7] Ibid., ad 3.

ations belong to the composite of body and soul. Therefore, since their souls have no *per se* operation, we conclude that their souls are not subsistent; for the operation of anything follows its mode of being.[8] We argue from the operations to the mode of being; but of course the order of nature is the reverse of this. Animals do not have subsistent souls, and therefore can perform no operations which transcend the conditions of materiality; therefore they have no universal conceptions, they cannot understand or reason. It is because man can perform these operations, which are essentially different from all sensory operations, that we know that he has a substantial soul. We shall, therefore, expand St. Thomas' simple argument by an examination of the intellectual operations which form its basis.

2. **Sensism.** The opponents of the spirituality of the human soul, when confronted with the evidence of the immaterial character of intellectual thought, generally meet the argument by denying the evidence; they maintain that there is no intellect distinct from sensation and imagination, that all acts of the mind are sensory in character, that ideas are merely sensory signs (for example, images or words) of the objects meant, that thinking is a function of the brain. These beliefs are the tenets of *sensism* or *empiricism*.[9] Some contemporary naturalists take a different line of argument, which we shall note later.

3. **Universal Ideas, or Concepts, Are Not Products of Our Sensory Powers.** Sensists deny that we have any universal, abstract ideas; what we call such, they say, are in truth simply the sensory images or phantasms of our imagination. The briefest comparison of ideas and images shows the falsity of this contention. The elements that make up an image or phantasm are the qualities of material objects as perceived by the external senses — qualities such as shape, color, temperature, size, weight, tone, loudness, movement, rest. Furthermore, these qualities are represented in the image with the concreteness which they have in external objects. Thus, an imagined color is not simply the abstract notion of color, but it is a concrete surface of red or blue, etc., appearing somewhere near or far in space, having a certain degree of vividness or paleness, and so forth. It is particular; that is

---

[8] *Ibid.*, 1, 75, 3, c.

[9] Some very good treatments of sensism are: Balmes, *Fundamental Philosophy,* Vol. 2. Bk. IV, "On Ideas"; Maher, *Psychology,* Chaps. XII–XIV; Lotze, *Metaphysics,* Bk. III; Blanchard, *The Nature of Thought,* Vol. I, Chaps. VII, IX, XV; Vol. II, Chap. XXVIII; Gruender, *Experimental Psychology,* Chaps. XIV–XVI.

to say, it is the representation of a singular patch of color, not the essence of color. It represents only a patch of color that it looks like, not every color; if you are imagining a patch of red, your image does not represent a patch of green, and no image can represent both. These, therefore, are three salient features of images: materiality, concreteness, and particularity.

Concepts, that is to say, universal ideas, are essentially different from both percepts and images. They have universal signification or reference, whereas an image has particular reference. The concept "building," for example, refers to any one of the millions of structures put up by men; it refers equally and accurately to the college library, St. Patrick's Cathedral, the Empire State Building, and Farmer Brown's chicken house. Obviously no image of a building can refer to any two of these. The image is particular; the idea universal. Concepts and images do not have the same sort of content, that is, they do not represent the same type of thing. Concepts represent the essence, nature, or "whatness" of a thing; images represent the determinate, sensible qualities of a thing. The idea is abstract, the image concrete. The "three sides" of the conceptual triangle have no determinate length, color, etc. The idea is simply a complex of abstractions. The imagined triangle is pictured as having determinate lines, angles, etc., that is to say, lines of particular and definite length, color, position, and angular incidence to one another.

4. Concepts and Generalized Images. In their efforts to avoid admitting that men do have universal ideas, sensists have tried to show that such supposed ideas are really something else. Many have said that they are generalized images, that is to say, images with all the distinctive marks blurred over — something comparable to a composite photograph of a number of men, say, the Supreme Court justices. According to this view, the so-called concept of man is really a mental picture which is general and indeterminate enough to cover any man. It is difficult to believe that anyone can seriously hold this theory. A vague, blurred, all-purpose image is not a more universal image; it is merely a poorer image. The generalized image of a man is not the image of all men, but the image of an indefinite man who does not and cannot exist. Such an image does not fit any man accurately. A clear image fits one particular man accurately in respect to some of his external appearances; and the concept man fits every man accurately in respect to the nature underlying the appearances.

Generalized images do play an important part in our mental activity; but that part is in subordination to ideas, not in substitution for them.

5. **Universal Ideas Are Not Words.** Other sensists have said that ideas are but the words used to stand for certain things. Thus, I really have no idea "man," but I do have a word, *man,* which I use to designate all men. It is very hard to find any intelligible meaning in this theory. We apply words, that is to say, names, to objects. It is very difficult to believe that I call a certain perceived object an apple because when I compare it mentally with the word *apple* it corresponds. Do I compare it with the spoken, heard, or written word? Do I compare it with *apple,* while a Frenchman compares it with *pomme?* Do I taste the word in order to compare it with the object; or do I pronounce the object in order to compare it with the word? It is clearly impossible to compare an object and a word *in regard to anything except their meaning.* And their meaning is in each case an idea. We got the idea from the thing, and we gave it to the word by using the word as a symbol of the thing and of the idea of the thing. Words cannot replace ideas, because in order to name an object you have to think both it and the word. Words mean objects because they signify the ideas which the objects exemplify. Words are not thoughts, but signs of thoughts. In a broader sense, language is a sign of thought; our primary reason for believing that animals do not think is the fact that they do not speak. They do not use universal symbols for things because they do not *think* the things to begin with; signs are inseparable from meaning.

Some of those who say that universal ideas are merely words mean that ideas are images of words. The images of words, unlike other images, represent classes of things instead of particular things. Men think with images, and in order to think many things at once, they give to things of which they have similar images the same name, and then imagine the name instead of some particular thing. In this way, without any universal ideas, they are able to signify a whole class of objects. Those who advance this explanation of thought miss the point entirely. Whether we use an image, a word, or whatever the sensists imagine the non-sensists mean by a universal idea, to signify a universal class of things, we must, obviously, *think* the universal class in order to use anything to signify it. No image or word can signify to a mind what that mind cannot think. Nothing can signify triangles universally to any mind that cannot think triangles universally. Thinking things universally and abstractly is what we mean by having universal ideas. If men did not think things universally, there could be no discussions about what means they use to signify classes. They would not know classes and they would not use signs.

6. The Argument. The one fact that man does think in universals is sufficient proof of the immateriality of his intellect. Every material thing operates always and necessarily under conditions which are inseparable from matter: conditions of space, time, and concrete singularity. No acorn can engender a universal, eternally unchanging oak tree; nor can any sense image represent one. Material agents, the patients they act upon, and the effects which they produce are always spatio-temporal and singular; they are here and now and this, or there and then and that. Never are they "anywhere and anywhen and anyway"; never can they be non-spatial, non-temporal, abstract, and universal. But man does think the non-spatial, non-temporal, abstract, and universal every time he thinks intellectually, every time he asserts a certain predicate of a subject, every time he applies a name to an object. Therefore, we must conclude, intellectual thought is the act of a power which is not material and is not operating in essential dependence upon any material instrument.[10]

From this conclusion there follows of necessity a further one: man's soul is a spiritual substance. One of its operations, intellectual thought, is intrinsically independent of matter. But operation follows being; an agent can act only according to the mode in which it exists. Since it operates in essential independence of matter, man's soul must exist in essential independence of matter. That is to say that it is a spiritual substance.[11]

7. Comparison, Judgment, and Reasoning. In a comparison of two objects of thought, e.g., "This light is brighter than that one," or in any judgment which attributes a predicate to a subject, e.g., "John Smith is a white man" or "John Smith is not a Negro," an act is performed which is no mere association of sense images, and which in fact transcends the power of any material agent or instrument. In the first proposition above the two lights must be cognized by the one, identical knowing subject at the same moment, and each must be cognized distinctly as itself. Otherwise they could not be compared. Both are known separately, though at once, and a new idea which is

[10] S. Theol., I, 75, 5, c; Con. Gen., II, 66, 67; De Spirit. Creat., II, c; Q. D. De Anima, I; In II De Anima, 12, No. 377; In III De Anima, 7, Nos. 687–688.
[11] S. Theol., I, 75, 2.

neither of them nor any merger of them arises in the intellect. This is the idea of the *relation* between the two brightnesses. It is not a brightness, nor is it any material thing or quality that could possibly affect any sense or any material organ. The same is true of all relations; they simply are not material. Yet most of our thinking consists in the intuition of relations. Therefore the intellect cannot operate by means of any material organ.

The same argument can be made from any judgment, such as the last two given above. To judge that anything is or is not anything else, the same, single knowing agent must know the two things at once and distinctly and see in the two taken together a third thing which is neither of them, namely, their identity or non-identity. This simple relation of identity or non-identity cannot be an affection of a material organ. The act of judging, therefore, is the act of a simple agent that grasps its objects in an immaterial, non-spatial manner, and pronounces an immaterial relationship between them. Therefore, the soul that judges is immaterial.

A reasoning process is far from being a mere series of propositions. Consider the difference between the following two sets of propositions:

A	*B*
No being with free will is wholly material.	Columbus discovered America.
Men have free will.	Shakespeare wrote Hamlet.
Therefore, men are not wholly material.	Napoleon was defeated at Waterloo.

In set *A* the intellect sees a relationship between the first two propositions which compels it to pronounce the third. The first two together *imply* the third. The perception of this logical relation cannot be equated with any material process in a material organ. The relationship cannot be sensed nor imagined, yet it is certainly real. All coherent thinking depends upon the reality of such logical relations or implications. Since in reasoning it is concerned with these immaterial relationships, the intellect in reasoning is operating immaterially.

8. **The Intellect's Knowledge of Itself.** The human intellect not only knows external objects and relations, but it knows the acts by which it grasps these objects and relations and knows itself as exerting these acts. In a word, we not only think things, but we know our own thinking as our own, and know ourselves thinking. In order to know

itself, the intellect must be subject and object in the one same act. No material thing can be agent and patient in the one act. At best one part of a material thing can act upon another part of the same thing. But self-knowledge, that is, reflex consciousness of self, demands the *total* identity of knower and known. If one part of the intellect knew another part, and that were all, there would be no self-knowledge. Hence, the intellect must be immaterial.[12]

9. Medical Evidence as to Relation of Brain and Thought. Although the nature of the intellective operation makes it clear that man's intellect does not reside in any corporeal organ nor use any as its immediate instrument, it is widely assumed that we think with our brains. Many efforts have been made to relate thought to particular parts or to general areas of the brain. T. V. Moore, professor of psychology at the Catholic University of America, makes a survey of the relevant evidence in his *Cognitive Psychology*. He defines consciousness as "a state or condition of the human mind, in which the individual can perceive and adequately interpret external reality, and in which past experience is fully available for the control of conduct."[13] This seems close enough to a definition of operating intelligence to serve our present purpose. Some of the interesting facts which he discusses, we shall merely list.

1. Neither the right cerebral hemisphere nor the left is necessary for consciousness as above defined. Dr. Moore cites two cases of women who were mentally normal after excision of the entire right hemisphere. One of them made approximately the same score on a standard intelligence test after as before the operation. He cites one case of a girl from whom the entire left hemisphere was removed, and who grew up mentally normal.[14]

2. Neither both nor either frontal lobe is necessary for consciousness. Moore cites cases of normal intelligence surviving removals of one or both frontal lobes of the cerebrum.[15] This seems to dispose of the once popular view that the frontal lobes are the organs of thought.

3. Passing from the cerebrum, or forebrain, down to the other parts of the brain, Dr. Moore shows that no evidence yet advanced warrants the designation of any particular part of the brain as the organ of consciousness. On the contrary, the evidence points to the conclusion that no definite region is necessary for consciousness.[16]

[12] *S. Theol.*, I, 87, 3.
[13] T. V. Moore, *Cognitive Psychology* (Philadelphia: Lippincott, 1939), p. 45.
[14] *Ibid.*, pp. 56–59.
[15] *Ibid.*, pp. 59–61.
[16] *Ibid.*, Chap. VII.

Efforts to relate definite conscious operations to definite parts of the brain have failed when they have gone beyond the special senses (sight, hearing, taste, touch, smell) and the special motor functions. As for thought itself, *there is no evidence at all* of any function which any part or the whole of the brain plays in it. The *manifestation* of thought depends upon the relative integrity of the brain; but this proves nothing since the manifestation of thought depends upon sensory and muscular operations. When a great enough impairment of the brain occurs, a man dies. This, again, proves nothing, since science can offer no evidence that thought ceases at death. Our general conclusion must be that there is no physiological evidence that we think with our brains, and that the psychological evidence makes it overwhelmingly clear that we do not possibly do so.

10. **Thought Uses the Brain.** Aristotle and St. Thomas both distinguished intellect very sharply from sense, but both insisted that all our knowledge comes originally from our senses. The intellect is, to begin with, a *tabula rasa,* a mere potency for knowledge. In order to know, it must be put in touch with external reality through the senses and their organs. From the data given it by the senses it forms its ideas and its judgments. It alone can think, judge, and reason; but of itself it has not anything to think, judge, and reason about. The material on which it exercises its operations it must obtain through the senses. As a consequence of the soul's status as form of the organism, all the operations of sense are prior to and presupposed by the operation of thought. The external senses collect data from the corporeal world, the internal senses correlate these data, perceive particular objects, and form and preserve sensory images of the perceived objects. It is from these images that the intellect derives its ideas by thinking, that is, conceiving the essential and universal elements embodied in them. The conception of the universal, and the subsequent acts of judging and reasoning are purely intellectual acts, but the intellect is nevertheless extrinsically dependent upon the whole sensory complex since it is from it that it obtains the materials upon which it works. This makes it extrinsically dependent upon the brain, for each of the external senses operates through an organ which has its nerve termini in the brain, and the brain itself, most probably, is the organ of internal sense. Wherefore, the human intellect is dependent upon the brain to get its primary data. In the second place, human thought is applied in exercise to the natural world in which man lives. This world of

nature is a world of corporeal particulars. Therefore, in the return of intellectual thought upon nature, thought must be re-materialized and re-particularized. Consequently, in every concrete application of his conception, judgment, and reasoning, man must again have recourse to his senses and his brain. He must, as St. Thomas repeats frequently, turn back to the phantasm (i.e., to the sensory image in the imagination) in order to know the singular. For these reasons human thought, whether in getting knowledge of the external world or in applying this knowledge, is extrinsically dependent upon the senses, the brain, and, in fact, the whole organism.[17]

We say that the intellect is *extrinsically* and not *intrinsically* dependent upon the brain (and the organism) because, while the intellect needs and uses the brain to get the materials for thought and to return thought upon the world, the act of thought itself, in all its three stages, conception, judgment, and reasoning, is effected solely by the intellect itself.[18]

IV. MEN AND ANIMALS

1. Do Animals Think? Animals do not work out differential equations. Of the many possible reasons why they do not, one which seems very probably true, is that they do not have to. They never come across situations which can be met successfully only by forming and solving a differential equation. Such situations can arise only in the environment of a rational mind. Because animals are capable of some very clever or intelligent responses to complex situations in their environment, or in the artificial environment created for them by animal psychologists, some persons have sought to erase the line of essential difference between the human and the animal mind. But it is a far fairer basis of comparison between the animal and human mind to point out that all normal men are capable of understanding the use of a differential equation, while no animal is, than to point out that animals and men behave in pretty much the same way when placed in problem-situations requiring escape from confinement or procuring food. Escaping and eating are needs which fall within an area common to men and animals. There are, however, plenty of human needs which fall outside this area. The human mind, for example, creates science; the animal mind does not; man creates

[17] *S. Theol.*, I, 85, 1; 86, 1.
[18] *Ibid.*, I, 75, 2, ad 3.

science in response to a need to understand the world he lives in; the evidence is overwhelming that animals feel no such need. Animals do not wonder. As far as the physical universe is concerned men and animals live in precisely the same world; yet the environment of man includes the environment of animals as only a part, the least part. The difference is made by the difference between the animal and the human mind.

Modern experimental psychologists, dealing with animal behavior, have shown that in certain circumstances animals perform actions which indicate that they "think." The famous ape experiments of Yerkes are a case in point. Faced with more or less complex problem-situations, some animals show capacity for the intelligent use of means for the attainment of an end. Thus, a chimpanzee procured a banana hung beyond his reach by piling one box atop another and climbing to where he could reach the banana; in another experiment a chimpanzee, after having tried unsuccessfully to reach a banana outside his cage with each of two short sticks, inserted one stick in the end of the other and then with this new long stick got the banana. The making of the long stick seemed to be more or less accidental, but once the chimp had made it, he seemed to realize immediately that he could now reach the banana; he seemed to think out the result before he performed the action. This use of "tools" in situations not part of the animal's natural environment seems to indicate a power more like thought than instinct. Some psychologists, therefore, have interpreted such findings as evidence that the animal mind is not essentially different from the human mind.

This interpretation, however, goes far beyond any conclusion warranted by the data; and it is, besides, based upon a very narrowly selected group of data. The most radical conclusion that can be validly drawn from the findings of animal psychology is that some animals think, if you are willing to define the term thinking widely enough. Some animals, when faced with problems similar to some problems which men have to face, solve the problems in ways similar to some of the ways which men use. This is hardly surprising. Whatever else man may be, he is partly animal in nature, and he lives the animal part of his life in the same world as the other animals. That world presents the problems, and presents also the conditions for their solution. But the problems common to men and animals are animal problems. If animals were not capable of wide variability and adaptability in meeting these problems, they would hardly have survived. None of the problems which animal psychologists think up in order to study the animal mind are peculiarly human problems; they must be animal problems or they would be useless for the psychologist's purposes. But the problem of thinking up ways to study the animal mind *is* a peculiarly human problem; so that in his very efforts to find out whether animals "think," the psychologist is giving an object lesson to the effect that men think in ways in which animals never do. Scientific problems are peculiarly human; animals do not have such problems. To put the situation rather crudely: it will be time enough to ask whether the ape mind operates like the human mind when we hear about apes putting psychologists in cages with bananas outside and then keeping records of what the psychologists do in order to get the bananas.

2. **Man's Distinctly Human Interests.** That man has many interests and modes of behavior in common with animals proves that man is partly animal in nature. That he is, is, of course, a truism as far as Thomistic philosophy is concerned. The evidence that man is partly animal should not be used, however, to attempt to show that he is wholly animal. If all man's interests, aspirations, and modes of behavior are considered, it becomes apparent that the most important ones are precisely those which the animals do not share with him. We may say that the distinctly human interests and occupations of man fall within the following fields, fields which do not exist for animals: science and philosophy, art and literature, society and politics, morality and religion. All these peculiarly human pursuits arise, more or less directly, from a need in man to understand the world and to express this understanding in explanation, representation, and action. These interests and needs are all concerned with goods and values which are not material, which do not serve man's bodily comfort, safety, or pleasure. The interests of animals, on the other hand, all seem to be concerned with bodily comfort, safety, and pleasure.

Both in individual men and in human civilizations, the more advancement there is, that is, the more "human" the individual or society becomes, the more preoccupation is turned away from the interests common to both men and the animals and turned toward those proper to man. Indeed we have come to name these pursuits of the cultured man or society "the humanities." In both individual and society, advancement is conditioned by — is, perhaps, identical with — the increasing subordination of material interests and pursuits to spiritual interests; the ideal is that the material needs of man be taken care of so systematically that little attention need be paid to them, so that man is freed to pursue spiritual values. Is it possible that a merely material being should have interests and aspirations which are immaterial, that these should be peculiar to this being of all natural beings, and that they should dominate all his material interests even to the extent of relegating the latter to the role of servants?

V. A GLANCE AT CONTEMPORARY NATURALISM

1. The Naturalist View. Naturalists reject our argument for the spirituality of the soul. Many contemporary naturalists, however, do not, like the older materialists, deny the fundamental difference between sensory operations and intellectual thought. They insist upon the difference, and, with rather exaggerated emphasis, they disavow the "reductionism" of the naturalistic schools of the past. By reductionism they mean the practice of defining every higher reality in terms of lower realities, of denying any real differences of levels of operation and activity; for example, thinking is "nothing but" chemical process, everything is "nothing but" matter in motion. Their new naturalism, they insist, is not a "nothing but" philosophy; the charge that it is, is a libel for which anti-naturalistic philosophers are responsible. The new naturalism, say its proponents, recognizes each kind of being or activity as itself, and does not attempt to reduce it to something on a lower level. But naturalists make a distinction between end-products and means or mechanisms, which anti-naturalists refuse to do.

It is, for the naturalists, all a question of evolution. Nature, in its evolutionary progress, regularly gives rise to operations and functions on new and higher levels. For example, consciousness and thought are end-products on a higher level than their natural antecedents: when matter began first to feel, something new, really new, had emerged; when it began to think, something new again had emerged. Consciousness and thought, however, have as their sole ground or cause the organism in connection with which they appear on nature's scene and the natural environment which makes up the world of this organism; no being, nothing "substantial," distinct from the organism and its natural environment, can be admitted in the explanation of consciousness or thought. To argue to a higher cause from the basis of a higher function is, in the logic of naturalism, a fallacy; it is a confusion of mechanisms with end-products. Nature may bring forth novelty and hierarchy in the realm of end-products, values, or activities; but there is unbroken continuity in the realm of the mechanisms which produce these new and higher values and activities. Thought, for example, is admittedly distinct and essentially different from any previous product of evolving nature; but the factors from which it arose are no different, except for their particular organization, from the factors whence physical, chemical, and biological laws arose. In other words, the old exiom that there can be no more in the effect than there is in the cause, is false. Hence, when thought emerges in certain organisms, this function, novel though it is, is yet a function of the organism.

2. **The Thomistic Answer.** We cannot agree with the naturalists. The account which they present involves a clear absurdity, namely, an action which is and is not a certain process at the same time. Physiologists accurately describe the function of the human organism, including the brain. No part of their description is a description of thought or even of sensation, feeling, or imagination, and it is unthinkable that any part should be; they are describing physiological processes. Their description is complete; and if they are asked, as physiologists, to describe thinking or feeling they have nothing to add. Yet, if thinking and feeling were merely resultants of certain processes of the organism, thinking and feeling would be flatly identical with the complexus of these processes, and the description of the processes would be a description of thinking and feeling. No one since the behaviorists has defended this thesis. If, on the other hand, thought and feeling are not flatly identical with the processes of the nervous system, and if there is nothing acting except the organism, how are thought and feeling related to the nervous processes? Nothing occurs in the organism except the physical process, and yet the distinct conscious act occurs also. In other words, my thinking is certain neural movements in my brain, and yet is not neural processes at all, but thinking.

Now, not only is this absurd, but we have heard it all before. We heard it from the old materialists, from the proponents of the double-aspect theory, from the epiphenomenalists, from the behaviorists — that is, from the reductionists, the "nothing but" philosophers, whom the new naturalist disowns. The naturalists disavow reductionism, but

it is not easy to see how they escape it or offer any real alternative
to it. The only real alternative is the doctrine of the soul.

What is the relation between conscious operations and the physical
processes which accompany and in some cases mediate them?[19]
Thomists believe that the axiom that there can be no more in the
effect than in the cause is perfectly true. Conscious operations have
causes higher than purely physical ones; their principle is the soul.
Some of them, namely, sensory operations, are performed through
physical organs. The processes which occur in these organs, some of
which are antecedent conditions to the sensory operation and some
of which are instrumental in that operation, are not to be confused
with the operation itself. The operation is an action; the processes
are motions. Some of these motions are caused by external agencies
affecting the organism, and some are caused by the organism itself
performing the vital operation of sensing or feeling. When the physiologist studies these processes, he is studying the effect of the vital
operation produced in the organism; he is not studying the operation
or action itself or its cause. The philosopher seeks the cause of the
operation, and he seeks an adequate cause. Hence, for any vital operation, that is, for any immanent action, he demands a cause which
is more than the matter of the body; he demands a soul. And for a
purely immaterial operation such as thought he demands a spiritual
soul.

3. The Poor Logic of Naturalism. The naturalists' doctrine is merely
a more subtle form of reductionism. Their law of continuity is based
upon an assumption, which in turn is based upon an inductive
fallacy. The assumption is that, when we are ready to take up the
study of spiritual operations and values, we have *already* established
the basic character of the world in which these emerge; and hence,
these must be explained and accounted for in terms of that basic
character. The inductive fallacy which led to this assumption is the
very common one of favoring certain kinds of data over other equally
evident kinds. The data favored are those of the natural sciences; the
data discriminated against are those of human activity and interests.
Thus the phenomena of consciousness, thought, free will, science,
philosophy, language, money, religion, etc. — all have to be fitted into
the conception of nature which has already been formed through
the natural sciences alone. When they cannot be fitted in, it is too bad

[19] See Chapter VIII, Section VI, "Process and Action."

for them. Thus, for example, although many naturalists are great defenders of freedom, they rarely believe in free will. It would have been a far better logical procedure for the naturalists to have refrained from formulating a conception of nature until they had considered all the kinds of data which nature offers for study.

VI. SOUL AND BODY

1. Aristotle and St. Thomas. This brings us full circle back to the question that puzzled Aristotle: How can immaterial, impassible mind be the form, that is to say, the first actuality of a material body? For St. Thomas the question took a radically different form. Instead of asking, "How can a spiritual soul be the form of a body?" he asks, "Why does the human soul have a body?" The difference between their two approaches to the question of the human soul and body springs from a fundamental difference between the general world views of the great Greek philosopher and the great Christian theologian.

St. Thomas believed (and proved) that the world, including matter itself, is created by God. Aristotle never attained to the concept of creation. Matter, according to him, is that out of which all nature is generated and which itself is not generated from anything but is eternal and imperishable. He wrote many times that matter exists for the sake of form; and St. Thomas borrowed this expression from him. But because the latter was a creationist and the former was not, there was a very great difference between the significance given by each to this expression. In a non-creationist philosophy, matter is an independent ultimate stuff existing in its own right and being the primary condition of all that occurs in nature. In a creationist world view, it is a creature and instrument of God, depending for its being upon Him, and made by Him for His purposes. Instead of an intransigent, ultimate fact which determines the limits of what the universe can be, it is a means created by God out of which He fashions the universe which He wants; it in no way limits Him in His creative activity, but He, on the contrary, makes possible through it creatures which would be impossible without it. Wherefore, when Aristotle writes that matter exists for the sake of form, he means no more than that eternally existing matter is the fundamental condition for the concrete existence of every form; form is the end of matter in the sense that it is the actuality in which the potentiality of matter is realized: but when St. Thomas writes the same proposition, he means that matter exists only in order that it may be the subject of certain forms; that is to say, certain forms of created being cannot subsist except in matter, and therefore, desiring that such forms should exist, God creates matter for them to exist in. Hence the Thomistic answer to the question why the soul has a body is simply that the soul needs a body. The need which the soul has for the body may be viewed in two different ways: metaphysically and psychologically.[20]

2. **Why the Soul Needs the Body.** Among the myriad forms of being which exist, the human soul has just that degree of perfection or actuality whereby it is able to subsist apart from matter but is not able so to exist in full possession of individual and specific being. The forms of being above man (i.e., the angels) are pure forms, unmixed with matter. Each single one of them is a complete species of being in itself, a single pure form which actualizes in its own individuality the full perfection of a whole species. Since it can so exist, it does not need to be repeated over and over in matter in order to fill out a specific degree of perfection. The human soul, on the contrary, is specifically incomplete; it is a form, but not a species. In order to constitute a species, it has to be united with a principle of repetition or numerical multiplicity. This principle is matter. The multitude of human individuals, composites of human souls and bodies, constitutes the species; and this species is not the soul, but man.[21]

The human soul is a spiritual substance and is intelligent. But it is not a pure intelligence. Its power of intellect is the lowest existing degree of intelligence and is not in itself fully adequate for its own exercise. It is capable of understanding, but it does not of its nature possess the ideas whereby it may understand. The intellects higher than it are created already endowed with the ideas whereby they understand; the soul is created with the power to understand, but without ideas through which to understand. Hence it needs an instrument which can put it in contact with intelligible essences from which it may obtain ideas; or to state the same fact in another way, it needs other powers which can administer to its power of intelligence and enable that power to attain to the intelligible natures which will actualize its power to know. Too imperfect, too dim in intellectual light to grasp by its own

[20] *S. Theol.*. I, 76, 5.
[21] *S. Theol.*, I, 75, 7, ad 3; *De Spirit. Creat.*, II, ad 5; ad 16; V, ad 8, 9, 10, 11.

power the pure intelligible forms that exist apart from matter, it can seek its ideas only in those forms bound up with matter. But in order to make contact with these it has to be receptive or passible in their regard. Being a spiritual substance it cannot itself be directly acted upon by matter. Thus without the body and its sense organs the soul would be cut off from all intelligible natures and could never formulate an idea. Hence, it has a body in order that through the sense organs of that body its intellective power may attain to its intelligible object. From the data supplied the soul by the senses, the intellect abstracts the intelligible natures of material substances.[22]

The question, Why did God give the human soul a degree of intelligence so imperfect that the soul needs a body in order to exercise its intelligence? might be raised. The simplest answer is that God willed to create men, and that no other spiritual substance could be the soul of a man. He made man "a little less than the angels"; if He had not done so, there would be no men. To ask why He did not make man a little more perfect is as pointless as to ask why triangles do not have four sides. God did make the being a little more perfect than man; it is the lowest of the angels.

3. A Word About the Angels. Can all this strange-sounding explanation of man's place in nature be proved? Enough of it can to make the rest credible. The substantial unity of a man and the spirituality of his soul we have demonstrated. The original emptiness of his intellect and its use of the senses to attain knowledge are facts of common experience. The need of the intellectual soul for the body follows as an immediate inference. Below man living beings without intellect are observed. Why not intellectual beings without bodies above him? If his form, so imperfect as to need a body for its natural operations, can yet exist apart from the body, is it unreasonable to think that more perfect forms, namely, angels, may exist naturally apart from any body? For St. Thomas it was more than reasonable; it was (even apart from revelation) practically certain. The imperfect in any genus always points to the more perfect in that genus, and ultimately to the absolutely perfect. Wherefore, it is impossible to believe that man's intellect, the most imperfect conceivable, should be the only intellect, or even the only created intellect. Intellect and matter are the opposite poles of being, and if, as in man, intellect is found united with matter,

[22] *S. Theol.*, I, 76, 5; *Con. Gen.*, II, 68; *De Spirit. Creat.*, II, ad 5; ad 7; V, c; *Q. D. De Anima*, 1, 7, 8.

then most surely it exists also separate from matter. Consequently, the existence of angels is perfectly credible on grounds of natural reason alone.[23]

VII. ORIGIN AND INDESTRUCTIBILITY OF THE HUMAN SOUL

The fact that man's soul is a spiritual substance carries two all-important implications: the soul cannot have originated from matter; and the corruption of the body with which it is united does not involve its own destruction. In these two respects it differs from every other substantial form in the world. Every other form, including plant and animal souls, is naturally generated from the potency of matter; it is merely the actuality of that potentiality. And it ceases to exist when the substance of which it is the form is corrupted; it lapses into the potency of the matter, which simply means that the matter in question is again only potentially what for a time it was actually.[24]

The human soul, a spiritual substance, cannot possibly originate from matter; matter may evolve into an infinite number of things, but they will all be material; it cannot evolve out of itself into the immaterial. Nor can the human soul be a derivative of a parent human soul, since every human soul is simple and indivisible. Therefore, every human soul is created by God from nothing. Yet, as pointed out in the last chapter, every human soul is different from every other one. The soul is not the complete substance; the man is. God creates each soul for a particular man whose body is produced by natural causes which determine its potentiality. The soul is created to actualize this potentiality in a living human person; wherefore, insofar as its organic powers and perfections are concerned, it is created precisely as the actuality of this potentiality, and every human soul is therefore as individually unique as the body which it informs.[25]

Since the human soul is a spiritual substance existing in its own right and independently of the body, there is no reason to believe that its existence is terminated by the man's death. No change occurring in any material thing can essentially affect the spiritual soul. Being a simple, immaterial substance, the soul is by nature incorruptible. It depends solely upon God's creative act for its existence. Nor may we

[23] *S. Theol.*, I, 50, 1; *ibid.*, 2; *Con. Gen.*, II, 91; *De Spirit. Creat.*, V.
[24] *S. Theol.*, I, 75, 4; *ibid.*, 6, ad 1; *Con. Gen.*, II, 82.
[25] Cf *S. Theol.*, I, 76, 5, c; *Con. Gen.*, II, 86, 87; *De Spirit. Creat.*, II, ad 8.

believe that God will ever allow it to relapse into non-existence; for it is incompatible with the wisdom of God that He should create a naturally incorruptible being only to destroy it in the end. Wherefore, true philosophy supports the Christian belief in the immortality of the human soul.[26]

[26] *S. Theol.*. I, 75, 6; *Con. Gen.*. II, 79, 80, 81; *Q. D. De Anima*, 14.

CHAPTER XI

HUMAN COGNITION

1. MAN'S COGNITIVE POWERS AND OPERATIONS

Among the powers of the human soul there are two genera of special interest to the student of human nature. These are the cognitive and the appetitive powers. By the former, man knows; by the latter, he desires. In the present chapter we shall study man's cognitive powers and operations, and in the next chapter his appetitive powers and operations. Our study of man's cognitive powers and operations will include: first, a descriptive study of the operations; second, St. Thomas' theory of the nature of knowledge; and third, an explanatory or causal study of man's cognitive operations and the powers of which they are the acts. This order of study will entail a certain amount of repetition, but it will in every case be repetition with a difference.

1. **The External Senses and Sensation.** All man's knowledge begins with sensation. So far as any evidence shows, we begin to know only when the material things around us or the movements in our own bodies affect our senses; that is to say, the first stage in knowing is seeing, hearing, tasting, smelling, and feeling things. We are equipped with five senses, sight, hearing, taste, smell, and various kinds of touch; and each of these senses has a special organ by which it receives some special effect or impression from material objects. Thus, we see the color of an orange and, through the color, its shape and size; we feel its texture, weight, shape, and size; we taste its flavor; we smell its odor; and if we tear it or strike it on something we hear the sounds it makes. All these sensations come to us through physical effects produced in our sense organs by the impact — direct or indirect — of external objects. Thus, we see an object only when light from the object is thrown upon the retina of our eye, producing certain physiological movements in the retina; and we hear only when some vibrating sub-

stance sets the tympanum of our ear in vibration. These physical movements in the sense organs, and the subsequent movements which they
cause in the nervous system and brain, are not sensations, but they are
the necessary physiological conditions of sensation. We have sensations
when physical causes in the world around us act upon our sense organs
and, through the physical changes produced in them, somehow produce in us conscious sensory apprehension of the things in the world
around us.[1]

It is from these sensations of external things that our mind builds
up all its ideas and judgments about the nature of the physical universe and, in fact, of all being. But before these ideas and judgments
are formed, the data received by the external senses are elaborated and
organized into purely mental, though still sensible, representations or
images of the external objects. This part of the work of knowing is
done by the *internal senses*.

2. **The Internal Senses and Their Operations.** St. Thomas, following
Aristotle, attributes to man four internal senses. They are so called because they have no external organs receptive of direct impressions from
the external world but instead receive their data from the external
senses and through the organs of these latter. The internal senses are
common sense, imagination, cogitative sense, and memory.[2]

Imagination. We picture in our mind things which we have
previously perceived, although at the moment when we picture them
they are not acting upon any of our external sense organs. This means
that we have a power or faculty for preserving the sensory impressions produced in our consciousness and of representing, in their
absence, the objects which produced these impressions. We exercise
this power whenever we imagine how a person, thing, or place looks
(visual imagination), or when, for example, we let a song "run through
our head" (auditory imagination), or similarly imagine how something
tasted, felt, or smelt. We may imagine a thing as we actually perceived it, or we may combine in one representation sense impressions
which were not actually perceived together, thus constructing "imaginary" objects. The mental representations which we form by this power
are called images or *phantasms*, and the power itself is called
imagination.

Sensus Communis. We have explained imagination first because its

<hr/>

[1] *S. Theol.*, I, 78, 3; *ibid.*, 84, all articles but especially 6; *ibid.*, 85, 1 and 3.
[2] *S. Theol.*, I, 78, 4.

familiarity clarifies what is meant by an internal sense, but it is not in fact the first of the internal senses. The first one is the *sensus communis*.[3] Our external senses give us only their proper objects — colors, sounds, odors, tastes, feels. Through these we perceive also certain common objects like shape, size, distance, movement, and time. We perceive these latter through the special senses but by the common sense. The special or external senses cannot combine or integrate into unified objects the various impressions which they receive, because each sense receives only its own special kind of impression and not that received by the other senses. Yet what we perceive is not a congeries of unrelated and chaotic colors, sounds, feels, etc., but unified objects or things having these colors, sounds, feels, etc., as determinations or attributes; for example, we perceive an apple which is round, red, sweet, and succulent. The power which does this work of organization and synthesis St. Thomas calls the *sensus communis* and some comtemporary psychologists name it the central or synthetic sense.

Cogitative Sense. The third internal sense is the cogitative (*vis cogitativa*). We perceive things not merely as objects having certain sensible qualities, but also as being good or bad, desirable or repellent, useful or harmful. That animals possess such a power is obvious. A lamb (to use a favorite illustration of St. Thomas) perceives a wolf not only as a thing with certain sensible determinations of color, size, odor, etc., but also as a dangerous thing, an enemy; and the lamb, without having to be taught, flees in terror when it perceives a wolf. This "dangerousness" is not a sensible quality which any external sense organ can perceive, and yet nature abounds in illustrations of the animal's ability to perceive things under just such non-sensible aspects. These aspects are called by Scholastic philosophers *species insensatae*. They may be defined as aspects of individual sensible bodies not perceivable by any external sense, yet grasped by the sentient subject in the total perceptive act. Among them, in the case of man, is the individual nature of the object perceived. Men as well as animals perceive such insensuous qualities sensitively; because it is a matter of common experience that men are attracted by some things and repelled by others instinctively, as it were, prior to any intellectual judgment about the thing in question. Hence, Aristotle and St. Thomas after him con-

[3] This does *not* mean "common sense" as we use that term in English, designating a kind of natural prudence; it means generic or general sense as contrasted with specific or special sense.

clude that animals and men have an internal sense by which these "insensate species" are perceived. They call it in animals the estimative sense (*vis aestimativa*) and in man the cogitative sense (*vis cogitativa*). This power is essentially the same in animals and in men, but its actual exercise in men is superior because in them it operates in subordination to and under the influence of reason, and this influence ennobles or elevates its action.[4]

Memory. The last of the internal senses is memory. It is similar to and yet different from imagination. The phantasms or images produced by the imagination are constructed out of the data received by the external senses and integrated by the central sense. Such images represent the object in only its sensate aspects — its color, size, shape, tone, loudness, timbre, etc. Memory phantasms or images represent more than this. In the first place they represent a past experience as such. To imagine the Statue of Liberty is simply to picture it before my mind's eye without any reference to time or circumstance or any past personal experience; to remember it is to picture it as I actually experienced it on a definite past occasion, so that the occasion and the experience are as much part of the memory as is the statue itself. In the second place, the memory-image of an object includes the insensuous aspects perceived through the cogitative sense. In imagination we merely represent to ourselves some object as it appears to the external senses supplemented by common sense; in memory we represent the object and recognize it for what it was in our experience of it. Thus, the cogitative power and memory connect our repeated sense experiences together, and so give rise to "experience" in the broader meaning of that term, namely, the knowledge or skill which arises from repeated contacts with a certain kind of object — as when we speak of an "experienced man."[5] Like the cogitative sense, memory is essentially the same power in animals and men, but in men its actual operation is superior because of the influence of the intellect to which it is joined and subordinated.

3. Order Among the Cognitive Powers. The four internal senses do not operate in isolation from one another and from the intellect. They are not separate agents but simply distinct powers of the same agent, the man. Their action is co-operative, and the highest product of sensory cognition is created by all of them working together, in con-

---

[4] *In II De Anima*, 13, Nos. 395–398; *In I Meta.*, 1, No. 15; *S. Theol.*, I, 78, 4, c; *De Ver.*, XIV, 1 and 9; *Con. Gen.*, II, 73; *In VI Ethic.*, 9, No. 1255.
[5] *In I Meta.*, 1, No. 15.

junction with the external senses, and under the directive influence of man's supra-sensory cognitive power, the intellect. This subordination of all the sensory powers to the intellect is an exemplification of a law which, according to St. Thomas, is universally operative in nature, namely, that the lower in any order exists for the sake of the higher — matter for the sake of form, the corporeal world for man, man's body for his soul, man's senses for his intellect. Through the co-operation, therefore, of all these powers there is formed in the man's imagination the supreme product of sensory cognition, namely, an image or phantasm, only potentially an idea, but elaborated and refined so that it is disposed to be made an actual idea by the action of the intellect. About its nature and function we shall study below.

4. **The Formation of Concepts.** In Chapter X we saw that man's intellect has three principal operations: simple apprehension (or conception), judgment, and reasoning. The latter two follow the first, since by them we manipulate the ideas which we attained in the act of conception. In what does this act of conception consist, and how is it related to the sensory operations which we have just studied?

Simple apprehension or understanding is the act whereby the intellect grasps and represents to itself the nature or essence of some object. The object may be a thing, an action, a relation, a quality, or any kind of being whatsoever. Simple apprehension is the act by which we know what something is; for example, what a circle or a man or beauty or life or motion is. It is not merely the act of perceiving a circle or a man or something beautiful or something living or something in motion — any of these things can be perceived without the percipient knowing what they are. In order to apprehend something intellectually, that is, to understand it, we have to form in our mind an idea or concept of it — an idea which represents, not how the thing looks or feels, but *what it is* (*quod quid est*). This representation of the "what it is," or *quiddity,* of something is what we call an idea or concept; and the content of such a representation is expressed in the definition of the thing represented.

We saw in Chapter X that ideas are radically different from images or phantasms. The content of the latter is sensible and concrete, representing how a particular thing appears; the content of the former is intelligible and abstract, representing what a thing is. This essential difference between the percept and image, on the one hand, and the idea on the other, becomes very clear in cases where we perceive something without at all understanding what it is; we can perceive and imagine the object clearly but we "have no idea what it is." Our intellect has not yet probed beneath the perceptible aspects of the thing to its intelligible essence. We have only a very general idea of the thing; we know that it is something, but we do not know what. A second essential difference between percepts and images on the one hand, and ideas on the other is the fact that the latter are universal while the former are particular. The concept "tree" represents the nature of every possible tree and represents every individual tree in so far as the latter possesses the nature common to all trees. The image of a tree, since it represents the individual appearances of a particular tree, cannot at the same time represent those of a different tree which is individually different; in so far as it becomes representative of a larger number of trees, it becomes a vaguer and less accurate image of any of them. In the preceding chapter we studied these contrasting characters of ideas and images, and we saw that the idea is an immaterial representation; we do not wish to labor this fact again, but rather we wish to stress another fact; namely, that universal, immaterial concepts are formed by the intellect from particular, material phantasms.

How the mind is able to derive universal, immaterial concepts of the natures of things from particular, material images of their appearances is not the point now at issue. *The fact that it does so* is what we are interested in now, and this fact is indisputable. We form ideas of things only after having perceived things, and in forming the ideas we are governed by the perceived aspects of things. Hence we may summarize the human cognitional process from sensation to conception thus:

(1) Man, affected in his various sense organs by external bodies, their qualities, actions, etc., perceives through his power of external sense, these bodies and their sensible determinations; (2) he forms by his internal senses sensible representations (i.e., phantasms) of these bodies with their qualities, operations, etc.; and (3) somehow, by his intellectual power, he grasps in and through these sensible representations the essence or quiddity of the bodies, their qualities, operations, etc., expressing these essences in purely immaterial, universal representations, viz., ideas or concepts.

All the above account of the human process of arriving at knowledge is purely descriptive. The explanatory account will constitute the third section of this chapter. Before entering upon this explanation of the real causes which operate in the human act of knowledge we must first understand something about the nature of knowledge itself.

II. THE NATURE OF KNOWLEDGE

1. What Knowledge Is. Every normal human adult knows what knowledge is, and yet the nature of knowledge has been one of the perennial problems of philosophy. It is in no sense to belittle philosophy or to exalt common sense to the level of philosophy to say that the normal man's spontaneous grasp of such an omnipresent fact as knowledge is more to be trusted than any philosophical explanation which disagrees with it. A common man, asked what knowledge is, might only be able to answer that, as everybody knows, it is what you do do when you know something. His unphilosophical answer would have stated very clearly the thing which every philosopher must keep in mind, and which some of them have not kept in mind, when trying to analyze the nature of knowledge. Knowing is always someone knowing something; it is always an act which joins a mind with an object in a relationship which is unique and incomparable with any other. Any explanation of knowledge which reduces the act of knowing to some other kind of act destroys what it is trying to explain.

St. Thomas' doctrine of human cognition is his answer to this question: What real causes in the essential order produce knowledge in the human mind? The answer which he gives is most remarkably integrated with his whole philosophical system. He does not, like some philosophers, erect his whole account of nature and reality upon his analysis of knowledge; nor, on the other hand, is his theory of knowledge a mere *ad hoc* theory specially formulated to solve a special problem. Instead, he deals with the problem of knowledge as it comes along in his studies of the various beings of the universe and their operations, and he finds that the very same principles which provide an essential explanation for the observable phenomena of the physical world provide it also for the phenomena of knowledge. Consequently, we shall find his account of human knowledge given in terms of principles with which we are already familiar; for example, his doctrine of causes, of potentiality and actuality, of substance and accident, of matter and form.

2. Knowledge and Immateriality. There is no such thing as knowledge without something known and someone knowing it. Every act of knowing is a synthesis of object and subject, an intersection or point of being where merge a knower and what he knows. The act of knowing is at once the subject knowing and the object known, and every theory of knowledge must begin from this fact, must still have it as a fact when finished explaining it, and must really explain it, that is to say, must state how the synthesis of knower and known is accomplished.

We are used to situations where two or more beings merge to form one being. Oxygen and hydrogen unite in water; the things which we eat become our body; forces merging at a point become a new single force. But in these and in all similar cases, the beings which merge in one lose the identity which they had before the merger, and the new thing is actually none of the things which were united to form it. In knowledge, on the contrary, the beings which merge retain their identity and the new being formed, namely, the knowing, is at once actually both of them. When I know something, the something must be actual and must be itself, and I must be actual and be myself, in the very act of knowing; for otherwise there would be no knowing, because there would be either no knower or nothing to be known. When, therefore, St. Thomas, following Aristotle, writes repeatedly[6] that in knowledge the knowing subject and the known object become one, he is not voicing a theory, but is merely stating a fact.

How can two beings become one while each yet remains itself? Certainly not in any material way. I cannot become one with a tree materially. I do not, when I get to know a tree, turn into a tree and sprout leaves. Yet there is a difference in me from what I was before I knew a tree, and that difference, the something new that has been added, is precisely "what a tree is." In every act of knowledge the knower and the known become one, but the unity is not effected in their respective matters.

Hence it is not surprising that St. Thomas finds *immateriality* at the basis of knowledge. Nothing can be known unless it has in itself something not matter which it can give to the knowing mind. Nothing, on the other hand, can know unless it has within itself something not matter which can receive the nature of another thing without losing its own. Therefore, the condition both of knowledge and of knowability is some degree of immateriality.[7]

---

[6] E.g., *Con. Gen.*, l, 77; *S. Theol.*, I, 14, 2, c; 55, 1, ad 2; *In I Sent.*, d. 3, q. 1, a. 1; *De Ver.*, I, 1, c.

[7] *Con. Gen.*, II, 49–50; *S. Theol.*, I, 84, 2, c.

Knowledge, or indeed communication of any sort, is inexplicable unless the immaterial be admitted. It is sometimes asked by students just becoming acquainted with St. Thomas' theory of knowledge how an object can give or communicate its form to the mind and yet retain the form and remain itself. The question arises out of a materialistic prejudice common to all of us. Because nothing material can be given without being given up — because I cannot give a man a dollar without losing the dollar — we wonder how something of the object can really be given to the subject without being lost to the object. A little reflection should suffice to show us that what we are taking as a general characteristic of being is in truth merely a peculiarity of matter. To give a friend my love is something better and more real than to give him a dollar; yet I certainly do not give up my love in loving my friend. To communicate to my students the knowledge and love of philosophy which I have is something very real; yet in doing it I do not lose that knowledge and love. Wherever we turn in life there are instances innumerable of communication which does not involve loss of the being communicated, of giving that does not entail giving up. Only when the thing given is material must it be given up. I cannot give a piece of my finger to someone without losing the piece myself; but I can give my fingerprints to a blotter without giving up my fingerprints. The fingerprints are forms, not matter. So, in knowledge, the object gives its forms to the subject without losing these forms; form is communicable; matter is not. The significance of all these facts is the clear indication of the utter inadequacy of materialism as a philosophy. Materialism is incompatible with the simplest and most familiar facts of human experience. Every effort, for example, to explain knowledge in terms of materialism is doomed to complete failure; knowledge involves communication without expropriation, giving without giving up, and matter cannot be communicated without being expropriated, cannot be given without being given away.

3. Form and the Knowable. There is, as a matter of fact, according to Thomistic philosophy, something immaterial in every actual being, even in every material being; this something is the form, or rather the forms — substantial and accidental. Every corporeal substance is, as we have seen, an essential composite of primary matter and a substantial form and is determined in many ways by accidental forms. Hence we find that St. Thomas' account of the nature of knowledge is bound up closely with his doctrine of hylemorphism. We cannot get the matter of things into our cognitive powers, but we can get their forms in. And it is by these forms of other things in us that we know these things. For form is what makes matter actual, giving it a determinate nature, and thereby making it knowable, since knowledge is always knowing something determinate. Anything, therefore, is knowable just to that degree to which it possesses form, and is unknowable to the degree to which it lacks form. Our mind responds to an object set before it, and can lay hold upon the object, just to the extent to which it can discern some form in the object. The more precisely it can discern form, the more precisely does it know what the object is; and the more formless it finds the object, the more it is left in the dark about its nature.

An utterly formless thing would be of necessity unknowable; but an utterly formless thing cannot exist, for in order to exist it is necessary to be something actual, and form alone determines actuality of being. If we imagine (what is in fact impossible) a material being bereft of all accidental forms such as color, size, shape, texture, it is clear that we could not know it, for such a thing would give our sensory powers no sensible forms by which to perceive it. On the other hand, if we were faced merely with accidental forms which did not manifest any definite substance as their reason and foundation, if, for example, certain colors, movements, sizes, and shapes, appeared in a juxtaposition which led the mind to no essential form underlying the combination of phenomena, our intellect would stand groping. Where the intellect can penetrate to a substantial form in a thing presented to it by the senses, it can formulate an essential idea of that thing; where it cannot penetrate to such a form, it either remains in a state of perplexity or employs some substitute for the substantial form, for example, invariable and distinctive accidents. Thus the intellect can pronounce clearly on the essence of a living substance and can accurately state its essential difference from a non-living substance, because it discerns in the living thing the essential form of immanent activity. But if it is asked what distinguishes a fly from a wasp, it can discern no essential form of being present in one and missing from the other, and it must, therefore, fall back upon external or accidental forms in order to distinguish the one from the other. In any case, form is what the mind seizes upon. Take away form, whether essential or accidental, and there remains nothing knowable for the mind to grasp.

Wherefore, St. Thomas makes a direct equation between form and knowability. The more a thing is formal, the more it is knowable; the more its form is immersed in matter, the less knowable the thing is. Matter itself, that is to say primary matter, is unknowable. We are able to speak and think of it at all only by analogy and negation. We cannot say what it *is* in itself, because it is not anything actual in itself; we can say that it is not this, nor that, nor any determinate thing; and we can say that it is made into this, that, or the other by the reception of this, that, or the other form. We know it only by relation to forms.

4. **Form and the Knower.** St. Thomas makes an equation not only between knowability and form but also between the power to know and form. When I know a thing, I have in some manner become that thing; that is, I have received its form. We have already become acquainted in preceding chapters with what it means for matter to receive a form. When some matter receives a substantial form, it becomes physically the substance determined by that form; thus, the food which I eat becomes my flesh. When some matter receives an accidental form, it is physically altered to that accidental determination; for example, it becomes hot or red or square. But my mind does not turn to flesh when I know what flesh is, nor does it become flat when I know what a plane is. Therefore, it must be concluded that it is not the matter in me that assumes the forms of the things which I know. In other words, I do not, in knowing things, assume their forms in my capacity of a composite substance; if I did I would literally turn into the things which I know. I receive these forms into my form as such, and consequently the modification wrought in me is not material.[8] From this St. Thomas concludes that only those beings whose forms are to some degree free from their matter are capable of having knowledge. "Free from matter" does not here mean separated from matter; certainly the substantial forms (i.e., the souls) of animals are inseparable from matter and yet animals have a certain degree of knowledge. Their soul may be said to be free from matter in the sense that although it can never exist or operate except in and through their body, yet its whole energy is not limited to or used up in forming and animating their own body but reaches also to the reception of the forms of other bodies in an immaterial way. Thus a kitten first possesses in itself cognitively and immaterially the milk which it is about to add to itself materially; the milk is part of the kitten's life in two distinct

---

[8] *S. Theol.*, I, 50, 2, ad 2; *Con. Gen.*, II, 50, fourth arg.

ways, but one of these ways, the cognitive way, is purely formal. The milk, on the contrary, can never contain the kitten formally but only materially. The form of the milk is to no degree free from matter, and consequently the milk cannot receive any purely formal determination by which it becomes something else while yet remaining itself; therefore it is incapable of knowledge.[9]

"Knowing beings are distinguished from non-knowing beings," wrote St. Thomas,[10] "in that the latter possess only their own form, while the knowing being is by nature capable of having also the form of another thing." And by receiving the forms of other things knowing beings become those things without ceasing to be themselves.

> In beings which have knowledge, each is so determined to its own natural being by its own natural form that it is nevertheless capable of receiving the species of all intelligible things. And so the human soul, in a certain manner, becomes everything through sense and intellect.[11]

5. Form and Intelligibility. Intelligibility means capacity to be understood or to be an idea. It is St. Thomas' teaching that forms are of themselves intelligible; that is to say, they are ideas, either potential ideas, when they are immersed in matter, or actual ideas, when they are free from matter. The form in anything is its idea, and this form, in the mind, makes the thing known to the mind.

> What is called *idea* in Greek is called *forma* in Latin. Whence by ideas we understand the forms of certain things existing apart from the things. Now the form of a thing existing apart from the thing can have a twofold being: it may either be the exemplar of that of which it is called the form, or it may be the principle by which the thing is known, for which reason the forms of things known are said to be in the one knowing.[12]

When a form is not actually intelligible, this is not due to anything in itself as form, but to its mode of existence in matter. Every form existing free from matter is actually intelligible, that is to say, is an actual idea.

6. Form and Intelligence. St. Thomas goes further than this. He not only equates form with intelligibility, but also with intelligence. Every form subsisting in itself apart from matter is an actual intelligence.

[9] *S. Theol.*, I, 84, 2, c.
[10] *S. Theol.*, I, 14, 1, c.
[11] *S. Theol.*, I, 80, 1, c.
[12] *S. Theol.*, I, 15, 1, c. Cf. *De Ver.*, III, 2, c.

How far the Angelic Doctor goes in identifying form with intelligibility and intelligence is made clear by the following passages:

> Just as matter is the principle of particularity, so is intelligibility due to form. For this reason form is the principle of knowledge. Wherefore, it follows necessarily that every form existing in itself apart from matter is intellectual in nature; and if, indeed, it subsists in itself, it will also be an intelligence. If, on the other hand, it is not subsistent but rather a perfection of some subsistent being, it will not be an intelligence, but a principle of understanding.[13]
>
> If there were a box subsisting in itself without matter, it would understand itself; because immunity from matter is the cause of intellectuality, and because of this, the box without matter would not differ from the intelligible box.[14]
>
> Every form subsisting in itself without matter is an intellectual substance; for immunity from matter confers intelligibility.[15]

7. Actuality, Intelligibility, and Intelligence. This teaching of St. Thomas is no special, peculiar doctrine, but is simply a particular application of principles which he constantly employs. Creatures are ordered in a hierarchy of degrees of perfection, and perfection itself is measured by actuality of being. Primary matter is pure potentiality; and consequently the more any form of being involves materiality the more potential and the less actual it is, and the more free the form is from matter the less potential and the more actual it is. Actual intelligibility is a high degree of perfection, attained by form only when it is completely free from matter, as a form is in an intellect. Hence, every form separated from matter and received in an intellect is an actual idea. But actual intelligence, being an operation, can belong only to a substance, since every operation must be attributed to some substance. Therefore, an actually intelligible form, if it is a substance, that is, if it subsists in itself, will also be an actual intelligence; for intelligence is simply subjective intelligibility. An idea which is *in* a subject, but is not itself a subject, is understood but does not understand; an idea which is itself a subject understands itself. In the final analysis intelligibility and intelligence are identical, because, as St. Thomas says so often, and as shall be explained below, "the intelligible thing in act is the intellect in act."

[13] *In I Sent.*, d. 35, q. 1, 1, c.
[14] *De Spirit. Creat.*, 1, ad 12.
[15] *Con. Gen.*, II, 91.

III. CAUSAL ANALYSIS OF HUMAN COGNITION

1. Man's intellect begins empty — a merely potential intellect. In order actually to understand something it must have within itself immaterially the form of a known object, since all knowledge is by means of some form determining a cognitive power. Consequently the explanation of human knowledge is the answer to the question: How does the human intellect acquire the intelligible forms by which it knows things?

2. The Sensory-Intellectual Character of Human Knowledge. Because man is an intellectual being and at the same time a composite of matter and form, his knowledge is sensory-intellectual. His soul is an intellectual form, but is the lowest or least perfect of all intellectual forms. Unlike the angels, it does not subsist as a complete being, but is only part of a being of which the body is the other part. The union of the soul with matter is not accidental, but is essential to the soul itself. Man's soul simply is not a form of sufficient perfection to constitute a completely determined being capable of existing separately and with the full exercise of its proper operations. It is futile to ask why it is not; if, *per impossibile,* it were, it would not be a soul at all and there would be no men in the universe. Man's body, therefore, exists because of the need which the soul has for it; and (a simple corollary) his senses exist because of the need which his intellect has for them.

What is this need which man's intellect has for his senses? An intellect is a power of knowing being; but in order actually to know, the intellect must actually possess the forms of the beings to be known. Of the many degrees of intellectual perfection, man's soul possesses precisely the lowest; it has the power to know beings, but it is not naturally endowed with the forms whereby this power is actualized in knowledge. If it is to know, it must receive these forms. It can receive them only through the senses; and that is why it needs the senses.[16]

3. Angelic and Human Intelligence. The case is different with the angels. In the Thomistic view of the universe, all creatures form a perfect hierarchy of degrees of perfection or fullness of being. Each creature is in its essence an imitation of the simple, absolutely perfect being which is its source, namely, God. The various species of creatures differ from one another by the degree of fullness with which they

---

[16] *S. Theol..* I, 76, 5.

reflect the divine perfection. Each higher form or species contains of necessity within itself all the perfections of the lower forms, and contains these lower forms themselves virtually though not actually, as we have seen. The angels are the highest forms of created being. Each angel contains naturally within itself the perfections of every angel lower than itself and every form of material being. Furthermore, since an angel is a pure form subsisting separate from matter, it is an actual intelligible and an actual intelligence; for, as we have seen above, every form free from matter is actually intelligible (i.e., is an actual idea), and every form subsisting separate from matter is an actual intelligence. As an actual intelligible and an actual intelligence an angel understands itself; but as possessing the perfections of all the lower forms of being, it understands these also, because they can be in it only as immaterial or intelligible forms since it is itself a form free from all materiality. The angels, therefore, are always in possession of the intelligible forms by which they know the various beings of the universe. They are, as St. Thomas expresses it, endowed by God with these forms at their creation.[17] If man's intellect were, like an angel, a separately subsisting form, it would naturally possess as intelligible species the forms of all beings inferior to itself. But it is only a power of man's soul. Man does possess the perfections of all lower forms of being, but he does not possess them intellectually as do the angels because he is not a subsisting actual intelligence. Therefore — and this brings us back to where we started — man's intellect, in order actually to know beings, must somehow *receive* the forms of these beings.

4. External Sense and Sensation. In order to receive the forms of other objects, man must have a certain degree of passivity; and whatever passivity there may be in his intellect is not sufficient, because the objects which man is primarily capable of knowing are the natures of corporeal things, and these cannot act upon his incorporeal intellect.[18] Passivity, properly speaking, is predicable only of corporeal things, and therefore whatever passivity is attributable to man's soul is so attributable only because of the soul's union with the body.[19] Consequently, the first step toward the intellect's reception of the form required to actualize it in knowledge is a material affection in man's body. This

---

[17] *S. Theol.*, I, 57, 2, c; *Con. Gen.*, II, 46, last par.; 99, third par.; *Q. Quod.*, VII, 3; IX, 7.

[18] *S. Theol.*, I, 84, 6, c.

[19] *De Ver.*, XXVI, 2, c.

affection takes place when an external body acts upon one of man's sense organs; for example, when a colored object reflects light into a man's eyes and produces a physical alteration in the retinas of the eyes. This alteration in the retinas leads to subsequent alterations in the optic nerve and to a final physical alteration in the visual region of the cerebrum. These physical alterations are requisite conditions for sensation, but they are not adequate conditions; a psychic or spiritual alteration must also occur. Both alterations are receptions of a sensible form of the thing-to-be-known, but the form is received differently in each case. St. Thomas expresses this as follows:

> There is, however, a twofold alteration,[20] one natural and the other spiritual. [There is] a natural one according as the form of the thing producing the alteration is received into the thing altered according to its natural mode, as heat is received in a thing made hot; [there is] a spiritual one according as the form of the thing producing the change is received into the thing changed according to its spiritual mode, as the form of color is received in the pupil of the eye, which is not thereby made colored. Now, the operation of sense requires a spiritual alteration, through which the intentio [i.e., the cognitional impression] of the sensible form is produced in the organ of the sense. Otherwise, if only the natural alteration sufficed for sensing, all natural bodies would sense, since all undergo alterations.[21]

5. The Essence of Sentiency. The above quotation expresses the very essence of St. Thomas' doctrine of the power of sense. Those bodies whose physical modifications, produced by other bodies acting upon them, are naturally transmuted into spiritual or intentional modifications have the power of sense; those bodies whose physical modifications remain merely physical are non-sentient. The natural forms of the latter bodies are entirely immersed in their matter, and are altered only inasmuch as the composite substance, that is, the body, is itself altered; the natural forms of the former are to some degree free of matter, and are capable of being altered precisely as forms. This formal alteration or affection is what St. Thomas calls the *intentio* or the *immutatio spiritualis*.

To illustrate what St. Thomas means is simple enough. A needle pressed into the back of my hand produces a physical alteration, namely, a pressure and a tearing of the flesh; but because the hand is a sentient body, that is, an organ or instrument of the power of feeling,

---

[20] "Alteration" here translates *immutatio*.
[21] *S. Theol.*, I, 78. 3, c.

there is in addition to the physical alteration a psychic or spiritual alteration: I feel a pain in my hand. If the needle were pressed into a dead hand, the physical alteration would be to a large degree the same, but it would not be transmuted into a spiritual alteration because the dead hand is not an organ or instrument of feeling; it is no longer a sentient body. Whatever substantial forms may be present in the dead flesh are entirely immersed in the matter of the flesh; they inform or determine the matter and have no other function. The form of the living hand — that is, the soul — is not entirely immersed in the matter; it informs the matter, but over and above this it has a function directed beyond the matter to things that can be felt. Because of this function the physical alterations produced in the hand by other bodies give rise to spiritual alterations in the sentient power of which the hand is the organ. Such a spiritual alteration is what St. Thomas calls the *intentio* and what later Scholastics have called the impressed species (*species impressa*).

In the sentient body this *intentio* is a cognitive modification or determinant; in the body causing it, it is a physical accidental form, for example, its color or shape. Every agent acting upon a patient communicates to or produces in that patient the form which is the agent's immediate principle of operation.[22] Therefore, the sensible species or *intentio* is a sensible form of the thing sensed, impressed upon the sense, and determining the sense cognitively. This form actualizes the sense power, making it one with the sensible object, and thus enabling the man to know this object.

> The knowledge belonging to the external sense is effected entirely through the alteration of the sense by the sensible object. Wherefore, it [i.e., the sense] senses through a form which is impressed upon it by the sensible object.[23]

This form or impression or *intentio* is regularly called the *species sensibilis*. For any actual knowledge to exist, the cognitive power must be assimilated to or made one with a knowable object. The function of the *species* is to effect this assimilation.

> All knowledge is accomplished through some species by means of whose information [i.e., act of informing or determining] there is effected an assimilation of the knower and the thing known.[24] Whence

[22] Cf. Chapter IV, Section VI, No. 7, pp. 73-74.
[23] *Q. Quod.*, V, 9, ad 2.
[24] *In I Sent.*, d. 3, 1, 1 ad 3.

it is said in Book Three of *De Anima* . . . that the sensible in act is the sense in act and the intelligible in act is the intellect in act. For we actually sense or understand anything by the fact that our intellect or sense is actually informed by the sensible or intelligible species.[25]

We saw in Section II that knowledge is always someone knowing something; there can be knowledge only where a knower and a known thing merge in one reality. We now see how this condition is fulfilled in sensation. The sense, before the act of sensation, is a power or potency to perceive some object, and the object is a potency to be perceived. In the act of sensation these two distinct potencies are actualized in one identical actuality; the sensing is the act of the sense's power to sense and the act of the object's potency to be sensed. The sense, actualized and determined by the form of the thing sensed, becomes that thing, in so far as the thing is sensed. *Sensus in actu est sensum in actu.*

6. The Internal Senses and the Phantasm. As the result, therefore, of the actualization and determination of his senses by the sensible forms of corporeal substances, man perceives these substances. All that his external senses grasp are the external sensible determinations of the substances, e.g., their color, odor, sound, and taste. These accidental forms, united in the external substance but received separately by the external senses, are reunited again in cognition by the *sensus communis.* From them, the imagination, aided by the other internal senses, forms a mental image or phantasm of the sensed object. It is from this phantasm, as we have seen, that the intellect abstracts its universal idea or concept of the thing perceived. In itself, the phantasm is a sensible representation of a particular thing. Its character as a representation is given to it by the forms received through the external senses into the organ of internal sense, namely, the sensorium. The sensorium is the whole physical sensory apparatus of man, but more particularly his brain. Just as various sensible forms determine each external sense to some individual quality of the sensed object, so the complexus of sensible forms from one subject determine the sensorium, and through it the internal senses, to a unified sensible representation of the object.[26] The man's active power of sense, through its determination by the spiritual *immutatio* or impressed form of the object, becomes the

[25] *S. Theol.,* I, 14, 2, c.
[26] *S. Theol.,* I, 84, 7, ad 2; 85, 1, ad 3.

object perceived, and expresses itself, thereby expressing the object, in a phantasm.

7. The Intelligible Species. The phantasm, residing in a corporeal organ, is both particular and material. Yet it is from it that the intellect must receive the immaterial and universal form by which it, in its turn, is to be assimilated to or made one with the object to be known. The intellect is an immaterial power to know, as we saw in Chapter X, but in order actually to know, it must be determined to one or another specific nature, since knowledge is always about something definite. Hence, it must receive a form which determines it, and this form must be free from matter and the conditions of matter, since it is to be received into the immaterial intellect. It is this form which is abstracted by the intellect from the phantasm, and which is called the *species intelligibilis*. How is it abstracted from the phantasm?

8. Abstraction. The simplest answer would be that just as the external object impressed its sensible form on the sense power through the sense organ, so the phantasm impresses the intelligible form which it embodies upon the intellectual power. But that answer is too simple, for two reasons: first, the intellect has no material organ through which to receive the impression, and a material image, like the phantasm, cannot produce any impression on a purely spiritual power; second, the form in the phantasm is not *actually* intelligible because it is not entirely free from matter. Consequently, the form or species embodied in the phantasm must be freed from all material conditions and made actually intelligible before it can be received by the intellect.

9. Agent Intellect and Possible Intellect. Nothing can be moved from potentiality to actuality in any respect except by something which is already actual in that respect. Therefore, the form in the phantasm can be made actually intelligible only by some agent which is itself actually intelligible. This agent is the intellect itself which, being an immaterial form, is actually intelligible. Consequently, the intellect itself makes the form embodied in the phantasm actually intelligible before it receives that form into itself. St. Thomas, therefore, following Aristotle, distinguishes two intellects or two distinct powers of the human intellect, namely, the active or agent intellect which *makes* things actually intelligible by freeing their form from its material conditions in the phantasm, and the possible intellect which *becomes* the intelligible object by receiving the form or species abstracted by the agent intellect.

10. The Active Intellect.[27] St. Thomas' argument for the active intellect is based upon two principles which find frequent employment in his philosophy. They are: (1) that the lower being in the order of perfection cannot act upon the higher, since the agent is always superior to the patient; (2) that whatever is moved from potentiality to actuality is moved by some agent already in actuality in the respect in which it moves the patient. Hence, according to the first principle, neither the sense impressions nor the phantasm can move the intellect from potential to actual understanding, because they are sensible and material, whereas it is spiritual. The intelligible form which is to determine the intellect is in the phantasm, but is not actually intelligible because it is not completely free from matter. It must be moved from potential intelligibility to actual intelligibility. But, according to the second principle, that which moves it must be itself actually intelligible and, therefore, immaterial. This mover is the active intellect. Here are St. Thomas' words:

> But nothing is reduced from potency to act except by some being already in act, as the sense is actualized by the actually sensible thing. Consequently, it is necessary to posit some power on the part of the intellect which makes actual intelligibles by abstracting the species from the material conditions. And herein lies the necessity of positing the active intellect.[28]

Let us try to summarize the situation and the argument. When the sensuous part of the cognitive process is completed, the intellect finds itself face to face with the phantasm. This phantasm embodies the essential form of some corporeal thing. In order to know what this thing is, the intellect must receive this form into itself as an intelligible form determining it to actual understanding. But the form itself, in order to be so received, must be actually intelligible. It is not in fact actually intelligible in the phantasm because it is involved with individual material conditions, and only a form free from material conditions is actually intelligible. Nevertheless, the intellect does succeed in receiving and being determined by the form, since otherwise we would not understand. Consequently it must itself first have moved the form from potential intelligibility to actual intelligibility by freeing it from

[27] *S. Theol.*, I, 79, arts. 3 to 5; *Con. Gen.*, II, Chaps. 76–78; *Q. D. De Anima*, 4 and 5; *In De Anima*, III, 10, Nos. 728–739; *Q. Quod.*, VIII, q. 2, art. 4; *De Spirit. Creat.*, 9 and 10.

[28] *S. Theol.*, I, 79, 3, c.

the material conditions of the phantasm. It is able to do this because it is itself actually immaterial and intelligible. Its power of doing this St. Thomas calls the active intellect and the operation of doing it he commonly calls abstraction.[29]

11. **The Possible Intellect and the Intelligible Species.** The universal form or species abstracted from the phantasm by the active intellect is then received into or impressed upon the possible intellect in a way analogous to the impression of sensible species upon the sense powers. The result of its reception by the possible intellect, since it is a form, is to determine that intellect to the nature of the being whose form it is. So determined, the possible intellect is made the intellect in act and is made at the same time and by the same token the intelligible thing in act.[30] "*Sensibile in actu est sensus in actu, et intelligibile in actu est intellectus in actu.*" For the intellect informed by the species is at once the actuality of the intelligibility of the object and the intelligence of the subject. Prior to the informing of the intellect by the intelligible species, the intellect is a power or potency for knowing, and the thing is a potency for being known. The intellect informed by the species is a new reality in which are actualized both these potencies; hence it is both of them at once — the *intellectum in actu* and the *intellectus in actu*.

12. **The Act of Conception.** When the possible intellect is actualized and determined by the intelligible species, it is fully disposed to perform its own operations. The first of these is the simple apprehension or understanding of the nature of some external thing. The intellect in apprehending, like the sense in imagining, produces a mental representation of its object. This is what we commonly call the concept or idea. It is not the intelligible species informing the intellect, any more than the phantasm is the sensible species informing the sense; it is a conscious intelligible likeness of the thing apprehended. It is the actualized intellect's expression of itself, and as such it cannot be anything other than the likeness of the thing whose form the intellect has received; because at the moment when the intellect produces this expression it is one with the thing by whose form it is determined. St. Thomas states this argument very clearly:

It ought to be further considered that the intellect, informed by the

---

[29] *S. Theol.*, I, 79; *In III De Anima*, L. 10; *Q. D. De Anima*, IV.

[30] *S. Theol.*, I, 85, 2 ad 1; 14, 5 ad 3; 85, 3 ad 1; *Con Gen.*, I, 55; *Q. Quod.*, III, 20, c.

species of the thing, forms within itself, in understanding, a certain idea of the thing understood, which idea is the nature of that thing, that which its definition signifies. This is necessary so that the intellect may understand the thing indifferently whether absent or present; in which respect the imagination is similar to the intellect. But the intellect has this further trait, that it also understands the thing as separated from material conditions, without which it cannot exist in the real order; and this would not be possible unless the intellect formed the idea spoken of above. This concept, however, since it is as the term of the intelligible operation, is other than the intelligible species which actualizes the intellect and which must be considered as the principle of the intelligible operation, although each of them is a likeness of the thing understood. For by the very fact that the intelligible species, which is the form of the intellect and the principle of understanding, is the similitude of the exterior thing, it follows that the intellect forms a concept similar to that thing; for everything acts according to its nature. And by the fact that the concept is like some thing, it follows that the intellect, forming such a concept, understands that thing.[31]

13. Knowledge Is an Immanent Action. The whole operation of knowing, although it depends upon prior external conditions, takes place within the knowing subject — it is an immanent and not a transient action. It has an essential relation to the external thing which initiates the process and which, in the end, it knows. This essential relation is what makes the act an act of knowledge — someone knowing something — and the relation is determined in the intellect by the form of the thing known informing the intellect itself. St. Thomas writes in the same chapter as the above passage:

It should be considered that the external thing understood by us does not exist in our mind according to its proper nature, but that it is necessary that its species be in our intellect, which is made an intellect in act through this species. Existing in actuality by such a species, as by its own form, it understands the external thing itself; not however in such a manner that the act of understanding is an act passing into the thing understood, as heating passes into the thing heated. On the contrary, it remains within the understanding subject itself, and has a relation to the thing understood, because the aforesaid species, which, as a form, is the principle of the intellectual operation, is the likeness of that thing.[32]

The concept, therefore, is a conscious likeness of the external thing, produced within itself by the intellect; it must be a faithful likeness of the thing, because it is determined in its intelligible content by the

---

[31] *Con. Gen.*, I, 53.   [32] *Loc. cit.*

very form of the thing informing the intellect and determining it to the production of this concept; the intellect is incapable of producing anything but a likeness of the thing whose form is at the moment its own form. And, of course, the intellect actually knows the thing by means of the concept, because to have consciously or cognitively in itself the likeness of something is nothing else than to know that something.

14. **Knowledge of Universals and Singulars.** The intellect is not finished with the phantasm when it has abstracted the intelligible species from it. On the contrary, it turns again to the phantasm each time it considers the thing known through the abstracted species. This dependence of the human intellect upon the imagination and the phantasm is a mark of its relative imperfection, but at the same time it renders possible the proper perfection of human thought. For the natural objects of the human intellect are the natures of sensible things, and if these natures were conceived with no relation to material individuals they would be misconceived as forms existing separate from matter. By conceiving them in the phantasm the intellect ties them to the sensible particulars of which they are the natures.

> Whence the nature of a stone or of any material thing cannot be known completely and truly except insofar as it is known as existing in a particular thing. Now we apprehend the particular through sense and imagination, and therefore it is necessary, in order that the intellect actually understand its proper object, that it turn back to the phantasm, so as to envision the universal nature existing in a particular thing.[33]

Because of its abstractive mode of knowing, the human intellect has as direct object not a particular thing but a universal nature. It knows by abstracting the form from individual sensible matter, and the form so abstracted loses the individuality which it has in nature where it is embodied in individual matter. Such a form can determine the possible intellect to knowledge of the universal species or genus, but not to knowledge of the individual thing:

> It must be stated that our intellect does not know the singular in material things directly and primarily. The reason for this is that the principle of singularity in material things is individual matter. But our intellect, as noted above, understands by abstracting the intelligible species from this kind of matter. Now, whatever is abstracted from individual matter is universal. Wherefore our intellect is able to know directly only the universal.[34]

[33] S. Theol., I, 84, 7, c. Cf. ibid., 85, 1 ad 5; Con. Gen., II, 60, 73.
[34] S. Theol., I, 86, 1, c.

This failure of the human intellect to understand the singular primarily and directly is evidenced by the fact that all our definitions and scientific laws are concerned with classes of things rather than with individual things. Yet our intellect is not cut off from all knowledge of singulars. We have *reflex* intellection of particular things. Our senses grasp the singular, and we represent the singular in the phantasm. From this phantasm our intellect abstracts the universal ideas, thus getting direct knowledge of the universal. But by reflecting upon its own act of abstraction it comes to a consideration of the phantasm whence it drew the intelligible species, and from the phantasm it is led to an indirect or reflex grasp of the individual thing whence the phantasm was formed. Hence, while we know universal natures directly in intellectual knowledge, we also know singulars indirectly by reflection on the phantasm from which we abstracted the universal:

> It must be said that the soul joined to the body knows the singular by the intellect, not indeed directly, but by a certain reflection; inasmuch, namely, as by the fact that it apprehends its own intelligible object, it turns to the consideration of its act, and the intelligible species which is the principle of its act, and the origin of this species; and so it arrives at a consideration of the phantasms. But this reflection cannot be accomplished fully except through union with the cogitative and imaginative powers.[35]

This teaching of St. Thomas on our reflective knowledge of the singular is very often misunderstood and misrepresented. If the Angelic Doctor meant to say — as, it must be confessed, he seems to say in several places — that the intellect does not apprehend the singular at all in our immediate perceptive acts, but only through a reflection which follows the universalizing abstraction, his doctrine would be open to several grave psychological and epistemological difficulties.[36] But a more thorough study of relevant Thomistic texts[37] makes it quite clear that his meaning is somewhat different. In perception, the human mind, which is sensio-intellective, apprehends a singular thing as having a certain nature; that is to say, the immediate object of the mind's

[35] *Q. D. De Anima*, 20, ad 1 of second series. Cf. *S. Theol.*, I, 86, 1, c; *In IV Sent.*, L. 1, 3, sol.; *De Ver.*, II, 6, c; *ibid.*, X, 5, c and ad 3; *ibid.*, XIX, 2, c; *In III De Anima*, No. 713.

[36] Some of these difficulties are discussed by Rudolph Allers in "The Intellectual Cognition of Particulars," *The Thomist* (January, 1941), Vol. III, No. 1, pp. 95–163. The primary epistemological difficulty is pointed out in Chapter XVIII, Section I.

[37] For example, *In II Post. Anal.*, l. 20; *In II De Anima*, 13, Nos. 395–398; *In I Meta.*, 1, Nos. 15–23; *S. Theol.*, I, 85, 1 ad 5; *ibid.*, 85, 3.

sensio-intellective act is a singular and an implicit universal given to-gether — "this thing so and so determined."[38] But the mind does not thereby *understand* the singular, either as to its generic or specific essence or as to its individual actuality. For these understandings, the intellect must abstract the quiddity or essence from the singular datum, thus explicitly universalizing it, or "giving it the intention of universality." Hence, the first thing *understood* or clearly known is the abstracted, universalized essence.[39] This kind of understanding is "science," that is, knowledge through causes, principles, essences, laws; and thus science is of universals. In order to see the singular in the light of this universal or scientific knowledge, the mind must return, in the reflection we have described, to the individual object whence the whole cognitive process started. Thus it attains reflective understanding of the singular.

[38] This is explained in Chapter XVIII below, where St. Thomas' doctrine of knowledge is explained from the epistemological point of view.

[39] Cf. *S. Theol.*, I, 85, 3.

CHAPTER XII

HUMAN APPETITE AND WILL

I. WILL AS APPETITE

1. Nowhere does the mysterious unity of matter and spirit which constitutes human nature manifest itself more clearly than in the voluntary actions of man. Every philosopher attempts a theory of the human will, and in many systems of philosophy the theory of the will is the place where wide cracks appear in the structure of the system, testifying to the shakiness of its foundation. Many, surprisingly many, philosophers of all varieties of belief end up by denying that man has any such power as will and that he has any freedom of action. The apparently unquestionable testimony of our own consciousness to the fact that we not only can determine our own courses of action but that we must do so, that in many important circumstances of life we have to "make up our mind" what we shall do, that nothing can settle matters which have to be settled except our own free decision — this testimony is set at naught for the sake of a philosophic system which, *a priori*, pronounces human free will impossible. Dr. Johnson once remarked of free will that the facts are all for it and theory all against it. Let us say rather that, since the facts are for it, we must test every philosophy by its ability to make room for the facts and to supply a theoretical explanation for them. From such a test St. Thomas' philosophy emerges unscathed and triumphant. For the Angelic Doctor's theory of the human will accounts for human freedom in terms of the same principles which are basic to the whole Thomistic philosophy of nature, of man, and of being in general. St. Thomas did not have to force a doctrine of free will into his philosophical system; his doctrine grows out naturally as an organic part of that system. Teleology, the four causes, movement, potency and act, the universal and the particular — of such basic stuff is the Thomistic doctrine of will compounded.

2. The Notion of Appetite: Inclination to the Good. Will, for St. Thomas, is one kind of appetite. An appetite is an inclination of a being toward what is *good* or suitable for it. Beings without knowledge possess merely *natural appetite;* that is, the tendency to act in determinate ways which accord with their natures. For example, certain elements tend to unite with certain others to form certain compounds; trees tend to capture and store energy from the sun by means of the chlorophyll substance in their leaves. These tendencies are unconscious, blind, and extrinsically determined by the natural laws of material substances. They are called appetite only by analogy, by virtue of a certain resemblance to appetite proper. Animals have *sensitive appetite.* Perceiving things around them, some of which appear good, some harmful, they tend to seek the good and avoid the harmful. This tendency is conscious; that is to say, it is real desire, or appetite properly so called. It is entirely on the sensory level, because the animal has no power of knowledge which surpasses sense, and consequently no desire for any suprasensory good, since he knows none. Besides sensory cognition, man has, as we have seen, intellectual or rational knowledge. Consequently, in addition to sensitive appetite, which he possesses in common with the animals, man has an inclination for the good which he knows through intellect or reason. This inclination is *rational appetite, or will.* Man's rational appetite is, like his intellect, an immaterial or spiritual power of his soul, and operates without the instrumentality of any corporeal organ. This immateriality is the reason for the will's freedom.

Appetite is the desire of a conscious being for a good. It is not the mere tendency of a power to perform its operation. Sight naturally tends to see, and hearing to hear; but it is not this tending which is called appetite. By appetite we mean the tendency, *consequent* to seeing or hearing, to get what we see or hear, or even to see or hear it again; we do not mean the tending, *prior* to seeing or hearing, to see or hear. Appetite is a tendency of the whole animal or man, and its object is, not what is good for one power of the animal or man, but what is good for the animal or man as such.[1]

3. Appetite Follows Knowledge Because It Follows Form. Every natural agent tends toward and acts for a definite end or good;[2] this is the universal principle of finality which we studied in Chapter V.

[1] *S. Theol.,* I, 80, 1, ad 3.
[2] *Con. Gen.,* III, 2 and 3.

And it is all that St. Thomas means by natural appetite. The natural tendency of every being is determined by its form; for its form, in determining a thing's nature, gives the thing an inclination toward what is suitable to that nature. We saw in Chapter XI that knowing beings are distinguished from non-knowing beings by the fact that their natural forms, as well as determining them to their own natural being, also make them capable of receiving the forms of other beings, while the forms of non-knowing beings merely determine each one to its own natural being. The inclination determined by an apprehended form is appetite properly so called:

> Therefore, just as in those beings that have knowledge forms exist in a higher manner and above the manner of natural forms, so there must be in them an inclination surpassing the natural inclination which is called the natural appetite. And this superior inclination belongs to the appetitive power of soul, through which the animal is able to desire what it apprehends, and not only that to which it is inclined by its natural form. And so it is necessary to assign an appetitive power to the soul.[3]

4. Appetite Is a Power Distinct From Cognition. The object of appetite must be the same as the object of cognition, since we can desire only what we know.[4] But that does not imply that appetite and cognition are not distinct powers:

> What is apprehended and what is desired are the same in reality, but differ in aspect; for a thing is apprehended as something sensible or intelligible, whereas it is desired as suitable or good. Now it is diversity of aspect in the objects, and not material diversity, which demands a diversity of powers.[5]

5. Sensitive and Intellectual Appetite Are Distinct Powers. Appetite is a passive power which is naturally moved by what is apprehended. Powers which are passive are distinguished by the objects which move them, for it is these objects which determine the distinctive movements of the powers; in other words, the appetite as moved takes its nature from the mover. Now sense and intellect have different objects, and it is these objects which, respectively, move sense appetite and intellectual appetite. Therefore these latter are distinct powers.[6] The

---

[3] *S. Theol.*, I, 80, 1, c (*Basic Writings of St. Thomas Aquinas*, Ed. Anton C. Pegis [New York: Random House, 1945], Vol. I, p. 769).

[4] *Ibid.*, Obj. 2.

[5] *Ibid.*, ad 2 (Pegis, *op. cit.*, Vol. I, p. 769).

[6] *Ibid.*, I, 80, 2, c.

object of the intellect is universal, while the object of sense is particular. Consequently, the proper object of intellectual appetite is the universal good, or the good as such, while the proper object of sensitive appetite is some particular good. The intellectual appetite does desire particular goods, as when a man wills to do a certain act, but it desires particular goods only under the universal notion of good; it is not the particular good thing which attracts the intellectual appetite, but the goodness of the thing. Thus, the man wills to do a certain act because that act appears to him to be in some way good.[7] Furthermore, although the universal or absolute good is what our will is naturally and always inclined to, our individual will-acts are always concerned with particular goods. There are two reasons for this: first, in our present state of life only particular goods are effectively offered to our choice; second, since we are human, our wills move us through our sensitive appetites, just as our intellect gains its ideas through the perceptions of sense.[8] In respect to will, as in all respects, St. Thomas refuses to confuse men with angels. This point is very important for an understanding of his doctrine of free will, and we shall return to it below.

II. SENSITIVE APPETITE: IRASCIBLE AND CONCUPISCIBLE

1. Sensuality or sense appetite, which is the inclination of our sensitive nature toward goods apprehended by sense, is divided by St. Thomas, following Aristotle, into two powers which are specifically distinct. These are called the concupiscible appetite and the irascible appetite. The concupiscible power is the inclination to seek what is good and suitable in things perceived and to avoid what is harmful and unpleasant. The irascible is the inclination to resist obstacles to the good and threats of the harmful. When a dog sniffs around, seeking a bone, it is his concupiscible appetite which is moving him; when he fights another dog who seeks the same bone, it is his irascible appetite which moves him. When he flees from a whipping, it is his concupiscible which inclines him to avoid what is hurtful; and when he fights back against an attack, it is the irascible which is operative.

Therefore, since the sensitive appetite is an inclination following sensitive apprehension . . . , there must needs be in the sensitive part

[7] *Ibid.*, ad 2.　　　　　　　　　　[8] *Ibid.*, ad 3.

[of man or an animal] two appetitive powers: one through which the soul is inclined absolutely to seek what is suitable, according to the senses, and to fly from what is hurtful, and this is called the concupiscible; and another, whereby the animal resists the attacks that hinder what is suitable and inflict harm, and this is called the irascible.[9]

Of the two powers, the concupiscible is the more fundamental, since it is related more immediately to things which bear for good or ill upon the man or the animal. The irascible is subordinated to it.

And for this reason all the passions of the irascible appetite rise from the passions of the concupiscible appetite and terminate in them. For instance, anger rises from sadness [being directed against some cause which deprives the animal of a good and thus renders it sad], and, having wrought vengeance, terminates in joy [at having conquered or destroyed the cause of the sadness]. For this reason also the quarrels of animals are about things concupiscible — namely, food and sex, as the Philosopher says.[10]

2. The Passions or Emotions. It is from the sensitive appetites — concupiscible and irascible — that the *passions* take their rise. Passion, properly so called, is found only where there is bodily alteration,[11] and consequently cannot be ascribed to the rational part of man. When we speak of love or hate in the will of man, this rational love or hate, though accompanied by and related in mutual influence with the passion of love or hate, is not itself a passion. Passion belongs to the sensitive nature, to the powers which require both body and soul for operation.[12] "Passion is a movement of the sensitive appetite under the imagination of good or evil."[13] Those passions which have a good or an evil as their immediate object or stimulus arise from the concupiscible appetite, which relates to good and evil directly. Such passions are love, sadness, joy, hatred. Passions occasioned by and directed toward obstacles to a desired good or threats of some harm arise from the irascible appetite. Such are *audacia* — the passion which leads us confidently to face up to danger — and its opposite, fear; hope and its opposite, despair. St. Thomas gives a classic treatment of the human passions in the *Summa*, I–II, questions 21 to 48; but we cannot even

---

[9] *S. Theol.*, I, 18, 2, c (Pegis, *op. cit.*, Vol. I. p. 772).

[10] *Loc. cit.* (Pegis, *op. cit.*, Vol. I, p. 773).

[11] For example, as modern psychology teaches us, change in pulse rate, in blood pressure, in breathing rate, increased or decreased activity of the endocrine glands, etc.

[12] *S. Theol.*, I–II, 22, c, ad 3.

[13] *Ibid.*, ad 4.

summarize it here. We can only state his teaching on the relation of the passions to the action of the will. The passions unquestionably influence the will, but they cannot move it of necessity; that is to say, they cannot determine its choice.[14]

3. Sensuality Is Under the Control of Reason. Man's sensitive appetite is subordinated to his intellect and will. Sensitive appetite in man has the same nature as in animals, but its actual movement differs. It does not move man necessarily to the sensuous good, as the animal's appetite moves the animal. There are two reasons for this. First, as we recall from the last chapter, the estimative sense in animals, and the cogitative in man, is the sense of the good and harmful. The external senses can grasp only sensible qualities, while good and harmfulness are non-sensuous. These non-sensuous aspects (*species insensatae*) are grasped by the estimative or the cogitative power. Now, since sensitive appetite is concerned with the good and the harmful, it is clear that this appetite is moved through the estimative power in animals and the cogitative in man. But we saw also in the last chapter that while the estimative and cogitative are the same in nature they differ in operation, since man's cogitative operates under the direction of intellect, whereas the animal's estimative does not. Consequently, since sensuality in man gets its movement from the cogitative power, and since this is directed in its operation by intellect, sensuality is under the control of intellect. This means that when any sensuous good attracts man's sensitive appetite, this good is always, or at least normally, apprehended by intellect as well as by sense, and consequently man is capable of judging about it rationally instead of being compelled to immediate action by his sensitive inclination for it.[15]

Second, sensuality in man is subject also to his will or rational appetite. An animal's appetites move him automatically to act because they are the ultimate springs of action in him, since his proper perfection is sentiency. But man's proper perfection is rationality, and consequently his sensitive appetites are not the ultimate sources of action in him but are subordinated to and dependent upon his will. Therefore, though a man may be incited to act by the inclination of a sensuous desire, he must first give consent of the will before he

[14] *S. Theol.*, I–II, 9, 2; *ibid.*, 10, 3.
[15] *S. Theol.*, I, 81, 3, c.

acts. The will, as the highest motive power in man, rules and controls all his other motive powers.[16]

It may happen that sometimes a concupiscible or irascible impulse is so strong and so sudden that one is surprised into acting before his reason has judged or his will consented or refused consent.[17] For the rule of reason over the sensitive passions is, as Aristotle said, politic rather than despotic. These passions have a certain autonomy, like free men under a just ruler rather than like slaves under a tyrant. They have ends of their own, which, in the present condition of human life, do not always conform to the ends of reason. For they are moved, not only by the cogitative power, but also by imagination and sense, and therefore they can incline us toward things which are pleasant for imagination and sense but bad for the man as a man and consequently forbidden by reason. Similarly, they can arouse in us disinclinations for tasks which are unpleasant for our sensuous nature, but which reason nevertheless pronounces duties. Thus, the concupiscible and irascible appetites can and do resist reason; but from this we must not conclude that they do not obey it.[18] The degree to which they obey reason depends, humanly speaking, upon the effective control over sensuous inclination which intellect and will have built up by repeated practice.[19]

III. THE OBJECT AND MOVEMENT OF THE WILL

1. **Nature of Will.** Appetite is desire for an apprehended good. Rational appetite, or *will*, is desire for what the *intellect* apprehends as good. The intellect, as we have seen, grasps its object under universal conceptions, and consequently the good apprehended by intellect is the *universal good,* or the good as such. It is this good-as-such which is the object of will. But since every particular good falls under the notion of the universal good, and because will is a power of the whole man, and not a mere function of intellect, any good, no matter how evil it may be in the clear light of reason, may be desired by the will. Thus, for example, rest is a sensitive good, but oftentimes rest and the fulfillment of duty are in conflict. When a sensuous good thus conflicts with a higher good, the sensuous good becomes actually an evil. Yet it still appears good to the sensitive appetite, and consequently it can still attract the will, since the scope of the will in

---

[16] *Loc. cit.*
[17] *S. Theol.*, I–II, 17, 7.
[18] *Ibid.,* ad 2.
[19] Cf. *S. Theol.*, I–II, 10, 3.

respect to the good is universal, and since a sensuous good is really good for a part of man's nature. We cannot will evil as such, because the will inclines only to the good; but we can will what is in fact evil if in some way it appears good.

2. The Will Necessarily Wills Absolute Good. The first question which St. Thomas asks about the will, in the *Summa,* is whether it desires anything *of necessity.* His answer is that it desires happiness, or the absolute good, of necessity. In a certain sense, this statement is a mere tautology; for if the will is defined as the rational appetite for the universal good, it is a contradiction in terms to say that the will can fail to desire the good as such. Yet it seems to many people that to say that the will desires something necessarily is equivalent to denying the will's very nature. For, they say, what is necessary is not voluntary, and voluntariness is the essential character of the will's movement; furthermore, to say that a man possesses will is to say that he is master of his own actions, but certainly we are not master of what is necessary.[20]

St. Thomas' answers to these arguments make his own doctrine of the nature of the will very clear. He distinguishes three kinds of necessity which are relevant to the problem. The first is necessity of coercion or force, which moves something contrary to that thing's own inclination. This may be illustrated by the forcible eviction of a man from his home, or of a people from their land. This *necessity of coercion can never be found in the will,* because the movement of the will is voluntary, and coercion destroys voluntariness. St. Thomas does not mean that we cannot be forced to act against our will; he means that when we do act against our will because we are forced, we do not exercise a will-act, for no movement can be both coerced and voluntary.[21] Therefore, the argument that there is no necessity in the will, since what is necessary is not voluntary, is valid in respect to necessity of coercion, but only in respect to that kind of necessity.[22]

The second kind of necessity, namely *necessity of end, is found in the operations of the will.* Necessity of end signifies the necessity which arises in regard to the means to a certain end once that end has been willed. Thus, if a young man wills to be a surgeon, he must will to attend medical school; people who refuse to take the necessary

---

[20] *S. Theol.,* I, 82, 1, Obj. 1 and 3.
[21] *Ibid.,* 1, c. Cf. *ibid.,* I–II, 6, 4.
[22] *Ibid.,* ad 1.

means for attaining the goals which they desire, do not really *will* those goals; they merely wish for them. This necessity of end does not destroy the will's voluntariness or freedom, because the necessary willing of the means arises from the will's own act of willing the end.

The third kind of necessity, namely *natural necessity,* is the one which is most relevant to the problem. This necessity arises from the nature of the subject or principle of movement, which in the present case is the will. *By its very nature the will necessarily desires the good as such;* for if it did not, it would not be will. This necessity is not contrary to voluntariness, as coercion is. Coercion moves something *against* its own natural inclination; but the will's necessary desire of the good *is* its natural inclination. In other words, the root of man's voluntariness is the necessary appetite of his rational nature for the good.[23] Hence this necessity does not take away our mastery over our own acts except in reference to the absolute good; in respect to all other goods we are master.[24]

3. **Happiness Is the Absolute Good.** The good as such, translated into terms of human psychology, is happiness. Happiness is good as such because its goodness is not determined by relation to anything other than itself; we may demand of someone that he give a reason why he wants power or wealth or even pleasure, but it would be absurd to ask why a man desires to be happy. The desire for happiness underlies all our desires for anything. Man is free to desire or not desire any particular good, but he is not free as regards happiness; it is of his nature to desire happiness. It is this necessary and unchanging desire for happiness that stirs man unceasingly to strive for one thing or another — to seek pleasure, fame, wealth, or, on the other hand, to spurn these when they conflict with duty. A sensuous man pursues pleasure because he wants to be happy; a man of character carries through an arduous and unpleasant task because he wants to be happy. A child cries for its mother because it cannot be happy without her; a young man wants to marry a certain girl because he thinks that he cannot be happy without her. Even a suicide is perversely seeking happiness in release from present misery. Why do they all want to be happy? The question has no more meaning than this other question: why is the good desirable?

[23] *Ibid.,* c.
[24] *Ibid.,* ad 3.

4. The Will Does Not Desire Any Particular Good Necessarily.
It would seem that if we will whatever we will because of our desire
for the absolute good, and if this latter desire is necessary, then we
will necessarily everything that we will. In less abstract terms: if
I *must* desire happiness, and if this necessary desire produces all my
other desires, then all my desires are necessary. To this argument two
more may be added. Since I cannot desire evil, then I *must* desire the
good proposed to my intellect, since not to desire it would be to will
the evil contrary to it. Again, will is related to intellect as sensuality
to sense; but the object of sense moves sensuality necessarily; hence
the good apprehended by intellect moves the will necessarily.[25]

The will's necessary willing of the universal good or happiness
does not necessitate its willing of any determinate particular good. The
universal good is willed as the end, and particular goods as means
to this end. Many particular goods, for example an automobile or a
college diploma, are not necessary for happiness, and consequently need
not be willed even though happiness must be willed. Other particular
goods are necessary for happiness; for example, the observance of
God's law. But a person can desire happiness without in fact willing
even these necessary means to it, *if he does not see that they are necessary means.*

The truth of the matter is that there is nothing at all — that is, no
concrete being or action — which man necessarily wills in this life. He
must, it is true, will the absolute good; but the only concrete things
presented to his will are particular goods — things good under one
aspect but not good under another. And for each good there is also
presented a rival good. Consequently, he is never necessitated to
choose any particular good. He does not will necessarily even to possess
God, in whom alone true happiness consists. Faith and reason may
tell him that God is the absolute good, but he does not *see* Him as
such, as do the blessed in heaven. God appears to man in this life as
one good in competition with others; and sometimes the demands
of God seem to be obstacles to happiness rather than conditions for
it. Therefore, although man necessarily wills to be happy, there is
not, in this present life, any particular means to happiness which he
necessarily wills.[26]

From this the answers to the arguments above are clear. It is true

[25] *S. Theol.*, I, 82, 2, Objs. 2, 1, 3.
[26] *Ibid.*, c.

that the will can desire only what is apprehended as good, but many different things appear good and consequently no one of them necessarily moves the will. Since the capacity of the will is for the absolute good, no particular finite good is capable of moving the will necessarily. Finally, sensuality is moved necessarily by the good object apprehended by sense because sense apprehends only one thing in one act. But reason compares different things with one another; hence rational appetite is not moved necessarily by any one thing.[27]

5. Intellect and Will Move Each Other. Since the will is a desire for the good, arising from an apprehended form in the intellect, it does not even exist as a power, to say nothing of actually operating, except in dependence upon the intellect's act of judging something to be good. It is clear, then, that the intellect moves the will by presenting it with its end or object. On the other hand, the will moves the intellect too. The will is one among several active powers in man, but it is the power which has the highest and most universal end, for its end is the good in itself, whereas the ends of all the other powers are particular goods. Now, just as in an army the general, who is charged with the ultimate end of the army, namely victory, has authority over all the lower officers, each of whom is charged with some particular end contributing to victory, so in the soul the will, whose end is the good itself, controls and moves all the other powers whose ends are particular goods contributing to the good in itself, or happiness. This control of the will extends even to the intellect, for truth, the end of intellect, is a particular good, and consequently we can will to think or not think about some truth. Hence, while the intellect moves the will as end, the will moves the intellect as agent.[28]

IV. FREEDOM OF WILL

1. The Thomistic Concept of Free Will. By freedom of will St. Thomas meant the power which men have of determining their own actions according to the judgment of their reason. We act freely, in his meaning of that term, when we mentally compare different possible courses of action in order to determine which one of them is preferable, and then choose our course of action in accordance with our rational judgment as to the comparative preferability of the various alternatives. Thus, for example, when a young man who, having

[27] *Ibid.*, ad 1, 2, 3.
[28] *S. Theol.*, 1, 82, 4.

compared the advantages of going to college with the advantages of not going, and the advantages offered by one college with those offered by others, finally decides to go to a certain college, he has made that decision freely; that is to say, he has exercised free will. A free act is one which we choose to do for reasons which we know, when we could choose otherwise, since we also know reasons for some alternate course of action.

St. Thomas never subscribed to the view of free will which looks upon it as a spontaneous, uncaused, non-rational choice. Our will, for him, always follows our reason; we act freely only when we consciously determine ourselves to a choice based upon known reasons. To be free means to be self-determining; but if a man's will were some spontaneous inner determinant of choice, not directed by his judgment and unpredictable even to himself, he would not determine his own actions, but would be at the mercy of this uncontrollable inner determinant; he would be liable to adopt any course of action at any moment, without knowing why he did so. Men who seem to us to act from some such unaccountable, magical, inner spontaneity we do not regard as the most free of men, but rather as slaves of impulse. To seek to free the will from reason is to seek to destroy the freedom of man.

2. **Reason Is the Basis of Freedom.** That the Angelic Doctor considered reason as the only basis of freedom he makes very clear in article 2, question XXIV, of *De Veritate,* where he is answering the question whether brute animals have free will. Appetite, he says, always follows knowledge; that is to say, it follows a judgment that something is good. If this judgment is determined to a particular good, appetite will necessarily be moved to this good, and its operation will not be free. This is the case with animals. They have, it is true, a certain faculty of judging which approaches a likeness of reason, but which is not truly reason. Their judgments are made by their natural estimative sense, and are determined by nature to what is sensed as good. These judgments deal only with particular sensible goods, and have no reference to universals, which animals cannot apprehend; consequently they cannot gather particular goods under the concept of the universal good in order to compare them as to goodness. Their judgments as to good or harm are determined for them by their own nature and the nature of the thing perceived. They naturally judge something to be good without knowing the

reason for this judgment. Consequently, the judgments which they make are not in their own power but are determined by something else; namely, the natural instinct implanted in them. Therefore their appetite, which follows judgment, and their operation, which follows appetite, are not in their own power either, but, like the judgment which they follow, are determined by something else.

3. Man Is Free Because He Can Reflect. The only case in which the judgment of an agent is in the agent's own power is when he can judge about the judgment itself; that is to say, when he knows not only what he judges but also the reason why he judges as he does. This ability to judge about one's own judgments belongs only to the rational power, or reason; for reason alone can reflect upon its own acts, and know the conditions and relationships of the things about which it judges and which are the reasons why, in any given case, it judges as it does. Knowing the reasons according to which it passes a certain judgment, it can weigh these reasons against other ones, which may warrant a contrary judgment, and thus it can call its own judgments up to be judged. Just as we approve or condemn the judgments made by other men, so we can approve or condemn a judgment made by ourselves; and in both cases we base the approval or condemnation upon our evaluation of the reasons on which the judgment in question is based. We can do this in the case of our own judgments because our intellect is capable of reflecting upon itself, upon its own acts, and upon the reasons for these acts. Animals cannot do it because they lack intellect, and consequently cannot reflect upon their own judgments and know the reasons why they made those judgments.

4. We Compare Goods to the Good. Appetite follows knowledge in us, just as it does in animals. But reason makes a big difference, and that difference is free will. We saw above that the only good which moves the will necessarily is the absolute good, or that which is good under every aspect. When we judge some particular thing or act to be good, we can, as has just been explained, hold this judgment itself up for judgment. When we do, we see that the reason on which we based the judgment is not the absolute good, but is one particular good among many, is mixed also with evil aspects, is not necessarily related to the absolute good, and may even be, under the circumstances, opposed to it. These considerations of reason leave our intellect free to pronounce a contrary judgment; and since these considerations are within our power whenever our judgment concerns a particular good, all such judgments remain in our power to accept or reject; that is, they remain free. Consequently, rational appetite or will, which follows judgment, remains free. Thus every agent which possesses reason possesses free will.

This same argument is given much more briefly in the *Summa Theologica*:[29]

> Man has free choice, or otherwise counsels, exhortations, commands, prohibitions, rewards and punishments would be in vain. In order to make this evident, we must observe that some things act without judgment, as a stone moves downwards; and in like manner all things which lack knowledge. And some act from judgment, but not a free judgment; as brute animals. For the sheep, seeing the wolf, judges it a thing to be shunned, from a natural and not a free judgment; because it judges, not from deliberation, but from natural instinct. And the same thing is to be said of any judgment in brute animals. Now man acts from judgment, because by his apprehensive power he judges that something should be avoided or sought. But because this judgment, in the case of some particular act, is not from a natural instinct, but from some act of comparison in the reason, therefore he acts from free judgment and retains the power of being inclined to various things. For reason in contingent matters may follow opposite courses, as we have seen in dialectical syllogisms and rhetorical arguments. Now particular operations are contingent, and therefore in such matters the judgment of reason may follow opposite courses, and is not determinate to one. And in that man is rational, it is necessary that he have free choice.

5. St. Thomas' Argument for Free Will. It is interesting to note that St. Thomas' appeal, in the first sentence above, to the efficacy of counsels, commands, rewards, punishments, etc., is not meant by him in the sense in which it is so often interpreted. The usual interpretation makes his argument purely pragmatic: we do and we must, it says, treat men as if they have free choice; we exhort them, threaten them, command them, promise things to them, in order to influence their choice; but we would not do this unless we considered them to be free agents; therefore, they are free agents. Now this is not what St. Thomas means. His argument is not at all pragmatic. He is not offering as evidence for free will the manner in which we treat other men; he is offering the rational factors which we consider in making our own choices. We actually weigh commands, threats, promises, etc.,

[29] I, 83, 1, c (Pegis, *op. cit.*, Vol. I, p. 787).

in our deliberations and they are real factors in influencing our final judgment; but they could not be — they "would be in vain" — if that judgment were determined to one thing; and therefore that judgment must be free. That is what St. Thomas means, as is made clear from the phrase, "In order to make this evident," by which he connects the two parts of the argument. His argument, therefore, may be briefly summarized thus: The will chooses according to a judgment of reason which compares several particular alternatives. These alternatives must be really contingent, because if they were not, the judgment would be, like the instinctive judgments of animals, determined to one thing. But if the judgment were determined to one thing, counsel, command, threat, promise, etc., could not be real factors in the deliberations leading up to the judgment, as in fact they are. Consequently, the judgment of reason about a particular act to be done is free. Therefore the will, which chooses according to this judgment, is free. "The fact that man is master of his actions is due to his being able to deliberate about them; for since the deliberating reason is indifferently disposed to opposites, the will can proceed to either."[30]

V. THE DETERMINATION OF THE WILL

1. The Root of Free Will. What is perhaps the most thorough single statement of St. Thomas' teaching on the freedom of the human will is found in *De Malo*, article 6. The Angelic Doctor begins by stating rather bluntly that the denial of free will is unphilosophical; for ethics, the science of the moral character of human actions, is destroyed if a man's actions are not freely determined by himself. The moral philosopher should no more waste his time arguing with someone who denies human freedom than the physicist should pay attention to someone who denies that there is any motion in the world. The philosopher and the scientist do not have to take into account, in their arguments, those who deny the subject matter and the first principles of philosophy or science. Then St. Thomas goes on to state succinctly the ultimate reason for human free will: since the form in the intellect which is the principle of the will's movement is a *universal,* and since actions pertain to *singulars,* none of which equals the universal principle, the movement of the will remains *indeterminate* in respect to many different things; only the man himself determines it to one or another of

[30] *S. Theol.,* I–II. 6. 2. ad 2.

them. The will, which necessarily desires the universal good, is free in respect to any particular good, just as a man who desires to build a house is still free to build a stone house or a frame house.

2. Specification and Exercise. In his further explanation Aquinas introduces the distinction between the *specification* and the *exercise* of the will-act. The determination of a power of action to actual operation is twofold: The power must be determined as to *what specific action* is to be done, and it must also be determined as to *whether to act or not act*, and in what manner to act. The former determination has to do with specification, and it comes from the object of the act; thus, when I see, it is the object seen which determines or specifies what color I see. The latter determination concerns exercise, and it comes from the subject; thus, it is the condition of my eyes that determines whether I see or not and whether I see well or poorly. In an act of will, that which moves the will as to *specification* and object is the intellect, since the intellect presents the will with the apprehended good which moves it to desire. In respect to *exercise*, the will itself is its own moving principle, for the will as agent moves all the powers of the soul, including itself.

3. Mutual Influence of Will and Intellect. The will in moving itself is not mover and moved, actual and potential, in the same respect; for it is by willing one thing that the will moves itself to will another, as a student, by willing to pass an examination, moves his will to will to study. Nor, again, is the will, in moving itself to will, moving itself without at the same time and in the same movement being moved by the intellect. Why does the student *will* to study? Because he first wills to pass the examination. But why does he will *to study?* Because he *understands* that to study is good for him since it is a means to pass the examination. The will, as St. Thomas expresses it, cannot move itself "without the aid of counsel."[31] Its act of willing the end moves it to a deliberation about the means to the end. So that even in the act whereby the will moves itself to will, or to exercise its act, the will is also moved by the intellect.

But if the intellect plays a part in the determination as to exercise, which is primarily the work of the will, so does the will play a part in the determination as to species, which is primarily the work of the intellect. Suppose there is a dance on a night when the students ought to study for the examination. Some students will choose to study;

[31] *S. Theol.*, I–II, 9, 4, c.

others will choose to go to the dance. Both groups desire to pass the examination, and both understand that under such circumstances to study is a good. But so is it good to dance. It really is not good, under the circumstances; *but you don't have to think about the circumstances.* You can follow the advice of the lad who says, "Aw, forget about the exam! Come on, get dressed." By thinking about the fun of the dance, and not thinking about the exam, the intellect is determining the will as to species, for it is presenting the dance as being *only* good and *not* bad, and thus inclining the will to it. But the will itself is not so innocent as it might like to appear. Why did the intellect forget the exam and turn its attention to the fun? Surely it got a little nudge from the will. You *thought* about the dance because you *wanted to;* and the more you thought about it the more you wanted to go. Maybe the examination tried to sneak back into your intellect, but your will was strong — you resolutely repelled the evil thought. Thus, by thinking, you determined the course your will would choose; but your will had had plenty to do with what you thought about. And, similarly, by willing the end, your will moved itself to the actual willing of the means; but even in moving itself it was moved by your understanding of the relation of the means to the end, that is to say, by deliberation, which is an act of the intellect.

4. The First Movement of the Will. How did the whole thing start? If you could move your will only by deliberating, and if each particular deliberation presupposed a prior act of willing to deliberate, you would never actually will anything, because you would always have to will something else first. You would be in the position of someone attempting to climb a ladder after having agreed not to step on any rung except after first stepping off another. The first rung would give you a lot of trouble. Of course, if you were smart, you would not have made the agreement before you were firmly planted on the first rung. The rest would be easy. St. Thomas, who was smart, maintained that the will must be, in fact, on the first rung to start with.

Prior to any movement which the will gives to itself by willing, it has a movement which is given to it by an extrinsic agent; so that every series of acts, in which the will successively determines itself to new acts, begins from a movement of the will to which it does not determine itself but to which it is determined by an exterior agent. This exterior agent is the author of the will's nature: God.[32]

This movement of the will by God, the First Mover of all movements, is not to be confused with the natural movement of the will to the absolute good or happiness. This natural movement is, of course, also from God; but it is not, strictly speaking, a movement. Rather it is the will itself, that is to say a *nature, form,* or *power* of man. As a power, it must be brought from potency to act in order to operate. The apprehended good presented to it by the intellect cannot, of itself, reduce the will from potency to act. In the first place, this apprehended good makes the will actual *as a power* or inclination, for the will is defined as the inclination for the good apprehended by reason; so that before the apprehension of the good the will is not actual even as an inclination. The apprehended good makes it actual in that respect, but something more is required to make it actual as operation. There is one good which, if directly apprehended, would actualize the will as both power and operation at once. This is the absolute good. But this good is never concretely presented to us in this life, as we saw above. Consequently, the object presented to the will by the intellect never moves it necessarily to will, but simply gives it an inclination to will. This means that the object or end leaves the will in potency in respect to the operation of willing. Consequently, the will still needs *to be moved,* since nothing moves itself from potency to act in the same respect. God moves it, as St. Thomas says, speaking here of God as agent or First Efficient Cause rather than as End or Absolute Good.[33]

5. God's Movement of The Will. By so moving the will, God does not destroy its own freedom of movement. To begin with, He moves it to act; but to act, for the will, means to will, that is to say, to act voluntarily. Second, He moves it according to the nature which He has first given it, just as He moves every agent according to its own nature — necessary agents to necessary acts and free agents to free acts. It is true that He moves the will to will necessarily the absolute good, but, as we have seen, no particular will-act in this life directly concerns the absolute good. The particular act is a choice of some particular good, chosen as a means to the absolute good, happiness. By moving the will according to its own nature, God moves it to the absolute good necessarily and to particular goods indeterminately,

[32] *De Malo, loc. cit.; S. Theol.,* I–II, 9, 4, c.
[33] *S. Theol.,* I–II, 10, 4, c, justifies the argument of this paragraph.

so that His movement leaves it free to choose or not choose, and free to choose one or another particular good.[34]

6. The Nature and Scope of The Will's Freedom. Since the human will, in order to act, needs to be determined both as to specification and as to exercise, it was not possible to define precisely the nature and scope of its freedom of action without having first understood how it receives both these kinds of determination. Now we are in a position to define what freedom the will possesses; indeed we need do little more than summarize all we have said above. In this summary, we still follow St. Thomas' exposition in *De Malo*, 6.

In respect to the specification of its act, what moves the will is something apprehended as good and suitable. If something appears good but not suitable, as, for example, pointing out to one's employer the less lovable aspects of his personality, it does not move the will. Now the will moves itself to choice through deliberation, and deliberation and choice are concerned with *particular* goods and actions. Consequently, for something to be apprehended as good and suitable, so as to determine the will, it must be apprehended as good and suitable *in particular;* that is to say, as this concrete action in these actual circumstances, and not merely as a certain kind of action in general. If, therefore, some object is apprehended as good and suitable in *every* respect and under all circumstances, it will move the will by necessity. Such an object is beatitude or happiness. Hence, beatitude determines the will, *as to specification,* by necessity: presented with beatitude, the will could not reject it or will something contrary to it. Yet even here, some freedom of choice is left to the will. For this necessary determination of the will concerns only specification, and does not concern exercise. While we cannot contemplate beatitude and choose its opposite, we are still not compelled to choose beatitude; *for we can will not to think of beatitude;* and if we do not think of it, we do not have to choose it. The reason why we can will not to think of the absolute good is the fact that our intellectual acts are themselves particulars, and the will, being free in respect to all particulars, can move the intellect to think of one thing rather than another.

---

[34] *De Malo, loc. cit.,* and other places. The many problems which arise concerning God's movement of the will and the will's freedom cannot be treated fairly before we have studied about God. Hence we have left them for Chapters XXIII, XXV, and XXVI.

So much for the absolute good. If a good which is not absolute, that is to say, which is not good and suitable in every particular respect, is presented to the will, it does not determine it necessarily either as to specification or exercise. Since such a good is not good and suitable in every respect, it is evil or unsuitable in some respect and its opposite is good and suitable in that respect. Studying is good and suitable in respect to passing the examination, but it is bad and unsuitable in respect to having fun with one's friends; and in just this respect going to the dance is good and suitable. Hence, when presented with the good object, namely, studying, the will can turn the intellect to the evil aspects of this object and to the good aspects of its opposite; and since it can always do this when presented with particular goods, no particular good can determine it necessarily. Consequently, in respect to particular goods, the will is free both as regards exercise and specification. In final summary: the will is necessarily moved by absolute good in regard to specification; but in regard to exercise it is not moved necessarily by anything at all.[35]

VI. THE WILL OF THE INDIVIDUAL

1. So far we have been speaking about the will in general, but, of course, there is no such thing; there is only your will and my will and every other individual person's will. Furthermore, we have spoken only about the will and the intellect, that is to say, the rational part of man; whereas in fact non-rational factors play an extremely important part in influencing our acts of will. It is they, more than anything else, which make the difference between your will and mine. St. Thomas treats of these non-rational factors, and once more the remarkable unity of his thought is apparent. Man is a composite being, an organism animated by a rational soul; he possesses a sensitive nature as real as that of any animal and as truly part of his person as is his rational soul. He lives in a material world and he is material himself, so far as his body is concerned. Nothing which affects him as a part of corporeal nature and nothing which occurs within his own corporeal organism, is without effect in his soul, and therefore in his will. Man is free. He is a "little lower than the angels." But if he is not careful, he can become a lot lower than the brutes. In making his decisions, his will is not only guided by reason but it is influenced by

[35] For perfectly clear statements of the above doctrine, shorter than that of *De Malo*. the student should read *S. Theol.*, I–II, 10, 2, and *ibid.*, 13, 6.

his habits or his character, by his sensitive passions, by the permanent and momentary dispositions of his temperament and his body and even by the external physical forces of the world. He remains free, but with a freedom subject to an infinity of extra-voluntary influences, such influences as modern psychology studies under the head of heredity and environment, organic predisposition, the subconscious, emotional stability or instability, etc.

2. **General Factors in Choice.** Why does the individual make the particular choices which he does make? In *De Malo,* 6, St. Thomas lists three general factors or influences. The first is the rational factor which we have already treated: we may choose one thing rather than another because it appears to reason to outweigh the other in goodness. This is the way in which we ought to choose and in which we always would choose if we were purely rational. If that were the case, our wrong choices would always be due to an error of intellect or a perversity of will. In truth, however, we do not always determine our choice according to the dictate of even our own fallible reason. We can use our reason so as to arrive at an unreasonable choice; for a second factor which influences our decisions is the direction in which we turn the attention of our intellect. Thus, as we have seen, by thinking of the fun that we would have at the dance and by not thinking of the examination which we have to pass we can determine our wills to choose the dance. When we now raise the question, Why do some of us think of the fun and others of the examination, and so determine our wills oppositely? we come to a consideration of the non-rational factors which operate when an individual determines his voluntary acts.

3. **Dispositions Arising From External Circumstances.** These factors may all be called dispositions of the agent willing, for they all are forces within the individual influencing his will. Some of these dispositions arise from external circumstances. Thus, the student who is invited to go to the dance just at a moment when all the injustices and stupidities of what is outrageously called higher education are torturing his sensitive soul, will be more likely to say yes, than will his roommate, who, having had recent sad proof of the unfairness and irrationality of the lovelier sex, is seeking solace in the soothing calm which a sane and rational philosophy book brings, sometimes. Other dispositions arise from the individual's nature, or his previous

actions, and these are far more potent influences upon his will. So let us give our attention to them.

4. Dispositions Arising From Internal Causes. Of these dispositions some are natural to man because they are inseparable from the absolute good, happiness. Thus a man is naturally disposed to desire to live and to know. Such natural dispositions incline the will of necessity; rooted in the very nature of the will, they are not under its free control. We can, however, choose to act in a way contrary to these necessary dispositions; as, for example, when a martyr chooses death rather than renunciation of the faith, or when a hero sacrifices his life to save another's, or when a man commits suicide. Yet the disposition itself and the inclination which it gives to the will are *necessary* even in such cases. We may, in some circumstance, choose to die because death seems, in that circumstance, necessarily related to happiness; but we cannot make death itself *seem* good and we cannot remove from our will its repugnance to death. We have to view death as life — the portal to the blessed life. So the grace-illumined reason of the martyr sees death; and so, too, the deranged reason of the suicide sees it. The hero sees it as the only means to fulfill duty and to remain himself; cowardice, in his eyes, is greater self-destruction than death.

Other dispositions do not necessarily incline the will, but are themselves under the control of reason. Those which have the greatest power over the will are habits, because habit affects the soul so intimately as to become virtually a second nature. Along with the passions of the sensitive appetites and the qualities of the body itself, habits constitute a man's character; and it is said that men make their choices according to what kind of men they are.[36] This is indeed true, if it is properly understood. Very obviously, different things appear good to a sensual man and to a spiritual man, or to a temperate man and an intemperate man.[37] The more often a man has chosen a merely sensual good, the more likely he is to do so again; and the more often a man has chosen the rational good in preference to the sensual good, the more likely he is to choose similarly again. Both men may deliberate in order to reach a final judgment as to which good is to be chosen, but, as we have seen, the will itself guides

[36] *De Malo*, 6, Obj. 3.
[37] *S. Theol.*, I–II, 9, 2.

deliberation by turning the mind to one aspect or another of the alternative goods proposed. The habits of the sensual man will press strong upon him to turn his intellect to the sensual aspects of the good proposed; while his passions, from many past victories, will exhibit an insolent disregard for the commands of his reason. The temperate or spiritual man, on the other hand, will find his habits inclining his will to the side of the rational good, and will find his passions, though present, under the control of his will. If, indeed, habit did not strongly influence will, man's pursuit of his final end would be most precarious; after many years of virtuous living, a good man would be just as liable as a degenerate to choose to sin. Habit is what makes progress possible, because it is by habit that we retain the fruit of our past good actions.[38] The other side of the picture is, of course, that each new evil choice fixes the evil man more firmly in his evil ways and blocks off for him the way to his final end, beatitude. Men choose, indeed, according to their characters; but if this is taken to mean that they do not freely determine their own actions, that is erroneous. It was, in the first place, chiefly by their own free choices that they formed their characters — building up habits, good or bad, and placing their passions in subordination to or in ascendancy over their reason; if it is true that we act as we are, it is also true that we are as we have acted.

In the second place, men retain command of will over their habits and passions as long as they retain the use of reason. It is hard for a drunkard to stop drinking, but he can do so just as long as drink has not yet driven him quite mad. Similarly, it is hard for an incontinent man to be chaste, but he can be so just as long as sexual indulgence has not stripped him of reason. For as long as he retains the exercise of reason he is capable of calling up before the bar of his own reflecting judgment his judgments about what is desirable; and, as we have seen, this ability of reason to judge its own judgments in the light of the absolute good is the root of freedom.[39]

We do not need to say very much about physical dispositions in the body and external physical forces acting upon the body. Only one view of the relation of these to the will was possible for St. Thomas, given his theory of man's nature. The will is a power of the rational soul, and the rational soul is the one substantial form of a man. With

[38] *S. Theol.*, I–II, 49, 4, c, ad 1, ad 3; 50, ad 1, ad 3.
[39] *S. Theol.*, I–II, 10, 3.

the body it makes the man a single hylemorphic substance — a fully natural being in the natural world, even though something more than this. Nothing affecting the body can fail to affect the soul, for body and soul are one in actual being. Hence no disposition of the body, nor any external force upon the body, can be without its influence on the will. Such dispositions and forces, it is true, affect sensitive appetite directly, rather than will; but the will is moved through the sensitive appetites.[40] Though all these factors influence the will, none of them determine it. To this truth we must devote the next chapter.

[40] *S. Theol.*, I–II, 9, 5, c, ad 2 and ad 3.

CHAPTER XIII

FREE WILL AND DETERMINISM

I. MECHANISTIC DETERMINISM, OR BEHAVIORISM

1. Behaviorism. Any doctrine of human action which denies the real ability of men to choose freely what acts they shall do is called by the general name *determinism*. We have already given St. Thomas' answers to the chief types of deterministic theory. Yet it will be well to say a brief word about some of the more popular doctrines opposed to freedom of will. We have chosen three: materialistic or mechanistic determinism, psychological determinism of the type taught by many contemporary naturalists, and intellectual determinism, taught by Leibniz and which some philosophers charge St. Thomas himself with teaching. A fourth doctrine, namely theological determinism, we must defer until our study in later chapters of God's action upon His creatures.

The philosophy of mechanistic materialism has no room for free will. Whatever exists is material, according to that philosophy, and therefore whatever occurs is a material event and is necessarily determined by physical law. Man's supposedly free actions are the results of purely physical forces acting upon his body and determining his reactions. The basic activity of man and of every animal is *reflex action*. Every movement of a man, every thought and decision which he makes, is an automatic response of his nervous system to some stimulus, either a natural stimulus or one to which the response has become associated through "conditioning." Strike a man just below his knee cap, on the patellar tendon, and his leg jerks out; wave something suddenly close to his eyes, and his eyelids automatically flicker down and up again, that is, he blinks; expose his nostrils to roasting beef, and his salivary glands step up their secretions and his appetite is aroused. Some of man's actions, like deciding whether to marry or whom to marry, or deciding to commit his nation to war against another great nation, or deciding whether to assent to the behavioristic philosophy (the one we are now explaining) or Thomistic philosophy or extreme idealism — some actions like these are more complicated than the knee jerk and the eye blink, that is, they involve more complex external stimuli and a more complex pattern of nerve discharges, but they are exactly the same kind of action. Thinking, for example, is merely the movements of the vocal organs; i.e., it is subvocal speech. Man is like a chewing-gum machine: push in a stimulus and out pops a response; or, perhaps, he is like an extremely complex calculating machine: put in all the numbers and out comes — inevitably — the right, the only, answer.

2. **Criticism of Behaviorism.** Behaviorism, or materialistic determinism, is a purely *a priori* theory based on the assumption that nothing but matter is real. It cannot be said truthfully that there is any evidence, even incomplete, inconclusive evidence, for it. Reflex action is, of course, a reality. But instead of being made the basis of a renewal of materialistic philosophy of human nature, its discovery and explanation should have had the effect of finally discrediting that philosophy. It was perhaps possible to believe that all human actions are automatic before any of them were definitely known to be so and before the characteristic traits of reflex action were known. But once these things became known, the excuse for behaviorism disappeared, for it was now possible to compare voluntary actions with actions known to be automatic, and to define precisely some, at least, of the irreducible differences between them. Many psychologists did just this. But the behaviorists chose to assume that voluntary actions are automatic and that their apparent differences from ordinary reflexes are merely the result of their greater complexity.

If there is no evidence for behaviorism, is there any against it? Every moment of conscious awareness is sufficient evidence to disprove behaviorism absolutely. Behaviorism identifies mind with body, mental with material; that is to say, it denies mind and the mental. John B. Watson, the founder of the behaviorist school of psychology, began by saying that *he did not need to consider conscious states or phenomena,* such as feeling, sensation, images, thoughts, desires, and volitions, but he ended by saying that *there are no such phenomena,* that nothing at all corresponds to the terms consciousness, feeling, sensation, willing, etc. All human behavior is merely movement — neural, muscular, glandular movement, and nothing more. If Watson or any behaviorist really means this, then he does not experience any feelings, sensations, desires, or decisions; he is not conscious of them or of anything. Clearly, then, argument with him is impossible. He neither hears you, nor thinks of what you say, nor thinks of what he answers. To convince him, you would have to have a perfect understanding of his nervous system and brain, so that you could bring to bear upon them the physical stimuli which would start a chain reaction in agreement with your argument. Logic, in such a situation, is identical with physics, anatomy, and physiology. Of course, you will not be able to get rid entirely of the suspicion that he really does see you, hear you, consider your arguments, and think of his own answers; but on the assumption of his sincerity and his honest desire to get at the truth, you will put these suspicions behind you. Even then, you may not be able to avoid wondering what *he* means by sincerity and honest desire. If these are movements of nerves, muscles, and glands, it is difficult to see why they are *better* movements than certain other movements, namely insincerity and dishonesty. Behaviorism, in a word, is absurd.

3. **The Lesson in Behaviorism.** Behaviorism is absurd, but the fact that such an absurdity should have captured considerable attention in psychological circles for even a short time is salutary. Materialism is a theory which is incompatible with the fact of conscious activity of any sort. The experimental psychologists against whose methods the behaviorists had revolted — psychologists like Wundt and his followers — had taken psychic or mental phenomena and states as the data for their studies and experiments. All efforts to build a purely materialistic theory out of these data, or to account for them on materialistic grounds, failed. So the behaviorists drew the natural conclusion that these are the wrong data, since it is self-evident that materialistic theory is capable of explaining everything real. At first they only said that their predecessors in scientific psychology were using the wrong data; that they should be measuring physical changes in the body instead of conscious changes in the mind. But it soon dawned on them that mental data, right or wrong, have no right to exist at all, on the materialistic assumption. So they took the final step and denied the existence of conscious phenomena, and thus they saved materialism. Therein lies the great service which they have rendered to human thought: they have shown clearly the price which it is necessary to pay in order to be faithful to the materialistic assumption.

If this lesson is applied to the question of free will, its directive is clear. We must start with facts, with data; and we must make a theory which fits the facts, not a theory which denies them. If we sometimes determine our own course of action by means of conscious deliberations, comparisons, final judgments, and decisions based upon reasons which we understand, then we must formulate a theory which explains this fact, but which does not explain it away. Even if we can formulate no theory which explains the fact, we must not deny the fact. Rather we must say: "On many occasions I freely make up my own mind what to do. I know why I choose what I choose on these occasions, and I know that I am quite capable of choosing otherwise. *How* I am capable of this, I do not understand. I understand it no better than I understand how, when light falls upon the retinas of my eyes, and starts a chain of neural processes which terminate in my brain, *I see*."

4. **Thomism and Behaviorism.** The Thomistic philosopher sees in behaviorism a truth perverted — perverted, as truth so often is, by being made exclusive. A corollary of the Thomistic doctrine of hylemorphism, taken together with the principle of causality, is that no action of a man which involves his body can fail to have, from the first movement of his sense organ by an external stimulus to the last ounce of the body's movement expended against some external thing, an unbroken chain of physical and physiological "causes"; for example, neural, glandular, and muscular processes. That the action in question is voluntary and free affects the situation not one whit. Man's will comes into action only in reference to some object known by his intellect; his intellect gets its object through his senses; his senses operate through his nervous system and special sense organs. The will, in turn, moves the body through the body's own organic powers, as we have seen in Chapter IX. The physiological processes involved in acting are only parts of the whole action; indeed, they are parts which are determined by the will-act itself as means to its execution. The belief that the discovery and the detailed description of these processes refutes the contention that the act proceeds from the free agency of the will, does not seem to have any sense or logic behind it at all. Behaviorism perverts the truth that man's voluntary acts are elicited in response to some external object sensibly perceived and are executed through his bodily organs, to the falsehood that these organs, moved by external forces, completely determine man's actions. The Thomistic doctrine recognizes fully the necessary part which physical stimuli, bodily

organs, and physiological conditions play in voluntary activity, but it refuses to ignore the immediate knowledge which each of us has on many occasions of freely and rationally choosing his own course of action.

5. **Physical Science and Free Will.** Mechanists have not all felt compelled to give any *evidence* that man does not have free will, because they have felt that science settles the question. They maintain that science rules out free actions as incompatible with the principles of inertia and the conservation of energy, principles which are essential to the very method of scientific research. A free act of a man would be one wherein he set himself in motion by an absolute start, physically speaking; no prior movement, no antecedent communication of energy, would be presupposed to this action. The man would move by just "willing" to move; that is, a body would begin to move without any physical force having been exerted upon it. But if any movement or any event could occur in the physical world without an adequate physical cause, no scientific principle could have any value.

In order to meet this objection it is not necessary to hold that physical laws apply any less rigidly to human actions, in so far as these actions are physical, than they do to any other material processes. No amount of "strength of will" will enable a man to lift a bag of potatoes without expending the same amount of physical energy, measured in horse-power units, which a machine would expend in lifting the same bag. If free actions could be carried out in the world without being subject to all the physical laws which operate in the world, every golfer would score 18 for every round. But to conclude from this that men are not free to lift potatoes or not, to play golf or not, is a gross *non sequitur*. The translation of a man's will-acts into bodily acts places these acts in the domain of physical law. This, as the examples above are meant to illustrate, is certainly so for the world outside our skins. Contrary to the prewar song, wishing will *not* make it so; to effect our will on the world outside our skins we have to exert precisely the amount of energy required to overcome the inertia of the materials with which we are working.

The situation may be the same for the world inside our skins. "You cannot, by taking thought, add to your stature one cubit." Our will must, in order to act, have motives; and motives are things known. The materials for all our knowledge come to us through our sense organs, and these are moved only by physical energies. Who is to say that any of the energy that comes to us from without is ever lost; or that any energy, even so much as is required to form the mental image of a desirable object, ever "starts up" within the organism? A typical voluntary act situation begins with some physical stimulus setting a sense organ in motion; this motion produces movement in the sensory nerve and then in the brain, where the physical organ of the internal senses is located. All these movements are the organic side of perception and of the formation of a phantasm; they are the physical processes which are instrumental in the performance of these conscious actions. The subsequent actions, namely, the understanding of the perceived object, the consideration, acceptance, or rejection of it as a suitable motive for choice, and the choice itself, involve no motion — no physical processes — because they are purely immaterial actions. But before the man can act in accordance with his choice, he must get back to the world of material particulars; he must re-translate the intelligible good into a particular object of action; he must form a phantasm. He can form it only out of sensory materials perceived and preserved in his imagination. This psychological truth seems to imply a corresponding physical truth, because the imagination uses a bodily organ. The physical truth would be that the organ of imagination cannot form the image except by using energy received in the past and stored up. This energy is sufficient to arouse movement in the motor nerves which govern muscular action. From there on, in the voluntary action, the motive powers of the body take over. Nobody supposes that they create any energy. Consequently, nowhere along the line is there any question of any new energy or any movement starting from an absolute beginning; every movement is accounted for by a prior movement; every expenditure of energy, by energy received and stored up in the organism.

This account would seem to be a necessary implication of man's hylemorphic constitution. Its denial would seem to imply that man's soul could, by itself, be the subject and agent of an *organic* power and operation, and that his sensory powers could operate without a bodily organ. Both these suppositions are quite contrary to St. Thomas' conception of the mode of union between body and soul and of the manner in which the soul "moves the body." The soul moves the body, we have seen, only through the powers which it, as substantial form, confers on the body: the animated body moves itself. Man's free will is his power to determine his own actions according to rational motives. But he is a composite of matter and form; and regardless of how free he is to choose between possible actions, he is quite incapable of effectuating his choice in the material world in which he lives except through his own corporeal self, and this corporeal self is obedient to all the laws of the physical world of which it is a part. We are free to do what we wish, within our power; we transcend physics and chemistry by virtue of our spiritual soul, but, as remarked in previous chapters, we do not skip them. We freely choose what we will do; but physical laws make the rules according to which we do what we choose. You may, if you wish, call this relation of will to physical and physiological forces mysterious. But it is no more mysterious than the fact that brain movements produce conscious images in the imagination or that neural movements originating when light strikes the retina produce seeing. No one ought to deny free will on the ground of the mysterious character of its relation to physics and physiology unless he is prepared to deny seeing, hearing, smelling, feeling, pleasure, and pain on precisely the same ground. Dogmatic materialism has no more room in its scheme of things for the humblest conscious phenomenon than it has for free will.

II. A CONTEMPORARY NATURALISTIC VIEW

1. **Rejection of Mechanism.** Some contemporary naturalistic philosophers reject mechanistic determinism of the behavioristic type, yet hold that determinism is universal in nature; men's voluntary actions are, they say, determined by causal law, and, though man is free, he does not possess free will in the metaphysical sense. Mechanistic determinism is wrong because it reduces all the apparently higher levels of being, operation, and law in nature to the one lowest level of matter in motion. This reductionism the new naturalists reject, as we have already seen. There is in nature, they hold, a real emergence of novelty, a real evolution which produces higher levels of being and novel sets of laws which operate on these higher levels and which cannot be reduced to the laws of the lower levels. Hence *mechanistic* determinism must be rejected. Yet *determinism* cannot be rejected. Determinism in its broadest sense means that all events in nature occur according to the principle of causality; and this means that every event is the outcome of prior events and conditions in such a way that its occurrence conforms to law, and consequently

is theoretically predictable. In other words, every natural event is determined by some law of nature, but there are different levels of law in nature. Human voluntary actions are determined, but they are determined by laws which are peculiar to human action and not by the laws of inert matter.

2. Rejection of Free Will. Hence, metaphysical freedom of will must be rejected. Metaphysical freedom of will would mean that our will-acts are not caused; that their occurrence is not determined by any law; that, with one single set of antecedent conditions leading up to a voluntary act, we might will one way or another or not at all. This belief cannot be accepted. It would place will-acts outside the order of nature, thus making them something supernatural. It would render impossible any systematic scientific study of human action, for no natural conditions would govern the occurrence of such actions. It would preclude the possibility of social control and direction of man's voluntary behavior, through which control alone we have any hope of bettering the condition of human society. It would preclude control of even our own actions, since we can control events only by controlling the causes and conditions which determine them. It would destroy the conception of responsibility for our voluntary behavior, for we cannot be held responsible for actions which simply spring into being spontaneously from no controllable conditions; all our actions would be accidents, and we are not held morally responsible for accidents. Finally, the metaphysical conception of free will is in itself philosophically untenable, holding, as it does, the existence in the world of uncaused, law-free events.[1]

3. Naturalist Interpretation of Freedom. Yet naturalism, so many of whose proponents are sincerely and seriously concerned with the social and political freedom of man, needs a doctrine of human freedom. Hence for the rejected conception of metaphysical freedom there is substituted an empirical account of freedom. This account seeks to study those factors in human behavior which lead to undesirable choices, and those which lead to desirable courses of choice.[2] The former study is concerned with freedom in a negative sense: an act is voluntary or "free" if it is not the result of coercive and undesirable

---

[1] From: *Philosophy: An Introduction*, by Randall and Buchler, pp. 234–238. By permission of Barnes and Noble, Inc., New York. Abraham Edel, *The Theory and Practice of Philosophy* (New York: Harcourt, Brace, 1946), Chap. 17.

[2] Edel, *op. cit.*, p. 229 ff., whence the present account is almost entirely drawn.

factors; it is involuntary if it is forced from us by undesirable pressures. When I hand a man my money because he is pointing a gun at me, my act is involuntary; when I pay money for an object which I wish to acquire, my act is voluntary. Just which undesirable factors are to be considered coercive, in the sense of destroying voluntariness, is decided by social values; thus, our present society would not hold me responsible for giving up to a gunman even someone else's money, but it would hold me responsible for killing a friend at the command of a gunman. Hence, "as a negative concept, freedom is . . . an indirect vehicle for social value judgments concerning the kinds of restraints people in a given society find effective but undesirable."[3]

Freedom as a positive concept means "the presence of traits of character that issue in or encourage desirable lines of choice. The content of freedom as positive is then social in origin and reference. The ideals of character which it embodies will differ with what a given society or group takes to be the desirable direction of choice." Even from individual to individual the concept of freedom will vary. A man who believes himself free because he is able to follow every impulse and desire, is regarded by a temperate man as a slave of impulse and desire, while he regards the temperate man as a slave to convention and timidity. Yet we can formulate an objective or universal concept of a "free man." He is the integrated man, the various parts of whose nature have been harmoniously developed:

> . He suffers no conflict of appetite and reason because his desires have become stably organized according to the system that is reason. . . . He knows himself and the direction of his aims and can estimate clearly the situations under which they can effectively be realized. . . . The aims of others are constituent elements of the pattern of his values. In short, his integration is not merely within himself, but with the physical and social environment. . . .
>
> In all these senses positive freedom is not something *given* to man, with which he is natively endowed. It is the product of careful nurture in well-ordered society. Some men more nearly approximate the ideal than others, but if the ideal is actually to be attained in a specific society, sanctions and influences will have to be so arranged as to guide men in that direction. In short, the problem of clarifying a positive conception of freedom is the problem of the direction of an educational system and the ideals of desirable character which it embodies.[4]

4. Critical Comment. A Thomist cannot but consider the above

[3] *Ibid.*, p. 232.   [4] *Ibid.*, pp. 233–234.

interpretation of man's freedom as a simple case of sidestepping the issue. In the first place, the man described is really "the good man," and naming him "the free man" seems only to be a sugar coating for the pill — the pill being the fact that naturalism has no definition of freedom, because determinism and freedom cannot be reconciled in the one conception. The man described is a good man according to the values of democratic society; but he is not, on the basis of the theory under discussion, a free man; he is, on the contrary, an inevitable product of physical, psychological, and social factors. That the factors in question produce a desirable product does not make that product free. Neither this good man, nor his opposite number, the bad man, ever once interposes himself freely into the process of the formation of his character or the determination of his actions; every single factor, internal as well as external, and including his will itself, which contributed to making him what he is, was determined antecedently to and independently of any choice he may have made. His "choices" may have felt like choices, but they were not really choices. In the second place, the empirical study and control of the traits of character leading to desirable lines of choice are irrelevant to the question of whether man has or has not free will. Such a study is an approach to another question, namely, how and to what extent society can direct the behavior of men into desirable channels. That society can do this to a very great extent, and that there is a social responsibility to do it, has never been questioned throughout the history of western civilization. The Catholic Church, the stanch defender of "metaphysical" free will, has always based her educational theory and practice upon belief in the possibility of directing human attitudes and behavior by means of psychological and social factors and forces. What naturalists do, in substituting the study of the factors influencing voluntary choices for the task of determining the nature of human volition, is to turn away from the latter problem. They have a right to do this; but they have no right to give the impression that they are solving the problem of freedom and determinism by doing it.

5. Naturalist Criticism of Arguments for Free Will. Abraham Edel[5] does something which few recent naturalistic philosophers bother to do; he gives a fair statement and criticism of some of the traditional arguments for free will. The first argument is based upon the fact that the act of willing involves in the agent the sense or feeling of

[5] *Ibid.*, pp. 221–229.

freedom, the sense of "dealing with *real* or *genuine alternatives*," of having been really able, when he chose, to have chosen differently. Mr. Edel answers by distinguishing between the feeling of freedom and the sense of real alternatives, and then giving a naturalistic interpretation of each. The feeling of freedom, from the point of view of psychological determinism, may indicate the conformity of the act willed with the general character of the person willing it; social forces, for example, acting upon the person over long periods, may become so internalized, so much a part of the person, that they are felt as his own will. Thus, though the act is determined, it feels as if it were freely put forth. The sense of genuine alternative is something different. Essentially it is the agent's recognition that he could have acted differently had he so willed. But this recognition, that I could have *acted differently* if I had willed differently, throws no light on the question of whether I could have *willed differently*. If the willing is determined according to causal laws, as the naturalist must assume, I could *not* have willed differently under the circumstances. Furthermore, the sense of genuine alternative is often absent from acts which men consider the highest acts of freedom: for example, when a man gives his life rather than betray his friends or country, or when a martyr dies rather than renounce his faith, these men feel that they have no genuine alternative, that they cannot choose otherwise. Hence, it is rather bad tactics for proponents of free will to use a sense of genuine alternative as evidence of free will.

6. **Critical Comment: Knowledge, Not Feeling, of Freedom.** What weight have these criticisms? Is it, to begin with, correct to speak of our immediate consciousness of freedom as a "feeling" of freedom? Is it not *knowledge* rather than feeling? Do we not often make choices while *knowing* that we can choose otherwise? And, indeed, are not some of these very choices accompanied by a feeling which is quite the opposite of a feeling of freedom? Maybe some fortunate men find that their free choices are always congenial to their inner selves — that what they choose is always what they feel like choosing — but the writer must confess that some of his own choices which go quite against the grain, and are accompanied by a distinct feeling of compulsion rather than freedom, are the ones he knows most certainly as free, because he knows how very possible, how easy, it would be for him to choose contrarily. If our consciousness of freedom were a feeling indicative of congeniality between the act and our character, no

act which gives us a feeling of distaste and a sense of being done under undesirable pressure should ever seem free to us. This, however, is not the case. Any normal parent who, after long deliberation, sets about chastising his wayward child, does so with an acute feeling of both distaste and compulsion, yet with perfectly clear knowledge that he is acting freely.

7. Alternatives as to Choice, Not Merely as to Consequences. Mr. Edel seems to be wrong in distinguishing between the feeling (i.e., knowledge) of freedom and the sense (again, knowledge) of genuine alternatives. My knowledge of the freedom of my action is ordinarily the same thing as my knowledge that I can act one way or another; the difference is merely one of abstract and concrete expression: I know I am free — I know I can do either this or that. And he is certainly wrong in his interpretation of the sense of genuine alternative. His interpretation is backward looking: "I could have *acted* differently, had I *willed* differently." The actual conscious judgment made by a person thinking himself free is forward looking: "I can will this or that." It is to be hoped that no one argues for free will on the grounds that "a man could have acted differently if he had so willed it."[6] The real argument is based on my consciousness, prior to willing, of being really able to make either of alternative choices.

Finally, the argument of Mr. Edel, that in some acts considered by men to be supremely free there is no sense of genuine alternatives, seems to be a bit disingenuous. The patriot keeps silent under torture because the alternative is to betray his co-workers and his cause. It is a clear alternative, and he knows only too well that he *can* choose it. His choice of fidelity and death rather than betrayal and life is eminently free because it is made in the face of powerful forces urging him to the opposite choice. That he is morally certain to will fidelity to his cause, even though the cost be death, does not indicate that he has no real alternative, but that his will is perfected by habit built up through a life of right choices. The moral certainty of his heroic choice is not the result of determinism; it is the result of his own ability, acquired by repeated free choices, to determine his will according to his rational judgment about relative and absolute values. His will is so much the more free as it is the more certainly directed to the rational good. If it were perfectly free, he would inevitably choose the higher good on every occasion, because will is the appetite

[6] *Ibid.*, p. 222.

for the good certified by reason. Growth in freedom is growth in knowledge of and fidelity to the good; it is not growth in irrationality or unpredictability of behavior. A man who is equally capable of lying or telling the truth is less, not more, free than a man who inevitably tells the truth. Thomism and naturalism agree on this; but on its significance they disagree. Naturalism, faithful to the postulate of determinism, defines freedom as growth in the determination of action by desirable factors, and refuses to admit metaphysical freedom. Thomism, faithful to its definition of will as the appetite for the good as such, defines freedom as the ability to choose the good, and growth in freedom as increasing facility in choosing the good which, under the circumstances, is good absolutely. For Thomism, will has a proper object just as sight has, and the more surely it attains this object the more perfect is its operation. It is free, not because it can act without determination, but because it can determine itself to that which is its proper object. It has the freedom of alternative choices because its proper object may be found, really or apparently, in different and mutually exclusive things at the same time.

8. **Freedom and Alternatives.** In the Thomistic scheme, the most perfect act of freedom — the choice of the Supreme Good seen as such — leaves no real alternative. This is a stumbling block for many. Freedom without alternative seems a contradiction. Reflection, however, shows that there is no real contradiction. The apparent contradiction arises from the belief that the will is determined by its object rather than that it determines itself to the object. Will follows reason, and desires the good. It "is determined" to the good in the sense that it is nothing else than the faculty of the good — none of it is left over for other functions. It tends to the good whenever it is actual; its actuality is this tendency. It tends to as many distinct goods as reason presents to it. Where two such goods are presented but cannot both be possessed, it can choose between them, and this is what we ordinarily mean by its freedom. Yet the choosing *between* is accidental; the choice is really the choice *of* one of the goods as good absolutely under the circumstances; and this choice would not be essentially different if the alternative were absent. Indeed, the presence of an alternative is merely one of the circumstances considered by the will in coming to its choice. Freedom is not, therefore, set aside or negated when reason presents one good alone as Goodness itself, so that the will cannot but fly to it and cleave to it. It is what the will was made

for, what it has always been seeking, glimpsing it from afar and in part; now, face to face with it, it embraces it with the total power of fully self-determined action. Now its freedom is perfectly realized, for it has now all that it ever desired in desiring anything.

9. **Moral Ideas and Free Will.** Moral ideas, traditionally put forward as primary evidence for free will, can be defended and interpreted in a naturalistic, deterministic setting, claims Mr. Edel.[7] Thus, praise for good actions and blame for evil actions need not imply that the one praising or blaming believes that the person he praises or blames could have done otherwise than he did under the internal and external circumstances of his action. Rather, praise and blame are given to bolster the factors which lead to desirable choices and to weaken or remove those which lead to undesirable choices. In the concrete, if I praise a boy for an act of generosity, I do so, not because I believe that he could have willed otherwise than he did at the time, but in order to make it more certain that he will choose similarly in the future; my praise encourages and increases in him the psychological or internal factors which determined his actual choice, thus making him more likely to choose to act generously on future occasions, when, perhaps, the external factors may give him less encouragement. Two comments on this interpretation seem to be in order. First, although we do use praise and blame in the manner described, we also give them quite disinterestedly and without any intention or hope of influencing anyone's future action. Indeed, some of our most deeply felt sentiments of admiration for virtuous or heroic actions, or disgust and reprobation for vicious actions, we do not even express. Second, our use of praise and blame is based upon the recipient's love of praise and dislike of blame. These feelings are bound up with the recipient's knowledge that he *merits* the praise or blame. Mr. Edel mentions merit, but passes it over without comment. Yet it is felt or known as something very real and as consequent only upon actions done freely, as is painfully apparent to anyone who has had to suffer the experience of helplessly receiving fulsome praise or scathing blame when he knew that it was not merited.

Similar remarks must be made about the naturalist interpretation of the sense of sin, repentance, conscience, remorse.[8] In Edel's discussion of them one important feature is overlooked. The consciousness

---

[7] *Ibid.*, pp. 225–229.
[8] *Ibid.*, pp. 224–225.

of these feelings — not other feelings sometimes confused with them, e.g., regret, grief, frustration — occurs only in cases where the action which gives rise to them is known by (or, at least, seems to) the agent to be a free action. The feelings attach to the will-act, not to the consequences. Not only children but grownups as well, in all sincerity, excuse themselves for the evil consequences of their actions by saying, "I could not help it," or "I did not mean it." And, we excuse them too, if we believe them. There may be a considerable complexity of factors determining what kinds of behavior produce a sense of guilt and what kinds produce a sense of self-approval in various societies, but the common belief which connects the two feelings with actions done freely seems to be quite independent of this complexity of factors; that the act be freely done seems to be the common factor present among the other factors which vary from one social context to another.

10. What Is Freedom? When the naturalist gets around to defining his own conception of freedom as opposed to the metaphysical conception, his definition is surprisingly like that of St. Thomas — or it would be, if it could be taken at face value. Free action is reasonable action, or action which is intelligently directed.[9] Reason or intelligence is not, of course, on the hypothesis of naturalism, a special faculty. Rather, reasonable or intelligently directed actions "represent an equilibrium of forces rather than the drive of isolated component forces. The mastery of reason over desire is not the domination of a master over his slave, but the organized strength of a stably organized system of desires over one or two aberrant desires."[10]

Reason is, therefore, "a quality of human behavior." Behavior has this quality when it is the resultant of a stably organized equilibrium of forces instead of the product of individualistic desires. The present writer must frankly confess that he does not quite understand this. It seems to him that on the deterministic theory *every* action must be the resultant of a complexity of forces and that where there were an *equilibrium* of forces there would be no action at all, a conclusion, by the way, from which Mr. Edel does not shrink.[11] Hence the quality of reason cannot lie in equilibrium of forces, but rather in the dominance and victory of *certain kinds of forces* over certain other kinds. The certain kinds in question are simply those motives of

[9] *Ibid.*, pp. 228–229. Randall and Buchler, *op. cit.*, p. 237.
[10] Edel, *op. cit.*, p. 229.
[11] *Op. cit.*, p. 223.

action which reason pronounces good. Reason, then, is not merely a quality of free behavior, but its principle and determinant, as Thomists have always held, and as naturalists recognize in practice whenever they appeal to a person's reason against his passion and prejudices. The naturalist may reply that reason is the quality which belongs to modes of behavior that are socially desirable; that reason is defined by the consequences of will-acts, not by their causation; that free and reasonable behavior is the behavior of a man who has attained stability of inner forces and of interaction with his society. But again the Thomist must answer that such stability is attained through the consistent judgment and application of reason; it is a stability effected by one certain kind of quality which is the dominant principle of the stability and not its mere outcome or resultant. In so far as a man does not merely give blind responses to the myriad forces and motives, inner and outer, which urge him toward one or another course of action, but instead brings these forces and motives up before the bar of reason in order to determine his course of action according to his judgment of their relative desirability, he exercises free will.

11. **Conclusion: Evaluation of the Naturalistic Arguments.** By the "metaphysical free will" which they reject, naturalists do not seem to mean free will as explained by St. Thomas and Thomists. They seem to mean rather the theory, rejected by St. Thomas, of some sort of irrational inner decider of choice. What the naturalist's argument against the Thomist doctrine would be, the present writer will not try to guess. It seems more profitable to point out that there is a possible road of approach between many contemporary naturalist views and the Thomistic view, in the naturalists' insistence upon the real difference between the laws of different levels of natural events — in the present case, between the laws of matter in motion and the laws of human choice. Naturalists are not yet free from the dogma of materialism, and, consequently, are still incapable of a fair study of the laws of human choice. Even the most tenuous form of materialism associates *determinism* with causality and lawfulness, so that to any one tinged with materialism, lawfulness in *free* actions seems to be a self-contradiction. Freed from the materialistic dogma, some naturalists might come to see St. Thomas' theory of free will as what it truly is, namely, an analysis of the causes and laws of free action.

The naturalists' technique in dealing with human action is specious and misleading. They do not really come to grips with the problems involved, but instead they substitute for the problem of the causation underlying free action a quite different problem, namely, the problem of describing or itemizing the empirical factors operative in human action. Thus they present an empirical and functional account of human behavior. They do this very well, but a comparison of their account with those of Aristotle's *Ethics* and St. Thomas' *Summa Theologica*, I-II, does not reveal any great advances which they have made. That they consider this functional account to be a refutation of the theory of free will can only suggest that they have a strange conception of what free will means and implies.

III. THE WILL AND "THE UNCONSCIOUS"

1. St. Thomas and Psychoanalysis. What would St. Thomas have had to say about the teachings of the modern schools of psychoanalysis? Since Sigmund Freud first brought psychoanalytic theories and methods to public attention, it has been widely granted that the "unconscious" or the "subconscious," that is to say, certain inner drives or urges of which we are not consciously aware, influence our voluntary actions. Certainly the Angelic Doctor would have rejected the exaggerated version of psychoanalytic theory, which makes our hidden desires and fears the *determinants* of our "voluntary" actions. He would have pointed out that it is not at all uncommon for us to determine what we shall desire and what we shall do by weighing and comparing motives and reasons of which we have full consciousness and understanding. But he would not have found anything disconcerting in the notion that unconscious forces within us *influence* our choices. He had himself written of such forces; he attributed them to "bodily dispositions" resulting from heredity, illness, and other such causes, as well as to all our past experiences, many of which have been forgotten. He would hardly have been willing to admit an *unconscious mind;* except, perhaps, in the sense that bodily conditions or movements bring about certain mental states which have no immediate conscious causes or antecedents, so that the person discovering them in himself does not know whence they arose. Movements within the body do give rise to phantasms, he said; and certainly we can add that along with some of these phantasms come ill-understood desires, fears, or anxieties associated with them in some forgotten experience.

He would have insisted that such phantasms are all related in some way to past experience, and in this he would be in agreement with the psychoanalysts. Probably he would have attributed to the work of the devil some of the phenomena brought to light by the psychoanalysts, and this would certainly not be strange. But even in this case he would insist that the devil himself can work upon our imaginations and appetites only by working on our bodies; that is, by causing bodily movements which would arouse imagery and incite passion; and that the imagery so aroused would be built out of past imagery and perception. But even when the devil is not giving us his personal attention, the marks left by our own past actions and experiences in our highly sensitive body-soul compound can move us in ways that are dark and secret.[12]

2. **Free Will and Psychoanalysis.** But what has all this to do with free will? It is certainly no evidence against the fact of free will. People go, or are sent, to psychoanalysts, because they have been doing things or desiring things from causes for which they cannot rationally account. If they considered this state of affairs normal, they would not seek medical advice. What they want from the psychoanalyst is some direction as to how to regain normal, rational control of their behavior, both mental and overt. The psychoanalyst tries to bring up to the level of their conscious mind the hidden root and motive of their abnormal behavior, so that they will understand why they have been acting as they have. This procedure often succeeds in aiding the patient to regain normal mental life and behavior. And why? Strange though it may be, St. Thomas Aquinas in the thirteenth century seems to have very accurately explained the causation which underlies the commonest procedure of twentieth-century psychoanalysis.

In question XXIV, article 2 of *De Veritate,* which we used extensively in the last chapter, the Angelic Doctor explains why men have free will whereas animals do not. Animals know the objects which move their sensitive appetites, but lacking reason, they understand neither the nature of these objects nor the reason why they judge them good, and therefore they cannot reflect upon their judgments about them. Man, possessing the power of reason, can understand the nature of the objects which move his appetites and can reflect upon his own judgments about the suitability of these objects as motives, comparing

[12] *S. Theol.,* I, 111, 2 and 3; I–II, q. 80.

them to the rational good itself.[13] Apply this to the psychoanalyst's patient. Driven by a subconscious fear or desire, he is not free in respect to it, *because he does not understand it and cannot, therefore, reflect upon it or upon its relation to his judgments and actions.* When the psychoanalyst succeeds in bringing the hidden motive out of the dark into the light of conscious recognition, the patient is now able to understand it, to reflect upon its nature and its relation to his behavior, and to compare it with the rational good; and thus he becomes free in respect to it because it has been brought under the compass of reason.

3. Summary: Thomism and Determinism. According to the Thomistic theory of human action we actually do all the kinds of behavior described by behaviorists, psychological determinists, and devotees of the subconscious urge. We respond automatically to physical stimuli; we act because of pain and pleasure, fear and sensual desire, like any animal; we respond unthinkingly to the pressures and value-judgments of our society; and we are moved, sometimes to the point of serious abnormality, by dark fears, desires, and anxieties of which we are only vaguely aware and which we do not understand at all. But these are only the acts which we do when we are not acting freely. In our free acts such factors as these influence us, but they are never determining, and often they are negligible; in fact we frequently act directly against such forces. We act freely when we knowingly determine our own actions on the basis of reasons which we understand. When the determining causation behind an action is something else than rational judgment and choice, our will has not entered the act at all. Studies of reflex action, of the influence of feeling, pleasure and pain, and social pressure, and of the function of subconscious forces within us, are all extremely important studies, because they reveal things which are essential to the understanding of man's behavior and nature (and, incidentally, the only theory of human nature to which they give any support is the hylemorphic theory). But so long as study is limited to these factors, the proper study of voluntary action has not even been begun.

IV. IS ST. THOMAS' DOCTRINE OF CHOICE DETERMINISTIC?

1. The Charge Against Thomism. It has sometimes been charged

[13] Cf. Chapter XII, Section IV.

by Scholastic philosophers outside the Thomistic group that St. Thomas' doctrine of the human will is actually a doctrine of determinism. This charge is based upon the Angelic Doctor's insistence that the final choice, when it is put forth by the will, is made according to the direction of a last determining judgment of the intellect. The will, in Thomistic teaching, never actually chooses except according to a judgment of the intellect which pronounces some particular act the one to do here and now. Therefore, the opponents argue, according to the Thomistic doctrine the will is not actually free, but is determined by motives offered it by the intellect so that it must always choose as the strongest motive dictates. In order to preserve real freedom of will, these philosophers say, we must insist that, contrary to the Thomistic doctrine, the will can, after the intellect has pronounced its last practical judgment, still choose otherwise; or as some others hold, that there is no need at all of any last practical judgment: in face of a number of goods the will can choose any, without the intellect first judging one as the one to be preferred.

2. The Determinism of Leibniz. Gottfried Leibniz, who though not a Scholastic, studied Scholastic writers and saw the problem of free will as they saw it, adopted a position of psychological determinism. Every choice of the will is determined by the weight of known motives; for the will to choose anything but what is presented to it as the greatest good, given all the actual circumstances, would be for it to defy the principle of sufficient reason. The act of will must have a sufficient reason, because everything must have. A choice made contrary to the intellect's judgment as to which good is, at the moment, the greatest good offered would be a choice made without any sufficient reason. Believing that self-determination on the part of the will is incompatible with the principle of sufficient reason, Leibniz chose to stand by that principle. He therefore denied what Scholastics call "liberty of indifference." He insisted, however, that his doctrine, according to which our will-acts are determined by the motives presented by our intellect, is truly a doctrine of free will.

3. Liberty of Indifference. The will is said to have liberty of indifference inasmuch as when it chooses, and until it has made its choice, it is not determined to one thing rather than another, but, on the contrary, makes its choice by freely determining itself to one thing. Leibniz denied that there can be any such freedom: "There is indifference, when there is no more reason for one [choice] than for

the other. Otherwise, there would be determination. . . . A liberty of
indifference is impossible . . . creatures are always determined by
internal or external reasons."[14] Indifference could arise only from lack
of a sufficient reason for acting one way or another, Leibniz believed;
but in such a situation no choice would be made at all. Many critics
of St. Thomas seem to believe that his doctrine is the same as that of
Leibniz, but that Thomists will not admit this. These critics maintain
that the will is truly free only if it is freed from the judgment of
reason. We wish to show, in what follows, that the Thomistic doctrine
is far from being the same as that of Leibniz; that it is truly a doctrine
of free will, answering the argument of Leibniz, and allowing the
will liberty of indifference; and, finally, that to free the will from
the judgment of reason, as St. Thomas' critics wish to do, would,
instead of preserving man's free will, destroy it utterly.

4. St. Thomas' Doctrine. The argument of St. Thomas that his doctrine of the will assigns a sufficient reason for choice, yet avoids
psychological determinism and maintains liberty of indifference
may be briefly stated as follows: *The will always chooses according
to a last practical judgment of the intellect; but this choice is made
with true freedom of indifference because this judgment was itself
made freely: the intellect made the judgment without having had to
make it, because it made it only as moved by the will, which did not
have to move it.* This brief statement requires considerable explanation.

By a practical judgment is meant an order from reason to act or
not act, to do this or that. Practical judgments concern individual acts
to be actually exercised by the person making the judgment. They are
not merely speculative judgments about the character of some action,
but are directives of reason determining what is actually to be done.
They do not take the form, "This is right to do"; but the form, "Do
this." They are acts of intellect determining what is to be willed.

The last practical judgment which determines the will to its choice
is a free judgment, made because the will moves the intellect to
pronounce it. Reason, as such, is never *necessitated* to judge any particular good or motive as the one to be chosen here and now. Reason
as such assents necessarily only to propositions whose subject and
predicate are seen to be necessarily related, either by themselves, as
in self-evident propositions, or by a middle term necessarily joining

[14] Quoted by Bertrand Russell. *The Philosophy of Leibniz* (London: George Allen
and Unwin, Ltd., 1937), pp. 193–194, n. 2.

them, as in demonstrated propositions. When reason does give assent to a proposition without being necessitated to do so either by self-evidence or by demonstration, it gives this assent only because it is moved by will to do so.[15] Such assent is, therefore, free; we will to give it or not give it. Aside from one case, which never occurs in this life, our practical judgments are always free judgments, never necessary ones. Our deliberations about what to do always concern *particular* goods; and no particular good is ever seen to be equal to or requisite for the universal good; hence, no judgment pronouncing a particular good to be suitable and desirable absolutely, so that it is here and now the thing to be chosen, can be a necessary judgment. When, therefore, the intellect pronounces a judgment that such and such a thing is to be willed or chosen here and now, it can do so only because the will moves it to do so. Consequently, when the intellect, by so judging, determines the will, it does so no more than the will determines it. The intellect gives the will the object to be chosen; but the will has itself moved the intellect to present that object.

5. The Last Practical Judgment Is Required for the Act of Choice. Though this judgment of the intellect is freely made, it is nevertheless a necessary condition for the will's act of choosing. St. Thomas never tires of repeating that the will's movement of the intellect and the intellect's movement of the will belong to different genera or orders of causation, and that both orders of causation are required for the complete free act. Intellect moves will by specifying its act; that is, the intellect is formal cause relative to the will-act. The will is efficient cause or agent in respect both to the intellect and itself. It moves the intellect to judge and itself to choose. It is a radical power of choice needing for the exercise of its operation no extrinsic efficient mover (save God); but this operation must have a determinate form and end before it can be exercised in actuality. This formation of the power is given it by the intellect, by means of which man "possesses the forms of other things." Just so long as no particular known good is judged as suitable here and now, man's power of choice remains undetermined, and so remains potential. Without the final practical judgment of the intellect, the will remains without sufficient reason for one act rather than another, it remains without a determinate form, without a determinate end. An act of will made independently of an ultimate command from the intellect is a metaphysical mon-

---

[15] Cf. *S. Theol.*, II–II, 1, 4, c.

strosity: it is something which has no sufficient reason; it is an agent acting for no definite end; it is an indeterminate actuality.

6. This Judgment Is Required for the Freedom of This Act. If we ignore these metaphysical difficulties, and suppose that the will can act without an ultimate command of the intellect, or that it can choose contrary to such a command after reason has issued the command, we face other difficulties. The will is not itself a cognitive power; it does not think or judge. Therefore to say that, presented with two alternative goods, we can choose either one without a determining judgment of intellect first deciding between them, is to say that we can *choose* without *thinking* that "this is the thing to be done." Perhaps we can, but such a choice would not be free; we would not be determining our own choice — we would, instead, simply find out that we had chosen, or rather, that something in us had chosen for us. If, on the other hand, the will were "free" to choose contrary to the ultimate practical judgment, again we might call such choice voluntary, but we cannot call it free, because we would not have it in our own control. *We would not know why we made it.* Instead of making our own choices as intelligent free beings, we would have all our choices made for us by a hidden interior choice maker which we call "our will." The freest of men would be the man who could never account for his actions. We must conclude, with St. Thomas, that the judgment of intellect determines the act of will.

7. Will Is Not Determined by the Strongest Motive. But this is not to conclude, with Leibniz, that the will is necessarily determined by the weight of the strongest motive. In the interplay of mutual movements by will and intellect, the will at all times has the initiative. This fact is made clear by reflection upon the relations of efficient and formal causality in any action. The work of each is necessary for the action; because the action must be actually exercised, and it must be a specific action. In voluntary action, exercise is the function of will, specification the function of intellect. Intellect and will give each other the ultimate required determination in one act; intellect as formal cause, will as efficient cause. It is only because the will has the initiative in this reciprocal determination that psychological determinism is avoided. Let us see how this is so.

Formal causation, that is, determination to a definite species, is necessary in any causing or acting; but formal causality is never operative in an action except as applied by an efficient cause. An action exists only by virtue of the movement of an efficient cause. Hence, though formal and efficient causality are mutually dependent, the efficient cause is prior in the order of causality. The formal cause is a cause only in so far as the efficient cause applies it to action by acting under its formal determination. In a voluntary act, will has the role of efficient cause, and intellect the role of formal cause. The will has priority. Having willed to act, it submits itself freely to some determining form supplied by the intellect; or, as we have expressed it so often above, it moves the intellect to pronounce the final, determining, practical judgment.[16] The act by which the will moves the intellect to its last practical judgment is merely *one phase of one total act* of which this practical judgment and the ensuing choice are the other phases. There are not three agencies — will, intellect, and will again — producing three distinct acts — movement, judgment, and choice — but one agent, the man, moving himself to judge and to choose according to this judgment. *Choice is the act by which a rational agent voluntarily determines its own action by means of a free judgment.* Will and intellect, in one act, give each other the ultimate determination required for actual choice: will as efficient cause, intellect as formal cause. And because will, as efficient causation, and as the first moving power in man, moving itself and the intellect and all the other powers over which man has control, has the absolute priority, intellectual determinism is avoided.

8. **Choice, Though Free, Has a Sufficient Reason.** This priority of the will's movement to the intellect's formal determination by judgment saves liberty of indifference and avoids psychological determinism. But does it really show that there is a *sufficient reason* for the choice made? A free choice, like anything which is in any way real, needs a sufficient reason for its being. The principle of sufficient reason cannot be sacrificed in order to save freedom of will. Thomists say that they do assign a sufficient reason for the choice. It is the particular good chosen. This is a *sufficient* reason because it is a good; it is not a *necessitating* reason because it is not The Good, which is the only perfectly adequate object of the will. By being sufficient, it enables the will to act; by not being necessitating, it leaves it free to act or not act, to do this or that. One who seeks more reason than this has already unconsciously denied the will's freedom.

[16] Cf. Garrigou-Lagrange, *God — His Existence and Nature* (St. Louis: Herder, 1936), Vol. II, p. 317.

Difficulties still remain. Prior to choice, but after deliberation, the will has before it *several* potentially determining goods or motives, none of which is (actually or potentially) necessitating. For actual choice, one of these must be made the actually determining motive. Now such determination is formal determination, which is the work of the intellect. So the will moves the intellect to judge that one of these motives is the one to be acted upon now. This it can do, Thomists say, because each of them is a *sufficient* motive. But opponents argue, how can the will move the intellect to judge in favor of one motive rather than another? *Must not the will already have formal determination to that one in order to do this?* And if we suppose a prior determining judgment, we are starting along an infinite regress.

If to the above italicized question we answer, "No," we will remove all remaining difficuties. But can we defend this answer? We can. The will has sufficient formal determination to any particular good offered to it for choice, because it is formally determined to the Absolute Good. Particular goods are not more specific determinations of Absolute Good, as isosceles is a more specific determination of triangle: they are related as *means to* Absolute Good. Hence, every one of them, among which the choice is to be made, is potentially a sufficient formal determinant of choice because it is a means to Absolute Good, to which the will is always formally determined. The will needs only to submit itself to one of them to make it the actual formal determinant. By virtue of its movement to The Good, it can freely move itself to any particular determination of the good, by freely moving the intellect to the last determining judgment. Only then is the will adequately determined to choice; but it has determined itself. To ask what determined it to submit itself to one of the proposed goods rather than to another, is to require a *necessitating* as well as a sufficient reason; and to require this is to leave the will's own freedom of movement out of the inventory of the reasons for its action. But surely its freedom is the most fundamental of all the reasons for the way in which it acts. There is a strange anomaly in some of the criticisms of St. Thomas' doctrine of free choice. Because the Angelic Doctor assigns to the will, at each step, a *sufficient* reason for its movement, his critics accuse him of intellectualistic determinism; then when St. Thomas' followers point out that the reasons assigned are never necessitating, the critics answer that he does not, in that case, assign any sufficient reason. The attitude of these critics is intelligible only on the hypothesis that somewhere in the course of the argument they have forgotten that they began by agreeing that the will is free; for a free agency is one which can have for its action a sufficient reason which is not necessitating: having the reason, it *can* act; being free, it can *refrain* from acting. The precise point of the argument which they have forgotten is that the only possible necessitating cause of the will's action is the good as such or happiness, which is never in question in any choice, so that as the Thomistic analysis develops no question of a necessarily determining cause can ever arise.

9. The Person Chooses Rationally. In order to explain the roots of freedom of choice, we have been forced, in the above, to speak of intellect and will almost as if they were separate agencies. In truth, of course, there is only one agent, namely the man. In order to choose, he must be determined to a specific choice and to the actual exercise of choosing. In order to *explain* this twofold determination we must use the will-intellect terminology; and by doing so we run the danger of seeing separations where in fact there are mere distinctions. If we now describe a case of free choice in terms of a person rather than of a will and an intellect, the Thomistic position may be made clearer.

A young man who has willed to go to college cannot actually go to college without first deciding what college to go to. Although he has already willed to go before he makes this decision, he cannot effectively choose to go to college without his choice first being determined by a final practical judgment terminating in one particular college. Now, it is clear that this judgment determines him without in any way removing the freedom of his choice or subordinating the choice to the judgment. For the judgment was made freely, to begin with; and, furthermore, in the whole complex of volitions and judgments, the choice-aspect remains prior to the judgment-aspect in two ways: first, he willed to go to college *before* he deliberated and judged which one to go to; second, the judgment determining the final choice of a particular college served as a *means* to the realization of the original volition to go to college — whatever college he decided on, he chose as a means of going to college. Now, for the terms "going to college," "deciding," "particular college," "choosing," substitute the good as such, last practical judgment, particular good, and choice, and assign each of these to the proper faculty, intellect or will — and you have the Thomistic account of free will.

According to that account, the will (i.e., the man by his power of will) is naturally determined to the good as such, but every choice in this life concerns some particular good. The will cannot choose without choosing a determinate good; and consequently it cannot choose without the determining judgment of reason intervening. This condition in no way destroys its freedom or subordinates it to the intellect in the act of free choice. For the will remains prior in two ways: first, The Good is willed before any particular good is judged the one to be chosen; second, this judgment itself serves the will as a means to its choice. It is a *necessary* condition without being a *necessitating* condition, and it remains subservient to the will; it no more deprives the will of freedom of choice than the pencil which I need in order to write deprives me of the freedom to write or not write. Again, it *formally determines* what the will wills; but it no more deprives the will of freedom to will this or that than the thoughts which I put on paper deprive me of freedom to put them or other thoughts on paper. If I write, I must write something determinate; so I must think what to write in order to write at all. But I can think this or that as I choose, and therefore I can write this or that as I choose. Finally, whatever particular good the intellect commands the will to choose, it commands it in order that the will may move itself through this choice to The Good itself. The judgment is a means used by the will to effectuate its own original volition of the Absolute Good through the choice of a particular good contributory to the Absolute Good. What we want first of all is to be happy, and all our practical judgments and the choices that follow them are brought to birth by the will's primary determination to seek happiness.

10. Different Choices in the Same Circumstances. One last difficulty remains. Given that the will in choosing follows the judgment of the intellect, then if the will is placed twice in precisely the same circumstances, with exactly the same rival goods soliciting its choice, will not the same judgment inevitably be pronounced and the same choice inevitably follow it? The intellect, on the second occasion, would have the same reasons for its judgment, and the will would have the same motives for moving the intellect to the same judgment to which it moved it on the first occasion. Hence the same choice would necessarily be made. For every being and every action must have a sufficient reason, and, *since all the reasons in the two cases are precisely the same, there is no sufficient reason for any change of judgment or choice in* *the second case.* But if under the same circumstances a man *must* make the same choice, then the circumstances are what determine his choice, and he has no freedom of will. Hence, Thomists must either renounce the principle of sufficient reason or confess that the Angelic Doctor's doctrine of will is a form of determinism.[17]

Father Garrigou-Lagrange[18] gives a convincing answer to this argument. Thomists maintain that the human will placed twice in identical circumstances can choose one way the first time and another way the second time. The will has a sufficient reason for each choice; namely, a particular good seen as a means to the good as such, which the will always desires. But since no particular good is a necessitating reason for choice, one choice can be made one time, another the other time. The particular good chosen on each occasion is sufficient because it is related to the Absolute Good; it is not necessitating because it is not the Absolute Good.

To this reply of Father Garrigou-Lagrange another may be added. The argument given above has a catch or trick in it, and is, much weaker than it first seems. What is really being argued by those who advance this objection is that the Thomistic doctrine assigns no sufficient reason for the *change of choice* from the first to the second case. This, however, is nonsense; *because there is no change.* A change occurs only when something becomes something else. The first choice does not become the second choice. Once it has been made, it becomes part of history and can never be changed. The second choice is not made out of the first — which is what is meant by "change of choice." It is a new choice having no genetic relation to the first. There are, therefore, simply two choices made on separate occasions and having nothing to do with each other. We cannot change a choice, as we sometimes sadly realize. Therefore, to demand, as the argument in question does, a sufficient reason for the change from the first choice to the second, is to demand a *raison d'être* for a nonentity. All that can be asked of the Thomistic doctrine is that it assign a sufficient but non-necessitating reason for each choice; and this it does. It does not need to assign a reason for the non-existent change of will. The sufficient reason why we can choose differently the second time is the freedom of our will.[19]

[17] *S. Theol.,* I–II, 13, 6, Obj. 3.   [18] *Op. cit.,* Vol. II, pp. 336–338.
[19] As a matter of fact, the will can never be faced twice with identical circumstances. The choice made on the first occasion and the consequences of that choice will be a new and important circumstance on the second occasion.

PART THREE

KNOWLEDGE AND BEING

CHAPTER XIV

IDEALISM AND REALISM

---

1. METAPHYSICS AND EPISTEMOLOGY

The crowning part of St. Thomas' philosophy is his metaphysics. Metaphysics is the science of immaterial being, or the science of being-as-such. In Thomistic metaphysics we study being and its first principles, which are the ultimate foundations of all knowledge and thought; and we also study such vital questions as the existence and nature of God, the creation of the world, the divine government of all creatures, and the mystery of evil. This study of God and His creatures is purely rational and is not to be confused with our beliefs about God derived from divine revelation. Yet it is not altogether unrelated to Christian faith in the truths revealed by God. For among the things which Thomistic metaphysics studies are the questions of the possibility of a supernatural communication from God to man of truths which unaided human reason could not attain, and of the relation between faith in such truths and the rational knowledge attained in philosophy.

The temper of large numbers of contemporary philosophers is radically opposed both to metaphysics and to the possibility of a divine revelation. These philosophers regard belief in divine revelation as a superstitious survival of ages when the human mind had not yet awakened to knowledge of its own nature or the nature of the world, and they consider metaphysics as empty and futile speculation, which has no real object and which is dangerous because it tends to encourage the "superstitious" belief in supernatural being. For such philosophers, who call themselves naturalists, there is only one valid method of seeking truth; namely, what they call the scientific method.

The principal errors which have led to modern naturalism in philosophy have all been *epistemological* errors. *Epistemology* is the study of the nature, scope, and validity of human knowledge. An error made in epistemology works itself into the whole foundation and structure of a system of knowledge and, termite like, eats away the supports of the system. Three epistemological errors have dominated the development of modern philosophy and have brought it to its present naturalistic position. They are (1) the subjectivistic postulate of René Descartes, (2) the radical sensism or phenomenalism of David Hume, and (3) the transcendental criticism of Immanuel Kant. The end-result of these errors has been the undermining of every system of realistic and spiritualistic metaphysics, such as Thomistic metaphysics. The epistemology implied in these errors allows the human mind no knowledge of anything except subjective sensible phenomena; objective real being and supra-sensible or immaterial being are quite beyond its reach. It is our present task to examine this false epistemology, to disclose, if we can, the errors whence it arose, and to defend the Thomistic epistemology to which it is opposed. This is no easy task, and will take several chapters. In the present chapter we shall examine and evaluate the epistemology of Descartes and his idealistic followers, and in two succeeding chapters the theories of Hume and Kant. Then in the remaining chapters of Part Three we shall try to establish on a firm epistemological foundation the fundamental principles of Thomistic metaphysics. Entailed in this task are two subordinate problems, each of which will require a chapter; these problems are the relations between science and philosophy on the one hand, and between reason and faith on the other.

II. IDEALISM VS. REALISM

1. Modern philosophy, since the time of René Descartes, has been dominated by the epistemological problem. This is the problem of the truth-value or objective validity of human knowledge. We perceive external things, form ideas of them, and make judgments about them. But do our perceptions, ideas, and judgments truly attain to real things as these exist independently of our mind? Is a tree as perceived and thought by me anything like a tree as it exists in itself, apart from and independent of my perception or idea of it? Does the human mind, in knowing, transcend itself and grasp external or extramental reality and at the same time know that it does so? Or does it, in fact, never cross the boundaries of the subject, that is, itself, and so attain only to its own states or impressions? Philosophers who believe that in knowl-

edge men attain real extramental being are called *realists;* philosophers who believe that a man's knowledge never transcends the boundaries of the man's self and attains only intramental being are called *idealists.*[1]

2. **Descartes.** The great French philosopher, René Descartes (1596–1650), held a position which was later to receive the name "reasoned realism." He held that we know extramental reality, but that we have to demonstrate that it exists and that we know it. All that we know *immediately, directly,* and without need of demonstration is our own ideas. This belief is the subjectivistic postulate. How he "demonstrated" the reality of being outside his ideas we shall see later; what is relevant now is that he started with his ideas and reasoned to other things, and particularly to the reality of material things.

3. **Leibniz (1646–1716).** This reasoned realism did not satisfy Descartes' successors. But if they rejected his solution, they still had his problem: How can the mind know the material world? Leibniz and Spinoza did not even pretend that the mind in any way gets extramental reality into itself; all knowedge according to both of them is purely internal. The self-conscious monad which, according to Leibniz, is the human soul, represents all the other monads which make up the world, but this representation, which is knowledge, is not the result of any interaction between the mind and external things or of any presence of external things to the mind for every monad is perfectly self-contained and interacts with no other. The mind's representations correspond with — i.e., represent — the external world of the other monads, because God has created all monads in "pre-established harmony."

4. **Spinoza.** For Spinoza (1632–1677), ideas and things are different modes or aspects of the one same reality. Man's body is a system of parts, and there is an idea of each part, and the soul is the system of these ideas. To every mode of extension there corresponds a mode of thought. Each part, each cell, of the body is a finite mode of extension and all together make up the body; and to each there corresponds a mode of thought, or an idea, and all these together make up the soul. Hence every affection or modification of the body is also an affection or alteration of the soul. Knowledge, that is to say, these idea-alterations in the soul, is directly concerned therefore only with modifica-

[1] This terminology is not exact. *Objective idealists,* while believing that we know only ideas, regard ideas as objective, extramental realities. For the purposes of this chapter, however, we do not need to distinguish between idealists of various sorts. This should become clear as the chapter unfolds.

tions of the body; things outside the body, causing these modifications, are not known in themselves but only in the effects they occasion in the body's state of movement and rest. Knowledge is purely subjective for Spinoza.

5. The British Empiricists. The three great British philosophers, Locke, Berkeley, and Hume, reacted against the extreme rationalism and innatism of the Cartesian school, and sought to make experience the base of their theory of knowledge and reality, but they did not succeed in escaping the shadow of Descartes' subjectivism. John Locke (1632–1704) was a realist: he maintained that we do know extrasubjective being; but he constructed his realism upon the subjectivistic postulate that the immediate and direct objects of our knowledge are our ideas or perceptions. The first chapter of Book IV of his *Essay Concerning Human Understanding,* entitled "Of Knowledge in General," opens with a clear statement of the basic subjectivity of knowledge:

> Since the mind, in all its thoughts and reasonings, hath no other immediate object but its own ideas, which it alone does or can contemplate, it is evident that our knowledge is only conversant about them. Knowledge then seems to me to be nothing but the perception of the connection and agreement, or disagreement and repugnancy, of any of our ideas. In this alone it consists.[2]

A true realism cannot be built upon this subjectivistic basis, and Locke is driven to confess that we do not have any clear idea of substance; substance "is but a supposed I-know-not-what, to support those ideas we call accidents. . . ." This doctrine is nearer to phenomenalism than to realism.

George Berkeley (1685–1753) did not see why we had to "suppose" an unknown substance underlying our ideas of the accidents of bodies, since we have at hand a very competent support of these ideas, and one which we know immediately, namely, our own mind. The belief that the things which we perceive have some sort of reality outside our perception is not only an unnecessary hypothesis, it is an absurd one:

> For what are the forementioned objects, i.e., houses, mountains, rivers and all sensible objects but the things we perceive by sense? and what do we perceive besides our own ideas or sensations? and is it not plainly repugnant that any one of these, or any combination of them, should exist unperceived?[3] Their *esse* is *percipi;* nor is it possible that

---

[2] J. Locke, *Essay Concerning Human Understanding,* Bk. IV, Chap. 1.
[3] G. Berkeley, *Principles of Human Knowledge.* I. 4.

they should have any existence out of the minds or thinking things which perceive them.[4]

From what has been said it is evident there is not any other Substance than *Spirit*, or that which perceives. But, for the fuller proof of this point, let it be considered the sensible qualities are colour, figure, motion, smell, taste, and such like, that is, the ideas perceived by sense. Now, for an idea to exist in an unperceiving thing is a manifest contradiction; for to have an idea is all one as to perceive: that therefore wherein colour, figure, and the like qualities exist must perceive them. Hence it is clear there can be no unthinking substance or *substratum* of those ideas.[5]

Thus did Bishop Berkeley abolish the material world.

David Hume (1711–1776) saw no reason why the same trick should not work on the world of spiritual substance. We do not know spiritual substance any more directly than we know material substance; we simply "suppose" it as underlying our ideas, just as we suppose material substance underlying material qualities. The supposition in the one case is no more valid than in the other. If we rule out all those items of our "knowledge" which we do not know immediately and directly but which we suppose or infer, then there is left nothing but our ideas themselves, or rather nothing but *impressions of sensation* and the *ideas* which are the less vivid relics in consciousness of these impressions. Our beliefs in an external, material, substantial world and in a substantial mind or self grow out of mental custom: the repetition in consciousness of impressions leads us to *imagine* a permanent material source of these impressions and a permanent spiritual self by which the impressions are perceived. Neither belief is warranted by any evidence; all we *know* is the flux of impressions.

Immanuel Kant made a mighty effort to rescue thought from the rationalistic idealism of Leibniz and Spinoza and the empiricist phenomenalism of Hume, but since we shall devote another chapter to Kant we need say only this about him here: he might have succeeded in saving modern philosophy if he had gone back far enough for his starting point, that is, if he had gone back before Descartes; but he did not do so.

6. **Thomistic Realism.** The philosophy of St. Thomas Aquinas is realistic. St. Thomas believed that we know *things* — things which exist and have natures quite independently of whether or not we know them. He did not believe that our knowledge never reaches beyond

---

[4] *Ibid.*, I, 3.   [5] *Ibid.*, I, 7.

our own mind, nor did he believe that our mind creates or constructs its objects.

No explicit attempt to demonstrate realism or to refute idealism is found in the writings of St. Thomas, because the issue had not been raised in his age in the form which it took in the hands of modern philosophers. He states[6] his realistic position clearly, and in a few sentences points out the absurd consequences of the subjectivistic postulate: if *what* we know were the sensible and intelligible impressions in our mind, then all science would be about the affections of our minds instead of about the world around us; contradictory beliefs would be true at the same time, because different men have different mental impressions, and true knowledge would consist only in each knowing his own impressions, which, of course, he cannot help doing; thus every sort of opinion would be equally true. Modern thought has seen these consequences sadly realized. St. Thomas was more interested in making a carefully study of *how* we attain knowledge of the real, than in discussing *whether* we attain it; but his analysis of the how goes a long way toward indicating a convincing answer to the whether.

In the Thomistic analysis, contrary to the dictum of so many modern philosophers, our percepts and ideas play primarily the role of unobserved media of knowledge.[7] They are not *what* we know, but means *by which* we know things. In order to know the ideas and images themselves, we have to turn our mind inward in a reflection upon itself. I know that I have an idea of a tree only because I know that I know what a tree is; I knew what a tree is long before it ever occurred to me that I had ideas at all. In the inverted logic of modern philosophy, according to which my ideas are the primary objects of my knowledge, I know a tree because I know my idea of a tree; I know the idea first, and the tree from the idea. It is difficult to see how anyone can escape the admission that St. Thomas is right and the moderns wrong on this point. Knowledge of our own ideas comes late; knowledge of things from infancy. In each particular knowledge something is known and then later, perhaps, the idea of it may also be made an object of knowledge, when I realize that, since I do know the thing, I must have some likeness of it in my mind.

The reason[8] why we know things in themselves is, in the philosophy

[6] *S. Theol.*, 1, 85, 2.
[7] *Loc. cit.*
[8] See Chapter XI.

of St. Thomas, because our knowledge of them is entirely determined by what they are. The thing itself, existing in us, is what we know. To know anything we have to become it, and we become it by receiving its form. The mental image or phantasm by which we consciously represent the thing is made out of forms impressed upon our senses; we cannot make forms up, and consequently we cannot imagine anything which we have not in some manner perceived. We can, of course, put together in one phantasm forms which we have received from different objects. If we do this unknowingly, and think that the thing represented by this phantasm is real, then we are in error. This possibility of error does not imply that we can never be free from error or fear of error, but only that we have to be very careful.

On the intellectual level we find a similar situation. We can form concepts only in so far as our intellect is determined to a given nature by an intelligible species; and this species is the very form of the object which is acting upon our senses and whose phantasm is in our imagination. The concept which we form is universal, but we do not predicate this universality of the thing which it represents; we grasp that thing as a singular through our senses, and we know that the nature conceived in the intellect belongs to the singular thing perceived.[9] The act of conception, when dealing with simple essences, cannot err, because the intellect cannot express in an incomplex idea anything else than the nature of the thing whose form it has received. It may, however, combine in one complex concept essences never in fact found together in reality; and in its second act, judgment, it may affirm of something a nature which really does not belong to it, or deny of it a nature which it really has. Again, these possibilities of error call for caution, not for skepticism. Exercising this caution, letting ourselves be forced by the evident, but never forcing evidence, our minds, from sensation to the most complex reasonings, will be *formed by things;* it will not form them. Then it will conform to reality, and will know that it so conforms; that is to say, it will possess truth.

7. **Truth and the Epistemological Problem.** Truth is the conformity or agreement of being and intellect. St. Thomas finds the true definable in three different ways: (1) according to that in which truth is grounded, namely, being, wherefore, as St. Augustine says, "The true is that which something is"; (2) according to what formally perfects the notion of truth, namely, the relation of being and intellect, and hence

[9] *S. Theol.*, 1, 85, 2, ad 2.

Isaac defines truth as "the agreement of thing and intellect" (*adaequatio rei et intellectus*); (3) according to the effect following from truth, namely, the knowledge of the true, and so Hilary defines truth as "evident and assertive being."[10]

Whether we attain truth is the point at issue; but that we seek it is beyond question: the end of all our thinking is to put our minds in conformity with reality, to grasp things as they really are. Even the skeptic who concludes that there is no truth, comes to this conclusion after trying to attain truth; that is to say, after trying to conform his mind with reality, and failing. He has no doubt what truth is — the intellect's grasp of being itself. And because he cannot satisfy himself that he grasps being, he says that truth is unattainable. The real question, therefore, for the epistemologist to answer is: Can man ever know with certitude, when he makes a judgment about real being, that this judgment is true? Are the three definitions of truth given by St. Augustine, Isaac, and St. Hilary ever realized in a judgment? Is the intellect ever in possession of real being — *that which something is?* Does the intellect conform to that being — *adaequatio rei et intellectus?* And does it know both the being and its own conformity — *evident and assertive being?* We shall try to answer these questions through a critical examination of Descartes' search for certain knowledge.

III. DESCARTES' QUEST FOR TRUTH

1. **Cogito, Ergo Sum.** All philosophers were once little boys, and much knowledge went through their heads before they ever thought of examining what knowledge itself is, and what it bears upon. Before they thought of that, they thought of things. Many of the things were *evident:* for the future philosopher who was a farm boy, the soil, the sun, the rain, the cows, the horses, were evident; that is, they were known in and by themselves and not through something else. They were not inferred or proved, but experienced. Nothing at all was more evident than they. No defense of them had to be given: they needed but to be pointed at, if, as is unlikely, their reality was questioned.

Knowledge begins with things which are, or at least seem, evident in and by themselves. It goes, eventually, far beyond what is evident in itself, but all its advances into the realm of the not immediately evident start from and rest upon something which is immediately evident. In

[10] *De Ver.*, I, 1, c.

any science or in any thinking about practical affairs of life, conclusions, if they are valid, are reached by processes of induction, analysis, and inference which begin from something known in itself without any analysis or inference. In every science and in every sort of systematic thinking, a conclusion has an inalienable claim to assent if it is seen to follow by logical necessity from something which is evident in itself; conversely, any conclusion must be forthwith rejected as false when it is seen to be incompatible with anything which is evident in itself. Evidence is the touchstone. Before the philosopher began to reflect about knowledge, a very great number of things were evident to him and appeared to be valid starting points for thought processes. But when René Descartes turned his attention to the problem of knowledge, he did not take any of these evident *things* as his starting point. Instead, he rejected them all, and took his own thought as his point of departure: *Cogito, ergo sum* — "I think, therefore I am."

Descartes' aim was to arrive at knowledge so clear and so absolutely certain that it could not possibly be questioned. He began in his *Meditations on First Philosophy*,[11] by doubting, or rather by rejecting as false, everything which he had hitherto held as certain; for example, the existence of his own body and of the external world, and the reliability of his senses. The First Meditation sets forth the reasons which make this universal doubt possible and necessary. In the Second Meditation, he comes upon a truth which defies doubt, namely, his own existence; for no matter what he doubts, no matter how completely he is deceived, he must needs exist in order to doubt or be deceived. Hence, he has an *indubitable* starting point; namely, the famous *Cogito, ergo sum* — "I think, therefore I am." From this he goes on, in the same meditation, to demonstrate the nature of the human mind. It is a being which thinks — just that and nothing more. For we must attribute to anything only what is clearly and distinctly contained in the idea of it; and the sole idea I have of myself is that I think. "But what then am I? A thing which thinks."[12]

In the Third Meditation, starting again from his own thinking, that is, *from his idea of God*, Descartes proves the existence of God. The idea of God which he has is the idea of an infinite and perfect being. Now this idea, like anything else, must have an adequate cause to account for its existence. Neither Descartes' mind nor any finite

---

[11] *Descartes — Selections*, ed. Eaton (New York: Scribners, 1927), p. 84 ff.
[12] *Ibid.*, p. 100.

mind is an adequate cause for the idea of an infinite being. Indeed, the only adequate cause for the idea of an infinite being is an infinite being. Therefore, God must exist, since He alone can cause the idea of Him which Descartes has. From this point, Descartes goes on, in the Fourth Meditation, to establish the validity of his own power of reason. His proof starts from the perfection of God. God, who is my creator, is all-perfect; hence He cannot be a deceiver. But if He had given me a reasoning power such that, even when I use it perfectly, accepting as true only what is absolutely clear and distinct, and rejecting as false whatever is in the least doubtful, it would still inevitably lead me into error — if He had given me such a reason, He would be a deceiver. Hence, my certainty of the validity of my reason is as strong as my certainty that God exists. Therefore, that material things exist and that men possess bodies can now be proved; for it is not only my senses and imagination which testify to these, but my reason, whose validity is as certain as God's existence and perfection. This last is in the Sixth Meditation.

2. **The Wrong Starting Point.** Nothing, certainly, is more evident than "I think." But neither is any starting point for an inquiry into knowledge less likely to lead to an understanding of knowledge, and by adopting it, Descartes started modern philosophy down the road that led inevitably to idealism. The starting point, pure thought, effectively excluded external, non-mental beings from the inquiry right from the start. Every inquiry must begin from something which is evident in itself, and must constantly refer back to this self-evident, just as an army advancing must maintain constant communication with its supply depot. No matter how far the inquiry progresses, it gets its whole force only from the immediate evidents from which it starts. An evident which is entirely *subjective,* that is, within the mind, can never give to an inquiry starting from it the force to get beyond the mind. Consequently, modern philosophy, taking its signal from Descartes, was doomed to end in idealism. Hence, we find repeated, in some form or other, by nearly every great modern philosopher the dictum of Descartes, that *all we know immediately and directly are our own ideas.* Some, like Descartes himself, tried to show ways in which, from this direct knowledge of our own ideas, we can and do attain certain, though indirect, knowledge of other things. But their attempts are all failures.

It may be objected, in defense of Descartes, that he actually did start with knowledge other than the *Cogito,* but rejected this other knowledge, one item after another, because he found reason for doubting everything which he had previously considered certain, except the *Cogito,* which he could not doubt. His whole First Meditation examines other possible starting points, but shows that none of them is certain; the second shows that the *Cogito* is certain; indeed, is not that precisely his great contribution to human thought? The answer is: Yes, that is what Descartes did, but his great contribution to human thought was a two-edged sword. The *Cogito* refuted the universal skeptics, for which purpose St. Augustine had used it centuries before; but it tied later philosophers up in their own egos. It is a false starting point because it is not and cannot be a real first datum at all. Descartes thought, all right, but whenever he thought, he thought some *thing;* even when he doubted, he doubted something. If he had really abolished from his mind every *thing* that he thought, he would have annihilated every thought that he had; if, in his doubt, he still thought, it was only because he still thought something. He had no right to affirm the thought without affirming the thing; there is no thought without an object, and knowledge of the object is prior to knowledge of the thought. A man must think something before he can know his thought.

3. **"Cogito" Is Not Descartes' Sole Starting Point.** Descartes did not, as a matter of fact, actually use "I think" as his only first piece of positive knowledge. Some of the things that he knew before he enunciated his *Cogito, ergo sum* are implied in that enunciation and become quite obvious in the chain of reasoning which follows from it. One of them is of primary importance, for it is, according to Thomists, the first evident principle in all knowledge. It is the principle of identity, namely, that everything is what it is, or, in another formula, that that which is, is. It was the undeniable certainty of this principle that allowed Descartes to escape from his doubt through the doubt itself. His existence was indubitable because in order to doubt he had of necessity to exist: to doubt is to be, and that which is, is; I doubt, therefore I am. My idea of my own existence is so clear and distinct that it cannot be doubted; therefore, it cannot be doubted, for clearly nothing can *be* doubted and *not be* doubted at the same time. Whatever is, is what it is; "I think," therefore "I am a being which thinks."

Descartes also knew the principles of sufficient reason and causality as immediately as he knew that he thought. He uses these principles constantly in his argument. His rule that nothing is to be attributed to any being except what is contained clearly and distinctly in the idea of the being is nothing else but his own formula of the principle of sufficient reason. And his proof of God's existence is based explicitly on the principle of causality; as is his vindication of his reason on the ground that its cause (Creator) is all-perfect. I cannot be the cause of my idea of the infinite being because I am finite, and "that *there is nothing in the effect, that has not existed in a similar or in some higher form in the cause,* is a first principle than which none clearer can be entertained."[13] If anyone wishes to understand Descartes' arguments, he "must accustom his mind to put trust in ultimate principles, than which nothing can be more true or more evident. . . ."[14]

It will, of course, be objected, as Descartes himself objected,[15] that these principles are not known prior to the *Cogito, ergo sum,* but in it and by means of it, so that it remains the very first starting point of all knowledge. But Descartes' First Meditation negates this claim. All through the First Meditation he piles reason upon reason for doubting all that he had previously held certain; and in advancing every one of the reasons, he assumes the self-evidence and absolute certainty of the principles of identity, contradiction, sufficient reason, and causality; *and he does not reach the Cogito until the Second Meditation.* Descartes' doubt was, by his own testimony, a *reasoned* doubt based upon indubitable evidence: "at the end I feel constrained to confess that there is nothing in all that I formerly believed to be true, of which I cannot in some measure doubt, and that not merely through want of thought or through levity, but for reasons which are very powerful and maturely considered. . . ."[16] Clearly Descartes exempted from his doubt the reasons for his doubt. He saves himself from the absurd position of the skeptic, who offers indubitable evidence that everything is doubtful, only by his later explicit statement that there are ultimate principles, for example, the principle of causality, "than which nothing can be more true or more evident."

4. An Impossible Starting Point. What concerns us chiefly, however, is not the fact that "I think" was not Descartes' real point of departure, but the fact that *"I think" is impossible as a first starting point of*

[13] *Meditations on First Philosophy,* Replies to Objections (*Descartes — Selections.* ed. Eaton, p. 181).

[14] *Ibid.,* 181.

[15] *Ibid.,* 186.

[16] First Meditation, *ibid.,* p. 93.

knowledge. It is impossible because I cannot know that I think before I know what my thought is about. Thought is always about something, and the mind always goes to this something — that is to say, it thinks of it — before it goes to or thinks of its own thought. In more technical language, "I think" expresses a *reflex* cognition of the mind — the thought of its own thought — which presupposes a *direct* cognition — the thought of something other than its own thought. Aristotle and St. Thomas were right in saying that the mind knows itself only by knowing its act of knowing something other than itself; and because they were right, Descartes was wrong in trying to make *Cogito* the first positive starting point of all knowledge.

5. **The Right Starting Point: "I Know."** Where, then, should he have started? Since he wished to study knowledge, he should have started with *the act of knowing;* just as one who wishes to study biology starts with living bodies. Starting with the act of knowing is not at all the same thing as starting with the act of pure thought. In the first place, there are no acts of pure thought to start with; and in the second place, if there were they would tell the inquirer nothing about knowledge. Now Descartes' First Meditation was full of acts of knowing, from which he might have started the positive side of his inquiry. For each doubt, he gave a reason; for example, he doubts that the things which he perceives now, when he is awake, are real, because *he knows* that unreal things have seemed quite as real when he was asleep and dreaming. He doubts that he is awake now, because *he knows* that he has dreamed and mistakenly believed himself awake. Everything that he doubts, he doubts because *he knows a sufficient reason* for doubting it. He knows that nothing is certain without a sufficient reason for its certainty. And he knows — this is the absolutely first principle of his whole philosophy — that that which is in any way doubtful is not certain; that is to say, he knows, as the first principle of all thought, the principle of contradiction, expressed under the formula that that which is doubtful cannot be certain. None of these truths can wait upon the *Cogito* — not even in Descartes' own order of exposition.

6. **Knowledge Is Someone Knowing Something.** If Descartes had started with *Scio* — I know — rather than with *Cogito* — I think — the whole history of modern philosophy might have been different. The study of knowledge ought, it would seem, to take as its point of de-

parture the act of knowing. Knowledge is always someone knowing something; it is as unthinkable without the something as it is without the someone: a man does not know, if he knows nothing. The reason why Descartes started with *Cogito* rather than *Scio* is that he did not feel certain that he knew, whereas he could not doubt that he thought, since doubting is itself thinking. He was confused even at this point; either he did know, or he had no right to start at all. What gave him the right to start as he did (wrong way though it was) was not the fact that he doubted or that he thought, but the fact that he *knew* that he doubted; because only something known can be the starting point of a demonstration. Consequently, Descartes should have started with "I know."

7. Why the Subjectivistic Error Is Possible. Among the great number of things which I know, my own thinking does not have the favored position which Descartes gave it. When I know that I think, my knowledge is no clearer nor more distinct than when I know that the rain is falling. Yet it is not difficult to understand why it seemed to Descartes to have a favored and, in fact, a unique position. The object upon which our mind is immediately turned is always at that moment most evident to the mind. What Descartes was engaged in was the study of his own ideas, and it was upon those that his mind was immediately bent; since he was studying these ideas, they were far more evident to him at the moment than were the things of which they were ideas. Hence he assumed that he knew his own thinking more clearly and distinctly than he knew anything else. Of course he did — when he was thinking of his thinking; and, of course, he had to think of his thinking whenever he wanted to study his ideas to see which of them were absolutely clear and distinct. In other words, what Descartes did was to take as the type of our knowledge in general that very special kind of knowledge which consists in the reflection upon our own ideas.

8. Substitution of Intramental for Extramental Object. Descartes and the idealistic philosophers who followed the way broached by him needed, in order to enter upon their inquiry, a self-evident truth to start with. Since they were studying their own minds, they seized upon a self-evident truth which they found within their minds; and that seemed fair enough. This self-evident was, for each of them, his own thought, his own ideas. Now suppose that one of them tries to compare that thought with something else, as to their respective clarity and distinctness to his mind; for example, suppose that he compares his own ideas with a big, vicious dog encountered on a lonely country road. Which will be more clear and evident? On the road, when the philosopher is face to face with the dog, the dog (*not the idea of the dog*) will possess for him a clarity and distinctness — a self-evidence — which nothing else in the world will ever surpass. But even idealists do not pursue their inquiries into the nature of knowledge when confronted by big, evil-intentioned dogs; they wait till they get home. But when they get home the dog is not there, and they are alone with their memories. Their mind can have only one object in clear focus at a time, and when it is a mean dog, it is the dog. When they are studying their ideas, it is their ideas. Their error — without doubt it is an error — is to forget that the knowledge which they should be inquiring into is every kind of knowledge which they have, including the kind they had of the dog when his real, extramental presence before them was terrifyingly evident and impossible to doubt, instead of only that kind of knowledge which they have when they are engaged in studying knowledge. They lose sight of the distinction between knowledge whose object is extramental and knowledge whose object is intramental, because they actually study only the latter kind.

Some idealists answer that we have no right to speak of two kinds of knowledge. We do not and cannot, they say, distinguish between extramental and intramental objects of our knowledge, since all objects must be intramental, that is, in our mind, in order to be known at all. This argument smacks of pretense. Acts of knowing, as they are experienced by the one knowing, have either of two sorts of objects: extramental or intramental. *We know whatever we know either as a thing within our mind or as a thing outside our mind:* horses, trees, men, as outside our mind; our thoughts, decisions, doubts, hopes, fears, as within our mind. To say that we do not and cannot distinguish between intramental and extramental objects of knowledge is to speak recklessly and irresponsibly, because it is to ignore the one immediate evidence which is relevant to the point at issue, the evidence, namely, of the act of knowing. Only confusion is gained by calling an object of knowledge intramental in any other sense than that it is known as an affection or action of the mind. Only psychic entities are intramental objects of knowledge; and only mine are of my knowledge.

IV. THE STARTING POINT OF EPISTEMOLOGY

1. The Proper Data to Start From. Like every inquiry, the inquiry into the truth value of human knowledge has to begin somewhere. Where any inquiry is to begin is determined by the data which occasions the inquiry; that is to say, we start with what is given and needs to be explained. The reason why there is an epistemological inquiry at all is the fact that in some of their thoughts and judgments men are spontaneously certain that they possess truth. The inquiry has for aim to ascertain whether or not they actually do possess truth, as they naïvely think they do. Hence, the only useful starting point for this inquiry is those acts in which men are spontaneously certain that they have laid hold upon truth itself. They have this spontaneous certitude in those judgments wherein their mind is in presence of a being so evident that doubt about it is impossible and they are therefore impelled to assert it to be what it is; the "truth" which they have is the being itself, manifesting and asserting itself in their minds. At any rate, that is the way it seems at the time.

Consequently, to start the inquiry from thought, as if thought were something separate or separable from the being which is thought, is to begin from a wrong point of departure, and to determine from the outset that the true goal of the inquiry will not be attained. That is what Descartes did. If there is any thought separate from something thought, it is not the act with which epistemology is concerned. Epistemology aims at ascertaining whether human knowledge attains what truly is; and when men are certain that their thought is identical with what is, they say "I know," not "I think." The proper starting point of an inquiry into the validity of human knowledge is the act of knowing, the act wherein someone knows something.

Of various kinds of acts of knowing, one kind is the most suitable point of departure for epistemology. This inquiry is concerned with the *objective validity* of our knowledge; hence its primary interest and its only fertile datum is the act in which the object known is known as something which is real independently of the mind. In other words, epistemology ought to start from acts of knowing whose objects are known as extramental. The commonest and most primary type of such acts is the perceptive judgment, the act in which the mind affirms the being of something directly perceived through the senses. We make such a judgment when, for example, we judge that the tree we are now looking at is there.

In the third place, some selection must be made even among such objects; some of them are more important than others. For the Thomistic philosopher there is no question which are the most important: they are those which are the basis of all philosophy; those which are the primary subject matter of the queen of the sciences, metaphysics. If being, substance, causality, potency and act, essence and existence, the principles of identity and sufficient reason, are not extramentally valid notions, then Thomistic metaphysics is not a science but a game, and should be classified with jigsaw and crossword puzzles — fascinating and futile. Consequently, when we turn in a later chapter to a more positive study of the validity of our ideas and judgments, it is with these fundamental ideas that we shall concern ourselves.[17]

2. The Proper Procedure at the Beginning. How is the inquiry to be carried out? There are some who maintain that it cannot even be started. Real being, says one group, is given as self-evident in knowledge, and to question it is to question the only possible datum upon which an inquiry could be founded. Hence, it must not be questioned, if there is to be any philosophy at all. Epistemology, in other words, is not a part of philosophy, but a disease of the modern mind. Reason, says another group, is what epistemology calls up for judgment; but the judgment can be pronounced only by reason herself; hence the judgment is worthless, since the judge is uncertified until she certifies herself; and how can she?

3. Reason Must and Can Judge Herself. Both these objections must be met by the same answer. The philosopher simply cannot exempt any department of being or of experience from his study or from his critical examination. If, in order to subject human knowledge to his critical examination, he must adopt a critical attitude even toward the self-evident data of experience, well, then, he must, and that's that. If, in order to examine the reliability of his reasoning power, he must use that power to prosecute the examination, well, again, then he must, that's all. A convalescent will never walk if he will not start for fear that his legs will not hold him, nor will he ever find out whether they will hold him. If he tries, and they will not, he will collapse; if he tries and does not collapse, they will hold him; he has "proved it by walking." The philosopher will never know whether his reason can stand up under critical examination unless he uses it to make that examination; if it cannot stand up, it will fall down; if it does not

[17] We do this in Chapter XVIII, "Our Knowledge of First Principles."

fall down, it has stood up. No one has ever denied that reason can try; she must, then, be allowed to try.

Another answer can be given. What right has anyone to assume that reason is incapable of judging herself, that her self-certification is a vicious circle? Reason judges the other faculties; witness the skeptic's arguments based upon the errors of sense. Reason, as a matter of fact, is nothing else than the faculty of judgment; she is judgment pure and simple. In civil life we do not let a judge sit in judgment upon himself; but that is because he is not all judgment — he is often mostly self, and only a little bit judge. A judge who is pure judgment would judge himself as competently as he judges anyone else, and more competently than anyone else could judge him. In a word, *it is as unnecessary as it is absurd to demand beyond the faculty of judgment a judge to certify that faculty.* Reason must certify herself, because no one else can; and she can certify herself. We saw in Chapter XII that St. Thomas finds that reason's ability to judge her own judgments is the root of our free will. That same ability, which reason has because of her power of reflecting upon herself, is the root of our ability to know truth and know that we know it. "Wherefore, the intellect knows the truth by reflecting upon itself," wrote St. Thomas, in a passage which we shall cite and explain below. Because of her ability to reflect upon her own acts, reason can judge her own judgments and certify herself.

4. The Establishment of Realism. Spontaneous certitude about the objective reality of known things — e.g., the certitude of a man confronted by a mad dog as to the extramental reality of that dog — is not philosophical certitude; it is not a philosophical position at all. But it is the point of departure for a philosophical inquiry, because it is the relevant datum of that inquiry. In the spontaneous-certitude situation there are always three data distinguishable upon reflective analysis: something known, the act of knowing it, and the self performing this act. In other words, what we know in knowing anything is (1) the thing, (2) the act of knowing, (3) the knowing self.

In many cases — these are the relevant cases — the *thing* is known as extramental; that is, as *being* independent of my mind or even of my whole self. The first question is, Can I know, after critical reflection, that this thing *is* independently of my knowing it? One view answers that I must not make this critical reflection on the very being of the thing that seems to be, because that being must be my starting point; if I question my starting point I shall never get started. Another view — Descartes' — is that I must doubt this being and must then start from the doubt and not from the being. The first view enables me to construct a positive metaphysics, but a dogmatically based one; that is, one in which I have carefully examined and certified everything except its foundation. The second view — history proves it — leads to skepticism. Is there a third way possible?

According to simple logical division there ought to be a third way. I may start at once from the being (first way), or I may doubt the being and start from the doubt (second way), or I may doubt the being, dispel the doubt, and then start from the being (third way). Not only is this last way the only one which holds out hope of attaining a position of justified realism, but it is also the only way which is truly critical. The first way is not critical at all, but dogmatic. The second way is ostensibly critical, but its criticism is too selective; it is critical of knowledge, but not of doubt.

Critical reflection upon any spontaneous-certitude situation, that is, upon a common experience in which we judge, on the grounds of its own immediate and undeniable evidence, that some real extramental being exists, reveals these three facts: (1) that we cannot doubt about the absolute evidence of the objects of our common experience when our attention is directly upon these objects; (2) that we can doubt about the absolute evidence of these objects when we turn our attention away from them to our ideas of them; (3) that this doubt can be accounted for on grounds which have no bearing upon the real evidence of the objects of common experience but only upon certain limitations of our own mind; indeed, the reasons which have made the doubt possible disappear when they are noted and critically reflected upon. These three facts warrant the adoption of direct realism as a philosophical position. We shall now show that this is so.

It is psychologically impossible to doubt, in the act of perception, the independent reality of an object perceived as extramentally real. Doubt about a perceived object presupposes a reflection upon the perception — a reflection which once begun puts an end to the direct perception itself; the validity of the perception can be questioned only by an act different from the perception itself. While I sit at my window entranced by the spectacle of a pair of robins dive-bombing a squirrel to keep it away from their nest, I do not and cannot question the existence, out there on the campus, of robins and squirrels. But when

I begin to reflect upon my experience, I can doubt the extramental being of its objects. Even while 1 still watch the robins diving at the squirrels, I can fall to wondering whether such things can really be, outside my mind. Am I, perhaps, dreaming them up? Are they anything besides my own ideas? But when I pursue such wonderings, I am not really *perceiving* the robins and squirrel any longer; I am thinking about my previous perception and spontaneous judgment. This is what Descartes did, as he looked at his hand and wondered if it were really there. In such reflection my immediate object of thought is my own previous cognitive act, and not the thing which was *its* immediate object. The mind always seeks an *evident;* in reflection the new object is now the evident and, in comparison with it, the old object, now known only mediately, is not an evident at all. The new object, by the very nature of reflection, is an intramental object; and this gives to intramental objects a specious superiority over extramental realities, since epistemological inquiry is of necessity reflective. But a truly critical epistemology will recognize this superiority as spurious.

5. **The Reflection Must Really Have the Perception as Its Object.** Finally, the doubt made psychologically possible by the shift of direct attention from the thing to the act of knowing it — i.e., by the substitution in reflection of the *act* for the *thing* as immediate object of the mind — is logically untenable, and, as a matter of fact, psychologically anomalous, when the reflection is correctly made and has for its object what it really ought to have; namely, *the previous act of knowing the extramental thing as undeniably evident.* That is why we have insisted above that Descartes should have started with *Scio,* I know, instead of with *Cogito,* I think. If there is any thinking which is not knowing, it is irrelevant to the epistemological inquiry. If knowing is confused with some real or non-existent pure thinking, the epistemological inquiry is routed down the wrong line and dispatched to inevitable wreckage. If I wish truly to reflect upon my perception of the robins fighting off the squirrel and my spontaneous judgment of their reality, then that perception and that judgment, *with their full measure of real, evident, and undeniable robins and squirrel,* are what I must reflect upon, and not some plausible substitute, such as a mere present imagining of the robins and the squirrel. When the original act *remembered,* and not an impostor act *imagined,* is reflected upon, all its unquestionable certainty is seen in it; because it is known now, reflectively, as an *act of knowing,* not merely as an idea.

This point is so important that we must risk becoming tiresome in seeking to make it clear. The reflective act and the original act of perceptive judgment are alike in one respect and different in another. Both are acts of knowing: in both the mind knows something. But in the perceptive judgment the immediate object known is known as an extramental thing; whereas in the reflective act the immediate object is, and is known as, an intramental thing, namely, the original direct judgment. Now, if we are going to be critical, we must be critical about both acts. While subjecting the first act to the critical reflection of the second, we must be sure that the second one really has the first as its object; if it has any other object it is not merely useless but deceptive. But it does not have the first as its object except when it clearly grasps the first as giving to the mind, evidently and undeniably, an extramental thing. If it does give the mind such an object, the mind will see that it has no grounds for doubting the objective validity of its spontaneous perceptive judgments about the real existence of extramental being.

6. **How We Know That We Know the Truth.** But this removal of doubt it not quite enough. The intellect, in order to possess truth fully, must not only know something, but must also know that it knows the thing truly, that is to say, that it conforms to it. The intellect must know real being: *verum est id quod est;* it must be itself conformed to that being: *veritas est adaequatio rei et intellectus;* and it must know its conformity: *verum est manifestativum et declarativum esse.* This last full measure of truth the intellect attains by reflecting upon itself. There were, remember, three data in the original perceptive judgment which the mind made its starting point for the epistemological inquiry: the thing known, the act of knowing, and the intellect which performs the act. This last, the intellect itself, must also be subjected to reason's critical reflection; only by knowing its own nature as the principle of its operation can the intellect become absolutely certain of its hold upon truth.

The human intellect cannot study its own nature except by studying its own behavior: *operatio sequitur esse;* we learn what a thing is by first learning what it does. And when the intellect turns its attention upon its own operations, it very quickly sees that it does only one thing, wants to do only one thing, and can do only one thing. That thing is to put itself into conformity with reality; *to reproduce, generate, or conceive within itself what beings are in themselves.* In other words, it seeks the truth about things. To become in itself what things are in themselves — that is the sole function of intellect. An intellect may do this well or poorly, completely or partly, just as an eye may see well or poorly, completely or partly; but it does not and cannot do or seek to do anything else, any more than an eye can do anything but see. Man has within him an appetite and a power for truth; and the truth, whether found or merely sought, never poses as anything but understanding things as they are. Because he has this appetite and this power, he started upon his quest for truth, his pursuit of that which is; and it was this same appetite and power which gave him pause and made him question whether he can actually attain to the knowledge of real being; therefore he turns the power in upon itself, and he asks, What is it? What is my intellect in itself, as it really is? Then he sees that it is the very appetite which has been driving him along from the beginning of his quest; it is that whose nature it is to conform itself to being; it is that whose thirst will not be quenched while there is being left to become one with; it is that which naught can command but being, that whose assent is compelled only by evident being.

Then shall we ask, how does the intellect know that it knows the truth? It possesses truth and knows that it possesses it, because it knows that of its nature it cannot be compelled by anything but a being to which it is conformed. In some of its judgments it is compelled by an evident being. Knowing itself now, and knowing itself judging that something is, it knows that it so judges because there is present in it a being manifesting and asserting itself, and conforming the intellect to itself, so that the intellect is compelled to assert that that being is what it is.

We have not cited St. Thomas very often in the above inquiry into truth, but the thoughts expressed have been his. Here is one passage from *De Veritate*, on which the entire last section of this chapter has been a commentary:

> For [truth] is in the intellect as following upon the act of the intellect and as known by the intellect. For it follows upon the operation of the intellect according as the judgment of the intellect is about a thing inasmuch as it is; but it is known by the intellect insofar as the intellect reflects upon its act, not only according as it knows its act, but according as it knows the relation of the act to the thing. But it cannot know this unless it knows the nature of the act itself; which, again, cannot be known unless the nature of the active principle is known. But this

[principle] is the intellect itself, in whose nature it is to conform to things. Wherefore, the intellect knows the truth by reflecting upon itself.[18]

Two things remain to be said. First, the realistic conclusion of the above argument can be escaped only by denying the data; that is, only by denying: (1) that we naturally and inevitably distinguish, among the objects of our ideas, objects which are known as extramental and objects which are known as intramental; (2) that in direct-experience situations we spontaneously affirm with unquestioning certitude that real things exist outside ourselves and are perceived by us, (3) that we can ever remember such spontaneous and certain judgments, or (4) that we can analyze these judgments reflectively. Anyone who wishes to make these denials is welcome to do so. Second, we have not, in the above paragraphs, really entered upon a Thomistic epistemology; we have merely determined the proper point of departure and the initial procedure for the epistemological inquiry. We have not, that is to say, proved that robins or squirrels or mad dogs are real; we have only indicated how one ought to approach the examination into their reality, if one cares. The present author does not care very much; what he cares about is whether being and the principle of identity, substance and accident, cause and effect, and all the primary notions which are the foundations of metaphysics are real. Dogs and squirrels and robins seem to be quite sure of themselves, and even idealists and skeptics seldom challenge their right to exist. But being itself, and metaphysics, the science of being, are in ill-favor in many circles today; and consequently a defense of the realities which form the basis of metaphysics is in order. However, before we enter upon this defense, we must examine another effort to save metaphysics from idealism and skepticism — an attempt which failed, and of which the final result, up to the present date, has been rather the destruction of metaphysics than its salvation.

[18] *De Ver.*, I, 9, c.

CHAPTER XV

HUME, KANT, AND CONTEMPORARY NATURALISM

I. HUME AND KANT

1. In the first section of the last chapter we saw that the subjectivism which Descartes made the starting point of modern philosophy, instead of producing the certain and indisputable knowledge which he expected from it, led to the radical empiricism and skepticism of David Hume. Descartes, rejecting the testimony of his senses, had tried to prove that the external world exists. Hume showed that it can't be proved. We remarked, after we had indicated this final result of the Cartesian experiment, that Immanuel Kant made a great effort to rescue philosophy from the evil days upon which it had fallen, but that he failed because he did not go far enough back for his own starting point — he did not go back beyond the subjectivistic postulate of Descartes. The real villain of the piece, in the drama of modern philosophy, is subjectivism. The philosophical structure erected by Kant is a work of genius and is truly awe inspiring in its magnitude and systematic articulation; but its timbers are rotten with subjectivism.

To hold that the Kantian philosophy is fundamentally erroneous, and that it gave birth to two of the most pernicious errors of the modern mind, namely positivism and modernism, is not to hold that the Sage of Königsberg was not one of the world's great thinkers. His primary objective was to rescue the perennial philosophy from the extravagances of extreme rationalism on the one hand and of skeptical empiricism on the other. If, in his fight against these enemies of true philosophy, he fell into great extravagances himself, we need not conclude that his effort was altogether futile. If he did not succeed in reestablishing the true metaphysics, he did start philosophy on a fresh quest for metaphysical knowledge — a quest which would have been considered futile if the skepticism of Hume had been allowed to hold the field unchallenged by anything better than the innatist rationalism which he had so badly crippled. Thomists recognize Plato as a savior of the human intellect in an age when Sophism seriously threatened to discredit it entirely, although they also believe that Platonism is itself fundamentally erroneous. A similar attitude would seem proper toward Kant; he did turn skepticism aside for a long time, even though the seeds of naturalism were in his own philosophy.

Unfortunately, in the present chapter our emphasis will be almost entirely on the harmful things which arose from Kantian philosophy, and not upon the good things. The characteristic feature of contemporary thought which is most opposed to the *philosophia perennis* is naturalism; and our present task is to see how contemporary naturalism is a logical result of Kantianism. We shall probably overstate our case, since many factors besides Kantianism helped to give rise to naturalism, but this seems to be unavoidable without writing a whole history of modern thought. By presenting the story from the point of view of the effect of Kantian philosophy we shall be able to keep always in close touch with the metaphysical issues involved.

Kant was born in 1724 and died in 1804. His three greatest works, *The Critique of Pure Reason, The Critique of Pracitical Reason,* and *The Critique of Judgment,* were all written in the last quarter of the eighteenth century. In his early years as a teacher of philosophy he had followed the rationalistic *a priori* system of Leibniz and Wolff, but later on he became acquainted with the teachings of the British empiricists, especially David Hume, and his philosophical views underwent a complete transformation. He was, he wrote, "awakened from my dogmatic slumbers" by the penetrating attack of Hume upon all the principles that were the indispensable basis of the traditional rationalistic philosophy.

2. Hume's Attack on Metaphysics. Hume had argued, with great appearance of success, that the fundamental metaphysical conceptions, such as causality and permanent substance, are all unfounded assumptions, validated by neither reason nor experience, and owing their hold upon men's minds entirely to mental habit. Causation, for example, we never experience, nor can we rationally demonstrate its existence. We experience only certain unvarying sequences of events; for example, event A always followed by event B. When we have seen B follow A a great number of times, and no cases where A

is not followed by *B*, we come to expect *B* whenever we experience *A*. Our expectancy regularly fulfilled, we get to thinking of *B* as *following from A* and of *A* as *producing B*. Then we form the judgment that *B* must follow from *A,* and we call *A* the cause and *B* the effect. In cold fact we have never experienced the production or causation at all, but only the sequence of events; and we have no right to assume that the former event produces or causes the latter.

We are not even satisfied with invalidly creating this notion of cause. We erect it into a universal principle, which we call the principle of causality: every event must have a cause. Hume examines each of the arguments supposed to establish this principle and rejects them all. He subjects to like criticism other notions which stand as the foundation of metaphysics, and comes to the same conclusion: none of them is given in experience and none can be rationally demonstrated. The only data of experience are particular, contingent events. Permanent substance, whether material or mental, causation, universal and necessary principles, all fall outside experience and outside demonstration. Metaphysics is idle speculation, and the whole of knowledge is sense experience of the flux of individual phenomena. Whether there is a substantial material world which causes our experience, and whether we have a substantial soul or ego of which our experiences are the changing states, we cannot possibly know.

Kant saw that Hume's philosophy destroyed not only metaphysics but science as well. Now, you may be able to doubt the validity of metaphysics, but you cannot doubt the validity of mathematics and physics. At any rate, the intellectual world of Kant's day, dominated by the great mathematical physics of Isaac Newton, could not question for an instant the certainty of mathematical and physical truths. Yet you had to doubt them if Hume was entirely right, for the laws that constitute them are universals which can never have been experienced. Kant, therefore, decided that what must be done was to push the inquiry of Hume further until some final result would be reached concerning the possibility and the requisite conditions for both science and metaphysics.

II. "THE CRITIQUE OF PURE REASON"*

1. Kant's Inquiry. Kant's way of going about this inquiry into the

* I have used both the *Critique* and the *Prolegomena* in the explanation which follows. All quotations are from the Meiklejohn translation of the *Critique.*

possibility of and the conditions for science and metaphysics was to examine, not the things in the physical world, but the mind of man. After all, if you want to answer the question, What things can man know? you must first answer the prior question, not, What things are there? but, What kind of mind has man to know with? It is just because philosophers have not started off by answering this question first that philosophy has floundered around for centuries getting nowhere while science has been making rapid strides forward. If we begin by finding out *how* the human mind knows those things of whose certainty there is no question, we can then determine what it is capable of knowing and what is outside the limits of its knowledge. Fortunately we have a starting point for our inquiry, for the knowledge that is embraced in the sciences of mathematics and physics is certain knowledge. In order, therefore, to discover the conditions of valid scientific knowledge we need only to discover the conditions which make it possible for us to construct the two sciences of mathematics and physics. When we have discovered these conditions we can then see if they are present also in the realm of realities studied in metaphysics. If they are, then a science of metaphysics is possible; if they are not, no such science is possible.

Kant carries out this inquiry in his *Critique of Pure Reason* and summarizes it more briefly and in different form in his *Prolegomena to All Future Metaphysics*. Let us try to follow the major steps in his argument.

2. Synthetic "A Priori" Judgments. The primary reason why Hume had rejected the principle of causality, substance, and other such conceptions is that in formulating them the mind *adds* something to what is given in experience. For example, the universal proposition that "every event must have a cause" is not a merely *analytic* proposition, that is, one whose predicate merely *names* something already implied in the subject, like the proposition "all bodies occupy space." On the contrary, it is a *synthetic* proposition, that is, one whose predicate really *adds* something to the notion of its subject. This is obvious, for the subject "event" does not include in its conception the notion "having a cause." On the other hand, this proposition is not *a posteriori*, that is, it is not given in experience, like the proposition, "I feel warm." We do not *experience* every event and its necessary production by a cause. In fact, we cannot possibly experience anything universal and necessary, because our senses are capable of receiving only the particular and contingent. Every universal and necessary proposition, therefore, is *a priori,* or *independent of experience.* Consequently, the proposition "every event must have a cause" is *a priori* and *synthetic,* it is independent of experience and it adds something to the subject. Such propositions, *synthetic a priori* propositions, are the only ones that can form the laws of a science. For these laws are both universal and necessary and they actually add something to our knowledge of their subject matter. Consequently, if we are willing with Hume to reject all synthetic *a priori* judgments, we reject mathematics and physics. This, however, is absurd, and therefore synthetic *a priori* judgments must be possible. Since they are, metaphysics may be possible. At any rate, it is clear to Kant that he now knows how to approach the problem of the possibility of metaphysics. We need but answer the question, *How* are synthetic *a priori* judgments possible? and then go on to examine whether the conditions that make them possible are present in the subject matter of metaphysics. If they are, metaphysics is possible; if they are not, it is impossible. In order to find out how synthetic *a priori* judgments are possible, that is to say, what the conditions are which make them valid, we need simply to examine how our mind forms the judgments of mathematics and physics. Having thus found out *how* our mind knows, we can easily answer the question of *what* it is able to know.

That sounds very simple, but it was, in Kant's eyes, a revolution in philosophy. Hitherto, all philosophers had assumed that the mind must conform to the objects it knows, and had consequently directed their study and speculation to whatever objects they conceived, without first determining whether the human intellect can know them. Kant makes the contrary assumption, that the objects of knowledge must conform to the mind, and, consequently, the first thing that he sets about doing is to determine the conditions of knowledge inherent in the mind itself — the *a priori* conditions of knowledge. Obviously, only such objects as can conform to these conditions can be known. What are these conditions?

3. Sensibility and Understanding. To begin with we can and must, according to Kant, distinguish two different powers that operate in our knowledge. These are sensibility and understanding. By sensibility we receive data and perceive objects, and by understanding we form judgments concerning these objects. Both must operate in knowledge, because if we had merely the perceptions of sense, and did not classify them under the conceptions of the understanding, we could not be said to know anything; perceptions without conceptions would be blind. Neither would we know anything if we had only the conceptions with no objects of experience to which to apply them; conceptions without perceptions would be empty. Knowledge or judgment occurs, therefore, when the understanding spontaneously organizes under its conceptions the perceptions presented to it by sensibility.

4. The "A Priori" Forms of Sensibility: Space and Time. Let us examine sensibility. The first thing that strikes our attention is that there are two universal and necessary conditions in all our sense experience. All the perceptions of external sensation — what we see, hear, touch, etc. — are spatial in character. Their objects are here or there, near or far, left or right; they are all located in what we call space. All the percepts of internal sensation — what we feel within ourselves; our thoughts, pains, hopes, pleasures — though not spatial like the objects of external sense, are temporal; they form a time series. Men have always assumed that space and time are real characters of the external world, and that both men themselves and the objects they perceive truly exist in space and time. But that, says Kant, is impossible. Space and time are universal and necessary characters of the objects of all sensation. Now, as Hume had conclusively shown, experience can give only what is particular and contingent. Therefore, space and time cannot possibly be given in experience. Besides, the fact that we can imagine space as empty of all objects but can neither imagine objects not in space nor imagine space itself away proves that our intuition of space is independent of our experience of sensible bodies. Similarly, we cannot imagine any experience except as part of a time sequence. Kant concludes that space and time are contributed to perception, not by experience, but by the mind itself. They are the two *forms of sensibility* into which sensations are received.

5. Phenomenon and Noumenon. Here, then, is what happens in every act of perception: sensations (that is, mere chaotic, formless impressions of color, heat or cold, taste, etc.) are given to the faculty of sense; sense imposes upon these sensations, in receiving them, the two *a priori* forms of space and time; the sensations now organized under these two forms constitute the object of perception, namely, the perception or phenomenon. What is such an object of perception? In other words, what sort of thing do we perceive? The *matter* of the object is what is given by experience, namely, chaotic sense impressions;

the *form* is what is contributed *a priori* by sensibility, namely, space and time. Very clearly, then, the object itself is nothing that belongs to the real world apart from our mind. It is something constructed by the mind out of formless impressions. It is not any "thing-in-itself"; it is a "thing-as-it-appears-to-us." Thing-in-itself, that is, the source and cause of the sensations, Kant calls noumenon; things-as-they-appear-to-us, that is, the objects constructed by sense, he calls phenomena. *We can never,* he insists, *know noumena; all our knowledge bears upon phenomena.*

6. The First Condition for Synthetic "A Priori" Judgments. It is clear now how the synthetic *a priori* judgments of mathematics are possible. They can be synthetic and not merely the analysis of concepts, because the matter of the percept, the sensation, is given in experience. And they can be *a priori,* or necessary and independent of experience, because the forms of the percept, space and time, are contributed by sensibility itself, independently of the particular experience. It is also clear why the judgments of mathematics have apodictic, unqualified certainty and universal validity. Every phenomenon *must* conform to the laws of mathematics, which are the laws of the nature of space and time, because space and time are the forms of perception itself, and without them there can be no perception. The mind, in perceiving, makes the data given it by experience spatial and temporal. Finally, it is clear — and this is all-important — that we can never perceive things as they are in themselves, i.e., noumena. We can perceive only things as they appear to us, clothed in our mental forms of space and time, i.e., phenomena. Thus, an object that I perceive through external sense, for example a lemon, is not a thing-in-itself, a noumenon; it is merely a thing-as-it-appears-to-me, a phenomenon. Likewise, that object which I perceive by my internal sense, the empirical or experienced ego that I call myself, is not myself as I am in myself but myself as I appear to me. My ego-in-itself I cannot know, because it is noumenal not phenomenal.

7. The "A priori" Forms of the Understanding. That we do form valid synthetic *a priori* judgments about nature is unquestionable, since we do have a pure science of nature, namely, physics, a science in which there "are actually universal laws which subsist completely *a priori.*" Examples of such laws are: substance is permanent; every event is always previously determined by a cause according to constant laws. If, therefore, we discover how the understanding arrives at these laws of nature (i.e., physical laws) we can determine the conditions in general for synthetic *a priori* judgments.

In the first place, it is clear that such judgments can pertain only to "possible objects of experience," for nature means the complex of all the possible objects of experience together with the laws governing their relations. Now only phenomena, never noumena, are possible objects of experience. Here, then, is a first condition: objectively valid universal judgments can be made only about phenomena. Second, it is just as clear that we do not derive the laws of nature from experience, since experience is never of the universal and necessary. This gives us a second condition: the laws by which phenomena are necessarily related are given to the phenomena *a priori* by the understanding. One thing then remains: to discover the *a priori* forms by which the understanding organizes phenomena into laws of nature, just as we have already discovered the *a priori* forms by which sensibility forms impressions into objects of experience, or phenomena.

In order to find what these *a priori* elements are we must abstract from the *matter* of judgments and fix our attention upon their *form,* or the manner in which the judgment produces its synthesis. Consequently, it is by examining the various types of judgments that we shall discover the forms of the understanding. According to their quantity, judgments are singular, particular, or universal; this gives us the three *a priori* forms, or categories, as Kant calls them, of quantity: *unity, plurality, totality.* The division of judgments into positive, negative, and infinite discloses the underlying categories of quality; namely *reality, negation,* and *limitation.* The categories of relation underlie the distinction of categorical, hypothetical, and disjunctive judgments; they are *inherence and subsistence, causality and dependence,* and *reciprocity.* Finally the forms of thought which produce problematical, assertatory, and apodictic judgments are the categories of modality: *possibility, actuality,* and *necessity.*

8. Causality and Substance. We cannot here follow Kant's deduction of all the categories but we must get some idea of how he deduces two which are basic concepts in metaphysics, namely, cause and substance.

Examine the difference between a mere subjective judgment, for example, "The sun shone on the rock for some time and the rock became warm," and an objective universal judgment, for example, "If the sun shines upon a rock, it warms it." The former merely states a particular conjunction of two phenomena in my experience; the latter asserts a necessary connection between two phenomena. Now under what condition can this assertion of necessary and universal connection be justified? Certainly only on condition that the understanding join or unify the two phenomena under the form or conception of cause and effect; if, and only if, the sun-shining and the rock-becoming-warm are conceived as cause and effect, can the understanding assert that always and necessarily a rock will become warm when the sun shines on it.

It is evident that the conception of cause and effect is not derived from experience. If it were it would be *a posteriori,* contingent, and particular, whereas cause and effect are conjoined universally and necessarily; furthermore, we never experience causality but only phenomena. Hence, cause and effect is a *pure concept of the understanding,* an *a priori* form under which the understanding subsumes perceptions when it forms a conditional judgment of the type, "If *x,* then *y.*" Only a mind which judges under the category of causality could possibly form such a judgment.

In a similar manner, from the categorical judgment Kant derives the pure conception, subsistence and inherence (substance and accident). The type of the universal (or objective) categorical judgment is, *A* is *B.* The only condition that can possibly justify this universal conjunction is the condition that *A* and *B* are conceived as substance and accident. Hence, only a mind that has in itself the pure conception of substance and accident can possibly join a subject and predicate as they are joined in *a priori* synthetic categorical judgments.

9. The Schemata of the Imagination. Kant recognized the need of some medium between the phenomena and the categories of the understanding in order that the latter, which in themselves are perfectly abstract and universal, might be brought into contact with the former, which are concrete and particular. This medium is the productive imagination. It consists in the pure intuition of time, and therefore it is precisely the medium required, since like experience it is intuitive and like the categories it is *a priori.* Because it is *a priori* the understanding can bring it under the categories independently of experience; and because it is intuitive as well as *a priori,* it furnishes *a priori* conditions of all intuition, and therefore of all possible experience. The understanding, by applying its categories to the productive imagination, forms the *schemata* of judgment. Each category (unity, totality, plurality, substance and accident, cause and effect, etc.)

forms its own *schema*. *This schema is the condition under which that category is possible of realization in experience;* it is, in other words, the condition for the particularization in phenomena of the universal pure conceptions of the understanding.

This mediation by the productive imagination seems to work somewhat as follows (using for illustration the categories of substance and causality): Because my intuition of time is *a priori*, I can formulate from it by the aid of the categories certain *a priori* principles of possible experience. Thus, I formulate the principle of permanence in time (or substance): "In all changes of phenomena the substance is permanent, and its amount is neither increased nor decreased in nature." Similarly the principle of determinate succession (or causality): "All changes take place according to the law of connection between cause and effect." What Kant seems to mean is that my intuition of time enables, or rather compels, me to formulate these principles as the only conditions under which a mind constructed like mine could ever find application in actual experience of its *a priori* conceptions of substance and cause, or ever recognize phenomena as subsumable under these conceptions. The reason why time is the necessary mediator is that temporal sequence is the indispensable condition of all human experience, since it is the form of internal sense.

Still, how is the understanding led to apply a given category to a given experience? We can illustrate this in respect to causality, a category in which we are particularly interested. All representations of objects of experience are perceived in temporal succession, necessarily, since time is an *a priori* form of sensibility; but in some representations I can reverse the order of succession of parts, as when, for example, I let my gaze wander over a field from east to west and then from west to east; while in other representations I cannot change the order in which I perceive the parts, as when, for example, I watch a plow cutting furrows through the field, I see the various positions of the plow and the appearance of new furrows in a certain order and I cannot reverse this order or in any way change it. In the first experience the representations have no determinate order, wherefore the parts of the object of experience cannot be conceived as determining one another as successive events; but in the second case, they have a determinate order, not the mere subjective order of representation, but an order determined by the object itself, which must, therefore, be conceived as a series of phenomena successively determining one another — that is to say, these phenomena must be subsumed under the category of cause and effect.

10. Knowledge and Reality in Kant's Philosophy. Before proceeding further, it will be well to emphasize to ourselves how far removed, in Kant's philosophy, valid knowledge is from reality. The first remove occurs in perception. Reality or noumenon is not perceived at all; formless sense impressions are given in sensation and are formed by sensibility into phenomena through the imposition of the subjective forms of space and time: What is perceived is consequently mere subjective constructions whose relation to reality can never be known. The second remove occurs in understanding. To begin with, not reality but appearances (phenomena) are given to the understanding; in themselves, that is, in perception, these are utterly unrelated to one another; by subsuming them under its own subjective conceptions the understanding relates them and so constructs nature. The relations are purely mental. Nature, consequently, is a congeries of appearances which are not real and have no discoverable relation to reality nor to one another, but are united in sets of purely mental relations imposed by the human understanding. Thus has Kant "saved" science from the attack of David Hume.

11. How Physics Is Possible. The twelve categories lie within the understanding and are the forms in which it does and must think phenomena in forming its judgments. It is clear that every experience we can ever have, every object that we can possibly know, must, with absolute necessity, correspond to these categories of the understanding. The understanding forms judgments, and judgments constitute knowledge. But it is only through the application of the categories that we can have knowledge; hence it is utterly impossible that we can ever experience any object that is not in conformity with the categories; knowing an object means bringing it under the categories. But it is just as clear that the validity of the categories, that is to say, of the laws of thought, *is limited to phenomena.* The understanding applies the categories only to phenomena presented to it by the senses; the categories, *a priori* forms, or pure conceptions of the understanding, have no relation whatsoever to noumena or things-in-themselves. We cannot know things-in-themselves, and we have no reason to believe that they have to conform to the laws that are universally valid for phenomena, for example, to the principle of causality.

12. The Transcendental Unity of Apperception. Though it is by

the application of the categories to phenomena that we construct nature and the pure science of nature, the categories are not the ultimate principle of the synthesis or unity by which knowledge is possible. Just as perception is possible only by the unification of the manifold of sensation under the pure forms of intuition, namely, space and time; and just as judgment is possible only by the subsumption of perceptions under the pure *a priori* concepts of the understanding; so is knowledge itself possible only by virtue of an underived and transcendental unity or principle of synthesis. This ultimate principle Kant calls the transcendental unity of apperception.

Apperception is consciousness or self-consciousness. Empirical apperception is inner sense, whose *a priori* form is time. It has merely subjective validity, enabling us to perceive representations as coexisting or as succeeding one another in time. Transcendental apperception is not inner sense, which presupposes it and depends upon it. It is the ultimate condition of the necessary synthetical unity of the object. Without this necessary synthetical unity, there could be no objects, but only a manifold of representations; these representations would not be conjoined in an object. We "cannot represent anything as conjoined in the object without having previously conjoined it ourselves." Hence *all* our experience presupposes an original *a priori* synthesis which makes experience itself possible.

This original synthesis is that act of understanding which accompanies and makes possible all my representations. It is the judgment, "I think," which accompanies every judgment. In it, the mind recognizes itself as one and single, and recognizes all its experience as the content of the one consciousness. Nothing can be an object of my experience unless *I think it*. Hence, "I think" is a necessary *a priori* condition of all experience. "The *I think* must accompany all my representations, for otherwise something would be represented in me which could not be thought; in other words, the representations would either be impossible, or at least would be nothing in relation to me." The *I think* is, then, pure or primitive apperception. It is one and the same in all acts of consciousness, and, unaccompanied by it, no representation can exist *for me*. It is the transcendental unity of self-consciousness, and the ultimate *a priori* condition of all cognition.

This principle of the synthetical unity of apperception is the highest principle of all exercise of the understanding. "An object is that in the conception of which the manifold of a given intuition is united. Now all union of representations requires unity of consciousness in the synthesis of them. Consequently, it is the unity of consciousness alone that constitutes the possibility of representations relating to an object, and therefore of their objective validity, and consequently, the possibility of the existence of the understanding itself." The synthetical unity of apperception is prior to the categories, and their possibility presupposes and depends upon it; it accounts for the fact that all sensuous intuitions are subject to the categories. "All the manifold therefore, in so far as it is given in one empirical intuition, is determined in relation to one of the logical functions of judgment, by means of which it is brought into union in one consciousness. Now the categories are nothing else than these functions of judgment, so far as the manifold in a given intuition is determined in relation to them. Consequently, the manifold in a given intuition is necessarily subject to the categories of the understanding." "The synthetical unity of consciousness is, therefore, an objective condition of all cognition, which I do not merely require in order to cognize an object, but to which every intuition must necessarily be subject, in order to become an object for me, because in any other way, and without this synthesis, the manifold in intuition could not be united in one consciousness."

In summary: The first transcendental, *a priori* condition of all knowledge is the pure form or unity of thought itself, the unity of self-consciousness expressed in the judgment "I think." It accompanies every representation and judgment, and is the first condition of all experience and knowledge, prior to all the empirical data of knowledge. By virtue of it, it is possible for the mind to synthesize these data as objects of experience, and to cognize all possible objects of experience, subsuming them under the categories in a system of nature. This is the transcendental unity of apperception.

This whole examination of the understanding explains why we can have a science of nature, or physics. Our understanding creates nature by unifying the manifold of phenomena under the *a priori* forms of thought. Since we can know phenomena only under these categories, phenomena *must* obey the laws of nature, which are the laws of our minds imposed upon the phenomena in our very act of knowing them. Hence the apodictic certainty and the universal necessity of the laws of physics.

13. **Is Metaphysics Possible?** Kant had said that in order to discover whether metaphysics is possible we had to answer these questions:

1. How is a pure science of mathematics possible?
2. How is a pure science of nature possible?
3. Whether a metaphysics of the suprasensible is possible?

He has answered the first two by discovering the conditions which make synthetic *a priori* judgments possible. It now remains for him to answer the third and all-important one by examining whether these conditions can exist in metaphysics as they exist in mathematics and physics.

14. The Ideas of Reason. Metaphysics is concerned with the suprasensible. The faculty which deals with the suprasensible is *Reason,* which Kant distinguished from both sensibility and understanding. These two latter are concerned with what is; Reason, the faculty of Ideas, is concerned with what should be, what lies beyond all existence. The Ideas are regulative, never constitutive, that is to say, they regulate how we must think but they do not constitute any "what" that we can know. They are transcendental, never immanent; that is to say, they are ideal ends or goals of experience but do not stand for anything that can ever present itself in experience. Reason, in its demand for unity, gives us three transcendent, regulatory Ideas. It posits the Psychological Idea because it demands that all our experiences be reduced to a unity by being referred to the pure Ego as subject. It gives us the Cosmological Idea by its demand that all phenomena be unified by reference to one absolute system, the world. It posits the Theological Idea by its demand for a being which is the totality of perfection, a necessary being which is the unconditioned condition of all being, and to which all being and thought are referred for the ultimate unity which Reason demands. These three absolutes, the Pure Ego, the World-System, and God, are ideals of the pure reason, and transcend all possible experience.

15. The Illusions of Traditional Metaphysics. The traditional philosophers, Kant says, made the error of taking these transcendent Ideas to be objects known by the understanding instead of ideals postulated by Reason. Thus, they made Reason's postulate of the unity of self-consciousness, the basis of their proof of the immateriality, freedom, and immortality of the soul. To do this was to be guilty of applying the demands of Reason relating to the Pure Ego, which is noumenon, and never an object of experience, to the soul, or empirical ego, which is phenomenon and an object of internal sensibility. This rational psychology as they called it, is really an illusion, for the Ego and its immortality are not phenomena, and do not fall within the reach of the understanding. Hence, pure reason cannot demonstrate them, but neither can it disprove them.

They did the same sort of thing with the Cosmological Idea and the Theological Idea, producing the pretended metaphysics of rational cosmology and rational theology. In rational theology they treat the transcendent Idea of God as an object of knowledge for the understanding, which it is not and cannot be, and then they advance "proofs" that God exists. This is clearly erroneous, since the postulates of Reason are simply regulative ideals and cannot be objects of knowledge. In brief, the traditional metaphysics is merely a tissue of illusion, pretending to be certain knowledge about what, in fact, cannot possibly be known.

16. The First Critique and Positivism. The answer to the question, "Is a pure science of metaphysics possible?" must, it is evident now, be in the negative. The suprasensible Ideas posited by Reason are never objects of knowledge. The soul and God are above proof and disproof by pure reason because they are above knowledge. Pure reason, however, has shown them to be conceivable, and possibly some other faculty can establish them. Here, then, are the conclusions attained by the *Critique of Pure Reason:*

1. We do not and cannot know noumena, things-as-they-are-in-themselves; we can know only phenomena, things-as-they-appear-to-us.
2. Since all our knowledge is concerned with phenomena, and since phenomena are produced by the application of space and time to the data of sensation, we can know only what is spatial and temporal.
3. Since metaphysics pretends to be the science of the suprasensible and since only the sensible can ever be an object of knowledge, a metaphysics of pure reason is impossible.

These conclusions clearly leave men but one type of valid knowledge, namely, the conclusions of the natural sciences, and but one valid method of attaining knowledge, namely, the method of the natural sciences. These conclusions and the consequences which follow from them constitute precisely the postulates of positivism. Kant himself was not a positivist, but the positivistic implications of his philosophy worked themselves out in history. Parallel with the great stream of idealistic philosophies that sprang from his system was a smaller but no less continuous stream of philosophies that developed the positivistic and materialistic implications of his philosophy.

III. "THE CRITIQUE OF PRACTICAL REASON"

The Critique of Practical Reason contains Kant's doctrine of morality. It attempts to discover what can be laid down *a priori* concerning human conduct. It seeks to answer the question, "How is the moral law possible?" Whereas the first critique studies the pure reason, the faculty of human knowledge, the second studies the practical reason, or the will, the faculty of moral activity.

1. The Categorical Imperative. Kant finds that morality presents itself to man in the form of an unconditional command, which he calls the categorical imperative — categorical because it contains no ifs or buts, but is a clear and unequivocal "Thou shalt," which subjectively is received by men as an unconditional "I ought." This categorical imperative Kant expresses in various ways, the most general of which is: so act that the maxim of thy action may be a principle of universal legislation; or in other words, act only in such ways as you would wish all men to act. From this principle he attempts to derive all right and wrong in human conduct. We are not now interested in the details of his moral system, but rather in how it appeared to give back to men the suprasensible realities of which the *Critique of Pure Reason* had deprived them. Kant restored these suprasensible realities by showing that on the basis of the categorical imperative, the freedom and immortality of the soul and the existence of God are necessary postulates of practical reason.

2. Freedom of Will. In the first place, the practical reason, whence the categorical imperative arises, is autonomous, that is, it is the independent *source* of the moral law, not merely its interpreter or messenger. Consequently, man both gives and receives the law. He gives it as noumenon and he receives it as phenomenon; the Pure Ego gives it, the empirical ego receives it. The moral law speaks as an unconditional imperative, and this fact leads to a very important conclusion. The imperative says, "Thou shalt," and I feel that *I ought.* Now I cannot feel that I ought unless at the same time I feel that I *can.* Therefore, the *can,* that is, freedom, cannot be denied without denying the *ought,* which would mean the denial of morality. But the moral law cannot be denied, since it is categorical. It follows, therefore, that I am certain of my freedom as a necessary postulate of practical reason. This, of course, does not make freedom an object of knowledge. Knowledge is the act of pure reason; the act of practical

Categorical imperative; it's always wrong to lie

Apriori necessary

Hypothetical Imperative; if → then

reason is will or faith. Kant, however, concedes practical reason the primacy over pure reason, so that the fact that freedom is not a matter of speculative knowledge makes it no less certain as a postulate of morality. I cannot accept morality without accepting freedom along with it. It should also be noted that this freedom belongs to the noumenal or pure Ego, not to the empirical ego, which, being a phenomenon, is spatial and temporal, and bound by the iron laws of natural science.

3. **Immortality and God.** Immortality and the existence of God are also necessary postulates of morality. The goal of all moral action is the highest good, that is, the union of perfection and happiness. Perfection is the end that we ought to seek, and happiness is the end that we naturally seek. Unless the moral law and nature are in ultimate opposition, perfection and happiness must ultimately be united, with perfection the condition of happiness. This happiness-as-a-result-of-perfection is obviously not realized in this life; nature does not serve morality. We must therefore postulate a life wherein this union will be realized. Hence, practical reason postulates the soul's immortality. It must also postulate a ground or condition of this adjustment between nature, which aims at happiness, and morality, which aims at perfection. This ground can lie only in the author of both, namely, God. Therefore, through practical reason, we are certain of the existence of God.

4. **Faith.** This acceptance of principles because without their assumption it is impossible to act morally Kant calls faith. He claims that it is not a blind, subjective act: in the first place, the objects of this faith had already been shown to be conceivable, although unknowable, as transcendent Ideas of Reason; in the second place, these assumptions are not made to fulfill any personal, selfish need, but are the demands of practical reason itself. In this way, Kant restored to faith, in his second *Critique*, what he had denied to knowledge in his first. Was the restoration valid? To a good part of the theological and philosophical world it seemed to be so. But if we can judge a tree by its fruit, the *Critique of Practical Reason* was as evil a tree as the *Critique of Pure Reason*. Kant might protest loudly that his "faith" did not rest on a merely subjective basis, but his second *Critique* gave birth to subjectivism in theology just as his first *Critique* had sired positivism in philosophy. What he had done was to set up as the sole basis of religious belief the moral needs of men, and thereby to take

away from religious belief any basis in objective, knowable fact —
such as revelation claimed to be in traditional theology and metaphysics in traditional philosophy.

IV. THE DEVELOPMENT TO NATURALISM

Today, over a century since the death of Immanuel Kant, both
religion and philosophy still reel crazily under the impact of his
thought. What is at root the same disease afflicts both of them. It manifests itself in religion as the perversion of dogma, and goes by the
name *modernism*. In philosophy it consists in the denial of the ability
of man's mind to attain knowledge of any reality beyond sensible
phenomena, and it goes by many names, of which the most proper is
positivism. These errors have many sources, are nourished by many
factors, and have grown out of the whole movement of modern
thought from Descartes on through Kant and after him. But they
were most deeply implanted in the scientific, philosophic, and religious
mind by Kant's philosophy. His apparently successful demonstration
that knowledge is limited to spatio-temporal phenomena and relations gave a pseudo-scientific foundation for positivism. His substitution of practical reason for speculative reason, and his foundation of
faith upon moral needs instead of upon objective truth, furnished
modernism with its irrationalist basis.

1. **Modernism.** The essence of modernism in religion is the contention that religious dogmas are not to be understood as literal
truths or statements of fact, but are to be taken as formulas expressing
a truth or value of the moral order which corresponds to an essential
religious need or experience of man. Modernists believe things which
they do not think are true; thus many of them believe in the divinity
of Christ, but do not believe that He is God. By believing in His
divinity they believe that, morally speaking, the Godhead was manifested to men in the person of Jesus of Nazareth; this manifestation
is both an experience of the Christian people and a need of the individual Christian. But actually, they think, Jesus was a man and was
not God. Such a belief, such an idea of faith and dogma, find very easy
expression in Kantian terms: the divinity of Christ is a necessary
postulate of the practical reason, but it is not a "fact" as physical events
are facts; it is a regulative demand of Christian belief, but it does
not constitute any literal truth that we may know. Modernism developed directly out of Kantian philosophy through Schleiermacher

and Ritschl, two German Protestant theologians primarily responsible for modernist theology. We shall treat more fully of this in a later chapter on reason and faith.

2. **Positivism.** John Dewey, in Baldwin's *Dictionary of Philosophy and Psychology,* gives the following definition of positivism:

> Positivism: The name applied by Comte to his own philosophy, and characterizing, negatively, its freedom from all speculative elements; and, affirmatively, its basis in the methods and results of the hierarchy of positive sciences; i.e., mathematics, astronomy, physics, chemistry, biology, and sociology. It is allied to Agnosticism . . . in its denial of the possibility of knowledge of reality in itself, whether of mind, matter or force; it is allied to Phenomenalism . . . in its denial of capacity to know either efficient or final causation, or anything except the relations of coexistence and sequence in which sensible phenomena present themselves.
>
> The term is used more loosely to denote any philosophy which agrees with that of Comte in limiting philosophy to the data and methods of the natural sciences — opposition to the a priori and to speculation by any method peculiar to metaphysics.

In the following chapters we shall use the term positivism in the second or wider sense given by Dewey, meaning not particularly the philosophy of Auguste Comte but the general attitude that limits the meaning of knowledge to the data, methods, and results of the natural sciences, and whose prevalence in modern thought is traceable far more to Kant than to Comte.

It is clear that this doctrine involves the denial of the possibility of metaphysics as Thomistic philosophers understand that study. Positivism denies the power of the human intellect to know anything except what is sensible and material; it limits knowledge to the phenomenal as opposed to the substantial. For a thorough-going positivist such a statement as "God exists" is not true or false; as a supposed statement of fact it is meaningless, because there is no way of subjecting it to experimental test. The same is true of all metaphysical statements. They may have or lack pragmatic value; but they have no relation to truth or falsity. Positivism is worse than a philosophical error; it is the suicide of philosophy. It gives the whole field of knowledge over to the natural sciences, leaving to philosophy nothing at all of the knowable. It makes philosophy a mere hanger-on in the court of the sciences. Positivism allows the philosopher to mull over the findings of the scientists; and while the results of this mulling may have some relevance in the realm of values, it can have none in the realm of fact.

3. **Pragmatism.** In the United States the positivistic tendency in philosophy took a special turn. What developed from it was a philosophy considered peculiarly American, although it had considerable influence in European circles as well. This was pragmatism, formulated by the great American psychologist, William James. It was a frank abandonment of the effort to attain to any absolute truths. It made truth something relative to particular situations. The truth of a belief was held to consist, not in any accord between this belief and reality, but in the fruitfulness which the belief showed when used as a principle of action. An idea is really a *purpose;* it places before the mind a given course of action with a certain desired result; it is true when the thinker acts and really attains the desired result; it is false when the action is not in fact followed by the desired result. An idea which has produced desired results in many situations and for a long time may later fail to be fruitful. In that case it has become false. This is what has happened to many scientific theories, philosophical beliefs, and religious doctrines; they were true in their day because they gave rise to real satisfactions or values, but their day is done and now they are useless impedimenta in the mind. In such a theory of truth, it is clear, the *will* is more relevant to thought and truth than is the intellect, for truth is something in the realm of actions and ends. Practical reason has the primacy over speculative reason. James's doctrine of the "will to believe" is not altogether unlike Kant's "practical reason."

4. **The Outcome: Naturalism.** What of the future? Leaving unforeseen factors out of consideration, it is not difficult to forecast. Indeed, it is hardly a forecast, because the inevitable end of Kantianism has already been reached by many molders of contemporary thought. Out of Kant's philosophy sprang modernism, a religious heresy that has an inevitable tendency toward the denial of dogma, and positivism, a philosophical heresy that is more than a tendency, that is, in very truth, the denial of philosophy. The union of the two produces utter materialistic naturalism, the rejection of the supernatural and the spiritual altogether, the confining of man's interest to this world entirely, and the seeking of all human ends in this world.

Modernism and positivism have been highly successful in their respective fields, and this success has very largely been due to the peculiar way in which they were contained in Kant's philosophy. Outright denial of dogma, bursting suddenly into the religious world, can arouse only shock and rejection, and could not have succeeded as has modernism. The Kantian distinction between knowledge and the necessary postulates of man's moral nature enabled modernism to retain dogma while, in fact, radically altering its whole nature. It eventually leads to the denial of all dogma, but that was not too easy to see at the outset. In like manner, honest, forthright sensism or empiricism of David Hume's brand arouses philosophers to antagonism and rejection. Just as Kant's philosophy seemed to allow room for religious truth, so it also seemed to allow room for metaphysical truth. In fact it did neither, since in both cases the "truths" were rationally unknowable; but because it seemed to, the real denials of dogma and metaphysics that it contained were able to succeed. Today it has become clear that Kant's postulates of the practical reason saved neither religion nor metaphysics; and the two errors that he sired so successfully are now uniting in inevitable, if incestuous, wedlock, and their offspring is naturalism. Modernism has destroyed revealed dogma, and positivism has destroyed metaphysics, and there is nothing left but science.

Our whole presentation of the philosophies of Hume and Kant and of the positivism and modernism which resulted from them has been, thus far, merely explanatory. In following chapters we shall examine these philosophies critically, starting in the next chapter with an examination of the doctrines of Hume and Kant concerning substance and causality.

CHAPTER XVI

EXAMINATION OF HUME AND KANT

I. HUME ON CAUSALITY AND SUBSTANCE

1. A certain great ambiguity has characterized much modern philosophy since the days of David Hume and Immanuel Kant. Hume advanced arguments against the validity of the notions of substance, efficient cause, and the principle of causality. The ultimate effect of these arguments, if they are regarded as valid, is the demonstration of the impossibility of both philosophy and science. Kant saw this very clearly and undertook to rescue science and philosophy from Hume's destructive criticism by instituting a more penetrating constructive criticism. The upshot of his critique (as he thought) was to validate the notions of cause and substance and the principle of causality in regard to the sciences of nature, but to demonstrate at the same time their invalidity in respect to metaphysics. As a matter of fact, he failed to validate these conceptions at all, except as purely subjective modes of thinking about nature. Indeed, his philosophy if taken seriously implies the non-existence of nature outside the human mind. Some of his successors took it seriously and constructed the grandiose systems of absolute idealism that prevailed during a great part of the nineteenth century. Other philosophers, however, were more impressed by Hume's arguments and by the purely negative side of Kant's critique, and they accepted as quite unquestionable the final disappearance from philosophy of the concepts of efficient causality and substance. They went right ahead, however (and this is the great ambiguity), constructing sciences and philosophies which at every turn of thought assume these conceptions as absolutely certain and valid.

2. *David Hume,* we saw in the last chapter, argued that the notion of causation has no objective validity because we neither experience real causation nor can we demonstrate it. Yet we unavoidably believe

in the reality of causes and in the principle of causality. The case is the same in respect to material substances and our own spiritual self or ego. These, too, we naturally and unavoidably believe in, but this belief cannot be justified by either sensation or reason. On the contrary, it is produced by our imagination.

Sensation certainly cannot justify our belief in external things or substances which exist independently of our perceptions and which continue in existence while we are not perceiving them. If we judged solely according to the evidence of our senses, we would believe only in our perceptions themselves, and we would believe that these exist only when we perceive them. Sensation gives us no more than pure impressions existing at the moment when they are sensed; it does not give any slightest hint of some thing or subject hidden behind the impression and continuing to exist even while we are not perceiving it.

The case is no different for reason. No reasoning process can carry us validly from perceived impressions to unperceived things of which they are the impressions. What we actually perceive are transient and intermittent sense qualities and groups of qualities; and if reason has anything to tell us about their distinct and continuous existence, it is simply that belief in such existence is, on face value, absurd and self-contradictory, for it is belief in unsensed sense impressions or unperceived perceptions.

Yet there is a constancy and a coherence in our experience which relates various separate perceptions so closely that our mind is compelled, as it were, to bridge the gap between them with something permanent and distinct — something which goes on existing between our separate perceptions and which we perceive now and again later. Each day I come up to the college and I find the hill the same, the buildings the same, the trees the same, the quadrangle the same, the instructors and my classmates the same. That is the way it seems to vulgar thought. The fact, of course, is that each day when I come to the college I experience perceptions very similar to the perceptions I experienced the day before, and the day before that, and so on. My perceptions, in other words, though interrupted, are constant. They are also coherent. If I approach the college from different directions, I get different perceptions. If I start from the north end and walk south, I get one succession of perceptions; if I start at the south and walk north, I get a different succession. But it is not merely different; rather it is the reverse of the first set. The two sets, therefore, are coherent; each, as it were, accounts for the other, given the reversal of direction of my view. Because of this constancy and coherence it is difficult, very difficult, for me to imagine that each perception and each set of perceptions is entirely new and unconnected causally with the others. Yet I cannot believe that perceptions perceived on different days are identical; that would be absurd. Now, here is where my imagination steps in. I can easily connect the series of similar impressions by imagining that the hill, the buildings, the trees, the quadrangle, my instructors, and classmates are things or substances which exist distinct from my perceptions, which continue to exist while I am not perceiving them, and which I can perceive whenever I place myself in the proper position for doing so. So lively and vivid is my imagination of these objects as existing continuously and distinct from my perceptions, that I *believe* that they really do so exist. Thus our belief in the existence of permanent material substances — the external world — arises neither from experience nor reason, but from imagination.

Hume gave a similar account of our belief in our own substantial spiritual selves, but he later confessed himself dissatisfied with it and omitted it altogether from the later editions of his *Enquiry Concerning Human Understanding.* It had, however, quite the same influence upon subsequent empirical philosophers as if its author had never renounced it. If Hume was not quite the skeptic that he is most frequently represented as,[1] it was nevertheless the apparently skeptical elements of his teaching which had the greatest influence upon later thinkers.

II. CRITICISM OF HUME

1. **Sensism.** Hume's original error, which led to his rejection of substance and causality as valid philosophical concepts, was sensism. He considered experience as the sole ultimate source of valid human knowledge, which it is, but by experience he meant pure sensation, or at very best perception, and nothing more. *Impressions of sense* and their less vivid relics in the mind, namely, *ideas,* are the only data of knowledge for which experience vouches, according to Hume. We have no *impression* of causality or substance; therefore, he argues, these are not given in experience.

Hume mistakes an analysis of the factors in perception for an

[1] Cf. N. K. Smith, *The Philosophy of David Hume* (London: Macmillan, 1941).

account of the perceptive act. The data of *pure sensation* are, as he says, fragmentary and intermittent sense impressions. But the act which he is analyzing is not an act of pure sensation. What I *perceive* is not these fragmentary impressions, but the things of which they are accidents. It is doubtful that even animals perceive merely sensory qualities. Substances (i.e., particular, concrete substances) are the data of perception. They are incidental sensibles immediately perceived by means of internal sense co-operating with external sense. In his analysis Hume takes as the immediate datum of perception something which is actually known only as a result of a difficult abstraction, namely, the pure sensation. Then his problem is to discover how, starting from pure sensations, we come to believe in objective substances which exist unperceived and permanently. It is a false problem.

2. **Human Experience Includes Understanding.** Hume is right in saying that we never have a sensory impression of causality or substance. But he is wrong in saying that we never experience causes or substances. Efficient causes are immediately experienced every time we observe anything physically influencing anything else, every time, for example, that we see a hammer driving a nail. But the cause *qua* cause is never sensed directly; cause, like substance, is only sensed *per accidens*. The cause as a sensible object, its movement, and the subsequent movement of the object acted upon are the immediate data of sense. But to limit experience to the sensible data perceived is to imply that man perceives without ever at the same time understanding what he perceives. When I perceive a hammer descending upon a nail and the nail moving further into the wood, I also understand that the hammer is *something* and is *driving* the nail into the wood. Both perception and understanding are equally parts of the experience. To exclude the understanding is to reduce all human experience to uncomprehending sense awareness. Not only is this not the only kind of human experience, but, at least in the case of adults, it never normally occurs at all. We simply do not perceive without *some* understanding of what we are perceiving; we do not perceive phenomena without perceiving them as the phenomena of something; nor do we perceive one thing acting upon another without at the same time understanding the former as a cause of the effect produced in the latter.

3. **Understanding in Perception.** There is surely a crystal-clear distinction between mere perceiving and understanding. The domestic animals of the battlelands of Europe are no more spared the bombing

and the fire, the hunger and the cold, the noise and the stench, than are their human owners. But they have no understanding of what is going on; no *reason* for what is happening is known to them, *and none is sought*. Their minds do not grope for reasons the way their parched tongues crave for water. The darkness that their eyes suffer when they are driven in the midst of night through strange lands is matched by no darkness of intellect seeking a reason which it cannot find — that awful darkness which is so often the lot of man. Failure to understand could no more be a privation and a suffering in man if his intellect were not made for grasping the reasons and causes of things, than blindness would be a suffering if sight never grasped the visible. A man who does not understand feels frustrated, because his mind is made for understanding; he suffers when he cannot grasp the reason, because he knows that there is a reason. Perception is not understanding; but normally some understanding occurs together with perception: we could not possibly have the experience of failing to understand what we perceive, if we did not have the prior experience of understanding what we perceive.

4. Cause Is "Given" to the Intellect. Cause is something that we grasp intellectually in the very act of experiencing action — whether our own action or another's. We understand the cause as producing the effect: the hammer as driving the nail, the saw as cutting the wood, the flood as devastating the land, the drill as piercing the rock, the hand as molding the putty, ourselves as producing our own thoughts, words, and movements, our shoes as pinching our feet, a pin as piercing our finger, our fellow subway travelers as pressing our ribs together. We do not think that the nail will ever plunge into the wood without the hammer, the marble shape up as a statue without a sculptor, the baby begin to exist without a father, the acorn grow with no sunlight; if something ever seems to occur in this way, we do not believe it, or we call it a miracle (i.e., we attribute it to a higher, unseen cause). In a similar manner, substance is given directly to the intellect in the very act of perception; the substance is grasped as the reason for the sensible phenomena.

5. The Subjectivistic Postulate. The arguments of Hume are based on the subjectivistic postulate, namely, that we know nothing directly except our own ideas. From this starting point, certitude about real causality can never be reached. The only causality that could ever possibly be discovered if the primary objects of our knowledge were our

own ideas would be causal relations among the ideas themselves. No such relations are as a matter of fact found, since none exist and since the subjectivistic postulate is false to begin with. Causal relations exist between objects and the mind, and between the mind and its ideas, but not between ideas and ideas. Hume places causality in our mind, as a bond between ideas, when he accounts for our idea of causality by attributing it to mental custom. Whatever his intention, he actually presents similar successions of ideas as the cause of our ideas of causality and the principle of causality. As a matter of fact, such causality would not account for our belief in causality, because it would never be an idea, but only an unknown bond connecting ideas. It is only because Hume is already in possession of the concept of causality gained through external experience that he is able to formulate the theory that invariable succession of ideas *produces* mental custom, which in turn *gives rise to* the idea of cause.

6. Imagination and Causality. It is, perhaps, this locating of causality among our ideas that leads Hume to a very peculiar argument against the principle of causality:

> We can never demonstrate the necessity of a cause to every new existence, or new modification of existence, without showing at the same time the impossibility there is that anything can ever begin to exist without some productive principle. . . . Now that the latter is utterly incapable of a demonstrative proof, we may satisfy ourselves by considering, that as all distinct ideas are separable from each other, and as the ideas of cause and effect are evidently distinct, it will be easy for us to conceive any object to be non-existent at this moment, and existent the next, without conjoining to it the distinct idea of a cause or productive principle. The separation, therefore, of the idea of a cause from that of a beginning of existence, is plainly possible for the imagination; and consequently the actual separation of these objects is so far possible, that it implies no contradiction nor absurdity; and it is therefore incapable of being refuted by any reasoning from mere ideas; without which it is impossible to demonstrate the necessity of a cause.[2]

This argument, even if we overlook the flagrant *petitio principii* in the statement that "all distinct ideas are separable from each other," is no argument at all. What Hume says is nothing more than that he can imagine a thing beginning to exist without a cause, and that consequently no argument from mere ideas can ever prove the necessity of a cause. We can agree with him that no argument from mere ideas

[2] *Treatise of Human Nature,* Bk. I, Part III, Sec. III.

Petitio Principii (begging the question); the conclusion is implied in a premise

can ever prove real causality; but we will add that that is why Hume could never prove it — he started with mere ideas, or rather images. Aside from this, the argument is utterly unrelated to the subject of causality. Imagination has nothing to do with causes or with beginnings of existence. I never imagine anything as beginning to exist, or even as existing; I simply imagine the thing, and in my image there is no reference to existence. The thing which I imagine may as easily be a fire-breathing dragon as my own brother. The reference to existence lies in thought, not in imagination. The words of Hume, "The separation, therefore, of the idea of a cause from that of a beginning of existence, is plainly possible for the imagination," have no real meaning, because the imagination *never* possesses the idea of a beginning of existence. *Thought* judges whether a thing conceived exists or not, and thought (even Hume's "natural belief")[3] judges that nothing begins to exist without a cause. Surely, I can imagine a situation in which a certain thing is *not* an element and then a situation in which it *is*. To do this is not to conceive the thing as beginning to exist; it is merely to imagine it after not imagining it. Such imaginative play has no connection with causality, except in the obvious sense that I could not imagine anything, to say nothing of making imagination experiments, if I had not the power of producing, that is, causing images in my mind; and presumably that is not the sense in which Hume intended his illustration to be interpreted.

7. **Loaded Dice.** The subjectivistic postulate prejudices the whole issue as to the reality of causes before examination of the question even begins. If knowledge cannot attain to anything real and extramental, it cannot attain to real, extramental causes. The only causality it could possibly discover would be causal relation among images in the mind. If the object is read out of court by the postulate that we know only our ideas, objective causality is read out with it. It is not surprising that sensism and subjectivism should lead to the explicit denial of the principles of causality, sufficient reason, and substance, since they begin with their implicit denial. Sensations, impressions, images separated from any *being* arousing them must be viewed by any intelligent mind as so many phenomena *without any sufficient reason* for existing. Normal men cannot abide sensory experiences without objective reasons. They regard a person who has such experiences as a psychopathic case; they say, "He imagines things," and suggest a psychiatrist.

---

[3] See No. 8 below.

(margin note) Hume is a picture thinker

8. Sensism Bars Recognition of the Self-Evident. David Hume was far from psychopathic, and therefore he never really doubted causality or the principle of causality. Such doubt he considered absurd:

> But allow me to tell you, that I never asserted so absurd a Proposition as *that anything might arise without a Cause:* I only maintained, that our Certainty of the Falsehood of that Proposition proceeded neither from Intuition nor Demonstration; but from another Source. . . . There are many different kinds of Certainty: and some of them as satisfactory to the Mind, tho perhaps not so regular, as the demonstrative kind.[4]

That every event has a cause we know, according to Hume, by "natural belief." But "natural belief," though it is a good enough basis on which to construct practical conduct, has nothing to do with metaphysics. Hume's natural belief is in fact rational self-evidence under a name which conceals its intelligible character. The self-evident for Hume was never intelligible; only the demonstrated was. The self-evident in his scheme could mean only the subjective sense impression or image — than which, in fact, there is nothing less self-evident or intelligible, if it be not understood by reference to a substance and a cause, that is, to an objective reality grasped by the intellect as the source of the impression, in the same experience in which sense receives the impression. Because he did not recognize the self-evident, Hume demanded, in philosophy, that everything be demonstrated. It is as great a defect in the philosophical mind to be unable to recognize the self-evident as it is to be unable to recognize what needs to be demonstrated. The existence of the external world is self-evident to us by common experience; but all modern idealism is based upon the demand to demonstrate this indemonstrable, self-evident starting point of human knowledge.

III. THE POSITION OF KANT

1. Substance and Cause in Kant's System. In Kant's philosophy substance and cause are pure conceptions of the understanding, not derived from experience but imposed by the mind in experience upon all possible objects of experience. Consquently these concepts and the two principles of substance and causality are universally valid for all

---

[4] From a letter written in February, 1754, probably to John Stewart, professor of natural philosophy at Edinburgh. Stewart's attack and Hume's letter are to be found in N. K. Smith, *The Philosophy of David Hume,* pp. 411–413.

possible objects of experience, that is to say, all spatio-temporal phenomena. But the use of these concepts and principles in reference to transcendental objects, that is, to noumena, is invalid. They cannot, for example, be used in a proof of the existence of God or the immortality of the soul. They have no metaphysical use. In Thomistic metaphysics they are fundamental principles.

It would be futile to attempt any special refutation of Kant's doctrine of substance and causality. His doctrine on these two conceptions is an integral part of his entire critical philosophy, and if we are to show the falsity of his teaching on substance and cause, we have to attempt nothing less than a critical examination of his philosophy as a whole.

2. The Argument of the First Critique. The whole argument of Kant's *Critique of Pure Reason*, stripped of all the evidences and proofs which he offers in its support, may be summarized briefly enough:

a) Man's faculty of scientific knowledge, pure reason, is constituted by his powers of sensibility and understanding.

b) Since we cannot experience any object except as existing in space and time, space and time are *a priori* conditions of our experience. Consequently, they are forms of our faculty of experience, that is to say, they are *a priori* forms of sensibility.

c) Since we can have no scientific understanding of objects of experience except in so far as these objects are understood as standing in categorial relations with one another, thus constituting nature, the categories under which the objects are so related are *a priori* conditions of our understanding of nature. Consequently, these categories are forms of our faculty of understanding. Among these categories are substance and accident, cause and effect.

d) Since the objects of our experience, in the very process of being perceived and understood, thus receive their necessary sensible and intelligible forms from our faculty of knowledge, we cannot experience or understand things as they are in themselves (noumena) but only things as they appear to us (phenomena). Consequently, scientific knowledge (i.e., knowledge by pure reason) has to do only with phenomena.

e) Since scientific knowledge deals only with phenomena, that is, with possible objects of experience, we cannot prove or disprove anything about the objects which we conceive as transcending the conditions of experience.

f) Since metaphysics deals with the transcendent Ideas of Reason, which are not possible objects of experience, and to which, therefore, the categories of the understanding have no application, metaphysics cannot be a science of pure reason.

g) Since nothing can be proved or disproved by pure reason about the transcendent Ideas of Reason (e.g., the World, the Transcendental Ego, God), the way is left open for a critical inquiry about these objects from some other source than pure reason.

3. Kant's Conception of the Universe. The conception of the universe as a whole, implied in this argument, can also be stated briefly.

> According to Kant, the world which we know fills space, and lasts through time, and is composed of permanent substances acting upon one another in accordance with the laws of cause and effect. This world is common to all human beings and is explored by science: yet it is a world, not of things as they are in themselves, but only of things as they appear to us; or, in Kant's language, a world of phenomena or appearances.[5] This world is called 'objective,' since it is an object common to all men. . . .[6]
> Kant never questions the reality of things-in-themselves, never doubts that appearances are appearances of things-in-themselves. The appearance is the thing as it appears to us, or as it is in relation to us, though it is not the thing as it is in itself. That is to say, things as they are in themselves are the very same things that appear to us, although they appear to us, and because of our power of knowing must appear to us, as different from what they are in themselves. Strictly speaking, there are not two things, but only one thing considered in two different ways: the thing as it is in itself and as it appears to us.[7]

The world which is the object of our knowledge, that is to say, the world of appearance, is the resultant of conditions from two sources, from things as they are in themselves and from our mind:

> the thing in itself is the condition . . . of the appearance.
> It is not, however, the only condition. The other condition which determines the character of appearances is the mind. . . . The character of the human mind (with its human sensibility and understanding) determines (along with things-in-themselves) our common objective world. It determines in short how things-in-themselves must appear to us.[8]

Our examination into the validity of the philosophy of the Sage of

[5] H. J. Paton, *Kant's Metaphysic of Experience* (New York: Macmillan, 1936), Vol. I, p. 59.

[6] *Ibid.*, p. 59, Note 1.

[7] *Ibid.*, p. 61.

[8] *Ibid.*, p. 62.

Königsberg shall adhere closely to the above outline of his fundamental position, and shall be as brief as possible. We may organize that
examination under two questions:

1. Did Kant prove his central thesis? Do his conclusions explain the
facts which he is trying to explain, and are they the only intelligible
explanation of those facts? Are they at least consistent with the facts?

2. Is his over-all conception of reality as it is related to human
knowledge intelligible?

IV. KANT FAILED TO PROVE HIS CENTRAL THESIS

1. What Kant had to do in order to set in place the keystone of his
whole philosophy was to *prove* that space, time, and the categories are
a priori (i.e., innate) forms of human cognition and are not extracognitional determinations of real things. His method was to start by an
analysis of experience, and to discover through this analysis the necessary presuppositions or implications of both the fact and the character
of human experience.[9]

Kant's analysis of experience yields three elements: (*a*) sense qualia,
e.g., red, sweet, soft; (*b*) space and time; and (*c*) categorial relations,
e.g., substance and accident, cause and effect. The first is the matter of
experience, and the two latter are the forms of experience. It is worthy
of note that Kant found in the matter of experience, namely the
sensible qualities through which anything is perceived, no implications
at all as to the nature of either the external source or the subject of
experience. One would think that the primary data of all human
experience ought to have some significance relative to the source and
the subject of experience; but Kant's only inference from ·what he
considers the "pure given" of perception is that sensation is possible
only in so far as an extracognitional thing-in-itself is its source. From
the form or forms of experience he concluded that, "Experience is
possible only on the assumption that the formal features found in
experience are *a priori* conditions *of* experience."[10]

The argument by which he reaches this conclusion depends entirely
upon the equation which he sets up between "universal and necessary"
and "*a priori* form of the mind." Whatever is universal and necessary
in experience is *a priori*; and whatever is *a priori* in experience is con-

[9] Cf. Ledger Wood, "The Transcendental Method" in *The Heritage of Kant*, eds..
G. T. Whitney and D. F. Bowers (Princeton, N. J.: Princeton University Press, 1939).
pp. 3–35.

[10] Wood, *op. cit.*, pp. 10–11.

tributed to the object of experience by the mind — and not given to the mind in experience. Consequently, since space and time determinations are features of every possible object of perception, they are innate forms of the power of sensibility, not extramental forms of the reality which we perceive. Similarly, since the understanding cognizes necessary and universal features among the objects of experience only in so far as these are related according to the categories, the categories are *a priori* forms of the understanding and are not extramental determinations or relations of the things which we understand.

2. The Mental Apriority of the Forms Is Not Proved. This equating of the necessary and universal in knowledge with an innate form of the knowing mind is an assumption, pure and simple, and an unwarranted assumption. The contrary assumption, namely, that the universal and necessary features of the objects of our experience are objective determinations of all the things which we experience, is, on face value, just as likely as Kant's assumption. Space, time, and categorial relations would appear as universal and necessary in all the objects of our experience if they were in fact features of those objects prior to our experiencing the objects. As a matter of fact, the initial advantage lies with this hypothesis, because the forms in question *seem to be* forms of the things experienced rather than forms of the subject experiencing. They could, of course, be universal forms of both; and that would go a long way toward explaining why such subjects perceive only such objects. This, indeed, was St. Thomas' theory; he believed that men directly perceive only spatio-temporal things because they experience by means of their bodily senses; they are themselves spatio-temporal beings living in a world with other spatio-temporal beings.

3. Assumptions at the Base of Kant's Argument. If the realistic view of space, time, and the categories is (at least) as likely at the outset as Kant's idealistic view, why did he make the assumption that his view alone could account for the formal characters of experience? The answer is that this assumption resulted from a prior assumption, a dogma taken over from the very philosophers whose views he was combating. The pure empiricists held that there is nothing in knowledge which is universal and necessary; and the pure rationalists held that the universal and necessary is known innately; but both agreed that nothing universal and necessary can be derived from experience. Kant was busy refuting the extreme views, but it does not seem to

have occurred to him that the reason why each side adopted an erroneous extreme might be because the mean which both rejected was the
truth. A possible middle road between pure empiricism and pure
rationalism is the theory that the universal is derived from the empirical data of sense perception; or, differently expressed, that form as well
as matter is given in experience. Kant's hypothesis of the mental
apriority of form is another possible middle road, but one not a whit
preferable on first sight.

Why did Kant uncritically accept the common assumption of the
two schools of thought which he was trying to refute? His belief that
the universal and necessary can never be derived from experience
seems to have arisen from assuming the subjectivistic postulate and
an exaggerated separation of the sensory and intellectual parts of the
act of experience. We have already pointed out how these errors lay
at the root of Hume's phenomenalism. If intellection is a separate, second act following sensation, and if the data of sensation are subjective,
the intellect never can, as Hume made clear, attain to a valid universal
principle or even a valid universal concept; because the intellect could
never do more than manipulate the singular and subjective data of
sense — the *impressions* of Hume and the *manifold of sensation* of
Kant. In criticizing Hume, Kant did not attack either his subjectivistic
assumption or his separation of sense and understanding, and as a
result he, too, accepted the "given" of experience as a pure phenomenal
manifold. Hence he concluded that the forms by which it is unified in
experience must be forms of the experiencing mind, since no unifying
forms are given in the manifold itself.

4. **The Thomistic View.** If, as seems certain and as we have maintained above, sense and intellect co-operate in one act in common perception or experience, intellection is not limited to manipulating or
unifying some manifold of sensuous representations, because these are
not what the intellect seizes upon directly at all. Our sensory impressions are not *what* we know, but means by which we know. What the
intellect attains directly in the perceptive act is a reality which is the
subject and reason of the sensible determinations perceived in sensation.
It is by reference to this directly cognized reality that the intellect
"unifies the manifold of sensation," not by reference to some innate
but unknown forms of its own constitution. This object, namely, the
being, substance, and nature of the thing, is the foundation of the
intellect's universal conceptions and judgments. The nature of the per-

ceived thing is grasped as implicitly universal, and is immediately universalized by the intellect, though the intellect does not dream, of course, of attributing this mode of universality to the perceived thing itself. It does, however, see that what belongs to this particular instance of the nature, not because it is this instance but because it is an instance of this nature, must belong to every instance of the nature. Therefore, it is able to make universal and necessary judgments on the sole basis of the data of experience — *sole* basis because such judgments do not add any elements not experienced; they simply assert what the mind understands in the experience.[11]

5. Kant's Theory Fails to Explain Some Features of Experience. So far we have been arguing merely that the theory of knowledge just stated is a possible alternative to Kant's. We may now go further and say that it accounts far better than his for certain features of experience. The account given in section 4 is certainly an account of how it *seems* to us that we form universal conceptions and judgments; we seem to set our intellect to work upon the object presented in perception, seeking in that object the answer to the question, What is it? and we seem to interpret the *What,* when we have found it, as being also the *What* of an infinite number of other possible individual objects, and we seem to judge that the characters belonging to the *What* of the first individual, rather than to its individuality, must belong to all possible individuals with the same *What.* We may often do this carelessly and, as a consequence, make false universal judgments; but there can be no doubt that it seems to be what we try to do and do do, well or ill. On the other hand, Kant's account of the unification of sensory data under *a priori* sensuous forms of space and time and the unification of these spatio-temporal representations into judgments of experience under the *a priori* categories never seems to be what we are doing.

a) Particular Formal Determinations. In addition to this feature of experience not accounted for by Kant's theory there are several others. Kant's conception of the mental apriority of space, time, and categorial relations may account for the *general* spatio-temporal and categorial character of the objects of experience, but it does not seem to account for the *particular* spatio-temporal and categorial determinations of particular objects of experience. Each object that we perceive has its own individual spatial determinations differing from those of anything else, and its own particular temporal and categorial determina-

---

[11] The contention of the above paragraph is presented more fully in Chapter XVIII.

tions. The universal forms of space, time, and the categories are given to each object in experience, but what determines the individual, concrete pattern which they take in each case? Kant ought to have held that it is not determined by what is given in experience, since this is mere matter without form, a pure manifold. The sense impressions given in different experiences have no spatial character at all prior to their unification by sensibility; hence there is nothing in different matters of sensation to account for different particular spatial patterns. Similarly, since representations bear to one another no categorial relations prior to their subsumption under the pure conceptions of the understanding, nothing in different representations can account for different particular categorial relations. But if particular spatio-temporal and categorial determinations are not derivable from the matter of experience, neither are they from the form, since the *a priori* forms of sensibility are mere undifferentiated sensuous continua and the *a priori* forms of the understanding mere universals.

b) *Differentiation of the Categories.* An analogous difficulty exists for Kant in respect to the selectivity exhibited by the understanding in subsuming phenomena under the categories. Why does the intellect relate some phenomena as substance and attribute, and others as cause and effect? By the Kantian hypothesis there is nothing of these relations in the representations presented by sensibility to the understanding; they arise entirely from the synthesis effected by the understanding. The consequence would seem to be that in subsuming a set of representations under a certain category the understanding gets no hints from the representations themselves; nothing about *them* helps to determine how the categorial scheme shall be called into play. If this is so, then Nature, as Kant conceived it, is not a rational construction, and its laws, far from having universal objective validity even in the Kantian sense, are most precarious; not only is Nature a subjective construction, but it is an irrational and unpredictable one.

Of course, Kant's account of the schematization of the categories through the work of the mediating imagination is intended to explain why the categories are applied as they are. But the schematized category is quite as *a priori* as the pure conceptions of the understanding, and unless some particular determination in the representations themselves is given to the understanding, it still has no ground for selection in subsuming representations under the categories. Now, this ground would seem to be, according to Kant, the particular time-determinations of particular representations; thus, for example, we apply the category of cause and effect when the representations are presented in a time sequence which follows a determinate rule of succession.

At first sight, this theory seems to meet the objection which we have raised; but in truth it does not bear analysis. To begin with, the origin of the particular time-determinations remains obscure. Second, it must be remembered that the categories are not known objects of the understanding prior to experience, but become known only by virtue of being applied to the data of experience, unifying it. To express Kant's view in Thomistic terms, the categories are potentially known forms of understanding which become actually known only by reflection upon the operations of understanding. We do not, for example, first know cause and effect and then pigeonhole certain phenomena under this idea; we instinctively relate certain phenomena as cause and effect, and then we get to know both the pure conception of cause and effect and the fact that it is an *a priori* form of our understanding. Consider the significance of this in relation to Kant's account of the application of the schematized category. When we *first* judge that certain phenomena are related causally, we have not previously known anything of causality; and therefore we must actually make this judgment because sensibility presents the phenomena to us in a certain temporal sequence. Now that is just what David Hume had maintained.

The order of Kant's exposition prevented him from seeing that in the end he was back where he started. Before treating of the schemata of the imagination and the schematization of the categories, he had already made his deduction of the categories, and he now treats them as known conceptions when he is explaining how we apply them to the objects of knowledge. But, according to his explanation, *we* do not have them as known conceptions when we actually apply them to the objects of experience. Kant, we may now conclude, gives no explanation of how such conceptions as cause and substance can be validly applied to objects of experience, if they are not given to the mind in experience. We have no right, as Hume made clear, to go, for example, from the perception of determinate succession in time to the conception of causal relation. But that is just what Kant says that we do. He has not succeeded in answering Hume, and he actually returns to Hume's position without realizing that he is doing so.

c) Valid, Universal, Synthetic Judgments. The full significance of the above is that Kant failed to account for what it was his chief business to account for. He did not explain how we can pronounce universal and necessary judgments which are not purely analytic. That every event must have a cause is a universal and necessary judgment. It is clear that nothing can validate this judgment except the perception of a necessary relation of event to cause. According to the Thomistic theory, I pronounce the judgment because I do perceive a necessary relation of real events to causes which produce them. My judgment is not analytic in Kant's sense; the concept of event does not contain that of cause. But the real nature or quiddity represented by the concept event is seen to involve a reference to a reason extrinsic to itself; if I do not see this reference in the real nature of an event, then my judgment, the principle of causality, is simply invalid. Kant's categorial theory will never validate it. If the concept *cause* is entirely outside the concept *that which happens,* and arises from the fact that, because of an *a priori* form of my understanding, I understand events only as standing in relation to prior events which determine them, there is no reason why I should ever judge that every event *must* have a cause, and certainly no reason for thinking the judgment valid in case I did somehow pronounce it.

d) *Sensible Quality.* Kant's doctrine does not explain the *matter* of experience, that is to say, the sense qualia with which all experience begins. Whether they be regarded as objective determinations of phe-nomena or as subjective affections, as Kant and most modern philoso-phers regard them, they need some sort of explanation. Since they are not forms of intuition, like space and time, the thing-in-itself is respon-sible for them. But a thing-in-itself which cannot be known is hardly a satisfactory explanation for such an all-pervasive character of human experience as sensible qualities. We might go so far as to say that Kant offers no explanation of experience itself. The thing-in-itself and the mind are the conditions of experience, but how are these two condi-tions related in producing experience? A causal relation, that is to say, some action of the thing-in-itself upon the mind, would be an answer; but that answer is ruled out by the fact that causal relations can be predicated only of phenomena.

V. THE UNIVERSE OF KANT IS UNINTELLIGIBLE

1. **Relation of Noumena and Phenomena.** The phenomenal world, that is to say, the spatio-temporal and categorized world which we live in and know and of which we as men are parts, somehow arises

out of prior conditions which themselves belong to a world of noumena, or things-in-themselves, which we do not know. That is the
basic meaning of Kant's philosophy if that philosophy means anything
at all. The most fundamental criticism that can be made of this philosophy is that the universe which it posits is unintelligible and incredible.
This charge will be made and proved in what follows. The charge is
based upon the impossibility of discovering any intelligible relation
between noumena and phenomena. In order to grasp the force of the
argument supporting the charge, it is necessary to keep three facts
about Kantian philosophy constantly in mind: (1) that the real existence of noumena (or noumenon) distinct from the world of our
experience was never doubted by Kant and is essential to his whole
philosophical construction[12]; (2) that we do not know anything about
noumena as they are in themselves; and (3) that the objective world
of phenomena is the resultant or product of some sort of action or
influence of the noumena upon the human mind, the character of that
phenomenal world being specifically determined by the *a priori* forms
of sensibility and understanding in that mind.

There seem to be four possible interpretations of Kant's conception
of the relation of noumena and phenomena. We shall state all four, but
shall say no more than a word on those which Kant certainly did
not intend.

a) There is *one noumenon,* and it somehow gives rise to the phenomenal world. This doctrine amounts to an absolutistic appearance-
reality theory. We need spend no time on it, because: first, Kant certainly did not intend such a doctrine; second, it takes all meaning
from his doctrine of the function of the *a priori* forms of the mind in
producing the world of phenomena; and third, it explains nothing at
all of either the appearance or the reality.

b) There are a *plurality of noumena, none of which are conscious
selves or egos,* but which nevertheless give rise to phenomenal egos and
the phenomenal world which they experience. Again, Kant did not
intend this; it is the most incredible of all possible interpretations of
his philosophy; it renders purposeless his explanation of the role which
the *a priori* forms of the mind play in producing objective phenomena;
and, finally, it quite destroys his central idea of the transcendental unity
of apperception as the first condition of any knowledge.

c) There are a *plurality of noumena, all of which are conscious selves*

[12] Paton, *op. cit.,* I, p. 61; II, Chaps. LV–LVI.

or egos, and which give rise to the world of phenomena by appearing to one another. Kant does not seem to have intended this view although he does not reject it. We need not treat it separately from the fourth view (which follows) for two reasons: first, nothing in Kant's system would ever enable us (or him) to decide between the two views, since we cannot know noumena; and second, the criticisms which we shall direct against the fourth view apply equally to the third.

d) There are a plurality of noumena, some of which are conscious selves or egos and some of which are not; the phenomenal world arises from the influence of noumena (of both kinds, probably) upon those noumena which are selves or egos. This view is the least unlikely of all, and seems to be what Kant generally was thinking of when he mentioned noumena. We shall therefore direct our criticism against this view. The difficulties which we shall point out in it apply equally to the third view and *a fortiori* to the first and second. These difficulties all hinge upon the most characteristic feature of Kant's philosophy, namely, his theory of the *a priori* forms of space, time, and the categories.

2. What Kant's Doctrine Really Means. Before explaining the difficulties of this theory, we may state summarily and bluntly its real significance. Are space, time, and the categories phenomenal or noumenal? Kant's insistence that we know nothing of things as they are in themselves forbids us to say that these *a priori* forms of the human mind are noumenal; for if they were, they would be known characters of a noumenon, namely, a human mind, and would give us a considerable knowledge of that noumenon as it is in itself. They must, therefore, be considered phenomenal. But then, since (together with the noumena which are the source of the matter of experience) they determine the world of phenomena, they are phenomena which are the prior conditions of all other phenomena. Hence, they must be themselves phenomena resulting entirely from noumenal conditions. These noumenal conditions are prior to and produce the human mind; and then the noumena themselves appear to the human mind, giving rise to the world of objective phenomena. Thus Kant's philosophy reduces itself to an appearance-reality theory in which the human individual falls on the side of appearance. This, in historical fact, was what some post-Kantians made of it.

3. Absurdities in Kant's Doctrine. Never mind the significance of the theory; let us examine its internal structure. Can it hold together?

It cannot. It falls apart at its precise center, its doctrine of the *a priori* forms. According to this theory some conditions existing among things-in-themselves give rise to the phenomenal world, the world in which phenomenal egos experience objective phenomena. The *a priori* forms of sensibility and understanding, as we have seen, are, according to Kant's intention, forms of the mind of the empirical ego. But it must be remembered that these forms play an essential part, the all-important part, in conditioning or producing the world of phenomenal objects. In view of this, Kant's theory really means the following: conditions existing in the noumenal world give rise to phenomenal egos with certain *a priori* forms of sensibility and understanding; and then things-in-themselves, appearing to these phenomenal egos, give rise to the objective world of phenomena. Does that make sense? It means that noumena interact with noumena (thus falling, by the way, under the categorial scheme) and also with phenomena; that is, they interact with the resultants of their mutual interactions. To express the situation in another way: noumena act upon (or, perhaps, appear to) noumenal egos, thus producing phenomenal egos; then they appear to (or, perhaps, act upon) these phenomenal egos, thus producing objective phenomena. Nature is the appearances of things-in-themselves to their own appearances.

This interpretation of Kant's teaching seems closest to his real intention, because it seems to be necessarily implied in his distinction between the noumenal and phenomenal ego and in his assumption that noumena are in fact a plurality. It seems quite unintelligible and impossible, since it makes the essential prior conditions of the whole phenomenal world — space, time, and the categories — themselves phenomena. It breaks down, in other words, because of the double distinction between the empirical ego and noumenal ego and between the empirical ego and objective phenomena. That fact suggests two ways to save the theory while holding to the same general interpretation. The first is to do away with the distinction between the phenomenal ego and the objective world of phenomena thus making all phenomena affections or ideas of the ego. But this would be precisely the kind of idealism which Kant rejected and tried to refute. The other alternative is simply to eliminate the empirical ego as a knowing mind, thus making the noumenal ego the immediate subject of experience, and phenomena the appearance of noumena to the noumenal ego. This alternative, unlike the others, does make sense; its only undesirable feature is that it abolishes the central doctrine of the *Critique of Pure Reason.*

If the noumenal ego is regarded as the immediate subject of human experience, Kant's doctrine ceases to have any specially Kantian character. The *a priori* forms — space, time, and the categories — would have to be considered as forms or natures in the noumenal or real ego, that is to say, in a thing-in-itself. In that case we should know a good deal about a supposedly unknown thing-in-itself. But the worst damage that would be done to the critical philosophy would be the freeing of the human mind from the fear, planted in it by that philosophy, that it is not really itself, that it is merely a phenomenal appearance of itself or of some other self. Once it tasted this new freedom, there would be no stopping it till it had torn its erstwhile prison down entirely. At once it will see that there is no need at all for the whole noumenon-phenomenon baggage and the limitation of knowledge to the so-called phenomena. Knowing itself as a thing-in-itself, it will now assert what it suspected all along: that it acts and produces changes in things, that things act upon it and produce changes in it, that it and the things it experiences are permanent entities which undergo accidental changes as they mutually affect one another, that it is a unity unifying manifolds of various sorts and recognizing other unities more or less similar to itself; that it understands in terms of categorial relations because such relations are very real features of itself and the things around it; and that its forms of sensibility are space and time for the very simple reason that it is itself material as well as mental, changeable as well as permanent, just as it seems to be. In a word, once it were admitted that the so-called *a priori* forms of sensibility and understanding in the human mind belonged to the real ego, and that it is this real ego which experiences and understands the world, Kant's whole philosophy would be undermined. For my real ego would be just about what it appears to me to be, making allowance for the fact that I do not know myself fully. After that, only blind devotion to Kant's system could keep me from concluding that the case of the world I experience is pretty much the same as my own case: it is the real world, or part of it at any rate, and in knowing it I know it as what it is, allowance being made for the obvious fact that I never know all about it.

There seems to be no need of adding any special criticism of Kant's doctrines of substance and causality. If our argument against his philosophy as a whole has succeeded, we have disposed of his doctrines of substance and cause. Kant's contention that substance and causality are, so far as we know, limited to the phenomenal world, stands or falls with his whole doctrine of critical idealism. On the positive side, we may simply add that in so far as Kant, like Hume, started from a subjectivistic and sensistic assumption, many of the remarks we have made concerning our knowledge of real substances and causes in connection with Hume are equally applicable to Kant. We may also add that Thomists, since they derive the principles of substance, sufficient reason, and causality, not from any particular slice of being, for example, sensible being, but from being as such, from the principle of identity, and from such primary determinations of being as essence and existence, potency and act, know that they may confidently use these principles throughout the whole realm of intelligible being.

CHAPTER XVII

BEING AND TRUTH

I. METAPHYSICS AND ITS OBJECT

1. Metaphysics and the Other Sciences. In contrast to Hume, Kant, and our contemporary naturalists, Aristotle and St. Thomas considered metaphysics not only as a science but as the supreme science. Aristotle called it First Philosophy, Theology, and Wisdom. The question, whether there is such a science, is settled by determining whether there is any distinct formal object proper to such a science. If there is such an object and if a body of truths about it can be demonstrated, there must be a science of metaphysics.

According to the *philosophia perennis,* there is an object proper to metaphysics alone: it is being-as-such. This object not only is studied by no other science, but it underlies the object of every other science; and, consequently, not only is metaphysics a true science, but it is the most fundamental and the supreme human science. It is the ultimate foundation of all the other sciences and it has by nature the right to regulate and govern these others. None of the sciences which deal with particular pieces or slices of being, nor all of them together, can ever attain to the unitary goal of the mind, namely, truth — the all-embracing truth to which all the particular partial truths make their contribution and in which they achieve their proper intelligible setting — unless they are governed by a master-science which studies, not some slice of being, but being itself. Metaphysics is this master science. Its principles are the absolutely first principles of all science; and hence they are presupposed by and support and regulate the special principles of all the other sciences.[1]

The reason for this is that while the other sciences study being, each studies it from some partial point of view. So long as a science studies being in respect to some particular aspect, its study cannot

---

[1] Aristotle, *Meta.,* I, 1 and 2; III, 2; St. Thomas, *In Meta., Proem.* I; *Con. Gen.,* I, 1.

reach the very foundations of being. The conclusions of all the special sciences taken together will constitute all the secondary and relative truths about being, but will have nothing at all to say of the primary and absolute truth about being. Only the science which brushes aside, so to speak, the particular conditions of particular types of beings and probes into the heart of being itself can give the primary and absolutely universal truth about being. And clearly such a science will be the first of sciences — wisdom itself — since its object will embrace all the objects of all the other sciences and its principles will judge and support all the others.

The special sciences take for granted, without establishing or justifying them, certain universal principles and starting points; for example, being itself, the principle of contradiction, the ability of the human mind to know reality, the principle of causality, the existence of nature. These are among the very things which metaphysics, instead of taking them for granted, must examine and justify. Consequently, since these truly first principles underlie the more particular "first" principles of the particular sciences, only metaphysics can supply the ultimate ground of validity for all the sciences. Without metaphysics the mansion of human knowledge would rest on something less stable than bedrock. Metaphysics does not zoom inspiringly but insecurely into ethereal realms, as many moderns think; on the contrary, it is primarily concerned with foundations.

2. Being-As-Such. Sensible being considered as changeable is, as we have seen, the formal object of the philosophy of nature. The intellect attains to this object by an abstraction which pierces through the individual marks and the individual matter of perceptible beings to their common and universal status as changeable, sensible substances. By a second abstraction the intellect leaves out of consideration the mobility and sensible quality which arise from the object's materiality and seizes upon the note of quantity which affects every sensible thing. This second abstraction gives the mind a second formal object, quantity; and a second science, mathematics. By a third, and highest, abstraction the intellect discerns a still deeper common note possessed by all its objects: whether mobile or not, whether quantified or not, whatever is, is *being*. It thus attains a further formal object and a further science; namely, metaphysics, the science of being-as-such, or of immaterial being.[2]

[2] *In Boet. de Trin.,* V, 1 and 4.

In the act of making this third degree of abstraction, the intellect realizes that changeableness, sensible quality, quantity, and indeed, materiality itself, are not necessary characters of being: ["to be" does not of itself entail materiality, quantity, perceptibility, or changeableness.] In other words, the mind now arises to the concept of immaterial being. It sees that while all the objects of its immediate experience are mobile, perceptible, and quantified, being, as such, is not so. It sees also that *being* is the very first of concepts, that it is implied in all other concepts, and that all other concepts are further determinations of it. *That which is,* is prior to *that which is material* or *that which is changeable: material* or *changeable* can be left off and *that which is* still makes sense; but material or changeable, or for that matter, any concept whatsoever, makes no sense unless *that which is* be understood along with it and prior to it. Being alone makes anything intelligible; being alone can affect the intellect; being is the proper object of the intellect, the only stuff on which it feeds.

Therefore, metaphysics, since its object is being-as-such, studies the primary and most fundamental object of thought, the object without which no other object can be thought. What it learns about this object is true about everything that exists or can exist; because nothing exists or can exist except in so far as it is being; in so far as it is not being, it is nothing. Consequently, the principles established in metaphysics are absolutely and universally true. Such are the principles of identity, of contradiction, of sufficient reason, of causality, of finality. Similarly, the primary determinations which metaphysics discovers about being-as-such will of necessity apply in some manner to everything in the universe, since they are determinations of whatever is or can be. Such primary determinations of being are potentiality and actuality, essence and existence, substance and accident. Finally, the attributes which metaphysics discloses as belonging to being-as-such must of necessity belong to everything in so far as it is being. These transcendental attributes of being are unity, truth, and goodness.

Aristotle and St. Thomas both define metaphysics sometimes as the science of being as such and sometimes as the science of immaterial being. The two definitions are not contradictory; rather they involve and imply each other. Being-as-such, considered as the formal object of a science, is being free from materiality; for so long as a science studies properties, for example, quantity and mobility, that determine beings in so far as they are affected by materiality, that science has not for its object being-as-such but being-as-material. The study of being-as-such must prescind from all material conditions and consider its object in freedom from materiality. Hence being, unity, substance and accident, potency and act, and all those determinations of being which are not of their nature bound to matter are considered apart from matter, or as immaterial, by the metaphysician. Such objects are called negatively immaterial; they exist indifferently in or apart from matter. They are studied in *General Metaphysics* or *Ontology*. Beings which are positively immaterial, that is to say spiritual substances, are studied in *Special Metaphysics* or in one branch of it, *Natural Theology*. Another branch of special metaphysics, *Epistemology*, studies knowledge, which is an immaterial operation of being.

3. The Concept of Being. The metaphysician's concept of being is attained only as the result of an abstraction that is on the highest level of thought. Yet obviously the least tutored and least thoughtful mind has a concept of being. The "being" represented by both concepts is the same but the representations, that is to say, the concepts, are very different. Being is a first principle, or rather *the* first principle, of intellectual knowledge. It is known naturally, by itself and necessarily, just as soon as the intellect is first brought into contact with it through the senses. The intellect knows being directly and in itself, and knows whatever else it knows by means of being: it knows being as naturally as sight knows color; and, just as sight is defined in relation to color, so is intellect defined in relation to being. The intellect's first response to experience is the judgment that the thing experienced *is*, and is *something*. In this judgment there is contained — very vaguely, perhaps — the concept of being-as-such. The intellect may not *explicitly* distinguish between "being" and that which it pronounces a being, but it could not possibly affirm the one of the other unless, at least confusedly, it conceived them as distinct. This same object, vaguely grasped in our first intellectual act, is the object which the metaphysician seizes in a clear and distinct concept, the concept of being-as-such.

The purely logical concept of being is the emptiest of all concepts; every other concept adds something to it. It is attained by sloughing off determinations from other concepts until only the least determinate and most poverty-stricken concept is left — a concept signifying merely to be without being anything in particular. It has, we say in logic, the widest extension and the least comprehension; it means so little that it means anything. The metaphysician conceives being in the richest of concepts, not in the poorest. His idea does not exclude everything except mere being; rather it embraces in itself everything that can possibly be. The first vague idea of being was its seed, and the logical concept a stage through which it had to pass; but this stage must be passed through and left behind if there is to be any science of metaphysics. Metaphysics is the science of The Full, not of The Void.[3]

The term "being" has three equally fundamental usages. (1) It is the present participle of the verb "to be," just as "painting" is the present participle of the verb "to paint." So used, it expresses the actual exercise of the act of existing, just as "painting" expresses the actual exercise of the act so named. (2) "Being" is used as a noun, just as "painting" is of (a) a painting, or (b) the whole collection of paintings, or (c) the common nature of all paintings. So used, the term "being" designates (a) a thing which exists or is at least capable of existing; (b) the totality of all such things, and (c) that which all such things possess in common. (3) "Being" is used as the copula or connective between a subject and predicate in a proposition, as when we speak of blindness being a great misfortune. When it is so used, it applies as well to that which is not anything, as in the example given, as to that which is something. Hence, in this third usage it does not signify absolutely the object of metaphysics, which is being as opposed to non-being; yet it does affirm the identity of two concepts, which while negative, are yet intelligible and consequently conceived in relation to being, and therefore it does signify being at least relatively. It signifies logical being (*ens rationis*) in distinction from real being (*ens secundum se*). It is the object of logic rather than of metaphysics.

The metaphysician uses the term "being" in sense (1) where "being" means existence, and in all senses of (2), but especially (2c), where "being" means being-as-such, or that which is common to everything that is. In medieval Latin two different words expressed these two principal meanings. Being-as-such, or that by virtue of which whatever is real, is real, was expressed by *ens*. Existence, or that by which something is actual, was expressed by *esse*. *Ens est id cujus actus est esse.* "Being is that whose act it is to exist," wrote St. Thomas. *Ens* expresses

[3] Cf. J. Maritain, *A Preface to Metaphysics*. Second Lecture (New York: Sheed and Ward, 1939).

the subject of existence, and *esse* expresses the act of the subject by which it exists.

II. THE DIVISIONS OF BEING

1. Being and Other Concepts. The concept of being — that which is — is amazingly fertile in yielding further concepts and principles. If human knowledge is to have any ultimate and solid foundation, then all human knowledge, that is to say, all demonstrations and all definitions or conceptions, must be reducible to a principle (or principles) known by and in itself — *per se notum*. If we had to go on always giving one thing as evidence for another, we could not avoid an infinite regress in demonstrations; we would, indeed, be unable truly to demonstrate anything, and all science and knowledge would be destroyed. Fortunately there is a first conception whose object is evident in itself, so that the intellect does not need to seek beyond it for any token of its certainty. This concept is that of being; it is *per se notum*, and all other conceptions are reduced to it.

The human intellect cannot conceive of anything unless it conceives of it as "being this or that" or as "this or that mode of being." Consequently all other conceptions are formed by some addition to being. Thus, substance is conceived as being *per se* and accident as being *per aliud*. Even "nothing" is conceived as the negation of being. In no case, however, is that which is added to being in forming another conception added from outside being itself; for, as we have seen, every nature is essentially being, and therefore every nature added to being is itself being. What is added is a *mode of being* which is not expressed in the name "being."

This addition of a nature to being in order to form another conception occurs in two ways: (1) the mode expressed may be some special mode of being designating a distinct grade or manner of the possession of being; (2) it may be something that belongs of necessity to every being, though it is not expressed in the name being. The conceptions formed by additions of the first sort to being represent the *predicaments* or the essential divisions of being. The conceptions formed by additions of the second kind represent the transcendental attributes of being, or the *transcendentals;* these are not divisions of being, but transcend all divisions; indeed, each of them is equivalent to being itself.[4]

* *De Ver.*, I, 1.

2. The Predicaments. When the mode added to being is a special mode signifying a distinct grade or manner of possessing being, it names one of the divisions of being; that is, it signifies one of the genera into which being is divided. Thus, the conception of substantial being adds to being the special mode of existence in and through self; hence substance is *ens per se*. The conception of accident adds the special mode of being in and through another; thus, accident is *ens per aliud*. Accident is itself divided into nine special modes. These, together with substance, are represented by the ten predicamental conceptions; they are the highest genera of being. They are: substance, quantity, quality, relation, place, time, action, passion, posture, and habit. These genera really divide being, since every being is in some one of them and not in any of the others.

The predicaments, as the term itself indicates, are taken from the various ways in which a predicate may be related to its subject. Every predicate asserts of the subject that it *is* in some way or other. Even predications in which the term "is" does not appear still predicate being. There is no difference between saying, for example, "The man is convalescent" and "The man convalesces." Consequently, to every mode of predication there corresponds a mode of being; and the predicaments are not only the modes of predication but also the supreme genera, or the categories, of being.[5]

The predicate may be related to the subject in three ways: as signifying what the subject itself is, as in "Socrates is an animal"; as signifying something which is *in* the subject, as in "The apple is red"; and as signifying something external to the subject, as, "Macy's is at 34 Street." The first mode of predication, signifying the subject as to its essence, gives the first predicament, namely *substance*. The predicate signifies the ultimate subject of predication, the "first substance" or particular substance, of which all the predications in every genus are ultimately made. The other nine predicaments are of the genus *accident*, and accident has being only in a substance; consequently the substance is the subject of the accident and therefore the ultimate subject of every predicate signifying an accident.

The second relation of the predicate to the subject — signifying something in the subject — has three divisions. It may signify something which is in the subject (*a*) absolutely, as consequent upon the subject's matter, or (*b*) absolutely, as consequent upon its form, or

[5] *In V Meta,* 9, Nos. 890, 893.

(c) which is in the subject in respect to something other than the subject itself. A predicate signifying something in the subject following from its matter is in the predicament *quantity*, as, for example, "The baby is sixteen pounds." A predicate following the form is in the predicament *quality*, as, for example, "The boy is intelligent" or "The flower is pink." When the predicate is attributed to the subject because of a relation which the subject bears to something else, as, for example, "John is my friend," it is in the predicament *relation*.

There are also several subdivisions of the third mode of predication, where the predicate is taken from something exterior to the subject. A predicate signifying something of a subject, but altogether outside the subject, as for example, "John is dressed," is in the predicament *habitus*. Three predicates express something outside the subject, but measuring it: first, temporally, as, "John arrived on Thursday"; second, as to its location, for example, "Macy's is at 34 Street"; and third, as to the disposition of its own parts, for example, "Willie is standing on his head." These give three predicaments of *time, place,* and *position*. Finally, a predicate may attribute something to a subject according as *something else* is in the subject; and then we have the two predicaments which refer to causation. In every causal situation something acts upon something else, which is acted upon. When the predicate signifies what belongs to the subject as principle of causation, for example, "John wrote the poem," the predicament is *action*. When it signifies what belongs to the subject as terminus of the causation, the predicament is *passion,* as, "The poem was written by John."[6]

III. BEING IS TRANSCENDENTAL AND ANALOGICAL

1. Being Is Not a Genus. Whatever is in any genus is being, and all the species of every genus are being, and all the differences that divide one genus from another and one species from another are being. Being is not a genus, because a genus is always divided into species or subgenera by differences which are not included in the concept of the genus as such. Thus the genus "animal" is divided into "man" and "brute" by the differences "rational" and "non-rational," neither of which is included in "animal," but which are added to it from outside itself. There are no differences outside being which can be added to

[6] *Ibid.,* Nos. 890–892.

being, because every difference, if it is real, is being.[7] Being, then, is not a genus, but a *transcendental*. It is not one kind of anything, but is everything. A genus is a division of being; being is not a division of itself. A transcendental concept is one whose object stands over and above all divisions and determinations of the real because it is proper to every part of any division that may be made. The primary transcendental is being itself.

That beings differ from one another in a great variety of ways is a matter of experience which is beyond dispute. If, then, beings *differ really* from one another, can there be any *single real object* represented by a concept which embraces them all? Or to put the question another way: if the intellect forms a single concept which embraces a multitude of things which differ essentially from one another, can that concept have any true essential unity?

A generic concept, for example, animal, has true essential unity because it represents a real essence shared by several species and *does not represent* (i.e., it leaves out) *the differences which are added to this essence*. By ignoring the differences which determine the several species, it preserves the unity of the generic essence common to them all. But we have seen that being is not a genus, and that its concept cannot leave out the differences that divide it, because these differences are themselves being. How, then, can the idea of being have any essential unity? How can there be a real unitary object corresponding to this idea? The answer to this question is that the concept of being has essential unity, but that this unity is *analogical* rather than univocal.

2. Univocal Unity. An idea possessing univocal unity designates several things in precisely the same way: the essence which it represents as common to them, it represents as belonging to each one in the same way, or as the same in each. Thus when I say that a man and a brute are animals I mean that each possesses the one generic nature called animality, although each also possesses a different extrinsic determination of that nature. A man and a brute agree in being sentient organisms, and this common nature is what the generic concept represents. They differ in respect to rationality, but the concept "animal" does not include any reference at all to rationality, and consequently it represents the generic nature of man and brute univocally. The reason why the concept of animal can univocally represent essentially

[7] *Ibid.*, No. 889. Cf. *S. Theol.*, I, 3, 5, c.

different animals is the fact that it leaves out of its representation those things whereby one animal differs from another and includes only that whereby they are the same, namely, sentiency.[8]

3. Analogical Unity. A concept which possesses *analogical unity* represents several different things as having a common essence but having it differently. An analogical concept, to state the same thing in other words, represents a certain essence which each of the things to which the concept applies possesses within itself, but which is differently possessed by each; and the reasons for the differences lie within the essence itself instead of being added to it from without; and these differences, therefore, are also embraced within the concept which represents the essence. Because the concept embraces these differences instead of excluding them, it does not have univocal unity.

Take, for example, the concept "skill." It represents a definite single object of thought, namely, the ability to perform some activity with precision, ease, and effectiveness. Yet, although the concept has this one meaning, it does not have univocal unity. Different skills are not different determinations of one common genus, skill, as different species of animals are determinations of one common genus, animal: skill in writing, in automobile mechanics, in golf, and in piano playing differ from each other right down to the bottom. They are grasped under one concept, not by excluding the differences of the several activities in order to reach a common nature, but by grasping the several different activities, with their differences, under a single relationship or ratio found equally in each one. Bobby Jones is to golf as Paderewski is to the piano. The specifically different objects of a univocal generic concept differ essentially down to a certain point in their essences, but below that point there is an absolute sameness of essence, and it is this which the generic concept represents. The different objects of an analogous concept have an essential sameness plus an essential difference both of which go all the way down into their being and both of which are embraced in the analogous concept. Thus, the intellect, observing the several activities of several men, abstracts a single essence, skill, which is present in all these activities. But the activities in which this essence is found possess it in absolutely different ways, and the intellect in conceiving the idea "skill" does not exclude, but on the contrary embraces, all these differences. Hence, the unity of the concept "skill" is not univocal. It represents a single

[8] *In IV Meta.*, 1, Nos. 535–536.

essence within the several activities. The essence is *a relationship between absolutely different terms in the several cases, but nevertheless proper to each case and the same in each case.* Hence, the unity of the concept "skill" is analogical. The meaning of the concept, when applied to different skills, is both the same and different — about as much the same and as much different as the meaning of "half" in half an apple, half a mile, and half an hour.

The natures represented by an analogous concept are, in Scholastic terminology, different *simpliciter*, or "absolutely speaking," and the same *secundum quid*, or "from a certain point of view." Various skills, each considered in itself, are different; hence, absolutely speaking, they are different. Yet when each is considered from a certain point of view, it is found to embody within itself a real principle or ratio which each of the others also embodies, and by means of which it can be seized in a single concept together with the others. This principle is a relationship which is real and is the same in all, although the things which it relates are different in each case. The concept of skill represents this relationship. The case is the same with the concept "half." It is clear that the intellect has before it a real and single object when it conceives of skill or of a half. Similarly, it has before it a real and single object when it conceives of being-as-such; and this object is the formal object of metaphysics. We must now show that this is so.

4. The Analogy of Being. Two great analogies of being are of primary importance for the metaphysician. The first analogy is between God (*ens a se*, self-existing being) and creatures (*ens ab alio*, caused being). The second is between substance (*ens per se*, being existing in itself) and accident (*ens per aliud*, being existing in another).

5. God and Creatures. God is being and a creature is being, but being cannot be a universal essence common to the two and differentiated in them by a determination added from outside itself, as rational and non-rational differentiate animal into man and brute. If being were a univocal genus divided into two subgenera, self-existing and caused being, then in itself it would be related to self-existing being and to caused being as a potency to two alternate acts. This is absurd. In the first place, it would mean that a potentiality is the first source of everything actual, and a complete indeterminateness the first source of all determinate being. This would be equivalent to making nothing the matrix of being, since potentiality not grounded in any actuality and indeterminateness not grounded in any determinate being are nothing. To consider the concept of being as univocal is, therefore, to equate being with nothing. If we try to remove both self-existence and caused existence from the concept of being, we leave nothing thinkable; and so we destroy the concept.

In the second place, to consider being as univocal destroys the notion of self-existent being or pure actuality, that is to say, God. For it would make self-existent being a determination of something prior to itself, and would introduce potentiality into the Pure Actuality. God, instead of the origin of all being, would be Himself a derivative of being; instead of Being Itself, He would be a division of being. Consequently, the concept of being which embraces both God and creatures cannot possibly be a univocal concept. No common generic being can be divided into *ens a se* and *ens ab alio* without destroying the concept of *ens a se*. Hence, no common generic being can be found in God and creatures; the being of God and the being of creatures differ to the last drop.[9]

Yet there is a concept of being which possesses true essential unity and which embraces both God and creature. Being is that whose act it is to exist: this concept is clearly verified both in regard to *ens a se* and *ens ab alio*. The actuality of God is "to be" and the actuality of a creature is "to be"; and herein lies the *ratio* or principle by which these two beings can be grasped under the same concept. The ratio is real, and is the same in each case, and consequently the concept which signifies it possesses essential unity. But since this *ratio* is not a common generic nature, the concept has not univocal but analogical unity. Being, when predicated of God and creatures, is analogous, because while it expresses an identical relation to existence in both cases, both the subject of existence and the act by which this subject exists are essentially different in the two cases. To be, for God, is to be of Himself (*a se*) and to be God; to be, for a creature, is to be caused (*ab alio*) and to be a creature. In the two propositions, "God is," and "The creature is," the two predicates are precisely as different as the two subjects, but the relation of predicate to subject is identical in both.

6. **Substance and Accident.** The case is parallel in respect to substance and accident. Being is truly a single concept which embraces both substance and accident; yet being cannot be a univocal essence

[9] *S. Theol.*, I, 3, 5, *Sed contra* and c.

divided into substantial being and accidental being. If being were a genus divided into two subgenera, substance and accident, it would have to possess some determination prior to the two dividing determinations, *per se* and *per aliud;* but there is no conceivable determination prior to these and indifferently determinable to one or the other. In other words, nothing is conceivable of which substance and accident are two kinds. Just as in the case of *ens a se* and *ens ab alio,* so substance, *ens per se,* and accident, *ens per aliud,* are not related to each other as alternate determinations of a common nature. They are different natures all the way through. They have in common a *ratio* or principle by virtue of which they can be designated by a single unitary concept, namely, being; this *ratio* is that the act of each of them is to exist. But their two modes of existence are not varieties of any common nature; both the subject of existence and the act of this subject differ essentially in the two cases, and differ in precisely the same way in both cases. Strictly speaking, only substances are subjects of existence and only substances exert acts of existence, for it is of some substance that all predications are ultimately made. As subject — that is, as to its essence — a substance is that which has the capacity of existing in itself; and as to existence, a substance exists by an act of existence (*esse*) which is its own act. An accident, on the other hand, is, as to essence, that which can exist only by inhering in a substance; and, as to existence, an accident has no act of existence — no *esse* — of its own, but exists only by the act of existence of the substance in which it inheres — it is in fact only a mode or determination of the substance's act of existence.[10] No effort of abstraction probing deeper and deeper into substantial and accidental being will ever come upon some ultimate core of univocal sameness; the deepest abstraction will attain being-as-such, but this will be analogous.[11]

7. **Résumé.** To summarize: Being is an analogous concept. Being is common to everything, because it is embraced in every nature; but it is not a common part of every nature, because it embraces every nature. The being of anything is that by which it is, just as the half of anything is one of two equal parts into which it is divided; and just as half an apple and half a mile are radically different yet truly

[10] *Nam accidentis esse est inesse. In V Meta.,* 9, No. 894. Cf. Gerard Smith, S.J., in a review of Gilson's *Le Thomisme,* 5th ed., in *The Modern Schoolman* (March, 1946), Vol. XXIII, No. 3, pp. 169–170.

[11] *In XI Meta.,* 3, No. 2197.

halves, so the being of God and the being of a creature, the being of substance and the being of accident, are radically different, yet each is that by which its subject is. St. Thomas' definition of being, "that whose act is to exist," is verified exactly in every being, yet is realized in different beings in natures which are *simpliciter* different. But while the object conceived as "being" is *simpliciter* different in different things, it is *secundum quid* the same, because each is a subject whose act it is to exist. This is precisely what is proper to a concept having analogical unity.

8. **Analogy of Proportionality and of Attribution.** The kind of analogy we have been explaining is *analogy of proportionality*. In it a concept is predicated of several things as belonging to each of them intrinsically, though in ways which are *simpliciter* different. Thus, being is predicated of God and creatures as intrinsically possessed by each; and while the being of God is entitatively different from that of creatures, yet it is to God as a creature's being is to the creature. A second kind of analogy, called *analogy of attribution,* predicates the essence properly or intrinsically of one thing, called the primary analogue, and extrinsically of others, called secondary analogues, because of their relation to the first. Thus, health is properly and intrinsically predicated of a man as being really possessed by him, and it is extrinsically and analogously predicated of his complexion in relation to him, that is, as a sign of his health.[12]

IV. THE TRANSCENDENTALS

1. The predicaments, or the divisions of being, were formed by adding to being a mode designating a distinct grade or manner of being. The second way, we have seen, in which a nature is added to being is when the mode expressed in the concept signifies something which belongs of necessity to every being, although it is not expressed in the name being. There are two ways in which some nature may belong of necessity to every being: (*a*) something may belong to every being when the being is considered in itself; (*b*) something may belong to every being when the being is considered in reference to something else.

The first thing that may be predicated of every being considered in itself is its *essence;* whatever is, is some definite thing. From this absolutely universal predication everything is given the name *res* or

---

[12] *In V Meta.,* 8, No. 879.

thing. Thing (*res*), wrote St. Thomas,[13] differs from being (*ens*) because *ens* is taken from the act of being while *res* expresses the quiddity (*quod quid est*) or essence of being.

Res is formed from being by *affirming* of every being its own essence. There is likewise something that can be *denied* of every being considered in itself. This is division, for nothing is a being except in so far as it is undivided; to divide a thing is to destroy it. When we add the notion of indivision to being we conceive of being as one (*unum*). Every being, therefore, is called *one* in so far as it is undivided in itself.

In reference to something else we may consider being (1) according to the division of one thing from another; and inasmuch as every being is divided off from, or is not, something else (*aliud quid*), it is called *something* (*aliquid*). Thus a man has an essence (*res*), he is undivided in himself (*unum*), and he is something distinct from anything else (*aliquid*).

We may consider being in reference to something else (2) according to the agreement of one thing with another; that is to say, we can so consider being provided there is something which by its nature agrees with or conforms to every being. Now there is such a thing, namely, the human soul, which by its cognitive and appetitive powers is in some manner everything. Since the soul by these two powers is related to every being, these two relations must be predicated universally of every being. Now the cognitive power is that by which the soul knows being, and since by its intellect the soul is capable of apprehending being as such, every being, in so far as it is being, is conformed to the intellect. This conformity of being to the intellect is called truth; and, consequently, every being, inasmuch as it is related to intellect, is true (*verum*). Finally, being in so far as it is desirable is called good (*bonum*), for "the good is what all things desire" as Aristotle says. Now, desire is the act of appetite, and consequently it is by virtue of its relation to appetite that anything is good.

2. We may summarize St. Thomas' deduction of these transcendental conceptions in the diagram on p. 372.

Three of these transcendentals call for further discussion. If one, true, and good are truly transcendental, then they are equivalent to being itself, or as St. Thomas expresses it, they are convertible with being. But each of them has an opposite, viz., many, false, and evil.

---

[13] *De Ver.*, I, 1, whence is taken the whole present account of the transcendentals.

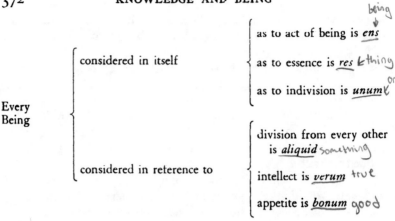

It would seem to follow that these latter must be non-being, since each is the opposite of that which is equivalent to being. This, indeed, is exactly the position which the Angelic Doctor takes: multiplicity, falsity, and evil are non-being. Anything is being in so far as it is one, in so far as it is true, and in so far as it is good; in so far as it is many, false, or evil, it is non-being. Of the three transcendentals and their opposites, we shall treat here of truth and falsity; in later chapters we shall give St. Thomas' teaching upon the one and the many in connection with our discussion of creation, and his teaching on good with our proof of God's goodness, and on evil in relation to the problem of evil.

V. TRUTH AND FALSITY

1. **The Meanings of "Truth."** Truth is being as it is related to intellect. We saw in Chapter XI that all knowledge is brought about by the mind's being made like or assimilated to the thing known. This assimilation of thought and thing is, therefore, the cause of knowledge. But this assimilation or conformity of being and intellect is what truth formally consists in. Truth, consequently, is prior to knowledge and is its cause. But the being of the thing known is prior even to its truth, for its being is the foundation of its truth. Taking all this into consideration, we find that truth has been defined in three ways. Augustine defined it according to its foundation or ground; namely, being. *The true,* he wrote, *is that which is.* Isaac defined it according to what formally constitutes its notion. *Truth,* he wrote, *is the agree-*

ment of thing and intellect. And Hilary defined it according to its effect; namely, knowledge. *The true,* he wrote, *is being manifesting and declaring itself.*[14]

2. Truth Is Predicated Primarily of Intellect. Though being is the cause or ground of truth, truth is not predicated primarily of things, but primarily of intellect and secondarily of things, St. Thomas holds. Truth, he argues, is to be predicated primarily of that in which its full nature is found. Now truth is what the intellect by its nature tends to, just as appetite tends to the good. But the terminus or end of the movement of intellect, as of every cognitive power, is not something outside the soul, as in the case of the appetitive powers, but something within the soul; for the terminus of cognition is the known object, and an object is known only according as it is in the mind of the knower. Consequently truth is to be found primarily in the intellect in so far as the intellect in its act of knowledge is conformed to the being which it knows. This agreement of intellect with thing has been called by Scholastics *logical truth.*

Truth is also found in things. When an intellect is conformed to a thing, the thing is, of necessity, conformed to that intellect. The form by which the thing is what it is, is in the intellect, and is affirmed by the intellect of the thing. The thing is what it is and is true, by virtue of the same form. But since it is only because this form is predicated of the thing by the intellect conformed to it that the thing is called true, it is clear that truth in the thing is subsequent to truth in the intellect. Hence, truth, as St. Thomas says, flows from the intellect to the thing by virtue of the thing's conformity to the intellect. Therefore, the truth of intellect is primary and the truth of things (called by Scholastics ontological truth) is secondary.

3. Truth of Things Is Transcendental. The truth of things is twofold. The truth of anything is its being in so far as that is conformed to an intellect. The being of anything is of necessity conformed to any intellect upon which it depends, since it must be whatever that intellect ordains it to be. Consequently, in relation to the intellect upon which its being depends everything possesses truth by nature, or absolutely. Such is the truth possessed by a house in relation to the mind of its architect. Such also, but far more perfectly, is the truth of natural things in relation to the divine intellect, the mind

[14] *Verum est manifestativum et declarativum esse (De Ver.,* I, 1, c). In Chapter XIV I have rendered this as "evident and assertive being."

of the Creator. Such truth is of necessity possessed by everything; and in relation to the divine intellect nothing can contain falsity, since everything is as the divine intellect ordains it. In other words, absolutely speaking, whatever is, is true, and nothing is false. It is clear that in this sense truth is transcendental, that is, convertible with being.[15]

In the second way, a thing is true in relation to an intellect upon which its being does not depend, but for which it is a possible object of knowledge. In this way also, every being is true. For any being is known by virtue of its form, in so far as this form is in the intellect. Now everything is a being just to the extent to which it possesses form. Since, therefore, it is the same principle, namely, its form, by which a thing is being and by which it is an object of knowledge, it is clear that everything that exists has a relation to intellect, or is, as we say, intelligible. Now this intelligibility is precisely what is meant by the truth of the thing. Consequently, since the soul, by intellect, is in a certain manner, all things, so all things, as intelligible, are conformed to the soul, that is, to the human intellect, and are true. In order for something not to be true in the second way, it would be necessary for it to have no form at all, in which case it could have no actual being. Hence, the truth of things, in this second sense also, is transcendental and convertible with being.

4. Truth of Thought Is Transcendental. Not only is the truth of things convertible with being, but so also is the truth of thought. The two, however, are convertible with being, or transcendental, in different ways. The truth of things is convertible with being by predication and in respect to substance; we can say flatly of the thing that *it* is true, because that by which a thing is conformed to intellect is nothing else but its being and substance. The truth of thought, or of an intellect, on the other hand, is convertible with being, not in respect to the substance of the intellect, but in respect to its agreement with a thing. It is related to being as the manifestation to that which is manifested. It is transcendental because an intellect has truth only in so far as it is conformed to being; and every intellect is in fact conformed to every being either actually or potentially, because the same form which makes anything a being is also what conforms the intellect to that being when the intellect possesses that form.[16]

15 *S. Theol.*, I, 16, 1, c; *De Ver.*, I, 2, c.
16 *S. Theol.*, I, 16, 3; *De Ver.*, I, 2, ad 1.

5. Truth in Respect to Negations. Sometimes what the intellect knows is not a being but rather a non-being, that is to say, a negation or a privation, for example, blindness. But how can truth of thought be said to be convertible with being when that which the intellect knows, and by which it is true, is non-being? Is not this the case when a true judgment of the intellect is about a negation or a privation? Even here, St. Thomas answers, it is being which is the measure of the intellect and of its truth. In these cases the truth of the intellect corresponds to the being of which the negation or privation is predicated. The latter, which are not-being, have nothing in themselves whereby they are known; yet they are made knowable by the intellect itself, which makes of them logical beings (*entia rationis*). It does this by conforming itself to their subject, which is a defective being, and by recognizing the principle of the defect in the being. The defect itself is nothing, but as compared with the being it is an *ens rationis*. Thus, blindness is a defect, or non-being, in man; and the intellect, by its own conformity, on the one hand, to man with sight as a property, and, on the other hand, to man, lacking sight, renders blindness an *ens rationis* and knows it. A privation is measured by the possible being which it negates and the actual being in which it resides; and although a privation cannot, strictly speaking, have truth, since it has no being, yet the intellect can have truth in respect to a privation by conforming itself to the measure of the privation, that is to the being which is the subject of the privation compared with the being which that subject ought to have.[17]

6. All Truth Is From the First Truth. From these considerations another one follows very clearly, namely, that both the truth of things and the truth of human intellects are from and depend upon the first truth, that is to say, the truth of the divine intellect upon which things depend for their being. This intellect measures or determines the truth of things, since it gives them their being and the relation of that being to itself. It gives them also their truth in reference to human intellects, since in this respect they are true in so far as they are knowable, and they are knowable by virtue of their forms; and these forms, which are the principles by which things are what they are, are from the divine intellect, the Creator, who is the exemplary and efficient cause of all things. Finally, since human intellects are true in so far as they are in conformity with things and since they are in such conformity

[17] *S. Theol.*, I, 16, 3, ad 2; *De Ver.*, I, 8, c; ad 7; ad 9.

only in so far as they possess the forms of things and predicate these of the things, it is manifest that their truth is from that intellect whence these forms are, and whence their own nature, power, and operation are — the creative intellect of God. Hence the divine intellect is the first truth and the source of all truth.[18]

7. **The False.** In speaking of the false we must make exactly the same distinctions we have made in regard to the true. There are falsity of the thing and falsity of the intellect; and falsity of the thing must be considered in respect to the divine intellect, on the one hand, and human intellect, on the other. There can be no falsity in the divine intellect because things depend upon that intellect and consequently it can never fail to conform to them. For the same reason there can be no falsity in things in respect to the divine intellect, because things, since they depend upon this intellect for their being, must conform to it; and this conformity is truth.

But there can be falsity in things in respect to the human intellect, and there can be falsity in the human intellect. In regard to the human intellect, things are called false when they present sensible appearances which naturally cause them to be taken for something which, in fact, they are not, for example, false teeth or artificial flowers. Such falsity, however, is not essential but only accidental. Things of this kind do not lead the intellect necessarily to judge them to be what they are not; they are likely to beget a false opinion in the intellect, but the latter need not form this false opinion if it is careful enough. Nothing can be false *absolutely*, even in respect to the human intellect, because everything, no matter how likely its sensible appearances are to suggest to the mind a nature which it does not have, does have, in fact, its own nature or form by which, absolutely speaking, it is true in respect to every intellect, at least potentially. In other words, what deceives the mind is never what the false thing is in itself, but rather the sensible likeness which it bears to something which it is not. False teeth are true artificial substitutes for natural teeth, and fool's gold is true iron pyrites.[19]

8. **Truth and Falsity Are in the Judgment.** The question of falsity in the mind is more complicated. To begin with, truth and falsity, in the full meaning of those terms, do not occur in sensation or simple apprehension, but only in judgment. An external sense cannot be de-

---

[18] *S. Theol.*, I, 16, 6, c; *De Ver.*, I, 8, c.
[19] *S. Theol.*, I, 17, 1; *De Ver.*, I, 10.

ceived about its own proper object, for example, sight about color, because the only power any sense has is to apprehend the proper sensible appearance presented to it. In other words, each of the senses has only one possible act, namely, to apprehend a certain class of sensible qualities; in order to apprehend them falsely, or otherwise than they are presented, it would have to perform some other act; but this is impossible, because the sense is nothing but a power to perform this one act. Yet error can occur in perception in regard to those things which are not the proper objects of a special sense; for example, common objects like shape or distance, or accidental sensibles like substance. Furthermore, internal sense can err in forming the phantasm, by putting together in one phantasm things not actually perceived in one object. Although perception can be right or can err in these ways in grasping its objects, we do not properly say that there is truth or falsity in sense. There is either a likeness or a false impression of the object in the sense, by which the sense conforms or fails to conform to the thing; but the sense never knows this conformity or lack of conformity, and hence it does not know truth or falsity.

Much the same thing holds true of the intellect in its first act, simple apprehension. It cannot err in respect to that which is its proper object — essence or quiddity. Hence, it can never be false in respect to a simple or incomplex essence, as, for example, being. It can, however, accidentally err in respect to complex essences. The reason why it cannot err in respect to simple essences is the fact that it is wholly determined in its act by the form which it receives, and hence it cannot fail to apprehend the nature of which that form is the likeness; therefore, it either apprehends an incomplex essence rightly or not at all. But it can accidentally be in error concerning a complex essence, since it may combine in one conception simple essences which are not, in fact, found together in nature. Hence, error can accidentally be found in simple apprehension just as it can in sense, and for the same reason, namely, that composition and division enter accidentally into apprehension just as they do into perception. Yet truth and falsity are not, properly speaking, found in simple apprehension.

The intellect is, indeed, conformed to an essence when it has a correct conception of that essence, and is out of conformity when it has an incorrect conception; and therefore the intellect may, in a manner, be called true or false in simple apprehension. But so long as it has not made any judgment, it has not placed itself alongside any real thing for comparison, and consequently cannot be called true or false in the full sense of those terms — the sense they have when we speak of the truth or falsity of thought. The intellect, in other words, possesses truth or falsity as soon as it asserts something about some being, but not before it does. St. Thomas summarizes all this in his commentary on Aristotle's teaching about truth and falsity in the sense and intellect:

> But although in sensitive cognition there can be a likeness of the thing known, yet to know the reason for this likeness does not pertain to the sense, but only to the intellect. And therefore, although the sense can be true about the sensible object, yet the sense does not know truth, but only the intellect; and for this reason it is said that true and false are in the mind.
>
> But the intellect, on its part, has the likeness of the thing understood according as it conceives the natures of incomplex things, yet it does not on this account judge about the likeness, but only when it composes or divides [i.e., affirms or denies]. For when the intellect conceives what a rational, mortal animal is, it has in it the likeness of man; but it does not by this fact know that it has this likeness, because it does not judge man to be a rational and mortal animal; and therefore truth and falsity are only in this second operation of the intellect, according to which the intellect not only has the likeness of the thing understood, but also reflects upon that likeness, knowing and judging about it. From these considerations, therefore, it is clear that truth is not in things but only in the mind, and, moreover, [only in the intellect's act of] composition and division.[20]

The present chapter has explained the character of the science of metaphysics as understood by St. Thomas and has briefly presented some of the principles and basic conclusions of that science. Before we proceed to the more special conclusions, those concerning God, we must return to the problem of knowledge which occupied us in the preceding chapters, and we must show that the metaphysical principles expounded in the present chapter are objective truths which we know with certainty. This is our task in the chapter to follow.

[20] *In VI Meta.*, 4, Nos. 1235–1236. Cf. *S. Theol.*, I, 17, 3; *De Ver.*, I, 9, 11, 12; *In III De Anima*, 2.

CHAPTER XVIII

OUR KNOWLEDGE OF FIRST PRINCIPLES

I. METAPHYSICS AND EPISTEMOLOGY

1. Thomistic metaphysics is nothing more than a logical exercise in deducing the implications of ideas, unless we know to begin with that through these ideas our minds have hold upon existing realities. We have seen that this is denied by idealists, and that it is denied also by Kant and by naturalists when the idea in question is the conception of a suprasensible or immaterial being. The most important part of Thomistic metaphysics is concerned with immaterial, infinite being, that is to say, with God. If our study of this metaphysics is to be a study of reality and not merely a logical exercise, we must establish, before entering upon it, the certitude and the objective validity of our knowledge of those ideas and principles which form its foundation. This is the task of epistemology. We have already begun that task: in Chapter XIV we criticized the Cartesian and idealistic approach to the problem of knowledge, and we established the beginnings, at least, of the Thomistic approach; in Chapters XV and XVI we examined and criticized the phenomenalism of Hume and the critical idealism of Kant and carried a little further our argument for the Thomistic position. In the last chapter we studied the ideas and principles which form the basis of Thomistic metaphysics. In the present chapter, leaving the criticism of others aside, we shall try to demonstrate positively the validity of our knowledge of these ideas and principles.

The general problem which epistemology attempts to solve may be formulated thus: How do we know that we know the truth? A Thomist need not get lost in the maze of post-Kantian disputes carried on by proponents of the coherence theory, the correspondence theory, the pragmatist theory, and others, as to the nature of truth;

St. Thomas' doctrine, explained in the last chapter, that truth is being or reality itself, conforming the mind to itself and manifesting and asserting itself in the mind, stands on a plane above all these conflicting theories. To possess truth is, for a mind, to know being, to know what really is; no theory can deny that.

2. The Problem. We have no intention of developing a whole science of epistemology, so let us determine our special problem further. The metaphysics which we are studying depends upon certain facts and principles. Our problem, then, is: How do we know the truth of these facts and principles? The simplest and clearest way to approach the solution of this problem would seem to be to list those facts and principles and then examine whether and how we know them. The following list seems to include all the essential ones:

a) Extramental being
b) Being as such
c) The principles of identity and contradiction
d) Essence and existence
e) Possibility and impossibility
f) Actuality and potentiality
g) Substance and accident
h) Cause and effect
i) Universal natures
j) The principles of sufficient reason and causality
k) Spiritual being

This list is not the result of any deduction, but is made up of the things out of which St. Thomas actually constructs his metaphysical system. If we do not really *know* them to be true, that system has no real foundation. Do we know them, then; and if so, how?

3. A First Condition for a Solution. In order to show that we have certain knowledge of all the principles and facts which we use in metaphysics, we have to show that all these facts and principles are contained, either explicitly or implicitly, in those acts of knowing which are the most primary and immediate and from which all our subsequent knowing acts follow. In other words, the starting points of our knowledge must be such as to account for and justify whatever we claim to know by means of any subsequent thought processes. In Thomistic theory, perceptions are the primary acts, and all the other cognitive operations, such as generalization, induction, and deduction merely elaborate what is given explicitly or implicitly in perceptions. Anything which the mind itself might add over and above the explicit and implicit content of the immediate cognitive act would not truly be knowledge, because it would not be founded upon the being or reality immediately known. This principle, that our valid knowledge cannot reach beyond what is contained at least implicitly in the primitive knowing situation whence all our knowledge gets its start, was what motivated Descartes in his quest for indubitable knowledge. Hume and Kant both used it in their criticism of *a priori* rationalism. All three were right in affirming the principle. Their error lay in failing to see what really is explicitly and implicitly contained in acts of direct perception.

4. False Points of Departure. Certain epistemological points of departure render the effort to fulfill the condition stated above futile from the start: (1) To regard the subjective idea or image as the immediate object of knowledge is to separate thought from extramental being from the outset and to render hopeless any effort to establish as certain that we *know* extramental being. Descartes, the idealists, and a great many modern philosophers made this false start. (2) To accept as the immediate and sole content of perception discrete, particular, sensuous impressions — sensations or bare sense qualities — is to rule out of the primary cognitive act any understanding of the extramental reason or ground of these *sensa* and to enclose oneself in an unbreakable circle of pure phenomena with no knowable substance or cause as their ground. This is the road taken by Hume and all sensists, and the road which Kant tried to escape, but unsuccessfully. (3) To affirm that direct experience gives only particulars, with nothing at all of the universal, is to cut oneself off from all hope of justifying any inferential knowledge, whether inductive or deductive, since both depend upon the universal. This is the error of nominalism and it is, of course, closely allied to the sensist error. (4) To regard the universal divorced from the particular as the first and proper object of the understanding or intellect is to condemn oneself to imprisonment in the world of ideas or essences, shut out from the world of concrete existents, for universals do not exist. Some interpretations of St. Thomas' account of the process of abstraction seem to commit this error. Historically, it is the error of Plato.

We have, of course, anticipated in calling these four positions errors; we have to show that they are errors. But if they are not errors, there is no hope of laying an epistemological foundation for a metaphysics which deals with real and immaterial being. Such a metaphysics requires that the mind attain in its primitive, direct cognition an immediate grasp of reality as extramental, substantial, existent, and implicitly or potentially universal. If any of these characters is lacking from what is directly given to the mind, there is no legitimate way in which the mind can ever introduce that character into its knowledge. The mind might fabricate the idea of the missing character, but it could never honestly affirm this idea of anything that it knows. That is what Hume saw so clearly.

II. THE PRIMITIVE KNOWING ACT AND
THE REFLECTION

1. We have maintained, in Chapter XIV, that the only relevant point of departure for the epistemological inquiry is the spontaneously certain perceptive judgment; that is, the act by which we affirm without question that a thing now directly perceived is really there. In section 3, above, we referred to this act simply as perception. In normal human experience, perception and judgment about the thing perceived form one act. From such perceptive judgments we derive *all* our knowledge of the external world, and even our knowledge of our own mind goes back ultimately to such acts for its start. Our task, therefore, is to show that in such acts we know either explicitly or implicitly all that we need in order to work out a realistic metaphysics of whose principles and primary conclusions we are certain.

2. "Scio Aliquid Esse." Every perceptive judgment has an immediate extramental and an immediate intramental object. The immediate extramental object is *something which is;* and the immediate intramental object is *the act of knowing* this something. Maritain[1] expresses this in the formula, *"Scio aliquid esse,"* I know that something is. In the very act of affirming the existence of a sensible thing directly perceived there is a consciousness of this knowing act itself. In other words, the "I" which knows is aware of itself knowing. Descartes recognized this truth in pronouncing his *Cogito*, but he failed to recognize the even more obvious truth that the thought which is prior to all my other thoughts is a *thought that knows a thing*. Consequently, he left extramental reality out of the starting point of his epistemology, and neither he nor any of his followers was ever able to get it in at any

[1] *Degrees of Knowledge* (New York: Scribners, 1938), pp. 91–93.

later phase of the knowledge process. That we do in fact know existing objective being as well as our own thought in the primary direct
knowledge act was shown clearly in Sections II and III of Chapter XIV
and does not need to be repeated here.

3. **Truth Is Known by Reflection.** That we also know the act of
knowledge in that act itself is what enables us to make the reflection
on our own intellect, explained in the last pages of Chapter XIV, by
which we come to the full possession of truth: knowing truth and
knowing that we know it. This reflection would not be able to guarantee that the *truth* which we know is identical with the *being which is*
unless this being and our knowing it were from the start given to the
intellect in the one primitive act of knowing. The reflection of the
intellect upon its own act and its own nature is the operation by which
the philosopher turns his spontaneous unreflective certitudes into
critical, fully possessed certitudes. The intellect sees that in certain of
its acts it is forced by evident being to assert something about that
being; to see this it must see itself and the being and its relation to
the being. What it sees is (1) that it itself is nothing at all but a power
which man has of thinking what is, and (2) that in certain acts of
thinking, for example, direct perceptive judgments, it thinks what it
thinks because a being compels its thought. We have only been repeating what we have already stated at greater length in Chapter
XIV. Let us repeat also the succinct statement of St. Thomas which
we have been explaining:

> For [truth] is in the intellect as following upon the act of the intellect,
> and as known by the intellect. For it follows upon the operation of the
> intellect according as the judgment of the intellect is about a thing
> inasmuch as it is; but it is known by the intellect insofar as the intellect
> reflects upon its act, not only according as it knows its act, but accord-
> ing as it knows the relation of the act to the thing. But it cannot know
> this unless it knows the nature of the act itself; which again cannot be
> known unless the nature of the active principle is known. But this
> [principle] is the intellect itself, in whose nature it is to conform to
> things. Wherefore, the intellect knows the truth by reflecting upon
> itself.[2]

This reflection of the intellect upon itself, its act, and the relation of
the act to the thing, which we have here presented in reference to the first
knowing act, the perceptive judgment, is repeated for each more complex judgment. When the intellect makes a universal judgment as the

[2] *De Ver.*, I, 9, c.

result of an induction, or when it makes a deduction from a universal, it knows that it is judging truly because, by knowing itself reflectively, it knows that its judgment is forced from it by the thing which is asserting itself in it and conforming it to its (i.e., the thing's) own being. Reason has the ability to judge its own judgments.[3] When, for example, we check over the chain of reasoning by which we have reached a conclusion, we are making a reflection on our own judgments. If we see by this reflection that the premises whence our reasoning started are forced upon our judgment by their own self-evidence, or by their relation to self-evident principles, or by perception, and that the implication of the conclusion in the premises is such that we cannot affirm the premises and yet deny the conclusion except at the cost of denying a self-evident principle of being — the principle of identity or of contradiction — then we know from our reflection that our judgment is true, and the touchstone of its truth is being itself.

The above account, together with the lengthier treatment of Chapter XIV, takes care of the first of the foundations of metaphysics listed above, namely, extramental, real, existing being, and refutes the subjectivistic position of Descartes and the idealists. The second foundation, being as such, is obviously taken care of in the same account. Both the extramental object and the intramental object of perception are known as "being" — as being in the sense of existing, and as being in the sense of that which exists. The more or less confused grasp of these two aspects in one idea is, indeed, our first idea; that is to say, we know that things are and are something before we differentiate, classify, or attempt to define them. Every other concept includes the prior concept of being.

III. FIRST PRINCIPLES AND BASIC CONCEPTS

1. **The Principle of Identity.** Being, therefore, is first known by the human intellect in the act wherein the whole mind is given, through the senses, a perceived thing. This thing is grasped by the intellect as a being and as existing. In other words, the proper object of the intellect — being — is grasped immediately under two aspects: as an intelligible subject of existence and as existing. These two aspects, in Thomistic terminology, are named *ens* and *esse: Ens est id cujus actus est esse.*

The mind asserts both these aspects when it judges that *this being is.*

[3] *Ibid.,* XXIV, 2, c.

In pronouncing this judgment, the mind is also affirming that *every being is what it is*. This is the formula of the first principle of all thought and being, namely, the principle of identity. It is implied in every judgment pronounced by the intellect; because the intellect cannot assert any predicate of a subject except in so far as it sees that the subject, of necessity, is what it is. In grasping its object as being, it sees that it is being because it is itself; that is, because it has its own essence and is what it is. That which is not what it is, for example, a circle which does *not* have equal radii, is nothing. If a subject were not what it is, it would offer the intellect nothing whereby to grasp it. If, *per impossibile,* the intellect did grasp an object without at the same time seeing that the object must of necessity be what it is, it could never assert with certitude that that object exists, since any affirmation assumes the identity of the subject with itself. Consequently, the intellect can never, with certitude, affirm anything to be or to exist unless it simultaneously affirms as absolutely certain the principle that everything is what it is.

We do not, of course, *explicitly* formulate the principle of identity in all our perceptive judgments, and we had made many such judgments before we formulated it for the first time. Although it is implied in every judgment, it is itself attained as an explicit principle only through abstraction, induction, and reflection. Just as judgments about particular men are made before the conception of man as such or judgments about man as such become explicit, so we affirm that this thing is itself, that a circle is a circle, that to eat is to eat, and so on, before we make the abstraction of highest generality, namely being as such, and affirm that whatever is, is, and is what it is.

2. **The Principle of Contradiction.** The act by which the intellect asserts the principle of identity follows from its conception of its first and proper object, being. The human intellect attains truth only by "combining and separating" ideas (*componendo et dividendo*); it naturally and necessarily judges — that is the kind of intellect it is. Having attained the concept of being, and having by nature — having as its very essence — an ordination and appetite for truth, it must seek the truth about being. Hence it compares being with being, and it affirms being of being: being is being; that which is, is; that which is something, is that something; everything is what it is. All these primary assertions are formulas of the principle of identity. The principle of contradiction is merely the negative form of the principle of identity,

and it is asserted when the intellect compares being with non-being. Being is not non-being; that which is, is not that which is not; that what is something, is not what that something is not; nothing is what it is not; nothing can be and not be something at the same time. The intellect not only necessarily asserts these principles, but it knows that it must assert them and that it cannot be mistaken in asserting them. If, perchance, it suffers a moment of doubt, fearing that they may be only necessities of its thought and not necessities of being, it need only reflect upon itself and its act, and revert to that immediate, primary, sensio-intellectual perception of the self-evident being which first forced these principles out of it; then it cannot doubt that they are absolute principles of thought only because they are absolute principles of being.

3. **Essence and Existence.** Everything that we experience in a really human way we judge *to be* and to be *something*. This judgment is prior to any judgment classifying things as different kinds of being, because it is impossible to judge things to be different without first judging them to be; the distinction of different kinds of being presupposes at least a vague and confused idea of being as common to the several kinds. Hence our first judgment, when our intellect is aroused to operation by an object given us through sense experience, is that "this thing is and is something."

When we judge some perceived object to be and to be something, we may note that we are really making two affirmations: that the thing is, and that it is something. But as soon as we do reflect on our judgment, new ideas begin to appear in it, and these are as firmly grounded in the perceived object as is the original affirmation. Two of the most primary of these ideas are the notions of essence and existence. As soon as we analyze the judgment that something is and is something, we see that *being* is asserted in it in two distinct ways or senses. To assert that a thing is, is to assert that it *exists;* and to assert that it is something is to assert that it has an *essence.* The simple judgment, "something is," contains the concepts of a subject and the act whereby it exists. The subject must be conceived as real, that is, as a determinate, intelligible object, or else the intellect could not have and would not have grasped it in a concept. This aspect gives the intellect, upon analysis, the concept of essence, namely that whereby a thing is what it is, or that whereby it is a certain thing (*res*). The other aspect of the judgment is that it asserts, on the evident testimony of the senses, that this thing *is;* that is to say, that it exerts a certain action, namely, that it exists. Hence, the reflective analysis of the intellect's most primitive judgment yields explicitly the concept of essence, i.e., the determinate, intelligible character of a being which makes it a fit subject of existence, and the concept of existence, i.e., the act whereby this subject is an actuality in the real order of being.

4. **Possibility and Impossibility.** As soon as the intellect explicitly considers essence and existence, it sees their logical separability; that is to say, it sees that something may be conceivable or intelligible without thereby necessarily existing. What is conceived is necessarily some essence, but conceiving it does not depend upon knowing it to exist. Yet, if something can be conceived at all, it can be conceived only as being, that is, as a determinate subject of existence (*ens* and *res*), and hence as related to existence; it is conceived as able (*posse*) to exist. Reflection upon the being so conceived gives rise to the explicit notion of possible being as compared with existing being, and to the more abstract notion of possibility.

The notion of possibility suggests that of impossibility, just as being suggested not-being. By comparing possible and impossible and by seeking illustrations of each, the intellect discovers that just as the possible means the intelligible, that which has an essence, so the impossible means that which is unintelligible, that which has no essence, that which is not-being, for example, a circle with unequal radii. The impossible cannot exist because it is not, to begin with, a fit subject for existence.

5. **Actuality and Potentiality.** The concept of being as essence and existence is sufficient by itself for the attainment of that of possibility; but the experience of change is necessary for the formation of the idea of potentiality. Change in the concrete is known by direct experience; our sensio-intellective mind is given change as directly as it is given being, although the understanding of change presupposes the understanding of being. The intellectual grasp of change implies the notions of potentiality and actuality, which become explicit upon analysis of the concept of change.

Beings are perceived to change: we see the leaves stirring in the wind; we see them appear, open out, and grow in spring; we see them change color and fall to the ground in autumn. Whatever we perceive we grasp under the aspect of being; the green leaf of May and the red leaf of October are both beings. We see the green leaf come into being out of the branch, and we see the red leaf come into being out of the green; and in the winter we do not see the leaf at all. Last winter, the leaf I see now in spring did not exist; it was not; it was not-being. But it was a certain kind of not-being — a kind which, I see now, was to be a leaf. It was not not-being as the impossible is not-being; it was possible, at least. It was, in fact, something more than possible. Possible being is related, in the mind, only to thought, not to experience. The non-existent leaf of winter was, I see in spring, definitely related to experience. It had a relation to existence which is quite different from the relation which a mere possible has; it had a relation to a concrete future existence grounded in some concrete present existence. Even while it does not exist actually, it is rooted in the actual being of something which does exist and which is capable of becoming it. It possesses potential being.

Thus, by analyzing the changing being given to it by immediate experience, the intellect attains the concepts of actual being, or being which has present existence, and potential being, or being which has a real capacity for existence rooted in some actual being. From these concepts it forms the abstract notions of actuality and potentiality. Quite as important, by a simple comparison of actual and potential being with the principles of identity and contradiction, it arrives at an immediate judgment which is one formula of the principle of causality — that something can come to be only from something which is, or, in other words, that every potentiality presupposes an actuality. And still another principle of importance in Thomistic metaphysics follows this one — that every changeable being is a mixture of actuality and potentiality.

6. Substance and Accident. Substance means being which is, or exists, in itself; accident means being which is, or exists, in another. Immediate experience gives substance to the mind and analytic reflection testifies to the reality of substance and accident, while making the two conceptions explicit.

Our first notion is "being — that which is," and we probably make no distinction at first between being in itself and being in another. Rather, the intellect, on the presentation to it, through the senses, of a sensible thing, immediately grasps the intelligible being of the thing, the *reason* for the sensible phenomena, without, however, clearly distinguishing this reason — i.e., the substance — from the phenomena of which it is the reason. Very shortly, nevertheless, the distinction is made when the intellect perceives the permanence and unity of the being underlying the multiplicity and succession of the phenomena. Then "that which is" takes on two new distinct significations: that which is in itself, one and permanent throughout phenomenal alterations; and that which is in this permanent unity as its changing determinations. To express this more concretely: to a baby, Mother does not always look or sound or feel the same; but whatever confusion this may cause at first is soon cleared away, and Mother comes to be known as Mother whether she appears this way or that way. Later the realization arises that the different ways of Mother's being need Mother in order to exist or be known at all. Their being is entirely in Mother's being: their *esse* is *inesse*.[4] Then the distinction of substance and accident has become known; and, it is a safe wager, this distinction is never forgotten or repudiated in fact, no matter what philosophy we may adopt, because it is a distinction which we cannot do without; the world does not make sense without it.

Father Garrigou-Lagrange gives a very clear account of the close relation of our knowledge of substance and accident to our knowledge of being and the principle of identity:

> . . . one of the formulas of the principle of identity is that "every being is one and the same with itself." *To say of a being that it is a substance, is to assert that it remains one and the same under its multiple and changing phenomena.* The principle of substance, therefore, is simply a determination of the principle of identity and the idea of substance a determination of the idea of being. In the acquisition of its knowledge the intellect proceeds from the idea of being — in which that of substance is *de facto* implicitly included — to the somewhat confused ideas of the manner of being implied in phenomena, multiplicity, and change. It seeks to render these new ideas intelligible in the light of the idea of being, and comes to recognize the "something which is" as one and a permanent subject, as a *being* in the full sense of the word, as *something which exists in itself or subsists* (a substance). The intellect is now in a position to narrow down the concept of the manner of being implied in the phenomenon, which cannot be defined except in terms of what exists in itself, for it is an *ens entis*, "an entity of an entity." Thus, the confused concept of the phenomenon adds to the definiteness of the concept of substance, and is in turn more clearly defined by it.[5]

7. Cause and Effect. The notion of efficient cause is the notion of a being which, by its action, brings about or produces another being; and the notion of effect is the notion of a being produced or brought

---

[4] *Nam accidentis esse est inesse. In V Meta.,* 9, No. 894.
[5] *God — His Existence and Nature,* I, pp. 178-179.

about by the action of another. The basis of belief in cause and effect is twofold. (1) As we stressed in Chapter XVI, experience of things causing other things, or of events causing other events, is all-pervasive in life. Everything that we experience and understand is an instance of the cause-effect situation; what is experienced, but not as an instance of it, we do not understand. Our experience of the cause-effect situation is virtually infinite in extent, and is ever present. We believe that things are produced by other things because we see and feel things producing other things, because we produce things ourselves and are conscious of doing so, and because things act upon us and produce effects in us. (2) The principle of identity, namely, that which is, is, and its obverse statement, the principle of contradiction, forbid us to believe that anything comes from nothing. That which is not, since it is not, cannot become something; and that which is something cannot of itself become what it is not. That which is potentially something, since in itself it is *only potentially* that thing, cannot of itself be it; it may become it, but only by receiving the actuality which it lacks. Therefore, our mind demands a cause for whatever occurs, and perception, in the generality of cases, fulfills this demand by showing us events as following from prior events.

Cause and substance are what Aristotle and St. Thomas called accidental or incidental sensibles (*sensibile per accidens*). No external sense has them for proper object as sight has color or hearing sound, for they are not directly sensible (*sensibile per se*); yet in the very perceptive act whereby the mind grasps a group of phenomena or a phenomenal occurrence, the substance underlying the phenomena and the cause of the occurrence are seized also. The perceptive act is sensio-intellectual, and its object is a sensible thing. Where that being is acting as a cause, it is sensibly perceived as a sensible object, though not *qua* substance or *qua* cause; and in the same act the intellect knows it as a substance and a cause. In order for something to be an accidental sensible, it must, first, occur in or be a concomitant of something that is directly sensible; thus substance is *sensibile per accidens* because its color is visible *per se* and its texture can be felt *per se*. Second, it must be apprehended by the intellect immediately upon the sense's apprehension of the proper sensible of which it is a concomitant; that is to say, it is not known by some reasoning process but is known at once in the sensible object. It is thus that the intellect grasps substance and cause in common perceptive experience. In the same act in which I

see a certain color-shape pattern and hear certain sounds, I see my
friend (substance) and hear him talking (cause).[6]

IV. THE FOUNDATIONS OF DEMONSTRATED KNOWLEDGE

Thus far, in the present chapter, we have seen how the most general
principles of metaphysics are known with certitude, and are known
to be valid objectively. These principles and conceptions are all phases
of or immediate determinations of being as such, and are known
either explicitly in the perceptive judgment itself or by a simple and
immediate reflective analysis of that judgment. Most of our knowledge,
however, in metaphysics as well as in the other sciences, is not so
direct and immediate, but is the result of reasoning or demonstration.
Besides the first general principles of knowledge and being, we must
also have knowledge of the specific and generic natures of many things
in order to attain the demonstrated knowledge which makes up
philosophy and science. And we must so attain this knowledge of
the different natures of things that it is validly attached to our immediate knowledge of the particular existing objects of perception, for in
human knowledge only those ideas and judgments which find their
ultimate ground in perception are relevant to real being. We shall,
therefore, now turn our attention to St. Thomas' teaching upon our
knowledge of the natures of things, or universals.

1. **The Natures of Things.** How do we know the differences of
things? If the perceptive judgment did not contain the *natures* of
things, we would have no way of ever getting to know these natures,
or at least we would never be able to assert any natures, which we
might somehow get to know, of the existing beings which we perceive.
*We must perceive the thing and the nature together, or we can never
legitimately join them.* Another way of saying this is that primitive,
direct cognition must give the mind explicitly and in one act both
the particular thing and its nature. If the particular alone is given, as
is assumed in the third false position listed at the beginning of the
chapter, definition and all universal knowledge, and therefore all scientific knowledge would be impossible. If the nature as a universal alone
is given, scientific knowledge would not have any reference to the
existing world and would not, indeed, be *knowledge*. The Thomistic
theory of the abstraction of universals from phantasms and of the reflection necessary for the grasp of the singular, as this theory is ordi-

[6] St. Thomas, *In II De Anima*, 13, Nos. 387, 395-396. Cf. *S. Theol.*, I, 12, 3, ad 2.

narily explained and as St. Thomas himself explained it in the *Summa Theologica*,[7] seems to separate, in knowledge, the particular existing thing from its nature and to present the intellect as grasping first and directly the nature as a universal, while sense, which does not know the nature, grasps the singular thing. The mind then gets the two of them together through a reflection which joins the universal nature to the particular thing through the medium of the phantasm. This will not do, if we are to lay an epistemological foundation for a realistic metaphysics. *The mind must grasp the thing with its nature from the start.* And that is just what St. Thomas, following Aristotle, says it does. He says this in a context which lends it great significance, for the issue is how we attain the first principles or premises which are the basis of all demonstration. Among these are our universal ideas of the natures of things. These natures are grasped as implicit or potential universals in the perceptive judgment itself. St. Thomas' statement is the following:

> It is evident that the singular is sensed properly and in itself (*per se*), but nevertheless there is in some way also a sensing of the universal itself. For it [i.e., sense] knows Callias not only inasmuch as he is Callias, but also inasmuch as he is *this man*, and, in like manner, Socrates inasmuch as he is this man. And thence it is, that from such an antecedent grasp by sense, the intellective soul can consider "man" in both of them. But if, on the contrary, the case were that sense apprehended only that which belongs to particularity, and in no manner apprehended the universal in the particular, it would not be possible that knowledge of the universal could be caused in us from the apprehension of sense.[8]

St. Thomas is commenting on the following words of Aristotle:

> We conclude that these states of knowledge [i.e., knowledge of primary immediate premises from which demonstration can begin] are neither innate in a determinate form, nor developed from other higher states of knowledge, but from sense perception. It is like a rout in battle being stopped by first one man making a stand and then another, until the original formation has been restored. The soul is so constituted as to be capable of this process.
> . . . When one of a number of logically indiscriminable particulars has made a stand, the earliest universal is present in the soul: for though the act of sense-perception is of the particular, its content is universal

[7] Cf. above, Chapter XI, Section III.
[8] *In II Post. Anal.*, l. 20.

— is man, for example, not the man Callias. A fresh stand is made among these rudimentary universals, and the process does not cease until the indivisible concepts, the true universals, are established: e.g., such and such a species of animals is a step toward the genus animal, which by the same process is a step toward further generalization. Thus it is clear that we must get to know the primary premises by induction.[9]

In this teaching of Aristotle and St. Thomas it is clearly stated that in the perceptive judgment the first principles of demonstration are implicitly present, as are universal concepts in general, or the terms by which demonstration is carried out. The principles and universals are attained through *induction,* which is made possible by the co-operation of external sense, internal sense, especially cogitative and memory, and intellect. Along with the particular existent, the rudimentary universal is given in immediate experience, and from it are developed the real or actual universals, whence in turn are developed the primary and secondary principles of demonstration.

We may summarize this teaching of Aristotle and St. Thomas as follows. The extramental object of the direct perceptive judgment contains *explicitly* a concrete existing singular having a determinate nature. The act whereby this object with its three aspects (the singular, its existence, its nature) is grasped, is sensio-intellectual. Man is neither brute nor angel. His mind grasps what is presented through the senses to the understanding as something existing. St. Thomas writes that *sense* apprehends the nature or implicit universal; but he does not mean sense in isolation from intellect. In the perceptive judgment there are not a sensitive act *and* an intellectual act; there is a sensio-intellectual act. Because this one act is sensitive it grasps the material particular; because it is intellective it grasps the being and nature of this particular. The nature is grasped as a potential, fundamental, or implicit universal and is grasped *in* the individual — "Callias as this man." This ability to grasp the individual as having a certain nature St. Thomas assigns to the cogitative sense; but if we remember that in his teaching man's cogitative power differs from the animal's estimative power in its operation only, and not in its nature, and that this difference of operation is due solely to the permeation of the cogitative operation by the intellectual operation, it is clear that the act of grasping the singular as existing under a common nature is not merely a

[9] *Post Anal.,* II, 100 a–b.

sensitive act but a sensio-intellectual act.[10] The operation of abstraction *follows* the grasp of the singular; after grasping "Callias as this man" and "Socrates as this man," the intellect frees the nature "man" from the individual conditions in which it is originally presented, and makes it an explicit or real universal, that is, gives it "the intention of universality," which "is due to intellectual abstraction."[11] The reflective return to the singular through the concept, the intelligible species and the phantasm, which we have explained in Chapter XI, is now seen to be truly a *return*. The mind grasped the singular and its nature confusedly or unscientifically in direct perception; it returns to the singular reflectively, not to get a first understanding of it, but to apply to it the universal or scientific concepts and principles which it has attained through abstraction. If the mind had not, from the outset, grasped the particular and the universal together, nothing could give it the right thereafter to attach the universal to the particular.

2. **Demonstration: Abstraction, Induction, Definition, Deduction.** Demonstrative syllogistic reasoning moves from premises which are certain to a conclusion which is necessarily implied by these premises. Thus, the two premises, "All men are mortal" and "Socrates is a man," necessarily imply the conclusion "Socrates is mortal." The major premise itself, however, must have been attained by the mind as a certain truth before the syllogism is formulated. There is no use saying that we got it from a previous syllogism, for that way of thinking can lead only to an infinite regress of syllogisms. What is needed, if any syllogism is to be demonstrative, is some truths which are not themselves syllogistically demonstrated but which are yet certain and which can stand as starting points for syllogistic demonstration. Such truths are universal propositions and are the principles of demonstration. Some of them, for example, that nothing can be and not be in the same respect, are *first principles*, because they are presupposed by every other principle and are operative in every demonstration. Others are special principles, such as the major premise of the above syllogism. How do we get to know them?

In the two passages quoted above, Aristotle and St. Thomas are telling us how we form our universal ideas and judgments and how

---

[10] For St. Thomas' statements on the cogitative power see: *In II De Anima*, 13, Nos. 395–398; *S. Theol.*, I, 78, 4; *De Ver.*, X, 5, c; XIV, 1 and 9; *In VI Ethic*, 1, No. 1123; 7, No. 1215; 9, No. 1249; *Con. Gen.*, II, 73, 76; *Q. D. de Anima*, 20, ad 1 of second series; *In I Meta.*, 1, Nos. 15–23. Cf. Chapter XI, Section 1, No. 2 of this book.

[11] *S. Theol.*, I, 85, 3, ad 1.

we arrive at knowledge of first principles. We may call the process *abstraction* or, as Aristotle does, *induction*. Or we may distinguish two parts in it, and call the former abstraction and the latter induction. Then we have an answer to the problem which perplexes so many of our contemporary philosophers and scientists; namely, What is the basic justification for inductive judgments? Many of these philosophers and scientists start from the third false position noted at the beginning of this chapter, that is to say, nominalism. In the perceptive act they admit the grasp only of particulars; but a true and certain induction requires a universal; since, therefore, they cannot see how the mind can justify its passage from the particular to the universal, they cannot see how induction is really warranted. Yet, of course, they must go on making and using inductive generalizations if they wish to pursue philosophy or science. Many have chosen to consider every inductive conclusion as incomplete and provisional in theory, though usable as a true universal in practice. There is no need, however, of adopting this merely pragmatic attitude, because the fact is, as we have seen above, that the particular and the universal are given together in the perceptive judgment.

3. **Abstraction.** When we perceive something, we perceive it as an individual "existing under a common nature," that is, we know Callias "not only inasmuch as he is Callias, but also inasmuch as he is *this man*, and, in like manner, Socrates inasmuch as he is this man." Because *man* is given as well as Callias and Socrates, the mind apprehends a determinate nature or character as well as a particular thing. It can consider this nature separately, and that is what we mean by abstraction. From the complex object, *this man* or Callias, the mind abstracts or considers apart one aspect only, namely *man*. "And thence it is, that from such an antecedent grasp by sense, the intellective soul can consider 'man' in both of them." Clearly, we could not abstract *man* from the data of perception if *man* were not in those data. St. Thomas was fully aware of the difficulty that nominalists must find in respect to induction: "But if, on the contrary, the case were that sense apprehended only that which belongs to particularity, and in no manner apprehended the universal in the particular, it would not be possible that knowledge of the universal could be caused in us from the apprehension of sense." Abstraction is possible only because the universal is given fundamentally in perception; and induction is possible only because abstraction is possible.

4. Induction. The fundamental universal given immediately in perception is not a "real" or explicit universal. It is the nature which will be the real universal, but it is not yet conceived as a universal, that is, it has not "the intention of universality — viz., the relation of one and the same to many." For example, the mind knows the nature man, but has not yet explicitly viewed it as the one same nature of Callias, Socrates, and every man. How does the mind pass from the implicit universal to the full-blown universal? Aristotle's account is very vivid, as well as being grounded in our actual experience. We have memory as well as perception, and therefore as each perception flees from the mind not everything of the perception is lost. Callias is gone, and Socrates, but they are remembered. Because they can be remembered together they can be compared. They are remembered as this *man* and that *man;* and other men are remembered too. And, although *this* and *that* differ in every case, *man* is grasped as the same in each. Then since *man* is apprehended in this particular and in that particular, *man* is seen to be one and the same in relation to many. *Man* is now a real universal.

5. Definition. The idea *man* has a meaning or intelligible content. In the mental life of any particular knowing subject this idea, like all ideas, undergoes growth or development. At first, when we are very young children, our ideas are extremely confused and poor in content. At the very first, we probably throw everything we experience under one highly confused idea, *thing* or *being*. But we very soon start making distinctions, attaining more and clearer ideas, and building up some sort of system of ideas. We become more distinctly aware of the meanings of ideas and of the relations among our ideas and among the things which we apprehend. Different universals reveal common natures just as different individuals did. At some stage of our mental growth, we begin to *define* things and ideas. Callias is a man and Socrates is a man, but what is it to be a man? Callias and Socrates and others differ in many ways, but all exist under the common nature *man*. To discover what constitutes this common nature is to define man. The definition is reached by induction. The induction discovers what there is in the several individuals by virtue of which they are men. It is not anything in which they differ from each other, for example their color, manner of speech, personal peculiarities, ways of acting and thinking. Rather it is something of which these are individual determinations and manifestations. Callias, Socrates, and the others, we finally see, are men because they are living bodies which think. To be a man, we say, is to be a rational animal. We need not stop here; we can ask ourselves what it is to be rational, what it is to be an animal, or even, at the highest level of abstraction what it is *to be*. The answer, in every case, is attained through a process which is abstractive and inductive, which yields a new idea related as a "one and the same to many."

6. **Deduction.** Thus we know that "all men are mortal" because we have learned by induction, not merely that this man has died and that one and all who were born before, say one hundred fifty years ago, but rather that to be a man is to be a complex living organism which is naturally corruptible. The true conclusion of our induction, and the true premise of our syllogism, is not "all men are mortal," but "man as such is mortal." In other words, we can attain to certain knowledge of universal principles only because by abstraction and induction we can discover the essential constituents of the natures first grasped confusedly in perception. This fact, that we do know the nature as implicitly universal in the primitive act of cognition, is the only basis for the validity of inductively attained principles. It also answers an argument frequently put forward against the syllogism: namely, that the major premise cannot be affirmed unless the conclusion is already known; we cannot say that all men are mortal unless we already know that Socrates is mortal; hence we cannot use the former proposition to prove the latter. This argument is based on nominalism. It assumes that a universal can be established only by a complete numeration of particulars; hence, since Socrates is still alive, we cannot know that all men will die. In truth, the real major is that man as such is mortal, and it is known by the knowledge of man's nature attained by abstraction and induction. The conclusion is not that Socrates will die, but that he is mortal, that he liable is to die.[12]

V. THE PRINCIPLES OF SUFFICIENT REASON
AND CAUSALITY

1. The self-evident principle which governs the entire structure of a philosophy of nature and a metaphysics is the principle of causality.

[12] The above paragraphs were written before the appearance of Bertrand Russell's *History of Western Philosophy*. Compare them with pp. 197–198 and 199, (3), of that book.

It may be variously stated: for example, everything that begins to be has a cause, every contingent being has a cause, every being which is not its own sufficient reason for being has a cause. This last formula shows the close relation of this principle to a prior self-evident principle, namely, the principle of sufficient reason. The latter may be stated: everything which is, has a sufficient reason for being. This principle is absolutely universal, because it applies to every being — to a being which is its own sufficient reason (i.e., self-existent being) as well as to a being which has its sufficient reason in something other than itself (i.e., a caused being). The principle of causality refers only to beings which are not self-existent; such beings, it states, cannot exist without a cause, that is to say, without a sufficient reason extrinsic to themselves.

So understood, the principle of causality is neither more nor less than the principle of sufficient reason limited in its application to those things that have within themselves no adequate reason of being. To deny it is to deny the principle of sufficient reason, and to doubt it is to doubt that principle. For that which has no reason of being within itself and none outside itself has no reason for being at all; hence, to say that a non-self-existent being can exist without a cause is to say that it can exist without any reason for existence whatsoever.

A reason may be a cause or it may be a ground of being which is not a cause, at least not an efficient cause. It may be in the being of which it is the reason, or it may be extrinsic to it, as an efficient cause is. A self-existent being, if there is any, is its own sufficient reason for being. Consequently, it is necessarily existent, incapable of not not-being; *what* it is, is sufficient reason for its existence. Hence, self-existent being is either an impossibility, a contradiction in terms, or else it is eternally and necessarily existent. Which it is in fact, we cannot say *a priori* from any inspection of the phrase "self-existent," because we do not really understand the supposed essence signified by the phrase. A being which is neither impossible nor necessary, which is capable of either existing or not existing, is not its own sufficient reason for existing. *What* it is does not require existence. The principle of sufficient reason states that everything which is has a sufficient reason for being, either in itself or extrinsic to itself. Therefore, every being is either self-existent (i.e., necessary) or it is caused; no being just happens to exist and no event just happens to occur. Nothing comes from nothing.

2. **The Practical Validity of These Principles.** Everyone, of course, admits that men naturally believe in causes and in the principle of causality. But many philosophers have refused to grant to causality any philosophical or rationally demonstrative value. "Causation," wrote William James, "is indeed too obscure a principle to bear the whole structure of theology." Causation does indeed bear a great deal of the weight of natural theology, but before we are frightened into abandoning it as a foundation, it will be well to consider briefly what else causation and the principle of causality support and what besides traditional natural theology we would have to abandon if we reject our belief in causality.

Every scientist, no matter what his philosophical views about causation, pursues his quest for the explanation of natural phenomena because he knows that they must have explanations. He may call the explanations "invariable antecedents" instead of causes, but he has no right to assume that anything is invariably antecedent to anything else unless he believes in the principle of causality. We have seen above that the principle of causality cannot be rejected without rejecting the principle of sufficient reason, since it is necessarily implied in that principle. If the principle of sufficient reason is not objectively true, the order of nature is an illusion, and science is nothing more than a word game. For if things and events do not need any sufficient reason for being, all the following become real possibilities in the physical sphere: (1) that something begins to exist from nothing and with no antecedents whatsoever; (2) that something begins *not* to exist at any time and for no reason; (3) that something has any properties at any time; (4) that something performs any operations whatsoever, needing no particular nature to determine its operations nor any particular circumstances to call them forth. If any one of these propositions expressed a real possibility, science would be impossible.

The case is very much the same in the logical and practical order. If a sufficient reason is not needed for everything, then (1) any belief about anything may be held, since no reason is required; (2) no "demonstration" proves anything, since no reason is needed for holding the contrary of what is "demonstrated"; (3) all arguments are mere word games, because if reasons are not required neither are they relevant; (4) thinking does not exist, but only unrelated successions of ideas, since thinking proceeds from reasons to consequences or vice versa, and reasons do not require consequences or vice versa; (5)

communication is an illusion, since the words of another can produce no effect in me; (6) education, penal law, social-betterment projects, efforts "to remove the causes of war" — all are futile except perhaps as entertainment, because human conduct does not need nor spring from causes and reasons; crime and war may just "happen," like anything else. Ethics and politics, like science and logic, are merely word games.

3. **Value of Hume's Arguments Against Causality.** Among the most striking of all practical vindications of the principles of sufficient reason and causality are the arguments against them. No one has argued more forcibly against these principles than David Hume; *but his whole argument is a great effort to make us see that we have no sufficient reason for holding these principles as demonstrable truths and therefore ought not so to hold them.* He goes so far as to set down what in his opinion is the *cause* of our belief in causality — it is a habit or custom of mind. Denying that we have sufficient rational grounds for holding the principle of sufficient reason, he still feels the necessity of advancing a sufficient reason of some sort for this belief of ours. This is indeed a strange way to argue against the principle.

4. **The Ontological Validity of the Principle of Sufficient Reason.** Everyone, in all his thinking and acting, takes the principle of sufficient reason for granted. But how do we know with certainty that it is absolutely and universally true? Obviously it cannot be demonstrated, because every demonstration presupposes it. It is either self-evident or else a philosophically unjustified assumption. Can we show that it is self-evident? In the order of thought it is unquestionably self-evident. Its truth is what makes us reason, that is, think; it is the principle of reason. Reasoning is impossible without this principle — not merely in the sense that without it we would not know what to conclude from premises, but in the much more fundamental sense that without an intuitive knowledge of it we simply would not reason at all, we would never ask a question or try to answer one, we would never give or seek a reason for anything. To reason is to apply the principle of sufficient reason to objects of knowledge; to be rational is to be able to grasp this principle. But is the principle *objectively* valid? Is it a principle primarily of being, and a principle of thought only because thought is about being? The answer is found through the intellect's reflection upon itself and its act.

The intellect, reflecting upon its own nature, sees that it is an appetite and a power for conforming itself to being; and reflecting upon its acts and the relation of these acts to being, it sees that, when it judges with certitude that something is, it does so by reason of the compulsion of being itself. The intellect cannot think anything without a reason; whatever it thinks with certitude, it thinks by compulsion of the principle of sufficient reason. When it withholds judgment, it does so because it has no sufficient reason for an assertion. But thought — true thought — is *being in the intellect*. The intellect is actual as thought only by virtue of some being in it conforming it to what is; whatever the intellect knows as certainly and necessarily known, it knows as the self-assertion of a being in it. This being which compels the intellect to judge does so as a sufficient reason of judgment. Nothing, therefore, is more certainly known than the principle of sufficient reason, because this is the principle of thought itself, without which there can be no thought. But by the same token the intellect knows that the principle of sufficient reason is a principle of being because it is being, asserting itself in thought, which compels thought to conform to this principle.[13]

5. No Direct Demonstration of These Principles Possible. David Hume denied that the principle of causality is either given to us in sense experience or is rationally demonstrable. In both cases he was right. The principle of causality is neither sensibly experienced nor demonstrable, but is self-evident to reason. We do directly experience actual concrete causes producing effects; this we have seen above as well as in Chapter XVI. From our perceptions of cause-effect situations we attain, through abstraction and induction, the universal conceptions of cause and effect and the universal judgment which we call the principle of causality. This judgment, namely, that every contingent being and every event must have a cause, is self-evident because the mind, working over the data of perception in the light of the ideas abstracted from this data, sees that a cause is a necessary element in every situation involving a contingent being or an event; the meaning of contingent being and of event involves a necessary relation to a cause. Sensists and nominalists, like Hume, rule out of perception all direct grasp of the fundamental objective universals which are the basis for abstraction and induction, and consequently cannot see how a universal principle like that of causality can be intuited by the mind

[13] Cf. J. Maritain, *A Preface to Metaphysics.* pp. 97–99.

so as to be self-evident. Consequently, they demand that it be demonstrated.

Nothing should be clearer than that not everything in a demonstration can be demonstrated.[14] Every demonstration presupposes *some* starting point. If there are no self-evident starting points there can be no demonstration at all. To seek to demonstrate everything is to start upon an infinite regress of demonstrations and to sink into a bottomless quagmire of things to be proved before anything is proved. The self-evident cannot be demonstrated because demonstration presupposes a starting point more evident than the thing to be demonstrated, and there is nothing more evident than the self-evident. Every effort therefore to *prove* the principle of causality must end in failure. What we can attempt, however, instead of a proof, is a manifestation that no one can seriously deny or doubt the principle without committing himself to the absurd, the impossible, the self-contradictory. This is an indirect demonstration.

6. Indirect Demonstration of the Principle of Causality. "Being is that whose act it is to exist." A being may have one of two relations to actual existence. It may exist of itself, that is, be itself essentially the actuality of being, or it may not exist of itself, that is, be itself essentially only a possibility of being. In the former case it is self-existent or necessary being, and its sufficient reason is itself. In the latter case it is contingent being, and is not its own sufficient reason for being. The question is whether a being of the latter sort, in order to exist actually, *must* have a cause. The answer is that it must, for a contingent being existing without a cause is a self-contradiction. The essence of a contingent being does not itself determine that being to existence; what the being is in itself is insufficient for its actual existence. Consequently, to affirm that it can exist without an extrinsic determinant of its existence, that is to say, without a cause, is to affirm that it is what it is not. By definition such a being is one which in itself, apart from any extrinsic determinant, has only possible existence; to affirm its uncaused existence is to affirm that such a being is one which in itself, apart from any extrinsic determinant, has actual existence.[15] There can be, therefore, no such thing as uncaused contingent being; whatever exists is either self-existent, eternal, and necessary, or else it is caused.

[14] Aristotle, *Meta*, IV, 4.
[15] Cf. Garrigou-Lagrange, *op. cit.*, l, pp. 181–194.

VI. SPIRITUAL BEING

1. The Soul Knows Itself Knowing. There is no need for us at this point to give any lengthy justification for the entry into Thomistic metaphysics of the notion of spiritual being and the affirmation of its real existence. The whole of Chapter X above was devoted to the demonstration of the spiritual nature of man's soul. The brief truth about our knowledge of spiritual being is that we have attained its conception and have affirmed its existence because we directly experience it in the primitive perceptive judgment. *Scio aliquid esse* contains the idea of the soul quite as clearly as *Cogito ergo sum.* It differs from the latter by considering the whole of knowledge instead of merely its subjective aspect; but it does not neglect the subjective aspect. The formula, *Scio aliquid esse,* is Maritain's, but it is quite faithful to the teaching of St. Thomas. According to the Angelic Doctor, and according to Aristotle, the soul knows itself in its act of knowing a sensible thing. It knows primarily the thing perceived, secondarily its own act of cognition, and thirdly its own nature. The last knowledge is not immediate and direct, but comes only as the result of reflection upon the act of understanding, a reflection in which the nature of the principle of understanding is known from the nature of the act: *operatio sequitur esse.*[16] The second knowledge, the intellect's knowledge of its act, is direct; that is what Maritain means by *scio* in his formula. In immediate perception the soul confusedly knows itself knowing, just as it confusedly knows being as such and the natures of things. From this primitive cognition of itself it develops its knowledge of its own spiritual nature — we did this in Chapter X — just as from the primitive, confused grasp of real being it develops all the principles of being discussed in the present chapter.

From the soul's knowledge of itself and its own spiritual nature, it can attain to some, though very imperfect, knowledge of purely spiritual beings above it. St. Augustine had written: "As the mind itself acquires the knowledge of corporeal things by means of the corporeal senses, so it gains through itself the knowledge of incorporeal things." St. Thomas' commentary on this is as follows:

> Augustine may be taken to mean that the knowledge of incorporeal things in the mind can be gained through the mind itself. This is so true that philosophers also say that the knowledge concerning the soul

[16] *S. Theol.,* I, 87, 3.

is a principle for the knowledge of separated substances. For by knowing itself, the soul attains to some knowledge of incorporeal substances, such as is within its compass; not that the knowledge of itself gives it a perfect and absolute knowledge of them.[17]

Even from material things we attain some knowledge of spiritual being. When we have reached the highest level of abstraction, starting from the data of perception, we attain the clear and explicit concept of being as such, and we see that this concept in no way requires that being be material. Hence, we form the concept — very imperfect and more negative than positive — of immaterial being.[18] Thus we have two ways of approaching the nature of immaterial being and of proving that such being exists. This subject, however, belongs not to the foundations of metaphysics, but to its highest part, namely natural theology.

[17] *Ibid.*, 1, 88, 1, ad 1 (*Basic Writings of St. Thomas Aquinas*, ed. Anton C. Pegis [New York: Random House, 1945], Vol. I, p. 846).
[18] *Ibid.*, I, 88, 2, ad 1 and ad 2.

CHAPTER XIX

SCIENCE AND PHILOSOPHY

I. THE PROBLEM OF THE CHAPTER

1. Background of the Problem. Throughout Part Two of this book it was necessary on several occasions to draw a distinction between the natural science and the philosophy of nature, and to explain some principles concerning the differences in the objectives and procedures of the two. But the whole question of the relations between science and philosophy is such an important problem for both disciplines today that it warrants separate treatment. The place for that treatment is in this part, Part Three, of our book which is concerned with knowledge and being, for, as we shall show, it is precisely as different kinds of knowledge concerned with different aspects of being that science and philosophy essentially differ. Philosophy itself, if we omit practical philosophy,[1] falls into two divisions, namely the philosophy of nature and metaphysics. Our last chapter was a vindication of metaphysical knowledge, and for that reason, as well as for the more important one that the relations between science and the philosophy of nature are closer and give rise to more acute problems, we shall be concerned chiefly with the philosophy of nature in the present chapter. The whole chapter itself is part of metaphysics, for it is a function of that supreme science to define and order the lower sciences.

Only during the modern scientific age, which began with the great scientific rebirth of the sixteenth century, has the question of the relations of science and philosophy been given any great attention by

---

[1] The problem of the relations between science and practical philosophy, that is to say ethics or the theory of values, is, of course, of primary importance; but the scope of the present book does not embrace it. We ought, however, to note that the solution of that problem depends largely on the solution of the problem of the relations between science and speculative philosophy.

either scientists or philosophers; and the attention given it today far exceeds that of any previous age. For a long period since the sixteenth century few scientists or philosophers were conscious of the problem because they had unconsciously settled it, and settled it erroneously. They simply regarded natural science as being itself the philosophy of nature. If there was any problem for them at all, it was concerned with the relations of science and metaphysics.

One characteristic of modern science which has played a large part in determining the shape which the problem of science and philosophy has taken is the "mathematization" of science. The importance of exact measurement, the possibility of expressing natural phenomena in mathematical formulas and of developing procedures enabling the scientist to predict phenomena through the use of mathematical laws and formulas is one of the great discoveries which made our scientific age possible. But misuse of the discovery has had evil effects in philosophy.

2. The Domination of Physics. The great scientific revolution affected physics first. Indeed, if the ideal of a science of phenomena is to submit itself as completely as possible to the regulating influence of mathematics, then physics and the physical sciences such as astronomy are the only ones that as yet approach the ideal with any degree of proximity. Whether or not this mathematization is in truth the ideal of science, it was in fact taken as such during many generations following the sixteenth century. As a result, physics became the pattern or model of the natural sciences, and many scientists took it as axiomatic that all the science of nature would become more advanced and more perfect in form the more they became able to adopt the methods and concepts of physics. This attitude had a strong influence upon the philosophical views that became current during these centuries.[2]

3. Mechanism and Behaviorism. One of the earliest and most enduring philosophical attitudes that was nourished by the priority conceded to physical methods and concepts is mechanism. Mechanism denies any true substantial differences among different kinds of bodies, and any true intrinsic changes; bodies are different only by being different arrangements or organizations of identical unit-particles, and all changes in bodies are only extrinsic movements of

[2] Cf. E. G. Salmon, "Philosophy and Science," *The New Scholasticism* (April, 1942), pp. 130–149.

these unit-particles, which, aside from moving locally, never change in themselves. For three centuries physics was able to march from triumph to triumph through the use of this view of bodies, and it seemed quite clear that the other sciences would accelerate their progress just to the degree to which they could take and employ this view in their procedures. And, as a matter of fact, they have been able to adopt physical concepts and theories more and more, and through their use to arrive at fruitful hypotheses mathematically expressible. The ideal of some scientists and philosophers became the reduction of all science to physics. For such thinkers the object of biological science, the living organism, was to be viewed as simply and solely the sum or resultant of its smallest parts, that is, its indivisible unit-particles; vital phenomena were assumed to be in no way different from mechanical phenomena — to be, in fact, simply complex mechanical processes; and, of course, no real life-principle was admitted. The "dead matter" with which physics dealt became the pattern or type of all matter.[3] This same *reductio omnium scientiarum ad physicam,* applied to psychology, gave rise to behaviorism.

Such philosophical theories as mechanism and behaviorism would not have arisen if the distinction between natural science and philosophy of nature had been understood and kept in view by modern philosophers. But it was not kept in view, and from the time of Descartes down to recent years physics was widely regarded as being a philosophy of nature. Physics-minded philosophers were very certain that physics was a veritable science of the ultimately real in nature. The particles and forces which they imagined seemed as real as anything that anyone could reasonably ask for.

4. Positivism. As physics itself refined its concepts, it became clear that certain notions which were basic in traditional philosophy, notably substance and cause, were not really necessary at all in physics. Physical entities could be adequately determined and defined in terms of properties and operations, and physical events in terms of antecedent and consequent phenomena.[4] The questions whether the properties and operations belong to and manifest any underlying substances, and whether the invariable links between phenomena are

[3] E. F. Caldin, "Modern Physics and Thomistic Philosophy," *The Thomist,* Vol. II, No. 2 (April, 1940), pp. 208–225.

[4] The term "phenomenon" here, and throughout this chapter, is not used in the peculiarly Kantian sense, but in its more general signification, meaning the sensibly observable.

causal, did not have to be answered in order for physics to continue its march of progress; consequently physicists ceased asking them. Physics, the natural science, does not, in fact, have to ask or answer these questions, but philosophy of nature does; and when physics thinks itself to be philosophy of nature, the step from ignoring substance and cause to denying them is short and easy. And while the physicists were discovering that they do not really need the notions of substance and causality, some philosophers, on quite other grounds, were attacking the validity of these notions. We have already seen how David Hume led this battle against substance and cause and how Immanuel Kant's great effort to outflank him failed. Add now the philosophers' dictum that you cannot really know any substance or cause to the scientists' assertion that you do not have to use these notions anyway, and it is not very surprising that the attitude soon became general that the only knowledge which we can have of nature is knowledge of phenomena and their relations; in other words, that in nature the observable alone is an attainable object of true knowledge. Again, the step from the affirmation of the unattainability of substance, essence, and cause to the denial of their reality was short and easy. And so there developed the philosophy so widespread today — positivism or naturalism. This philosophy denies that there is any knowledge of anything besides what is experimentally verifiable, and affirms that the sole method of attaining knowledge is the empirical-experimental method used in the natural sciences. Philosophy of nature, if you wish to use that name, is, according to naturalists, simply a summary of the findings of natural science up to date; metaphysics is a game played in the land of nowhere — a dangerous game which perpetuates the superstitions of a pre-scientific age.

Has modern science overthrown and replaced the Aristotelian-Thomistic philosophy of nature, with its substances and causes, its hylemorphism and its teleology, its doctrine on souls? And are Scholastics, in retaining and expounding the latter philosophy, guilty of clinging obstinately and blindly to an outmoded, discountenanced "science" of the past? Many modern scientists and philosophers think so. They are gravely mistaken; but in order to make it clear that they are, it is necessary for us to inquire into the nature of science and the nature of philosophy and to determine, if we can, the relations of these two forms of knowledge to each other.

II. THE DEGREES OF ABSTRACTION AND THE
DIVISION OF SCIENCE

1. **Science and Its Divisions.** The word *science* in its broader and more ancient sense includes both philosophy and what we call science today. Science in this broader sense means knowledge that is certain because the reasons of its truth are known; it is *cognitio certa per causas*. The causes or reasons with which the knowledge is concerned may be primary causes or secondary causes, they may be real causes of the order of substantial being or regular antecedents of the phenomenal or accidental order. Where the causes in question are primary, real, and of the order of substance, the certain knowledge of them is philosophy; where they are secondary, merely logical, or of the phenomenal order, the certain knowledge of them is science (in the narrower sense of that term). In any case, both these knowledges are what Aristotle called science because both are certain knowledge through causes.

We have seen that Aristotle distinguished three speculative sciences, the basis of distinction being the objects which they study. These objects are themselves determined by the degree of abstraction with which the mind views the things which fall under its ken. Abstraction is an act by which the intellect selects a certain real aspect of a thing presented to it and makes that aspect the object of its thought, leaving out of consideration the other real aspects of the thing. The aspect so selected or abstracted becomes the *formal object* of the mind. This formal object, it is clear, is not identical with the "thing," but is the thing viewed under a particular aspect. And if different formal objects can be abstracted from the same order of things or beings, then different sciences can be constructed about these same beings.

The things which first fall under the ken of the human mind are material things, that is, corporeal substances. Each of them is a particular thing, differing individually from all the others. In order to have any science of them at all, the intellect must abstract from their individual and contingent peculiarities and direct its gaze to their universal and necessary characters; for science, since it is *certain* knowledge and aims at deductions, cannot deal with the contingent, the uncertain, and the particular, but must concern itself with what is necessary and universal. But whatever belongs to an individual inasmuch as it is individual belongs to it by virtue of its particular matter, and consequently belongs to it contingently; only what belongs to it by virtue of its form or nature belongs to it necessarily. When, therefore, the mind ignores the individual differences of corporeal substances and regards them under their universal aspects, it is ready to embark upon the pursuit of science, that is, *cognitio certa per causas.*[5]

2. **Physica.** By a series of abstractions the mind is able to distinguish clearly three different universal aspects of natural substances. In the first degree of abstraction the mind prescinds only from the individual matter and peculiarities of corporeal substances, and regards them in their universal character as sensible or mobile being. The formal object of the intellect in this degree of abstraction is sensible or mobile being (*ens sensibile seu mobile*). Mobility and sensible quality are inseparable from matter both in existence and in thought; for example, color and motion cannot exist except in a material thing. As Aristotle wrote, they have no separate existence (i.e., separate from material substance) and are subject to change (i.e., to the changes of the material substance in which they inhere); and for this latter reason they cannot be understood apart from material substance. The science which studies nature under this aspect, that is, as *ens mobile seu sensibile,* is called by Aristotle and St. Thomas *Physica.*

3. **Mathematica.** In the second degree of abstraction the mind prescinds not only from the individual peculiarities of natural substances, but also from their sensible quality and changeability, and considers them solely under their character of quantity, that is, as quantified being. Quantity cannot exist apart from sensible matter, but it can be conceived apart from it and as unaffected by its mobility and sensible qualities. Although bodies are constantly changing in their quantitative determinations, I can formulate unchanging principles of quantitative relations. Again, although numbers are real (i.e., not merely logical beings) only inasmuch as *things* are numbered or counted, I can formulate a science of numbers without any reference to the things numbered. The second degree of abstraction, therefore, yields to the mind a second necessary and universal aspect of corporeal substance, a second formal object, viz., quantity, and a second science, of which quantity is the formal object, viz., *Mathematica.*

4. **Metaphysica.** The mind can rise to a still higher abstraction. Both in the things presented to it by experience and in other things to which

[5] Aristotle, *Posterior Analytics,* I, 31; St. Thomas, *In I Post. Anal.,* lects. 42 and 44.

it attains by thought, which while starting from experience rises above it, the mind finds a basis for a third degree of abstraction. It prescinds from mobility, perceptibility, quantity, and, in fact, from every material condition, and considers immaterial being, or simply being as such (*ens qua ens*). Unlike mobility and quantity, being can both exist and be conceived separate from matter, and it is this immaterial being, or being as such, which is the formal object of the third and highest science, wisdom properly so called, namely, *Metaphysica.*[6]

III. NATURAL SCIENCE AND THE PHILOSOPHY OF NATURE

1. Neither Aristotle nor Aquinas explicitly distinguished between the natural sciences and the philosophy of nature, although the former was a great natural scientist as well as a great philosopher of nature, and the latter, while not a scientist at all as we would apply the term today, yet shows by certain remarks that the distinction in question must have more than once occurred to him. Both of them theoretically located the pursuits which are today distinguished as science and philosophy of nature under *physica,* without marking them as distinct pursuits. Most modern Scholastic philosophers, however, maintain that the distinction must be made — that, indeed, it is of prime importance to both science and philosophy. Foremost among contemporary Thomistic philosophers in expounding this view is Jacques Maritain, and the present chapter is greatly indebted to his analysis of the problem.

The problem is this: whether that scientific knowledge of nature which Aristotle called *physica* is in fact two distinct knowledges, one philosophic and the other scientific (using that word in its modern, narrow sense). And since sciences are distinguished by their formal objects, the solution to the problem lies in the answer to this question: In the formal object of *physica,* sensible or mobile being, are there in fact two distinct formal objects, one an apt object for a philosophical discipline and the other an apt object for a scientific discipline?

2. **The Object of the Philosophy of Nature.** "Mobile or sensible being" is obviously a complex conception, and the mind in contemplating it may give priority and stress to either "being" or "mobile or sensible." If the mind gives stress to "being," it will study corporeal

---

[6] Aristotle, *Meta.,* VI, 1; St. Thomas, *In Boet. de Trin.,* q. 5, art. 1; Maritain, *Degrees of Knowledge* (New York: Scribners, 1939), pp. 44–49.

substance under the aspect of its real or ontological essence and causes, that is, the first real principles, both intrinsic and extrinsic, which constitute it as being, substance, corporeal, mobile, and sensible. The sensible qualities of the object will be data and starting points for the mind's activity, but will not be goals. Similarly the movements or "processes" of bodies will be data for the mind to analyze and explain in terms of real causes, but the mind will not aim at any detailed account or formula of the processes as such. In a word, the object (*ens mobile seu sensibile*) will be regarded as *being,* manifesting itself through certain sensible phenomena; and what the mind will be seeking is demonstrative knowledge of the being, not of the phenomena. Approaching corporeal beings in this way, the mind formulates the philosophy of nature, the science of the essence and real causes of mobile or sensible being. This we have done in Chapters IV to IX.

3. The Object of Natural Science. Clearly the mind can approach the same thing (sensible being) in another way. Corporeal substance manifests itself to the human mind through sensible phenomena. These phenomena, because they are the manifestations of real essences, embody a definite order and regularity among themselves. The mind can make this phenomenal order its formal object, and, while not denying the real essences which are its true or ontological causes, can choose to ignore them. Then its formal object is *ens mobile seu sensibile* with attention given to the *mobile seu sensibile.* Approaching corporeal beings in this way, the mind formulates natural science, the science of the phenomenal order which obtains among the things and processes of nature. The phenomena and processes are not only its starting points but its goal.[7]

4. The Speculative Sciences. With this distinction in mind we may draw a new chart of the speculative sciences:

Material Object	Formal Object	Science
All being	being as such	Metaphysics
Material being	quantity	Mathematics
Material being	sensible being	viewed ontologically — Philosophy of Nature
		viewed empiriologically — Natural Science

[7] J. Maritain, *op. cit.,* pp. 48 ff.; Y. Simon, "Maritain's Philosophy of the Sciences," *The Thomist,* Vol. V, (Jan. 1943), pp. 85–102.

5. Comparison of Procedures in Science and Philosophy. Both philosophy of nature and the natural sciences begin with phenomena which are sensibly observable, since all our knowledge has its origin in sense perception. But the philosophy of nature goes from the observable phenomena to the real essences or causes which underlie and account for the phenomena, while natural science goes from the observable phenomena to a formula expressing some regular order in the occurrences of the phenomena and, eventually, through the application of this formula, to the prediction of future phenomena. For example, both philosopher and scientist observe that elementary substances in nature unite to form compound substances; from this fact the philosopher reasons to the conclusion that corporeal substances are essentially constituted by a determinable, potential principle the same in all of them and a determining, actual principle specifically different in each; whereas the scientist, after examining a great number of such combinations and applying exact measurements to the substances involved in them, formulates the laws of chemical affinity and of the combining weights of elements. The philosopher has arrived at the essential intrinsic principles of corporeal substance; the scientist has arrived at a law expressing the regular order that obtains among the chemical processes of nature.

Both the philosopher of nature and the natural scientist study being which is sensible and movable. But, as we have seen, it is "being" which dominates the study for the former and "sensible and movable" which dominates for the latter. The philosopher of nature considers the whole complex object under the aspect of *being;* consequently his primary question is, What *is* it? And he asks this question even about the sensible and mobile aspect. Thus, his interest in regard to the movement of natural things leads him to inquire about the essence and ultimate cause of motion itself: what, precisely, is motion, and why does anything move? Is motion self-generating? Or does it require a cause? The natural scientist, on the other hand, tends to consider the complex object, movable, sensible being, under the aspects of motion and sensible quality. He finds that natural things are, as a matter of fact, in movement. What motion is and why anything moves, he does not ask. His task is to discover the relations that exist among observable movements. He goes from movements to movements, not from movements to the essence of motion. He tends to treat being itself under the category of movement, and to regard substances as identical with their processes. In like manner he subordinates being to sensible quality, identifies substances with their observable properties, and does not inquire concerning the real nature and cause of these properties.

The philosopher of nature moves from the observable facts to his conclusion through the medium of the universal principles of being established by metaphysics. The natural scientist reaches his conclusions through hypotheses, which are provisional, universalized statements of the constant relations holding among the observed facts themselves. Thus, in the illustration used above the philosopher applies to the fact of substantial change the principles of identity, sufficient reason, and causality, and arrives at a new principle peculiar to the realm of material being, namely, the composite essence of all corporeal substance; the scientist formulates, on the basis of a number of measurements of chemical changes, the hypothesis that elements combine with certain other elements in constant proportions by weight, and when he tests this hypothesis by new measurements, which in all cases conform to it, he considers it verified, and it becomes a law of chemistry.

6. Facts in Science and Philosophy. From the last two paragraphs it should be clear that, while philosophy of nature and natural science both start from sensibly observable facts, they do not start from precisely the same facts. When sodium and chlorine combine to form common salt, $NaCl$, that is one event. But this one *event* can be several distinct *facts,* depending on the interests of the mind observing it. It is: (1) the fact that two sorts of stuff have combined to form a third sort; (2) the fact that two corporeal substances have undergone a change resulting in a new substance different from both of them; (3) the fact that sodium and chlorine have combined to form a compound; (4) the fact that sodium and chlorine have combined in a ratio of one to one; (5) the fact that two atoms each with its own internal structure and physical properties have combined to form a molecule with still another internal structure and other physical properties. The first fact is observable by common experience unenlightened by and uninterested in any philosophical or scientific knowledge; the second is close to common experience, but presupposes that the event has been observed in the context of ontological principles and philosophical interest; the last three demand a progressively more

special scientific knowledge and interest, and presuppose no explicit context of ontological principles. Facts of the first type (though the one offered is rarely experienced) make up the materials of our everyday non-philosophical and non-scientific thinking. Those of the second type may be called philosophical facts, and the last three kinds scientific facts. The mind, face to face with any thing or event, views it as a different sort of fact depending on the interest which the mind brings to its observation. Hence, common experience, philosophy, and science each has its own facts as well as its own procedures; and nevertheless the same natural events and things are their common ultimate foundation. As a consequence, although common sense, philosophy, and science may move on very different intellectual levels, they can never be entirely unrelated and indifferent to each other. Finally, philosophy of nature remains closer than science to common sense because its facts are closer to those of common experience, demanding reflective analysis, but no specialized technical aids, in order to be derived from facts of common experience.[8]

7. Analysis in Philosophy and Science. Philosophy of nature and natural science both analyze the data presented to experience and both seek, through this analysis, to reach universal conclusions concerning the data. But just as their aims are different (philosophy seeking the real causes and essences which underlie and explain the data, and science seeking the law expressing the phenomenal order among the data), so, too, do they employ different kinds of analysis. Maritain calls the analysis of the philosopher of nature *ontological* analysis and that of the scientist *empiriological* analysis. The philosopher abstracts from the complex of observable phenomena the intelligible core or essence which manifests itself through this complex and without which the phenomena are without sufficient reason and are unintelligible; his analysis moves *up* from the perceptible and accidental to the intelligible and substantial. This analysis leads to an explanation of the object of investigation in terms of more universal, or higher, intelligible objects, culminating, if it is carried far enough, in explanation in terms of the most universal and intelligible of all objects, being itself. The scientist, on the other hand, when he employs analysis, analyzes the original complex phenomenon into more elementary phenomena; he moves, not from the sensible up to the

[8] Cf. Maritain, *op. cit.*, pp. 64–66 and 71–73.

intelligible, but from the complex sensible object *down* (as far as possible) to the primary sensible or perceptible units which constitute it.[9]

8. The Method of Natural Science. The method of science begins
and ends with observations. Between its beginning and its end it
utilizes classification, hypothesis, and deduction; but the hypothesis
and deduction have as their purpose to predict or suggest additional
observations, and when the observations so predicted are actually made
as they were predicted the hypothesis is verified. Observations always
deal with the empirical or phenomenal. They cannot reach real causes,
substances, or essences. They, and the hypotheses, theories, and deductions which are formulated from them and used to predict con-
firmatory observations, yield regularly related phenomena, but do not
yield true causes or ultimate explanations. The aim of science is to
formulate the observable events of nature in a coherent system. That
is why we call its method empiriological.

The result of the different aims and methods of science and philosophy is that there cannot be any real conflict between them so
long as neither is mistaken for the other. The philosophy of nature,
seeking the ultimate real causes of natural processes, analyzes the real
or essential producing factors of these processes into four genera of
cause — the material, the formal, the efficient, and the final cause —
and singles out two of these as causal constituents of the substances
which undergo the process, namely, primary matter and substantial
form. Physical science, seeking to systematize the observable processes
of nature in a regular order which permits of prediction based upon
recorded observations and measurements, analyzes the processes into
chemical and physical motions and formulates these motions in
chemical and physical laws. No matter how deeply the chemical and
physical inquiry is extended, it gives nothing besides smaller scale and
more generalized observations and measurements in the place of
larger scale and less generalized ones. It does not *explain* the phenomena of nature, but only describes them more completely and relates them to one another more universally. Its goal is a complete
description of nature's myriad movements in terms of the fewest possible and most general possible formulas. Thus, the theory of atomic
structures, which enabled chemists to state the observed facts of

---

[9] Simon, *op. cit.*, pp. 90–91. Cf. J. Maritain, "Science, Philosophy and Faith," in
Science, Philosophy and Religion, a Symposium (New York: The Conference, 1941),
pp. 162–183.

chemical affinity in terms of one principle or formula, was a true advance in science, although it has nothing to do with real causation. Similarly, if biophysicists and biochemists succeed in stating all vital processes in terms of atomic and subatomic processes, they will have made a great advance in the science of biology,[10] but they will not have explained life or the activities of organisms. What they will have done is to have restated larger-scale processes in terms of smaller-scale ones and a variety of particular processes in terms of basic general processes.

9. **The Method of Philosophy.** The philosophic method cannot be described in any series of steps, like observation, classification, hypothesis, verification, or something of the sort. It is simply the application of the intellect, in the light of self-evident truths, to an object offered it by experience until it finds a true principle by which it can understand the object. Its rules are simple: respect the facts, and infer only what is necessarily implied by them. The philosopher who has carried through his study of a being to its last point understands the being and its operations because he has discovered the real or ontological causes and essences which account for the phenomenal manifestations of the being. He is not and cannot be satisfied with explanations of phenomena or events which are themselves only prior related phenomena or events; because, while these give a close insight into *how* the subject of his inquiry comes into being, they do not give any insight into what causes it to be. The piling up of phenomena antecedent to the phenomenon which he is seeking to explain gives him, not an ultimate explanation, but rather more things demanding explanation. What he is seeking is *understanding* of nature. It is only a rather childlike delusion to think that he understands nature better by passing from the facts of chemical changes to the facts of atomic movements which "explain" them. The scientific quest for laws of higher and higher generality does not lead to the philosopher's goal of causal explanation. The utopian scientific law would be one formula which would express the relationships of antecedence and consequence in nature's movements with a universality applicable to every kind of natural process. It would be, however, a descriptive law, not an explanatory one. It would no more explain nature than a compendium of English grammar, rhetoric, and poetics would explain English literature. A study, detailed and thorough, of why "Hamlet" is a

[10] Cf. Schroedinger, *What is Life?* (New York: Macmillan, 1945).

masterpiece does not explain "Hamlet"; the only explanation of "Hamlet" is Shakespeare. Science explains what nature is like; the philosopher wants to know what causes natural things to be and to be like that. He wants to know the real causes and essences which underlie natural processes.

10. Illustration of the Differences. Two examples will serve to illustrate the difference in object, method, and aim between natural science and philosophy.

a) The philosopher of nature, observing that corporeal substances have specific unity with individual multiplicity, undividedness with divisibility, actual nature with capacity to change, infers, through the medium of the principles of identity and sufficient reason, that they contain a real, essential principle of determinateness, unity, and actuality; and another real principle of determinability, divisibility, and potentiality. The former principle he calls substantial form, the latter primary matter. The analysis is a resolution into being: determined being and determinable being, actual being and potential being. The scientist, observing that material substances are changeable, divisible, and endowed with specific properties, devises methods of observing the inner physical constitution of the substances — and analyzes bodies into molecules, molecules into atoms, atoms into protons, neutrons, electrons, etc., and accounts for the properties and processes of bodies by the structures and movements of these molecules, atoms, electrons, etc. This analysis resolves an observable whole into parts which are also (directly or indirectly) observable.

b) Observing corporeal substances which have the property of immanent activity (e.g., self-determining movement, nutrition, growth, sensation), and observing that corporeal substance *as such* does not have this property, the philosopher of nature concludes that a real principle of immanent activity is part of the essential constitution of those substances that do have it, that is, of living substances. His analysis of a living organism follows immediately, and is very simple: an organism is a corporeal being with the power of immanent activity, and contains as an essential part, really distinct from the matter of the organism, a principle of life called a soul. The anlysis goes from the observable to the essential and is based on the principles of being and sufficient reason. The natural scientist, observing certain processes, called vital processes, in some material things and not in others, institutes a search which carries him from observation of the general whole-aspect of some vital process, e.g., nutrition and growth, to observation of more particular part-aspects of the same process, e.g., cell metabolism and division. He goes from organism to organ to tissue to cell; from the vital activity of the whole plant or animal, to the contributory vital processes of the organs that make up the organism, and finally to the separate cells that make up the organs and the organism. He need not stop at the cell, because cell metabolism is carried on by reactions between chemical substances, so that the scientist's search carries him all the way to elements and compounds, molecules and atoms, and even to subatomic particles, if he cares to go that far. But all along the way his progress is from observable to observable, from phenomenon to phenomenon. As far as he is concerned, living bodies differ from non-living bodies (a tree from a stone) because a certain type of process is invariably manifested by the former and invariably absent from the latter. The essences underlying and causing these processes are none of his concern as a natural scientist. Hence he does not speak of a soul in living things, and he does not seek to give an essential definition of life, being content to point out the phenomena which always mark it in nature and to analyze these phenomena into their ultimate observable elements. Vital processes are analyzed into chemical processes, and chemical processes into physical processes, and life is defined only in the empiriological order, that is, by the observable processes which manifest it.

11. **Process and Action.** Often, when the natural scientist and the philosopher are commonly said to be studying the same thing from different points of view, they are in fact actually studying different things. The former is studying a series of processes and the latter a series of actions; and the two series, while reciprocal, are by no means identical. This distinction seems basic in reference to the respective natures of natural science and natural philosophy, but this fact is seldom, if ever, noted today. Some of the problems in reference to which we have above employed this distinction and relation of process and action are: the nature of efficient and material causality (where the distinction is first discovered), and the nature of motion (Chapter IV), the relations of final causality and mechanical causality (Chapter V), the relations of hylemorphism and scientific mechanism (Chapters VI-VII), the nature of vital activity in an organism and the reconciliation of the scientific and philosophical study of organisms (Chapter VIII), and finally, the relations in man of thought, sense activity, and

physiological processes (Chapter IX) and of free will and biological and psychological determinism (Chapter XIII). These sections, especially Section VI of Chapter VIII, should be reread now in reference to our present problem.

12. Deduction in Philosophy of Nature and Natural Science.[11] Every science (using that term in its broader sense to include both philosophy and the natural sciences) aims at being *deductive;* that is to say, it strives to develop to the state wherein, from causes and essences, it can deduce effects and properties. Metaphysics is the supreme deductive science because its primary principles are self-evident and are of absolutely universal application, and because its formal object, being as such, is the most intelligible of all objects, the most self-contained since it is its own reason, and the most universal and primary since all other objects are resolvable into being under one aspect or another. Mathematics is purely deductive, but for a quite different reason. It deals with objects of the abstract conceptual order, with logical, not real, beings, and consequently is free from the contingencies and particularities that arise from the material, sensible element in the real beings of nature; it proceeds from definition and principle to universal and necessary conclusions without taking any account of individual contingencies, because it neither starts from nor returns to the real order of individual existents: a triangle is a three-sided plane figure, and its interior angles total 180 degrees whether there is any triangular thing in the world or not.

13. Philosophy of Nature and Natural Science Both Depend on Metaphysics. The case is different with philosophy of nature and natural science. Both, because they are sciences, deal with the universal and necessary, but both live in a world of the individual and contingent. From this world they take their starting points and to this world they apply their conclusions. Both start as inductive: they begin with particular facts and from these they formulate universal principles. Thus, to use illustrations already employed, the natural philosopher, after many observations, reaches the universal conclusion that material substances are essentially changeable; and the chemist, after many observations and experiments, concludes that elements regularly combine with certain others in constant proportions by weight. Both, having attained these universal principles, now seek to deduce further conclusions from them. The philosopher, applying metaphysical prin-

[11] Cf. Maritain, *Degrees of Knowledge,* pp. 41–43.

ciples such as those of identity and causality, reaches a conclusion about the intrinsic essence of material substance — that it is composite of matter and form. The chemist, applying mathematical principles, is able to predict the product of given quantities of given elements brought together under given circumstances. He is also able to employ the principle as a basis for a further hypothesis, from which he then makes deductions which, if regularly verified, support the hypothesis. In this way Dalton formulated the atomic theory from the law of combining weights.

It should be noticed that both philosophy of nature and natural science become deductive through the use of the principles of one of the strictly deductive sciences, metaphysics and mathematics. Philosophy of nature consciously and explicitly places itself under the regulation of metaphysics by borrowing and applying to corporeal being the metaphysical principles which concern being as such. The natural sciences tend more and more to place themselves under the domain of mathematics, though all of them have not yet done so equally. It should also be noted that all the natural sciences are, willy-nilly, under the regulation of metaphysics, since the scientist must respect and apply the primary universal principles established by metaphysics even though he never explicitly thinks of them, or, possibly, even though he denies their ontological validity. Science would be in fact impossible if the principles of sufficient reason and causality did not have universal validity. The same thing is true for the principles of identity and contradiction. These truths must be true both logically and ontologically; if they are not respected logically, thought becomes impossible; and if they did not in fact hold ontologically, the only possible objects of scientific thought, real beings, would be unintelligible. The scientist may take a merely pragmatic view of them, using them simply because they work; but, in fact, if they did not work in nature, outside his mind, he could never formulate a science of nature. In other words, the logical necessity of these universal first principles is a consequence of their ontological necessity. Every scientific procedure rests on the beliefs that everything is what it is, that nothing can be and not be something at the same time, that there is a reason for everything, and a cause for every event; and scientific procedures are successful because these beliefs are, in fact, true in the world that science deals with.

14. The Natural Sciences Submit Themselves to Mathematics. But

although the physical sciences are of necessity regulated at least remotely by metaphysics, the special character of their deductions tends
more and more to be given them by mathematics. The consequences
of this fact are important. Mathematics itself deals with logical constructs — things created by the mind (*entia rationis*) instead of with
real being. Therefore, the more a physical science submits itself to
mathematics the more it introduces *entia rationis* into its structure.
Furthermore, these rational entities enter into the science precisely in
the core of its deductive function, since it is by the mathematical
formularization of its observations and measurements that a science
is able to form mathematically expressed hypotheses, and it is through
its hypotheses that a natural science is able to make deductions (i.e.,
predictions). The phenomena which physical science studies and the
order that it discovers among these phenomena have real causes, the·
essences which underlie and manifest themselves through the phenomena. The mathematical formulas and laws of the natural sciences
do not reveal or express these essences, but they do derive their validity,
that is, their applicability to physical phenomena, from these stable
essences. They presuppose and indicate, without revealing, the stable
entity which, to physics, remains unknown — the ontological *x*, as
Maritain calls it.

15. Natural Science Pertains to Reality. This view of the function of
theories and laws in the natural sciences saves modern physics from
a charge not infrequently leveled against it in recent years — that it
is not directly concerned with the real world at all. If theories and
laws, and even formulas that are taken to function for simple entities,
are substitutes for real essences, but do not pretend to express these
essences, it is not necessary to conclude that the science embodying
them is entirely cut off from the physical world. The formula or law
expresses a regular relation between phenomena, and the essence for
which the formula is substituted is the cause of this regular relation.
However little real connection the formula has with the essence itself,
it still expresses a real fact when it expresses the relation between the
phenomena. The science of physics, as Maritain expresses it, remains
materially physical even though it becomes formally mathematical.
The *entia rationis* which it employs have a real foundation in the
physical order. The mathematical formula which enables the physicist
to predict future phenomena from present ones is a logical being, but
the phenomena are real beings; and if the formula had no foundation

in reality it would not be of any use in the attempt to predict events in the real order.[12]

IV. SOME SPECIAL PROBLEMS FROM MODERN PHYSICS

1. Some of the more recent discoveries and theories in physics have been generally regarded as incapable of reconciliation with the rigidly mechanistic and deterministic outlook of the classical physics of the past three centuries. Whether these new facts are in truth irreconcilable with physical mechanism is not a vital question for the Scholastic philosopher of nature, however interesting he may find these facts. Neither a rigidly determined nor a partly undetermined system of mechanical causes on the level of physical processes, and in the sense in which physicists use the terms *determined* and *undetermined*, seems to be a necessary correlate of the Thomistic philosophy of nature. Hylemorphism and the principle of causality certainly demand an unbroken series of mechanical — material and efficient — causes in natural processes; but that they demand that these causes be always amenable to precise measurement and related in a system of determinism mathematically expressible does not seem at all self-evident. Determinism and indeterminism are terms which take different meanings when translated from philosophy to physics. In philosophy they have to do with necessary and free causes; in physics they refer to the possibility or impossibility of precise measurements and predictions. Hence, when a physicist speaks of an event, for example the popping of an electron out of a radioactive atom, as undetermined, the philosopher has to make sure, before he can know the significance of the physicist's statement, whether by undetermined the latter means (1) uncaused, (2) freely caused, or (3) unpredictable. What the physicist really means — though *he* may use the term uncaused or free — is that there is no possible way of determining when a given electron will pop or which one will next; only a statistical prediction can be made: so many will be emitted under such circumstances in such and such a time. Efforts to represent the unpredictable movements of individual electrons as "free" are based upon a very strange idea of freedom. Since we cannot discover any cause or reason for the particular movement of the particular electron, it is assumed

[12] Cf. Maritain, *Degrees of Knowledge*, pp. 51–57; V. E. Smith, "The Nature of Scientific Theory," *Proceedings of the American Catholic Philosophical Association* (Washington, D. C.: The Association, 1942), pp. 96–103.

that there is no particular reason or cause for it; so then it is called free. Freedom, then, instead of meaning the ability to determine one's actions by intelligent control, means the plight of being likely to do anything at any moment for no reason at all.

2. **The Principle of Indeterminacy and the Principle of Causality.** From the fact that it is physically impossible to determine at once both the position and velocity of an electron (Heisenberg's principle of indeterminacy) some philosophers and scientists have concluded that the principle of causality does not reign universally among natural processes, indeed, does not hold in regard to those processes which are most basic. In order to predict the future course of a moving particle, it is necessary to know both its position and its velocity and direction at a given moment. But for particles as small as an electron these two factors cannot be determined for the same moment, because in order to determine either one the electron must be subjected to an outside force or energy, and the minimum quantum of energy in nature is great enough to create such a disturbance in the state of the electron that the other factor cannot possibly be determined within any useful limits of accuracy. Hence, the future course of an individual electron cannot be predicted. From this it is concluded that the course of the individual electron is not causally determined. It ought to be clear that this conclusion is reached only through a patent equivocation. What cannot be *determined* (i.e., ascertained by an observer) is said not to be *determined* (i.e., necessitated by causes). In addition to this purely logical error, the argument involves a very strange bit of overlooking the obvious. The argument concludes that in the case of physical particles of the lowest order of magnitude causal law does not hold; and the basis for the conclusion is the unascertainability of both position and velocity at the same moment. But the reason for this unascertainability or indeterminability is precisely the causal action of the quantum of energy that must be used in order to make either determination. It is only because it is assumed that this energy will *always* affect the electron, that the impossibility of determining both velocity and position at once is made into a general and necessary principle, instead of being regarded merely as a difficulty to be overcome. In other words, the principle of indeterminacy is based immediately upon the principle of causality, and cannot, therefore, be used as evidence against it.

3. **Wave-Particles and the Principle of Contradiction.** Another find-

ing of modern physics, said by some to contravene the principle of contradiction is the fact that the same entities (e.g., photons and electrons) exhibit both the properties of particles and the properties of waves. Now a particle is not a wave. Therefore, if something is a particle and a wave, it is at once a particle and not a particle. But the principle of contradiction states that the same thing cannot at once be and not be something Hence, modern physics proves that the principle of contradiction is not universally valid. This argument is a *non sequitur*. (1) If particles and waves were essences of the substantial order, then to be at once a particle and a wave would be to defy the principle of contradiction. But we have seen above that physics does not attain to scientific knowledge of substantial essences. Wave and particle in physics mean certain observable and measurable phenomena. (2) If these two groups of phenomena are truly incompatible so that their simultaneous presence in an identical subject would be contradictory — as red and green, or cubical and spherical are incompatible in the same subject — then, again, for something to be at once a wave and a particle would be an exception to the principle of contradiction. But (3) if it is possible that wave properties and particle properties can reside in the same ontologically real subject — as red and spherical, or green and cubical — then the principle of contradiction is as yet untouched by modern physics. It should also be added that the particle-character and the wave-character of photons and electrons are not known by direct observation but are operationally determined: when one type of operation, devised for detecting wave properties is employed, photons and electrons give the responses expected of waves; when another type, devised to detect particle properties is used, they give the responses expected of particles. By future findings and by further clarification of their concepts, physicists will probably dispel all the aura of apparent contradiction that today surrounds wave-mechanics, and the philosopher may confidently leave the task to them. They really are no more fond of contradiction than he.

V. THE PRIMACY OF METAPHYSICS

1. The primary tenet of naturalism as a philosophy is that the only knowledge which really is knowledge is that which is attained through procedures which use the methods of the natural sciences — "the scientific method." This whole book may be considered as one long argu-

ment against naturalism. For the remainder of the present chapter we wish to present that argument in its barest terms. And our first point is this: *that every operation and judgment in the other sciences presupposes certain metaphysical principles* which no other science can establish but which Thomistic metaphysics does establish. We have established them in Chapter XVIII.

a) Epistemological Realism. Scientists study the world, and do not think that they are studying the insides of their heads or the states of their minds. They do study these latter in special sciences, but then they study them as parts of the real world. Along with a real outside world they accept their sense faculties and their intellects as organs whose primary function is to acquire knowledge of this world, and they do not question the native general capacity of these organs to perform that function. .

b) First Principles: Identity, Reason, Causality. Scientific research and procedure imply, in every step they take, the identity of things with themselves and the impossibility of a thing's not being itself. Data would be utterly without significance, nothing at all could be inferred from them, if things were capable, while being what they are, of also not being what they are; because it is only in so far as the data are what they are that they imply anything rather than anything else. Similarly the scientist's unrelenting quest for the regular antecedents of events is meaningless if he does not accept as certain that nothing occurs without a sufficient reason or cause. No matter how uninterested he may be in the essential nature of causality, his life as a scientist is a constant application of the principle of causality.

c) Ontological Validity of Rational Inference. Scientists, if they are also naturalists, may say that they believe only in observation and experimentation, and that an inference is validated only by experimental verification; but in fact they trust rational inference *in itself* and *unreservedly.* If they did not, they would have no reason for rejecting hypotheses when necessary deductions from these hypotheses are not borne out by experiment; they would always be able to say that the hypothesis might still be true, since *what is necessarily implied in something need not actually follow from it.* Though this italicized proposition is the basic principle of systematic naturalism, naturalists never use it except for one purpose, namely, to reject *a priori* any metaphysical judgment. For all scientific purposes they use, and they must use, its contradictory as unassailably true. The only reason why they test theories and hypotheses experimentally is because they know that what is implied in a proposition must be true if that proposition is true, and that what is implied in a true existential proposition is true in the existential order.

d) *Essence and Existence.* The method of science, utilizing hypothesis, deduction, and experimental verification as complements of induction, presupposes essence and existence as real divisions of being. Deductive forecasting from an hypothesis is purely in the realm of essence, since it is a rigid demonstration of the nature of the consequences of a certain supposed property or operation, which property or operation is not given in existence but only in hypothesis; unless essence were recognized as ontologically distinct from existence, nothing could be deduced from the hypothetical. On the other hand, unless existence were recognized as a phase of being ontologically distinct from essence, the demand for experimental verification would be unjustifiable. Furthermore, the induction-deduction-verification procedure of scientific method assigns to the human cognitive faculties precisely the function that Thomistic philosophy assigns to them: existence is given to the intellect through sense experience, and essences are grasped and their implications deduced by intellect. Only the intellect can apprehend the essence, but the intellect can know the essence to be an existing essence only by the voucher of the senses. Third, essences known to belong to existents are assumed to have implications in further existents; whence science's final appeal to sensible verification. That natural science does not apprehend essence as such does not affect the present argument. The substitutes which it uses for real essences function in the place of essences, and, like essences, are, of themselves and apart from experience, in the logical and not the existential realm; only the facts from which the hypothesis is formulated and the facts which verify it connect it with the existential realm.

2. **Metaphysics and "Scientific Method": Appeal to Experimental Verification.** The last sentence above expresses a truth which is at the very basis of the difference between procedure in natural science, and in philosophy. Natural science goes from facts to hypothesis to perceptible facts. The substitute for the existing essence, the hypothesis, is connected with experience both before and after it is used as the basis of deduction. Metaphysics goes from facts to existing essence to facts not within the reach of experience. The essence is not connected to experience by *new* deductions made from it, but only by the same

sort of facts by which it was first made known. It is precisely here that metaphysics refuses to be limited by the conditions of "scientific method," and it is precisely this refusal which leads many scientists and philosophers to reject the claim of metaphysics to be real knowledge. Their attitude may be expressed (mildly!) as along the following lines: The conceptions, hypotheses, and theories formulated from facts in natural science cannot be accepted as valid before they are tested by further experimental data; they must, in a word, produce verifiable results in experience. No one denies this, not even any metaphysician. Then what right has a metaphysician to claim that in his science essences may be abstracted from experienced facts and accepted with certitude as really existent and as a basis for further deductions about existents when they have not been put to the test of producing verifiable results in experience?

3. **Philosophy Deals With Existing Essence.** The answer to this challenge involves the most profound difference between knowledge of the philosophical order and knowledge of the order of natural science. Philosophy, as we have said above, is concerned with real causes and essences; natural science with phenomena and logical substitutes for real causes. From the real existence of phenomena given to the senses, the intellect, in philosophy, attains the existent essence which is manifested through the phenomena and is their real cause. It is known with certitude to be existent, because it has been proved to be the real cause of existing phenomena. It is apprehended, therefore, by the intellect as an existing essence. Consequently, when it is used as a basis of deduction, its necessary implications are known with certitude to be valid in the order of existence. Thus, for example, being-in-motion is known by experience to be an existent. Next, it is proved that motion demands as its necessary first cause a being which is pure actuality. But if the essential cause of being-in-motion is being which is Pure Act, then being which is Pure Act exists, since being-in-motion exists. Pure Act is known, therefore, as an existent. If anything further can be necessarily deduced from what is known of its essence, that is, from the fact that it is pure actuality, this further knowledge concerns the realm of the really existent. Thus, for example, we establish the attributes of God. The order of existence is attained at the outset *and is never left,* because the reasoning is from a perceived existent to its necessary cause, and from this existing cause to its necessary property. Hence, the conclusions are valid in the existential order, even though

they cannot be used to predict experimentally verifiable consequences.

4. Science Deals With Phenomenal Relations. One difference between the natural sciences and philosophy makes all the difference in the world between the conditions which their methods must fulfill. The sciences start from existing phenomena, but for the essence which is the real cause of these phenomena they substitute an hypothesis which is a provisional expression of an invariable relation among the phenomena or of a supposed invisible entity, for example, electrons in certain formations, operative throughout the stream of visible phenomena. In the former case no one supposes that the hypothesis (i.e., the formula) represents any real existent; in the latter case it is a provisional or hypothetical representation of a supposed or postulated phenomenal cause about whose real essence the scientist does not pretend to know anything; all he knows is its operational value in accounting for the relations among the observed phenomena. In neither case is the hypothesis meant to represent the essence of the necessary real cause of the phenomena, and consequently in neither case is the real existence of any determinate being, represented by the hypotheses, guaranteed by the real existence of the phenomena from which the hypothesis was formulated. And when deductions from the hypothesis yield verified results, no determinate cause is yet certified as a real feature of the existential order, because the hypothesis does not express a necessary real cause.

5. Sensible Verification Plays a Different Part in Each. Because of this difference between philosophic and scientific knowledge, sensible verification plays an entirely different part in each. Scientific laws, in themselves, do not touch substantial existence directly. Their truth consists in their ability to relate and predict phenomena. Even a scientific law which expresses the only conceivable hypothesis consistent with the facts still remains a logical statement of phenomenal relations — the only possible statement, but not the statement of a real cause. At best it states phenomenal antecedents of the phenomena to be explained. And since its truth is measured by its congruity with phenomenal facts, it must always make appeal to those facts and always remain provisional as long as the possibility of the discovery of new facts remains.[13] St. Thomas came very near to expressing this truth about the nature of scientific theory:

Reasoning may be brought forward for anything in a twofold way:

[13] V. E. Smith, *op. cit.*, pp. 101–103.

firstly, for the purpose of furnishing sufficient proof of some principle, as in natural science, where sufficient proof can be brought to show that the movement of the heavens is always of a uniform velocity. Reasoning is employed in another way, not as furnishing a sufficient proof of a principle, but as showing how the remaining effects are in harmony with an already posited principle; as in astronomy the theory of eccentrics and epicycles is considered as established, because thereby the sensible appearances of the heavenly movements can be explained; not however as if this proof were sufficient, since some other theory might explain them.[14] For although, when such hypotheses have been made, they appear to account for the phenomena, it is still not necessary to say that these hypotheses are true; because possibly the appearances of the stellar movements may be explained according to some method not yet understood by men.[15]

The two illustrations given by St. Thomas are interesting. The uniform velocity of the heavenly bodies is supposed to have been necessarily proved; the astronomical theory of eccentrics and epicycles, to be an hypothesis which all the known phenomena support. The latter illustration is well-nigh perfect, and St. Thomas' remark on it is perfect. The epicyclic theory postulated *invisible* spheres moving in such a way as to "explain" the *visible* movements of the heavenly bodies, and the supposed invisible movements were expressed in mathematical formulas. The theory accounted for every known visible movement. But even if *all* the visible movements were assumed to be known, the hypothesis of the invisible ones remains provisional; because some other explanation not yet dreamed of might explain the visible movements as well or better. The former illustration is less fortunate. It reveals that St. Thomas admitted necessary demonstrative proof into natural science; that is, that he admitted purely scientific laws which are known in final, unconditional form. Leaving aside the context of medieval physics in which he was thinking, the truth about his illustration would seem to be this: science, that is, astronomy, might prove the uniform velocity of the heavenly bodies in two ways; first, by recording these velocities repeatedly at different times and always getting the same results; second, by "explaining" these identical results by a mathematized theory of gravitation. The first way would not be what we ordinarily call a scientific law, but would be only the empiric data for the law; the second way would be a true empiriological law, but

---

[14] *S. Theol.*, I, 32, 1, ad 2.
[15] *In II De Caelo*, 17.

history testifies to how little hope we have of ever formulating such a law in final, unalterable form. The law will always get its truth-value from its congruity with the phenomena, and there will always remain the possibility of new phenomena or of a new explanation. That is why scientific method must always have recourse in the end to the phenomena.

Natural science, nevertheless, remains *science,* that is *cognitio certa per causas.* The causes which it deals with are in the phenomenal order, but they are truly determining conditions of the phenomena of which they are the causes. Their expression in a law or formula, tested and verified, does give to the mind an intelligible reason for the observed behaviors of things. This reason is descriptive rather than explanatory, giving no more, to explain what happened later, than something that happened before; or, in other words, giving phenomena of one level of observation to account for phenomena of another level. Nor is this reason ever final even on its own level, inasmuch as it always remains subject to adjustment. But within these limits it may have a very high degree of certitude. Only when its limits are forgotten, does a scientific law become unscientific.

6. Our Knowledge of Real Essences. The reason why philosophical conclusions do not have the provisional character which scientific conclusions have is, as we have repeated several times, the fact that philosophy attains true causes and essences in its conclusions. But this fact is precisely what many modern philosophers and scientists challenge. Essences and true causes can be known only by induction from phenomena. But inductive methods, say these moderns, can do no more than progressively narrow the field in which the essence and true cause are to be sought; they can never fix finally upon any single property as *the* essence or any single condition as *the* cause. That there is some truth in this contention, no one who understands inductive methods as they are actually used in science will deny. But the truth is a very partial truth. Methods like those formularized by J. S. Mill, for example, are not the beginning of induction, or its end. Induction begins with the immediate, though confused, grasp of some determinate nature in a perceived thing, and it ends with the attainment through abstraction of an explicit universal.[16] The methods of agreement and disagreement, and so forth, come in between, and function chiefly in

---

[16] Cf. Chapter XVIII, Section IV.

clearing the road for the final abstraction. The question is: Do we in this final abstraction ever grasp true essences and causes? The answer is: Yes, but not very many of them.

Essences are not known to us in themselves, that is, in their pure intelligibility. They are known to us, however, as they manifest themselves through sensible appearances, through the proper accidents of the substance. The essence as manifested through the sensible appearances is the *quiddity*. This quiddity is what we express by the definition. Essences are not known to us *per seipsas* because we do not directly apprehend the substantial form of a thing, its root principle of intelligibility. Yet we do conceive the essences of natural things because they are presented to us in their sensible effects, which we perceive and from which our intellect abstracts them as quiddities. Therefore, to say that we do not know essences in themselves means only this: that our intellect has no immediate, intuitive presentation of them like the immediate intuition which sight has of color. Yet it has a true conception of the essence in its grasp of the quiddity. While our conceptual knowledge does not exhaust the intelligibility of the essence, since it has no direct intuition of it, it does, through abstraction from its sensible species, attain to it as it is in itself. For the quiddity *is* the essence, in so far as the essence manifests itself through sensible appearances.[17]

7. **What Essences Do We Know?** Many of those who attack philosophy have an exaggerated conception of the claims of philosophy, and especially of metaphysics. Thomistic philosophy claims to know the *specific* essence of very few things in the natural order, and the *specific* cause of very few phenomena. But it claims that we can know *something essential* about a great many things, and that we can reach some *certain knowledge* about the real causes of things. We cannot, by any inductive methods or in any other way yet discovered, isolate the specific essence of a fly or a blade of grass or of oxygen; but we can say with certitude that it belongs to the essence of the fly to be sentient, to the essence of the grass to be alive, to the essence of oxygen to be capable of chemical combination with other substances. Similarly, we can say of man that he is both a material organism and a spiritual mind, we can say of all natural things that they are movable, of all events that they are caused, of all phenomena that they are grounded

---

[17] Étienne Gilson, *Realisme Thomiste et Critique de la Connaissance* (Paris: Vrin, 1939), pp. 222–224.

in some substance, of all natural operations that they are actualities of some power, and of everything that it is what it is. It is such essential notes as these, the broad unmistakable ones, that philosophy claims to know with certainty and finality; and it is on these that she erects her superstructure of demonstrations. She insists upon her just claims, but they are modest enough.

8. **Concluding Remarks.** Three remarks ought to be added. The first is that, just as natural science deals with materials which are more specialized, more complex, and more numerous than those dealt with by philosophy, so the philosophy of nature deals with more specialized, more complex, and more numerous data than does metaphysics. Consequently, the conclusions reached in the philosophy of nature, while they are in the order of real essences and real causes, do not have as great clarity, certainty, and finality as do the conclusions of metaphysics. The second remark is that we have not tried in the above paragraph to demonstrate the certain knowledge of real causes and essences which philosophy attains. That is the task of the separate chapters of the book. Some of those demonstrations may be faulty, but the way to show that is to point out the particular fault in any given case; it cannot be shown by legislating *a priori* that demonstration in the philosophy of nature and in metaphysics submit to every condition relevant to demonstration in the natural sciences. The third remark is that there is a certain lack of meaning in asking philosophy to verify its conclusions by new observations. The observations which it has used are limited to the general or universal characters of all perceptible and experiential things; these characters are verified by every observation. Since it did not take its start from a special group of measurable and numerically formulable phenomena, it cannot produce new and different phenomena to test its conclusions; yet these conclusions are constantly being verified by every new experience which exemplifies the contingency, the materiality, the passivity, and activity of natural things, by every new act of life, by every new sensation, thought, and free decision. To ask the philosopher to produce new phenomena is to ask him to destroy the order of nature and create a new order.

The metaphysician — or the sort that Thomists are, at any rate — is often accused of intellectual arrogance; of appealing to a superior kind of knowledge, a higher faculty which places itself above the tests and criteria to which the lesser breeds of knowing must submit. The metaphysician, it is said, appeals ultimately to his own thinking, and will submit that thinking to no controllable test. The metaphysician, of course, denies the charge. What he appeals to, he answers, is not his own thinking but certain evident principles common to and essential to all thinking and employed by the scientist in all his thinking. These principles, he says, can be used in thinking about other things than those which the scientist has chosen to think about. The metaphysician begs men to test his thinking by these principles. He is grieved when some of them refuse to do so on the ground that they have a method which is the only valid method of thinking and knowing, and if he will not use it, they will not bother with him. Then he is tempted to call *them* arrogant.[18] He has the greatest respect for their method; they will not even examine his. They use all the principles which he establishes, and then they discredit the science by which he established them. He is tempted to call them dogmatic; because he does not see how anyone can pronounce one method of attaining knowledge the only valid one, especially when this method voluntarily limits itself, by self-imposed conditions, to dealing with only a small part of all the things which invite man's investigation; he believes that it is permissible to stake out a limited field, but not to make believe afterwards that there cannot be anything beyond the stakes. He is asked, and he himself asks, questions which are perfectly intelligible and quite important and which no one has been brash enough to pronounce answerable by "the scientific method"; and he does not think that it is very much in accord with the true scientific temper of mind to pretend that such questions are meaningless because "scientific method" cannot answer them.

[18] These remarks are directed, of course, not against scientists, but against philosophers who seek to limit philosophy to the methods of the empiriological sciences.

CHAPTER XX

REASON AND FAITH

I. THE PROBLEM

1. If philosophy is something distinct from natural science on the one hand, it is also distinct from religion on the other. Yet a glance at the chapter headings of Part Four of this book will make it very clear that philosophy treats of many subjects which we are accustomed to think of as belonging to the province of faith or religion; throughout Part Four we shall be concerned with God and His action in the world. Furthermore, philosophy, by defining itself as the science of first causes, seems to set itself up as a universal wisdom, as if it were the ultimate knowledge. Where does this leave religion? Does philosophy presume to replace religion? Or, if we look at the matter conversely, since religion gives us the truth about God and man, what need is there for philosophy at all? If philosophy and religion are both concerned with God, what distinction is there between them and how are they related to each other? Can philosophy disagree with religion? Does philosophy have anything to say about revealed religion? Is philosophy of any service to religion? Can there be any such thing as a Christian philosophy?

Every philosopher who professes faith in revealed religion must face such questions as the above; indeed, today every philosopher must face them. They are essential problems for philosophy in a world where a religion makes a serious claim to be the revelation of God. The ancient Greeks, who gave us so much of our philosophy, never had occasion to inquire into the relations between philosophy and revealed religion because they never heard of revealed rligion. Not that the idea of divine revelation was unknown to them — it was rather perverted into a superstitious belief in the word of the oracles. But the *fact* of a divine revelation of religious truth for all men to accept and believe did not occur among the Greeks, but among the Jews. Some of the Greek philosophers, however, may have felt a need for, and reasoned to the possibility of, divine revelation. When Socrates, in the *Phaedo,* is advancing his proofs of the soul's immortality, Simmias, expressing his doubt of their absolute cogency, agrees with Socrates that the sincere man must carry this discussion as far as human reason can take him: "For he should persevere until he has achieved one of two things: either he should discover or be taught the truth about them; or, if this be impossible, I would have him take the best and most irrefragable of human theories, and let this be the raft upon which he sails through life — not without risk, as I admit, *if he cannot find some word of God which will more surely and safely carry him."*[1]

This word of God had long before been given to the Jews; and four centuries after Plato wrote the *Phaedo,* the Word of God Himself came among men, becoming a man to teach men the truth which would more surely and safely carry them. This truth contained all that man needed to know in order to please God and save his soul. But philosophy seemed to contain a great deal of truth too; and its truth came, not from God, but from men — from men, indeed, who were pagans. Every believer in the word of God, therefore, who wished also to possess the philosophical wisdom of the Greeks faced the problem of reconciling this human wisdom with divine wisdom. Within Jewish, Christian, and Mohammedan circles, for a good part of the early Middle Ages, controversy was waged over what the true relations are between philosophy and religion, between reason and faith.

2. Medieval Views. Five distinct doctrines may be distinguished among the Christian theologians up to the thirteenth century. Some theologians were simply anti-philosophical. Divine revelation was the truth, and human reasonings were presumptuous pretenders inspired by Satan; Christ had destroyed "the wisdom of the Greeks." A second group, the "rationalists," took a diametrically opposite position: Divine revelation is the truth, but human reason is capable of understanding and demonstrating this whole truth. A third group, the Augustinians, subordinated rational truth entirely to revealed truth; they had no contempt for human wisdom, but they gave it no function other than that of supporting, defending, and clarifying the truths of revelation. Philosophy became for them, simply a tool of Sacred Science; or rather Sacred Science became the sole true philosophy. In the thirteenth cen-

[1] Plato, *Phaedo,* 85.

tury a new conception, inspired by the Arabian Averroes, was propounded. Philosophical truth and religious truth, this opinion held, are entirely independent — so independent that the same thing may be true philosophically and false religiously. Thus, for example, Aristotle had proved that the world always existed, while religion teaches that it had a beginning. Both "truths" are true: one is known by reason, the other believed by faith. This remarkable doctrine made St. Thomas quite angry. It is not merely an error, but the canonization of falsehood. It strikes at the heart of both reason and faith, because it makes the true identical with the false and thus corrupts the very object of reason and faith. It was Modernism in the High Middle Ages, making its first bid to corrupt the intellect of man. St. Thomas, St. Bonaventure, and their supporters defeated it — for the time being. It found a better reception in the nineteenth century, after the irrationalism of Rousseau and the "criticism" of Kant had prepared men's minds for assenting simultaneously to contradictories. The fifth solution of the problem — the solution which has become the traditional Catholic attitude — was that reason and faith, philosophy and religion, both give the truth. Revealed religion gives all the truths which man needs to know in order to save his soul, and among these are many which reason could never have discovered. Reason gives truths about nature and about God, the Cause of nature; but of God as He is in His essence it can say very little. Besides, it gives many truths about nature and man which have not been revealed by God because they have no relations to man's salvation. Finally, the truths of reason and the truths of revelation can never be in conflict, because only the false can contradict the true. This was the position adopted by St. Thomas.

3. **Contemporary Views: Naturalism or Secularism.** There are many conflicting views on the question today. Dogmatic naturalists, of course, deny the possibility of any such thing as divine revelation, and consider religion as merely superstition or "the opium of the people." On the other hand, many naturalists believe that religion has a real and valuable role to play in the lives of men, but they reject the possibility that any religion can have been made known by a revelation from God. Belief in such a revealed religion is, indeed, the ultimate heresy against the naturalist faith. According to this faith, religion is good if by religion you mean belief in and loyalty to the ideals and values which have proved their worth in the actual lives of men and society; but it is evil if you mean that it is something supernatural.

Many persons who cannot be classified under any philosophical label believe pretty much what naturalists believe; that is, that religion is the sum of all the beliefs, ideals, and purposes which have proved themselves to have an uplifting influence upon individual and social life.

The question, whether these beliefs and ideals are true, that is to say, whether they correspond to fact, receives different answers. Some naturalists answer that the question is a false question, because it uses the term "true" with a significance that is irrelevant to the context or universe of discourse in which the question is asked. Truth in reference to religious belief does not mean agreement with fact; fact is the province of science, not of religion. Truth in the context of discourse about religion means the valuable, that is, what is good for man and society; religion has values, not facts, for its province. What does it matter, for example, whether two men agree or disagree about whether God exists, in the sense in which the physical world exists, as long as they do agree that tolerance is Godlike and bigotry is diabolical? Does not history show that insistence on the fact-character of religious beliefs has divided men and produced intolerance and persecution? A prime duty of religious men in our atomic age is to destroy forever this dogmatic "true fact" conception of religion; only when it has been destroyed can true religion come into its own. What is true religion? It is men of good will co-operating in the work of improving human life all over the world. This view of religion is fairly common today. It is the religion of secularism. Secularism is the perennial enemy of supernatural religion, but it is only in fairly recent times that it has become a widespread and conscious philosophy of religion.

4. Modernism. Another answer to the question, whether religious beliefs and doctrines are true, is given by *modernists*. A modernist might be defined as someone who professes belief in divine revelation and who belongs to a church which claims to teach the truths of divine revelation, but who does not exactly believe that the revealed truths of his faith are true or that they are revealed. Modernism among Catholics had a brief but spectacular life at the end of the last and the beginning of the present century. It died a sudden death with the publication of Pope Pius X's letter *Lamentabile,* his encyclical *Pascendi gregis,* and the excommunication of those modernist leaders who refused to retract their teaching. But modernism within Protestant churches antedated Catholic modernism and has outlived it; indeed, contemporary Protestantism becomes ever more modernist in character. Further, the

thinking of many Catholics is not unaffected by the conditions which make for modernism among Protestants. In a word, modernism is a very present evil.

Modernism gets its name from the fact that it is an effort to modernize religion, that is, to bring dogmas and ecclesiastical institutions into harmony with modern scientific knowledge and with modern social needs. Its aim is, in the words of one of the Catholic modernists, Abbé Loisy, "To adapt Catholicism to the intellectual, moral, and social needs of the day." "All Catholic theology, even in its most fundamental principles, the general philosophy of religion, divine law, and the laws that govern our knowledge of God, come up for judgment before this new court of assize." The "new court of assize" is modern science and philosophy. The apparent conflicts between the old religious beliefs and the new scientific "knowledge," for example, the Darwinian doctrine of the evolution of living species, and the thoroughly mechanistic character of scientific theories in the nineteenth century, plus the influence of the "Higher Criticism" of the Bible, seemed to certain Liberals, both Catholic and Protestant, to open a yawning abyss between the modern mind and the traditional religion. No longer could they take the revelations of the Scriptures literally. Some deserted religion. Others, and these were the modernists, clung to the old faith, but "reinterpreted" it to bring it into harmony with the "new knowledge." The traditional conceptions of revelation and dogma had to be radically changed so that they would not conflict with science, so that they would be able to remain valid in a world of changing needs; and, especially, they must be brought under the universal law of evolution.

5. The Essence of Modernism. The primary condition for the modernist reinterpretation of dogma is to bring religious beliefs under the "new philosophy." Now, according to this new philosophy, science, which is the only real knowledge, deals entirely with material, sensible things, that is to say, with phenomena. The suprasensible and immaterial is entirely beyond man's grasp. Consequently, the conception of faith as a free intellectual assent to objectively true, but supramundane realities, must be abandoned. Faith in the supernatural must find some other foundation than intellect, for intellect is competent only in the realm of the material and sensible. This new foundation is feeling — man's feeling for God, his inner aspiration for perfection. There is no such thing as Revelation in the sense of a direct communication of supernatural truths from God to man. Rather, it is man's feeling for

God that is the source of revelation. The human soul, reaching upward toward the unknowable God, endeavors to interpret its spiritual experiences and sentiments in intellectual formulas. These formulas, approved by the Church, are our ecclesiastical dogmas, or truths of faith. They are not literally truths; they merely symbolize the unknowable, but can give us no real knowledge concerning it. Their value lies in their usefulness in preserving faith, and they preserve it as long as they are relevant to man's needs. When they have outlived their usefulness they ought to be abandoned. Hence, the truly religious soul will strive constantly to bring the Church to modernize its teachings.[2]

From this account it is clear, as Father Vermeersch writes,[3] that the essence of modernism is the perversion of dogma. The only source of dogma, according to modernists, is private consciousness; dogmas come into being with the rise of new needs and pass away with the passing of these needs. The truth of a dogma is not its conformity to a real fact or object, but its capacity to satisfy a momentary need of the religious sentiment. The inevitable result of modernism is the destruction of dogma.

It is true that before Kant, Jean Jacques Rousseau had spilt the poison of irrationalism and romanticism into the European mind, and he, perhaps, has had the greatest single influence in producing the strange mentality which was capable of conceiving and accepting modernism. But Kant had supplied the modernists with a philosophical foundation for their heresy. In the *Critique of Practical Reason* he restored to the human mind the access to the suprasensible which he had taken from it in the first *Critique,* but he restored it not to the intellect but to the will. By this maneuver, and by making the moral needs of man the sole source of faith in God, he laid down the foundation on which the modernists were to build. He had taught them (1) that the intellect can attain no knowledge of the suprasensible, and (2) that the foundation of faith is the heart rather than the mind. He had even anticipated the whole doctrine of modernism in his *Religion Within the Bounds of Mere Reason.* Finally, the direct historical connection between Kantianism and modernism is obvious in the two Protestant theologians who are called founders of modernism, namely, Friedrich Schleiermacher (1768–1834) and Albrecht Ritschl (1822–1889). Both

[2] *Catholic Encyclopedia,* Vol. XIII, p. 1, article, "Revelation."
[3] *Ibid.,* Vol. X, pp. 416 ff., article, "Modernism."

were Kantians in philosophy and used Kantianism as essential elements in their theology.

6. **Schleiermacher.** There were two primary factors in the development of Schleiermacher's religious philosophy. The first was his deep sense of the intensity and primacy of the individual's feeling. The second was his devotion to the critical philosophy of Immanuel Kant. More emphatically even than Kant, he asserted that all ideas which transcend experience possess *symbolic value only,* do not constitute objective knowledge. His new theology was the harmonization of two convictions: that the innermost life of man is lived in feeling, which alone can bring man into immediate relationship with God; and that the Kantian philosophy has established the definite conditions and limits to which human knowledge is subject.

To combine these two convictions he had to reinterpret radically the ideas of Christian theology. His fundamental conception in this reinterpretation — the conception that makes him the father of modernism — was his view that that which philosophy allows no objective validity as speculative truth, need not on that account lose its religious value, if it can be interpreted as the symbolic expression of an experience lived by man in his innermost life of feeling.[4] Hence, the dogmas of religion, since they are not phenomena, must be reinterpreted so as to be understood, not as statements of objective facts, but as symbols which may be used in deepening and liberating the individual's life of feeling. Feeling, or religious experience, is the dogma-creating principle. Dogmatic formulas are merely intellectual symbolizations of these experiences.

The true meaning of this new notion of dogma appears in Schleiermacher's application of it to particular doctrines. Take, for example, the existence of God. In what way does God come into experience? Religion, says Schleiermacher, consists in immediate consciousness that everything finite exists in and through the infinite. In feeling, one's full individuality can unfold itself, while at the same time this individuality is penetrated by the infinite. The culmination of this experience of one's own individuality penetrated by the infinite is the feeling of absolute dependence, which is the purest religion. As soon as reflection, following feeling, seeks an expression of that on which our entire being is dependent, the feeling becomes the consciousnesss of God, so

[4] Höffding, *History of Modern Philosophy* (London: Macmillan, 1924), Vol. II, p. 195.

that, Schleiermacher writes, "the true God denotes the *whence* of our sensible and self-active existence." In a very similar way individual feeling gives us the idea of Christ, the divine, sinless, Redeemer. The Christian soul in its innermost life feels something which hinders its consciousness of God and causes it to suffer. The experience that that which so hindered it has now been cleared away is the experience of redemption. Only by regarding Christ as the historically revealed, sinless prototype of Christian souls can the Christian explain his consciousness of redemption. Just as God is the *whence* of the absolute feeling of dependence, so is Christ the *whence* of the feeling of redemption.

Schleiermacher similarly reinterprets all traditional Christian doctrines. All dogmas are deduced from reflection on states of immediate feeling. The impulse for expression causes us to seek words and images to express the feeling, which is in itself inexpressible. Religious conceptions, therefore, are symbolizations of immediate feeling-states. Hence, all those symbols which cannot be traced back to immediate feeling-states must be rejected. Among those that Schleiermacher rejects on this ground are the personality of God, Creation, the first man, and the story of the origin of sin in the human race.

7. Ritschl. Albrecht Ritschl holds almost as important a place in modern liberal Protestant theology as does Schleiermacher. He conceived religion as a *value theory*. Following Kant, he abandoned the attempt to obtain theoretical knowledge about reality. We can know only how reality acts in our experience. Since the human reason has not the power of arriving at a scientific knowledge of God, religion can have only a practico-moral foundation. Religious knowledge, or faith, is derived from the practical needs of our soul, and rests upon judgments of value. These judgments of value affirm nothing concerning the nature of divine things, but are concerned solely with the usefulness of religious ideas; not what a thing is in itself, but what it is for us, is what matters. The reality that God is in Himself remains forever unknown; the important thing is that in our experience the divine reality acts like a father toward his children. The "truth" of a religious doctrine lies in its *value* in satisfying our need for spiritual happiness. Christian faith exists only through personal experience, and therefore the objects of faith are not presented to the mind from without by a divine revelation as an authoritative rule of faith, but become vividly present for the Christian through subjective experience. Man is consciously religious if he has a moral purpose to which he has committed himself. By adhering to the hypothesis of a God working with him, he can make the world a means to his own spiritual growth, and thus verify that hypothesis and actually find God. God is that power which brings us the moral victory, and since we find such a principle and power in Christ's gospel, for us Christ is divine.[5]

It is hardly necessary to point out how strong the influence of Kant's philosophy is in this system. The truths of faith arise out of man's moral struggle; they are less truths than postulates of the moral life. God and Christ are Kantian transcendent Ideas which are not objects of knowledge but are the unifying conceptions that give meaning to the moral life. Ritschl's value theory of religion had and still has tremendous influence.

II. BASIS FOR A CORRECT SOLUTION OF THE PROBLEM

At the time when St. Thomas Aquinas lived, the problem of reason and faith presented itself in a somewhat different form from that in which it presents itself to us today. Today, superficially, religious faith seems to be on the defensive, threatened by reason; whereas in St. Thomas' day it was reason that seemed on the defensive, trying to save itself from being swallowed up by revealed religion. The mental environment of the learned in the thirteenth century was thoroughly Catholic and theological; today it is largely nonreligious and scientific. But it is only superficially that the problem has changed; essentially it is the same. And the solution set forth by St. Thomas is just as valid today as it was in the thirteenth century. The basis of that solution is a right understanding of the nature of reason, revelation, and faith.

1. **The Nature of Human Reason.** The first step in the solution of the problem is an understanding of what reason is. Modern philosophers have ignored or denied the distinction between the senses and reason, and that is one of the chief causes for the utter confusion about the relations of reason and faith. Reason, or intellect, St. Thomas taught, following Plato and Aristotle, is essentially different from the senses. Intellect or reason is concerned with the essence and being of things, while the senses are concerned with their appearances. The intellect is capable of forming ideas of immaterial things, such as democracy, equality, virtue, liberty, the soul, God. The senses form no images of these. The intellect *judges,* saying, for example, that lying is wrong;

[5] Cf. J. H. Randall, Jr., *The Making of the Modern Mind* (New York: Houghton, Mifflin, 1940), pp. 563–564.

the senses do not judge — a lie sounds the same as the truth. If lies sounded wrong no one would ever be deceived by a lie. The intellect *reasons*, proving, for example, that the square on the hypotenuse of a right triangle is equal to the sum of the squares of the other two sides. The senses do nothing that even faintly resembles reasoning. All these things we have studied at length in Chapter X.

Reason or intellect, therefore, is not, as the ancient Sophists held, and as Hume, Kant, and the modern positivists held, limited to sensible, material objects. It can know spiritual or immaterial things. It can and certainly does form ideas of them, and, therefore, it certainly has the right to ask whether any realities corresponding to these ideas exist. And finally, it can actually prove the reality of some of these spiritual things. Here, then, is the first step toward the solution of the reason-faith problem: Man is rational; his knowledge is not confined to the sensible and the material, but can grasp the spiritual; his reason is not a mere instrument for dealing with phenomena or appearances, but its true object is being or reality or the essence of things in themselves.

2. The Limitations of Human Reason. The second step is an understanding of the limitations of human reason. Emphatic as St. Thomas was in maintaining that man has intellect as well as sense, he was just as emphatic in holding that all man's knowledge *begins* in his senses; or, in other words, that man's intellect gets all the materials for its thoughts through his senses. Man is partly material himself, since he is not pure spirit but part body, and he lives in a material world. He is not born with his ideas ready made; but, as the whole process of learning shows, he must, in order to think and exercise his intelligence, collect data from the world around him by using his eyes, ears, and hands. So whatever beings his mind may reach out to in its reflections and speculation, it always begins with data collected by the senses from material things.

This fact is very important in the philosophy of St. Thomas and in connection with the reason-faith problem. It means that man has no direct experience of purely spiritual or immaterial things. The nearest that he comes to it is in his knowledge of his own soul; but even this knowledge is indirect, for he does not grasp his soul in itself, directly perceiving its nature, but grasps it only through its acts of thinking, feeling, desiring, willing, etc. That is why, although he is conscious of his soul, he does not clearly see its nature. To know its nature he must reflect upon its actions, and reason out what kind of thing it must be in order to perform the kinds of acts that it does perform. The difficulty is still greater in regard to other spiritual beings, for example, God. Man can reason to a certain knowledge of God's existence, but he cannot reason to anything like an adequate knowledge of God's nature. To form an adequate idea of the nature of anything it is necessary to grasp the thing as it is in itself. But since man knows spiritual beings only through his knowledge of material things, he never grasps them in themselves and consequently his ideas of them are very inadequate.

In summarizing the above we can say that St. Thomas' teaching about human reason in relation to spiritual being is the following: (1) man, through reason, is capable of knowing immaterial or spiritual beings; (2) but, because man has no *direct* experience of purely spiritual beings, the knowledge that his reason can attain about them is very limited and inadequate.

3. **The Nature of Revelation.** So much, for the present, on the Thomistic doctrine of reason. We turn now to the other factors in the problem, revelation and faith. We ask first, What is revelation? We have seen that the modernists conceive revelation to be the individual's inner experience of spiritual need and of a basis for its fulfillment. This certainly is not the historical Christian conception of revelation. To Catholics, and to Protestants who have not "liberalized" and "modernized" their religion, revelation means the manifestation or disclosure by God to men of some truth about Himself, a truth which He proposes to their intellects and obliges them to accept on the ground of His own supreme authority. Such truths, for example, are the three great mysteries of the Christian religion: the Holy Trinity, the Incarnation, and the Redemption. Christians accept and believe such revealed truth, not because of some inner feeling of insufficiency which belief in these doctrines removes, but because they have God's own word for the truth of the doctrine. And when they say that these doctrines are "true," they do not mean that they are valuable in satisfying some spiritual need, but that they express what are actual facts: it is a fact that God is one God in three Persons, Father, Son, and Holy Ghost; it is a fact that the Second Person, the Son, was incarnated as the God-Man, Jesus Christ; it is a fact that this God-Man redeemed the fallen human race from everlasting banishment from God by His death on the cross.

Two questions arise in respect to revelation, and both are relevant to the problem of the relations of reason and faith. The first is: Is revelation possible? The second is: What is the nature of the act of faith by which man assents to revealed truth?

4. The Possibility of Revelation. The first question may be answered briefly. Revelation is possible from the side of God, because, as philosophy itself can prove, God knows Himself perfectly, and being Man's Creator and Ruler, can manifest His knowledge of Himself to man. It is possible on the side of man, because man is endowed with intellect or reason, which is itself an immaterial faculty capable of grasping, though inadequately, the nature of immaterial being. Hence, divine truth is not something entirely disproportionate to man's nature, and though this nature may not be capable of demonstrating *by itself* a given divine truth, it can receive and accept this truth. Man can, therefore, by an act of faith, accept divine revelation. Though man's acceptance of revelation is a supernatural act, it is founded upon man's natural faculties; for if man did not have reason, no revelation could be made to him, since he would have no power to grasp truth, whether aided or unaided. Hence, the essential condition for faith is reason, and St. Thomas never forgot that in solving the problems of the relations of reason and faith.[6]

5. The Nature of Faith. St. Thomas located the intellectual assent given in the act of faith, or believing, midway between two other assents, knowledge and opinion. We *know* a truth scientifically or demonstratively when the reasons for its truth are understood by us and our intellect has no choice but to pronounce it true; the assent of the intellect is necessitated by the intrinsic evidence of the truth itself, and is given with certitude and firmness. We have an *opinion* about something when, because of evidence which is only partial and not compelling, or because of conflicting evidence, we hesitatingly and provisionally assent to something as true, while fearing that the opposite may be true. Faith agrees with knowledge inasmuch as its assent is certain and firm, not hesitant and fluctuating like opinion. But it differs from knowledge and resembles opinion inasmuch as it is an assent given to something not understood and not evident.[7]

6. Part Played by the Will. An act of will moving the intellect to give its assent is required in an act of faith, whereas in the case of knowledge it is the evidence of the object itself which alone moves the

---

[6] *Cf. Con. Gen.*, I, 3.
[7] *In Boet. de Trin.*, III. 1, c: *S. Theol.*, II–II, 2, 1, c.

intellect. Knowledge is of things seen, but "faith is of what appears not." In an act of faith or belief the intellect assents, not because it sees the truth to which it assents, either in itself or as reduced to other truths already known, but because the will commands it to assent.[8]

> Faith signifies the assent of the intellect to that which is believed. Now the intellect assents to a thing in two ways. First, through being moved to assent by its very object, which is known either by itself (as in the case of first principles, which are held by the habit of understanding), or through something else already known (as in the case of conclusions, which are held by the habit of science). Secondly, the intellect assents to something, not through being sufficiently moved to this assent by its proper object, but through an act of choice, whereby it turns voluntarily to one side rather than to the other. Now if this be accompanied by doubt and fear of the opposite side, there will be opinion; while, if there be certainty and no fear of the other side, there will be faith.
>
> Now those things are said to be seen which, of themselves, move the intellect or the senses to knowledge of them. Therefore it is evident that neither faith nor opinion can be of things seen either by the senses or by the intellect.[9]

7. Faith Is Not Blind. To say that in an act of faith the intellect assents because the will moves it to do so is not at all the same as saying that faith is an act of will and is blind. In the first place, the actual assent to the truth proposed is an act of the intellect. Second, the will, before it can move the intellect, must be itself moved by some motives; and these, like any motives, are presented to it by the intellect. In the third place, a true act of faith, as understood by St. Thomas, is always made on account of intelligible reasons or grounds of belief, and never blindly. These reasons are not rationally compelling, as a geometrical proof or a physical demonstration is, since they do not make the truth proposed for belief evident in itself. They are extrinsic to that truth rather than intrinsic. They adequately vouch for its certainty, yet do not explain it. They make clear why it ought to be believed without making clear why it is true; just as the word of the scientific authority makes clear to the non-scientist that he must accept as true the proposition that the terrible power of the atom bomb is due to the fission of uranium or plutonium atoms, though it does not make clear why this is so. The scientist's word is sufficient ground for

[8] *S. Theol.*, II–II, 4, 2, c and ad 1.
[9] *Ibid.*, II–II, 1, 4, c (*Basic Writings of St. Thomas Aquinas*, ed. Anton C. Pegis [New York: Random House, 1945], Vol. II, p. 1060). Cf. *In Boet. de Trin.*, III, 1, c.

belief, although an extrinsic ground; and the non-scientist's assent is not blind, although he does not understand the proposition to which he assents. The act of religious faith, as understood by St. Thomas, is always made for good reasons known by the intellect; an act of faith made without good reason would not be an act of the virtue of faith, but a sin against that virtue.[10]

8. Supernatural Faith. The nature of belief may be summarized thus: We believe a truth when, lacking understanding of its intrinsic reasons, we firmly hold it to be true because of some ground of credibility external to the truth itself, for example, the word of an authority; in belief our intellect does not assent necessarily, but freely, under the movement of our will, which is itself moved by some extrinsic movement. In *supernatural faith,* that is, belief in divinely revealed truth, the psychological character of the act remains the same as in belief in general, but supernatural factors must come into play in order that the act may be done. For the act of faith raises man above his own nature and hence requires more than his natural powers. It is impossible without the help of God moving man inwardly by grace.[11] In the act of faith the believer's intellect, enlightened by the supernatural light of faith and moved by the will, which is itself prompted by the grace of faith, freely assents with complete certitude, on the ground of God's infallible testimony, to a truth which it cannot understand or demonstrate.

9. Conclusions. Up to this point we have merely been laying down a basis upon which to attack the problem of the relations of reason and faith. We may, however, here draw two conclusions from the above considerations. First, the act of believing something which we do not understand and cannot demonstrate is a common human act and is often done with perfect rational justification. Second, if God

[10] Comparisons, such as the one above, of religious faith to the belief given on the word of experts in science, history, etc., are helpful, but can be very misleading. My assent to a scientific proposition on the word of a scientist is superficially similar to my assent to a religious proposition on the word of God, since in both cases I believe on the word of one who knows; but the two acts are really worlds apart. I assent to the scientific proposition because it has been demonstrated and verified by men, and could be by me; I assent to the religious proposition while knowing that neither I nor any man can demonstrate or verify it in this life. "Faith is of things which appear not," and any explanation of it which would strive to make it similar to an assent whose object is demonstrable would falsify its very nature. The point of the illustration above is merely to show that unquestioning assent to what is not in fact demonstrated or understood is a common and perfectly rational human act.

[11] *S. Theol.,* II–II, 6, 1, c.

exists, and if there are adequate signs[12] that He has revealed to men some truths which surpass their power of demonstration and understanding, assent to these truths on His word is a perfectly rational act and, indeed, an obligatory one.

III. THE RELATIONS OF REASON AND FAITH

1. The Necessity of Revelation and Faith. When we speak of the necessity of divine revelation, we do not mean any absolute necessity which compels God to manifest Himself to man. God is perfectly free and nothing can compel or necessitate His action in respect to creatures. By the necessity of divine revelation we mean a hypothetical necessity contingent upon God's own plan for men; we mean that it is necessary for man that God reveal certain divine truths to him if man is to attain the end for which God created him. We mean that man's natural reason alone is an insufficient instrument for the attainment of the truths which man must know in order to save his soul, and that man requires, in addition to his reason, faith in the divinely revealed word. This necessity of revelation and faith arises, not from man's nature, but from the end or destiny appointed to man by God, an end far surpassing the power and competency of human nature.[13] The necessity of faith, therefore, arises from the infinite generosity of God toward men; if man were destined for nothing beyond what befits his nature, he would have no need of faith for he would have no need to know what lies beyond human reason.

The end of man is beatitude, which consists in the full vision of divine truths. This is an end beyond the grasp of reason. Yet, in order to direct his actions toward this end man must know it to be his end and must know what is required of him that he may attain it. Furthermore, he must possess this knowledge of his end and the things pertaining to it from almost the beginning of his life, since even in childhood he is obliged to seek his end, long before he can come to know by reason even those truths about God which reason can attain. Hence, it is clear that the light of reason is insufficient, and that man needs the light of revelation.

> Since, therefore, the end of human life is beatitude, which consists in the full knowledge of divine truths, it is necessary that human life

[12] Inquiry about these signs and evidences is the work of apologetics, not philosophy. Philosophy treats only of the essence of the problem, that is to say, the rationality of the act of faith.

[13] *In Boet. de Trin.*, III, 1, ad 2.

be directed to this beatitude by a possession of divine truths by faith from the start, truths which man can hope to know fully in the ultimate state of human perfection.[14]

2. Revelation of Truths Attainable by Reason. In the revelations which God has made to man and which are to be found in Christian doctrine, there are some truths which are attainable by natural reason; such, for example, are the existence, unity, omnipotence, and providence of God. There are others which are above the grasp of reason, such as the Trinity and the Incarnation. It is easy enough to see why the latter must be revealed: man must know them, and he cannot know them by reason alone. But what about the former? Why should those be revealed, since they are demonstrable? In his commentary on the *Trinity* of Boethius, St. Thomas gives five reasons, repeating them from the great Jewish philosopher Maimonides, why these truths are revealed. First, even though these truths are attainable by the light of natural reason, they are deep, and subtle, and the reasonings required to establish them are difficult and not within the capacity of all men. Therefore, lest any man be without some knowledge of them, they are revealed so that all may hold them by faith at least. Second, no one can attain these truths by reason until he is mature; whereas some knowledge of them is required of him at all times. Third, the rational knowledge of God is the highest knowledge that human reason can attain, and much knowledge of natural things must precede it. Even this preliminary knowledge is never acquired by a great number of persons; yet all are required to know about God. Hence, revelation of these truths is necessary. Fourth, many men are not so fitted with intellectual gifts as to be able ever to attain rational knowledge of God. And, finally, most men are too occupied with the affairs of life in this world even to pursue the studies necessary to know God through reason.[15]

3. Answers to Objections. Against these views of St. Thomas many objections were offered. A few of them have a remarkably modern sound. One objection is directed against the revelation of truths knowable by reason, and is based on the nature of knowledge and faith. We *know* something when we know it to be true and understand the reasons for its truth; but we *believe* something when we assent to its

---

[14] *In Boet. de Trin.*, III, 1, c, translation of Sister Rose Emmanuella Brennan, *The Trinity and the Unicity of the Intellect* (St. Louis: Herder, 1946), p. 77. Cf. *S. Theol.*, I, 1, 1, c.

[15] *In Boet. de Trin.*, III, 1, c. Cf. *Con. Gen.*, I, 4.

truth without understanding the reasons for that truth. Consequently we cannot know and believe the same thing; and therefore no truth can be at once an object of reason and faith. Hence, those divine truths knowable by reason cannot also be revealed to faith. St. Thomas answers that, while it is true that the same person cannot know and believe the same truth at the same time, yet he can believe it at first and later come to know it; as, for example, one who first believes in God's existence and later demonstrates it. Furthermore, the same truth may at the same time be an object of faith for some, for example, the ignorant, and an object of knowledge for others, for example, the learned.[16]

4. The Rationality of Faith. The more modern sounding objections attack the very right of man to accept any truth on faith, and even the right of God to impose the obligation of faith upon man. They represent faith as the abdication of reason. Their basic thought, put in modern terms, is this: man has a certain instrument and method of attaining truth; the instrument is his natural powers of perception and reason, and the method is to accept as true only what is evident to experience and reason; to adopt any other instrument or any other method is to abandon and betray reason and to cast aside his only means of attaining truth; and he does just this when he accepts something as true through faith. One antagonist of St. Thomas expressed it as follows: "As Dionysius says, it is evil for man to exist apart from reason; but man in adhering to faith departs from reason, and in this he is even accustomed to despise reason; therefore it seems that such a way is evil for men."[17] Another expressed it even more clearly:

> Whenever there is acceptance of knowledge without judgment, the road to error is easy; but we have in ourselves no ability by which we are able to judge of the things which we accept by faith, since our natural judgment does not extend to truths of this kind, as they exceed reason; therefore evidently the road to error is an easy one for us, and so it would appear harmful rather than useful for man that he should be directed to God by the way of faith.[18]

In answering this objection we shall direct our remarks to our own modern opponents rather than to the medieval opponents of St. Thomas; yet it is the thought of St. Thomas which we shall express.[19]

[16] Cf. *S. Theol.*, II-II, 1, 5, c and ad 4. Cf. *ibid.*, I, 2, 2, ad 1.
[17] *In Boet. de Trin.*, III, 1, obj. 5, trans. Brennan, *op. cit.*, p. 75.
[18] *Ibid.*, obj. 4.
[19] Cf. *Con. Gen.*, I, 5, 6, and 7; *In Boet. de Trin.*, III, 1, answers to objections.

The Christian stand on faith is perfectly rational, given its premises. Man's reason is limited, and consequently there are truths about God which man can neither demonstrate nor comprehend. If God has chosen to reveal these truths, natural reason itself demands that assent be given to them. It would be a mark of stupidity for man, seeking the beatitude for which God has destined him, to ignore the easiest and most certain way to it. This certain way is the way of faith in God's word; for reason flounders in error and uncertainty when it seeks by itself to discover the ultimate purpose of human life. What the Angelic Doctor wrote in the thirteenth century can be supported by much more evidence today:

> No one can attain to such knowledge without danger, since human investigation, because of the weakness of our intellect, is prone to error; and this is clearly shown by reference to those philosophers who, in attempting to find out the purpose of human life by way of reason, did not find in themselves the true method, and so fell into many and shameful errors; and so greatly did they differ among themselves that scarcely two or three among them all were in agreement on any one question; yet, on the other hand, we see that by faith many peoples are brought to the acceptance of one common belief.[20]

5. Faith Has Adequate Grounds. We can hear the modern naturalist answer that disagreement in freedom is better than agreement in imposed belief. We can only reply that we do not agree with him, since the belief in question is the one truth, imposed by the word of God. It is almost impossible for Christian and naturalist to argue the question. The latter does not believe that there has been any divine revelation, or at any rate, that there is any way of telling what it is if there has been. The Christian believes that there has been, and that there are signs by which it can be recognized. From the naturalist's position, his arguments against the rationality of faith seem compelling; and many naturalists must be sincerely puzzled that anyone can fail to see the cogency of these arguments. But from the Christian position, the naturalist's arguments are puerile and his position absurd. If God has granted man a revelation of divine truth, of the purpose and end of human existence, and has set certain signs by which this revelation may be known, then the contention that disagreement in freedom is better than agreement in imposed belief amounts to the absurdity that it is better to be lost on bypaths than to pursue the one road to your

[20] *In Boet. de Trin.*, III, 1, ad 3. Cf. the quotation from the *Phaedo* in Section I above.

desired goal. And to hold, as naturalists do, that the acceptance by faith of truths which cannot be demonstrated is the betrayal of reason, seems to the Christian both silly and blasphemous. It seems silly because it sets up an opposition between reason and truth and attempts to protect the freedom of reason from the tyranny of truth. Reason wants no such protection; a scientist, having at long last discovered some difficult truth, asks no freedom to reject it. Reason is perfectly docile to truth, and only the irrational parts of man's mind want to be free in respect to truth. The believer's assent in his act of faith is given in docility to truth, and he wants no freedom which would enable him to reject the truth. The naturalist view seems blasphemous; because, ruling out *a priori* the legitimacy of faith, it is really placing a restriction and a condition upon God rather than upon men. It is equivalent to telling God that if He wishes us to believe His word, He must meet the same standards of evidence and proof that we require of anyone else; it places God even below the expert, whose word we accept in the field of his competency.

The obvious reason why the non-believer cannot understand the true relations of reason and faith is the fact that he has not faith. He is dealing with two terms, one of which he does not understand. It will inevitably seem to him that the assent given in the act of faith is an assent given on grounds known to be insufficient; because the only kind of assent which he recognizes is that given because of the evidence of the object assented to. Since this assent is an act of knowledge or demonstration, where the evidence is compelling and clearly understood, then the assent of faith must be, he thinks, simply a certain and unhesitating acceptance of something as true when in fact there are admittedly no sufficient grounds for such a firm acceptance. Naturally he considers such an assent as irrational. What he fails to consider is that faith has its own grounds for assent, as clearly seen and as valid as those of demonstrative knowledge but of a different sort. The act of faith is not the accepting of something as if it were demonstrated when you know that it is not demonstrated; it is the acceptance of something as true because of adequate grounds for assenting to its truth even though this truth is not demonstrated. But in order to see the adequacy of the grounds for assent, the light of faith illumining the intellect is necessary; and in order to put forth the assent in spite of the absence of demonstration, the grace of faith moving the will is necessary. Because the non-believer has not faith, he lacks this light and grace; and hence he cannot see that the assent of faith is based on clearly understood reasons and adequate motives.

Those things that come under faith can be considered in two ways. First, in particular, and in this way they cannot be seen and believed at the same time, as was shown above. Secondly, in general, that is, under the common aspect of credibility; and in this way they are seen by the believer. For he would not believe unless, on the evidence of signs, or of something similar, he saw that they ought to be believed.[21]

The light of faith makes us see what we believe. For just as, by the habits of the other virtues, man sees what is becoming to him in respect of that habit, so, by the habit of faith, the human mind is inclined to assent to such things as are becoming to a right faith, and not to assent to others.[22]

6. Faith Perfects Reason. Far from doing any violence to reason, faith protects and perfects reason. There is no surer way of making clear to man the limitations of his own reason and God's infinite transcendence over him and all his powers than to compel him to accept from God truths which he cannot himself understand or demonstrate. God created man for a glorious destiny far surpassing the competency of his own nature, and from the very start the greatest obstacle to man's attainment of this destiny has been his own pride and presumption. His first sin was to try to grasp his beatitude by himself, to become like unto God, to have, of himself, "the knowedge of good and evil." Man can make no greater error than to think that he can, with his finite intellect, comprehend the infinite God. He would be wrong about himself, for he would be ignoring his own limitations. He would be wrong about God, for we do not know God truly unless we know that He is infinitely superior to all that we may think of Him. And, finally, faith, after thus protecting reason from presumption, crowns and perfects it by giving it knowledge of those sublime truths for which its own unaided searchings have created so great a thirst — a thirst which reason itself is unable to quench.

7. The Certainty of Faith. If supernatural faith is necessary and rational, as we have tried to show, there remain still other questions: How certain is faith? How certain ought it to be? Does a man truly have faith who believes in the teachings of the Christian religion because they seem to have more sense to them than paganism or agnosti-

---

[21] S. Theol., II–II, 1, 4, ad 2 (Pegis, op. cit., Vol II, p. 1060).
[22] Ibid., ad 3 (Pegis, loc. cit.).

cism or atheism; who believes in the Catholic Church because "it has more on the ball" than any other religion?

In comparing the certainty of faith with the certainty of reason, St. Thomas distinguishes between absolute and relative certainty. The absolute certainty of any proposition comes from its cause, and the more certain its cause, the more certain is the proposition itself. Now, the cause of our belief in an article of faith is the divine truth itself; and consequently the absolute certainty of faith is greater than that of any truth whose cause is merely human reason. Relative certainty, on the other hand, is measured not by the cause of certainty but by the degree to which the subject, that is, the man's intellect, lays hold of the truth. In demonstrative knowledge, or knowledge by reason, the intellect does lay hold of the truth, knowing it by its own evidence; whereas the truths of faith are above the grasp of the intellect. Hence, reason is more certain than faith relatively to the subject. As a mode of human knowledge, therefore, reason is more perfect, since it makes its object seen, while faith is of things unseen; but as to absolute value, faith is more perfect since its truth is guaranteed by God Himself and since its object is of a higher order.[23] This situation is not without parallel in purely human knowledge:

> Other things being equal, sight is more certain than hearing; but if the person from whom we hear surpasses greatly the seer's sight, hearing is more certain than sight. Thus a man of little science is more certain about what he hears on the authority of an expert in science, than about what is apparent to him according to his own reason; and much more is a man certain about what he hears from God, who cannot be mistaken, than about what he sees with his own reason, which can be mistaken.[24]

8. What Is Requisite for Faith. Belief in the articles of faith because of their intrinsic probability, or adherence to the Catholic religion because the Church seems to be "the best horse to put your money on," does not constitute faith. One of the results of the modernist heresy has been a widespread confusion between opinion and faith. Belief in the truths of faith because they seem to be true can only be opinion, since, in the case of most of them, there is no question of demonstration. Belief is truly supernatural faith *only when the reason for belief is the formal object of faith,* namely, the First Truth or God. Super-

[23] *S. Theol.,* II–II, 4, 8, c; I, 1, 5, c and ad 1.
[24] *Ibid.,* II–II, 4, 8 ad 2 (Pegis, *op. cit.,* Vol. II, p. 1107).

natural faith does not consist merely in accepting certain truths, *but in accepting all that God has revealed because He has revealed it.*

> Now the formal object of faith is the First Truth, as manifested in Holy Scripture and the teaching of the Church, which proceeds from the First Truth. Consequently, whoever does not adhere, as to an infallible and divine rule, to the teaching of the Church, which proceeds from the First Truth manifested in Holy Scripture, has not the habit of faith, but holds that which is of faith otherwise than by faith. So, too, it is evident that a man whose mind holds a conclusion, without knowing how it is proved, has not scientific knowledge, but merely an opinion about it. Now it is evident that he who adheres to the teaching of the Church, as to an infallible rule, assents to whatever the Church teaches. Otherwise, if, of the things taught by the Church, he holds what he chooses to hold and rejects what he chooses to reject, he no longer adheres to the teaching of the Church as to an infallible rule, but to his own will. Hence it is manifest that a heretic who obstinately disbelieves one article of faith, is not prepared to follow the teaching of the Church in all things; but if he is not obstinate, he is no longer in heresy but only in error. Therefore it is clear that . . . a heretic in regard to one article has no faith in the other articles, but only a kind of opinion in accordance with his own will.[25]

9. Conflicts of Faith and Reason. The absolute certainty which St. Thomas accorded to faith required no sacrifice on the part of his reason. As all the above discussion has been seeking to make clear, the act of faith was, for the Angelic Doctor, the most rational of acts. Above both faith and reason there is truth; and the first loyalty of the mind is to truth. It was because of his single-minded devotion to truth that Aquinas could pursue the path of natural reason and the path of faith to their very ends without fearing that the double pursuit would ever set his mind in conflict with itself. He recognized no possibility of conflict or contradiction between reason and faith. Both have truth as their goal, and "only the false can contradict the true."[26] Consequently faith and reason are in necessary agreement. The doctrine of the "double truth" — that what is true theologically may be false philosophically — he greeted with scorn when it was proposed and he would greet with as much scorn today the form it takes in modernist theology. This doctrine locates contradiction in the divine Wisdom itself, for the principles of reason as well as the

[25] *S. Theol.*, II–II, 5, 3, c (Pegis, *op. cit.*, Vol. II, p. 1112).
[26] *Con. Gen..* I, 7, first paragraph.

articles of faith come to us from God, the Author of our nature.[27] Siger had argued that the intellect can be proved to be one in all men, and that the philosopher must accept this unity of the intellect as a demonstrated truth; but that, since it is a teaching of the Church, the Catholic philosopher must believe that each man has his own personal intellect. St. Thomas' reaction is as follows:

> However, what he subsequently declares is even more reprehensible: "By reason I conclude of necessity that the intellect is numerically one; nevertheless I firmly hold to the opposite by faith."
> Therefore he judges that faith is concerned with doctrines the contrary of which can be concluded "of necessity." Since, however, what I conclude of necessity can be only what is necessarily true — the opposite of which is false and impossible — it follows that faith must be demanded in what is false and impossible: a demand which not even God could make. But the ears of men who have faith cannot endure such words.[28]

There may, as is clear from the history of thought, be *apparent conflicts* between reason and faith, between science or philosophy and theology. But all such conflicts arise because someone has made a mistake. Reason is infallible, since its sole object is truth; and faith is infallible, since its source and cause is God; but no man is infallible because no man is pure reason or pure faith. Men draw false conclusions in science and philosophy, and men also misinterpret articles of faith. Obviously, scientific or philosophical error can contradict theological truth, and (which seems to be the case most often in recent years) scientific error can contradict theological error; but true science or true philosophy can never conflict with theological truth: only the false can contradict the true.

10. Reason Serves Faith. Not only does human reason not conflict with Christian faith, but it renders it valuable service. The science of theology would be impossible without the work which human reason does in it. This science receives its principles from divine revelation and does not prove them; but by arguments of reason it does prove other truths from these principles. By such argumentation the theologian is able to render the truths of religion more intelligible to us, and thus give to the Christian believer illuminating glimpses into

---

[27] *Con. Gen.*, I, 7.

[28] *De Unitate Intellectus*, translated by Sister Rose Emmanuella Brennan, S.H.N., in *The Trinity and The Unity of the Intellect* (St. Louis: Herder, 1946), p. 276. The author has altered the wording of the clause, "a thing which not even God could do."

the profundities of the divine mysteries. Two of the world's greatest books, the *De Trinitate* of St. Augustine and the *Summa Theologica* of St. Thomas, are just such piercings of reason into the obscure depths of revelation. Reason also serves faith by defending the Sacred Science against the attacks of heretics and infidels. Reason can show the heretic the self-contradictoriness of holding to some doctrines of the faith while rejecting others; and, while it cannot prove the principles of theology to the infidel, it can refute all his arguments against them. Objections against faith are always fallacious, since faith rests upon infallible certitude, and truth cannot contradict truth.[29]

We saw earlier in the chapter that the truths of faith fall into two classes: those which are above reason and could not be known at all except that they are revealed; and those which are attainable by reason but which are yet revealed so that all may know them easily and hold them firmly. Reason in its service to faith has a function in respect to each kind. The philosopher or theologian should not attempt to advance demonstrative proofs for those truths which exceed the competence of human reason, for such proofs must of necessity fail in their objective, and this failure would harm religion. It would offer the enemy of religion an opportunity to discredit religion, especially in the eyes of the less mature and learned, by showing the error in the supposed proof in such a way as to seem to be showing an error in religion itself. On the other hand, while no demonstrative proofs can be given for the articles of faith, the philosopher or theologian should not hesitate to advance *probable* proofs from reason, as long as he carefully marks them as only probable. Such proofs make the truth of faith more credible in our eyes even though they do not demonstrate it. In respect to those truths of faith which are also attainable by reason, philosophy serves religion by demonstrating them. These truths, such as the existence, unity, and omnipotence of God, are the preambles of faith.[30] Their demonstration aids faith by showing men the possibility and suitability of divine revelation, thus strengthening the faith of believers and leading unbelievers to a sincere examination of Christian doctrine.

11. **Faith Aids Reason.**[31] Have the religious beliefs of the Christian

---

[29] *S. Theol.*, I, 1, 8, c and ad 1.

[30] *S. Theol.*, I, 2, 2, ad 1.

[31] The debt I owe in the following paragraphs to the writings of Étienne Gilson will be obvious to anyone who has read his works.

philosopher any influence upon his philosophy? Many writers on philosophy, even some Catholics, have upheld the view that a man's philosophy should be quite uninfluenced by his religious beliefs. This is psychologically impossible, for a man has but one intellect with which he both believes and reasons. Were his beliefs and his reasoning completely indifferent to each other, he would be a victim of split personality, which, far from being a correct philosophical attitude, is a mental disease. As a matter of fact, the Catholic philosopher's faith helps him immeasurably in his philosophy. Just as the natural virtues of a good man are not destroyed by the presence in his soul of supernatural grace, but are perfected by it and raised to a higher level, so also the rational operations of the Catholic philosopher are not contaminated by his faith but on the other hand are perfected and elevated by it.

Faith as a mode of knowledge is inferior to demonstrated knowledge because it leaves its object in obscurity, but, absolutely speaking, supernatural faith is superior to any human knowledge because it puts the intellect in possession of an object to which reason of itself could never attain. Herein lies one of the benefits it confers upon reason. A Christian philosopher's faith, by revealing to him objects and truths which his reason of itself could not grasp, prompts his reason to higher and more fruitful efforts; knowing the object of faith darkly and as through a veil, his intellect is incited to strive for a clearer view of it. In this quest he often discovers new philosophical truths. Thus, out of the reflections and discussions of the theologian-philosophers of the patristic and medieval periods upon the relations of the Three Persons of the Blessed Trinity, and the relations of the human and divine natures in Christ, came much valuable philosophical truth concerning human nature and personality.

Oftentimes, too, it happens that a Christian philosopher, reflecting upon a truth revealed by faith, discovers that he can prove that truth by reason. A most striking case of this in the history of philosophy is the introduction into philosophy of the conception of *Creation*. Not a single one of the great pagan philosophers, not even Plato or Aristotle, though they both proved the existence of God, arrived at the notion of the creation of the universe out of nothing by God. But Christian philosophers, who received the notion of creation from the Bible, were able to show that the creation of all things from nothing by God can be demonstrated by reason. They had the *fact* of creation from revelation, and that set them to inquire whether it can be proved by reason. Plato and Aristotle might have proved it if they had ever thought of it, but they seem never to have thought of it, although Plato came close to it, and the principles of Aristotle's philosophy supply all that is necessary for its proof.

A striking illustration of this service that faith performs for philosophy is found in a comparison of the philosophy of Aristotle and St. Thomas Aquinas. The latter's purely rational teaching upon God and man, although based thoroughly upon principles borrowed from Aristotle, far surpasses that of the Greek philosopher in both extensiveness and profundity; and the broader compass and deeper insight of St. Thomas can be most often traced to the fact that he possessed the Christian revelation that Aristotle lacked.

Another and very important service that faith in the true religion performs for philosophy is to give it a *negative* norm or guide. Human reason perfectly used will infallibly attain truth, if only the truth contained in a confession of ignorance; but men are not pure intellects, and they often exercise reason imperfectly. Hence human thinking is always liable to error. It would be a great misfortune to err in regard to something vital to man's salvation. The Christian philosopher has the great advantage of possessing through divine revelation all those truths necessary for salvation. If in his reasoning he reaches a conclusion that contradicts a revealed truth, he knows at once that his conclusion is wrong, since truth cannot contradict truth. Hence, he will go back over his reasoning to discover the error that must be in it, and his philosophy will be the better for this warning signal given it by his faith.

PART FOUR

GOD AND CREATURES

CHAPTER XXI

THE EXISTENCE OF GOD

1. THE NATURE OF THE THOMISTIC PROOFS

Philosophy is the rational study of first causes. If there is some one first cause of all things, this universal first cause is assuredly the supreme object of the philosopher's quest. Thomistic metaphysics demonstrates that there is such a first cause and that it is God. It is the God who spoke to Moses from the burning bush: "I am who am. Say to the sons of Israel, 'He who is has sent me to you.'"

1. **Whether God's Existence Needs to Be Demonstrated.** Before giving his own proofs of God's existence, St. Thomas treats of two preliminary questions; namely, whether God's existence needs demonstration, and whether it can be demonstrated. In discussing these questions he makes clear what, in his mind, is essential to a rational proof of God's existence. On the first question he notes several arguments which pretend to show that God's existence is self-evident and hence needs no demonstration. We need note only one of them here. It is equivalent to the famous "ontological argument" of St. Anselm, based upon the idea of God. It is stated as follows: The existence of God is a self-evident truth. A self-evident proposition is one whose truth is known as soon as the terms in which it is stated are understood; as, for example, "the whole is greater than any of its parts," or "no circle is square." That God exists is such a proposition. By God we mean the being than which no greater being can be conceived. But a thing existing both in our mind and in reality is greater than one existing in our mind alone. Hence, since when we understand the word "God," God forthwith exists in our mind, it follows that God also exists in reality; for if He existed only in our mind, He would not be the being than which no greater can be conceived. Therefore, it is self-evident that God exists.[1]

[1] S. Theol., I, 2, 1, obj. 2.

463

2. Meanings of "Self-Evident." Before answering this and the other arguments separately, St. Thomas gives a general explanation of self-evident truth that is both important and enlightening. A truth, he writes, may be evident (1) both in itself and to us, or (2) in itself but not to us. A proposition is evident in itself if its predicate is included in its subject. But in order for it to be evident to us it is further required that *we* comprehend the nature of the subject and predicate; for if we do not, we shall not see that the one is necessarily connected with the other. For example, the proposition, "Incorporeal beings are not located in space," is evident in itself, but is not evident to one who does not know the nature of incorporeal being. Now the proposition "God exists" is evident in itself, because God is His own being; but it is not evident to us because we do not see the essence of God, and hence do not see that He is His own being. Hence, we have to demonstrate the existence of God from things which, while less knowable in themselves, are more knowable to us, namely, His effects.[2]

To the argument of St. Anselm, Aquinas replies: In the first place not everyone understands by the term God the being than which no greater can be conceived. Second, even if we grant the definition, the argument does not prove that God exists in reality. This conclusion does not follow unless it be first granted that there actually exists some being than which no greater being can be conceived; and that is just what the atheist denies. From the definition or idea of a being whose existence is not previously admitted we can deduce properties befitting the being so defined, but these properties, having been deduced from a mere idea, will be mere ideas themselves. Thus the *conception* of the greatest conceivable being must include the *notion* of necessary existence, but from this you cannot conclude that such a being really exists; you can conclude merely that *if it exists*, it exists necessarily and not contingently.[3]

3. Can the Existence of God Be Demonstrated? Consequently, if we are to know the existence of God we must demonstrate it. But can it be demonstrated? A second series of objections[4] argue that it cannot:

a) One objector states that the definition or essence of a thing is the

[2] *Ibid.*, 1, c.

[3] *Ibid.*, ad 2. Cf. *Con. Gen.*, I, 10–11. In connection with Kant's "refutation," we shall examine in more detail the full meaning of the ontological argument and why St. Thomas rejects it.

[4] *S. Theol.*, I, 2, 2, objs. 2 and 3. Cf. *Con Gen.*, I, 12.

THE EXISTENCE OF GOD

basis of demonstration; that is, from the definition we deduce the properties, as, for example, in geometry. Now, we cannot know the essence of God, that is to say, what God is. Wherefore, we cannot demonstrate His existence.

b) Second, if we could demonstrate the existence of God we could do so only through His effects. But God's effects are in no way comparable with or proportionate to God, since they are finite whereas He is infinite. And, since a cause cannot be demonstrated through effects not proportionate to it, God's existence cannot be demonstrated.

c) God's essence (i.e., what God is) and His existence are identical. It is impossible for us to know God's essence. Therefore, His existence must remain unknown to us.

d) The principles of demonstration are derived from sensible knowledge, as Aristotle teaches. Consequently, whatever transcends the sensible is indemonstrable. God transcends the sensible. Hence His existence is indemonstrable. This objection embodies the whole argument of modern positivists against proofs of God's existence and against all metaphysical truth.

4. Two Kinds of Demonstration. Before replying to these arguments St. Thomas expounds his own view. There are, he writes, two kinds of demonstration. One takes the cause as its starting point, and is called demonstration *propter quid* (*a priori*). The other argues from the effects, and is called demonstration *quia* (*a posteriori*). In itself the cause is prior to the effect, but in demonstration we must start with whatever is prior as far as we are concerned; hence when the effects are more evident to us than the cause, we proceed *from* knowledge of the effects *to* knowledge of the cause. From any effect we can demonstrate the existence of its cause, for since every effect depends upon its cause, every effect presupposes the existence of its cause. Hence, the existence of God, which is not evident to us, can be demonstrated through His effects, which are evident to us.

This leads directly to the answer to the first objection. When we are demonstrating a cause through its effects, we have to use the nominal definition of the cause, that is to say, what is commonly understood by the cause, instead of the essence of the cause. The demonstration of the essence of the cause follows the demonstration of its existence. Hence, in demonstrating the existence of God through His effects we can use in our proof the meaning of the word *God* instead of the essence of God, which we do not know.

To the second objection St. Thomas replies that while we cannot derive perfect knowledge of a cause from effects which are not proportionate to it, we can nevertheless demonstrate the *existence* of the cause from any of its effects, since, as was said above, an effect of its nature depends upon its cause and therefore presupposes its existence.

To the third objection St. Thomas replies that although the essence and existence of God are identical, and therefore His proper mode of existence must remain as unknown to us as His essence, nevertheless the simple fact of His existence, which we express when we say, "God exists," is demonstrable from His effects.

Finally, to the fourth argument Aquinas answers that although God exceeds the senses and all sensible things, nevertheless His effects, from which we proceed in our proof of His existence, are sensible, and it is to them that we apply our principles of demonstration. Our knowledge begins with sensible things, but extends to the cause of these things, since the effect always implies the existence of the cause.

5. **Method of the Thomistic Proofs.** From the above discussions it becomes clear that St. Thomas requires certain definite conditions for a proof of God's existence. These conditions are imposed on him by his own theory of knowledge. The proof must start from empirical or observable facts; that is to say, from things, characters, or events in nature directly experienced by men. Because he rejects the doctrine of innatism, and maintains that all our knowledge in this life has its source in sense perception, St. Thomas cannot base a proof of God's existence upon any innate idea of God which some philosophers suppose us to have. The proof must start from the world, not from the essence of God. The first condition, therefore, for a proof of God's existence is a basis in data evident to human sensio-intellectual experience. The second condition is that the proof reach its conclusion through the principle of causality, by showing that these data necessarily demand God as their explanation; it must show that the existence of God is the only possible explanation of these data.

6. **The World Is Explained, Not God.** The data which, it appeared to St. Thomas, cannot be accounted for except by positing God are motion, action, being, perfection, and order. Each of these is an unquestionable part of the experienced world; but each exists in nature in a mode which is not self-explanatory; each presents itself to human experience as existing in a mode that is intelligible only as the effect of

a cause existing in an entirely different mode. This cause is God. Consequently the proofs are explanations of the world, not explanations of God. Incidentally they answer some of our questions about God, but if they are understood as primarily intended to do this, they will not be well understood. If they are regarded as *explanations of God,* they will not be understood at all. God appears in them as the *explanation,* not as the thing explained. We learn, in mastering the proofs, that God is self-explanatory; but since we do not see God, we do not see the explanation.

II. "THE FIVE WAYS" OF PROVING GOD'S EXISTENCE

St. Thomas gives five proofs of God's existence. We shall give them here in his own words.[5]

1. **The Argument From Motion.** The first and more manifest way is the argument from motion. It is certain, and evident to our senses, that in the world some things are in motion. Now whatever is moved is moved by another, for nothing can be moved except it is in potentiality to that toward which it is moved; whereas a thing moves inasmuch as it is in act. For motion is nothing else than the reduction of something from potentiality to actuality. But nothing can be reduced from potentiality to actuality, except by something in a state of actuality. Thus that which is actually hot, as fire, makes wood, which is potentially hot, to be actually hot, and thereby moves and changes it. Now it is not possible that the same thing should be at once in actuality and potentiality in the same respect, but only in different respects. For what is actually hot cannot simultaneously be potentially hot; but it is simultaneously potentially cold. It is therefore impossible that in the same respect and in the same way a thing should be both mover and moved, i.e., that it should move itself. Therefore, whatever is moved must be moved by another. If that by which it is moved be itself moved, then this also must needs be moved by another, and that by another again. But this cannot go on to infinity, because then there would be no first mover, and, consequently, no other mover, seeing that subsequent movers move only inasmuch as they are moved by the first mover; as the staff moves only because it is moved by the hand. Therefore it is necessary to arrive at a first mover, moved by no other; and this everyone understands to be God.

[5] *S. Theol.,* I, 2, 3, c (*The Basic Writings of St. Thomas Aquinas,* ed. Anton C. Pegis [New York: Random House, 1945], Vol. I, pp. 22–23).

2. The Argument From Efficient Causes. The second way is from the nature of efficient cause. In the world of sensible things we find there is an order of efficient causes. There is no case known (neither is it, indeed, possible) in which a thing is found to be the efficient cause of itself; for so it would be prior to itself, which is impossible. Now in efficient causes it is not possible to go on to infinity, because in all efficient causes following in order, the first is the cause of the intermediate cause, and the intermediate is the cause of the ultimate cause, whether the intermediate cause be several, or one only. Now to take away the cause is to take away the effect. Therefore, if there be no first cause among efficient causes, there will be no ultimate, nor any intermediate, cause. But if in efficient causes it is possible to go on to infinity, there will be no first efficient cause, neither will there be an ultimate effect, nor any intermediate efficient causes; all of which is plainly false. Therefore it is necessary to admit a first efficient cause, to which everyone gives the name of God.

3. The Argument From the Contingency of the World. The third way is taken from possibility and necessity, and runs thus. We find in nature things that are possible to be and not to be, since they are found to be generated, and to be corrupted, and consequently, it is possible for them to be and not to be. But it is impossible for these always to exist, for that which can not-be, at some time is not. Therefore, if everything can not-be, then at one time there was nothing in existence. Now if this were true, even now there would be nothing in existence, because that which does not exist begins to exist only through something already existing. Therefore, if at one time nothing was in existence, it would have been impossible for anything to have begun to exist; and thus even now nothing would be in existence — which is absurd. Therefore, not all beings are merely possible, but there must exist something the existence of which is necessary. But every necessary thing either has its necessity caused by another, or not. Now it is impossible to go on to infinity in necessary things which have their necessity caused by another, as has been already proved in regard to efficient causes. Therefore we cannot but admit the existence of some being having of itself its own necessity, and not receiving it from another, but rather causing in others their necessity. This all men speak of as God.

4. The Argument From the Degrees of Perfection. The fourth way is taken from the gradation to be found in things. Among beings there are some more and some less good, true, noble, and the like. But *more* and *less* are predicated of different things according as they resemble in their different ways something which is the maximum, as a thing is said to be hotter according as it more nearly resembles that which is hottest; so that there is something which is truest, something best, something noblest, and, consequently, something which is most being, for those things that are greatest in truth are greatest in being, as it is written in Metaph. ii. (993^b 30). Now the maximum in any genus is the cause of all in that genus, as fire, which is the maximum of heat, is the cause of all hot things, as is said in the same book. Therefore there must also be something which is to all beings the cause of their being, goodness, and every other perfection; and this we call God.

5. **The Argument From Design in the World.** The fifth way is taken from the governance of the world. We see that things which lack knowledge, such as natural bodies, act for an end, and this is evident from their acting always, or nearly always, in the same way, so as to obtain the best result. Hence it is plain that they achieve their end, not fortuitously, but designedly. Now whatever lacks knowledge cannot move toward an end, unless it be directed by some being endowed with knowledge and intelligence; as the arrow is directed by the archer. Therefore some intelligent being exists by whom all natural things are directed to their end; and this being we call God.

This fifth argument as here presented is based upon intrinsic finality, or the attainment by each natural being of its own end and good. In the *Summa Contra Gentiles* St. Thomas bases the argument on extrinsic finality, or the general order which exists among the diverse beings of nature:

It is impossible that things which are contrary and dissimilar in nature should harmonize in one order always or for the most part except by the government of a being which directs all together and each one separately toward a definite end. But we see in the universe things of different natures harmonizing in one order, not rarely and as if by chance, but always or in the most cases. Therefore, there must exist some being by whose providence the universe is governed. And this being we call God.[6]

[6] *Con. Gen.*, I, 13, last paragraph.

III. COMMENTS AND FURTHER EXPLANATION

Later in the chapter we shall examine and answer the most important arguments which have been put forward against these proofs of God's existence. First, however, it will be well to attempt to clarify the full meaning of three of the proofs, namely, the First, Third, and Fourth Ways.

A. CONCERNING MOTION AND THE UNMOVED FIRST MOVER

1. Two contentions of St. Thomas in the First Way have been questioned and these contentions form the very heart of his proof. They are: (*a*) that whatever is in motion is moved by something else, and (*b*) that we cannot regress to infinity in the series of moved movers. These two propositions are far from evident to many modern thinkers. A reason for this is the failure of modern science and philosophy to have any clear idea of what motion is. St. Thomas' argument is based upon the nature of motion, which we have already studied in Chapter IV, Section VI. Recalling Aristotle's analysis of motion, let us now explain and defend the two key propositions above.

Motion is not *thing,* but *process.* It is the actuality of the potential as such. Whatever is in motion, that is, whatever is in any way changing, is at each moment of its change gaining new actuality; the motion is the continuing actualization of the potential. Consequently, everything that is in motion is in potency in some respect and anything that moves something is in act in precisely that respect in which what it moves is in potency. Nothing, therefore, can move itself; because in order to do so it would have to be in act and in potency in the same respect, that is, in respect to one identical movement. Nor can anything be in motion simply by its nature or essence. The "movement" of such a being would be a complete actuality, not the continuing actualization of a potency. But to conceive of motion as a complete actuality is to destroy the concept of motion; it is to hypostatize motion, thus leaving only thing, and eliminating process from nature; and therefore it is to accept the changeless One of Parmenides. *Therefore, since nothing can move itself and since nothing can be in motion by its essence, whatever is in motion is moved by something else.*

Since everything that is in motion is moved by something else, the cause of any particular motion will always require a cause of its own motion, if it is itself in motion. Consequently no moved mover — no mover which is itself in motion — is a true cause or source of motion; it moves something only by virtue of the motion which it has received, and it is, therefore, merely a transmitter of motion rather than a cause of motion. Consequently, all the movers-in-motion which make up the world require as the true cause and source of their movement an unmoved mover, that is to say, a first mover which is not itself in motion.

2. **Motion Cannot Be Taken for Granted.** *This conclusion cannot be escaped by the hypothesis of an infinite series of moved movers.* In such a series, it is argued, every movement has an adequate cause; namely, the movement prior to it. Hence there is no need to posit a first unmoved mover. This argument will not stand examination. To say that each member of an infinite series of causally connected movements is in motion because a prior member moves it, is not to explain its movement. It is not to explain anything, but is merely to repeat that the series is a series of moved movers. It does not answer the question why the beings in the series are not in static instead of dynamic relation; that is, why any of them move at all. It is analogous to believing that a watch will go without a spring if only you make sure to have a wheel in front of each wheel. It amounts to taking motion for granted, assuming that motion and rest are equally primal and equally in need of (or in no need of) explanation. But this is not so. Motion is the actualizing of potentiality, and as such it implies an actuality prior to any movement. What implies something prior to itself cannot be taken for granted.

To accept an infinite series of moved movers without an unmoved mover outside the series causing its movement, is to accept motion within the series as an absolute, a starting point of explanation not to be itself explained. When we regard motion from the physicist's point of view, and consider the law of inertia, it is clear that the motion in any series of moved movers does not arise from anything in the series, but is a given fact for which no member of the series accounts. Because a physicist takes his stand within the phenomena of nature, he regards motion as an ultimate, a starting point; he can, *qua* physicist, accept an infinite series of moved movers without demanding any further cause. A philosopher cannot. For while motion can, for the sake of method, be taken as an ultimate *within* a series of motions, it cannot be taken as an absolute ultimate, because it necessarily involves a reduction of potency to act and so implies a prior actuality. The proof of God from the movement in the world is not an effort to explain motion, which, failing to find any natural explanation, falls back upon God. It is, on the contrary, the manifestation and explication of what every motion ultimately presupposes and implies, namely, a mover which is not itself in motion — a Pure Actuality. God is not dragged in, in default of a natural explanation; He comes in as a reality rigidly implied by nature's mode of being, which is being in process of actualization.

B. CONCERNING CONTINGENT AND NECESSARY BEING

3. There is, it must be admitted, a certain obscurity in St. Thomas' third proof as presented in the *Summa Theologica*. After showing the contingency of natural things from the fact that they are generated and corrupted, St. Thomas argues that what is able not to exist, that is, possible or contingent being, must at sometime actually not exist; and, therefore, if *everything* were contingent, at some time nothing at all would exist, and from then on nothing would ever exist; but, since something does exist now, there must be not only contingent beings, but a necessary being which cannot not-exist. We might ask several questions, to none of which the argument seems to have a satisfactory answer: Why must that which is capable of not-existing actually not-exist at some time? And if we do grant that *each* contingent being must not-exist at some time, why would it follow that all of them together should not-exist at some same time? Granting even this last, why should the time at which nothing exists be *now?* If the argument means merely that the contingent is of necessity transient, then it implies a time when something exists as well as a time (if this is really implied) when nothing does. The time when something exists might be now. If, on the other hand, the argument means that the contingent has, of necessity, a *beginning* of existence, it must be confessed that St. Thomas has chosen a very strange way of saying this, that he offers no demonstration of it, and that it conflicts with what he says elsewhere.[7]

This obscurity need not destroy the real value of the proof, however. Its deeper significance is that that which does not exist by necessity of its own essence requires a cause of its existence; and, since no being which is itself dependent upon another can be an ade-

[7] *S. Theol.*, I, 46, 2.

quate explanation of either itself or the things which depend upon it, we must admit, since contingent things do exist, that some being which is necessary in itself exists and accounts for the existence of all the contingent things.

4. **Thomism a Philosophy of Existence.** If we succeed in understanding St. Thomas' proof of a necessary being, we will at least have begun to understand what is meant by calling Thomism a philosophy of existence; we will have begun to grasp the position which "being" holds in that philosophy. The term *necessary* has several different meanings.[8] When we say that something is necessary we frequently mean that someone could not live or that something could not exist without it. Thus, air, water, and food are necessary for us that we may live. This is the first meaning of "necessary." Its opposite is "unessential." The second meaning is not very far removed from the first; it relates to the attaining of some good or end. Thus it is necessary to study in order to become learned; it is necessary to obey the laws of God in order to save one's soul; it is necessary to travel in order to get to Europe. The opposite of "necessary" in this sense is "unnecessary." Third, we call something or some act necessary when it comes about because of force or violence, or from a cause from which it *must* follow. Thus, if a man is blown off a roof by a sudden wind, his fall is necessary; whereas if he jumps off purposely, it is "free." Fourth, something is necessary when it cannot be otherwise than it is. Thus, it is necessary that a triangle inscribed in a circle with the diameter as its base be a right triangle; it is necessary that an animal be sentient and that a man be rational. However, it is not necessary, in this sense of the term, that anything triangular or animal or human *exist*. Consequently, this last meaning of necessary breaks down into two meanings, one of which is relevant to essence and the other to existence; and so we must add to the other definitions of necessary the one that is the most fundamental of all: that is necessary which must exist, which cannot not-be. It was St. Thomas' firm grasp of this significance of "the necessary" that made his metaphysics a metaphysics of existence rather than merely of essence; and it is this significance that "necessary" has in the Third Way.

The opposites of "necessary" in these last two senses are "accidental" and "contingent." Thus, while a triangle must have angles adding up to one straight angle, it need not be white and it need not have an

[8] *Cf. In V Meta.*, 6, Nos. 827–840.

area of six square inches; these things are accidental. While an animal must be sentient, it need not be in good health; this is accidental. And while an animal, if it exists, must, by necessity of its essence, be a sentient, living substance, it need not exist at all. Every animal sometimes exists and sometimes does not; hence, as to existence, an animal is contingent. The contingent is that which is capable of non-existence, that which need not exist.

Only that being is absolutely necessary which, of itself, unconditioned by anything else, must exist, cannot not-exist. St. Thomas' Third Way argues that if there were not in fact such a being, then nothing at all could possibly exist. There would be nothing which is of itself the act of existing, and so there would be no actual existence. For anything else, no matter what its essence, not being itself the act of existing, could exist only by participating or receiving that act; but there would be no act to receive or participate. The proof, therefore, means that the only possible explanation of any and all being is Being Itself subsisting of itself, that is to say, a being whose essence is to exist. For any explanation short of this could point only to an essence which needs to receive existence if it is to be actual. Nothing is actual except by virtue of existence, and hence there could be nothing if there were no Self-Subsisting Existence:

> But everything which belongs to any being is either caused from principles of the being's nature . . . or it comes to it through some extrinsic principle. . . . But it cannot be that existence itself should be caused by the very form or quiddity of a thing; caused, that is, as by an efficient cause, since if it were so something would be the cause of itself and something would bring itself into existence; but this is impossible. Therefore everything which is such that its existence is different from its nature must needs have its existence from another. And because everything which exists through another is reduced to that which exists through itself, as to its first cause, there must be something which is the cause of existence in all things, because it is existence only. . . .[9]

That this is the significance of St. Thomas' third proof is made very clear by two passages, almost identical with each other, in the *Summa Contra Gentiles*. One of them is as follows:

> We see in the world certain things that are capable of existing or not existing, viz., things which come into and pass out of existence. Now everything which is a possible [i.e., contingent] being has a cause; be-

[9] *De Ente*, IV.

cause, since of itself it is indifferent to both, that is to being or non-being, it is required, if being is to belong to it, that this be due to some cause. But it is not possible to proceed *ad infinitum* in causes. . . . Therefore, it is necessary to posit something that exists necessarily. But every necessary being either has the cause of its necessity from some other source, or not, but is of itself necessary. But we cannot proceed *ad infinitum* in necessary beings which have the cause of their necessity in something else. Therefore, we must posit some first necessary being which is of itself necessary. And this is God. . . .[10]

C. CONCERNING PERFECTIONS AND SUPREME PERFECTION

5. The wording of St. Thomas' Fourth Way is hardly such as to make the cogency of his argument immediately obvious, especially to the modern mind tinged by materialism and relativism. Yet in structure the proof is identical with the first three. It starts with certain data of experience, certain perfections observed among the beings of nature, namely truth, goodness, nobility, and the like. ("And the like" may be taken to include all transcendent or *pure* perfections, e.g., life, intelligence, freedom.) As in the case of the first three proofs, something about the data stamps them as not self-sufficient, as implying something prior, whence they are derived and on which they depend. The argument then proceeds, by way of the principle of causality, to an adequate, self-sufficient cause of these data. It concludes that only absolute perfection, Supreme Being, subsisting in itself, can account for the limited and relative perfections found in nature.

This argument "from the degrees of perfection" has often been called "idealistic," "Platonic," even by some Thomists. There is this much truth in the charge: the Fourth Way can have little appeal to a mind which sees matter as more real than ideas, a mind for which stones have an edge in being over the ideal which forms them into a school, a hospital, or a church. But to a mind which has no hesitancy in asserting that the good and evil, the kindness and cruelty, the generosity and meanness, the joy and sorrow met in life are as real, nay, more real, than stones, than water, food and air even — to that mind the Fourth Way is the best way of all. It starts from the things in life which count, the things for which material things are mere means and conditions — life itself, goodness, beauty, truth, nobility,

[10] *Con. Gen.,* I, 15. This passage is part of a proof of God's eternity. The other passage, II, 15, is a proof of creation.

knowledge, love — and it proceeds to a God who is recognizable as God — a living, knowing, loving, good God. It is a proof, in a word, which demonstrates that God exists by the very reasons for which most men believe in Him anyway.

As to whether it really does *demonstrate*, the crux is whether the principle of causality can rightly be applied to the data from which the proof starts. And as soon as we see St. Thomas' reasons for holding that the principle does and must apply here, we see also that this proof, like the Third Way, is an exemplification of how completely Thomism is a philosophy of being or existence.

6. The Data for the Argument. What are the data of the argument? What is meant by saying that we see things which are more or less true, more or less good, more or less noble, and the like? In some cases it is easy enough to know what is meant. A good man and a good horse are both good, but the goodness of the man is on a higher level than that of the horse. Among men we find varying degrees of the same kind of goodness, namely, moral goodness. Both these examples, in different ways, illustrate "more or less good." Another easy illustration is in regard to life. Plants, animals, and men live, and in each of them life is a perfection. But it is a perfection possessed here in three distinct grades. What about truth? How can anything be more or less true, or how can one truth be more true than another? St. Thomas' example, taken from Aristotle, of two falsities, one of which is nearer the truth, does not seem relevant, for the "maximum truth" approached need in no sense be absolute truth, as is very clear from Aristotle's illustration ("nor is he who thinks four things are five equally wrong with him who thinks they are a thousand").[11] What is needed are examples of *truths* which are true in different degrees. Such examples are not lacking. A merely contingent truth in the physical order has not so full a degree of truth as a necessary physical law; thus, that it rained today in New York is true, but is true on a lower level than the truth that certain meteorological conditions of necessity cause rain. A physical truth, such as the latter, is again a truth of a lower order than a metaphysical principle such as the principle of causality. And even among metaphysical principles there are degrees of truth. The first principle of all, namely, that what is, is, possesses truth on a higher level than any of the others. Finally, there is the "maximum truth," namely, the Truth which of itself is and must

[11] S. Thomas, *Con. Gen.*, I, 13; Aristotle, *Meta.*, IV, 1008b, 33–35.

be, without which there would be neither being nor truth, the Necessary Truth upon which all other truths are contingent.

7. **The Use of the Principle of Causality.** After the data themselves, the validity of the argument depends upon the truth of two principles: (1) if one and the same perfection is found in several different beings, it is impossible that each should of itself possess it, and therefore the several beings must have received this perfection from some one cause; (2) a being which possesses in limitation a perfection which is not of its essence limited, possesses it from an extrinsic cause which is itself the highest degree of that perfection. St. Thomas enunciates the first principle in several places. In *De Potentia* he writes:

> It is necessary, if some one thing is found in several beings, that it be caused in them by some one cause. For it cannot be that the common thing belongs to each one by reason of itself, since each one, inasmuch as it is itself, is different from the others, and diversity of causes produces diverse effects.[12]

His clearest argument for the second principle seems to be the following, from the *Summa Contra Gentiles:*

> What belongs to something by reason of its own nature, and not from some other cause, cannot be in it in a lessened or deficient degree. For if something essential be taken away from or added to a nature, the latter will at once be another nature. . . . If, on the contrary, while the nature or quiddity of a thing remains intact, something [in it] is found diminished, it is at once evident that this latter does not depend simply upon that nature, but upon something else by whose removal it is diminished. Therefore, what belongs to something in a lesser degree than to some other things, does not belong to it by virtue of its own nature alone, but from some other cause. Consequently, that to which the predication of a certain genus is proper in the maximum degree will be the cause of everything else in that genus.[13]

We may add another argument to this. The perfections which alone are in question in this proof are *pure* perfections; that is to say, their essence implies no limitation. Some perfections are *mixed;* they are positive perfections but can belong, because of their nature, only to limited kinds of being. Sight and hearing, for example, are positive perfections, but can belong only to a subject which is an organism, and is therefore material, limited, and partly potential. Knowledge

[12] *De Potentia*, III, 5. Cf. *De Ente*, IV; *S. Theol.*, I, 65, 1; *Con. Gen.*, II, 15.
[13] *Con. Gen.*, II, 15, "*Amplius. Quod alicui convenit* . . . "

itself, however, of which sight and hearing are diminished forms, implies of itself no necessary organic subject and no necessary limitation of any sort in its subject. Thus, intelligence can belong to man, but also to a purely spiritual being, and even to an infinite being, since its conception is not destroyed by removing from it the limitations which are found in it in man. Since, therefore, these pure perfections are of themselves unlimited, the limitations found in them in nature must be due to the subject in which they are found. Thus, for example, human intelligence is limited by man's capacity for intelligence, not by any intrinsic limitation in intelligence itself. Therefore man must possess intelligence as the actuality of a potentiality of human nature. But if a perfection in a subject is the actuality of a potency in the subject, then the subject has received it from an extrinsic cause, since a potency is made actual only by a cause already in act.

With these principles in mind the validity of the Fourth Way is clear. The only adequate ultimate cause for truth or goodness in limited beings is Absolute Truth or Absolute Good. For any truth short of absolute truth is truth-in-a-subject, in which case the truth is less than the subject and is limited by it, while the subject is not true of itself but by virtue of something else. Truth limited by a subject cannot be the ultimate cause of truth, nor can a subject which is true by virtue of something other than itself. Hence, only Truth Itself, subsisting absolutely, can be the first cause of all truth. The same line of argument applies in the case of good, nobility, intelligence, etc. Thus the limited degrees of these attributes compel the mind to posit an unlimited absolute Truth, Goodness, Intelligence, etc.

Absolute Truth, Absolute Good, Absolute Intelligence, etc., are not so many distinct realities, but are one and the same Supreme Being whom we call God. Pure Goodness is absolute, simple, and uncaused, since it is, as the whole argument concludes, the uncaused good which is the cause of all limited goods. It is at the same time *real,* since it is the cause of the real but limited goods which we experience. Hence, it is absolute, simple, uncaused Reality or Being. The same thing holds for the Absolute Truth, and so on. Therefore, the ultimate conclusion of the argument is that there exists a perfect, uncaused, self-existent Supreme Being, God, who, because He is Being Itself, is absolute Goodness, Truth, Nobility, Intelligence, Life.

8. The Primacy of Being. Other great philosophers had used this

proof before St. Thomas, but he alone seems to have fully compre-hended the place of primacy which being, that is, existence, holds in the proof. The others got lost somewhere in the world of ideas and essences. Plato thought that The Good is primal: since everything is to be explained by an end, reason, or good, then the ultimate expla-nation is The Good itself. The logic is flawless; but something is over-looked: The Good is nothing and explains nothing unless The Good *is*. Plotinus placed The One first: since every multiplicity is derived from a prior unity, then everything emanates from Unity Itself. Yes, St. Thomas answers, provided that The One *is*. Aristotle's God is Pure Act, but Aristotle, thinking in terms of essence, conceives Him primarily as perfect action and perfect thought, not seeing that He must *be* in order to be action or thought. Even St. Augustine seems to have thought of God as Truth rather than as Being. Of course, all these great men were right—only they were not quite right enough. Certainly there would be no goods without The Good, no many without The One, no truths without The True, no movement without The Act. God is Pure Actuality, supremely One, True, and Good; but He is these because He is the perfect act of being. "I am who am," said God to Moses. "God is Subsistent Being," paraphrases St. Thomas.

> Being itself is the most perfect of all things, for it is compared to all things as that which is act; for nothing has actuality except so far as it is. Hence being is the actuality of all things, even of forms themselves.[14]
> But *being* is found to be common to all things, however otherwise different. There must therefore be one principle of being from which all beings, in whatever way existing, have their being, whether they are invisible and spiritual, or visible and corporeal.[15]
> . . . God is being itself, of itself subsistent. Consequently He must contain within Himself the whole perfection of being. . . . Now all the perfections of all things pertain to the perfection of being; for things are perfect precisely so far as they have being after some fashion. It follows therefore that the perfection of no being is wanting to God.[16]

IV. KANT'S "REFUTATION" OF THE PROOFS OF GOD'S EXISTENCE

In his *Critique of Pure Reason* Immanuel Kant attacked both the traditional proofs of God's existence and all attempts to give any cogent

[14] *S. Theol.*, I, 4, 1, ad 3 (Pegis, *op. cit.*, Vol. I, p. 38).
[15] *Ibid.*, 65, 1, c (Pegis, *op. cit.*, Vol. I, p. 610).
[16] *Ibid.*, 4, 2, c (Pegis, *op. cit.*, Vol. I, p. 39).

demonstration from pure reason of the existence of a Supreme Being. It has been generally assumed by philosophers of both the naturalistic and the idealistic schools since the time of Kant that his criticism effectually disposed, once and for all, of all rationalistic attempts to prove that God exists. Scholastic philosophers, however, have not been greatly impressed by the famous "refutation." They have repeatedly pointed out serious and fundamental flaws in Kant's argument, flaws which render the argument as a whole invalid. However, not many modern philosophers read the Scholastic defenses of the arguments, because they consider the whole question as a closed and settled one, and because the influence of Kant's philosophy has been so widespread and dominant that demonstrations based upon a pre-Kantian metaphysics and theory of knowledge are not often given very serious consideration today. Yet the truth is that the traditional Scholastic arguments and Kant's criticism are public property which anyone who wishes may examine and compare, so that there is no excuse for dispensing with such an examination and assuming that the question is forever settled against the arguments.

1. **Kant's Main Argument Outlined.** There are, Kant says, only three possible ways of attempting a demonstration by pure reason of the existence of God. These are: (1) the physico-theological (i.e., the teleological) proof, from the order and harmony of the world; (2) the cosmological proof, from the existence of the world; and (3) the transcendental or ontological proof, from the idea of God or perfect being (*ens realissimum*). The last proof can easily be shown to fail to establish God's existence; the cosmological proof can be shown to depend upon the ontological; and the teleological proof can be shown to depend upon the cosmological. Hence all three are invalidated by the ontological fallacy, and there is therefore no possible way of proving the existence of God by pure reason.

Following his exposition of this main argument Kant adds four independent arguments against the cosmological proof in particular. These are of interest because they embody practically every objection raised by modern philosophers against the Thomistic proofs. We shall examine them after we have examined his main argument.

2. **The Ontological Proof.** St. Anselm, Descartes, and Leibniz were among the philosophers who had used the ontological proof. St. Thomas, as we have seen, rejected it. The essence of the proof consists in the deduction of the real and necessary existence of God from

the idea or conception of God. To be definable as the most perfect conceivable being, or the totality of the real (*ens realissimum*), God *must* be conceived as possessing real and necessary existence, since without this He would obviously not be the most perfect conceivable being. But since we do mean by God the most perfect conceivable being, or the *ens realissimum,* He really and necessarily exists.

Kant's chief criticism of this argument is not entirely different from St. Thomas', though, as shall be shown below, Kant does not succeed in putting his finger on the heart of the error in the proof, as St. Thomas did. Asserting the existence of a being, Kant says, is not the same sort of judgment as attributing a predicate to a subject. The proponents of the proof pass from the latter sort of judgment to the former; and this is invalid. To affirm a predicate of a subject is to assert that that subject must be conceived as having that predicate; but it is to assert nothing at all about the real existence of the subject or the predicate. If the subject exists only in the mind, it must have the predicate — but only in the mind. If it exists in reality, it must have the predicate in reality; but that proves nothing about whether it really exists or not; the *if* remains, even though the predicate in question is necessary being. Hence, in the judgment, *"Ens realissimum is necessary being,"* I simply designate necessity as a proper predicate of the subject *ens realissimum,* but it still remains a question whether this subject with this predicate exists only in my mind or in reality. On the other hand, the judgment, *"Ens realissimum exists,"* does not affirm any predicate of any subject; it states that a certain subject with all its predicates, whatever they may be, really exists. It is clear that the passage from the first proposition to the second is unjustifiable. In a word, while it is self-contradictory to say that *Supreme Being is not necessary being,* it is not self-contradictory to say that *there is no Supreme Being.* Consequently the ontological proof has no value.

3. **The Cosmological Proof.** The cosmological proof is the proof of God's existence through the demonstration of the existence and attributes of a necessary being upon whom the contingent beings of the world depend. Of St. Thomas' arguments, the second and third come closest to what Kant has in mind. Kant's refutation consists in showing that this argument embodies the ontological argument and depends upon it; and, since he has already shown that the latter argument is fallacious, the cosmological argument is also fallacious.

Kant does not, at this point,[17] attack the first part of the cosmologi-

[17] Except in a footnote.

cal proof, that is to say, the argument from the world to a necessary being upon whom it depends. Instead he tries to show that the identification of this necessary being with God, the Supreme Being, is accomplished only through the same reasoning which constitutes the ontological argument. After we have established the existence of some necessary being, we proceed, according to Kant, thus: A necessary being can be determined in only one way; it must be *completely* determined in and by its own conception, that is to say, it must be self-existent and self-determining. It must, therefore, be the *ens realissimum* or Perfect Being, for such a being alone has within itself the entire condition of its own existence and nature. Consequently, Perfect Being or God necessarily exists.

This mode of demonstration, Kant maintains, involves the old ontological argument under a new guise. It starts from experience, but once it attains the concept of the necessary being, it must abandon experience altogether; for experience can tell us nothing at all of the properties which an absolutely necessary being ought to have. Reason, abandoning experience, falls back upon its own conceptions in order to discover from them what attributes a necessary being ought to have; that is to say, it seeks to discover "which among all possible things contains in itself the conditions of absolute necessity." Reason believes that it finds these conditions in the conception of an *ens realissimum*, and consequently that the necessary being is the *ens realissimum*. Now that last conclusion embodies the ontological argument. In making the conclusion, Reason assumes that "the conception of an *ens realissimum* is perfectly adequate to the conception of an absolutely necessary being, that is, that we can infer the existence of the latter from the former — a proposition which formed the basis of the ontological argument. . . ." What Kant means is this: in reaching the ultimate conclusion of the cosmological argument, namely, that a supreme being necessarily exists, we make the conceptions of supreme being and necessary being identical; but if these conceptions are identical then either of them can be deduced from the other — in Scholastic terminology, they are convertible; hence necessary existence can be deduced from the conception of the supreme being (*ens realissimum*); but that is the heart of the ontological proof, which we have already shown to be invalid. Hence, the cosmological proof is also invalid.

4. Criticism of Kant's Argument. Kant's presentation of the cosmological proof is a misrepresentation of it. According to him, when we have established the existence of some necessary being, we then cast around in the pool of all our conceptions of possible beings trying to hook one which fits the conception of an absolutely necessary being. We hook the conception of an *ens realissimum,* the big fish of the ontological argument. This conception of "the completeness of reality" fully determines in itself the object of which it is the conception, and thus fulfills the demand of the notion of a necessary being, namely, that it be fully determined in and by its own conception. Then we assert, without further ado, that the supreme being is necessarily existent. At this point, however, the fish slips off our hook; because if we were justified in making that assertion, we *could* validly demonstrate God's existence from the mere idea of the *ens realissimum,* and we have already seen that we cannot do this.

If Kant's presentation of the cosmological argument were really that argument, his conclusion could not be escaped. But the argument as Scholastics, for example, St. Thomas, give it bears no resemblance to Kant's version. In St. Thomas' proofs of God's existence, when we have demonstrated the existence of a necessary being (and a First Cause, First Mover, Supreme Truth, Goodness, Life, etc.), we by no means abandon experience, to cast around among the pure Ideas of Reason for a conception which fits the notion of necessary being. On the contrary, we turn back to experience at once. Our reason had been led, in the first place, to demonstrate that necessary being exists because experience had shown us evident marks of contingency in the beings of nature. Now that we know that a being which is necessary does in fact exist, we have a very clear road open — and it is the only road open to us — for determining something about the nature of this necessary being. Since it *is* necessary, we must deny of it those characteristics of natural beings which are the marks of their contingency. This is the "way of negation"; by means of it we demonstrate that necessary being is eternal, simple, immaterial, unlimited pure actuality, in contrast to the temporality, composition, materiality, limitedness, and potentiality of natural beings. Second, since this necessary being is the *cause* of nature, we must affirm of it every perfection which we find in its effect, that is to say, in nature; but since it is necessary, we must deny of it every admixture of imperfection which the contingency of nature introduces into the perfections found in nature. This is the "way of analogy"; by it we demonstrate that necessary being is supreme, original, unlimited unity, goodness, truth, life, intelligence, freedom, and activity.[18] Kant's contention that reason abandons experience when it seeks to determine the nature of necessary being is entirely false. In both "ways," the negative and the analogical, it is the objects of experience, the contingent beings of nature, which dictate to reason what predicates must be assigned to necessary being, to the Cause of the world.[19]

5. **Kant's Subsidiary Criticisms of the Cosmological Argument.** (a) *Transcendental Use of the Principle of Causality.* Kant's first contention is that the principle of causality is applicable only within the realm of phenomena and hence cannot be used to establish the existence of God, or an absolutely unconditioned and "transcendental" being. This dictum is based upon his own theory of knowledge. Thomistic philosophy rejects Kant's whole theory of knowledge, and along with it, its implications about the nature of causality. Thomistic philosophy maintains and proves that causality is a valid metaphysical principle of real being and not a mere subjective principle of human thought. Hence, Thomists feel no qualms about resting their proofs of God's existence upon the principle of causality. We may add, without taking up again our formal criticism of Kant's system of philosophy, that he himself makes the extra-phenomenal use of the principle of causality which he forbids others to make. Whatever words may shroud Kant's meaning, the central doctrine of his philosophy supposes causal action which involves noumena. The noumenon acting upon sensibility produces experience; and the *a priori* forms of the mind determine the character of that experience, giving rise to phenomena. Neither of these contentions of Kant is intelligible, as we saw in Chapter XVI, unless causal influence exerted between noumenon and noumenon or between noumenon and phenomenon is presupposed.

Kant's argument that the principle of causality cannot be employed in such a manner as to bring us beyond natural phenomena to a transcendent cause of nature is advanced by some modern philosophers in a way that makes it independent of Kant's theory of knowledge. Principal Caird, a British philosopher of the recent past, presents it as follows:

[18] This method of negation and analogy will be used and explained more fully in the next chapter.

[19] There is more than this to our reply to Kant's main argument. It is given below in our answer to his third subsidiary argument (italicized headings, (c) and (d) below).

You cannot in a syllogistic demonstration put more into the conclusion than the premises contain. . . . All that from a finite or contingent effect you can infer is a finite or contingent cause, or at most an endless series of such causes. But if, because the mind cannot rest in this false infinity, you try to stop the indefinite regress, and assert at any point of it a cause which is not an effect, which is its own cause, or which is unconditioned and infinite, the conclusion in this case is purely arbitrary.[20]

G. H. Joyce comments on this argument as follows:

It would seem as though he [Caird] had failed to see that not the contingent substances themselves, but the analytic proposition "Contingent being involves the existence of necessary being" provided the premises of the syllogism.

To Father Joyce's comment we may add another. Those philosophers who argue that you cannot prove God's existence from the existence of finite being, because in trying to do so you pass over from the finite to the infinite and from the caused to the self-existent, which passage is illegitimate, are unconsciously testifying to the validity of the proof which they are attacking. They are really saying that the only adequate cause of the series of finite caused causes of nature — the only cause which can adequately explain these finite caused causes — is an uncaused infinite cause, which, because it must be infinite and uncaused, cannot be seized in any human demonstration. They see, as clearly appears in Caird's argument,[21] that the world can be explained only on the supposition that God is its first cause; but then, because this throws no explanatory light upon the first cause itself, they become confused and forget that it is the world which they set out to explain, not God. Kant himself, as we shall see, made this error. It is also committed, in a more crude and less excusable manner, by those who object to the argument from causality on the grounds that it "fails to give an adequate reason why, though every cause must allegedly have had a previous cause, the 'first' cause is excepted from the rule."[22] No one in the whole history of philosophy has ever been so absent minded as to argue that every cause must have a cause, and that *therefore* there is a cause without a cause. What the proponents of the cosmological proof argue is that *caused causes, such as the ones we observe in nature,*

[20] *Introduction to Philosophy of Religion.* p. 129; quoted by G. H. Joyce, *Principles of Natural Theology*, p. 226, note 1.

[21] And throughout Kant's, see below.

[22] Randall and Buchler, *Philosophy: An Introduction*, p. 160. Used by permission of Barnes and Noble, Inc., New York.

depend ultimately on something which is not merely another one like themselves, that is, upon an uncaused cause; to explain them merely by other things like themselves, which also need to be explained, is not to explain them at all. If it is then charged against those who defend this proof that they do not explain this first cause,[23] they answer (1) that they never set out to do so, and (2) that to attempt to explain it in the only way in which *we* ever explain anything, namely, by determining the prior conditions whence it arose, would be to ignore what they are talking about, that is, the first cause. The First Cause is self-explanatory; if you saw it, you would see its explanation.

b) *The Possibility of an Infinite Series.* Kant's second subsidiary argument against the cosmological proof is one of the constantly recurring objections to that proof. The proof, it is argued, rests entirely upon the assumption that an infinite series of caused causes is impossible; but such a series is not impossible; therefore the proof fails to establish its conclusion, namely, that there must be an uncaused first cause.

All those who reject the theistic proofs on the grounds that these proofs assume the impossibility of an infinite series of causes, are themselves assuming that what the proponents of the proofs hold to be impossible is an infinite regress of causes into the past — a regress which in theory could always be followed back further without any beginning ever being reached. Now, whatever any other proponents may have meant by the impossibility of an infinite regress in causes, this most certainly is not what St. Thomas meant. He clearly states so, when he rejects, one after another, several arguments pretending to show that the world must have had a beginning.[24] There are two reasons why St. Thomas rejects an infinite regress of caused causes, moved movers, or contingent beings, and neither of them has anything to do with an infinite regress into the past or a necessary beginning of the world's existence.

The first reason, which he states in his first and second proofs of God's existence, we have already explained when treating of moved movers and contingent beings. This reason is that so long as we adduce only *caused causes* to account for an effect, we do not account for it merely by increasing the number of these causes, even if we increase this number to infinity. Caused causes are themselves effects, and an

23 *Ibid.*, p. 160.
24 *S. Theol.*, I, 46, 2.

increased number of them, instead of explaining what needs to be explained, only adds still more requiring explanation. Only the self-explanatory can adequately explain anything; only the self-existent can adequately account for the existence of anything. Without a self-existing being, or an uncaused cause, whence they derive their caused, existence, no contingent beings at all can exist. Surely, then, an infinite number of them cannot. An infinite series of contingent causes pre-supposes a self-existent cause outside the series just as certainly as does a finite series. No matter what relations of dependency contingent beings may bear to one another, each of them and all of them together depend upon a necessary being.

Those who object to the argument entertain a picture of the relationship of the uncaused cause and the caused causes in which God is merely the starter who gives the series of natural causes its beginning. Their picture might be represented thus:

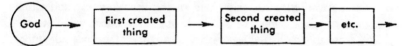

Since, on the supposition that the series might be infinite in regress, there would be no point at which God would have to act as starter, they argue that His existence is not, therefore, demonstrable. Their picture is very different from that of St. Thomas, in whose view God is the cause of every contingent thing, and of every action of every contingent thing upon another, and of every relation among contin-

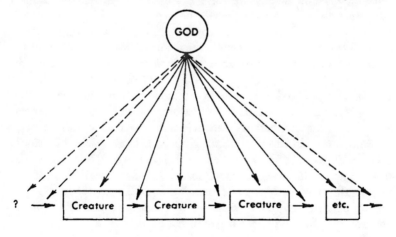

gent things — the universal cause of nature, not merely the starter of natural processes. St. Thomas' picture might be shown as in the second diagram on page 487. In the world represented by this pitcure it does not matter in the least whether there is a *beginning* of contingent beings, that is, a first caused cause; God is not stuck in at the beginning of a series of caused causes to give it a start; He is the cause of the series as a whole, of each thing in the series, and of the relations of causality between the members of the series.

The other meaning of St. Thomas' rejection of an infinite series of caused causes is quite simple. He is talking about essential and actual causes, that is to say, causes upon which the being of an effect essentially depends so that it cannot exist apart from the action of these causes giving it existence; the actual operation of these causes is a necessary condition for the existence of the effect. If the causes were infinite in number, an infinity of conditions would have to be fulfilled in order for the effect to exist. But an infinity of actual and simultaneous conditions cannot be fulfilled; hence the effect will not exist.

This reasoning will make no sense to anyone who does not understand St. Thomas' conception of being or existence, and it seems that there are very few who do. Most of us see readily that a thing which comes into existence must have a cause in order to come into existence. We do not see so readily that it must have a cause of its being at every moment in which it exists. We do not see this because we think of being statically; a thing is, to us, so much stuff which will go right on being or existing if only we leave it alone. St. Thomas, on the contrary, thought of being as action — the first action of a thing which is the foundation of its every subsequent action. By a contingent being he meant, therefore, one which is incapable of itself of exercising this action, one which (in barbarous terminology, necessary because our way of thinking does not afford us a suitable terminology) can exist only by being existed. Hence he says that every contingent being needs a present, actual cause of its being: its own act of existing is a potency actualized, and this potency can be actualized only by virtue of an efficient cause, already in act, acting upon it. If, therefore, one contingent being exists by the action of another contingent being, this other in turn needs the prior action of something else. But if there had to be an infinity of such actual actions at a given moment in order for something to exist, its existence would depend upon a condition impossible to fulfill, and hence it would not exist:

In efficient causes it is impossible to proceed to infinity *per se*. Thus, there cannot be an infinite number of causes that are *per se* required for a certain effect; for instance, that a stone be moved by a stick, the stick by the hand, and so on to infinity. But it is not impossible to proceed to infinity *accidentally* as regards efficient causes; . . . and it is . . . accidental to this particular man as generator to be generated by another man; for he generates as a man, and not as the son of another man. For all men generating hold one grade in the order of efficient causes — viz., the grade of a particular generator. Hence it is not impossible for a man to be generated by man to infinity; but such a thing would be impossible if the generation of this man depended upon this man, and on an elementary body, and on the sun, and so on to infinity.[25]

Now this is impossible, because it would mean that something is dependent on an infinity for its existence; and hence its generation would never be accomplished, because it is impossible to traverse what is infinite.[26]

In other words, if no ultimate condition can be reached which is *sufficient* for the existence of something, that thing will not exist; but if there is an infinite regress in the order of the causes actually and presently *necessary* for the existence of something, the sufficient condition is never attained.

St. Thomas supports this argument by a "proof" that an actually infinite multitude cannot exist, although a potentially infinite multitude can.[27] His proof may or may not be valid; but it does not seem to matter whether or not it is, for his general argument is independent of the possibility or impossibility of an actually infinite multitude. If there cannot be such a multitude, then nothing which by hypothesis depends upon one, can ever actually exist. If there can be such a multitude, then a being dependent upon it can exist, provided the multitude does. But if the multitude is made up entirely of contingent members there will not be in it any self-sufficient act of existence, and consequently it will exist only because it has been actualized by a prior self-existing being, an uncaused cause, the "unconditioned condition" of all being, the only *sufficient* condition of anything.

c) Inconceivability of a Necessary Being. The third "fallacy" which Kant finds in the cosmological proof reveals the fundamental error present in Kant's own mind throughout his whole treatment of the theistic proofs. The gist of his objection is that when we conclude,

[25] *S. Theol.*, I, 46, 2, ad 7 (Pegis, *op. cit.*, Vol. I, pp. 454–455).
[26] *Ibid.*, I, 7, 4, c (Pegis, *op. cit.*, Vol. I, p. 61).
[27] *Loc. cit.*

from the series of contingent or conditioned beings which make up nature, that there exists a necessary or *unconditioned* being which is the primary cause or condition of contingent beings, we remove from this necessary being all conditions; but in removing all conditions, we remove everything which would enable us to conceive of this being as necessary; we call the being necessary, but we cannot *think* its necessity, because we have excluded from its conception everything which might determine its necessity. Hence, our idea of necessary being is empty of all meaning.

In the pages where Kant explains this objection (Book II, Chapter III, Section 5 of the *Transcendental Dialectic*) he reverts over and over to the fact that I cannot "cogitate" an absolutely necessary being; I cannot *think* any object such that I see that it necessarily exists. I cannot avoid the inference that some necessary being exists, and yet whatever individual things I can conceive or think, I can conceive as nonexistent. Now this dilemma, Kant says, leads to only one conclusion: contingency and necessity are not properties of things themselves, but are merely subjective principles of reason, that is, pure conceptions by which the understanding synthesizes experience. If they were properties of things themselves, I would be faced with a clear-cut contradiction: something necessary exists, but every individual thing is contingent. If, however, contingency and necessity are subjective, regulative demands of reason, there is no contradiction; for then they simply lay down two rules for reason: one requiring us to seek a necessary ground for everything — a complete explanation; the other forbidding us ever to hope to attain this completeness, and commanding us to regard every experienced thing as conditioned. When we make the first regulative principle, viz., a necessary ground of all experience, into an existing being, viz., Necessary Being, we commit the fallacy of regarding a *regulative* principle of reason as a *constitutive* principle of knowledge. Then we get into the impossible position of trying to cogitate an unconditioned necessity — trying to conceive of a thing as necessary, while excluding the conditions which would enable us to conceive its necessity.

6. Kant's Fundamental Error. In this argument Kant is guilty, first of confusing the hypothetical necessity of thought and of physical law with the absolute necessity of self-existing being. When I think certain conditions, I must think certain consequences; for example, I cannot think that a figure is a triangle and yet think that its angles do not add up to two right angles. In nature, when given events occur, certain other events must follow. Both these necessities are hypothetical or conditional; a certain condition makes a certain consequent necessary. The necessity which we mean when we speak of a necessary being is entirely different. Such a being must exist *because of itself;* it does not depend on any conditions, but its essence is to exist. Kant realizes this, as he shows repeatedly; yet he ignores it in his objection. He equates "unconditioned" with "necessary," but then he goes on to use "necessary" as meaning "required by certain conditions." No man of Kant's intellectual stature could have fallen into such an obvious ambiguity unless some more fundamental error, some assumption which he constantly but unconsciously made, drove him into it. What was this unconscious assumption?

Kant's underlying error is the same as that of certain thirteenth-century philosophers against whom St. Thomas argued. It consists in the failure to distinguish between what is knowable in itself and what is knowable in respect to us. Because of this failure, Kant will not accept as complete any demonstration of the existence of a necessary being which is not at the same time a demonstration of the intrinsic ground of its necessity. Aware that any such proof would be the ontological proof under some guise or other, and rejecting the ontological proof, he rejects all proofs. This peculiar blindness of Kant is probably the root of his false statement of the cosmological proof: he casts the latter in such a way as to involve the ontological proof because he himself has made the unconscious assumption that any proof to be valid must do what the ontological proof pretends to do — exhibit the ground of the necessity of necessary being.

St. Thomas would have described Kant's error as the fallacy of assuming that wherever a demonstration *quia* is possible, a demonstration *propter quid* must also be possible. The former, we recall, proceeds from effect to cause, and often can establish little more than the *existence* of the cause. The latter goes from the cause to the effect or from the essence to the properties. The proof *quia* is *a posteriori* and the proof *propter quid* is *a priori*.[28] It is clear that the demonstration of the real properties of some real being by means of the *a priori* mode of proof is possible only when the real essence of that being is understood. But what Kant demands, both in his main argument against the cosmological proof and in his third subsidiary argument, is that

[28] *A posteriori* and *a priori* are here used in the Scholastic, not the Kantian, sense.

once the existence of necessary being has been established *a posteriori*, its property of necessity must be deducible *a priori*; he asks us to "cogitate" it as necessary, that is, to see in its conception the reason of its necessity. To demand this is to assume that the demonstration of the *existence* of a cause must be also the manifestation or explication of the *essence* of that cause.

St. Thomas, as we have seen, actually had such an argument as Kant's put to him.[29] God's essence is identical with His existence, since He is necessary or self-existent being; but it is admitted that we cannot know God's essence; therefore it is evident that we cannot know His existence. Kant is merely a little more subtle: if I know God's existence (*ens necessarium*), I must know His essence (*ens realissimum*); but if I knew the latter, I could demonstrate the former from it (ontological proof); I cannot do this; therefore, I cannot know God's existence. St. Thomas answered his medieval opponent by pointing out that we cannot know God's existence, if by His existence we mean the mode of being whereby He exists, which is identical with His essence. We can, however, prove the bare fact of His existence, so that we are certain that He does exist, without at all comprehending what His mode of existence, namely, necessary self-existence, is. Thus, we can know Him to exist, without knowing His essence and without, therefore, being able to demonstrate His existence from His essence.

d) An Illicit Passage Is Made From Logical Possibility to Real Possibility. Kant's fourth criticism of the logical structure of the cosmological proof is that it confuses the *logical possibility* of the totality of the real (*ens realissimum*) with its *real possibility,* passing without justification from the former to the latter. The criterion of logical possibility is the absence of contradiction in the conception of a thing; but the criterion for real possibility is that the thing can enter the synthesis of experience, that is, be a possible object of experience. Because the conception of the supreme being fulfills the first criterion, we assume that it is really possible; whereas this criterion establishes only its logical possibility.

The objection, of course, is not true. As Kant himself notes, the cosmological argument seeks to establish the *existence* of necessary being; and if it succeeds, it does not have to raise the question of the real possibility of this being. Kant's argument, instead of damaging the cosmological proof, throws a glaring light upon his own false as-

[29] *Con. Gen.,* I, 12.

sumption, the one pointed out just above. The fact is that we do not and cannot, in the cosmological proof *or in any other context,* make any use of the notion of the logical possibility of Supreme Being, because we simply cannot know *a priori* whether such a being *is* logically possible, since we cannot conceive the essence of that being. We know full well that our conception of God is only an analogous substitute for an unattainable idea of His essence; we would be very presumptuous to pronounce upon the logical possibility of a being which we cannot define. In giving the above criticism Kant shows again that the source of his misinterpretation of the cosmological proof is his failure to keep distinct in his own mind the pseudo-essence represented in our concept of perfect being and the real essence of that being.

This failure, indeed, is apparent even in his argument against the ontological proof itself. Here he argued forcibly that our conception of necessary being is, for all we know, quite empty of content. He should then have said flatly that the ontological argument is useless, since we do not comprehend the essence from which we are seeking to deduce necessary existence; but instead he bases his rejection of the argument on the fact that he is unable to form the slightest conception of a thing which, when annihilated in thought, with all its predicates, leaves behind a contradiction. This, of course, is true; but the real point of its truth Kant does not notice: namely, that what is annihilated in thought is *not* the conception of *ens realissimum,* but a substitute conception. The ontological proof arose out of the confusion of our conception of perfect being with the essence of that being. If my conception of perfect being were really the adequate representation in my mind of the essence of perfect being, I would see that this being necessarily exists and why — and the ontological proof would be valid, though no proof would be any longer needed. The reason why the ontological proof is not valid is not because the necessary existence of supreme being cannot be deduced from its conception, but because I can never have the conception of supreme being and therefore can never affirm *a priori* whether such being is even possible. When I have demonstrated *a posteriori* that a necessary being exists, I still know only the fact, not the essence of this being. My conception of supreme being has not been advanced one inch nearer the real essence of supreme being, and therefore I am as incapable as ever of starting my demonstration from that essence. But this in no way affects the validity of my *a posteriori* proof of the existence of a necessary being. Having proved that there is a being which exists by necessity, I go on from there; I do not go on from the still unknown essence of supreme being.

Kant carried his argument on to attack also the teleological proof, but the main principles of attack are the same as those of the arguments we have just examined; that is, he seeks to show that this proof calls to its aid, in order to reach its conclusion, the cosmological proof, and in doing so falls under the same strictures as does that proof, namely, that it is ultimately reducible to the invalid ontological argument. Instead of following Kant in his criticism, which would entail repetition of points already made, we shall examine some other attacks on the teleological proof.

V. ATTACKS ON THE TELEOLOGICAL ARGUMENT

The reader is reminded that we are not now about to explain the teleological argument for God's existence. We are merely going to examine certain objections urged against it. The four objections selected form a sort of crescendo of argument against the teleological proof. The first says that we cannot infer anything about nature's cause from the "order" of nature, because nature must have some order no matter what its cause. The second says that we cannot argue from the order of nature, because there is also disorder in nature. The third says that there is no design or finalistic order in nature to begin with. And the fourth caps the climax by maintaining that even if there is order or finality in nature, that gives us no right to conclude that there is an Orderer or Designer *of* nature.

A. One Order as Good as Another

The first objection offered is that we cannot use the "order" of nature as a proof of anything, because *any* arrangement is an order. Let us give the objection in the words of its authors:[30]

> Nature, it is maintained, is "orderly" and not "disorderly." But how significant is this assertion? If nature were "disorderly," would not that situation constitute merely a *different* order? Strictly speaking, it is self-contradictory to speak of nature as possibly lacking order. Any situation, any arrangement among existing things constitutes some kind of order. . . . Thus, if objectively speaking there can be neither greater nor less order in nature, the argument that the character which nature has requires us to assume an extra-natural architect collapses. Either

[30] From: *Philosophy: An Introduction,* by Randall and Buchler, pp. 163–164. Used by permission of Barnes and Noble, Inc., New York.

any order necessarily requires us to assume this, or no order necessarily does.

In Chapter V we developed the argument for teleology at some length. One primary point made was that the actual order of the universe is unmistakably directed toward the maintenance of life; it is an order with an end or goal. The argument is not merely an argument from order, but an argument from finalistic order. The above criticism is quite valueless in respect to such an argument. Suppose we agree that *any* arrangement is an order of some sort; in other words, that "arrangement" and "order" are synonyms. Does it then follow that no particular order is more significant than any other? Times Square is packed with many thousands of persons on any night of the year; these persons are, at every single moment, in some definite arrangement; consequently, there is a definite "order" among them. In January, 1946, there was a great military parade up New York's Fifth Avenue; at each moment there was a definite arrangement of the soldiers marching in the parade; hence, there was a definite "order" among them. Are the two orders equally significant or equally nonsignificant? The "order" of the crowd in Times Square does not lead the mind to infer a single orderer or governor; on the contrary, it speaks eloquently of independent determination of action. The parade, on the other hand, forbids the thought of independent determination of action and compels the mind to infer a single source of order. We might offer a similar illustration by comparing a metal scrap pile and a complex metal machine.

This answer is not a mere analogy; it is an illustration. Each illustration above instances two "orders" among similar things, and one of these orders gives no basis for an inference to a single orderer, while the other does. The argument in the objection, passing from the definition that any arrangement is an order to the conclusion that no order compels us to assert an external orderer, is a palpable *non sequitur*. It is especially futile when urged against the teleological argument, because that argument, as the data given in Chapter V show, is based on the peculiar character of the actual order of the world, an order which compels the inference to a single ordering agency.

B. Disorder as Well as Order in the Universe

The second argument states that we cannot infer a design in the universe from the order observable in the universe, because disorder is also observable.[31] This argument is as trivial as the one examined above. Suppose, to begin with, we ask for a few examples of the observed disorder. It is not easy to give any; in fact, if we put the question to almost any scientist he will tell us that there are no examples of disorder in the universe, so far as he knows. Indeed, he will point out, the complete orderliness or lawfulness of the material world is the base of all scientific research; it is a necessary presupposition of science, and a presupposition which the progress of science justifies more fully every day. Disorder in the universe would mean occurrences which are independent of or counter to physical laws. Nobody believes that, aside from miracles, there are any; and those who advance the present argument are hardly ready to adduce miracles in its support.

Those who advance the above argument, however, are probably using the term disorder loosely; and by disorderly phenomena they probably mean natural phenomena which are harmful to human life or to life generally. They mean, not disorder in nature, but conflict in nature. They mean that the same physical laws which produce and maintain life also destroy it, and that living beings prey upon one another. Earthquakes, floods, tornadoes, typhoons are all parts of nature's process, and they destroy thousands of human and animal lives. Virulent bacteria are living organisms, and they attack and destroy human life. The argument of the anti-teleologist is that if there were an all-powerful and all-good God who created and governs the world for the sake of life and especially human life, these harmful and life-destroying features would not be found in nature. There is one aspect of this argument which requires serious consideration and we shall give it that consideration in a later chapter on the problem of evil. For the present, however, let us simply examine the "logical" structure of the argument.

That structure is almost ludicrously illogical. That *we* cannot discover the perfection of the world's design does not prove that the design is not perfect. That someone *can* point out apparent imperfections in it does, on the other hand, prove that he discerns *some* design which these imperfections apparently mar, and which is his standard for judging the perfection or imperfection of the order of nature. Possibly, if we understood this design as a whole, we would see that the imperfections are merely apparent. At any rate, to argue that because

[31] A. Bahm, "Teleological Arguments," *The Scientific Monthly*, May, 1944, pp. 377–382.

the design seems imperfect to me, God cannot be the designer, is hardly modest; it amounts to saying: "God didn't make this world, because it is not made the way I would have made it if I were God." The Persian poet expressed the argument better than any atheistic philosopher:

> Ah, Love! could you and I with Him conspire
> To grasp this sorry Scheme of Things entire
> Would not we shatter it to bits — and then
> Remould it nearer to the Heart's desire!

Maybe we would, Love; but in truth we cannot say what we would do if we were to conspire with God; because in that case we would hardly be ourselves; we would see things as God sees them and do things as God does them, and we would please the pagan poet and the mechanistic philosopher little better than God pleases them now.

C. There Is No Design in Nature

1. This Objection Is Based Upon Evolution. Its meaning is this: all the evidences advanced by teleologists for purposive design in nature are taken from the evident adaptability of living things to their environment; they seem to be constructed as they are in order to be able to live in the conditions which nature supplies. But the real fact is that evolution does not produce *only* living beings which are fitted to live and adapted to their environment. On the contrary, it produces living forms in unlimited profusion, and, of all those produced, as many are unfitted to live and are destroyed by nature as are fitted to live and find a place in nature. The *appearance* of purposiveness in nature arises simply from the fact that unadapted organisms are killed off, so that only the adapted ones survive; then, when we look at the survivors, we think that nature produces only living things fitted to live, and we conclude that nature acts purposefully. Here is a clear statement of the argument:

> If we can free our minds from all prejudices, we find no evidence in nature of anything like a purpose or aim in creating life. We may therefore state that the appearance of life on the earth is nothing more than a cosmic event. In other words: just as mountains, rivers and oceans are formed by the play of the forces of nature, so also arise living structures on the surface of the earth.[32]

[32] R. Beutner, *Life's Beginning on the Earth* (Baltimore, Md.: William and Wilkins, 1938), p. 1.

It is quite obvious that the originators of all the elaborate terms such as vital force or determinism took it for granted that nature aims primarily at creating purposeful organisms. But in this regard these learned men were thoroughly mistaken since an unprejudiced investigation proves that enormous numbers of plants and animals with an inadequate make-up are constantly being formed. The late J. Loeb, biologist of The Rockefeller Institute, has demonstrated this fact through his studies on cross fertilization in marine animals; he showed that by fertilization of the eggs of one fish by the sperm of another fish, animals are generated in which some of the organs indispensable for life are absent. Since sperm or eggs of countless fish freely float in the ocean water and since cross fertilization frequently occurs, deficient creatures must be generated in a number probably equaling that of animals with adequate organs. Naturally only the latter survive.

The plain fact is that all plants or animals that have no organization adequate to meet the requirements for their existence have disappeared from the earth. This is why we see nothing but purposefulness in life. This statement seems to be so self-evident that it hardly requires further elucidation.[33]

2. Life Is Nature's Goal. Regardless of how self-evident the above statement may be, the conclusion which its author draws from it, namely, that nature presents no unmistakable signs of teleology, or working for definite ends, is far from self-evident. We have already pointed out in Chapter V that even if we regard the life of plants and animals upon earth as a struggle for existence — a struggle in which the fit survive and the unfit die off — we still must say that life itself is the end or goal of this struggle. Nature, perhaps, chooses comparatively few beings for successful living, but she calls many to life; and that is why there *is* a struggle for survival. We have also pointed out more than once that the inorganic substances and forces which constitute inorganic nature are in plain fact directed to the production and maintenance of life upon the earth; and that the probability that these substances and forces accidentally gave birth to life is so infinitesimally small that the mechanical processes which have in fact led to the emergence of life upon the earth are made intelligible only if we consider them as *intended for* that very end. That these forces and processes result in a profusion of living forms too numerous for the earth to bear, or that imperfect or deficient forms of life are produced along with efficient forms, is hardly evidence that nature is not directed toward the production of living beings upon the earth.

[33] *Ibid.*, pp. 3–4.

3. The Evolutionary Hypothesis. The view of nature upon which the argument now in question is based is the evolutionary view. According to this view, the original living things on the earth developed from non-living matter, and all the variety of living things which have ever existed on the earth developed from these original ones. Thomistic philosophy offers no theoretical objection to this hypothesis; and whether the hypothesis represents a fact is a question for natural science to answer. Let us, therefore, accept it now hypothetically in order to see where it leads us in reference to the question of whether there is purposive design in nature.

Let us suppose, then, that living beings of some very simple sort — say, unicellular or even sub-cellular organisms — originally evolved from non-living matter, and that all subsequent forms of biological life have evolved, through many intermediate stages, from these first simple forms of life. The forms of life which now exist as relatively permanent types are those which, because of their kind of structure, found a way of fitting into the environment which nature supplied. They, the survivors, were not *specially* produced; they were simply *some* forms among innumerable forms impartially produced; but, by the accident of a structure that jibed both within itself and with the world around it, they were kept alive while less lucky forms were destroyed. Even these survivors do not really *survive;* that is, they do not, for any very long time, remain unchanged. They are, in fact, changing in every generation, perhaps in ways so slight as to be imperceptible, perhaps by some sudden perceptible development or mutation; in any case, their offspring are never exactly the same as they. Some of the offspring change in a lucky way; that is, they differ from their parents by having some new structure that is better adapted to their surroundings. Some others change in an unlucky direction and fit less well into their surroundings. More of the former will live long enough to produce offspring themselves, so that the whole family tree will grow faster and bigger in the direction of its more fortunate branch, until the changes in that direction become so emphasized that we call some later generation of offspring a new species. Thus the present species of plants and animals in the world have come to be what they are.

What does it all mean? Why have some of the simple living forms remained simple? Why have some developed into highly complex organisms? Why have some become plants and some animals? Were the cells which began each of these lines of evolution different from one another, or were they the same? If they were the same, what caused their later differentiation? The probable answer to all these questions is environmental conditions and gene mutations. That answer explains hardly anything, but it leads to some fertile reflections concerning the emergence of the various forms of life. If the environment is the *external* condition of the forms of living beings, the *internal* conditions must be sought in the stuff which becomes the various forms. The cell which resists death by dividing and by becoming a multicellular organism, the cell which provides, as it were, for future contingencies by gene mutations, must have in it some mighty urge to live. The original simple forms, which are the first parents of all the complex forms of life, pursued their long road of self-differentiation because it was the only alternative to death; they had to evolve or die. That they have not died, that they have filled the earth with countless kinds of life, is evidence of the unthinkably rich potentiality for life which was originally locked away in them, and which the struggle to live has brought to actuality in so many different channels. Like June, nature's urge to live keeps "bustin' out all over"; life tries everything in order to avoid extinction.

4. Matter Is Urge to Live. But what of life's beginning? On the hypothesis which we have adopted, living things originally evolved from non-living matter. We must, consequently, locate the "urge to live" in matter itself. But can the non-living have an urge to live? It *must* have, for surely a becoming alive is as strongly indicative of an urge to live as is a fighting to stay alive. Then it is in matter itself that the urge to live resides. What is matter? Today the usual answer is that matter is energy; modern physics thinks in images of force and activity, rather than in images of bulk and chunk. Units of electrical charge have replaced solid particles of stuff. Every form of matter is some form of energy, and primary matter is indeterminate energy. And out of this matter or energy all living organisms have evolved. Perhaps, then, energy or matter *is,* fundamentally, "urge to live." However strange this may sound, it is, for one thing, not un-Thomistic. St. Thomas called it matter's appetite for the most perfect actuality attainable:

> But since, as was already stated, everything which undergoes motion tends as such toward a divine likeness in order to be perfect in itself, and since a thing is perfect in so far as it becomes actual, it follows

that the intention of everything that is in potentiality is to tend to actuality by way of movement. Hence the more final and more perfect an act is the more is the appetite of matter inclined to it. Therefore the appetite whereby matter seeks a form must tend toward the last and most perfect act to which matter can attain, as to the ultimate end of generation. Now certain grades are to be found in the acts of forms. For primary matter is in potentiality, first of all, to the elemental form. While under the elemental form, it is in potentiality to the form of a compound; wherefore elements are the matter of a compound. Considered under the form of a compound, it is in potentiality to a vegetative soul; for the act of such a body is a soul. Again the vegetative soul is in potentiality to the sensitive, and the sensitive to the intellective. This is shown in the process of generation, for first in generation is the fetus living a plant life, afterwards the life of an animal, and finally the life of man. After this no later or more noble form is to be found in things that are generated and corrupted. Therefore, the last end of all generation is the human soul, and to this does matter tend as its ultimate form. Consequently the elements are for the sake of compounds, the compounds for the sake of living things; and of these, plants are for the sake of animals, and animals for the sake of man. Therefore, man is the end of all generation.[34]

St. Thomas in the above passage, is not teaching evolution in the modern sense of that term, but someone coming upon the passage out of its context might well believe it to be an effort to indicate a metaphysical ground for the evolutionary process. The Angelic Doctor is teaching something that is very relevant to the problem of evolution, something which makes evolution intelligible. What he is teaching is that primary matter is appetite or urge to live and ultimately to live on the highest possible level, that is to say, as the body of man. The clear implication of this is that the first *cause* of the processes through which matter passes in its evolution is the *end* of those processes.

If, therefore, we could ask St. Thomas why matter becomes alive, he might answer: because matter is urge to live; life is the end of matter. From inorganic matter in the universe there was somehow produced living matter in at least this part of the universe, and, ever since, life has fought strenuously and successfully to keep itself in being and to attain to higher levels. In order to succeed, it had to adopt a million forms whose variety staggers the imagination; but succeed it did. If, now, we ask natural science why matter became alive, only one answer can be given: it had to. Any other answer would amount to a rejection of chemistry and physics. And the answer is the same if we ask

[34] *Con. Gen.*, III, 22.

why life evolved to its present variety of forms: it had to. St. Thomas' answer and the answer of science are in no way in conflict or disagreement; indeed, they amount to the same thing, although each states that thing from a different point of view. As always, the philosopher speaks from the point of view of action and the scientist from the point of view of process. The evolution of matter is a series of actions determined by the ultimate act which is their end; it is also a series of mechanical processes produced by the series of actions. The series of processes is necessary if the series of actions is to take place and attain its end. If matter is urge to live, it must go through the evolutionary process. If it must go through the process, it is urge to live. But if matter is urge to live, should not all matter become alive? No. The scientist, speaking in terms of process, will answer that all matter cannot possibly become alive in the present order of nature, because inorganic nature supplies the conditions for life. The teleologist, speaking in terms of ends and actions, will give what amounts to the same answer: all matter does not become alive because the urge to live is not suicidal; the end of nature determines means to its own attainment, it does not swallow up its means and thus destroy itself. The means which nature provides in order to attain its end are the physicochemical processes which science studies; and nature is so ordered that these processes culminate not only in life, the end of nature, but also in the inorganic conditions of life, the means to that end. In brief, mechanical and final causality are reciprocal in nature; that is the consistent Aristotelian-Thomistic position.

But if life is the end of nature, why does nature give birth to living things which are bound to fail in the struggle for life? When a sperm fertilizes the wrong egg and a deficient organism bound to extinction is formed, what design or purpose is there in that? We may answer that the egg and the sperm were each designed for successful life. An egg fertilized by the wrong sperm was an egg for which there was a right sperm. And its fertilization by any sperm is clear evidence of its urge to live. In any case, whatever becomes of it under any conditions is primarily determined by what it was naturally meant to be, just as the course of a deflected bullet is primarily determined by the target at which it was aimed. Perhaps nature's profusion in spilling out life all over so that some of it may survive is not very efficient; but let us not argue that way, for pretty soon we would find ourselves again saying that if God manages nature, He does not do it as well as we would if we were God. Instead let us remark that it is a very strange way to argue *against* nature's determination to produce living beings to offer as evidence nature's profligacy in producing them.

D. Even If There Is Design, That Does Not Prove That There Is a Designer

We saw in Section VII of Chapter V that many contemporary philosophers hold that finality or purpose is unquestionably at work in nature, but that we cannot conclude from this fact that an intelligent cause distinct from nature exists and moves nature to His own ends or purposes. These philosophers, to use the terminology we used in that chapter, admit immanent finality in nature, but hold that immanent finality does not necessarily imply *transcendent* finality. The final end and the agency which moves natural beings to this end may be *within nature,* that is to say, *solely* within nature.[35] This view, we pointed out in Chapter V, involves several insurmountable difficulties. We need not repeat them all here, but it will be worth while to restate one of them in slightly changed form.

To believe in finality in nature is to believe that ends are causes in natural processes. But we cannot believe that an end which is solely *in* nature can be a cause, for every such end is subsequent to the process of which it is the end. If it is in nature, it is in *time;* and in relation to the process of which it is the end, it is in future time — which means that during the process it has no existence. Now a cause must be prior to its effect. Therefore an end which is a cause must be in some way prior to the process of which it is the end. It is not prior in time; consequently, if it has being only in time, it is not prior at all. Therefore, belief in finality within natural processes entails belief in final causes or a final cause which is *timeless* or outside time. But a cause which is outside time transcends nature, since nature, being in process, is of necessity in time. Therefore, finality in nature demands a *transcendent* final cause or causes. That this transcendent final cause is *One* we may prove from the unity of order in nature; or, if that does not seem satisfactory, we may add a final step to the teleological argument, and prove, as we did in the Fourth Way, that even if there are a plurality of orders in the universe, they all demand one First Order and Ordainer as their ground or cause.

[35] In Thomistic doctrine this agency, which is God, is both immanent and transcendent; it is both within nature and above nature. This will be explained in Chapter XXV.

CHAPTER XXII

THE DIVINE ATTRIBUTES AND NAMES

===

I. OUR RATIONAL KNOWLEDGE OF GOD

1. We Know God as Cause of the World. Having proved the existence of God, it is now our task to inquire into His nature. This inquiry really forms part of, and the completion of, the demonstration of God's existence; because, until we have arrived at some determinate conception of what kind of being the First Mover, First Cause, Necessary Being, Supreme Being is, we cannot mean very much when we call it God. For the philosopher, the inquiry into the nature of God is the same thing as the ascertainment of the properties of the First Cause, the First Mover, the Necessary Being, the Supreme Being. The philosopher cannot start, as the theologian does, from the nature of God as He has Himself revealed it. The object of our study is not God as He is in Himself, but God as He can be known to us as cause of the world. Just as all proofs of His existence had to start from His effects, so His effects supply us with the only road to a rational knowledge of His essence. Direct, positive knowledge of God's essence as it is in itself is unattainable by human reason, because: (1) all our knowledge of God is inferred from His effects: we do not directly perceive the essence of God; (2) all our knowledge begins with sensory data, and the proper object of our intellect is the essence of material beings. God is purely immaterial.

> Our natural knowledge begins from sense. Hence our natural knowledge can go as far as it can be led by sensible things. But our intellect cannot be led by sense so far as to see the essence of God; because sensible creatures are effects of God which do not equal the power of God, their cause. Hence from the knowledge of sensible things the whole power of God cannot be known; nor therefore can His essence be seen. But because they are His effects and depend upon their cause, we can be led from them so far as to know of God whether He exists, and to know of Him what must necessarily belong to Him, as the first

cause of all things, exceeding all things caused by Him. Hence, we know His relationship with creatures, that is, that He is the cause of all things; also that creatures differ from Him, insamuch as He is not in any way part of what is caused by Him; and that His effects are removed from Him, not by reason of any defect on His part, but because He super-exceeds them all.[1]

2. Negative Knowledge. Negative knowledge of God is attainable. We can ascertain *what God is not.* We can with certainty deny of the divine essence any mode of being that is intrinsically limited and imperfect. The conclusion of each of the Five Proofs implies certain immediate negations; e.g., God is unmoved, uncaused, completely independent of any other being, utterly without imperfection. By probing into the significance of these conclusions we add other negations to these immediate ones and thus keep adding to our conception of what differentiates God from creatures; we determine ever more accurately what God cannot be. Is such negative knowledge truly knowledge? Yes; although it is very imperfect knowledge, it is not utter ignorance; we do know something, even though that something is a negation, a denial. Although it is not saying *what God is,* it is saying something true about Him to say that in Him there is no matter, no potentiality, no composition, no accidents, nothing distinct from His being, nothing defective. We do not show what He is, but we do show that He is different from all else.

3. Analogical Knowledge. In addition to this negative knowledge of God, we can also attain some analogical knowledge. Analogical knowledge of God is knowledge based upon the similarity, proportion, or analogy which exists between God and creatures. God, as the second proof has shown, is the cause of all creatures. Now the act of causing is always a communication or giving of something to the effect by the cause. Consequently, every effect receives something from its cause, and, therefore, no matter how much it may differ from its cause, it cannot fail to bear some resemblance to it. God is the first and total cause of all creatures, and, therefore, whatever they have that is positive and real they have received from God; and consequently their reality and perfection, howsoever limited it may be, gives them a similarity or analogy to God. This fact justifies us in making certain *analogical predications* about God.[2]

It is in connection with this question of predication about God that

[1] S. Theol., I, 12, 12, c; cf. 13, 1, c (*The Basic Writings of St. Thomas Aquinas,* ed. Anton C. Pegis [New York: Random House, 1945], Vol. I, p. 109).

[2] *Ibid.,* I, 4, 2 and 3.

the doctrine of the analogy of being, explained in Chapter XVII, reveals its importance. The being of God and the being of creatures are analogous. God is the cause of creatures, but not a *univocal* cause, as a human father is of his son. God is an *equivocal* cause of creatures, as an artist is of a picture or a watchmaker of a watch. The attributes of creatures cannot be simply predicated of God, their cause, any more than the qualities of a picture can be simply predicated of the artist, or those of the watch of the watchmaker. Therefore we cannot make any univocal predications of God and creatures. But just as we can attribute the beauty of a painting to the painter as existing in him in a mode quite different from the mode in which it exists in the painting, and just as we attribute intelligence to the watchmaker because he causes the intelligible design and function of the watch, so we can attribute to God, as being in Him in a different mode — that is, analogously — the perfections we find in His effects.[3]

All positive predications, therefore, that we make of both God and creatures are made analogously. When we say "Solomon is wise" and "God is wise," we are not saying two entirely different things about God and Solomon, nor are we saying precisely the same thing. Wisdom is an attribute which we predicate of the subject Solomon. It is not Solomon himself, but a quality of Solomon. Two realities are involved: the subject and the attribute. The attribute determines the subject; the subject participates in the attribute. The subject can exist without the attribute; and the same attribute can be found in other subjects. Our poor, faltering human language makes it sound as though we are saying the same thing of God. But in fact there is in this case no distinction of subject and attribute, no two realities involved. God's wisdom is not an attribute determining God and participated in by God; that is precisely what is impossible — that the Uncaused can be determined by anything, that the First Being can participate in anything. God's wisdom is God Himself. God does not *possess* wisdom; He *is* wisdom and the one source of all wisdom.[4]

To summarize: All our natural knowledge of God's essence is derived from our knowledge of creatures. The starting points of our quest into God's nature are the conclusions of the proofs of God's existence. We attain knowledge of God in two ways: the negative way and the way of analogy. By the negative way we deny of God

[3] *Ibid.*, I, 4, 2; *ibid.*, 13, 2.
[4] *Ibid.*, 13, 4.

all that we find to belong to creatures precisely because they are creatures; that is to say, all that is intrinsically limited and imperfect. By the way of analogy we affirm of God all those positive perfections which we find in creatures and which, although limited in creatures, are in themselves intrinsically unlimited. The basis of analogy is the fact that God is the cause of creatures, the source of all being, and the fact that the effect must in some way resemble its cause. When we predicate the same attribute analogously of God and creatures, we concomitantly deny of its existence in God all the modes of imperfection in which it exists in creatures.

Finally, whatsoever knowledge we attain philosophically of God does not reach to the intrinsic life of God — the Persons of the Trinity — but only to God as He can be known as cause of the world. We predicate of God only what we can see must belong to Him in order to account for the universe of which He is the cause. Whatever else He is, philosophy is incompetent to say — except that He is infinitely above all that man can say of Him.

4. The Method. The method by which we derive the divine attributes from the proofs of God's existence is simple enough. The marks by which we knew that the world is contingent, caused, and dependent led us to affirm a necessary, uncaused, and self-existent being upon which the world depends. Since this being is put forward as the adequate explanation of the world, it must not itself have the marks by which we recognized the contingency of the world; for in that case it would itself need to be explained in terms of some prior being. Hence, where the world is marked by movement, generation, dependency, and imperfection, this cause must be immutable, ungenerated, underived, perfect. These primary attributes were attained in the conclusions of the proofs themselves, but others follow necessarily from them, and by deducing these others we build up a conception of God, which, while phrased in negative terms, is nevertheless bringing us ever nearer to a knowledge of the nature of the First Cause. To this conception we add the attributes which we can discover by way of analogy.

II. THE SIMPLICITY OF GOD

1. God Is Pure Actuality. God can in no way contain in Himself any passive potentiality; He cannot be the actuality of a prior potentiality, and He cannot have in Him any potency for becoming:

The first being must of necessity be in act and in no way in potency. For although in any single being which passes from potency to act, the potency is prior in time to the act, nevertheless, absolutely speaking, act is prior to potency; for whatever is in potency is reduced to act only by some being in act. Now it has already been proved that God is the First Being. It is therefore impossible that in God there should be any potentiality.[5]

From the fact also that God is necessary being, it is clear that there can be nothing in Him in potentiality. For necessary being is being which is self-existent, self-actual. Whatever is in the divine being must be in act, since the divine being is necessary.

2. God Is Immaterial. From the pure actuality of God, it follows that God is absolutely simple; that is to say, that in Him there is no composition of any sort. He has not the composition of extended parts, which belong to a body, because any extended thing is divisible, and whatever is divisible contains potentiality. Nor can He be composed of matter and form. In the first place, He would be a body were He so compounded, for a composite of matter and form is a body. Second, matter, as we have seen, is pure potentiality; and therefore the Pure Act can contain no matter. Furthermore, it is impossible that the First Agent, or first efficient cause, which God is, should contain matter. For every agent acts by its form, and consequently must possess form in the same manner in which it acts. But God, as First Agent, acts by Himself without participating in any prior act; consequently, He does not participate in form, but is of Himself Form, and is completely immaterial.[6]

3. God's Essence Is Himself. From this fact, that God is pure form, it follows that there is no distinction in God between Himself and His essence. A man is not humanity; but God is Deity. Forms not received into matter are not, as in the case of natural forms, individuated by matter, but are individuated of themselves. They are themselves first substances or *supposita*.[7] Consequently, individual and essence are identified in them. God is Pure Form and consequently in Him, Self is identical with essence. God's essence is God Himself, and whatever is of His essence — life, wisdom, goodness, love — is identical with God Himself; whatever is in God is God.[8]

[5] *Ibid.*, I, 3, 1, c. Cf. *Con. Gen.*, I, 16.
[6] *S. Theol.*, I, 3, 1 and 2; *Con. Gen.*, I, 17, 20.
[7] Cf. Chapter VI, Section V.
[8] *S. Theol.*, I, 3, 3; *Con. Gen.*, I, 21.

4. God's Essence Is His Existence. In God *essence and existence are identical.* Anything whose essence is not itself existence can have existence only from an external cause. For whatever belongs to anything besides its essence belongs to it either by virtue of its own essential principles or by virtue of an external cause. Now, if the essential principle of something is not itself existence, it is not of itself actual, for existence is the actuality of essence. Therefore, of itself, it does not exist. So long as it does not exist, it cannot be a principle of any actual perfection; hence it cannot be a principle of existence, the first of all actualities. It must, therefore, receive existence from an external cause, if it is to exist. But God is First Cause, and receives existence from nothing. His essence, therefore, is His existence. Furthermore, any essence which is not itself existence, is potential in respect to existence. If, therefore, God's essence were not His existence, He would be potential in essence. But we have seen that He is Pure Act. Finally, something which *has* being, but is not itself being, is a being by participation. But God, as we have seen, is His own essence: *suppositum* and nature are identical in Him. If, therefore, He is not His own being, He will not be essential being but participated being; that is, He will exist by virtue of something else. In that case, He would not be the First Being — which is absurd. Hence, God's existence is His essence.[9]

5. God Is Not in Any Genus. God cannot be contained in any genus of being. The genera divide being, and whatever is in a genus is contained in one division of being and excluded from the other divisions. If God were in any genus, He would be in the genus being, since His essence is His being, and everything is located in a genus according to its essence. But being, we have seen, cannot be a genus.[10] Hence, God cannot be in any genus. Furthermore, the things in a genus differ from one another in being or existence and agree with one another in essence; and, therefore, in each of them existence and essence must be distinct. But we have seen that existence and essence are identical in God. Consequently, God is not in any genus or division of being, but is Being Itself.[11]

6. There Are No Accidents in God. God cannot be a composite of substance and accidents, as natural substances are. His action, for

[9] *S. Theol.*, I, 3, 4; *Con. Gen.*, I, 22.
[10] Chapter XVII, Section III.
[11] *S. Theol.*, I, 3, 5; *Con. Gen.*, I, 25.

example, cannot be distinct from His being, as our actions are distinct from our being. A subject which has accidents is related to those accidents as potentiality to actuality; the accidents are determinations added to the subject's substantial being, making it actual in some of the nine categories of accident. But God is pure actuality, and consequently nothing can be added to His substance actualizing it in some mode. Second, His essence is being itself, not being of some limited genus, and hence can have nothing added to it. Finally, if there were any accident in God, it would be something caused — either by an external cause or by His own constituent essential principles. Each alternative is impossible: nothing in the First Cause can be caused by an external cause; and nothing in God "caused" by His essence can be accidental, for His essence is its own actuality or being, which means conversely that His whole being is His essence.[12]

7. **God Is Absolutely Simple Being.** The absolute simplicity of God may be proved in many ways. The above arguments, for example, treated of each separate kind of composition and showed that it is not in God; hence, God is altogether without composition. Second, everything composite in any respect is posterior to its component elements and dependent upon them; but the First Being is absolutely prior and independent. Third, everything composite has a cause; for it is made by the union of diverse components, and diverse things are united only by the agency of a cause. God, however, has no cause. Fourth, there is potentiality in every composite being, for either one part actualizes the other (as accident actualizes substance, and form actualizes matter) or at least all the parts are potential in respect to the whole, having their concrete actuality only by virtue of the whole (as an eye, for example, is an eye only in a living organism). But in God there is no potentiality. Finally, nothing composite can be predicated of any of its parts, as we cannot say that a man's foot is the man, or that part of a quantity of some homogeneous substance, like water, is the whole quantity. Thus, in every composite being there is something which is not itself. But in a form there is nothing but the form itself, as in humanity nothing but humanity and in red nothing but red. Since God, therefore, is absolute form, or rather absolute being, He can in no way be composite.[13]

8. **God Is Not Only Simple in Himself, But Enters Into Composition**

[12] *S. Theol.,* I, 3, 6; *Con. Gen.,* I, 23.
[13] *S. Theol.,* I, 3, 7; *Con Gen.,* I, 18

With Nothing Else. St. Thomas mentions and refutes three ancient pantheistic theories — theories which make God in some way part of the world. According to the first, God is the soul of the world; according to the second, He is the form or formal principle of all things; and according to the third, He is primary matter. The first two may be reduced to one; namely, that God is the form of the world.

God, answers the Angelic Doctor, cannot be either the form or the matter of anything. First, He is the first efficient cause. Now the efficient cause of something is never numerically identical with its formal cause, as a father is not the form of his son, but only specifically the same, as the father as man generates a man. No efficient cause can be identical either specifically or numerically with primary matter, for an efficient cause exists actually while primary matter exists potentially. Second, it belongs to God, as *first* efficient cause to act primarily and essentially; nothing, however, in a composite acts primarily and essentially, but rather the composite in which it is does; thus a man's hand does not seize or his intellect think, but the man seizes by his hand and thinks by his intellect. Hence, God, since He acts primarily and essentially, cannot be something in a composite. Finally, no part of a composite can be absolutely first among beings, not even the first parts of every composite, namely matter and form. Matter cannot be first absolutely, because it is of itself potential, and the potential is posterior absolutely to the actual; if there were no first actuality, there would be nothing. Nor can a form which is in a composite be first absolutely; for, as we have seen above, a form which is in a composite is a participated form, since it does not have being of itself. But nothing which is participated being can be absolutely first. God, therefore, who is the absolutely first being, cannot be the form of any composite. Hence God in no way enters into composition with anything.[14]

III. THE PERFECTION OF GOD

1. God is absolutely perfect. By attributing absolute perfection to Him we mean that He possesses in its fullness and without defect everything positive and perfect which can belong to being; we mean that He is being itself, in its totality, without lack, limitation, or defect. We may prove God's perfection from His actuality. For actuality and perfection coincide; every perfection is, in the last analysis, a

[14] *S. Theol.*, I, 3, 8; *Con. Gen.*, I, 26, 27.

certain degree of actual being, and every imperfection a certain lack of actual being. Wisdom, for example, means being wise, and foolishness means not being wise. Now since God is being itself in pure actuality, He is absolutely perfect. Some have argued, not seriously perhaps, that since God's essence is being, He is most imperfect, for merely to be is the least of perfections. They confuse the logician's concept of being, which represents the minimum comprehension, with the metaphysician's concept, which represents the fullness of being. God is being itself in the real, actual order, not in the logical order. He is the First Being and the source of all other being. He is being itself in the sense that He is all that being is; and being is life, goodness, beauty, intelligence, freedom, and everything positive and real. God, the Pure Act, is not being at its most undefined and potential; He is being at its fullest and most actual. The logician, for his purposes, may consider life and intelligence as something added to and received by being; but the metaphysician knows that being is the perfection of everything — that life and intelligence are nothing if they have not being. Being is that which everything else *receives* in order to be actual and perfect; being itself is never the recipient; it is the actuality of all things.[15]

God, therefore, has all the perfections of all being. Not limited to any genus, He transcends all the divisions of being and possesses the perfection of every genus. He is not a slice out of being, but is being itself in its fullness. As the first cause of every other being, He contains the perfections of all, since the perfection of the effect must pre-exist in its cause. He contains these perfections in a higher manner, as does an efficient cause, which He is, and not in a lower manner, as does a material cause; all perfections are in Him in act, not in potency. God, therefore, contains all the perfections of all beings *eminently;* in God the perfection is original and identical with God; in the creature it is derived and participated in by the creature.

2. God Is Subsistent Being. St. Thomas' treatment of God's perfection brings out clearly the fact that Thomistic philosophy is the philosophy of being, or existence. The ultimate reason, according to the Angelic Doctor, why God is absolutely perfect and contains the perfections of all things is that He is being itself:

> God is being itself, of itself subsistent. . . . Since therefore God is subsisting being itself, nothing of the perfection of being can be wanting

[15] *S. Theol.*, I, 4, 1; *Con. Gen.*, I, 28.

to Him. Now all the perfections of all things pertain to the perfection of being; for things are perfect precisely so far as they have being after some fashion. It follows therefore that the perfection of no thing is wanting to God.[16]

It is thus that St. Thomas answers those who confuse being itself with the bare notion of being which is left when all other positive determinations have been stripped away:

> The same Dionysius says that, although being itself is more perfect than life, and life than wisdom, if they are considered as distinguished in idea, nevertheless, a living thing is more perfect than what merely is, because a living thing is also a being, and an intelligent thing is both a being and alive. Although therefore being does not include life and wisdom, because that which participates being need not participate in every mode of being, nevertheless God's being includes in itself life and wisdom, because nothing of the perfection of being can be wanting to Him Who is subsisting being itself.[17]

In brief, whatever is, is from being itself, the Original; and consequently there can be no perfection in any being which is not first and most properly in Being Itself.

3. The Analogy of God and Creatures. That God possesses properly and eminently the perfections of all His effects enables us to make certain predications about His nature, but at the same time forbids us to make these predications in the same manner in which we make them of creatures. All creatures are like God inasmuch as every effect is like its cause in communicating in some manner in the same form as the cause. But, at the same time, no creature is specifically or generically like God, for God is not contained in any species or genus. Hence the creature bears only an analogous likeness to God. God is not a univocal, but an equivocal cause. A man as father is the univocal cause of his son, producing an effect which contains his own form of human nature in the same manner in which he contains it; but a man as artist is an equivocal cause of a painting, producing an effect which contains the same form or idea which is in his mind, but in a manner different from the manner in which it is in his mind. This latter kind of causing is more like God's. The being or perfection of a creature is a likeness of God's being or perfection; but whereas it is simple, self-existent, and unlimited in God, it is composite, caused, and limited in the creature.

[16] S. Theol., I, 4, 2, c (Pegis, op. cit., Vol. I, p. 39).

[17] Loc cit. ad 3 (Pegis, op. cit., Vol. I, pp. 39–40). Cf. De Ente, IV; De Potentia. III. 5; Con. Gen., 1, 28.

For since every agent reproduces itself so far as it is an agent, and everything acts in accord with its form,[18] the effect must in some way resemble the form of the agent. If, therefore, the agent is contained in the same species as its effect, there will be a likeness in form . . . according to the same formality of the species; as man reproduces man. If, however, the agent and its effect are not contained in the same species, there will be a likeness . . . not according to the formality of the same species . . . but only in its generic likeness. If therefore there is an agent not contained in any genus, its effects will still more distantly reproduce the form of the agent, not, that is, so as to participate in the likeness of the agent's form according to the same specific or generic formality, but only according to some sort of analogy; as being itself is common to all. In this way all created things, so far as they are beings, are like God as the first and universal principle of all being.[19]

IV. THE GOODNESS OF GOD

1. **The Nature of the Good.** Something is called *good* inasmuch as it is desirable. What is first of all desired by anything is its own perfection. But something is perfect in so far as it is actual. Now *being,* as we have seen, is what makes anything actual. Consequently, in the last analysis, goodness and being are really the same. The two *concepts,* being and good, are not the same, because goodness adds, over the notion of being, the notion of desirability; but that which the concepts represent is the same thing, for that which is primarily desirable in anything is its actual being.[20] It might sometimes seem that non-being is desired, as, for example, by a suicide; and if this is so, it can hardly be maintained that the good, or the desirable, is identical with being. However, when any case where non-being is desired is considered carefully, it will be found that the non-being is not desired of itself but only relatively to being. For non-being is desired only inasmuch as it removes some evil; and the removal of an evil is sought by something because the evil deprives this thing of some being. A suicide, for example, may be seeking to escape through non-being from some shame or loss or fear which has deprived him of peace and happiness more than he can bear to be deprived. Therefore, it is only being which is desired in itself, and non-being is desired only relatively to being.[21]

From the fact that goodness and being are really identical it follows,

---

[18] This has been explained in Chapter IV, Section VI. No. 7.

[19] *S. Theol.,* l, 4, 3, c (Pegis, *op. cit.,* Vol. I, pp. 40–41); *Con Gen.,* I, 29.

[20] *S. Theol.,* I, 5, 1. Cf. *De Ver.,* XI, 1 and 2.

[21] *S. Theol.,* I, 5, 2, ad 3.

of course, that every being is good. Goodness, like truth and unity, is transcendental and convertible with being. Every being, in so far as it is being, is good; because as being it has actuality and is in some way perfect, since every actuality, as we have seen, is some sort of perfection and therefore is in some manner desirable. Although the concept of good is different from that of being, it does not limit being or divide it, because what goodness adds to being is simply desirability, that is, a relation to appetite; and this is proper to every being. If it be objected that evil could not exist if every being were good, we must answer that every being *in so far as it is being* is good, and something is evil only in so far as it lacks being; that is, in so far as it is a privation in being, like blindness in a man or untruthfulness in speech. A thing may exist without possessing all the perfections due it; in so far as it exists, it has some perfection and is good, and in so far as it lacks some due perfection it is evil.[22]

2. **God Is Good.** From all this it is clear that God is good, that He is the supreme good, that He alone is essentially good and that anything else is good only by virtue of His goodness. God is the first cause, that is, the first universal agent, and all the being and perfection in anything is from Him. Now what anything seeks first of all is its own perfection. But the perfection of an effect consists in its likeness to its cause, for every agent, as we saw above, reproduces its own likeness in its effect; and therefore the agent itself is desirable. Therefore, all things, by desiring their own perfection, desire God Himself, inasmuch as the perfections of all things are so many likenesses of the divine being. Hence God as First Agent is the first desirable and the first good. Some things, which lack knowledge, as minerals and plants, "desire" God only by natural appetite, being directed to their ends by Him; others, the animals, which have only sensitive knowledge, desire Him only by desiring certain likenesses of His goodness in sensible things; and rational creatures are capable of knowing and desiring Him in Himself.[23]

3. **God Is the Supreme Good.** God is absolutely the highest good because all perfections flow from Him as the first cause. We have seen that He is not a univocal cause which produces its likeness in an effect of the same species as itself, but an equivocal cause which is not contained in any species or genus and which produces effects

[22] *S. Theol.*, I, 5, 3, c and ad 2; I, 5, 1, ad 1. Cf. *De Ver.*, XI, 1, ad 9.
[23] *S. Theol.*, I, 6, 1; *Con. Gen.*, I, 37.

which resemble it by analogy and imperfectly. Therefore the goodness of God transcends, or superexceeds, the goodness of all His effects, and He is absolutely supreme good.[24]

God alone is essentially good, and all the good of other things is derivative of His goodness. Goodness belongs to anything by virtue of its being, its perfect operation, and its attainment of its end. Only in God, who is Being Itself, that is to say, Pure Act, are these three aspects identical with essence: God's essence is His being, His operation is His being, and He is His own end; consequently He is essentially good, and He alone has every kind of perfection by His own essence. In all other things essence receives being and operation, and has its end in something else; hence, although other things possess goodness, they possess it only by participation.[25]

That the goodness of other things is derived from the divine goodness does not mean that these things have no goodness of their own. Created things are not being by essence or good by essence; but they really are being and really are good, for what the first agent produces in them is a real participation in and a real likeness of His own being and goodness:

> . . . there is something first which is essentially being and essentially good which we call God. . . . Hence from the first being, essentially being and good, everything can be called good and a being inasmuch as it participates in the first being by way of a certain assimilation. . . . Everything is therefore called good from the divine goodness, as from the first exemplary, effective, and final principle of all goodness. Nevertheless, everything is called good by reason of the likeness of the divine being belonging to it, which is formally its own goodness, whereby it is denominated good. And so of all things there is one goodness, and yet many goodnesses.[26]

In this teaching of St. Thomas we see exemplified his clear rejection and avoidance of two opposite errors, naturalism and pantheism. He will not admit any goodness in the creature which is not derived from and caused by the goodness of God; but neither will he admit that the creature is not itself good in its own right. God's goodness is the exemplar, the efficient cause and the final cause of the creature's goodness; but the formal cause of this goodness is in the creature itself; it is the real created likeness of the uncreated good.

[24] S. Theol., I, 6, 2; Con. Gen., I, 41.
[25] S. Theol., I, 6, 3; De Ver., XI, 1, ad 1; Con. Gen., I, 38, 40.
[26] S. Theol., I, 6, 4, c (Pegis op. cit., Vol. I, p. 55); Con. Gen.. I, 40.

V. GOD'S INFINITY, IMMUTABILITY, AND ETERNITY

1. **The Infinity of God.** The infinity which we signify when speaking of God cannot be an infinity of multitude. As we shall prove below, God is one, and, as we have already proved, He is utterly simple; consequently He cannot be infinite in respect to either multiplication or division. Nor can this infinity refer to quantitative magnitude, or size, since God is immaterial and free from quantity. The infinity of God can only be an infinity of spiritual magnitude. Spiritual magnitude is measured by two factors, power and completeness of being. Of these two factors, the former is ultimately reducible to the latter; for power to act and produce follows and depends upon fullness of being: precisely to the degree to which something is actual is it active. Spiritual magnitude, therefore, means degree of completeness of being. Hence, when we ask whether God is infinite, we are asking whether He possesses being in its fullness without limitation of any sort.[27] By God's infinity we really mean the same thing as His perfection; yet it is well to treat of it separately, for the emphasis is different and the infinity of God arouses certain difficulties in some minds.

2. **Proofs of God's Infinity.** God is infinite. Whatever is finite is determined to some genus of being; but God, we have seen, transcends all the genera of being.[28] Second, whatever is limited, is limited by virtue of the limitations imposed upon it by the subject in which it is; thus all forms of corporeal being are limited because they are received in matter, and even immaterial forms are limited if they are received in a limited subject; as, for example, intelligence and freedom, though unlimited essentially, are limited in man. God is His own being, received in no subject, and consequently His being has no limitations.[29] That God is First Cause of the world is another proof of His infinity. In any causation, the active power of the cause must be greater, the greater the distance is from the matter on which the cause is acting to the effect to be produced. Thus, for example, it requires far less power to put an automobile together from parts already made than it does to produce the automobile from the original raw materials. Now the First Cause produces everything in the world, including even the matter out of which the world is made. Hence this produc-

[27] *Con. Gen.*, I, 43.
[28] *Loc. cit.*
[29] *Loc. cit.*

tion is a production of determinate being out of nothing; in other words, the distance from the starting point to the effect is infinite. Hence, the First Cause possesses infinite power. But since magnitude of power depends upon fullness of being, the First Cause, God, is infinite being.[30]

The most formal proof of God's infinity is taken from the identity of essence and existence in Him. God's essence and existence are identical. He is pure actuality, and is uncaused, simple being. Existence and actuality are limited intrinsically by essence and potentiality. Essence is to existence as a potency to its act. The being of anything which receives existence is proportionate to the essence receiving it and is limited by it; the existence received can be no more than the potentiality which it actualizes. In like manner, every caused being is limited by its causes; that is, it can be no more than its causes make it. But God's existence is not distinct from His essence, no potentiality limits His actuality, and He is uncaused. Therefore there is neither intrinsic nor extrinsic limitation upon His actuality. He is unlimited act.[31]

If a being possesses unlimited actuality in a certain respect, it may be called infinite in that respect, or relatively infinite. If, for example, any one man were to possess at one moment the complete perfection possible to the species man, he could be called, at that moment, relatively infinite, that is, unlimited in respect to human perfection and being. He could not, however, be *absolutely infinite* because many perfections of being are not possible to the essence of man. If, however, a thing possesses unlimited actuality, *not in a certain respect, but in regard to being itself,* that thing will be absolutely infinite, because the whole actuality of being will belong to it, the total perfection of being will be actualized in it. Now, it is precisely this that God possesses, namely, unlimited actuality in regard to being itself. He is, therefore, absolutely infinite being.[32]

3. God's Infinity and the Reality of Creatures. Many persons find it difficult to reconcile God's infinity with the existence of creatures which are really distinct from Him. If God is infinite, does it not seem that nothing else can exist? Would not other beings be something added to the infinite, and would not the infinite be lacking something

[30] *Loc. cit.*
[31] *Loc. cit., Amplius. Ipsum esse* . . . and *Adhuc. Omne quod.* . . .
[32] *S. Theol.*, I, 7, 2, c and ad 1.

if beings distinct from it exist? We must answer that creatures are not something added to the Infinite Being, nor does their existence imply any lack in God. Creatures are not God, but there is no being in them which is not in God in a more perfect way. Created being is analogous to God's being, a reflection of it possessing nothing not already contained in it. Because God is infinite, all being is in Him. More beings add no more being, because they contain nothing which the Infinite lacks and nothing not derived from Him.

The difficulty we have in grasping this arises, as do so many philosophical difficulties, from our habit of thinking in terms of material being. To an infinite quantity no further quantity can be added. So we say, "God is infinite; how, then, can He create something more?" In reality, quantity does not enter into the question at all, since there is no quantity in God. God's infinity is His possession of the full and absolute perfection of being in actuality and at once. No being can be added to Him because He is the fullness of being. Surely it is not contradictory to say that Infinite Being can cause to exist, distinct from Himself, imperfect, limited beings; or that Goodness Itself, Truth, Beauty, Life, can produce reflections or imitations of Itself, and that these add nothing to the Absolute Good, Beauty, Truth, Life, the Infinite Being, but only reflect it in diminished splendor. In brief, there is no reason why there cannot exist infinite self-existing Being and finite beings depending upon it, and it is clear that the Infinite Perfection is not increased or diminished in any way by the existence or non-existence of finite effects and imitations.

4. The Immutability of God. Immutability means unchangeableness. Change is an all-permeating trait of our own lives and of all that we experience; hence, we find it very hard to imagine anything as being completely unchangeable. Further, we are inclined to think of unchangeableness as a defect, for *we* must change or stagnate; life without change is, for us, life lost; growth and development are essential to life as we know it. And we are right in almost all of this. For where the starting point is potentiality and imperfection, change is the only way to actuality and perfection. But God is pure actuality, perfect and infinite being. He does not change — not because He is stagnant and inactive, but because He is the fullness of being, life, and activity. To change is to attain to being which was not yet possessed; or it is to lose being which is possessed. But God is Being Itself, subsisting in itself.

From what precedes, here is the proof that God is altogether immutable. First, because it was shown above that there is some first being,
whom we call God, and that this first being must be pure act, without
the admixture of any potentiality, for the reason that, absolutely,
potentiality is posterior to act. Now everything which is in any way
changed, is in some way in potentiality. Hence it is evident that it is
impossible for God to change in any way. Secondly, because everything
which is moved remains in part as it was, and in part passes away,
as what is moved from whiteness to blackness remains the same as
to substance; and thus in everything which is moved there is some kind
of composition to be found. But it has been shown above that in God
there is no composition, for He is altogether simple. Hence it is manifest
that God cannot be moved. Thirdly, because everything which is
moved acquires something by its movement, and attains to what it
had not attained previously. But since God is infinite, comprehending
in Himself all the plenitude of the perfection of all being, He cannot
acquire anything new, nor extend Himself to anything whereto He was
not extended previously. Hence movement in no way belongs to Him.[33]

Nothing could be further from the truth than to think that immutability is equivalent to inactivity; and that by an immutable God
St. Thomas means an inactive God. Motion and action, as we have
so strongly insisted in previous chapters, are by no means the same
thing. The only reason why action is invariably associated with
motion in the world of our experience is the fact that nothing in this
world is pure actuality. Everything in nature is a mixture of potency
and act; and one of the phases of this mixture is the relation of
operation to power and substance. The first actuality of a natural
thing is its substantial being; a further actuality is the power of this
being to operate in a certain manner; and the last actuality is the
operation or action. The operation is the act of the power, and consequently in order to operate a natural substance must pass, as regards
one of its powers, from potency to act. This passage is motion. Only
at the completion of the movement does the being operate. The movement from potency to act is not the action, but a condition which
must be fulfilled before the action can be exercised. Thus I see only if
my visual organs are moved by light rays, but it would surely be
absurd to confuse this movement with my act of seeing. The reason
why I must be moved is the fact that while I have the power to see —
or, more generally, to act — I am not myself sight or action. But God
is pure act; His action is Himself. He acts infinitely and always

[33] *Ibid.*, I, 9, 1, c (Pegis, *op. cit.*, Vol. I, pp. 70–71).

without ever moving to action: He is, He knows, He loves, He creates, He governs.

5. The Eternity of God. God is eternal as well as immutable. Eternity is that attribute whereby God always completely exists, without beginning, ending, or succession of parts in His existence. The first three proofs of God's existence all directly imply His eternity. As unmoved mover, He cannot have been moved from potency to act, nor can He be moved in any way; wherefore He has always existed, He exists unchangeably and He always will exist. As uncaused cause, He cannot have been brought into being by a prior cause, but must exist of Himself always. As necessary being, He necessarily always exists, and He not only exists always, but He exists unchangeably, possessing His whole being always and at once.[34]

6. Meaning of Eternity. When most of us use the term "eternity" we mean by it, very inaccurately, an unending time; thus we say that the human soul is eternal when we mean that it is immortal. Eternity properly understood, signifies more than unendingness; it signifies absence of beginning as well as of ending, and it also signifies lack of change and succession. That which is eternal, always and completely *is;* it has had no beginning of being, it will have no end of being, and it possesses its *whole* being always. We may, perhaps, understand the notion of eternity more easily by contrast with some temporal being. Besides having a beginning and an ending, the life of a man is parceled out to the man a moment at a time. I live, as it were, on a time-line. My life is a tiny point of illumination and activity moving along this time-line. All I possess of my life is the one tiny, moving, illuminated point. The part of the time-line over which the point of light has already passed is gone, and I can never possess it again; the part of the line stretching away in front of the light is not yet possessed —may never be possessed, indeed. Only the present moment of my life is mine; I have had the yesterdays and I shall have the to-morrows, but I actually have only today, only this moment. I live my life a piece at a time. My life, indeed, is as a thin edge of being ever moving forward between two nothings[35]—an edge of being which *is,* only by continually *becoming.* I live only by becoming alive; I possess life only as long as I can continue to get new life, for the

[34] *Ibid.,* I, 9, 1 and 2. Cf. *Con. Gen.,* I, 15.

[35] The figure is from Bergson. So indeed is the idea, though I do not think it dependent upon Bergsonism.

life which I get I at once lose. Change is the warp of my life and time is its woof: of them is my being compounded; but they are such strands as must unravel behind as fast as they are woven before. Because my soul is, in its essence, out of time, I can in mind grasp my life as a whole; but by doing so I only realize that I cannot really possess it as a whole; and I am mystified at its beginning, sad at its departed days, anxious for its days to come, fearful of its ending. Eternal life is not like this life of mine. Eternity is the perfect possession, altogether and always, of unending life. God's life is not lived along a time-line; none of it falls away into the nothingness of the past; none of it stands waiting on the non-existent future. God does not come into being, does not live a piece of His life at a time, does not move from beginning of life to ending, from part to part: God *is*, always and completely. There is no beginning or ending of His life; no past or future; no succession of moments; no parts, but always the ever present whole.[36]

VI. THE UNITY OF GOD

1. **The Notion of Unity.** Unity, like truth and goodness, is convertible with being; whatever is, is one. The concept of unity adds the notion of indivision to the concept of being, but what is signified by the two concepts is the same reality. Thus being and one are the same *in re* but differ *in ratione*.

> One does not add any reality to *being*, but is only the negation of division; for *one* means undivided *being*. This is the very reason why *one* is convertible with *being*. For every being is either simple or composite. But what is simple is undivided, both actually and potentially; whereas what is composite has not being while its parts are divided, but after they make up and compose it. Hence it is manifest that the being of anything consists in indivision; and hence it is that everything guards its unity as it guards its being.[37]

2. **The Unity of God.** The unity of God — that is to say, that there is only one God, not many — can be shown in three ways. First, it has been shown above that God is absolutely simple, that His essence is His being and Himself; that is, He is His own nature. From this it follows clearly that divine nature cannot belong to any other being:

---

[36] Cf. *S. Theol.*, I, 10, 4 and 5.
[37] *Ibid.*, I, 11, 1, c (Pegis, *op. cit.*, Vol. I, p. 85). A fuller explanation of St. Thomas' teaching on the one is given in Chapter XXIV, on creation.

deity is God Himself; to be divine is to be God Himself, no other. Second, God's unity is proved from His perfection and infinity, which we also demonstrated above. Since God is infinitely perfect, the total perfection of being belongs to Him. If there were two or more Gods, something would have to belong to one and not to another to distinguish them. But each, then, except one, would have to lack some perfection belonging to some other; hence none except one of them would be the totality of perfection, which God is. Therefore there is only one God. Third, all things in the world, though diverse, are ordered in relation to one another. This unity of order among diverse things could not exist in the world unless the cause of the world, namely God, were one.[38]

From a simple comparison of one and being, applied to the essence of God, it follows that God is not only one but is supremely one. Just as God is the Pure Act of Aristotle and the Good of Plato, so is He the One of Plotinus; and He is these because He is Being Itself.

> Since *one* is an undivided being, if anything is supremely *one* it must be supremely being and supremely undivided. Now both of these belong to God. For He is supremely being inasmuch as His being is not determined by any nature to which it is adjoined; since He is being itself, subsistent, absolutely undetermined. And He is supremely undivided inasmuch as He is divided neither actually nor potentially by any mode of division; since He is altogether simple, as was shown above. Hence it is manifest that God is *one* in the supreme degree.[39]

VII. GOD IS NOT MATTER OR NATURE

It was remarked in the very first paragraph of this chapter that the demonstration of the divine attributes is in fact part of the demonstration of God's existence. By proving merely that a first mover, a first cause, a necessary being, a supreme being, exists, we do not sufficiently prove that God exists. The materialist might accept all our proofs and then say: "Sure, a first cause and a necessary being exists; it is matter." The pantheist might accept them and say that God and Nature are one. The contemporary naturalist might accept them and maintain that Nature is the supreme being, the necessary being, the first condition of conditioned beings. As long as they could make such answers, we would not have proved that God — that is, God Himself, the true God — exists.

[38] *S. Theol.*, I, 11, 2; *Con. Gen.*, I, 42.
[39] *S. Theol.*, I, 11, 4, c (Pegis, *op. cit.*, Vol. I, p. 90).

If, however, the derivation of the divine attributes from the conclusion of the Five Ways is valid, then obviously the First Cause is not matter or Nature, nor is God one with Nature. God is one, simple, unchanging, immaterial, perfect, and purely actual. Matter is composite, dispersed, constantly changing, in no sense perfect, and the very stuff of potency. Matter, indeed, as the materialist uses the term, is not even a concrete being, but is an abstraction whose use as if it represented a concrete reality covers up the fact that it is in no way an explanation or a cause of anything. Things may be causes; but "matter" is not. "Matter" is a universal name for a vast number of particulars, these particulars being among the things to be explained. When we prove that there is a First Cause, we prove that there is a real concrete being who is the cause of all other beings; this first cause cannot be any universal abstraction. Nor can Nature be the First Cause, whether we simply call nature Nature or whether we call it God. If Nature is not an abstraction, like "matter," but is one concrete being, then it certainly is not a simple, perfect, immutable, immaterial, and purely actual being. Nor is it supremely good, since it embraces so much evil. In brief, what the derivation of the divine attributes has added to the Five Ways is the demonstration that the God whose existence is proved by these ways infinitely transcends nature. Thus the demonstration of God's attributes is at the same time the refutation of naturalism and pantheism. We shall, however, return to this subject in the chapter on creation.

VIII. THE NAMES OF GOD

1. **How We Can Name God.** In what manner may we speak of God and apply names to Him? Words are signs of ideas, and ideas are signs of things; consequently the words and names which we use are signs of things through the conceptions of our intellect. Hence we can give a name to something in so far as we understand that thing. In this life, however, we do not understand the essence of God, but we know God only through knowing His effects; that is, we know Him not in His essence, but only as cause of the world. Therefore we can name Him only from creatures, by way of negation and analogy. Hence the names which we can give Him do not express the divine essence itself; that is, they do not define what God is in Himself, and they fail to express His mode of being.[40]

---

[40] *S. Theol.*, I, 13, 1, c and ad 2. Cf. *Con. Gen.*, I, 30.

2. Some Names Are Predicated Substantially and Properly of God.

Yet, contrary to what some persons have maintained, not all the names which we apply to God signify merely a negation or merely a relation to creatures; some of these names, in fact, signify the substance of God. Such names are those expressing positive and absolute perfections, like *wise* and *good* and *living*. We cannot believe that these names express merely a negation or merely the relation of a cause; we must deny this for three reasons. First, if such were the only significance of these names, we could have no reason for applying any particular name to God rather than any other. If I say that God is good only because He is the cause of good in creatures, why do I not say He is a body, since He creates bodies? Or that He is blind, since He has no eyes? Second, if all names given to God signified only a negation or a relation to creatures, they would all be applied to Him only in a secondary sense, only by way of the analogy of attribution, and would belong primarily and properly to creatures. Then to say that God is a *living* God would mean only that He is the cause of life in creatures, just as we call medicine healthy because it causes health in a man. Third, this merely negative and relational meaning is not in fact what is intended by those who speak of God. When they say that God lives, they mean more than that He is the cause of our life, or that He differs from inanimate bodies.

> Therefore we must hold a different doctrine — viz., that these names signify the divine substance, and are predicated substantially of God, although they fall short of representing Him. Which is proved thus. For these names express God, so far as our intellects know Him. Now since our intellect knows God from creatures, it knows Him as far as creatures represent Him. But it was shown above that God prepossesses in Himself all the perfections of creatures, being Himself absolutely and universally perfect. Hence every creature represents Him, and is like Him, so far as it possesses some perfection: yet not so far as to represent Him as something of the same species or genus, but as the excelling source of whose form the effects fall short, although they derive some kind of likeness thereto. . . . Therefore the aforesaid names signify the divine substance, but in an imperfect manner, even as creatures represent it imperfectly. So when we say, *God is good,* the meaning is not, *God is the cause of goodness,* or, *God is not evil*; but the meaning is, *Whatever good we attribute to creatures pre-exists in God,* and in a higher way. Hence it does not follow that God is good because He causes goodness; but rather, on the contrary, He causes goodness in things because He is good.[41]

[41] *S. Theol.,* l, 13, 2, c (Pegis, *op. cit.,* Vol. I, p. 115).

From the above it follows that some of the names which we predicate of God are predicated *properly* of Him. Names like *good, living,* and *wise* signify certain perfections, and we know these perfections as they are found in creatures. When, therefore, we ask how these names are predicated of God, a distinction must be made between what the name signifies and the mode of signification. As for the perfections signified, these belong properly to God, more properly than they do to creatures; but as to the mode of signification, they do not properly and strictly apply to God, because signification follows the understanding of the one who uses the name, and we understand the perfections signified as they belong to creatures. As for names which essentially signify something corporeal, these cannot apply properly to God, but only metaphorically; they signify some perfection of God expressed metaphorically by analogy to some corporeal perfection, as to speak of the eye of God is to mean His omniscience, to speak of His arm is to mean His omnipotence.[42]

The names which we properly attribute to God signify a reality which is one and simple, since, as we have seen, whatever is in God is God. Consequently the attributes which these names signify in God are really identical in God. Yet these names are not synonyms; by predicating several attributes of God, we are not merely heaping up words to repeat the same idea. The attributes which are really identical in God are conceptually distinct in us, and, as said above the names we use acquire their signification through our conceptions. Unable to grasp the infinite reality and simplicity of God's being in one idea, we multiply different partial conceptions of it. Since we know God from creatures, we form conceptions of God proportioned to the perfections flowing from God to creatures:

> These perfections pre-exist in God unitedly and simply, whereas in creatures they are received divided and multiplied. Just as, therefore, to the diverse perfections of creatures there corresponds one simple principle represented by the diverse perfection of creatures in a various and manifold manner, so also to the various and multiplied conceptions of our intellect there corresponds one altogether simple principle, imperfectly understood through these conceptions. Therefore, although the names applied to God signify one reality, still, because they signify that reality under many and diverse aspects, they are not synonymous.[43]

[42] *S. Theol.*, I, 13, 3. c and ad 1.
[43] *S. Theol.*, I, 13, 4, c (Pegis, *op. cit.*, Vol. I, p. 118). Cf. *Con. Gen.*, I, 35.

3. Predication Is Analogous. We have already noted several times throughout this chapter that we can make no predication about God and creatures univocally. Since the names which we predicate are understood by us according as the perfections which they signify are found in creatures, they apply to creatures as in some degree circumscribing and comprehending the thing signified in the creature; when we say that a man is *wise*, we comprehend what we are predicating of the man. This is not the case when these names are applied to God. In that case they do signify something in God, but they leave this thing uncomprehended and as exceeding the signification of the name. We know what wisdom is in creatures, we know that God is wise with a wisdom super-exceeding every created wisdom, we know that the creature's wisdom is a dim reflection of God's, but what it is to be wise as God is wise we do not comprehend. Hence these names are not predicated univocally of God and creatures.

But neither are they predicated equivocally, that is, as carrying entirely different significations. If they were, the study of God's creatures could teach us nothing whatsoever about God. We could say, for example, that since God causes goodness in creatures, He is Himself good; but to say this would be to say nothing, for we would have no idea whatsoever of what the name good signifies in God. These names are applied neither univocally nor equivocally but as we have seen above, analogously. They are used of God and creatures according as there is some relation of the creature to God as its principle and cause in whom the perfections of all things pre-exist eminently.[44] In an analogy, the name used analogically is predicated primarily of one of the analogues and secondarily of the others as including a relation to the first. What is the case in respect to names predicated of creatures and God? If the name is used *metaphorically* of God, and not properly, then, of course, it is predicated primarily of the creature; as when God is spoken of as a lion because He shows strength in His works. The case of names used properly of God, like good, wise, living, is different. These names signify something which is in God essentially, though they signify it in the manner in which we know it in creatures. Consequently, as to *what* they signify, these names are predicated primarily of God and secondarily of creatures, because the perfections signified flow from God to creatures. But as to the imposition of the names, they are first applied by us to creatures,

[44] *S. Theol.*, I, 13, 5, c; *Con. Gen.*, I, 32, 33.

since we know creatures first; and therefore as to their mode of signification they are predicated primarily of creatures.[45]

4. How Relative Attributes Are Predicated of God. Some names given to God signify a relation to creatures; thus, for example. *Lord* and *Creator* signify God's dominion over creatures and His relation to them as their universal cause. Now there cannot be any real relation to creatures in God, since He is absolutely simple and whatever is in Him is Himself. Yet such names as these certainly express a relation, since God can be called Lord, Creator, Saviour only because there are creatures who are subject to Him, whom He creates and whom He saves; these names in fact are predicated of God temporally although God is eternal. How can something be predicated of God in virtue of a relation, if there can be no real relation in God?

A relation may be real or logical; and which it is, is determined by three conditions. Sometimes the relation stands between two extremes both of which are extremes in idea only, as when we compare a thing with itself and say that it is identical with itself. Obviously the thing is *two,* and so related to itself, only in our idea, not in reality. Other relations are real as regards both extremes: for example, quantitative relations like half and double have two real quantities as extremes; and agent-patient relations have two real extremes, one acting and the other receiving the action. Finally a relation may be real as regards one of its extremes, but only logical as regards the other; it is in one really, but in the other only in idea. Thus when I say that a tree is on my right, the relation expressed is real as regards me, but only logical as regards the tree. Knowledge and the thing known are related by such a one-sided relation. Sense and science refer to sensible and intelligible things, and this relation is real and essential in sense and science; but in the things it is nothing real at all. Things are what they are whether I know them or not; nothing in them is different by virtue of being known. Hence the relation between sensible things and sense, and between intelligible things and intellect, is real on the side of sense and intellect, but only logical on the side of the things; these things are relative only in the sense that something is related to them, not in the sense that they are related to it. Such also is the case of God and creatures:

> Since, therefore, God is outside the whole order of creation, and all creatures are ordered to Him. and not conversely, it is manifest that

[45] S. Theol., I, 13, 6, c; Con. Gen., I, 34.

creatures are really related to God Himself; whereas in God there is no real relation to creatures, but a relation only in idea, inasmuch as creatures are related to Him. Thus there is nothing to prevent such names, which import relation to the creature, from being predicated of God temporally, not by reason of any change in Him, but by reason of the change in the creature. . . .[46]

Nor is it incongruous that God should be denominated from relations really existing in things, provided that the opposite relations be at the same time understood by us as existing in God, so that God is spoken of relatively to the creature inasmuch as the creature is related to Him; just as the Philosopher says that the object is said to be knowable relatively because knowledge relates to it.[47]

5. God's Proper Name. All the attributes of God which we have demonstrated in the present chapter are true names of God, and all of them aid us to form some notion of God's essence. This notion, of course, does not adequately represent that essence, but nevertheless it does enable us to name in human terms what God is, even though we still cannot grasp what it is to be what we name. The idea of God to which these attributes add up is that of Simple, Perfect, Unlimited Being. In one, perfect, undivided, and indivisible actuality God is the fullness of being. Consequently, the most proper name of God is the name by which He named Himself when He sent Moses to rescue the children of Israel from the tyranny of Pharoh: "Thou shalt say to them, HE WHO IS hath sent me to you." The most proper name of God is *He who is.*

This name does not signify some form of being, but being itself. Therefore, it applies only to God, in whom alone essence is being itself; and of all names it most properly applies to God, since everything is named according to its essence. It is more proper even than the name *Good*, for God is called good inasmuch as He is a cause; whereas He is called being according to His essence. Furthermore, being is understood prior to cause. God is a cause only because He first is He who is.[48]

IX. MAN'S END: THE VISION OF GOD'S ESSENCE

The essence of God is hidden from us in this life, and we know God only from His effects. But the adequate object of our intellect is perfect truth or the ultimate reason of things. The thirst of our

---

[46] *S. Theol.*, I, 13, 7, c (Pegis, *op. cit.*. Vol. I, p. 124).
[47] *Ibid.*, ad 4 (Pegis, *op. cit.*, Vol. I, p. 125).
[48] *Ibid.*, I, 13, 11.

intellects for more and more truth, a thirst which dies not so long as the whole truth is not possessed, would be in vain and would be a torture if we could have no hope of ever attaining the fullness of truth, the Self-Explaining Truth which is the reason for everything. Let us use the Angelic Doctor's own words:

> Since everything is knowable according as it is actual, God, who is pure act without any admixture of potentiality is in Himself supremely knowable. But what is supremely knowable in itself may not be knowable to a particular intellect, because of the excess of the intelligible object above the intellect; as, for example, the sun, which is supremely visible, cannot be seen by the bat by reason of its excess of light.
>
> Therefore some who considered this held that no created intellect can see the essence of God. This opinion, however, is not tenable. For the ultimate beatitude of man consists in the use of his highest function, which is the operation of the intellect. Hence, if we suppose that a created intellect could never see God, it would either never attain to beatitude, or its beatitude would consist in something else besides God; which is opposed to faith. For the ultimate perfection of the rational creature is to be found in that which is the source of its being; since a thing is perfect so far as it attains to its source. Further, the same opinion is also against reason. For there resides in every man a natural desire to know the cause of any effect which he sees. Thence arises wonder in men. But if the intellect of the rational creature could not attain to the first cause of things, the natural desire would remain vain. Hence it must be granted absolutely that the blessed see the essence of God.[49]

[49] *S. Theol.*, I, 12, 1, c. Cf. I–II, 3, 8 (Pegis, *op. cit.*, Vol. I, p. 92). *Con. Gen.*, III, 50–51.

CHAPTER XXIII

GOD'S INTELLIGENCE AND WILL*

I. GOD'S INTELLIGENCE

1. The attributes of personality are life, intelligence, will, and freedom; any being which lacks these is not person, but merely thing. By God, Christians mean a personal being who is not only supreme being and first cause of all the world, but who knows, loves, and cares for His creatures. If philosophy cannot demonstrate that the First Mover, First Cause, and so forth, is a personal being endowed with life, knowledge, will and freedom, then it cannot in truth demonstrate the existence of God — at least a God such as Christians believe in and pray to. Hence, it is a very important part, indeed the crowning part, of natural theology to furnish rational demonstration of the fact and the mode (as far as that can be known by us) of God's intellect and will.

The simplest argument for God's intelligence takes as its starting point the conclusion of the fourth proof. God is the Supreme Being, the noblest of beings. To Him, therefore, must be attributed all perfections in their highest degree — He is the absolutely perfect being. But the highest and noblest of all perfections are those implied by intelligence. Without intelligence there can be no consciousness of self, no freedom, no love, no happiness. If God lacked these realities, it would be absurd to call Him the most perfect of beings. Man, who possesses them because he possesses intelligence, would be superior to God. Therefore, God must possess intelligence.[1]

2. **God Is Supreme Intelligence.** St. Thomas' favorite proof of God's intelligence takes as its starting point God's immateriality. The argument may be summarized thus: a being is possessed of intelligence

* Primary readings: S. Theol., I, qq. 14 and 19; Con. Gen., I, 44-88.
[1] Con. Gen., I, 44.

in direct proportion to the degree to which it is free from matter and material conditions; God is pure, unlimited immaterial being, and hence He is supremely intelligent. This argument may be explained and expanded as follows:[2]

a) Knowledge is clearly a community of being, a synthesis of knower and thing known. Matter, however, is precisely what renders being incommunicable, for it is the principle of limitation and individuation and encloses being within determinate and exclusive spatio-temporal boundaries.[3] In order to be known an object must be in the mind of the knower. It is not there in its physical individuality, because it is still outside the knower and may be also at the same time in the minds of other knowers. Its matter, therefore, is not in the knower; but since something of it must be in the knower, this something must be its form. Wherefore, St. Thomas writes:

> Knowing beings are distinguished from non-knowing beings in that the latter possess only their own form, while the knowing being is by nature capable of having also the form of another thing.[4]

The form of the known object, received by the knowing subject, determines the latter's power of knowledge to perform its operation, that is, to know the thing whose form it has.

b) It follows that the subject of knowledge does not receive the form of the object into itself as into a material substratum, because if it did the form would determine it physically, not cognitively; that is to say, it would determine it to a new mode of material being, either substantially or accidentally, depending upon whether it was a substantial or accidental form. Instead it determines it psychically; it stirs it to produce an idea. From this it is clear that the subject as knowing receives the forms of other things, not, so to speak, into its passive principle, its matter, but into its active principle, its form.

c) This, however, is impossible unless its own form is to some extent free from matter; because if it were not, any change affecting the subject would affect it as a composite of matter and form, and it could never receive the form of another without losing its own form. Hence, only those beings have knowledge whose forms are to some degree free from matter; and the more free from matter the form is, the more perfect will be the being's mode of knowledge, for the more

---

[2] *S. Theol.*, I, 14, 1 c; *ibid.*, I, 84, 2 c; *Con. Gen.*, I, 44, fourth arg.
[3] *In II De Anima*, lect. 5, No. 283.
[4] *S. Theol.*, I, 14, 1, c.

will it be able to possess the forms of other beings without ceasing to be itself. If its form is capable of existing and operating without using a material organ, it will possess intellect.[5] Wherefore, God, who is absolutely and supremely free from matter, is supremely intelligent.[6]

3. **The Simplicity of Divine Intelligence.** When we attribute intelligence to God, we do so by way of analogy. The only mode of intelligence that we know in its actual working is human intelligence. When we attribute intelligence to God, we mean that the perfection whereby we know and understand is not lacking in Him. But we do *not* mean that intelligence is in God in the same mode in which it is in us, only bigger. We have intelligence; God is intelligence.

a) *Human Knowledge.* The first striking fact about ourselves as intelligent beings is that we start off in ignorance; whatever we ever know is something we have learned. Originally we have a potency for knowledge, but no actual knowledge. Acquiring knowledge is actualizing this potency. Our intellect does not of itself possess its object. Furthermore, it is powerless to move itself to the possession of its object; it must be moved by external causes. Our knowledge is, therefore, dependent upon its objects. Natural things must act upon our sense organs, producing sensible impressions in those organs and in the powers of which they are the organs, before we can know anything. Our intellect is dependent upon these powers, organs, and impressions, for it needs the sensible representations of the objects that act upon our senses as the material whence it draws its own object, namely, the intelligible natures of these objects. Our intellect, therefore, is sense dependent.

Nor are these the only imperfections of our intelligence. We know what we do know piecemeal, by successive acts of intellect, each single act giving us only a single item out of all the intelligible world. We have to multiply ideas to get any considerable knowledge of being, and at the moment when one item is actually known the rest has slipped back into mere potential knowledge. And multiply ideas though we may, we never acquire an exhaustive knowledge of any one being, to say nothing of the totality of being. In a word, our knowledge is limited.

Even the things most suited to be the objects of *our* intellects, corporeal substances, we know imperfectly. In order to know their

[5] Cf. *In II De Anima*, lect. 5, No. 284.
[6] *S. Theol.*, I, q. 14, 4; *Con. Gen.*, I, 45.

natures we have to abstract their forms from the matter which embodies them in the concrete, and we thus universalize their natures by separating them from the principle which individualizes them. Wherefore, the natures of corporeal beings are understood directly by us only as universals, the concrete reality of the individual escaping the grasp of our intellect. When, therefore, we wish to apply this universal knowledge to the real world of singulars, our intellect must again have recourse to the senses.

Even when we have succeeded in grasping a truth, we are far from knowing all that is in that truth. Our mind has to run from one aspect of it to another, seeing its full unity only as a series of separate implications. Our thinking, in a word, is ratiocinative or discursive, rather than contemplative or intuitive; we do not see wholes as wholes, but we must run from part to part. We fill a book with separate theorems about so simple a thing as a triangle.

Finally, our knowledge of ourselves is very imperfect. We are unable to grasp our own nature directly and clearly. Our very soul seems to elude our vision. We do not see it in itself, but have to catch it in its acts. We are, of course, conscious of ourselves and of our soul, but we do not see directly what we are or what our soul is. Over what do men disagree more than over the nature of man? Only by very careful observation and very difficult reasoning can we attain a clear idea of the nature of our own soul.

b) Divine Knowledge. None of these imperfections can characterize God's knowledge. God never passes from ignorance to knowledge, for He is unchangeable. His intellect is not a potentiality for knowing, since He is pure actuality. God always knows whatever He ever knows. God's knowledge can in no way be dependent upon its objects, because God can in no way be dependent upon anything. Whatever is in God, is God; and He is self-existent First Being. His knowledge is not caused by its objects, for causes can affect only what has potentiality. It is needless to say that His intellect does not depend upon sense organs, since He is not a body. Succession of ideas cannot mark His knowledge, as it marks ours, for He is unchangeable. He knows what He knows all at once; none of His knowledge can ever be potential. Nor can any being elude His knowledge, since He is the cause of all being. Besides, if His knowledge were limited, He would be ignorant of some things; but infinitely perfect being cannot contain within itself the imperfection of ignorance. Finally, God's intelligence cannot be a power, that is to say, an accident of His being, for God is not composite of substance and accident. His intelligence is His being. God is infinite simple intelligence.

II. THE OMNISCIENCE OF GOD

The last paragraph above contains in essence all that we can say of God's knowledge. The answers to two questions: What does God know? and How does God know? are really an amplification of that paragraph. All that man can say of God's knowledge can be stated in this one sentence: *God knows Himself perfectly, and in that perfect knowledge of Himself He knows perfectly all other beings, possible and actual.*

1. **God Knows Himself Perfectly.** Three truths were made clear in our proof of God's supreme intelligence. (1) A being is intelligible to the degree to which it is immaterial; wherefore, whatever possesses form to any degree is to that degree intelligible. (2) A being is intelligent to the degree to which it is free from matter and the conditions of materiality; wherefore, any being whose form is to any degree capable of existing and operating independently of matter is to that degree intelligent. (3) Knowledge is actualized when the intelligible object and the intelligent subject are synthesized; that is to say, when they are in some way united so that the being of the intelligible object is added to the being of the intelligence. From these truths it follows that the degree of perfection of knowledge depends upon three factors: first, the degree of perfection of intelligibility in the object; second, the degree of perfection of intelligence in the subject; and third, the degree of perfection of union of subject and object.

Let us test these factors in respect to God. First, the essence of God, being absolutely immaterial, is supremely intelligible; second, God, pure and infinite Form, entirely free from matter and all material conditions, is supremely intelligent; third, God being perfectly simple and there being nothing in Him that is not His being, His essence is united with His intelligence in the most perfect unity, namely, identity. It is therefore abundantly clear that God, the Supreme Intelligence, must know Himself, the Supreme Intelligible, perfectly.[7]

2. **In His Perfect Knowledge of Himself God Knows All Things Perfectly.** It is true that the only object that God knows directly and of itself is Himself. For if something else could become the object of

[7] *S. Theol.,* I, 14, 2 and 3; *Con. Gen.,* I, 47.

God's intelligence, that intelligence would be changeable, imperfect, in potency to its object, and dependent upon its object. All this St. Thomas insists upon; but instead of drawing therefrom the superficial conclusion that God consequently can know nothing outside Himself, he shows that the opposite conclusion is in fact the one that follows.

Aristotle was right in maintaining that God knows Himself perfectly and that He alone, strictly speaking, is the object of His knowledge; for the introduction of any other object into the divine intelligence would destroy the divine simplicity. But it does not follow that God does not know the world. For what does it mean, to know something *perfectly?* It means to know it through and through, to know all that it is and all that it can do, all its powers and all its effects, its complete being and all that is related to or dependent upon that being. If the intelligence does not reach to all the powers and effects of its object, it certainly does not have perfect knowledge of that object. Now we have proved that God does know Himself perfectly. Wherefore, since God's power extends to all things, since He is the first efficient cause of all things, it follows of necessity that in knowing Himself perfectly He knows all things.

Whatever exists besides God is an effect of God. But every effect must in some manner pre-exist in its cause, since it receives its being from its cause. Hence, everything pre-exists in the divine essence. But God's essence *is* His intelligence, since whatever is in God is God. Wherefore, everything pre-exists in God's intelligence, and it is impossible that anything should exist if God does not first know it. The first being that anything has is this eternal being in God's mind. Prior to creation all things exist in the Divine Ideas. (This is the Augustinian doctrine of exemplarism which was adopted by St. Thomas; God is the exemplar of all created things, and they are imitations of God.)

God's knowledge of all things is, therefore, dependent upon nothing but Himself. He sees all things in Himself by seeing Himself; His ideas are not copies of things, but things are copies of his ideas. Any possible thing is possible because God conceives its nature as a reflection of His own. And actual things are actual because God wills to create some of the beings which His intellect conceives. Hence, He knows all possible things in knowing His own essence, and all actual things in knowing the decree of His own will. Wherefore, it remains a fact that the only immediate object of His intelligence is Himself, and that His knowledge of other things in no way depends upon those things.[8]

3. God Knows Every Particular Thing. Some philosophers maintained that God knows only the universal natures and laws of created things: He cannot know particulars, they argued, because (1) His knowledge follows His causality, and He is the *universal* first cause, and (2) particulars contain matter, and therefore only a being who possesses senses can know them, whereas God is purely immaterial. Therefore, He knows only universal species, e.g., "man," but not individuals, e.g., you and me. St. Thomas gives several answers to these arguments. (*a*) God is the universal cause of things in the sense that He is the total cause of their entire being. Therefore, since He knows His effects in His own causality, His knowledge extends as far as that causality, that is, to the entire reality of every being. Concrete individuality or particularity is the final determining reality of every being. Therefore God knows every particular being. (*b*) Everything in a being is a certain mode of participation of the divine essence. God would not know Himself perfectly, unless He knew every mode under which His essence can be imitated. Consequently, He knows all modes of being, particular as well as universal. (*c*) God is the cause of individuals, their matter as well as their form. Matter is not nothing, and therefore, like everything else, its possibility is founded upon the divine essence. Consequently, God knows particular composites of matter and form. To argue that He would need senses to know them is to forget that His knowledge does not depend upon its objects, but they upon it. God, therefore, knows every particular being which exists.[9] This knowledge is the basis of His loving providence toward men. If God did not know each one of us individually, He could not love us, aid us, and guide us toward our final destiny as individual persons. Prayer to a God who knew only universals would be a waste of time, for such a God, while knowing what prayer is, could not know any particular prayers.

4. God's Knowledge of the Multitude of Beings Does Not Destroy His Simplicity. It might be objected that God cannot have the ideas of all things in His intelligence, since this multiplicity of ideas is incompatible with the divine simplicity. This objection would be valid if God knew the multitude of things in such manner that each was

[8] *S. Theol.*, 1, 14, 5 and 6; *Con. Gen.*, I, 46, 48, 49, 50.
[9] *S. Theol.*, I, 14, 6 and 11; *Con. Gen.*, I, 50.

a distinct object of His intellect and was known by a distinct form derived from the object. But God knows the multitude of beings in the one simple act of knowing Himself. Knowing His own essence perfectly, he knows it not only as it is in itself, but as it is capable of being participated in through some similarity by creatures. The form of every creature is, in fact, its mode of likeness to the divine essence. Consequently, inasmuch as God knows His essence as imitable by a certain creature He knows it as the idea of that creature. Therefore, it may be said that the ideas of all things are in God without jeopardizing God's absolute simplicity.[10]

5. God's Knowledge Is Independent of Time. In the infinite richness of His own self-knowledge, God knows the whole course of events, past, present, and future. This does not mean that God's knowledge changes, or moves along with history; God does not have to wait to see what will happen; in one single act of infinite intelligence He sees the whole course of history. He knows all the causal and temporal relations of things and events. But He is Himself without time and temporal sequence, and all events are eternally present to Him. He knows them eternally because they are all eternally in Him as their cause. To suppose that God has to wait for something to happen in order to know it is to place the Eternal within time and to make the First Cause dependent upon its effects. God stands to the universe as an architect to the house he builds, not as a visitor strolling through it; the architect's knowledge is the cause of the house, not its effect, antecedent to it, not subsequent.[11]

III. GOD'S OMNISCIENCE AND HUMAN FREEDOM

1. God Knows Our Future Free Acts. Does God know the free actions that men have not yet performed? If He does know all the future choices of our will, then are not all these choices determined and necessary rather than free? To these questions Catholic philosophers and theologians unanimously answer: (1) that God *does* know all our future free acts, and (2) that this foreknowledge *does not* deprive these acts of their freedom.

There can be no doubt that God does know our future free acts. When these acts do occur, they will undoubtedly be known to God, since they will then be existing realities and since God's knowledge

---

[10] *S. Theol.*, 1, 15, 2.
[11] *S. Theol.*, I, 14, 8; *Con. Gen.*, I, 55.

extends to all reality. But if they are to be then known by God, they must always be known by Him. In the first place, all God's knowledge is eternally present to Him: He is above time, not in time, and He does not depend upon an event's happening in order to know it; He knows it always because He knows it in Himself. In the second place, if God did not know the free actions of men until they occurred, these acts would determine His knowledge: the First Cause would be dependent upon its effects, the Pure Act would be potential in regard to knowledge of its creatures' operations, the Immutable would be changed by every act of a free creature, the Absolutely Simple would be a constant stream of new mental states. We cannot escape the conclusion that God eternally knows all the free acts of all His free creatures.

2. **Yet These Acts Are Free.** How, then, can these acts be free? A free act is an act which a free agent may or may not produce, an act which he does not do of necessity. Before it is done, it is in no way determined, since its cause is free to do it or not do it; it may or may not be done; it is not certain to be done. Therefore, to say that God knows our future free acts, is it not to say that God knows as certain to occur what is in fact not certain to occur, that He knows as a determined reality what is in truth undetermined? Must we not admit either that God's knowledge of our future free acts is not certain, or that these acts are really determined and not free?

The way in which St. Thomas resolves this dilemma involves a truth about the free act and a truth about God. The act is in time; God is not in time. The temporal conditions that affect the state of the act do not affect God's knowledge of it. There are a before and an after in the act; there is no before or after in God. The act cannot be at once in its *before condition* and its *after condition;* but God can know it at once in both conditions. Before the act takes place, it is uncertain and undetermined, because its cause is a free cause and may or may not produce it. After it takes place it is certain and determined because it is now part of the actual world of events and no longer problematical. A free act, when once done, is as necessarily done as an act produced by the most necessary of causes. Time cannot be turned back, and what is done cannot be undone. Judas did not *have to* hang himself; but, having hanged himself, he necessarily *had* hanged himself. A free act, in brief, is one that is undetermined until it is done; after it is done, it is a determined reality. Now let us turn our attention to God. He is not in time and His knowledge does not depend upon time. An act future to us is not future to God, because all time is embraced in His infinite vision. The free act, which has two conditions at different times — undetermined before, determined after — is present always to God in all its conditions. He knows it at once in its undetermined state as a possible choice of a free will, and in its determined state as the actual choice of that free will. Only if He were subjected to His own creature, time, would He be unable to know such an act at once in all its states. Wherefore, the fact that God knows our future actions does not imply that they are now determined and not free.[12]

This explanation, however, does not solve the whole problem of the relation of free will to God, the Universal Cause. We cannot carry the problem any further until we first study God's will. We shall now proceed to that.

IV. GOD'S WILL

1. **The Notion of Will.** We see by experience that every being tends to what is in accord with its nature, to what perfects its being; in a word, to its own good. On the contrary, it struggles against what is harmful to its being, e.g., pain, death, destruction; in a word, evil. This tendency toward good and against evil is called by the general name appetite.

Appetite differs in different beings according as the beings differ in nature. Beings which lack knowledge tend to the goods of their nature blindly and unconsciously; this tendency is called natural appetite. Sentient beings tend toward what pleases their senses, and this tendency is called animal appetite. Intelligent beings tend toward that which their intellect apprehends as good, and this tendency is called rational appetite, or *will*.[13]

The proper act of will in relation to the good is love. The act has two modes of exercise: striving for the good when it is not possessed, and reposing in it when it is possessed. The proper act of will in relation to the evil is hatred.

Intellect considered in abstraction from will is purely speculative; it knows, but it produces nothing outside itself. Practical intellect,

---

[12] *S. Theol.*, I, 14, 13; *Con. Gen.*, I, 67, 68. Cf. Sertillanges, *op. cit.*, Vol. I, pp. 232–238.
[13] Cf. Chapter XII.

which results in actions or products outside itself, is intellect complemented by will. Any intellectual being which produces effects intelligently, produces them by will.

2. **God Has Will.** In the *Summa Theologica* St. Thomas bases his proof of God's will directly upon the Divine Intelligence:

> God possesses will, as He possesses intellect. For will is a necessary consequence of intellect. Just as a natural thing possesses being in actuality through its form, so it is through its intelligible form that the intellect is an actual intelligence. Every being is so related to its natural form that when it does not possess it, it tends to it, and when it does possess it, it reposes in it. And the same thing is true in regard to every natural perfection whatsoever which is a good of nature. This relationship to the good in beings lacking knowledge is called natural appetite. Whence, therefore, an intellectual nature has a similar relation to the good apprehended through the intelligible form; when it possesses it, it reposes in it; when, indeed, it lacks it, it strives to attain it. And both these activities are proper to will. Wherefore, in any being possessing intelligence there is will, just as in any being possessing sensation there is animal appetite. Therefore, it is necessary that there is will in God, since there is intellect in Him. And as His act of intelligence is His being, so also is His being His act of willing.[14]

That will in God is never a striving for the good, but only love of the good perfectly possessed, is brought out clearly by St. Thomas in answer to the argument that God cannot possess will since will is an appetite, and appetite implies imperfection since it is directed toward something not possessed. The Angelic Doctor replies that to appetite belongs not only the act of desiring what it does not possess but also the act of loving what it does possess and delighting in it. It is in this latter sense that will is predicated of God, who always possesses the good which is His object, since this good is nothing else but Himself, His own divine essence.

3. **The First and Principal Object of God's Will Is Himself.** Will, we saw above, follows upon intellect. In the second section of this chapter it was clearly established that the only direct and immediate object of God's intellect is His own essence. The object of will is the good apprehended by the intellect, but the only good apprehended in itself by God's intellect is His divine essence; wherefore, the first and principal object of His will is this same divine essence, which God loves as the Supreme Good. God wills Himself with an infinite act

[14] *S. Theol.,* 1, 19, 1.

of love. God's essence considered as the object of His will is called the divine goodness by St. Thomas.

4. God Wills Other Things in View of Himself. Some would seek to show that God cannot will anything but Himself, just as they sought to show that He cannot know anything but Himself. Three of their arguments are interesting inasmuch as they give St. Thomas occasion to clarify further his teaching about the divine will. It is argued, first, that if God willed anything other than Himself, this object would act as an end moving His will; but God cannot be moved by anything. Second, it is pointed out that every will has some object that satisfies it, so that it wills nothing in addition to this object; now God's own goodness fully satisfies His will, and He therefore wills nothing else but Himself. Finally, it is stated that acts of will are multiplied as additional objects are willed; and therefore that God's will-act would be multiple if He willed anything in addition to Himself; but this is impossible since His act of will is identical with His being, which is one and simple. For all these reasons it seems quite clear that God can will Himself only.[15]

To all three objections St. Thomas gives, in essence, the same answer: *God wills things other than Himself, but not for their own sake. He wills them for His own sake, and in the same act in which He wills Himself.* Wherefore, these objects do not move His will; His own goodness alone moves His will to will both Itself and those other things. For when something is willed only in view of some end, it is the end alone that moves the will; as when a man drinks a bitter medicine for the sake of his health. Therefore, just as in understanding His essence God understands other things, so in willing His goodness, He wills other things. Similarly, the fact that God's own goodness suffices to satisfy His will does not imply that He cannot will any other object, but rather that He cannot will anything else except by reason of that goodness; just as, although His intellect is completely perfected in knowing His own infinite essence, He nevertheless knows other things in knowing it. Finally, just as the divine intelligence is one because God sees the multitude of things only in the one act of seeing His own simple essence, so His will is one and simple because He does not will the multitude of things except in willing one thing, which is His own goodness.[16]

---

[15] *S. Theol.*, I, 19, 2, objs. 2, 3 and 4.
[16] *Loc. cit.*, ad 2, 3, and 4.

It is in the body of this same article that Aquinas advances the deepest reason why we must admit that it is proper to God to will other things than Himself. Everything, as we have seen above, desires its own good. But everything, by the very fact that it wishes its own good, wishes to expand and share that good; for is not the expansion of one's goodness in itself a good? Nature is full of examples of this self-expansiveness of the good — every plant and every animal fills out its own measure of perfection by reproducing itself; every good man seeks to share and spread the good he has. Only the mean, the miserly, the selfish, seek to keep their goods all to themselves, and when they succeed, their goods turn into curses upon their own heads. Good is self-propagating, self-expanding; evil propagates itself only under the guise of good. This tendency of the good to communicate itself should certainly belong most especially and most properly to the divine good, from which all other goodness and perfection are derived. Wherefore, much more than to natural things, is it proper to the divine will that it should communicate its own goodness to others in so far as that is possible. Therefore, St. Thomas concludes, "God wills both Himself and other things; Himself as end, other things as directed toward an end, inasmuch as it is fitting that the divine goodness, like other beings, should share itself." Consequently, God wills His own being and goodness, and wills in the same act that finite beings should participate in that being and goodness by representing and, as far as possible, imitating it.[17]

5. **God's Will Extends to All Being, Particular as Well as Universal, Possible as Well as Actual.** We saw in the previous section that God's knowledge is not limited to the universal, but reaches to every individual being. It follows that His will extends to particulars, too, for as soon as something is known by the intelligence as good, the will is inclined toward it. In like manner, from the fact that God knows all possible things and events, including future contingent events, it follows that He wills these, and wills each in its proper nature. He wills the possible as possible, the actual as actual, the necessary as necessary, the contingent as contingent. Nothing can exist, nothing can happen, without God's knowing it and willing it; and God does not know and will something *because it happens;* on the contrary, *it happens because He knows and wills it.* If the reverse were true, God's knowledge and will would be determined by created beings, and that needs but to be

[17] *Ibid.,* I, 19, 2, c.

stated for its absurdity to be seen, since God's knowledge and will are identical with His being.

6. God's Will and Our Free Acts. There are some who do not like this doctrine. They ask: "How can a contingent event be contingent, if it happens because God knows and wills it? How can any *free* acts be free? Are they not necessary, if God's knowledge and will causes them?" Those who speak thus forget that God is the transcendent source of all being. They forget that He created freedom and contingency as well as determination and necessity. They think that if I let His power reach too far, it will destroy my power; they fail to see that it is only because He has infinite power that I can exist or act at all. They see that that which God wills to be must be; they fail to see that that which He wills to be free must be free. They place God *among* created causes instead of seeing Him as the Creator of all causes. They conceive of His action as destroying His creature's freedom, forgetting that it is by His action that His creature's freedom exists. Shall we say that an apple tree does not produce apples because God wills apples? Or shall we say that man can do no free act because God wills each free act? Human free acts could not exist if God did not will them. How foolish, then, to argue that since He wills them, they do not exist.[18]

Let us summarize in St. Thomas' words:

> Since, therefore, the divine will is entirely efficacious, not only does it follow that those things happen which God wills to happen, but also that they are accomplished in that manner in which God wills them to be accomplished. But God wills that certain things should be accomplished necessarily, and certain others contingently. . . . And therefore He assigns to some effects necessary causes which cannot fail, and from which the effects proceed necessarily; and to other effects he assigns contingent causes which are capable of failing and from which the effects proceed contingently. It is not, therefore, because their secondary causes are contingent that effects willed by God occur contingently; but it is rather that because God wills them to happen contingently He prepares contingent causes for them.[19]

V. GOD'S FREEDOM

1. God Wills His Own Goodness Necessarily. God's will is free inasmuch as it is not by absolute necessity or by any determination of nature that He wills everything that He wills. There is one object

---

[18] Cf. *S. Theol.*, I, 22, 2; Sertillanges, *op. cit.*, I, pp. 255–268.
[19] *S. Theol.*, I, 19, 8, c. Cf. *Con. Gen.*, III, 94.

toward which His will is not free, but to which it has a relationship of necessity; this is His own divine goodness. But toward all other things it is free. God wills these things because He chooses to will them and for no other reason. Nothing in them and nothing in Himself compels Him to will them.[20]

To say that God wills Himself necessarily is not to detract in any way from His freedom; because it is the same thing as saying that He *has will*. God, being infinite intelligence and infinite good, cannot look upon this infinite goodness which is Himself and not love it supremely.

2. God Wills Whatever Else He Wills Freely. We have already seen that God wills whatever He wills for the sake of His own goodness. But this goodness exists and is complete without anything else, and consequently, there is nothing else that God *must* will for its sake. Hence, whatever He wills besides His own goodness, He wills freely. St. Thomas writes:

> Accordingly, as to things willed by God, we must observe that He wills something of absolute necessity; but this is not true of all that He wills. For the divine will has a necessary relation to the divine goodness, since that is its proper object. Hence God wills the being of His own goodness necessarily, even as we will our own happiness necessarily. . . . But God wills things other than Himself in so far as they are ordered to His goodness as their end. Now in willing an end we do not necessarily will things that conduce to it, unless they are such that the end cannot be attained without them; as, we will to take food to preserve life, or to take a ship in order to cross the sea. But we do not will necessarily those things without which the end is attainable, such as a horse for a stroll, since we can take a stroll without a horse. The same applies to other means. Hence, since the goodness of God is perfect and can exist without other things, inasmuch as no perfection can accrue to Him from them, it follows that for Him to will things other than Himself is not absolutely necessary. Yet it can be necessary by supposition, for supposing that He wills a thing, then He is unable not to will it, as His will cannot change.[21]

God, therefore, has free will:

> We have free choice with respect to what we do not will of necessity, or by natural instinct. That we will to be happy does not pertain to free choice but to natural instinct. Hence other animals, that are moved to act by natural instinct, are not said to be moved by free

[20] *S. Theol.*, I, 19, 10, c.

[21] *S. Theol.*, I, 19, 3, c (*The Basic Writings of St. Thomas Aquinas*, ed. Anton C. Pegis [New York: Random House, 1945], Vol I, p. 199).

choice. Since then God wills His own goodness necessarily, but other things not necessarily, as was shown above, He has free choice with respect to what He does not will necessarily.[22]

3. God's Will Has No Cause. Not even the necessary willing of His own goodness can be said to be the cause of God's freely willing created things. He wills the latter for the sake of the former, but He does so in the *one same act* of will. Now nothing can be the cause of itself; and therefore God's willing of His own goodness cannot be the cause of His willing created effects. Obviously nothing outside God can be the cause of His will-act, since He can in no way be determined by anything.[23]

One of the objections urged against this doctrine by some medieval opponents is still urged today. Many moderns argue that if God freely causes all the events of nature, then nothing in nature is due to natural causes, and science is a futile pursuit. Unwilling to give up science, they reject the Christian idea of a freely creating God. The argument, as St. Thomas formulates it in the *Summa Theologica*, runs thus:

> No other cause except the will of the agent may be assigned for those things that are produced by a voluntary agent who wills things without his own will having any cause. But, as has been shown above, the will of God is the cause of all things. If, therefore, there is no cause of His will, no other cause may be sought for all natural things except the divine will alone. In that case all sciences would be vain which seek to assign causes for any effects. This is unacceptable. Therefore, some cause ought to be assigned for the divine will.[24]

The answer of St. Thomas is just as good today as it was seven centuries ago; indeed, the bindnesses of contemporary naturalism give it added point:

> Since God wills effects to exist in such a way that they proceed from definite causes so that the order among beings may be preserved, it is not vain to seek other causes in addition to the will of God. *It would, however, be vain, if the other causes were sought as primary and not depending upon the divine will.* So spoke St. Augustine (*De Trinitate*, Book III, Chapter 2): "It pleases the vanity of the philosophers to attribute contingent effects to other causes, since they are altogether unable to see that cause which is superior to all others, that is to say, the will of God."[25]

[22] *S. Theol.*, I, 19, 10, c (Pegis, *op. cit.*, Vol. I, p. 211).
[23] *S. Theol.*, I, 19, 5.
[24] *S. Theol.*, I, 19, 5, obj. 2.
[25] *Ibid.*, ad 2.

4. God's Free Act of Will Is Eternal and Irrevocable. The act of *our will* is distinct from the will itself; in relation to its act our will is indeterminate and potential, and its act is its determination and actualization. When we will, our will moves from potentiality to actuality, from indetermination to determination, from power to action. Our will depends upon our intellect, and, through our intellect, upon beings other than ourselves. It does not act unless it has the requisite conditions, and in respect to these conditions it is dependent upon the intellect and other beings. Therefore, it sometimes wills and sometimes does not.

None of this is true of God's will. It is identical with its act, since there is no potentiality in God; therefore its act is not an actualization of its power. It depends upon nothing at all for the requisite conditions or dispositions for willing, because, as we have just seen above, no cause can be assigned for it; on the contrary, it possesses in its own goodness the one adequate condition for its action. For these reasons, it is clear that God's act of free will is eternally actualized: God always wills whatever He wills.

The same reasons make it clear that God's will is irrevocable. We reverse decisions of our will, either because circumstances have changed, or we have learned something that we did not before know, or because our original volition was itself defective, etc. No such causes for reversing His decisions could ever apply to God's will. His act of will arises out of His perfect knowledge of all possible and actual contingencies, so that nothing new can ever be introduced into that knowledge. Nor can any change of circumstance affect His will, since He is outside time, and all circumstances are always known to Him. And certainly His volition cannot be defective in the first place. In a word, God's will is irrevocable because it is completely self-determining and absolutely independent of anything else.[26]

God's will cannot change, but God can will change. He may will that I be sick today and well tomorrow; but He does not will today that I be sick, and will tomorrow that I be well. The change is in the thing willed, not in the will.[27]

It would be foolish to pretend that God's freedom of will is not shrouded in deep mystery for us. One aspect of the mystery may be expressed thus: If God is pure actuality, everything in Him is neces-

[26] *S. Theol.*, I, 19, 7, c.
[27] *Ibid.*, ad 3.

sarily actual. How, then, can He be free to will or not to will something? How can an eternally actual act be free? We can attempt an
answer. Freedom does not imply passive potentiality in the agent,
i.e., capacity to be changed, but rather active potentiality, i.e., power.
God's power to act is infinite and is identical with His action itself,
and hence is always actualized. Now God's freedom of willing does
not refer to His willing of Himself, which is necessary; it refers only
to His willing of other things. But the act by which He necessarily
wills Himself extends to whatever other beings He wishes; wherefore,
in reference to them it is free. By God's free will, then, He freely
determines, not something about His own act of will, but something
about the possible effects of that act; namely, which ones, if any, shall
be actualized. The act by which He freely wills these effects is, we
have seen, the same act by which He necessarily wills Himself. This
is, of course, eternal and necessary. The one act of will, therefore, is
necessary if considered in reference to God Himself, since it is identical with His essence and His intelligence; and it is free if considered
in reference to its external effects, since it does not produce these effects
by any necessity of nature, but God voluntarily determines whether
any effects shall be produced, and which ones. If this answer still leaves
the mystery as dark as ever, let us remember that we do not and cannot
comprehend God's infinite essence, and therefore we should not expect
to understand clearly His activity, which is, in fact, identical with
His essence.[28]

5. God's Will Is Always Fulfilled. In article 6 of question 19 of the
First Part of the *Summa,* St. Thomas raises the question whether the
divine will is always fulfilled. Does everything that God wills infallibly
occur, or is it possible for created things to frustrate the will of God?
The Angelic Doctor maintains that God's will is always fulfilled.

The effects of any particular cause can fail to occur, but not the
effects of the universal cause upon which all particular causes depend.
When a particular cause fails of its effect, the failure is due to some
other particular cause preventing the effect. This can occur, because the
latter cause does not come under the ordination of the former. But all
particular causes come under the ordination of the universal first cause.

> Therefore, since the will of God is the universal cause of all things,
> it is impossible that the divine will should not produce its effect. Hence,
> whatever seems to withdraw itself from the divine will according to

[28] *S. Theol.,* I, 19, 3, ad 1, ad 3, ad 4, ad 6.

one order, will be brought back to it according to another; as, for example, a sinner, who, in so far as he can, withdraws himself from the divine will by sinning, falls under the order of the divine will as long as, through its justice, he is punished.[29]

But if this be so, how can it be true, as St. Paul writes (*1 Tim.*, 2:4), that "God wills all men to be saved"? Some men are not saved. Is not God's will therefore frustrated? In reply to this, St. Thomas distinguishes between antecedent will and consequent will. God wills what is good. Now something may be good in the abstract; thus, it is good for a man to live. But the same thing may be evil in the concrete, that is, when considered in relation to the particular circumstances that actually attend it. Thus a man may be a murderer and very dangerous to the common good; in that case it is evil that he should live, and good that he should die. The antecedent will is the will considered in its relation to that which is good in the abstract before particular circumstances have been considered; the consequent will is the will in its relation to that which is good in the concrete when the particular circumstances have been considered. The will may be compared to a just judge. Antecedently the judge wishes all men to live; but consequently he wishes a murderer to be hanged. Similarly it may be said that God's antecedent will wishes all men to be saved; salvation being good in the abstract; but God's consequent will wills the unrepenting sinner to be damned, salvation being evil under the circumstances because contrary to God's justice, and damnation being good because in accordance with that justice.[30]

Now it is only consequent will which is actual will, because those things that we will in general before considering the circumstances, but which we reject when we have considered the circumstances, we do not in fact actually will at all. Hence, God's actual will is His consequent will and this is never frustrated. Strictly speaking, God has no antecedent will, since He always knows, and therefore wills, everything in particular and in all its concrete circumstances. Nevertheless, it is true, as St. Paul says, that God wills all men to be saved. He creates every man for the same end, eternal beatitude with Himself, and He gives every man sufficient grace to attain that end, and wills that he use that grace and actually save himself. Hence, He wills every man to be saved and enables him to be saved. But God knows that

[29] *S. Theol.*, I, 19, 6, c.
[30] *Ibid.*, ad 1.

certain men will abuse His grace to the very end and die unrepentant. He does not will that having done this they shall yet be saved; He wills that they be justly punished.

VI. GOD'S LIFE AND BEATITUDE

1. Life. Life is properly attributed to God; indeed, God is supreme life. A thing lives in so far as it operates of itself, and the more perfectly it operates of itself, the more perfect is its life. Thus, animals have a more perfect life than plants; for, whereas plants move themselves only with regard to the execution of their movement, while the form and end by which they are moved are determined in them by their nature, animals possess by sense the form and end by which they move, and consequently the more perfect their sense, the more perfect is their power of self-movement. Animals, however, cannot propose to themselves the ends for which they will act, but are moved by natural instinct to act for the ends presented to their senses. Man, possessed of reason, can propose to himself the ends for which he will act, and he is not moved necessarily by the goods which his senses apprehend; on the contrary, his intellectual power moves and controls his sensitive power. Since, therefore, not only the form and the end by which he acts are within him, but also the determination of this end, he has a higher power of self-movement and consequently a higher life than brutes. The life of God is still more perfect; indeed it is the perfection of life:

> But although our intellect moves itself to some things, yet others are set for it by nature, as are first principles, which it must accept, and the last end, which it cannot but will. Hence, although with respect to some things it moves itself, yet with regard to other things it must be moved by another. Hence, that being whose act of understanding is its very nature, and which, in what it naturally possesses, is not determined by another, must have life in the most perfect degree. Such is God; and hence in Him principally is life. From this the Philosopher concludes, after showing God to be intelligent, that God has life most perfect and eternal, since His intellect is most perfect and always in act.[31]

2. Beatitude. This life of God is a life of supreme happiness; it is the Divine Beatitude. Beatitude or blessedness is the perfect good of an intellectual being, and God, who is supremely perfect and intelligent, possesses beatitude in the highest degree. God is most perfectly — infinitely — happy.

[31] S. Theol., I, 18, 3, c (Pegis, op. cit., Vol. I, pp. 191–192).

Beatitude, as was stated above, is the perfect good of an intellectual nature. Thus it is that, as everything desires the perfection of its nature, so an intellectual nature desires naturally to be happy. Now that which is most perfect in any intellectual nature is the intellectual operation, by which in some sense it grasps everything. Whence the beatitude of every created intellectual nature consists in understanding. Now, in God, to be and to understand are one and the same thing, differing only in the manner of our understanding them. Beatitude must therefore be attributed to God according to His intellect. . . . [32]

VII. GOD'S LOVE

1. God Is Love. It cannot be denied that there is love in God, because love is the first movement or act of the will and of every appetitive power. Good is the essential and immediate object of the will. Now no power acts at all, unless it performs its first, proper act, for on this act depend all its subsequent acts; thus, the power of sight cannot see size or shape or any of its secondary objects except by seeing color, which is its primary object. Love is the first act of the will, since it is the will's natural movement toward the good, which is its first and proper object. Hence, no other act of the will, such as desire or joy, can be performed unless the will first loves something as a good. Consequently, in any being which has will, or performs any act of will, there must be love; because if this is missing, all the subsequent acts of will must also be missing, and the being would have no will at all. Since we have shown that God has will, we must attribute love to Him.[33] The primary object of this love is the divine goodness, i.e., God Himself, and it is in loving Himself that God loves all else.

Love, of course, is not bound up with sensitive passion and emotion in God, as it is in us. This aspect of love in us arises from our sensitive appetites, which in turn are due to our material nature; so that, just as our intellect operates through our senses, so our will operates through the movements of our sensitive appetites. But in God, who is absolutely immaterial, there is no body, no sense powers, and no sensitive appetite.[34] Passions, since they necessarily entail a sensitive and therefore bodily nature, are *per se* imperfect and limited, and consequently they cannot be predicated except metaphorically of God. But love and joy entail, of themselves, no other powers than intellect and

[32] *S. Theol.*, I, 26, 2, c (Pegis, *op. cit.*, Vol. I, p. 271).
[33] *S. Theol.*, I, 20, 1, c.
[34] *Ibid.*, ad 1.

will, and consequently they are not *per se* imperfect. They can therefore be properly predicated of God. This predication is analogous, as
far as we are concerned, because we actually experience love and joy
only in connection with the sensitive passions which accompany them,
while we must deny these accompanying passions when we attribute
love and joy to God.[35] Besides, God's love is not something in God,
but *is* God: *Deus est caritas.*

2. **God Loves All Things.** The object of love is the good, and good,
as we have seen, is identical in reality with being. Whatever has any
being, therefore, has to that extent some good. Further, all that is,
is created by God and therefore is good; and God, therefore, loves
whatever has any being. His love, however, is not caused or determined by the created good, as ours is; but on the contrary, His love
causes all things to be good, since His love for anything is simply His
act of willing good to that thing.[36] God loves even sinners, though
not *as sinners;* He loves them in so far as they are natures created by
Him, and therefore good.[37] He does not, of course, love evil or sin;
but evil is not-being, that is, privation of good and of being; God
hates evil because it is opposed to good, which He loves, as the privation of that good.

3. **God Loves Better Things More.** If we were to measure God's
love by the intensity of His act of will in loving different things, we
would have to say that He loves all things equally, since He loves
them all with the one infinite Act of Love whereby He loves His own
divine goodness. But there is another way of comparing God's love for
different beings. Since His love for them is what makes them good,
being simply His act of willing good to them, it follows that, of things
and persons, some of which are better than others, God loves the better
ones more; because He wills more good to them, and this is the reason
why they are better.[38] Thus, His love for rational creatures is different
from His love for non-rational creatures. Rational creatures, that is,
men and angels, are capable of communicating in love with God,
returning Him love for love; and so He loves them with the love of
friendship, willing that they share in His own love, so that they may
love Him in return for His love for them, and so attain to a final share
in His infinite beatitude.[39]

[35] *Ibid.,* ad 2.
[36] *S. Theol.,* I, 20, 2, c.
[37] *Ibid.,* ad 4.
[38] *Ibid.,* I, 20, 4.
[39] *Ibid.,* I, 20, 3, ad 3.

CHAPTER XXIV

*THE ORIGIN OF THE WORLD**

I. THEORIES OF THE WORLD'S ORIGIN

The world in which we live, of which we are part and which our natural sciences describe extends through unimaginable space and time, contains countless billions of different things of innumerable kinds, and yet has bonds of unity and order as remarkable as its multiplicity and variety. This world, again, is in constant movement and change; every part of it, we have reason to assume, always acts upon and is acted upon by every other part. Whence came this remarkable world? Men never tire of asking and trying to answer that question.

In the three chapters preceding the present one, we have already expounded all the elements of St. Thomas' answer to the question. The demonstration of God's existence is in truth the demonstration that the world's existence is due to a necessary, self-existent, supreme being. The demonstration that God is one, simple, immaterial, unchanging, and perfect is also the demonstration that the complex, changing, material multiplicity which makes up the world is something distinct from and different from God. Consequently, our question in this chapter is not, Where did the world come from? for we have already proved that it comes from God. Rather, our question is, How did the world originate from God? Our answer — St. Thomas' answer — is the Christian doctrine of creation: God produced the world out of nothing by a free act of His will.

1. Creationism. Creationism asserts four propositions: (1) that the world in its entirety, its whole substance, was produced by God; (2) that He produced it from nothing, that is, from no pre-existing substance whatsoever; (3) that He produced it by an intelligent and

*Primary readings: *S. Theol.*, I, qq. 11, 44, 45, 46, 47, 65; *De Pot.*, I, 5; III, 1–6, 13–17; *Con. Gen.*, II, 15–38.

free act of His will, and not by any natural necessity; (4) that God and the world are really distinct from each other as different substances are distinct, not merely as a substance and its modes, or reality and its appearances. Each one of these four propositions has been denied by various philosophers, and a theory of the world's origin has been based upon each denial.

2. **Materialism.** Atheistic materialism denies that God exists and, of course, denies that He created the world. In our day materialism takes the form of atheistic evolutionism. Its adherents believe matter to be eternal and attribute its existence to no cause other than itself; rather they regard matter as the first cause of everything. All existing things are modes of matter or functions of matter; matter, following necessary physical laws of motion, has evolved into the variety of beings now found in the universe. That is how the world originated.

We have already advanced adequate reasons for rejecting materialism. Self-existent or necessary being is, we have proved, immaterial, unchanging, pure actuality, personal, and infinitely perfect. Matter is the opposite of all these. Not only have we proved that the original being, God, is immaterial, but we have also demonstrated the immateriality of the human soul and the impossibility of its evolution from matter. Furthermore, we demonstrated that final causality is operative in nature and that this implies an intelligent cause of nature. We may add that materialism implies that intelligence can come from that which lacks intelligence, that the non-free can produce the free, that the higher can come from the lower, that something can come from nothing, since, according to materialism, the original being whence have evolved life, consciousness, intelligence, freedom, and moral responsibility is in itself non-living, non-conscious, non-intelligent, non-free, and non-moral. Finally, the fact, if it is a fact, that evolution takes place among living species is no evidence for materialism. Evolution is a process, not an explanation or a cause. It does not explain why matter exists, why it evolves, or why it evolves in the way in which it does. If evolution is a fact, it demands a cause; and if it is a progression toward higher and more perfect forms of being, it demands a cause that is both intelligent and good.

Many persons accept materialism because the doctrine of creation seems to them too incredible, too astounding for acceptance. Their minds recoil in unbelief from the idea of an eternal, self-existent, infinitely perfect personal God who created the universe. The idea of God is indeed astounding, and so is the conception of creation; but the universe is astounding too. No explanation of so amazing a thing as the world we live in ought to be rejected simply because it is itself amazing. But an explanation which is unintelligible and absurd ought to be rejected, and materialism is unintelligible and absurd. When materialists refuse to accept God as the source of the world, what do they accept instead? Matter, they say. But what is matter? In truth, it is a mere abstraction, not a concrete, unitary thing. Theism posits one self-existent being; materialism posits some trillions of trillions of self-existent beings; for matter, taken down from its ivory tower of abstraction, means every single electron and proton, every single photon of radiant energy, every single quantum of atomic energy, and possibly a great many more things we have yet to learn about. If "matter" is uncreated, it must exist of itself. If it does, then every single proton and electron is a necessary, self-existent, self-determined being. If one self-existent being is too astounding for credence, what are we to say of trillions of trillions of self-existent beings? And if it is incredible that the one self-existent, uncreated being should be intelligent and free, and should conceive and freely create the world, what are we to say of trillions of trillions of independent self-existing, non-intelligent, non-free beings all of which move and act and interact according to the same one set of physical laws, and by doing so give rise to intelligent and free beings as well as to material beings?

A man can be a materialist only so long as he does not understand what he is committing himself to when he believes in materialism. Suppose he is asked whether matter is necessary being; that is, whether matter *must* exist and be what it is. If he answers in the affirmative, he commits himself to the belief that each single particle of matter, each single quantum of energy, is absolutely necessary, and that every one of them is absolutely independent of every other; any effort to relate the separate particles in any sort of mutual dependence or single origin starts reason off on the road toward a unity and a power prior to matter, a road that leads to God. But if each particle is absolutely independent of each other one, how does it happen that each is also an embodiment of the same nature and the same laws as half the others, so that the two halves combine in atoms and molecules to form the amazing universe in which we live? Does it just happen? If the materialist places his faith in chance rather than in necessity, then he must believe that no single particle of matter is necessary, that none at all need exist, that others of different kinds might as well have happened to exist, that the proton-electron type of matter, with the physical laws concomitant thereon, is just a happy accident. The adoption of such a view is nothing else than the hopeless abandonment of all effort to seek out an explanation for nature. Materialism offers the inquiring mind nothing at all to account for the world we live in.

3. **Dualism.** Dualism (as an account of the world's *origin*) is the doctrine that the universe is the product of two independent eternal principles, matter and spirit; that matter is eternal and necessary like God Himself; and that the universe is the effect of God's action upon matter, giving it shape, nature, and order. Dualism differs from materialism inasmuch as it does not consider matter alone to be a sufficient cause of the universe. Because of the order, beauty, and goodness of the many things in the world, dualism believes that an intelligent mind, God, gave the universe its actual form. It differs from creationism because it considers God not as the universal and only first cause of all being, but merely as the architect, designer, and mover of the universe, the Artist who fashions the already existing matter into a harmonious work of beauty.

Dualism is open to the same objections as materialism, and others besides. Like materialism, dualism regards matter as uncreated and therefore either as necessary being or as something that just happens to exist; consequently, dualism involves all the absurdities involved in materialism. In addition, dualism, as the name itself indicates, introduces a radical duality into the heart of being: matter *is* and spirit *is,* and yet there is no community of origin or nature between them. "To be" in the two cases is utterly equivocal; the ultimate opposition of *being* and *not-being* disappears, and an opposition between matter and spirit or some other pair of contraries, for example, good and evil, replaces it, and "to be" loses all meaning. We shall return to the consideration of dualism in Chapter XXVI, when we discuss the origin of evil in the world.

4. **Pantheism.** Pantheism is the doctrine which holds that there is only one being or substance, namely, God; that the universe, or nature, is not distinct from God, but is part of God or the external manifestation of God; in other words, that God exists, and God alone exists. It is not so much an explanation of the world's origin as it is a denial of the world's real existence.

5. **Spinoza.** According to the most famous modern pantheist, Bene-

dict Spinoza, there is one infinite, unique reality, Substance; outside of this one reality nothing exists. The finite beings which seem to have distinct existence are merely finite modes or accidents of the infinite Substance. Substance has two names, God and Nature. Of its infinite number of infinite attributes two are known by men — thought and extension. In its infinite attribute of thought, Substance is God; in its infinite attribute of extension, it is Nature. God and Nature are in reality identical, because God is Substance and Nature is Substance, and Substance is one and simple. "God or Nature" is an expression frequently used by Spinoza. Spinoza's God is not a personal free being. Though God is Substance under the attribute of thought, he is not an intellect, for intellect is a limitation. He has no consciousness. Nor has he free will; by God's freedom, Spinoza means the absolute necessity of his operation, which is the precise contrary of what is universally understood by freedom.

Finite, separate individuals, in Spinoza's doctrine, do not exist as such; they are not things or *individuals,* but are modes or accidents of infinite Substance. They do not, however, proceed from Substance. From the infinite only the infinite can come. From Substance as God proceeds the infinite mode of thought, the Infinite Intellect. From Substance as Nature proceeds the infinite mode of extension, motion, and rest. These two infinite modes together constitute the totality of things (*facies totius universi*). The finite modes, namely, ideas and bodies, are determinations of the infinite modes, each idea being a finite mode of the infinite intellect, and each body a finite mode of motion and rest. The finite modes are not distinct beings, because determination is mere negation, and hence their finite individuality is unreal. Nor do finite modes proceed from the infinite modes; they produce one another by limiting one another, that is, every finite mode is determined by the other finite modes. In so far as they are real they are identical with God or Nature; in so far as they are finite determinations they are not real.

6. **Criticism of Pantheism.** To identify God with the contingent, finite, imperfect, ever changing, complex plurality that constitutes nature is to hold all human experience to be utterly worthless and all human life to be a complete illusion, and to be unable, at the same time, to account for the experience or the illusion. Even my consciousness of my own individual existence, my own self, is an illusion, because only God exists. To argue, as some pantheists do, that this conscious-

ness of self is not an illusion because I am real inasmuch as I am a manifestation of God, who is real, is futile. To whom am I a manifestation? To myself? Then I am a real individual. To God? Then where do I come in? If we call something a manifestation we mean that it is manifested to some mind; an appearance must appear to someone. According to pantheists there is no one but God for it to appear to. If my individuality is a deceit, then it is God who is deceived. The same thing may be said of evil and suffering. Are they real? Then God sins and tortures Himself. Are they illusions? Then God plays cruel jokes upon Himself.

7. Spinoza and St. Thomas on Finite Beings. An interesting comparison between St. Thomas and Spinoza can be made here. Both face the problem of explaining how finite things proceed from God, who is infinite. St. Thomas, who recognizes efficient causality, that is, one thing by its action producing another, regards finite things as distinct from God, though His effects. Spinoza, who rejects efficient causality, and admits only essential sequence, or implication by necessity of nature, denies that finite modes are realities distinct from God. St. Thomas[1] holds that the infinite *producing by necessity of nature* could produce only another infinite. Spinoza, admitting no other type of production, holds, without qualification, that only the infinite can proceed from the infinite. Because of their very different principles they give very different solutions to the problem. St. Thomas, who, besides admitting efficient causality, attributes intellect and free will to God, solves the problem by saying that God produces finite things as an efficient cause, their essences being determined by the imitability of His own essence and their existence by the free act of His will. Spinoza, admitting only causality by necessary implication of essence, and denying intellect and will to God, says that finite things are determined in being by other finite beings. "No single thing, i.e., having a finite and determinate existence, can exist and be determined to act unless determined thereto by some other cause also having a finite and determinate existence; which again cannot exist and act unless determined thereto by some other finite and determinate cause, etc., *in infinitum*."[2] At least two glaring fallacies mark Spinoza's argument. (*a*) He is trying to explain how *any* finite thing can exist; he explains it as due to *other* finite things. This is to offer as explanation the very thing to be explained. (*b*) He regards

---

[1] *S. Theol.*, I, 19, 4.
[2] B. Spinoza, *Ethics*, I, XVIII.

THE ORIGIN OF THE WORLD

finiteness and determination as negation — "every determination is a negation" — but he makes finite things *precisely as finite* perform the function of active causes.

Again, in seeking to explain how the universe *appears* to be made up of distinct, finite, individuals, when in fact it is not, Spinoza says that this is due to our "limited apprehension." If I had perfect apprehension, I would see nature as it is, a perfect, changeless unity; but because my apprehension is imperfect, I see it as a plurality of changing, finite individuals. But, we may ask, if distinct finite individuals are not real, then *who* has this finite apprehension? To explain how finite beings seem to exist when they really do not, limited apprehension is put forth; but unless finite individuals antecedently exist, there cannot be any limited apprehension. Here Spinoza does worse than offer as the explanation the thing to be explained; he offers the very thing he is denying.

8. Emanationism. Materialism, dualism, and pantheism all deny, in one way or another, that the world of real change and multiplicity is derived from the one unchanging God. The first two deny it explicitly, and the third denies it by denying any real distinction between the world and God. To change our terminology somewhat, we might say that to the age-old metaphysical question, How is the many derived from the one? these three philosophies answer, it is not derived from the one. Materialism denies the one, pantheism denies the many, and dualism relates the two only externally, allowing neither to depend on the other. In contrast to these three theories, two others affirm that the many is in fact derived from the one and depends upon it; these two theories are emanationism and creationism. They disagree with each other in respect to the manner in which the many — the world — is derived from the one — God. Emanationism holds that the world proceeds by necessity of nature from the substance of God: that the one is such that by the demands of its own essence it produces the many. We have already seen that creationism asserts that God produces the world, not by necessity, but by a free act of will; and not out of His own substance, but out of nothing. It is on these two points that creationism and emanationism disagree. Among emanationistic theories of note might be mentioned Neoplatonism[3] in ancient times, and Hegelianism and absolute idealism in modern times. We shall return to a consideration of emanationism below.

[3] Cf. Chapter III, section III, No. 3.

9. God-in-Process Theories.[4] Some recent philosophers have originated theories which might be described as emanationism in reverse and might be grouped under the general name of emergent or creative evolution. Whereas the classical emanationistic theories postulate a descending evolution or procession of the many from the one, or of the world from God, these later theories teach an ascending evolutionary process which begins from the many — from matter or space-time, for example — rises through successively more perfect forms of being, and culminates, or will culminate, in God. In doctrines of this sort, the movements of nature are the process of God getting created, or creating Himself, through nature. God does not exist as a separate actuality at any moment of the process prior to the final moment (if there is to be a final moment);[5] He is the end of evolution in the sense that He is what the whole evolutionary process is producing. We cannot exactly believe in God now, but we can hope in Him; and, perhaps, if we have charity one toward another, we shall aid in bringing the Kingdom of God to pass.

From the point of view of metaphysics, these theories of emergent evolution are indistinguishable from materialism and atheism, for they give no explanation of the world's origin other than matter or space and time, and they admit no God who now actually exists. Morally speaking, they are nicer theories than materialism, for their essential meaning seems to be that the original blind and lifeless stuff which is the matrix of nature, has an insatiable desire to get better and better all the time, so that it will not be satisfied until it becomes God. God, indeed, is definable, in the framework of such theories, as that which everything wants to become. In Thomistic philosophy, too, everything wants or tends to become like God, which is quite understandable, since in that philosophy God actually exists and created all things, giving to each a natural tendency toward its end. But in a philosophy according to which God does not actually exist, it is not understandable that matter or space-time or anything else should have a natural urge to become Godlike or to become God Himself. Indeed, the conception of an evolving God is nonsense; in a universe in which God is yet-to-be, there is no such thing as God-

---

[4] Cf. S. Alexander, *Space, Time, and Deity*, 1920, 1927. Summarized in Metz, *A Hundred Years of British Philosophy* (New York: Macmillan, 1938), pp. 622–651, especially 648–651.

[5] In S. Alexander's system no final moment when God *actually* exists is ever to be reached.

likeness or God Himself or tendency toward God, for there just isn't any God. Finally, these theories of an evolving God fall under all the criticisms which we made at the end of Chapters V and XXI of doctrines which posit immanent finality without transcendent finality in nature.

II. THE ONE AND THE MANY

The issue between emanationism and creationism is bound up with the age-old philosophical problem of the one and the many. Emanationism and creationism agree in recognizing the reality of both unity and multiplicity, and in holding that multiplicity is somehow derived from and dependent upon unity. They differ as to *how* multiplicity has proceeded from the one. Emanationism regards the procession of the many from the one as necessary, as required by the very essence of the one. Creationism holds that the production of the many by the one is free and is not necessitated or required by the essence of the one. A brief study of St. Thomas' teaching on the one and the many should aid us to understand the problem clearly and to see how it must be solved.

1. **Unity.** Unity, like truth and goodness, is a transcendental attribute of being; that is to say, whatever is, is one, true, and good, and the unity of anything is in reality identical with its being. To say that something is *one* is to say that it is *one thing,* that is, that it possesses undivided being. Obviously something can possess undivided being in many ways, but in every case its type of being is identical with its type of unity, and it is the being that it is just so long as it maintains the unity proper to that type of being. Water, for example, is a composite chemical unity of oxygen and hydrogen and it possesses being — it *is* water — just so long as it maintains this chemical unity. The human body is an organic unity of vital parts and functions, and it *is* a human body just so long as it keeps this organic unity. Thus *one* signifies undivided being, adding to the notion of being only the negation of division. There are, consequently, as many kinds of unity as there are kinds of division to be negated, or, from another point of view, as many kinds of unity as there are kinds of undividedness of being. A simple being is both undivided and indivisible, and its unity consists in its simple being. A composite being has parts, but it is a being only in so far as these parts are actually undivided from one another; only the actual union of these parts into one constitutes

the composite an actual being. Hence its unity and being are the same thing, and the loss of its unity is the loss of its being. Consequently, the actual being of anything consists in its indivision, and everything maintains its being in so far as it maintains its unity.[6]

2. One and Being. All this means that *one* and *being* are the same in reality (*in re*) but differ in conception (*in ratione*); they are different concepts which signify the same reality in anything of which they are predicated. When, for example, we say of someone that he *is* a man and that he is *one* man, we express two different concepts of him, but we do not predicate two distinct realities of him: to be a man and to be one man are the same thing. That thing is the man himself: his being is himself and his unity is himself; he is not a man *and* a being, or a man *and* one.[7] But if one and being signify the thing itself of which they are predicated, and are therefore identical *in re,* they signify this thing for different reasons, and therefore differ *in ratione.* The thing in question is called a thing (*res*) because of its essence, a being (*ens*) because of the act by which it exists, and one (*unum*) because of its undividedness. "But that which has an essence, and through that essence a quiddity, is the same thing as that which is undivided in itself. Wherefore these three, namely, thing, being, and one, signify precisely the same thing, but according to different reasons."[8]

3. Multiplicity and Unity. If in reality *one* is identical with being, then multiplicity would seem to be left outside being, or, in other words, to be non-being. Yet certainly multiplicity is as real as unity. St. Thomas takes the view that a multitude is real, but that its reality is founded upon some unity; that is to say, a multitude is being in so far as it is in some way one. An army, for example, is something only so long as it retains some unity; when utterly dispersed, it no longer exists. The unity of an army is a unity of organization, communication, and command, uniting a multitude of individuals. This is an artificial unity, and consequently an army is merely an artificial or accidental being. But there are several kinds of natural unity-in-multiplicity. A being may be one in subject and many as to accidents; as for example a man, who is the subject of many accidents, like his age, state of health, degree of intelligence, nationality. A

[6] *S. Theol.,* I, 11, 1, c; *De Ver.,* I, 1, c; *In X Meta.,* 3, Nos. 1974–1977.
[7] *In IV Meta..* 2, Nos. 549–552.
[8] *In IV Meta.,* No. 553.

being may be one as a whole and many as to parts; for example, an animal with its head, trunk, and limbs. Again, something may be one in species and many in individuals, like the human race. Still again, the unity may be a unity of cause or principle and the multiplicity a multitude of effects or products, like a parent and his progeny. In every case, the "many" is a being only by virtue of the "one," and apart from the one, it is nothing; for example, we can speak of the multitude of men as being something only because we consider the separate individuals under the unity of the species or race, and we can speak of a progeny only by virtue of a single progenitor.

Not only must we group a multitude under some unity in order to think of it as a being, but we cannot even grasp a multitude as a *many* without first understanding each separate member of it as a *one*. The concept of multitude or many comes after the concept of one. The first of all our ideas is *being* — whatever we conceive, we conceive as being; after the idea of being comes that of *division*, which we conceive when we understand that this being is not that being but is something (*aliquid*) else. When we then understand that each something, although divided from each other, is undivided in itself, we attain to the conception of unity or one. And only when we have thus judged each being to be one, do we understand that the divided ones constitute a many.[9] Thus, every multitude has a twofold dependence upon unity; it is a multitude only because it is made up of many ones, and it has being only in so far as it can be grasped in relation to some ground of unity.

4. Unity Is Proportionate to Being. Since *one* is identical *in re* with being, it follows that the kind of unity possessed by anything is proportionate to the kind of being possessed by it. The unity of a mineral, which can be broken into bits without losing its nature, is less perfect than that of a plant, which, in order to retain its nature, must retain something of its unity of organization. This becomes more evident the higher we ascend in the scale of natural beings; the higher animals are destroyed by comparatively slight disruptions of their bodily unity, while lower ones can be divided and yet live. The being of these latter, that is to say, their life, is of course divided, and in a sense destroyed, but it is not destroyed utterly; it splits with the splitting of their unity. Unity and being, then, are inseparable and

---

[9] *S. Theol.*, I, 11, 2 ad 4; *In IV Meta.*, 3, No. 566; *De Pot.*, IX, 7, ad 15.

directly proportionate to each other; hence the highest being possesses the highest unity.

5. God Is Supremely One. St. Thomas writes:

> Since the one is undivided being, it follows that in order for something to be one in the highest degree, it must be being in the highest degree and undivided in the highest degree. But both these are proper to God. For He is being in the highest degree inasmuch as He possesses being not limited by any nature which receives it, but is Himself subsisting being undetermined to any modes. He is also undivided in the highest degree, inasmuch as He is neither divided in act nor in potency according to any mode of division, since He is simple in every way. . . . Whence it is clear that God is to the highest degree one.[10]

6. The One God and the Many Creatures. Whence it is also clear, the Angelic Doctor might have added, that we have a real problem on our hands. If the Cause of all the beings of nature is absolutely simple and absolutely one, how have the multiplicity and composition so obvious in nature come into being? St. Thomas' solution of this problem affords another illustration of the remarkable coherence and integration of his philosophical system. The exigencies of his conception of the nature of God require him, as we saw in the preceding chapter, to insist that any activity of God relative to any being other than Himself must be absolutely free, must proceed freely from the divine intelligence and will. Now, when the concrete problem of the procession of the multitude of creatures from the absolute unity of the Creator is raised, it quickly appears that this problem is insoluble except on the postulate that creatures proceed from God — the many from the one — by way of a *free* determination and causation on the part of the one. .

This is clearly seen when we consider the different ways in which something may be one and many, and how the one and many are related to each other in these different cases. Something may be many in respect to its parts and one as a whole, as, for example, a man. But this kind of one and many cannot be attributed to God and creatures, because if creatures were parts of God, God would be a composite; but we have seen that He is absolutely simple. Nor can the one-and-many related as a substance and its accidents be attributed to God and creatures; from the side of God, we have seen that He is not a composite of substance and accidents; and, from the side of creatures, it is

10 *S. Theol.*, I, 11, 4, c.

obvious that the division of substance and accidents is *within* natural beings — they are substances determined by accidents, they are not accidents of some substance. Nor can the one-and-many of God and creatures be that of one species and many individuals, or of one genus and many species; because God is not a species or a genus, for species and genera are composite and potential, whereas God is absolute, simple, actual being. The only kind of one-and-many which can be the relation of God and creatures is the one-and-many of cause and procession from cause: God is the one cause and creatures are the many effects. The multiplicity is entirely within the effects; the cause is one, and is supreme unity because it is supreme being. But how do the effects proceed from the Cause? How can multiplicity be an effect of perfect unity? Whether we can ever arrive at an intelligible answer to this question, we can at least pronounce one answer unintelligible and self-contradictory: *it cannot be by any necessity of its own being that perfect simple unity gives rise to multiplicity.* Anything which *by the intrinsic demands of its own essence* becomes many or produces multiplicity, must have within itself an original multiplicity or composition. God produces the world; but if He produces it by necessity of His own essence, then the multiplicity which is visible in the world is antecedently, though invisibly, in the very essence of God. A principle which *must* produce a plurality of effects is a principle which contains within itself a plurality of needs.

7. The Fallacy of Emanationism. Yet philosophers throughout the ages have not tired of seeking to *deduce* the many from the one. It cannot be done. A one which implies a many is a composite one and is not the ultimate one. Absolute idealism, which is explicitly monistic, is basically a radical pluralism; because it posits in the heart of the one an original centrifugal urge which cannot belong to that which is perfectly one. The absolute idealists are faced with an insoluble antinomy: the many must have come from the one; but if the one *must* produce the many, it is not truly the one. They do not seem to see that because the many implies the one it does not necessarily follow that the one implies the many; they do not see that *just because the many does necessarily imply the one, the ultimate one cannot possibly imply the many.* A one which implies a many is itself a many-in-one. and implies a more ultimate One, an absolute One.

Deduction is possible only where the bond between the ground and consequent is necessary. All philosophers, like Hegel for example, who attempt to *deduce* the whole of actual reality from some primary principle presuppose that the relation between this principle and its consequents is necessary. This supposition entails something which no true idealist ought to admit, namely, that freedom is not characteristic of being at its highest level. It may be extremely difficult for the human mind to assent to the proposition that this world exists only because of a free decision of a personal Maker; but the alternative is to affirm that primary being is not free. Indeed, absolute idealism destroys freedom entirely, leaving only the delusion of freedom to man. If God's effects follow from Him by necessity, everything is what it is and does what it does by eternal necessity, and neither God nor any creature is free.

8. The Thomistic Solution. God, who is one and simple, created the world, which is multiple and complex. But how is it possible that from a single and simple cause, a multiplicity and variety of effects should arise? Spinoza and other monists deny that this is possible, and therefore they identify the world with God. Radical dualists also deny it, and hence they regard matter as the source of multiplicity and attribute to it eternal existence independent of God. Any philosophy that regards the emanation of the world from God as *necessary* cannot consistently explain how it can be truly a plurality and a variety. The situation is different in a philosophy which maintains that God produces the world freely and as something distinct from Himself. Creationism is such a philosophy.

St. Thomas finds the source of the multiplicity of creatures in the intelligence and the will of God the Creator. The end which God sets Himself in creating is the existence outside Himself of an imitation or reflection of His own essence, the sharing of His own goodness with His creatures. Since the divine essence is infinite, no one creature can be an adequate reflection of it; wherefore God wills a variety of creatures. The divine essence, being infinite and embracing within itself the total perfection of being, is capable of being reflected in an infinite variety of finite beings. This multiplicity of creatures, since it is an effect of God's knowledge and will, and since it is extrinsic to God's substance, in no way destroys the simplicity of that substance. Before their actualization in real existence distinct from God all creatures pre-exist in the divine intellect as ideas; but this pre-existence does not destroy the simplicity of the divine intelligence, because God knows all possible creatures in the simple, perfect knowledge of His own essence. Finally, in His perfect freedom and omnipotence, God can will to produce any combination, or order, of the possible imitations of Himself. That order which He chooses to produce is the universe as we find it existing.[11]

III. THE THOMISTIC DOCTRINE OF CREATION

1. Every Other Being Is Produced by God. Every multitude implies a unity, and the all-embracing multitude — the universe itself — requires an original and perfect unity as its principle. This primary unity, the One, is God, as we saw in proving God's existence. God is absolutely simple and is self-subsisting being. There can be only one self-subsisting being, as we have proved. Everything else, therefore, possesses being by participation. But everything which possesses any perfection by participation derives it from that which possesses it by essence. Since, therefore, God alone possesses being by essence — that is, is self-subsisting being — all other beings have derived their being from God. God is the first cause of everything that exists.[12]

God is not only the first efficient cause of all things, but also their exemplary cause and their final cause. Whatever He creates, God gives a determinate form; and the exemplar according to which He makes this form is His own divine essence. All things pre-exist in the divine wisdom as the divine ideas or exemplars. The divine ideas, although multiplied in relation to creatures, are one in the divine wisdom, for all the divine ideas are the divine essence itself in so far as the likeness of that essence can be shared by creatures.[13] God in creating is an agent, and every agent acts for an end. The end for which God acts is, as we have seen, His own divine goodness. He does not act so as to acquire this end, as if He lacked it; but so as to communicate and share it as far as that is possible. Consequently, the end of creation is the divine goodness communicated to and represented by creatures.[14]

2. God Produces Things From Nothing. Whatever comes to be, comes into being from the negation of what it becomes, since something cannot become what it already is. Now that which creatures receive from God is being itself, not merely this or that form of being,

---

[11] *S. Theol.*, I, 47, 1, c and ad 1; *Con. Gen.*, II, 45; *De Pot.*, III, 15 and 16.
[12] *S. Theol.*, I, 44, 1; *ibid.*, 65, 1.
[13] *Ibid.*, I, 44, 3.
[14] *Ibid.*, art. 4.

since they exist only by derivation from Subsisting Being. But the negation or privation of being itself is non-being, or nothing. Hence we say that God creates all things *ex nihilo*. We do not mean, of course, that nothingness is some sort of subject or material which God molds into creatures, as a carpenter molds a desk from wood. The expression "from nothing" signifies not a material cause but an *order of priority:* by creation, creatures become something, whereas prior to that they were nothing. The expression "from nothing" does refer to a material cause, but only in order to deny any such cause; it means that creatures are made *by* God but are not made *from* anything.[15] It is not a contradiction to say that God can make something from nothing. Those who call it a contradiction are thinking of every coming-to-be as a *generation* or change. In every generation there must be something out of which that which comes to be is generated. But creation is not a generation. If creation were a generation, it would presuppose some existing material or substratum which did not derive its being from God but existed independently of Him. We have seen that this is impossible, since everything which is not self-subsistent being must be derived from self-subsistent being, and since this supposed substratum cannot be self-subsistent being, because if it were it would be God Himself. Hence no subject or material can be presupposed to creation, and therefore God must create things from nothing.[16]

3. God Alone Can Create. Creation, and creation alone of all acts of production, is the production of being itself rather than of a change in being. Every creature possesses being only by reception; of itself, apart from God, the Source of Being, it is nothing. Clearly, then, it cannot be itself a source of being. A creature cannot be even an instrumental cause in creation, because the only reason why a principal agent uses something as an instrument is because that thing has a special quality making it apt for producing the desired effect when power is given to it by the principal cause. But no creature has any aptitude for the production of being itself. At best, the created instrument could dispose some material to receive being from God; but this is impossible since creation excludes any pre-existing material.[17]

4. Creation Is a Free Act of God. We have already proved this in

[15] *S. Theol.*, I, 45, 1.
[16] *Ibid.*, 2.
[17] *Ibid.*, 5.

Chapter XXIII when treating of the question of the freedom of God's will. We need only briefly restate the arguments now. These arguments dispose of every theory that is emanationist in character.

1. Whatever is ordered with a view toward an end is the product of a cause operating intelligently and freely; that is, a cause that can set up an end for itself and choose means for the accomplishment of that end. Nature is ordered with a view toward an end. Therefore, God produced it operating intelligently and freely.

2. If God produced the world by necessity, it would be (*a*) by necessity of His own nature or (*b*) by impulsion of the created good. Neither of these alternatives can be admitted. (*a*) Being infinite and undetermined being, God would, if He produced by necessity of nature, produce an infinite, undetermined being, since there would be no factors to limit or determine the effect. But (1) two infinite beings are impossible, and (2) as a matter of fact, God's effects are finite, determinate beings. Furthermore, God, being infinite and pure actuality, cannot be necessitated to produce anything, since such necessity would imply a lack in the infinite needing to be filled, a potentiality needing to be actualized, and a dependency of God upon His creatures for the filling out of His own perfection. (*b*) God, as we saw in Chapter XXIII, wills His own goodness in itself as an end and things other than His goodness for the sake of that goodness, as directed toward an end. But a means is willed necessarily only when the end cannot be realized without it. Since God's goodness is complete and perfect without anything else, He creates all finite beings freely and not of necessity.

3. Effects pre-exist in their cause according to the mode of being of the cause. God's being is identical with His intelligence. Therefore, His effects pre-exist in Him in the intelligible mode of being. Hence, they proceed from Him by way of intelligence, which means that they are freely produced effects and that their immediate cause is His act of will, since intelligence apart from will is not productive of anything outside itself.

4. As we have seen above, the doctrine that God produces the world by necessity of His nature deprives both God and creatures of freedom. God's freedom does not refer to His will in relation to His own being, which He necessarily loves and wills as Supreme Good; hence if He is not free in willing creatures, He is not free in any respect. But to deny freedom to God is to assert that the most

perfect of beings is not free. This is a proposition which no idealist or spiritualist can admit, and yet it is the idealists who most consistently maintain some sort of necessary emanation of the world from God. In the second place, if the world proceeds from God by necessity of the divine nature, then everything in the world is eternally fixed, and freedom can never arise among creatures.

IV. CREATION, TIME, AND ETERNITY

1. Problem of the Beginning. It is a revealed truth of religion that the world had a beginning in time. But it is one thing to believe a truth through supernatural faith and another thing to be able to prove it philosophically. The question of the demonstrability of the world's beginning was a much disputed one in St. Thomas' day. The issues involved in the dispute are quite as vital today as they were in the thirteenth century.

St. Bonaventure and others of the Augustinian school held that the fact of the world's beginning in time can be rationally demonstrated. The Latin Averroists taught the exact contrary, namely, that the eternity of the world is demonstrable. St. Thomas taught: (1) that we cannot prove either that the world always existed or that it had a beginning: (2) that we can prove that God could create either an eternal or a non-eternal world; (3) that, as a matter of fact, He did create a non-eternal world, as we know through divine revelation.[18]

2. God's Creative Act Is Eternal. As soon as we ask: Is creation eternal or non-eternal? it is clear that the question itself is ambiguous. It may mean: (1) Is creation, i.e., God's creative act, eternal[19] or non-eternal? or (2) Is creation, i.e., the created world, eternal or non-eternal? Taking the question in the first sense, the answer is that God's creative act is eternal. It must be so, because God's action is identical with His essence. Besides, if the creative act were not eternal, then God would at one time not act and at a later time act, which is impossible since God is pure actuality, changeless, and independent of time. But does it follow that because God's act of creating is eternal the thing created must be eternal? Many philosophers, both medieval and modern, say, "Yes, it does follow." St. Thomas says, "No, it does not." The point will be clarified if we study the

[18] *S. Theol.*, I, 46, arts. 1, 2, 3; *De Pot.*, III, 14 and 17.

[19] The term *eternal* wherever used in the paragraphs above in relation to the created world is not taken in strict meaning as applied to God, but has the sense of "existing without a beginning, without a first moment, yet in time."

arguments that are advanced to prove the eternity of the world, and the Thomistic answers to these arguments.

3. **Arguments for the Eternity of the World.** God is the adequate cause of the world. Whenever the adequate cause of an effect is actual, the effect must be produced. But God is eternally actual. Therefore, the world must be eternally produced. St. Thomas answers in these words:

> If God were acting by nature only, and not by will, the conclusion would necessarily follow. But because He acts through will, He can, through an eternal act of will produce an effect which is not eternal, just as an eternal intellect can understand a nature that is not eternal.[20]

The act by which God creates the world is eternal, but it does not follow that its effect, the world, is eternal. There is no contradiction in saying that a world created by an eternal act of God could come into being at a given moment, before which it did not exist. God creates the world, making it just what He wishes it to be: He gives it its existence, its nature, its beginning, and its end. Just as its being and its nature depend on His will, so does its time. In a word, God's act of creation freely establishes the world's existence, its nature, its spatial boundaries, and its temporal boundaries.[21]

God is immutable, and therefore His act of creation is eternal. The fact that the world is not eternal does not mean that God at one time did not will it and at another time did. *God does not exist and act in time. He is the creator of time, and no time existed before creation.* God did not exist a long time before creating the world, nor did He eternally will the world to come into being at some future time, because in Him there is no time. and His operation does not take place under the conditions of time. What is meant by saying that the world was created in time is simply that God willed it to have a beginning rather than always to be. When did it begin? In the first moment of time. Time is simply the measure of the succession of changes of state. That the world began means simply that there was a first state of the world before which it did not exist at all; or that if we could trace the states of the world back from the present one, we would come eventually to a first one and beyond that to the non-existence of the world and of time.

The following arguments for the eternity of the world are variations

[20] *In VIII Phys.*, 2. Cf. *S. Theol.*, I, 46, 1, ad 10.
[21] *S. Theol.*, I, 46, 1, ad 6.

on the same theme stated in the first argument. The refutation of
that one answers them all. For the sake of complete clarity, we shall
add a few words of comment on each:

Argument: The world must be eternal, because otherwise creation
would be a change in God, a passage from potency to act.

Answer: God is pure actuality, and His act of creation is identical
with His essence. He always creates, hence creation is no change in
Him. But what He creates is a world which has a beginning. His
effect does not proceed from Him eternally, because *He determines it
to have a beginning.*

Argument: The world must be eternal, because if the goodness of
creation moved God to create at one time, it would have moved Him
always.

Answer: This argument is based on the false supposition that something external to God, namely, the goodness of creatures, caused God
to create. Nothing extrinsic can cause God's action, because God's
action is identical with His essence, and He is absolutely uncaused;
He moves everything; nothing moves Him. God's "motive" for creation is His own goodness. Free to create or not create, He is free also
to determine whether the world should always exist or have a beginning. The argument also presupposes a false idea of eternity. It
considers the world, if it had a beginning, as coming into existence
at some moment in God's life, and asks, "Why did it not come into
being before that; indeed, why did it not always come to be?" It
overlooks the fundamental fact that God does not live or act in time,
that there are no successive moments in His life. The question, "Why
did not God create the world before He did?" is meaningless. There
is no before or after except in the created world itself. Before creation
there is no time, because time is merely a measure of change. Therefore, time began when the world began. God created time by creating the world.

Eternity is a duration not only without beginning or end, but
undivided and indivisible; it belongs only to uncreated being. Duration divided or divisible by a certain succession is proper to creatures.
Time exists only if there are created things; there can be no question
of a time anterior to the world. If we speak of a time before the
world, it is only an imaginary or possible time. Just as we can speak
of space outside the universe, so may we speak of time before it;
just as the universe might have been larger than it is, so might it

have been older. The question, *"When did the world begin?"* is not meaningless. "When" is taken in relation to the time that followed the first moment, not to the (non-real) time that preceded it. "When did the world begin?" means "How old is the world now?" It does not mean "How old was eternity when the world was born?" That question is meaningless.

The Reason Behind St. Thomas' Position. St. Bonaventure and other contemporaries of St. Thomas advanced several arguments seeking to prove that the world *must* have had a beginning. We shall not examine them or St. Thomas' replies to them. What is more important is to understand why St. Thomas stood opposed to them as well as to the arguments for the eternity of the world. The basic reason why St. Thomas stood ready to oppose every attempt to prove either the eternity or the non-eternity of the world was that such proofs as were given in his day would set a limit to either God's power or freedom. All the arguments advanced sought, by metaphysical considerations, to prove either that it is *impossible* for the world to be eternal or *impossible* for it to have had a beginning. If the first were true, then God would lack the power or freedom to create an eternal world; if the second were true, He would lack the power or freedom to create a world with a beginning. St. Thomas would not admit such limitation of God's omnipotence. His attitude might have been different in the face of scientific arguments such as are advanced today to establish the *fact* that the world had a beginning. These arguments, in so far as they are conclusive, prove only that the world *is* non-eternal, not that it *must be*. Hence their conclusions embody no implications concerning God's power or freedom. Whether St. Thomas would have considered any of these arguments conclusive, is another question.[22]

[22] *S. Theol.*, I, 46, 2.

CHAPTER XXV

*GOD IN NATURE**

I. THE DIVINE OMNIPRESENCE

No subject brings us more deeply into the heart of St. Thomas'
philosophy or gives us a clearer insight into the significance and
spirit of that philosophy than the subject of the relations that exist
between God and the things which He has created. In his treatment
of this subject the Angelic Doctor avoids all the extreme positions
into which it is so easy to fall and into which so many philosophers,
both ancient and modern, have fallen. In former chapters, especially
the preceding chapter, we have emphasized the *transcendence* of God
over creation; in the present chapter we must see the other aspect
of the relation of God and creatures, namely, God's *immanence* in the
created world. St. Thomas insisted upon both aspects.

1. **God Is in Everything, and Everything Is in God.** The immanence
of God in the world is emphatically affirmed by the Angelic Doctor.
He is present in all things, not as part of their essence or as an
accident of their being, but as an agent acting in them. God acts
immediately in every created thing, because the *being* of these things
is His proper and immediate effect, produced by Him alone and
directly, since, as we have seen, no creature can create or even be an
instrumental cause of creation. An agent may not be present in the
thing in which it acts, if it acts in that thing through a medium, as,
for example, when I speak to you over the telephone. But it must be
present in anything in which it acts without a medium. God, who
creates the being of everything without any medium, must therefore
be immediately present as an agent in every created thing. He is
above all created beings in reference to the excellence of His nature,

* Primary readings: *S. Theol.*, I, qq. 8, 21, 22, 82, 83, 103, 104, 105, 115; I–II, q.
10, art. 4; q. 75, art. 2; *Con. Gen.*, III, 64–69, 94; *De Pot.*, III, 7; V, 1 and 2.

but He is at the same time in them as the cause of their being. We call God's property of being present in all things His *omnipresence*.

2. God's Ubiquity. God is everywhere, and we speak of this divine property as His *ubiquity*. At first sight it would seem false to say that God is everywhere. First, God is indivisible, and hence cannot be in several places at once; second, wherever God is He is there totally, since He has no parts, and consequently He cannot be at the same time anywhere else. These arguments are easily answered. They arise from the belief that God, in order to be in a place, would have to be there as a body is. God, however, is a spirit, and a spirit is in a place, not by any quantitative dimensions in it which fill out the dimensions of the place, but by its power whereby it acts in the place. Consequently, the indivisibility of God does not, like the quantitative indivisibility of a point, prevent Him from being in more than one place; on the contrary, the infinity of His indivisible power enables Him to be at once in many places, indeed, in every place. Furthermore, He can be entirely in every place. "Entirely" or "totally" when used of a spiritual being cannot refer to quantitative parts and whole since a spirit has no quantity, but only to parts or whole of the essence. Now it is clear that something may be wholly in more than one place by its essence, although it cannot be by its quantity; the whole of whiteness is, as to its essence, in every part of a white sheet of paper, but, as to quantity, one part of the whiteness is in one part of the paper, another in another. God, purely spiritual, is wholly everywhere by His indivisible essence.

St. Thomas distinguishes three ways in which God is everywhere and in everything. He is in everything by His power, inasmuch as all things are subject to His almighty power; just as a king is said to be everywhere in his kingdom by his power and rule. He is, second, in everything by His presence, since everything is intimately known by Him and open to His gaze; just as a person is said to be present at something which he directly observes. Third, God is in all things by His essence, since He, essential being, is in all creatures giving them their being. He is not part of *their* essence: to hold that would be to fall into pantheism and to confuse uncreated, self-existing being with created, caused being. He is in things by *His* essence, inasmuch as His substance is the cause of their being.[1]

[1] *S. Theol.*, I, 8; *Con. Gen.*, III, 68.

II: DIVINE PROVIDENCE AND GOVERNMENT

God, acting as a free and intelligent cause, created everything that exists. But God's work in His creatures goes far beyond simply bringing them into existence. *Deism,* a doctrine widespread in the eighteenth and nineteenth centuries, admits God's existence and creative act, but denies that God has anything to do with the world now that it exists. Having created the world, God gave it physical laws by which it runs its own course. Deism denies *divine providence* and the *divine government* of the world. Christian dogma (and Thomistic philosophy) affirm divine providence and government.

1. Meaning of Providence. St. Thomas, following Boethius, defines providence as "divine reason itself, residing in the supreme ruler of everything, which disposes all things."[2] Providence is the divine reason ordering all creatures to the end for which they were created. Since it is the divine intellect and will, considered as governing creation, providence is eternal. But the execution of this order in creatures takes place in time. This execution is the divine government.

2. Proof of Providence. That God does govern the world, ordering all things to their end, is clear from the nature of creation; because, as we proved, God created by intelligence and will, and to act by intelligence and will is to act for an end. But from the fact that God created things for an end, it follows that He actually directs them to the end, as St. Thomas argues:

> For whenever certain things are ordered to some end, they are all subject to the disposition of the one to whom the end principally belongs, as appears in regard to an army; for all the parts of the army, and all their works, are ordained to the good sought by the general, viz., victory, as to their ultimate end; and because of this it belongs to the general to rule the whole army. . . . Since, therefore, all things are ordained to the divine goodness, as has been shown, it is necessary that God, to whom that good belongs principally, as being possessed, known and loved substantially, be the ruler of all things.[3]

It is also apparent from the nature and operations of created things that they are all directed to their end by God. St. Thomas, therefore, uses as another proof of divine providence the finality so evident in nature. Natural bodies are moved and operate for the sake of an end, and in order to do so they must be directed to this end by some

[2] *S. Theol.,* I, 22, 1, c.
[3] *Con. Gen.,* III, 64. Cf. *S. Theol.,* I, 103, 1, c.

knowledge, which they do not have themselves. If this knowledge which orders natural bodies to their end is anything less than the divine Wisdom Itself, it must be caused by and derived from that Wisdom, as the fourth proof of God's existence made clear. If it is not the divine Wisdom, it is a creature, ordered itself to the ultimate end of creation, and consequently it is not the First Orderer, but orders bodies to their end only because it is itself governed by Supreme Knowledge.[4]

3. **Universality of Providence.** The providence of God is, of necessity, as universal in its scope as the divine causality. The latter reaches to everything that has being in any mode; hence the former does also. In other words, absolutely everything in the created universe is subject to the divine rule. St. Thomas affirmed this universality of providence against those philosophers who denied providence altogether and against those who limited it to incorruptible beings or to universal species. According to the Angelic Doctor all things, corruptible as well as incorruptible, individual as well as universal, are created by God and known by God and therefore are governed and directed to their end by God; nothing which *is,* is exempt from divine rule:

> For since every agent acts for an end, the ordering of effects toward that end extends as far as the causality of the first agent extends. Whence it happens that in the effects of an agent something takes place which has no reference toward the end, because the effect comes from some other cause outside the intention of the agent. But the causality of God, who is the first agent, extends to all beings not only as to the constituent principles of species, but also as to the individualizing principles; not only of things incorruptible, but also of things corruptible. Hence all things that exist in whatsoever manner are necessarily directed by God toward the end. . . . Since, therefore, the providence of God is nothing other than the notion of the order of things toward an end, as we have said, it necessarily follows that all things, inasmuch as they participate being, must to that extent be subject to divine providence. It has also been shown that God knows all things, both universal and particular. And since His knowledge may be compared to things as the knowledge of an art is to the art-products . . . it follows necessarily that everything falls under His ordering just as all the art-products are subject to the ordering of the art.[5]

4. **The Infallibility of Divine Providence.** From the universality of divine providence it follows that nothing can occur contrary to or out-

---

[4] *Loc. cit.*   [5] *S. Theol.,* I, 22, 2, c; cf. *ibid.,* 103, 4.

side the order of the divine government of the world; that is, nothing that God has not foreseen and foreordained or at least permitted can possibly occur: divine providence and divine government are infallible. The only thing that can ever prevent any cause from producing its effect is some other cause over which it does not have control. But all causes in the universe are themselves caused by God, the First Cause, and can act only in so far as He moves them. Hence they can never so act as to prevent God's action from producing its effect, since their action depends totally upon His.[6] As we saw in Chapter XXIII, God's will is never frustrated, and whatever *seems*, from one point of view, to depart from the order of the divine government, is brought back under it from another point of view. Evil, which God never wills and cannot will, would certainly seem to be a departure from the order of providence; but even evils are departures, frustrations, or privations only of *particular* goods, and God foresees evils and permits them only because He makes them contribute to the greater good in the universal order, namely, the 'greater perfection of the whole universe.[7]

5. **The End of Divine Government.** What is the ultimate end toward which the divine government of the world directs and moves all things? It can be nothing else than the divine goodness itself; for, as we have seen, the first object of the divine will is the Divine Goodness, and God wills whatever else He wills only for the sake of this goodness. Furthermore, the ultimate end of anything is the same as its first beginning. Every agent acts for an end, and consequently in every causal operation the final cause is prior to all the other causes; it is the *causa causarum*. The first of all agents, God, who is the cause of all other beings, must be Himself the final cause for which He acts, since there can be nothing in any way prior to Him. Therefore, since God is the beginning of all things, He is also their end. Again, every end is a good; hence every particular end is some particular good; but the universal end, the end of all things, must be nothing less than the universal good, that is, the *bonum per se et per suam essentiam*, the very essence of goodness. This is the Divine Goodness Itself.[8] We may also call the order or perfection of the universe the end of divine government; but it must be remembered that this is not the ultimate end, but is itself ordained to the ultimate end extrinsic to the universe,

---

[6] *S. Theol.*, I, 103, 7, c; *ibid.*, 22, 2, c and ad 1.
[7] *Ibid.*, 103, 7 ad 1; 22, 2 ad 2.
[8] *Ibid.*, I, 103, 2, c.

namely, the Divine Goodness.[9] The perfect order of the universe, which represents the Divine Goodness, is created for the sake of that Goodness, so that the latter may communicate and share Itself as far as possible.

6. The Immediacy of Divine Providence. God not only cares for all things by His providence, but He cares for them *immediately*. In explaining this, St. Thomas applies his distinction between divine providence, which is the divine reason itself foreseeing and ordaining all things to their end, and the divine government of the world, which is the execution of the order of providence.

> In respect to the former, God immediately provides for everything, because He has in His intellect the exemplars of everything, even the least; and He gives to whatever causes He provides for certain effects the power needed for producing these effects. Wherefore, He must have beforehand in His intellect the order of these effects.[10]

Thus providence, or God's foresight and ordering, is immediate in respect to every being; God foresees and foreordains *in itself* every detail of the created world. But the case is not the same with the execution or carrying out of this ordination:

> In respect to the second, there are some intermediaries of God's providence, because He governs lower beings through higher ones — not because of any defect in His power, but because of the abundance of His goodness, so that He communicates also to creatures the dignity of causation.[11]

Therefore, as the last phrase indicates, the immediacy of divine providence does not, as an opponent of St. Thomas had argued, suppress the causal activity of creatures. God's immediate provision of an effect includes provision of the natural causes through which the effect will be produced.[12]

7. The Effects of the Divine Government. Considered from the point of view of its end, which is the divine goodness itself, the effect produced in creatures by the government of God is the likeness of this divine goodness; in other words, God, by moving all creatures toward himself as their ultimate end, produces in each of them, according to its own nature, a reflection of or a participation in His own Essential Goodness, and produces in all taken together the most per-

[9] *Ibid.*, ad 3. [11] *Ibid.*, cf. 1, 103, 6.
[10] *Ibid.*, I, 22, 3, c. [12] *Ibid.*, I, 22, 3, ad 2.

fect created reflection of His own perfection, namely, the order of the universe. This assimilation of creatures to God is accomplished in two respects; God is good, and so the creature is made like God by being made good: God causes goodness in others, and so the creature is made like God by being made able to move other creatures to good. Hence, there are two universal effects of the divine government of things: the conservation of things in good and the movement of things to the good. These two effects of Divine Providence are called the *Divine Conservation* and the *Divine Concurrence.*[13]

III. DIVINE CONSERVATION

1. **Borrowed Being.** The Hudson River seems a very stable thing indeed. The greatest city in the world came into being because the Hudson was there, day in and day out, year after year, broad and deep, solid and dependable. The city has to be cared for and governed, repaired, and rebuilt; if men neglected it for long, it would crumble into ruin. But the river takes care of itself — or so it seems. A thousand tiny brooks tumble out of hills and join in little streams, and these join again into bigger streams and all the bigger streams come together to make the great Hudson River. Some of the tiny brooks dry up when the rainfall is light; many more of them dry up when a few weeks pass without rain; and sometimes some of the streams run very low. If all the tiny brooks dried up for any considerable time, all the streams would run lower and lower until they did not run at all; and after a while the Hudson would no longer flow majestically down to the sea. For the lordly Hudson is not what it seems. It cannot support itself for an instant. Its air of utter stability and self-sufficiency is only a mask which covers up a fundamental precariousness and dependency. It lives on borrowed being. So does the whole world.

What the Hudson River needs, in order to continue in existence, is a constant influx of water. Indeed, its very being consists in the water which flows into it from its thousand tributaries. The latter do not make it and leave it; for them to stop making it would be for it to cease to be. Nor did God make the world and leave it; for Him to stop making it would be for it to stop being. Its very existence consists in the being which constantly flows into it from God, its cause. Perhaps St. Thomas' own illustration is better than the Hudson River. The sun, shining upon the air, makes it lightsome. But it does not stay

[13] *Ibid.*, I, 103, 4, c.

lightsome when the sun stops shining on it. For its lightsomeness is the effect of the sun's action upon it; and when there is no such action, of course there is no such effect. Similarly, the being of every creature is the effect of God's action; and were this action to cease, so, of course, would its effect. Hence, when, in Article One of Question 104 of the First Part of the *Summa,* St. Thomas asks "whether creatures need God to preserve them in being," he answers in the affirmative.

2. **Direct and Indirect Conservation.** St. Thomas distinguishes two ways in which something is conserved in being by something else. The first way is *indirectly* or *per accidens.* Something conserves another in being in this way when it removes the causes which would bring about the corruption of the thing; as, for example, when a child's guardian keeps him away from fire, water, automobiles, etc., or when a gardener keeps a perishable plant in a hothouse to save it from the inclemencies of the winter weather. God conserves corruptible beings in this way, but not incorruptible, that is, spiritual ones, since these do not need to be so conserved. The second way is *directly.* A thing is conserved in being directly when it depends upon its conserver and cannot exist without it; as a statue is directly conserved in being by the power of the marble to retain the shape given to it. All creatures need to be conserved by God in this way; every one of them would collapse into non-existence instantaneously unless the divine operation directly conserved it in being.[14] In the paragraphs which follow we shall be at all times speaking of *direct conservation.*

3. **The Proof of Divine Conservation.** Every effect depends upon its cause in precisely that respect in which the latter is its cause. Some agents are the causes only of the *becoming* or generation of their effects, and not directly of their *being.* Such causes we call causes *in fieri,* or *causae fiendi.* A builder, for example, causes a house to *come into being,* but he does not cause its very being; he assembles certain materials in a certain order or form, and these materials by their natural powers retain this form. Hence he can go away when the building is finished and the house will continue to exist without him, since only its becoming and not its being depends upon him. On the other hand, if he stops building before the house is finished, it will not fully become a house; because its becoming a house depends directly upon his operation of building, so that at the very instant that this operation ceases the becoming ceases. If an effect, besides having a cause of its becoming, has

[14] *Ibid.,* I, 104, 1, c.

also a cause of its being, then its being or existence depends upon the operation of this latter cause just as intimately as its becoming does upon the operation of the former cause. Consequently, just as the becoming or generation ceases instantaneously when the operation of the *causa fiendi* ceases, so the being of the effect will cease instantaneously when the operation of the cause of its being (*causa essendi*) ceases. But, since God is the cause of the being of everything that exists, God must conserve everything in being by acting in it at every moment of its existence.

Against this conclusion it is argued that the causes of being of any natural thing are its intrinsic essential principles, namely, its matter and form; and that since these conserve it in being, it does not need any efficient cause to conserve its being. This argument is inadequate. The efficient cause which induces the form of a substance in the matter is the cause of the thing's becoming, for the induction of the form *is* the generation of the substance. Now the being of the thing, as well as its becoming, obviously depends upon the form which is induced in the matter. Hence, if this form itself presupposes an efficient *causa essendi* distinct from the *causa fiendi* which induces it in the matter, the thing of which it is the form will depend upon this efficient cause for its being, even after it has been generated. This is the case, as we shall now show.

A natural agent which generates a thing of the same nature as itself can never be the *causa essendi* of that thing, but only its *causa fiendi*. In order to be the *causa essendi* it would have to be *the cause of the thing's form as such*. But every cause producing an effect of the same species as itself, for example, an animal producing offspring, presupposes, as prior to its operation, the existence of the form which it gives to the effect, because it has that form itself and the form in it and in the effect are distinguished only by being in different matters. Cause and effect, by having the same form, belong to the same species. Now, to be the cause of the form as such would be to be the cause of the species; but it is clear that no individual in a species can be the cause of the species since it would, in such case, be its own efficient cause, which is impossible. Therefore, whatever agent induces its own form in matter so as to produce an effect of the same nature as itself is not the cause of the form induced but only of its induction, and, consequently, is not the cause of the effect's being but only of its becoming.

It follows clearly from this that no *corporeal agent* can ever be more than a cause of becoming, since it can cause a thing only by inducing in matter a form which, considered in itself, is necessarily in being prior to this operation and which, therefore, is never caused by the operation. Therefore, the cause of the forms which are the principles of being in natural things must be some *incorporeal agent*. It is upon this agent that the forms as such depend, and consequently they are principles of being only in so far as the operation of this incorporeal agent gives being to them. Now the induction of a form in matter ceases just as soon as the inducing agent, the corporeal generator, ceases to operate; similarly the existence of that form in the matter would cease just as soon as the operation of the cause of its existence, the incorporeal agent, ceased. Furthermore, no natural agent can give being to matter itself; hence material things require an immaterial *causa essendi*.

Now this incorporeal agent, by whom all things, both corporeal and incorporeal, are caused, is God, from whom all things derive not only their form but also their matter. For God alone is being by essence, i.e., self-existing or uncaused being, and all creatures are beings by participation, i.e., caused beings. As such they depend upon the cause of their being, God, and they can exist only so long as God's operation conserves them in being.[15]

The conservative action exercised by God in relation to His creatures is not a new act distinct from the creative act. It is the continuation of the action of giving them being. To say that it is a continuation does not mean that God keeps doing it a long time, for the action is without motion or time. What is intended by the term is to emphasize the fact that the divine conservation is the endowment of continued being upon creatures, and consequently is not a different act from creation itself.[16] And since the divine operation conserving things is the same operation as creating them, it is clear that God could not possibly enable a creature to keep itself in existence without His assistance; to do so would be to cause something to be uncaused. To say that He cannot do so is not to deny or limit His omnipotence, because

God's omnipotence does not imply that He can make two contradictories true at the same time. Now the statement that God can produce a thing which does not need to be upheld by Him involves a contradiction. For

[15] The above argument as presented here combines three statements of it by St. Thomas: *S. Theol.*. I. 104, 1. c; *Con. Gen.*. III, 65; *De Pot.*. V. 1.

[16] *S. Theol.*, I, 104, 1, ad 4.

we have already proved that every effect depends upon its cause in so far as it is its cause. Accordingly, the statement that a thing does not need God to uphold its existence implies that it is not created by God; while the statement that such a thing is produced by God implies that it is created by Him. Wherefore, just as it would involve a contradiction to say that God produced a thing that was not created by Him, even so it would involve a contradiction were one to say that God made a thing that did not need to be kept in existence by Him.[17]

IV. DIVINE CONCURRENCE

1. **Meaning of Divine Concurrence.** Divine concurrence, the second part, as it were, of divine providence, is the action of God in the action of every created agent, giving it its power to act, moving it to act, and producing the effect which it produces. When water is placed over a flame and brought to a boil, God, says St. Thomas, (1) gives to the heat the powers by which it boils the water, (2) moves these powers to the actual operation of boiling the water, and (3) boils the water. And St. Thomas means exactly what he says: he is not talking in metaphor or hyperbole. Every agent in the created universe is an instrument in the hands of God, an instrument through whose powers (which He has given it and which He conserves in it) and through whose operations (in which He operates) He produces, as First Cause, the effects which this natural agent produces as secondary cause.

2. **Proof of Divine Concurrence.** (a) *Every Agent Acts by God's Power.* In the first place it is clear that no agent can produce *being* except in so far as it acts by the power of God. Now all created agents produce one effect common to whatever multitude of effects they may produce, since every effect has this in common, that it is actual being. Whatever is a certain nature by essence is the proper cause of what has that nature merely by participation. Now God alone is being by essence, while all other things are merely by participation, since they can either be or not be. Consequently, the being of anything is more properly the effect of God than of any other cause. Therefore, every agent which produces something in being does so inasmuch as it acts by God's power.[18]

(b) *God is the Cause of Operating in Everything That Operates.* From the fact just established, namely, that nothing causes being except

[17] *De Pot.*, V, 2, c. Cf. *S. Theol.*, I, 104, 1 ad 2.
[18] *Con. Gen.*, III, 66.

in so far as it acts by the divine power, it follows that God is the cause of operating in everything that operates.

> For everything that operates is in some way a cause of being, either of substantial being or of accidental being. But nothing is a cause of being except in so far as it acts by the power of God, as was shown. Therefore everything that operates, operates through the power of God.[19]

Furthermore, God is clearly the cause of the operations of everything from the fact that it is He who gave them the powers by which they operate and who conserves them and their powers in being. We saw in the preceding section of this chapter that if God's operation of giving being to all things should cease, these things would at once cease to be. Hence both their being and their operation depend on the continuance of the divine operation. Therefore, every operation of every agent is reduced to God's operation as its cause.[20]

(c) *God Operates in Every Operation of Created Agents.* It might be objected that these arguments do not quite prove the point. They rather prove that nothing can operate without God conserving it in being and conserving also the powers by which it operates; but that is not quite the same thing as saying that God operates in every operation of every created agent. Therefore it is necessary to show that God operates in the very operation of the created agent and produces the very effect which this agent produces. St. Thomas proves these things in several places,[21] but his fullest treatment is found in *De Potentia,* question III, article 7. The following argument is the second half of the body of that article summarized.

3. How Does God Cause the Actions of Creatures? One thing may be the cause of another thing's action in several different ways. (1) *It may give the thing the power to act,* as a knife grinder gives a knife the power to cut by giving it its sharp edge. We have already seen that God causes the actions of all things in this way, since in creating them He gave them the powers or forces whereby they are able to act. (2) *It may preserve the thing's power to act,* as the hardness of the steel in the knife directly preserves its sharp edge, or as its owner indirectly preserves the edge by protecting the knife from moisture which would rust it and contacts which would blunt it. God (and again we have already shown this) is the cause, not only of the be-

[19] *Ibid.,* III, 67.
[20] *Loc. cit.*
[21] For example: *S. Theol.,* I, 105, 5; *Con. Gen.,* III, 66, 67.

coming of all things and their powers, but also of their being; and therefore in this second way, namely, by conserving in all things their powers of acting, He is the cause of the actions of all things.

The third and fourth ways in which God is the cause of the actions of all agents answer directly and in the affirmative the question, Does God actually operate in the operations of all created agents? (3) Something may be the cause of the operation of something else *by moving it to act.* The powers of all created things are potencies in respect to their operations, and the operations are the actualities of these potencies. No potency moves itself to act, and every potency that is moved to act is moved primarily by the First Cause which is Pure Act. Hence, everything that acts is moved by God to act, not only in the sense that He causes and preserves its power of acting, but also in the sense that He applies this power to the action; just as the knife's owner moves the knife to cut by applying its sharpness to the act of cutting. Hence, God operates in the operation of every agent.

Something may operate in the operation of another (4) *as a principal cause operates in an instrumental cause, causing the action and the effect of the instrument.* In this way the knife's owner is the cause of the action of the knife and the handiwork which he produces through the use of the knife; this handiwork is his effect, although it is also the effect of the knife. Indeed, it is much more his effect than it is the knife's, for it is he who determines what the effect shall be and who moves the knife to produce it, while the knife is the cause of the effect, only through its participation in the power of the workman. Hence, in every case where a principal and an instrumental cause operate, the effect is due to each of them, but primarily and chiefly to the principal cause. God operates in the operations of all natural agents in this fourth way, namely, as a principal cause using them as instrumental causes and causing their action and its effect. This is proved by two facts which we have already noted: first, that God causes the action of every natural agent by moving its power to the action; and second, that that which is first and most common in every effect is *being,* and this is most properly the effect of God. Consequently, whenever a natural agent produces an effect, God (*a*) moves the agent, applying its power to the production, as does any principal cause, and (*b*) He produces in its effect what is primary and most common, namely, being. Therefore, since the natural agent acts only by the power of God in which it participates, and since the effect which it produces is due primarily and chiefly to God, God operates in the operation of every natural agent as a principal cause in an instrumental cause.

Let us summarize in St. Thomas' own words:

> If, then, we consider the subsistent agent, every particular agent is immediate to its effect. But if we consider the power whereby the action is done, then the power of the higher cause is more immediate to the effect than the power of the lower cause, since the power of the lower cause is not coupled with its effect save by the power of the higher cause; wherefore . . . the power of the first cause takes the first place in the production of the effect and enters more deeply therein. . . . Consequently, we may say that God works in everything forasmuch as everything needs His power in order that it may act. . . . Therefore God is the cause of everything's action inasmuch as He (1) gives everything the power to act, and (2) preserves it in being, and (3) applies it to action, and (4) inasmuch as by His power every other power acts. And if we add to this that God is His own power, and that He is in all things, not as part of their essence, but as upholding them in being, we shall conclude that He acts in every agent immediately, without prejudice to the action of the will and of nature.[22]

V. THE REALITY OF SECONDARY CAUSES

1. Occasionalism. There seems to be no truth among all the truths that men have discovered which has not, by someone at some time, been overemphasized and "ridden to death" to the exclusion of other truths equally valid. This error of exaggeration and exclusiveness constitutes the tragedy of the history of philosophy: all major philosophical errors have been overstressed truths. It was a characteristic of St. Thomas — one that it is difficult not enthuse about — that he seemed incapable of falling into this error of exclusivism. Every truth was to him something wonderful and precious; nothing else was so wonderful and precious — except some other truth.

When, therefore, some philosophers and theologians, overwhelmed, as it were, by the universality and intimacy of God's operation and causality in natural things, made such use of this truth as to deny that natural things have any operation or causality of their own, we find St. Thomas taking a firm and unequivocal stand against them. God operates in every operation of His creatures and produces the effects which they produce; nevertheless they, too, really operate and really produce these effects: that is St. Thomas' position.

This position was denied and attacked not only by philosophers and

[22] De Pot., III, 7.

theologians of St. Thomas' own age but by some important modern
philosophers, notably Nicolas Malebranche and Gottfried Leibniz in
the seventeenth century. The former, a French Catholic priest, a great
lover of St. Augustine, and a philosophical disciple of René Descartes,
regarded the Thomistic view as a species of naturalism. Malebranche
denied all causality to corporeal substance; what seemed to be causal
action on the part of a material thing, as, for example, when one body
sets another in motion, is in truth only an *occasion* for God, the only
cause, to cause the effect apparently produced by the material thing.
He got around St. Thomas' argument[23] that if corporeal agents do not
really cause anything the whole world is a conspiracy against man's
mind, since man's senses show him one thing acting upon another, by
asserting that the senses are not cognitive powers whose functions is to
discover truth, but simply biological mechanisms for the protection of
the body. Leibniz, of whom we have already studied something, denied
all action of one substance (monad) upon another, attributed to each
only internal activity, and attributed the apparent cause-effect character of natural events to a universal harmony of activity pre-established
by God.

2. **Arguments Against the Reality of Secondary Causes.** Those
medievals who denied the reality of the operation and causation of
natural agents did so on either or both of two grounds: (1) that natural beings, that is to say, corporeal things, are of their nature incapable
of acting or of producing any real effect; (2) that to attribute real
activity and real causation to created beings is to detract from the
infinite power and activity of God. They supported the first proposition
by the argument that corporeal things, being the very lowest members
of the order of being and most remote from God, who is pure activity,
must be pure passivity; hence they can only be acted upon and cannot
act. The arguments in support of the second proposition were many,
but they all reduce to one, namely, that since God operates in every
operation and since His power is infinite, it is superfluous and, in fact,
contradictory to attribute any operation or any effect in any way to
any agent other than God.

3. **Reply to These Arguments.** In reply to the first set of arguments,
St. Thomas gives the following answers. (1) That which is lowest in
being and most remote from God, and hence is pure passivity, is not
any actual corporeal substance, but is primary matter. Corporeal sub-

[23] *Ibid.*

stances are composites of substantial form and primary matter; because they possess form, which is the principle of activity in anything, they can act; and because *other* corporeal substances possess matter, which is the principle of passivity, they can act upon these other substances. (2) One corporeal substance, acting upon another one, can induce in the latter, if it is suitably disposed, a likeness of its own substantial form as well as of its own accidental forms; it can do this because the forms of natural substances are not separated forms, as the Platonists held, and are not brought into the substances from outside, but are educed by the generating agent from the potentiality of the matter of the patient. The form which is potentially in the matter is moved to actuality by the corporeal agent which already possesses it in actuality. Hence, corporeal agents are real causes of the substances which they produce.[24]

To the second set of arguments the Angelic Doctor opposes one reply, which he repeats as often as the arguments are put forward. God acts adequately in every operation of a created agent, but He does so as first cause; and the operation of the created agent as second cause is not on that account superfluous. The same effect may have two causes, each adequate in its own order, as long as they are causes in distinct orders. In every operation of a created thing God is the first and principal agent and cause, while the creature is the secondary and instrumental agent and cause.[25]

4. Proofs of Secondary Causality. Having thus turned aside the arguments which pretend to show that if God operates in all the operations of created things these things do not themselves really operate, St. Thomas goes on to advance positive arguments showing why we must attribute real activity and real causality to natural things. He treats the subject most fully in Chapter 69 of Book III of the *Summa Contra Gentiles.* Here he advances several proofs, based variously upon the principle that diverse effects come from diverse causes, upon the wisdom, power, and goodness of God, and upon the order of nature and the validity of natural science.

1. If God alone works in everything, His operation will not be diversified by any diversity of secondary causes, since there will in fact be no secondary causes; hence there will be no diversity of effects following from diverse causes. But this latter is just what we experience;

---

[24] *Con. Gen.*, III, 69; *De Pot.*, III, 7, c.
[25] *S. Theol.*, I, 105, 5, ad 1 and ad 2; *De Pot.*, III, 7, ad 3, ad 4 and ad 16.

for freezing never follows from the application of heat, nor elm trees from acorns.

2. If God alone wrought everything, and created causes did nothing, their employment by God in producing diverse effects would be futile and meaningless, which is certainly incompatible with the divine wisdom. All the powers, forms, and forces of natural things would be given to them in vain, for powers are to no purpose in a being which never operates.[26]

3. Those who wish to deny real causation to creatures think that by so doing they exalt the power of God. In fact they detract from it; for they regard it as a power capable of producing only an inert mechanical world, not an active organic one. They conceive of God as able to produce only creatures which can be pushed around, but which cannot act. Instead of exalting God's power, they belittle it:

> The perfection of the effect indicates the perfection of the cause, since a greater power produces a more perfect effect. Now God is the most perfect agent. Therefore things created by Him must needs receive perfection from Him. Consequently to detract from the creature's perfection is to detract from the perfection of the divine power. But if no creature exercises an action for the production of an effect, much is detracted from the perfection of the creature; because it is due to the abundance of its perfection that a thing is able to communicate to another the perfection that it has. Therefore this opinion detracts from the divine power.[27]

4. This opinion also detracts from the divine goodness:

> Just as it belongs to the good to produce a good, so it belongs to the highest good to make something best. Now God is the highest good. . . . Therefore it belongs to Him to make all things best. Now it is better that the good bestowed on someone should be common to many than that it should be private to one. . . . . But the good of one becomes common to many if it is communicated from the one to the others, and this can be only when the one, by its own action, communicates it to them; but if it has not the power to transmit it to others, that good remains private to itself. Accordingly, God communicated His goodness to His creatures in such wise that one thing can communicate to another the good it has received. Therefore, to deny their proper actions to things is to belittle the divine goodness.[28]

[26] Cf. De Pot., III, 7, c.
[27] Loc. Cit. (The Basic Writings of St. Thomas Aquinas. ed. Anton C. Pegis [New York: Random House, 1945], Vol. II, p. 125).
[28] Loc. cit.

5. The order of nature also demands that we recognize the proper operations of created things:

> To take order away from created things is to deprive them of the best thing they have. For while single things are themselves good, all together are the greatest good for the sake of the order of the universe; for the whole is always better than the parts, and is the end of the parts. If, however, their actions are taken away from things, the order of things in respect to one another is done away with. For there is no binding together of things of diverse natures in the unity of order except by this, that some of them act and some are acted upon. Consequently, it is inadmissible to say that things do not have actions of their own.[29]

6. Natural science is no more than the playful building of a pretty dream world if natural things do not truly have their own powers, actions, and effects:

> If effects are not produced by the action of created things but only by the action of God, it is impossible that the power of any created cause should be manifested through effects; for an effect does not show the power of a cause except by reason of an action which, proceeding from the power, terminates in the effect. But the nature of a cause is not known through an effect except in so far as through the latter a power is known which follows from the nature. If, therefore, created things do not have actions producing effects, it follows that the nature of no created cause will ever be known through an effect. And, consequently, we are deprived of all knowledge of natural science, in which, pre-eminently, demonstrations are made through the effect.[30]

VI. PROVIDENCE AND CONTINGENCY

1. **The Problem.** The most difficult problem connected with divine providence and concurrence is concerned with contingent and free effects. A contingent event is one which occurs but need not have occurred; its causes are capable of producing it or failing to produce it; it is not necessary. A free act is one performed by a free agent, for example, a man or an angel, which this agent need not have performed; which he does while able not to do it or to do its contrary. It is an act over which the agent has dominion, an act which he determines himself to do of his own free will. It is not an uncaused act; the agent is its cause, and he acts from definite motives; but he causes the act freely, remaining (until he does it) capable of not doing it. Now it would certainly seem that if everything, down to its last drop of

[29] *Loc. cit.*
[30] *Loc. cit.*

being and action, is subject to divine providence, that there is no room in this world for contingency and freedom. Divine providence is infallible in its working, because since all other causes are themselves subject to it and ultimately caused by it, no cause can so act as to prevent its effect. Consequently what is ordered by divine providence must occur. Therefore, the opponents of providence or of free will argue, providence imposes *necessity* upon all things. Hence, either providence is not infallible or else there is no contingency or freedom in the world.

2. The Thomistic Solution. Before answering this argument St. Thomas explains why, even if we did not directly experience contingent events and free actions, as we obviously do, we would yet have to admit contingency and freedom in the world from the very nature of providence itself. The intrinsic end of creation is the perfection of the universe taken as a whole. This perfection will be best realized if the universe contains *all grades of being* arranged in one perfect order. Now, necessary things and contingent things are two grades into which all possible being may be divided. Therefore, God created both these grades for the sake of the perfection of the whole universe. And therefore, finally, by His providence He directs to the ultimate end of creation all beings, whether necessary or contingent, in such manner as their necessary or contingent nature calls for. Consequently, He "prepares for some effects necessary causes, so that they occur necessarily; and for some, indeed, contingent causes, so that they occur contingently, according to the condition of the secondary causes."[31]

To the argument that if divine providence is infallible then whatever providence ordains *must* come about, and that therefore everything that occurs must occur necessarily, St. Thomas gives the same answer again and again:

> The order of divine providence is unchangeable and certain in this, that those things which are provided by it happen, every one, *in that manner in which it provides,* whether necessarily or contingently.[32]

God, in other words, is master of contingency and necessity because He is master of being, of which contingency and necessity are two modes.

> And it must be considered that the necessary and the contingent properly follow upon being as such. Wherefore, the mode both of contingency and necessity fall under the provision of God, who is the

---

[31] *S. Theol.,* I, 22, 4, c. Cf. *Con. Gen.,* III, 94.
[32] *S. Theol.,* I, 22, 4 ad 2.

universal provider of all being, although they do not fall under the provision of any particular provider.[33]

We use beings and events as we find them, necessary or contingent; God makes them as He wants them, necessary or contingent. He stands at the head of all being — *in summo omnium principe* — and all being is subject to Him. The necessity and contingency of created beings do not bind God; they are not *conditions of* God's operation, but *conditions produced by* that operation. What He foresees and wills, must be; but it must be as He foresees it and wills it. If He provides that something come to be, it will infallibly come to be; if He provides that it come to be contingently, it will infallibly come to be contingently.

Our inability to comprehend the infinite power of God is what gives rise to the problem which we have been discussing. Because God's power is infinite, it must, as we have seen, extend to every creature and to every act of every creature, and it must infallibly produce its effect. By so doing, it seems to our finite minds to destroy the contingency and freedom which it has first created. But if the infinite power of God gives rise to the problem, it also points the way to the answer. It is just because God's power *is* infinite that He, and He alone, can cause both that something infallibly occur and at the same time occur through causes that might have failed to produce it; or that He can determine a man to perform a certain act while at the same time determining him to perform it freely. The ultimate resolution of the mystery lies in the infinite power of God, which is identical with His ineffable essence, and which is inexpressibly above the comprehension of our finite reason.

Certain strong objections concerning free will must, nevertheless, be noted and answered. St. Thomas explicitly holds that God, acting both as an object of desire and as a moving agent, moves the created will to its operation.[34] His opponents argue: (1) Whatever is moved from without, is forced. The will cannot be forced. Hence, it cannot be moved from without, that is, by God. (2) God cannot make contradictories true. But the will would at once move voluntarily and nonvoluntarily if it moved itself and were at the same time moved by God. (3) If God moved the will, the movement would be more attributable to Him as the mover than to the will as the thing moved. In that case no merit or demerit could attach to the will for its actions. (4) Further-

[33] *Ibid.*, I, 22, 4, ad 3.
[34] *Ibid.*, I, 105, 4; I–II, 10, 4.

more, if God moves man's will, that will is moved necessarily and is not free, for that which is moved by another is not free.[35]

Now the basic error in all these arguments is this: after starting correctly by attributing to God an action which God alone can do, because He is God, they then go on to argue as if the one doing the action were not God. The first argument, for example, starts with the fact that God moves the will; then it goes on to say that whatever moves something from without forces it. The author of the argument forgot, somewhere in the middle, what he was talking about. He has switched from "God" to "whatever," which is precisely the switch which you cannot legitimately make in the present context. For it is true that whatever moves a thing from without forces it, that is, moves it against its own inclination, *unless in moving it, it gives it a natural inclination to that toward which it moves it;* but that *is* exactly what God does and what God alone can do. God moves the will by naturally inclining it to the good; His movement of it makes it a will. God's movement of the will is not against the natural inclination of the will, because that natural inclination has its origin in that movement.

The same answer disposes of the second objection: the supposed contradiction is not real, because God so moves the will that it is able to move itself and to move itself voluntarily. The will moves by an intrinsic principle, viz., its natural inclination to the good; but this intrinsic principle exists only by virtue of the extrinsic principle which gives it being and moves it, viz., God's operation in it. Hence, the will's movement is at the same time voluntary and due to an extrinsic principle. This takes care of the third objection: God's movement of the will does not exclude, but rather makes possible, its own movement of itself; hence, its acts are voluntary and imputable to it for merit or demerit.[36]

The answer to the fourth objection is similar. Man's will is free as long as it truly moves itself, determining its own action. It is not necessary that it be the *first* cause of its action in order for it to be free. God, in moving all creatures, moves each according to the nature which He has given it and conserves in it; He made man's will free, and therefore He moves it in such a manner as to guarantee the freedom of its move-

---

[35] These objections are collected from: *S. Theol.*, I, 105, 4; I, 83, 1; I–II, 10, 4; I–II, 79, 2; and *De Pot.*, III, 7, objs. 13–15.

[36] *S. Theol.*. I, 105, 4, ad 1, 2, 3. Cf. *De Pot.*, III, 7, ad 13, 14

ment. If He moved it necessarily, He would destroy the nature that He has Himself created.[37]

VII. THE ORGANIC UNITY OF NATURE

St. Thomas had a distinctly *organic* conception of nature as a whole, and perhaps Thomists ought to stress this aspect of his thought more than they have done hitherto. This organic conception of nature is most apparent and unmistakable in the Angelic Doctor's account of the relations between divine causation and the being and action of creatures; that is to say, what we have studied in the present chapter.

1. Mechanisms and Organisms. When we conceive nature merely as a collection of discrete substances moving one another by universal physical laws, we ascribe to it a certain unity, but it is the unity of a mechanism rather than of an organism. Both a mechanism and an organism are wholes composed of parts, but they are very different sorts of wholes composed of very different sorts of parts. The parts of a mechanism are inert, and move only by being pushed. The parts of an organism have their own proper activity. A mechanism is an artificial whole composed of essentially independent parts externally related; an organism is a natural whole composed of essentially interdependent parts. The parts of a mechanism do not depend upon the whole in order for each to be what it is; the parts of an organism are not themselves, and do not have their separate natures, except in the whole. The energy of a mechanism is entirely external and is merely received and transmitted by the parts, which have no energy of their own. The energy of an organism is a unified, internal energy to which the whole as whole and the parts as parts contribute; each part has an energy which, though inseparable from and animated by the energy of the whole, is yet its own, just as each part, though not itself when apart from the whole, is yet distinctly itself in the whole. A mechanism has one motion divided up throughout the parts and homogeneous in all the parts; an organism has one activity complete in each part and different in each part. A mechanism is a groupment of automata; an organism is a society of autonomies. The parts of a mechanism are moved by one movement; the parts of an organism live by one life. A mechanism does not act; it merely moves. An organism acts.

2. Nature Is Organic. The unity which belongs to the world, as the

---

[37] *S. Theol.*, I, 83, 1 ad 3; I–II, 10, 4 ad 1, 2, 3.

world is described in St. Thomas' philosophy, is much more akin to the unity of an organism than to that of a mechanism. The doctrines of hylemorphism, efficient causality, teleology, and the universal penetration of created causation by divine causation explicitly call for a universe in which, while all the parts are moved by one primary agency and energy, yet each part has its own proper energy and action. What does hylemorphism mean in relation to natural processes, if it does not mean, in opposition to the mechanistic theory, that the parts of the world do not merely transmit motion which they receive, but on the contrary determine and transform this received motion by their own intrinsic proper activity? Certainly, hydrogen and oxygen are "pushed" when they unite to form water; but their own natures determine where they shall go when they are pushed.[38] They act only under external impulsion, but the action which they perform under this impulsion is their own proper action, springing from their own natures and powers. They are more like cells in a living body than like cogs on a wheel.

Furthermore, all the parts of the world have their own proper natures only in the whole which is the world; just as a living cell in a body has its own proper being and life only in the whole which is the body. The things in this world, according to St. Thomas, form an *order*. and each thing is itself only in so far as it fills its place in that order. None of the parts of nature are independent of any of the other parts or of the whole. Nature could not be "taken apart," like a watch or an automobile; each isolated part would lose its nature, for it has its nature from interaction with the other parts. The realm of living things in nature depends for its being and its conservation upon the inorganic substances and forces in nature; the compounds depend upon the substance and operations of the elements, and the elements depend upon the energies of subatomic units. Our own part of the world, namely. the earth and its immediate neighborhood, was produced and is sustained by the outside world around it; the processes of this outside world gave rise to the conditions which make the earth a home for living things, and those processes continue to supply those conditions now. But the energies coming from this outside world are not received passively by the world of living beings; the latter, on the contrary, supply new conditioning factors of their own, and make their own use of the energies which larger nature supplies them. Each living being

[38] Cf. *De Pot.*, III, 7.

has its own form, its own autonomous idea or plan, and it embodies into this plan the substance and energy which other things give it. The order of nature is teleological and mechanical at the same time; higher levels of being build themselves out of lower levels, utilizing the physical forces and laws of the lower levels for their own self-attainment and self-fulfillment. Surely this world has far more analogy to an organism than to a machine.

3. **Nature Is an Organism.** Nature contains both organisms and mechanisms. What is it itself, then, organism or mechanism? In Thomistic philosophy nature is not precisely an organism, if that term is used *univocally*, because every organism is one single substance, whereas nature is a multitude of substances. But nature certainly is not a mechanism, since it contains organisms. A mechanism cannot allow autonomy and spontaneity of action in its parts; spontaneous action in a part of a machine would wreck the machine or would at least make the final resultant of the machine's operation unpredictable. On the other hand, an organism can contain mechanisms, as do all the organisms which we know. Nature contains both stable, predictable processes and novelty-producing, unpredictable processes. If nature is not precisely and univocally an organism, it at least is *like* an organism; we can call it organic. We might call it a society of more or less autonomous substances unified after the fashion of an organism.

Perhaps we may go even further, and name nature, outright, an organism. The term will be used *analogically,* but not equivocally. Nature is, obviously, unique; and no term applied to it could be applied with precisely the same significance that the term has when applied to some part of nature. When we call nature an organism, then, we mean that, of all the things in nature, those which most perfectly mirror the whole of nature are living organisms. To understand this rightly, we must now bring God into the picture.

4. **Nature's Organic Unity in God's Activity.** Divine conservation is the being and action of God in creatures sustaining the being of the creatures. No creature exists except God exist in it giving it existence. Divine concurrence is the action of God in creatures producing the action of creatures. No creature acts except God act in its action. The one activity of God energizes all nature. Nature is one with a unity only less perfect than the unity of God because every being and every activity in nature, and the being and activity of nature as a whole, spring from the one activity of God. Yet the being and action of each

part of nature is truly its own and truly distinct from the action of God, though inseparable from it and impossible without it; just as the life and activity of each cell in an organism is distinct and to some degree spontaneous, though inseparable from the life and activity of the whole organism and impossible without it. If God had created an inert universe, which moves only by being pushed, nature would be a mechanism. That conception of nature is Cartesian, not Thomistic. It dominated scientific and philosophical thought for two and a half centuries; but today scientists and philosophers in large numbers are deserting it to return to the organic conception of nature. Unfortunately, too few of them realize that they are returning to an old conception with a long and honorable history.

St. Thomas was as emphatic, we have seen, in asserting the reality of created activity as he was in asserting the universality of divine causality. God creates things and their actions; but He creates things which act. He does not create things just to push them around. He creates men with free wills, and He creates free acts which are really the acts of those wills. He creates causes and the effects that those causes really cause. When we seek an analogy for God's creative activity in nature, the best one we can find is the activity of the vital principle of an organism in the whole organism and in its parts. Each act of the organism is done by some part of the organism; for example, the eyes see. But each act is done by the whole organism; the animal sees. The first principle of every vital operation is the vital principle or soul of the animal. The soul has the power to see, and when this power moves to operation, the eyes see and the animal sees; and yet there is only the one seeing. Similarly, on a broader scale, every part of the organism lives with a life of its own, yet there is only one life in the organism, and this life is from the soul. An organism has one life in a million lives; and a million lives in one life. Nature has one activity in a million activities; and a million activities in one activity. Wherever there is life and operation in a living body, its single first principle is the life and operation of the soul, and yet it is the life and operation of the organ or cell of the body. Wherever there is being and action in nature, its single first principle is the being and action of God, and yet it itself is the being and action of the individual substance of nature.

5. Nature's Energy Is Goodness and Love. An organism is made one by its substantial form, or soul. This form, this vital principle, is the single first principle of life within the organism. But it is a generous principle. In actualizing the body's potentiality for life it gives to it a whole-life and makes it one, which is to say, makes it a being; but it gives also to each of its parts a part-life. Form, that is to say, good, is expansive — *diffusivum sui* — and in expanding itself it does not expend itself; in sharing its goodness it loses none of it. It can multiply itself without losing its unity. That is because goodness is love, and love does not divide itself up among its objects, but falls fully upon each: a mother does not love each child less for having more children. Love is like that because God is love, and created love imitates creating Love.

Love falls fully upon each of its objects, not in the same manner upon each, but upon each one according to that one's nature.[39] Just so does the soul give life to each part of the organism, but to each according to its nature and potentiality. And just so, again, does God's creative causation bestow real causation upon every secondary cause according to the nature which God has given it. God's causation moves natural things by communicating a proper causation to each natural thing; it has the nature of the good and of love, and therefore it is self-communicating. Power can move a machine, but only love can move an organism.

6. " 'Tis Love That Makes the World Go Round." The love, that is, the vital tendency to its good, that makes an organism live, not only goes from the whole-life to the part-lives, but is given back again. The parts of a machine fulfill the end of the machine by being pushed; they have no natural tendency to do it. Not so the parts of an organism; each has an end or good of its own, and each does what it naturally tends to do, but what it naturally tends to do is what is good for the organism. There is a mutual bond, love-like at least, between whole and parts. Life is given and given back and mutually shared and supported. God created the world out of love, love for His own infinite goodness and glory, but a self-love which infinitely abounds and expands and produces an extrinsic glory which mirrors His intrinsic glory. God's creative act is an act of love, and so " 'tis love that makes the world go round," since that creative act is in every created act, in every movement of nature. First Causality makes nature nature, makes it one and a being, falls fully upon each part of it according to the potency of that part, gives to each thing its proper activity. And

[39] Cf. Chapter XXIII, section VII.

nature as a whole is made up of its parts, each with its proper good and activity contributing to the unified good and activity of the whole. There is giving and giving back, mutual sharing and supporting — activity that is love-like. And this love-likeness is the extrinsic end of creation, the mirroring of Love Creative.

CHAPTER XXVI

DIVINE LOVE AND THE MYSTERY OF EVIL

I. THE PROBLEM OF EVIL IN THEISTIC PHILOSOPHY

1. The Setting of the Problem. The presence of evil in the world presents serious problems to the theistic philosopher — the hardest problems, perhaps, which he has to face. Naturalists are quick to point them out; but it is doubtful that the naturalist realizes their full force, since he has no adequate conception either of evil or of the goodness of God. God is all-good and all-powerful, and God created and governs the world, giving to everything in the world not only its being but its action — and yet this world that God made and rules is full of evil. Why does evil exist? Why does God permit it? What is its nature, and what are its causes? What is its significance in human life? Can we reconcile this world in which we live with the idea of an all-good God? Could God have created a world which would have no evil in it? If He could not, then is His power not finite? If He could, why did He not? How is evil even possible in a world which is produced in its entirety by an all-good Cause? No theistic philosopher may avoid such questions; if his philosophy is of no use when faced by them, it is of no use at all.

We wish, therefore, in the present chapter to see what the philosophy of St. Thomas Aquinas has to say about the presence of evil in the world. In order to understand the Angelic Doctor's teaching we shall have to introduce into our account the whole supernatural framework in which the natural world is set. In so far as we do introduce supernatural elements and truths known only through divine revelation, we shall be going beyond philosophy, which is defined as purely rational or natural knowledge of the ultimate causes of things. Our reason for introducing the supernatural framework may be expressed in two ways, though the basic reason is one. First, the purely philosophical account of any phase of reality, in so far as this account must refer to God, is always incomplete because of the inherent limitations of our natural knowledge of God. In regard to most problems this incompleteness raises no particular feeling of dissatisfaction, because it is a mere incompleteness; what the philosophical account cannot explain lies beyond reason's reach, but does not produce a real conflict within reason itself. In regard to the problem of evil, however, the purely philosophical solution leaves not only a feeling of incompleteness, but a feeling of positive unsatisfactoriness. Consequently, it would be very unfair to St. Thomas, and to the student, to present only the purely philosophical solution to the problem of evil, thus giving, perhaps, the impression that this solution is all that St. Thomas had to say about the matter or that it is the full Christian teaching upon the mystery of evil. Second, although the solution of the problem of evil in the world is reached largely by means of metaphysical considerations, the actual data of the problem, namely the world, man, suffering, sin, are, as a matter of fact, all parts of a supernatural order of things; so that a treatment of them which excludes all supernatural considerations is not merely incomplete but is, in fact, partly a falsification.

St. Thomas approached his consideration of the problem of evil through a prior consideration of the multiplicity, inequality, and imperfections found in nature. As we saw in Chapter XXIV, he finds the reason for the multiplicity and variety of creatures in the intelligence and free will of the Creator. The end of creation, namely the manifestation of the divine glory in an extrinsic imitation and reflection of itself, is eminently realized in the world which God chose to create: a world rich in multiplicity and variety of perfections, a world which imitates God in His action, love, and creativity as well as in His being and beauty. Yet, just because this world is what it is, imperfection and evil seem to be inevitable ingredients in it. Because it is rich in variety, it embraces great inequalities; because it is not inert but active, it embraces conflict and corruption; because it contains creatures capable of feeling, it contains creatures capable of suffering; because it contains free agents, it contains agents capable of rebellion.

2. The Inequality of Creatures. Nothing is more obvious than the inequality that prevails among creatures. Things are not equally valuable: why did God make the less valuable ones instead of only the most valuable?

Before trying to answer this question we must state a warning. No question asking why God did this rather than that can receive an *ultimate* answer from us. We have seen that God's act of free will has no cause. No extrinsic motive can move His will. God sees within His own infinite goodness a reason for what He does, but even that reason is not compelling, since He is infinitely free and infinitely self-sufficient. It follows that we can never assign a compelling reason why He created at all or why He created this order of things rather than another. We can only say that He did so because He is good, and that He could have done something else instead as long as it too would be good to do.

However, while we cannot assign any other reason than His free will for the actual order that God has created, we can show that in any order of creatures in which there is true variety there must be inequality. Every distinct species of creature is a different imitation of God's essence. But since that essence is absolutely simple and has no different aspects or parts to be imitated, it can be differently imitated only by being more or less perfectly imitated. Species of being are differentiated from one another by their substantial forms. Substantial forms are, in the last analysis, reflections of or participations in the infinite perfection of the Form of forms, God. They differ from one another precisely in the degree of perfection with which they reflect this simple, infinite Form. Wherefore, there cannot possibly be two equally perfect and yet different substantial forms. Now, variety of beings arises from difference of species, and species is determined by substantial form. Therefore, it is clear that any order of creatures that includes variety of being must of necessity include inequality of perfection; and if God wills to create a variety of beings, He must create beings of unequal perfection.[1]

Material beings are of their very nature corruptible. Would it not have been better, therefore, ask some persons, if God had created only the immaterial, incorruptible beings, for example, the angels? St. Thomas gives two answers. In the first place, even if a world with only incorruptible creatures were better than the present world, God would not *have* to create it. If He creates, He must create what is good, but not necessarily what is absolutely best (if there be any meaning at all to that expression when used of creatures); for He is absolutely free. In the second place, such a world would not in fact be better than the present world. As St. Augustine pointed out, incor-

[1] *S. Theol.*, I, 48, 2, c; *Con. Gen.*, II, 44; III, 97.

ruptible creatures alone are better than corruptible creatures alone, but both together are better than either alone. It may not be much to be a dog, but dogs seem to like it. Each creature, no matter how humble, is some reflection of the divine being and occupies a definite place in the whole cosmic order. Now it is this cosmic order viewed as a whole which is the highest actual imitation of God, not any part of it, even the most perfect part.[2]

3. **Imperfection in Creation.** St. Thomas disposes of one more objection before he takes up the problem of evil itself. Many creatures are admittedly imperfect. Now, a cause is judged by its effects, an agent by the work he turns out. Therefore, does not imperfection among creatures imply imperfection in God, their cause? St. Thomas answers that the excellence of a cause is measured by the excellence of its total effect. When an excellent cause acts, the effect produced must be excellent when viewed *in toto*, but each part need not be excellent when viewed in isolation from the whole. Thus, a great painter will produce a great picture, and if you stand where you can see the picture as a whole you will see its excellence and beauty. But if you look only at one square inch of it at a time, you will see nothing but shapeless blobs of paint. So to regard a picture is to falsify it, because in reality no blob of paint stands as a thing alone; on the contrary, each tiny area of color has its being and significance only in relation to all the others and to the total effect of all taken together. In like manner, each part of God's creation need not be excellent in isolation, since it does not exist in isolation; what is necessary is that it be excellent in view of its place and function in the total effect. God, therefore, has so created that the unequal perfection of creatures insures the perfection of the universe as a whole.[3] This answer of the Angelic Doctor gains added force when we consider it in relation to his organic conception of nature as explained in the preceding chapter. To judge the value of an organ as if it were an isolated thing would be absurd; it is only in respect to their function in the whole organism that the perfection of the separate organs can be justly estimated. Similarly the various beings which make up the organism which is nature can be judged only by reference to the whole organism.

4. **The Problem and the Mystery of Evil.** The above discussions have made it clear that God's intention in creating, namely, His own

[2] *S. Theol.*, I, 48, 2, c and ad 3; *Con. Gen.*, II, 45.
[3] *S. Theol.*, I, 47, 2, ad 1 and ad 3; *Con. Gen.*, II, 45; III, 97.

glory, manifested through a fitting reflection of His own perfection outside Himself, is admirably realized in the world which He actually chose to create, a world rich in multiplicity and variety of perfection. Yet this world that God created seems to be one in which evil must inevitably occur. The very laws of its architecture make the destruction of great masses of its inhabitants necessary for the life of others: many animals live only by feeding upon other animals; and in many cases it is the less valuable that destroys the more valuable, as when, for example, the malarial parasite completes its life cycle at the cost of tremendous human suffering and millions of human lives. More important still, man, the lord of the visible creation, is a being of such nature that sin and suffering seem to be inevitable accompaniments of his life.

These facts give rise to two acute questions: (1) Why did God choose to create a world in which evil is inevitable; does it not seem that He, the All-Good, wills evil? (2) How is it possible for a partially evil effect to have come from a cause that is totally good and infinitely powerful? The first question embodies what we may call the *mystery* of evil. You cannot "solve" a mystery; all you can do is to try to get some comprehension of its significance and its reason. The second embodies the *problem* of evil, and it is our task to solve it. We shall give a brief and incomplete answer to the first question now, and then return to it after we have treated of the second question.

5. Why This World? Why did God choose this world, with all its evil? This is another "Why did God . . ." question which cannot be finally answered. We can give a partial answer. God chose this world, evil and all, because it is best adapted as a means to whatever ultimate good He has made His aim or end in creating. No other world would have been so good a means to that end. We may say this because God's infinite wisdom requires that if He chooses an end and means to it, He must choose the means that will best accomplish it. If someone still insists upon asking, "Why did He choose an end in whose attainment the possibility of evil is involved instead of an end which could be realized without any chance of evil?" we can only reply that His will is absolutely free and no extrinsic cause can be assigned for His choice. We can also endeavor to show that the end which He chose is worth the evils involved in its attainment.

6. God Does Not Will Evil. Does the fact that evil exists in the world created by God mean that God wills evil? It is impossible that

God, who is infinitely good, should will evil. God cannot will evil, but He can permit it to occur. He wills the being and the good of His creatures and the end of creation as a whole. That some creatures fall short of their proper good is due to their own finiteness and imperfection, and not to God's will. If this very falling short, or evil, can be made by God to contribute to the realization of the ultimate good, He does, in fact, make use of it for that purpose. It does not at all follow that God wills the evil as a means to the good, but rather that, the evil having occurred through the imperfection of finite causes, God wills to make a greater good come out of it. A close analogy exists between God's relation to evil and man's. We are never allowed to will evil for the sake of the good, but under certain conditions we are allowed and even obliged to pursue a good end even when we foresee that, through no fault or intention of our own, certain evils will arise from our pursuit of that end; we are never allowed to use evil means for a good end, but when evil has occurred we are bound to "make the best of it," that is, to strive to turn it to good purposes. In summary we may say with St. Augustine that God never wills or causes evil, but He does sometimes permit it to arise from other causes because He knows how to make it contribute to a greater good.[4]

II. THE NATURE AND CAUSES OF EVIL

The problem of evil, in contrast to the mystery, is purely metaphysical rather than religious. It is a problem in cause and effect: How can a universe containing evil come from an infinitely good and perfect God? Some systems of philosophy show their inadequacy by their utter failure to give even a partially satisfactory answer to this question. Pantheism, identifying God and the world, can give no explanation of evil that does not amount to a denial of the fundamental principle of pantheism. The same thing is true of emanationism, which regards everything in the world as the necessary result of the nature of God. Many modern absolutists have tried to get out of this impasse by denying that evil is evil.

1. **Manicheanism.** The most direct effort to solve the problem of evil is that form of dualism known as Manicheanism. This doctrine maintains that the world is the joint product of two, eternal, independent principles, one of them the source of all good, namely, God, and the other the source of all evil, namely, matter. Matter is the absolute

[4] *S. Theol.*, I, 2, 3, ad 1; 48, 2, ad 3; 49, 2, c.

Evil, eternally existent, underived from any cause. Just as God is the *Summum Bonum* (Supreme Good) so is matter the *Summum Malum* (Supreme Evil). In man, the soul or spirit is the product and manifestation of the good or God, and the body is the manifestation and product of the evil or matter. Between these two an unceasing, unrelenting warfare goes on.

2. **The Nature of Evil.** St. Thomas gives to the question, "What is evil?" essentially the same answer given before him by Plato, Aristotle, Plotinus, and St. Augustine. Evil is not a positive being. Evil is the lack in something of a good which is proper to it and which it ought to possess. Evil is an absence, a defect, a negation, a privation. We have already seen that good, like unity and truth, is convertible with being; that is to say, that being and good are identical in reality, though different in concept. The good means the desirable, that which is in some manner an end. Everything, however, desires its own being and perfection, that is to say, its proper form; and, therefore, it must be said that the being and perfection of every nature is a good. Hence evil cannot signify any form or any nature or any being, but on the contrary signifies a certain absence of being, form, or nature. Evil, therefore, exists only relatively to good, being a deprivation of good.

That evil can be nothing but a non-being follows, furthermore, from St. Thomas' whole demonstration of God's attributes and of creation. The proofs of God's existence demonstrate not only that He exists, but also that He is the original Being, the supreme Good, and the universal Cause of all other reality. Everything that is real, in so far as it is real, is caused by God, and God can cause only what is good since He is absolute perfection. But every created being is a being only in so far as it is an effect of the divine causality and a reflection of the divine essence. It follows of necessity that goodness is exactly equivalent to being. The infinite being is infinite goodness; every finite being is a participation in the infinite being and is, therefore, good exactly to the extent to which it is being. In a word, in everything that exists, its being and its goodness are identical. What then is evil? What can it be but non-being?[5]

Does this mean that there is no such thing as evil? Not at all. It means that evil has no *positive* reality, no *positive* being, but exists

[5] *De Malo,* I, 1; *S. Theol.,* I, 48, 1.

only as a negation of good and of being. Evil is as real as the missing of a rung in a ladder, as the failure of a man to aid a sufferer, as the surgeon's not getting there on time, as the breakdown of a man's character. It is a physical evil for a man to have only one leg. The leg he has is not evil. Nor is the missing leg evil; indeed it is a good which he would greatly desire to have. It is the absence of this good which is evil. Again, a lie is a moral evil. The words are not evil, for they are the regular instruments of human communication. The thought expressed in the lie is not evil, for it is a product of one of the masterpieces of God's creation, the human intellect. Even the will-act determining the lie is not, as an act, evil, for it too is the product of a wonderful thing, the human will. What *is* evil is the failure of the will in acting to accord with the moral law. This accord of the will, or rectitude, is a good due and proper to a human act, and when a man acts without this rectitude there is sin or moral evil.

Evil then is a negation, but not a mere negation. Sheer nothingness is not evil. Evil is *privation* rather than mere negation. Privation differs from mere negation in that privation is the lack of something in a being which that being ought to possess; it is a negation in a subject of something due the nature of that subject. Blindness is a privation in a man or in a dog because sight is something which a man or a dog ought to possess; sightlessness is not a privation in a stone, but a mere negation, because sight is not something proper to a stone's nature. Similarly, we do not call an infant lame because it cannot walk, dumb because it cannot speak, stupid because it cannot understand what we say. Lameness, dumbness, stupidity are privations, and are predicable only of beings who naturally ought to be able to walk, speak, or understand but cannot in fact do so.

Evil, therefore, is not a mere absence of good, but a defect in a good. This means that nothing can be totally evil. Evil can exist only in a subject, and cannot subsist in itself: it can exist only in and supported by a substratum of good. Were an evil completely to consume its subject, the good would disappear; but the evil would disappear along with it, since there could no longer be a defective good or a defect in a good where there was no longer any good. As long as a being retains any shred of nature no matter how defective, it retains some shred of good; and if it loses every shred of nature, it no longer exists and hence cannot be evil. Men show that they realize this when they shoot sick or injured dogs and horses to put an end to their suffering. Animal suffering is an evil because it is truly a defective good — there *is* an animal and it is suffering. A dead animal is not an evil because it is no more an animal than sheer nothingness is. A suffering cow is an evil, but roast beef is good.[6]

To sum up: The being and perfection of every creature is good, and consequently evil has no positive being, no degree of essence or reality. It is purely negative, a certain lack of being and good. It is a negation in a substance or action, a deprivation of something which the substance or the action ought to possess. Consequently, the existence of evil is impossible without a positive and real good as its substratum or vehicle. It is, therefore, impossible that there should exist anything which is pure evil, absolute evil.

This analysis of the nature of evil disposes of Manicheanism. This doctrine, attributing all evil to an original, absolute evil existing independently of the good, makes evil a positive, self-sustaining reality, which is precisely what it cannot be.[7]

3. The Cause of Evil. We saw in Chapter IV that four kinds of causes co-operate in the production of natural things. Since evil is a negative reality, it will not be surprising to find that some of the four causes are entirely lacking to it and the others are its causes only accidentally, that is, contrary to their nature rather than because of it.

a) Formal and Final Cause. Evil has neither formal nor final cause. Form is the principle that gives a thing its proper nature; whereas evil is a defect in a thing's nature. Hence, evil is never caused by any formal principle in its subject, but is itself a defect in the subject's formal constitution. Final cause is the end or goal for which some being exists, acts, or is made. Evil is precisely the missing of the proper end or intention of the subject's being. Hence, evil has no final cause, but is precisely the privation of that order or perfection that would accomplish the final cause, or the end of the subject.

b) Material Cause. Evil has, *per accidens,* a material and an efficient cause. *Per accidens* means outside the nature and intention of the subject. Evil is a defect in a good, and therefore the good, that is to say the subject, is the substratum or material cause of the evil. It is so, however, only *per accidens,* since it is the subject of evil only in so far as it fails to attain the nature and end due it. Nothing is naturally and intentionally the proper vehicle of evil. No man as

---

[6] *S. Theol.,* I, 48. 4. c; *ibid.,* 49. 3; *Con. Gen.,* II.

[7] *S. Theol.,* I, 49, 3; *Con. Gen.,* III, 15.

man is naturally blind; it is only accidentally and by a defect of nature that a man is the subject of blindness. Similarly, the will, which in its very essence is an inclination to the good, is the subject, or material cause, of sin only by not conforming itself to its natural and proper end, the moral good.

c) *Efficient Cause.* The efficient cause, that is to say, the producing agent, of evil is a good; but the good causes evil only accidentally, not by nature or intention. Since the evil is a non-being, a deficiency, no proper or intentional efficient cause need be or can be assigned for it. The proper cause of the good in which the evil resides is the accidental cause of the evil. When a carpenter makes a defective desk, he is properly the cause of the desk and accidentally the cause of its defect. His action, in so far as it is action, causes everything positive about the desk; but in so far as it is imperfect action, it accidentally causes the defect in the desk. Similarly the efficient cause of suffering and sickness are certain things good in themselves but out of harmony with the organism upon which they are acting; and they are able actually to cause suffering only because of the operation of the same natural physiological laws of the organism which are normally the causes of health.

4. The First Cause of Sin. In the case of moral evil, that is, sin, man himself is the efficient cause. The sinful act is not entirely and purely evil; like every other evil it is a defect in a good. A sin is a human act that is contrary to the moral law. As a human act it is a good, because it is the proper operation of one of God's noblest creatures, a rational and free man. It is so good that God Himself will not destroy it by depriving man of his freedom even though man abuses this freedom to offend Him. Inasmuch as it is contrary to the moral law it is evil. The man who sins is, therefore, the proper cause of a good, viz., a human act, and the accidental cause of an evil, viz., a human act not conformable to the moral law.

Sin raises a difficulty in connection with divine concurrence. God, as we learned in Chapter XXV, acts in every action of the creature; He is always first mover and first cause. But how can God concur in sin? How can He move a man's will to do what is evil? In meeting this difficulty St. Thomas distinguishes between the causation of the act and the causation of the sin. God is the first cause and first mover of every act of a man's will; the man could not act, rightly or wrongly, unless God moved his will to action. God, therefore, moves man's will even when the action of the will is sinful. This does not, however, make Him first cause of the sin. The sin, as such, is a negation, a nonconformity of the act with the law. As a negation it does not require, and cannot have, a positive first cause; its first cause must be itself a negation, a privation. What is this first cause of sin? St. Thomas answers that it is the nonconsideration of the law or rule of action. There is a law to which man is obliged to conform his actions. He does not have to constantly think about or consider this law, and consequently the mere nonconsideration of it is not a sin. But he does have to make sure that, when he acts, his action conforms to the law; therefore, to act without considering the law is a sin. The nonconsideration itself is a pure negation — a mere not doing something — yet it is voluntary, since it is in the will's power to consider the rule and it does not do so. It is the first cause of sin, because when the will acts without considering the rule, that is sin. The first cause of the will-act as a physical reality is God; the first cause of its sinfulness is the man's nonconsideration of the rule of action. A voluntary defect in the created will is, therefore, the first cause of sin — a purely negative cause, which is the only kind of first cause that evil needs or can have.[8]

5. Answer to the Problem of Evil. All the above reflections put us now in a position where we can answer the second question which we asked above; the question expressing the problem of evil: *How can evil exist in a world created by an all-good God?*

1. Evil is not a positive reality. Hence, it can have no *proper* cause. Therefore, we do not need to, and we cannot, account for it by tracing it back to some positive absolute cause of evil, as the Manicheans did.

2. Since evil is a privation in a good, its cause is to be sought, not in any beings which naturally and properly give rise to evil, but in beings which are naturally good but are capable of failing to attain to their full measure of goodness. All creatures, because they are finite and contain potentiality, are capable of failing to actualize their full measure of proper good. From this failure arises evil.

3. God is in no way the cause of evil. All that He creates is good. He has created a great variety of creatures of every conceivable degree of perfection. Among them are beings liable to fall short of their full physical perfection because they are corruptible, and others liable to

---

[8] *De Malo,* I, 3; *S. Theol.,* I, 41, 1 and 2; *ibid.,* I–II, 79, 2; *Con. Gen.,* II, 15; *De Pot.,* III, 7, ad 15. Cf. J. Maritain, *St. Thomas and the Problem of Evil.*

fall short of their full moral perfection because they are finite. Their falling short and the evils that result are not caused by God but by their own finiteness and imperfection. And even from this evil good is produced by God. Because of the good that He brings from it God permits the evil to occur.

III. THE MYSTERY OF EVIL

1. The last sentence above brings us back to our first question: "Why did God choose to create a world in which evil, both physical evil (suffering, sickness, death) and moral evil (sin, everlasting ruin), are inevitable?" Shall you console a tortured invalid by telling him that his suffering is no real evil if viewed in its proper place in the universal order? Do you comfort a mother who has lost her child by explaining to her that it is only natural that some children should die, man being one of the corruptible degrees of perfection? Can it contribute to the perfection of the natural order that some of God's creatures should rebel against God Himself by sinning? Is not the sin itself worse than the destruction of the whole order of nature? What perfection of the natural order can balance the eternal ruin and misery of free spirits created to God's own image and likeness? Not the whole world is worth my soul — not to me!

2. **Sin Is the Price of Beatitude.** No metaphysics of the natural order can ever explain God's permission of moral evil and suffering in free rational beings. If St. Thomas' teaching upon evil did not go beyond what we have presented thus far in this chapter, it would be indeed "stale, flat, and unprofitable." It does go far beyond it, but in doing so it takes us out of the province of philosophy into that of theology. The justification for the existence of creatures capable of sinning and of suffering eternal damnation cannot be found in any end or good of the natural order. Free creatures exist in order that they may attain to supreme happiness in the beatific vision of the divine Essence and in the union of mutual loving friendship with the divine Persons. Such vision and such friendship are possible only to beings endowed with intelligence and free will.

> Friendship cannot exist except toward rational creatures, who are capable of returning love and of communicating with one another in the various works of life. . . . But irrational creatures cannot attain to loving God, nor to any share in the intellectual and beatific life that He lives. Strictly speaking, therefore, God does not love irrational creatures with the love of friendship, but, as it were, with the love of

desire, in so far as He orders them to rational creatures, and even to Himself.[9]

Hence, if God is to share a love of friendship with any creatures, they must be rational, that is to say, intelligent and free. But a free *finite* being is of necessity a fallible, peccable being, and creatures are of necessity finite. Therefore, free creatures naturally incapable of sinning are metaphysical impossibilities. Wherefore, we may conclude, *it was impossible for God to share His own beatitude, His own divine life, without creating beings naturally capable of sinning against Him and of encompassing their own eternal ruin.* Sin, and the misery consequent upon sin (which is, according to Holy Scripture, all human misery) is the price of Beatitude.[10]

It is essential for an understanding of this Christian view of the mystery of evil to remember that in Christian teaching sin is the cause of all other evils in human life. Original sin, the sin of Adam, deprived Adam and all his race of the supernatural gift of grace, which God had given to Adam at his creation, and of the effects of this gift. It deprived man of special gifts of divine illumination and divine motion directing him to his supernatural end, God. It deprived him of gratuitous excellencies of intellect and will far surpassing those of fallen man. It produced an internal disorder in man, destroying the natural subordination of his sensitive passions to reason. It deprived him of immunity from sickness, suffering, and death. The personal, or actual, sins of men through the ages add to the evils first brought into the world by original sin. Every man who sins brings suffering and unhappiness into his own life and the lives of others. If the misery caused by lies, greed, lust, pride, hatred, sloth, envy, drunkenness, and selfishness of all sorts were removed from the human scene, there would be surprisingly little suffering left to blame God for. At the present moment we are all greatly impressed by the terrible evils consequent upon war. But all wars arise from somebody's sins; not only in the vague sense that war is a visitation of divine vengeance for human wrongdoing, but in the very precise sense that wars are brought about by specific acts of injustice, by particular lies, by concrete actions arising from greed, hatred, and lust for power on the part of certain men, and by slothful and cowardly acquiescence on

[9] *S. Theol.*, I, 20, 2, ad 3 (*The Basic Writings of St. Thomas Aquinas,* ed. Anton C. Pegis [New York: Random House, 1945], Vol. I, p. 218).

[10] Cf. J. Maritain, *St. Thomas and the Problem of Evil.*

the part of a great many more men. So it is with the other great social evils which afflict man: economic injustice, oppression of the weak, racial conflict — all are direct results of someone's actual sins. So far as man is concerned, therefore, if the Christian philosopher can advance a satisfactory answer to the question why God permits sin, why He created a world in which sin is possible, he will have fully "justified the ways of God to man."

Why, then, has God created a world in which sin is possible? Sin is a misuse of free will; only a rational, free agent can possibly commit sin. That there might be no possibility of sin in the world, there would have to be no rational, free creatures in the world. It is the teaching of Christian religion, as of Thomistic philosophy, that the end of man is Beatitude, or perfect happiness, and that this beatitude consists essentially in the sharing in the very life and happiness of God by the direct vision of the Divine Essence and Goodness Itself: "We shall be like unto Him because we shall see Him as He is," wrote St. John. In order to create beings capable of sharing in His own life and happiness, capable of knowing Him, of returning Him praise and gratitude for His gift of being, of giving Him love for His love, of being united with Him in mutual knowledge and love, God had to create free beings, that is to say, persons. Then, because these creatures are free, they can determine their own actions; and because they are finite, they can choose badly in determining their actions. Hence, the price of beatitude is the possibility of sin.

Even in this world of free creatures, it was theoretically possible that no sin should ever have been committed. Adam and Eve could have chosen always to obey God; and so could the angels who sinned. Many of the angels did so choose. So also could every man, if Adam had not sinned. Against this theoritical possibility, however, stands the practical certainty that, given a very large number of beings, each of whom is really capable of sinning, some are sure to sin. In any case, the trials of the angels and Adam were real trials, not "setups." Because they had free will and finite natures, they could actually commit sin; they could, that is to say, choose a lesser good, themselves, to the Supreme Good, God, to whom they owed obedience. The obedience demanded of them was supernatural, requiring powers beyond those of their own natures; but they had the gift of grace which supplied the power lacking to their natures. It was, and is, really possible for every man either to triumph in his trial or to fail. The whole point of the Christian view of life is that triumph is well worth the risk of failure, and that the triumph of those who win is worth even the loss of those who fail. Sin, with its consequent evils, is the price of beatitude, but beatitude is worth the price.

3. **Is Evil Necessary in the Created World?** These considerations should enable us now to return to the question with which this section of the chapter opened: Why did God, who is infinitely good, choose to create *this* world, in which evil seems to play such an inevitable part? The general tenor of our answer should now be clear. Any of an infinite number of possible worlds would have attained the general end which God has in creating, namely, His own glory; but the particular end, namely, the manner in which this glory is to be manifested, is realizable only by *this actual world*. And in this actual world sin and the evils that follow from it are possible, and, practically speaking, inevitable. But the end of creation is worth all the evils incident upon its realization. Thus, the final stand of the Christian philosopher in regard to the mystery of evil embodies two contentions: (1) the particular end which God has in view in creating can be realized only at the cost of the possibility of moral and physical evil; (2) this end is well worth the cost.

Against the first of these contentions many objections are advanced. Three of them raise points of great importance concerning the relation between nature and the supernatural, and it will be worth our while to examine these three. The first holds that the Christian account of evil, failing to show how the evil in nature can be reconciled with the absolute goodness of the Creator of nature, falls weakly back upon a supernatural explanation. The second holds that sin, which is the crux of the whole Christian account of the mystery, could never actually have occurred in such a world as God, according to the Christian teaching, is supposed to have originally created. The third asks why God, who according to Christian doctrine is omnipotent, could not have created men and angels in possession of beatitude from the start, and thus have dispensed with the evil which Christian teaching represents as involved in the attainment of beatitude in the present order of creation. These three objections are serious and require serious answers. It is the author's hope that the answers now to be proposed will bring out with added clarity the profundity and the beauty of the Christian conception of the order of creation.

4. **First Objection: Nature Is Patched Up by Grace.** The proponents

of the first argument point out that, in Christian and Thomistic teaching, man and even the angels are parts of the natural order of created things. They are free finite persons and they are consequently capable of sin. Without them the order of nature would not be complete. Therefore, their existence is demanded for the perfection of the natural order without any reference to the supernatural, since it would be unbecoming to God to create an order of beings in which the most perfect parts should be missing. St. Thomas himself uses this principle as an argument to prove the existence of the angels.[11] Consequently, the order of creation actually selected by God is one in which the most perfect parts are of necessity liable to revolt against the Creator and to incur thereby irreparable misery to themselves. Such a revolt and such misery constitute an evil so great that no natural good can possibly compensate for it — the revolt of a creature against God, the utter ruination of an immortal spirit, can never be remedied by any act that any creature or any number of creatures can ever perform. Wherefore, the conclusion is inescapable that God has created a natural order in which evil will inevitably outweigh good. To say that God imposes on top of this natural order a supernatural order in which the good realized far outweighs the evil of the natural order is to depict Him as a clumsy worker who patches up a poor job by pulling miracles out of His sleeve.

5. Answer: The Supernatural Order Is the Only Order. The answer to this objection introduces us to the most profound truth that can be stated about the created order of things. There is no such thing as "the natural order." Order is the arrangement or disposition of things in view of an end. God did not create nature in an order of its own and then impose supernature upon it. If He had done so, the natural world would have some ultimate natural end of its own distinct from the supernatural ends of free, personal creatures. According to St. Thomas and according to the teaching of Holy Scripture and the Church, the natural world does not have any such ultimate natural end. The whole material universe exists for the sake of man, and man has only a supernatural end. Nature, therefore, was created only for supernature; God created nature only for the sake of grace. The only actual order of created beings has its end in a supernatural good, a good of grace, namely the attainment by created free persons of ecstatic bliss in perfect union of love with the uncreated Persons of the

[11] *S. Theol.*, I, 50, 1; *Con. Gen.*, II, 46.

Trinity. All nature is subordinated to that end. Consequently, not only is the meaning of the existence of moral evil not to be found in any good of nature, but on the contrary the significance of all the inequality and evil in nature is to be found in this good of supernature. "The natural order," that is, the physical universe considered in independence of the universe of grace, is a sheer abstraction; no such thing has ever existed. Hence, that natural evils should be swallowed up in supernatural good is not the patching up of a poor job; from the start creation was only one job, the supernatural job, and nature, with its goods and evils, exists only because of the supernatural ends which it was created to serve.

6. Second Objection: The First Sin Cannot Be Accounted For. It is the teaching of Catholic (and Thomistic) theology that the angels and the first man were created in a state of integral nature in which their whole being was naturally ordained by God to its last end and supreme good and, in the case of man, in which the lower or sensitive parts of his nature were fully subordinated to the higher or rational part. Now every nature necessarily seeks its own good, and only a nature which is already corrupted or de-ordained could tend to what is contrary to its natural good or end. This fact creates a difficulty in regard to the sin of the angels and the first sin of man: a sin is the choice of something opposed to the agent's true end; but having perfect natures, the angels and Adam could not have made such a choice. Some have stated the difficulty this way: How could evil have originated in free beings created by God, and therefore good, and ordered by God to their own proper good and end through a natural appetite for the good? How could they ever choose evil for the first time, before their ordination to the good was corrupted?

7. Answer: The End of Rational Creatures Surpasses Their Natures. The answer of St. Thomas[12] would seem to be along the following lines: no rational creature, while retaining its original ordination to the good, could have chosen an evil opposed to its own natural good; such a choice would be unnatural and hence would presuppose some corruption. But no rational creature was ever created for an end which was merely its own natural good, that is to say, a good proportionate to its nature. Hence, no turning away from its natural good ever occurred in the case of the angels or the first man. These creatures were assigned a supernatural end far surpassing the competency of

[12] Cf. *S. Theol.*. I, 62, 2, c and ad 2: 63, arts. 1 and 3.

their natures to attain. Hence they were by nature capable of turning from it in favor of some other good. Their trial was fully real: they were capable by nature of choosing an apparent natural good in preference to their real supernatural end; and they were capable, by virtue of the gift of grace, of choosing their supernatural end.

According to St. Thomas, the precise sin of the fallen angels was the effort to attain beatitude by their own powers, as if it were a good due their own natures.[13] The essence of Adam's sin would seem to have been the same. The biblical account does not show him turning to anything opposed to his nature; rather it shows him choosing something forbidden by God but apparently good, and which the serpent promised him would make him like unto God. Is not this the root of all sin: the desire to seize beatitude by oneself, independently of God? Hence, again we must say that the price of beatitude for creatures is the possibility of sin. Because God made rational creatures for an end which only He can give to them, they are capable of seeking to grasp it by themselves, of seeking to "be as gods"; and this is sin. In His infinite love, God made possible for men and angels a destiny surpassing all proportion to any nature save His own; namely, a sharing of His own divine life and happiness. So great is His goodness that He did this even though the cost was the rebellion of many of these favored creatures against Him.

8. Third Objection: Why Not Heaven Without Earth? We cannot admit that God can permit any evil except for the sake of some good. But God could have created man and the angels in possession of the beatific vision without subjecting them first to a trial, since He is infinite and since there is no contradiction in the notion of a creature created in actual enjoyment of the vision of God. God did, as a matter of fact, create man and the angels in possession of grace; He could as easily have created them in possession of glory. It seems, therefore, that all the evils that resulted from their trial, namely, all sins, all suffering, the damnation of many angels and men, are needless, since the end could have been attained without them. That God should permit such evil in order to attain an end attainable without it seems incompatible with infinite goodness and wisdom.

9. Answer: Not This Heaven Without This Earth. This objection does not go quite so deep as at first reading it seems to go. Is it true to say that God could have accomplished the end of creation without

---

[13] *S. Theol.*, I, 63, 3, c.

permitting the evils that actually do occur in the course of the attainment of that end? The ultimate end of creation is God's own glory, but that could have been attained by a thousand created goods different from the one that God has actually chosen. We may call God's glory the general goal of creation; but we must say that the *particular goal of creation* is the particular way in which that glory is to be realized through creatures. This particular goal we do not fully know. We do know something about it, however. Part of it is our own eternal happiness in the possession of God in heaven. Exactly what that happiness will be like we do not know. But whatever it is, its nature will be conditioned by and in part determined by the type of creation of which it is the result and the goal. God could have given us eternal happiness without first testing us upon earth, as the objection declares. *But such a happiness could not have been the same as the happiness that He actually has prepared for us.* The trial that we shall have gone through, the evils we shall have suffered and overcome, the very damnation we shall have escaped — all these shall enter as essential ingredients into the happiness we shall possess, so that it could not possibly have been the same without them. The life of St. Francis of Assisi in heaven could not possibly be exactly what it is if the life of St. Francis on earth had not been exactly what it was. Francis must be what he is in order to enjoy the happiness he enjoys. In a word, it is metaphysically impossible for God to create the heaven which He has created without creating the earth which He has created, because that heaven necessarily presupposes that earth, just as "the effect of *A*" presupposes "*A*."

There is nothing abstract or impersonal about heaven; happiness is possible only to *persons*. Each one there shall be himself; and what he shall be there, he shall be because of what he was upon earth. Beatitude is personal to each one of us. At each instant of our earthly life we are *making ourselves,* forming our characters, both naturally and supernaturally. What we do makes us what we are, and nothing of what we do is ever lost. I, if I get to heaven, shall. be myself in heaven, and the self which I shall be will be the effect of all that I have previously been and done. What I am now, at this moment on earth, is the result of my whole previous past life; with another past I could not now possibly be what I am. The same will be true in heaven. *My* beatitude will be possible only as the outcome of *my* whole life, and it will be possible *only for me.* Into it, as essential causes and ingredients, will go the good acts I shall have done, the sins I shall have repented and renounced, the sufferings I shall have undergone, the temptations I shall have overcome, the faith I shall have maintained against difficulties, the hope I shall have clung to when discouragement beckoned me, the love of God and neighbor I shall have practiced.— and even the hell, the particular, personal hell, I would have fallen into had my free acts been different. Such beatitude, such an end of creation, is possible only as the outcome of this world. This we may be certain of, because it is absolutely impossible for God to permit evil except for the sake of the good, since otherwise He would be permitting it for its own sake.[14] Therefore, if the particular good which He has chosen as the end of man's life were capable of realization without the probation of man in a world full of evils, God could not have permitted that probation or those evils.

10. A Note on Animal Suffering. Much has been written in recent years, in connection with the problem of evil, about the sufferings and pain undergone by animals. To many persons this is the phase of earthly life hardest to reconcile with belief in an all-good and all-powerful Creator. Animal sufferings are not directed toward any eternal bliss for the animals, as human sufferings are for men; even if we were willing to admit the possibility of a future life for animals, it could not be a life of beatitude. Without repeating what others have well written on the subject of animal suffering,[15] the present author wishes to call attention to one point which, though generally neglected, seems worthy of consideration.

Suffering presupposes self-hood in some degree. There can be no suffering where there is no "I." Pain divorced from a subject who feels the pain as its own is nonsense. That animals are able to suffer at all is due to the fact that they enjoy some approach to or some degree of self-hood; each is in some sense an "I." Like humans, they cherish life and self-identity very highly. They certainly seem to feel it worth the pain it costs them. God could have created a world in which there would be no animal suffering; He need merely have made one in which there would be no animals. If the world were very much different from what it is, there would be no animals; and if it were even a little bit different, there would not be the actual

---

[14] This principle, which suggested all the reflections of the last few paragraphs, I owe to E. I. Watkin, *The Catholic Center.*

[15] Cf. G. H. Joyce, *The Principles of Natural Theology,* pp. 584–592.

animals which there are; as it is, there are these animals and they inevitably suffer. Now it seems to the writer that the real animals of this real world should be given a voice in the controversy as to the wisdom of this world's creation. Their voice, indeed, is very loud in favor; they love their lives, such as they are. They, I am sure, prefer these lives to some theoretically better lives *for some other animals*. It is understandable that a tenderhearted person might pity a sick, injured, or hungry dog, but his pity should be tinged with logic. He should not so hate the suffering as to be willing to dispense with dogs altogether — which is truly what he seeks in demanding a "better world." Insistence upon a better world in which animals would not suffer is hardly fair to the animals of this world. Some human beings would be more comfortable if there were no animals to suffer, but the animals probably like the world better as it is; just as the poor among men prefer to live, even though their poverty and squalor embarrass some of their more comfortable brethren — advocates of birth control notwithstanding.

IV. DIVINE LOVE AND THE MYSTERY OF EVIL

1. God Is Love. *"Deus est caritas,"* wrote St. John. God is Love. Infinite subsistent Love lovingly wills to share Itself precisely as love. This is possible only if there are creatures who can love, creatures who have intelligence and free will — but then, also, creatures who can sin, being finite and being free. Love is the beginning of creation and its end. Truly, " 'tis love that makes the world go round"; not only rational creatures but all creatures are created so that rational creatures may attain to union with God in love. Love is the Alpha and the Omega.

God, who is infinitely good and holy, who loves each of us with a love surpassing any love that man or woman can experience or even understand, who could have created a different world with a different end, an end that would not have involved the possibility of evil, has looked, in His perfect foreknowledge, at all the evils of earth and hell, and has looked at the beatitude which He conceived for men, and has judged that this our destined glory is worth all the suffering, sin, and damnation which are its price. St. Paul, who was taken up to the third heaven, got some glimpse of what God sees: "The sufferings of the present time are not worthy to be compared with the glory to come that will be revealed in us." (Rom. 8: 18).

2. **Christ and the Mystery of Evil.** God has judged the end of creation worth the price. *And He Himself paid the price.* The second Person of the Blessed Trinity became man, lived, suffered, died in agony for men's sins, took all the evils of the world upon Himself that the end of creation might be attained. *"Et verbum caro factum est."* Christ elevated not only human nature by becoming man, but He elevated all nature, since all nature exists for man. *"Consummatum est."* Christ's sacrifice on Calvary redeemed not only man but the whole physical universe, which had fallen with man's fall since it is directed to man as its end. "So that whoever is in Christ is a new creature: the old things are passed away; behold they have become new! But all things are from God, who reconciled us to Himself through Christ, and conferred on us the ministry of reconciliation — that is, God reconciled the universe to Himself, in Christ, not holding men's sins against them; and He committed to us the message of this reconciliation" (2 Cor. 5:17-19). *"Resurrexit sicut dixit!"* "Death is swallowed up in victory. O Death, where is thy victory! O Death, where is thy sting!" On the first Easter Christ conquered not only His own death and the deaths of men, but also all the corruptibility and destructibility of the material universe; the world arose with Christ, for nature dies only to live again in the eternal beatitude of man. God formed the body of Adam from the slime of the earth; that is what He made the earth for. "Remember, Man, that thou art dust, and unto dust thou shalt return" — that is only half the truth. Indeed it is false if it be taken in separation from this: "For I know that my Redeemer liveth, and on the last day I shall rise out of the earth. And I shall be clothed again with my skin, and in my flesh I shall see my God. Whom I myself shall see, and my eyes shall behold, and not another. This, my hope, is laid up in my bosom" (Job 19).

"More was restored by Christ than was lost by Adam." Through the Incarnation man becomes eternally united in one nature with God; for the Word Made Flesh is man forever. We are members of the Body of Christ. The whole Christ is Jesus and His members. The Mystical Body of Christ is not to pass away with the end of time. Through all eternity we shall be one with the Father through Christ our Head whose members we are. "And He raised us up with Him and made us to sit in Heaven in Christ Jesus; that He might show in the ages to come the surpassing wealth of His grace by His kindness towards us in Christ Jesus." (Eph. 2:6-7). The Love by which the Son loves the Father and the Father the Son — the Substantial Love which is the Holy Spirit — shall live in us, making us one with the Father because we shall be one body with Christ, who is the Son.

3. Christian Optimism. It should now be abundantly clear that the great evils of the world, instead of being a source of discouragement, should be a great occasion for consolation and hope, and for love of God. "Eye hath not seen, nor ear heard, nor hath it entered into the mind of man to conceive the things that God has prepared for them that love Him!" So wrote St. Paul, who had been taken up to Heaven in vision. We cannot conceive the happiness that God has prepared for us; but we can get some idea of how great it must be if we reflect on what price it is worth. If we take that point of view, the horrible evils of the world will not overwhelm us. Instead of being led by them to morbidity, despair, and doubt, we will rather raise up our hearts and minds to God to love and thank Him, for He has prepared for us a glory and a bliss so great that it is worth all the wars and sufferings and sins of men, and the death of His beloved Son. This is true Christian optimism — not to deny evil, but to see it in its proper place in the work of divine providence. "Even Satan serves God."

READINGS

The lists of supplementary readings which follow are neither exhaustive nor highly selected. They are based more upon probable availability in college libraries than upon any other principle of selection. Only books and articles in English have been included. Teachers will supplement these lists with other writings which they may know to be available. The primary reading for each chapter should be, of course, the sections from St. Thomas' writings upon which the chapter is based; but these are sufficiently indicated in the footnotes and do not need to be repeated in the reading lists.

CHAPTER I

Gilson, E., *The Philosophy of St. Thomas Aquinas* (St. Louis: Herder, 1937), Chap. II.

Hocking, W. E., *Types of Philosophy* (New York: Scribners, 1929, 1939).

Maritain, J., *An Introduction to Philosophy* (New York: Sheed and Ward), Part I, Chap. V.

Rogers, A. K., *Student's History of Philosophy* (New York: Macmillan, 1932), Introduction.

Ryan, J. H., *Introduction to Philosophy* (New York: Macmillan, 1924), Chaps. I–III.

Stace, W. T., *Critical History of Greek Philosophy* (London: Macmillan, 1920), Introduction.

CHAPTER II

Bakewell, C. M., *Source Book in Ancient Philosophy* (New York: Scribners, 1907).

Burns, R. J., S.J., "Plato and the Soul," *The New Scholasticism*, XX (Oct., 1946), 334–343.

Nahm, M. C., *Selections from Early Greek Philosophy* (New York: Crofts, 1940).

Standard histories of Greek philosophy, especially W. T. Stace, *Critical History of Greek Philosophy* (London: Macmillan, 1920),

Standard histories of philosophy, sections on Greek philosophy.

Taylor, A. E., *Platonism and Its Influence* (New York: Longmans, 1927).

CHAPTER III

Azarias, Bro., F.S.C., *Aristotle and the Christian Church* (New York: Sadlier, 1888).

Brennan, R. E., O.P., *Thomistic Psychology* (New York: Macmillan, 1941), pp. 3–44 (on Aristotle's psychology).

Chesterton, G. K., *St. Thomas Aquinas* (New York: Sheed and Ward, 1933).

Conway, P., O.P., *St. Thomas Aquinas* (London: Longmans Green, 1911), a short biography.

D'Arcy, M. C., S.J., *Thomas Aquinas* (Westminster, Md.: Newman Bookshop, 1944), Chaps. I–III, X.

Farrell, W., *Companion to the Summa* (New York: Sheed and Ward, 1941), Vol. I, Chap. I.

Gilson, E., *The Philosophy of St. Thomas Aquinas* (St. Louis: Herder, 1937), Preface and Chap. I.

Grabmann, M., *Thomas Aquinas* (New York: Longmans Green, 1928), Chaps. I–V.

Maritain, J., *An Introduction to Philosophy* (New York: Sheed and Ward), Part I, Chaps. III–IV.

Meyer, H., *The Philosophy of St. Thomas Aquinas* (St. Louis: Herder, 1944), Chaps. I–III.

Mure, G. R. G., *Aristotle* (London: Benn, 1932).

Olgiati, F., *Key to the Study of St. Thomas* (St. Louis: Herder, 1924), Chap. I.

Pegis, A. G., *The Basic Writings of St. Thomas Aquinas* (New York: Random House, 1945), Vol. I, pp. xxxv–liii.

Ross, Sir W. D., *Aristotle* (London: Methuen, 1930).

—— *Aristotle-Selections* (New York: Scribners, 1938).

Sertillanges, A. D., *St. Thomas Aquinas and His Work* (London: Burns, Oates and Washbourne, 1933), an appreciation of St. Thomas.

Standard histories of philosophy on Aristotle.

Stocks, J. L., *Aristotelianism* (New York: Longmans, 1940).

Taylor, A. E., "St. Thomas as a Philosopher," *Philosophical Studies* (London: Macmillan, 1934), an appreciation by a non-Scholastic philosopher.

CHAPTER IV

Kane, W. H., "The Nature and Extent of the Philosophy of Nature," *The Thomist*, VII (Apr., 1944), 204–232.

Marling, J. M., *The Order of Nature* (Washington, D. C.: Catholic University Press, 1934), entire book, especially pp. 18–27, 44–120.

McCormick, J. F., *Scholastic Metaphysics* (Chicago: Loyola University Press, 1928), Vol. I, Chaps. IX–X.

McWilliams, J. A., "Ancients and Moderns on Motion," *Proc. Am. Cath. Phil. Assn.* (1945), 193–197.

—— "Aristotelian and Cartesian Motion." *The New Scholasticism,* XVII (Oct., 1943), 307–321.

—— *Physics and Philosophy* (Washington, D. C.: Catholic University Press, 1946), pp. 28–49, 53–67.

—— "The Bond Between the Physics and Metaphysics of St. Thomas," *The Modern Schoolman,* XXII (Nov., 1944), 16–23.

Meyer, H., *The Philosophy of St. Thomas Aquinas* (St. Louis: Herder, 1944), Chaps. XIX–XX.

Phillips, R. P., *Modern Thomistic Philosophy* (London: Burns, Oates and Washbourne, 1934; Westminster, Md.: Newman Bookshop, 1946), Vol. I, pp. 109–116; Vol. II, pp. 232–244, 255–259.

Renard, H., S.J., *The Philosophy of Being,* second ed. (Milwaukee: Bruce, 1946), pp. 17–30, 62–77, 116–167.

Sertillanges, A. D., *The Foundations of Thomistic Philosophy* (St. Louis: Herder, 1931), Chap. VI, pp. 159–174.

CHAPTER V

Coffey, P., *Ontology* (New York: Peter Smith, 1938), Chap. XV.

Garrigou-Lagrange, R., O.P., *God — His Existence and Nature* (St. Louis: Herder, 1934), Vol. I, pp. 199–206, 345–372.

Maritain, J., *A Preface to Metaphysics* (New York: Sheed and Ward. 1939), pp. 90–131, 141–151.

Marling, J. M., *The Order of Nature* (Washington, D. C.: Catholic University Press, 1934).

Mason, F. (editor), *The Great Design* (New York: Macmillan, 1939).

Aiken, R. G., "Behold the Stars!" 19–37.

Armstrong, H. E., "The Romance of Green Leaf," 187–206.

Crowther, J. A., "Radiation," 39–61.

Eve, A. S., "The Universe as a Whole," 63–91.

Fraser-Harris, D. F., "Unity and Intelligence in Nature," 257–279.

Gager, C. S., "Adaptations in the Plant World," 159–185.

Lodge, Sir O., "Design and Purpose in the Universe," 223–233.

Morgan, C. L., "The Ascent of Mind," 113–132.

Metcalf, M. F., "Intelligent Plan in Nature, Evidence From Animals," 207–222.

Willis, B., "The Earth as the Home of Man," 93–111.

McWilliams, J. A., *Cosmology* (New York: Macmillan, 1933), Chaps. II, XIV.

—— *Physics and Philosophy* (Washington, D. C.: Catholic University Press, 1946), pp. 61–64.

Phillips, R. P., *Modern Thomistic Philosophy* (London: Burns, Oates and Washbourne, 1934; Westminster, Md.: Newman Bookshop, 1946), Vol. II, pp. 245–254.

Sertillanges, A. D., *The Foundations of Thomistic Philosophy* (St. Louis: Herder, 1931), Chap. VI, pp. 178–184.

Thompson, W. R., "Providence," *The Thomist*, V (Jan., 1943), 229–245.

Chapter VI

Coffey, P., *Ontology* (New York: Peter Smith, 1938), pp. 123–135.

Gerrity, Bro. Benignus, *The Relations Between the Theory of Matter and Form and the Theory of Knowledge* (Washington, D. C.: Catholic University Press, 1936), Chaps. I–III.

Kane, W. H., "The First Principles of Changeable Being," *The Thomist*, VIII (Jan., 1945), 27–67.

McCormick, J. F., *Scholastic Metaphysics* (Chicago: Loyola University Press, 1928), Vol. I, Chaps. X–XI.

McWilliams, J. A., "Peripatetic Matter and Form," *Thought*, I (Sept., 1926), 237–246.

Meyer, H., *The Philosophy of St. Thomas Aquinas* (St. Louis: Herder, 1944), Chap. IV.

Phillips, R. P., *Modern Thomistic Philosophy* (London: Burns, Oates and Washbourne, 1934; Westminster, Md.: Newman Bookshop, 1946), pp. 22–55, 128–163.

Renard, H., S.J., "The Functions of Intellect and Will in the Act of Free Choice," *The Modern Schoolman*, XXIV (Jan., 1947), pp. 85–92.

—— *The Philosophy of Being*, second ed. (Milwaukee: Bruce, 1946), pp. 216–227.

Roo, van, W. A., "Matter as a Principle of Being," *The Modern Schoolman*, XIX (Mar., 1942), 47–50.

Chapter VII

Bittle, C., *From Aether to Cosmos*, second ed. (Milwaukee: Bruce, 1946), Chaps. XII–XIV.

Bonnet, C. L., "Note on the Thomistic Interpretation of Individual Bodies," *The Modern Schoolman*. XXII (Nov., 1944), 33–42.

Kilzer, E., "Efficient Cause in the Philosophy of Nature," *Proc. Am. Cath. Phil. Assn.* (1941), 142–150.

Klubertanz, G. P., "Causality in the Philosophy of Nature," *The Modern Schoolman*. XIX (Jan., 1942), 29–32.

Marling, J. M., "Hylemorphism and the Conversion of Mass Into Energy," *The New Scholasticism*, X (Oct., 1936), 311–323.

—— "A Neo-Scholastic Critique of Hylemorphism," *The New Scholasticism*, XII (Jan., 1938), 69–89. (An excellent discussion of hylosystemism, referring directly to the writings of its founder, Albert Mitterer, from whom Father Bittle [*q.v.* in present chapter] draws his material. Unfortunately I did not come across this discussion before my manuscript was in the publisher's hands.)

—— "Some Casual Notes on the Nature of Matter," *Proc. Am. Cath. Phil. Assn.* (1938), 36–45.

McWilliams, J. A., "Are Substantial Changes Instantaneous?" *The New Scholasticism*, XIV (July, 1940), 295–311.

—— *Cosmology* (New York: Macmillan, 1933), Chaps. XVII–XIX.

Nys, D., *Cosmology* (Milwaukee: Bruce, 1942), Vol. II, Chaps. I–III, pp. 3–54; VI–X, pp. 141–162.

Schmieder, L. R., "Some More Casual Notes on the Nature and Structure of Inorganic Matter," *The New Scholasticism*, XIV (Jan., 1940), 33–56.

—— "Substantial Changes in Inorganic Matter," *The New Scholasticism*, XVIII (July, 1944), 209–251.

Veldt, van der, F. J., "The Recognition of Individual Bodies," *The New Scholasticism*, XVII (July, 1943), 201–230.

Watkin, E. I., *A Philosophy of Form* (New York: Sheed and Ward, 1935), Part I, Chap. I, pp. 3–70.

CHAPTER VIII

Brennan, R. E., O.P., *Thomistic Psychology* (New York: Macmillan, 1941), Chap. IV, pp. 85–110.

D'Arcy, M. C., S.J., *Thomas Aquinas* (Westminster, Md.: Newman Bookshop, 1944), pp. 197–205.

Farrell, W., *Companion to the Summa* (New York: Sheed and Ward, 1941), Vol. I, Chap. XIII.

Hauber, U. A., "The Mechanism and Teleology in Current Biology," *Proc. Am. Cath. Phil. Assn.* (1938), 45–69.

—— "The Mechanistic Conception of Life," *The New Scholasticism*, VII (July, 1933), 187–200.

Mason, F. (editor), *The Great Design* (New York: Macmillan, 1939).
  Driesch, H., "The Breakdown of Materialism," 283–303.
  Fraser-Harris, D. F., "Unity and Intelligence in Nature," 257–279.
  MacBride, E. W., "The Oneness and Uniqueness of Life," 135–158.
  Thomson, Sir J. A., "The Wonder of Life," 305–324.

McCormick, J. F., *Scholastic Metaphysics* (Chicago: Loyola University Press, 1928), Vol. I, Chap. XII.

Meyer, H., *The Philosophy of St. Thomas Aquinas* (St. Louis: Herder, 1944), Chaps. IX–XI.

Moore, T. V., "Formal Causality and Fields of Force," *Proc. Am. Cath. Phil. Assn.* (1939), 216–235.

Phillips, R. P., *Modern Thomistic Philosophy* (London: Burns, Oates and Washbourne, 1934; Westminster, Md.: Newman Bookshop, 1946), Vol. I, pp. 173–210, 241–250, 321–327.

Ryan, J. H., *Introduction to Philosophy* (New York: Macmillan, 1924), Chap. V.

Schroedinger, E., *What Is Life?* (New York: Macmillan, 1945). (Very interesting discussion of life from point of view of the physicist.)

Sertillanges, A. D., *The Foundations of Thomistic Philosophy* (St. Louis: Herder, 1931), pp. 184–198.

Sherrington, Sir C., *Man on His Nature* (New York: Macmillan, 1941), Chaps. III–VI.

Windle, Sir B. C. A., *What Is Life?* (St. Louis: Herder, 1908).

Chapter IX

Brennan, R. E., O.P., *Thomistic Psychology* (New York: Macmillan, 1941), Chap. III, pp. 64–84.

Farrell, W., *Companion to the Summa* (New York: Sheed and Ward, 1941), Vol. I, Chap. XIII.

Gilson, E., *The Philosophy of St. Thomas Aquinas* (St. Louis: Herder, 1937), Chap. X.

——— *The Spirit of Medieval Philosophy* (New York: Scribners, 1940), Chap. IX.

Maher, M., *Psychology* (New York: Longmans Green, 1933), pp. 474–524, 545–578.

McCormick, J. F., *Scholastic Metaphysics* (Chicago: Loyola University Press, 1928), Vol. I, Chap. XIII.

Meyer, H., *The Philosophy of St. Thomas Aquinas* (St. Louis: Herder, 1944), Chaps. XII–XIV.

Phillips, R. P., *Modern Thomistic Philosophy* (London: Burns, Oates and Washbourne, 1934; Westminster, Md.: Newman Bookshop, 1946), Vol. I, pp. 304–311.

Reys. A. L., "Man a Substantial Unit: Vegetal and Animal Life of Man," in G. J. MacGillivray. *Man* (London: Burns, Oates and Washbourne, 1938), pp. 35–43.

Ryan, J. H., *Introduction to Philosophy* (New York: Macmillan, 1924), Chap. IV.

Schneiders, A. A., "The Unity of the Human Person in the Light of Evidence from Abnormal and Dynamic Psychology," *Proc. Am. Cath. Phil. Assn.* (1942), 112–116.

Sertillanges, A. D., *The Foundation of Thomistic Philosophy* (St. Louis: Herder, 1931), pp. 219–232.

Vonier, Dom A., *The Human Soul* (London: Burns, Oates and Washbourne, 1939), pp. 1–77.

CHAPTER X

Brennan, R. E., O.P., *Thomistic Psychology* (New York: Macmillan, 1941), Chaps. XI, XII, pp. 280–332.

Farrell, W., *Companion to the Summa* (New York: Sheed and Ward, 1941), Vol. I, Chaps. IX–X, XIII.

Gilson, E., *The Spirit of Medieval Philosophy* (New York: Scribners, 1940), Chap. X.

Grabmann, M., *Thomas Aquinas* (New York: Longmans Green, 1928), Chap. IX.

Heron, G., O.F.M., "The Spirituality and Immortality of the Soul," in C. Lattey, S.J., *Man and Eternity* (London: Burns, Oates and Washbourne, 1937), pp. 50–71.

Maher, M., *Psychology* (New York: Longmans Green, 1933), pp. 229–251, 459–473, 525–544, 579–594.

Meyer, H., *The Philosophy of St. Thomas Aquinas* (St. Louis: Herder, 1944), Chaps. XII, XIII, XV.

Phillips, R. P., *Modern Thomistic Philosophy* (London: Burns, Oates and Washbourne, 1934; Westminster, Md.: Newman Bookshop, 1946), Vol. I, pp. 252–263, 296–303, 312–320.

Vonier, Dom A., *The Human Soul* (London: Burns, Oates and Washbourne, 1939), pp. 1–77.

Williams, Dom R., "The Immateriality and Immortality of the Soul," in G. J. MacGillivray, *Man* (London: Burns, Oates and Washbourne, 1938), pp. 13–34.

CHAPTER XI

Allers, R., "The Intellectual Cognition of Particulars," *The Thomist*, III Jan., 1941), 95–163.

——— "The Vis Cogitativa and Evaluation," *The New Scholasticism*, XV (July, 1941), 195–221.

Bourke, V. J., "The Operations Involved in Intellectual Conception," *The Modern Schoolman*, XXI (Jan., 1944), 83–89.

Brennan, R. E., O.P., "The Thomistic Concept of Imagination," *The New Scholasticism*, XV (Apr., 1941), 149–161.

―――― *Thomistic Psychology* (New York: Macmillan, 1941), Chaps. V, VII, pp. 111–146, 169–209.

Coffey, P., *Epistemology* (London: Longmans Green, 1917), pp. 250–291.

D'Arcy, M. C., S.J., *Thomas Aquinas* (Westminster, Md.: Newman Bookshop, 1944), Part II, Chap. IV.

Farrell, W., *Companion to the Summa* (New York: Sheed and Ward, 1914), Vol. I, Chap. XV.

Gerrity, Bro. Benignus, *The Relations Between the Theory of Matter and Form and the Theory of Knowledge* (Washington, D. C.: Catholic University Press, 1936), Chaps. IV–VI, pp. 56–119.

Gilson, E., *The Philosophy of St. Thomas Aquinas* (St. Louis: Herder, 1937), Chaps. XI–XIII.

―――― *The Spirit of Medieval Philosophy* (New York: Scribners, 1940), Chap. XIII.

Grabmann, M., *Thomas Aquinas* (New York: Longmans Green, 1928), Chap. X.

Maher, M., *Psychology* (New York: Longmans Green, 1933), pp. 42–124, 163–178, 229–251, 292–313.

McKian, J., "The Metaphysics of Introspection According to St. Thomas," *The New Scholasticism*, XV (Apr., 1941), 89–117.

Meyer, H., *The Philosophy of St. Thomas Aquinas* (St. Louis: Herder, 1944), Chaps. XXV–XXVI.

Peghaire, J., "A Forgotten Sense, The Cogitative According to St. Thomas Aquinas," *The Modern Schoolman*, XX (Mar., 1943), 123 ff.; (May, 1943), 210 ff.

Pegis, A. C., "In Umbra Intelligentiae," *The New Scholasticism*, XIV (April, 1940), 146–180.

Phillips, R. P., *Modern Thomistic Philosophy* (London: Burns, Oates and Washbourne, 1934; Westminster, Md.: Newman Bookshop, 1946), Vol. I, pp. 212–240, 251–271.

Sertillanges, A. D., *The Foundations of Thomistic Philosophy* (St. Louis: Herder, 1931), pp. 10–44, 199–219.

Chapters XII–XIII

Brennan, R. E., O.P., *Thomistic Psychology* (New York: Macmillan, 1941), Chaps. VI, VIII, X, pp. 147–168, 210–237, 260–279.

Farrell, W., *Companion to the Summa* (New York: Sheed and Ward, 1941), Vol. I, Chap. XIV.

Garrigou-Lagrange, R., O.P., *God — His Existence and Nature* (St. Louis: Herder, 1934), Vol. II, pp. 284–338.

Gilby, T., "Thought, Volition and the Organism," *The Thomist*, II (Jan., 1940), 1–13.

———— "Vienne and Vienna," *Thought,* XXII (Mar., 1946), 63–82.

Gilson, E., *The Philosophy of St. Thomas Aquinas* (St. Louis: Herder, 1937), Chap. XIV.

———— *The Spirit of Medieval Philosophy* (New York: Scribners, 1940), Chaps. XIV–XV.

King, J. L., S.J., "The Soul and Its Faculties," in G. J. MacGillivray, *Man* (London: Burns, Oates and Washbourne, 1938), pp. 44–71.

Maher, M., *Psychology* (New York: Longmans Green, 1933), pp. 208–220, 378–424.

Maritain, J., "The Thomist Idea of Freedom," *Scholasticism and Politics* (New York: Macmillan, 1930), Chap. V.

Pace, E. A., "The Problem of Freedom," *The New Scholasticism,* X (July, 1936), 207–225.

Phillips, R. P., *Modern Thomistic Philosophy* (London: Burns, Oates and Washbourne, 1934; Westminster, Md.: Newman Bookshop, 1946), Vol. I, pp. 272–295.

Sertillanges, A. D., *The Foundations of Thomistic Philosophy* (St. Louis: Herder, 1931), Chap. VII.

Sheen, F. J., "The Moral Law and Freedom," in G. J. MacGillivray, *Man* (London: Burns, Oates and Washbourne, 1938), pp. 72–88.

Smith, G., "Intelligence and Liberty," *Proc. Am. Cath. Phil. Assn.* (1940), 69–85; Also in *The New Scholasticism,* XV (Jan., 1941), 1–17.

Taylor, A. E., *The Faith of a Moralist* (two volumes in one) (London: Macmillan, 1937), Appendix, Vol. II, pp. 409–433.

Veld, van der, F. J., "Psychology and Order in Action," *Proc. Am. Cath. Phil. Assn.* (1941), 102–113.

Chapter XIV

Coffey, P., *Epistemology* (London: Longmans Green, 1917), Vol. I, Chap. III; Vol. II, Chaps. XIV–XVIII.

Creaver, J. A., "Personalism, Thomism and Epistemology," *The Thomist,* VIII (Jan., 1945), 1–26.

D'Arcy, M. C., S.J., *Thomas Aquinas* (Westminster, Md.: Newman Bookshop, 1944), Part II, Chap. IV.

Eaton, R. M., *Descartes-Selections* (New York: Scribners, 1927). (On the Index, ecclesiastical permission required to read it.)

Gilson, E., *The Philosophy of St. Thomas Aquinas* (St. Louis: Herder, 1937), Chap. XIII.

———— *The Spirit of Medievel Philosophy* (New York: Scribners, 1940), Chap. XII.

———— *The Unity of Philosophical Experience* (New York: Scribners, 1940), Chap. V–VIII.

Maher, M., *Psychology* (New York: Longmans Green, 1933), pp. 252–291.

Sertillanges, A. D., *The Foundations of Thomistic Philosophy* (St. Louis: Herder, 1931), Chap. II.

Smith, G., "A Date in the History of Epistemology," *The Thomist,* V (Jan., 1943), 246–255.

Standard histories of philosophy for Berkeley, Descartes, Hume, Leibniz, Locke, and Spinoza.

Toohey, J. J., "The Mythical Doubter," *Thought,* VIII (Mar., 1934), 606–614.

Chapters XV–XVI

Coffey, P., *Epistemology* (London: Longmans Green, 1917), Vol. I, Chaps. VI–IX, XII; Vol. II, Chaps. XX–XXI.

Gilson, E., *The Unity of Philosophical Experience* (New York: Scribners, 1940), Chap. IX.

Kant, I., *Prolegomena to All Future Metaphysics,* trans. by Mahaffy and Bernard (London: Macmillan, 1915).

Paton, H. J., *Kant's Metaphysics of Experience* (New York: Macmillan, 1936), Vols. I, II.

Price, H. H., *Hume's Theory of External World* (Oxford: Clarendon Press, 1940).

Prichard, H. A., *Kant's Theory of Knowledge* (Oxford: Clarendon Press, 1909).

Smith, G., "Kant's Epistemology," *The Modern Schoolman,* XI (Nov., 1933), 3–4, 6, 19–20.

Smith, N. K., *The Philosophy of David Hume* (London: Macmillan, 1941).

Standard histories of philosophy on Hume and Kant.

Toohey, J. J., "Kant on the Propositions of Pure Mathematics," *The New Scholasticism,* XI (Apr., 1937), 140–157.

Whitney, G. T., and Bowers, D. F., *The Heritage of Kant* (Princeton: Princeton University Press, 1939).

    Bowers, D. F., "Kant's Criticism of Metaphysics," 139–159.

    Northrop, F. S. C., "Natural Science and the Critical Philosophy of Kant," 39–62.

    Scoon, R., "Kant's Concept of Reality," 117–136.

    Sheldon, W. H., "Some Bad Results of Kant's Thought," 163–179.

    Wood, L., "The Transcendental Method," 3–35.

Ziegelmeyer, E. H., "Kantianism: Faith versus Knowledge," *The Modern Schoolman,* XIX (May, 1942), 61–65.

Chapter XVII

Byles, W. E., "The Analogy of Being," *The New Scholasticism,* XVI (Oct., 1942), 331–364.

Coffey, P., *Ontology* (New York: Peter Smith, 1938), Chaps. I–VI, VIII.

D'Arcy, M. C., S.J., *Thomas Aquinas* (Westminster, Md.: Newman Bookshop, 1944), Chap. V, 1–4.

Garrigou-Lagrange, R., O.P., *God — His Existence and Nature* (St. Louis: Herder, 1934), Vol. II, pp. 203–225.

Maritain, J., *The Degrees of Knowledge* (New York: Scribners, 1938), Introd., Chap. IV.

——— *A Preface to Metaphysics* (New York: Sheed and Ward, 1939), pp. 17–89.

McCormick, J. F., *Scholastic Metaphysics* (Chicago: Loyola University Press, 1928), Vol. I, Chaps. II–VI.

Meyer, H., *The Philosophy of St. Thomas Aquinas* (St. Louis: Herder, 1944), Chap. VII.

Olgiati, F., *Key to the Study of St. Thomas* (St. Louis: Herder, 1924), Chap. V.

Phillips, R. P., *Modern Thomistic Philosophy* (London: Burns, Oates and Washbourne, 1934; Westminster, Md.: Newman Bookshop, 1946), Vol. II, pp. 116–124, 157–231.

Renard, H., S.J., *The Philosophy of Being*, 2 ed. (Milwaukee: Bruce, 1946), pp. 7–15, 78–115, 168–198, 199–215.

Sertillanges, A. D., *The Foundation of Thomistic Philosophy* (St. Louis: Herder, 1931), Chap. II.

Smith, V. E., "On the 'Being' of Metaphysics," *The New Scholasticism*, XX (Jan., 1946), 72–84.

Chapter XVIII

Bennett, O., "St. Thomas' Theory of Demonstrative Proof," *Proc. Am. Cath. Phil. Assn.* (1941), 76–88.

Bourke, V. J., "Experience of Extra-Mental Reality as the Starting-Point of St. Thomas' Metaphysics," *Proc. Am. Cath. Phil. Assn.* (1938), 134–144.

Coffey, P., *Ontology* (New York: Peter Smith, 1938), Chaps. III, XIV.

Creaver, J. A., "Personalism, Thomism and Epistemology," *The Thomist*, VIII (Jan., 1945), 1–26.

D'Arcy, M. C., S.J., *Thomas Aquinas* (Westminster, Md.: Newman Bookshop, 1944), Chaps. IV–V.

Garrigou-Lagrange, R., O.P., *God — His Existence and Nature* (St. Louis: Herder, 1934), Vol. I, pp. 111–241.

Grabmann, M., *Thomas Aquinas* (New York: Longmans Green, 1928), Chap. VI.

Joyce, G. H., *The Principles of Natural Theology* (New York: Longmans, 1934), Chap. II.

Lonergan, B., S.J., "The Concept of *Verbum* in the Writings of St. Thomas Aquinas," *Theological Studies*, VII (Sept., 1946), 349–392.

Mailloux, N., "The Problem of Perception," *The Thomist*, IV (Apr., 1942), 266–285.

Maritain, J., *The Degrees of Knowledge* (New York: Scribners, 1938), Chap. II.

——— *A Preface to Metaphysics* (New York: Sheed and Ward, 1939), pp. 43–61, 90–109, 132–152.

Meyer, H., *The Philosophy of St. Thomas Aquinas* (St. Louis: Herder, 1944), Chap. XXVII.

Munnynck, de, M., "Notes on Institution," *The Thomist*, I (July, 1939), 143 ff.

Phillips, R. P., *Modern Thomistic Philosophy* (London: Burns, Oates and Washbourne, 1934; Westminster, Md.: Newman Bookshop, 1946), Vol. II, pp. 1–7, 30–115.

Sertillanges, A. D., *The Foundation of Thomistic Philosophy* (St. Louis: Herder, 1931), Chap. II.

Smith, G., S.J., "A Date in the History of Epistemology," *The Thomist*, V (Jan., 1943), 246–255.

Taylor, A. E., "Knowing and Believing," *Philosophical Studies* (London: Macmillan, 1934), pp. 380–398.

Watkin, E. I., *A Philosophy of Form* (New York: Sheed and Ward, 1935), pp. 252–312.

Ziegelmeyer, E. H., "The Discovery of First Principles According to Aristotle," *The Modern Schoolman*, XXII (Mar., 1945), 132–143.

Chapter XIX

Adler, M. J., *St. Thomas and the Gentiles* (Milwaukee: Marquette University Press, 1936).

——— *What Man Has Made of Man* (New York: Longmans, 1938), pp. 3–30, 129–161.

Caldin, E. F., "Modern Physics and Thomistic Philosophy," *The Thomist*, II (Apr., 1940), 208–225.

Herzfeld, K. F., "The Role of Theory in Modern Physics," *The New Scholasticism*, VIII (Oct., 1934), 319–329.

Maritain, J., *The Degrees of Knowledge* (New York: Scribners, 1938), Chaps. I, III, IV.

——— *An Introduction to Philosophy* (New York: Sheed and Ward), Part I, Chap. VI.

——— "Science and Philosophy," *Scholasticism and Politics* (New York: Macmillan, 1940), pp. 25–55.

—— "Science, Philosophy and Faith," *Science, Philosophy and Religion* (New York: Conference on Science, Philosophy and Religion, 1941), pp. 162–183.

Marling, J. M., "A Neo-Scholastic Critique of Hylemorphism," *The New Scholasticism,* XII (Jan., 1938), 69–89.

McNicholl, A. J., "Science and Philosophy," *The Thomist,* VIII (Jan., 1945), 68–130.

McWilliams, J. A., "Mathematics and Metaphysics in Science," *The New Scholasticism,* XI (Oct., 1937), 358–373.

Phillips, R. P., *Modern Thomistic Philosophy* (London: Burns, Oates and Washbourne. 1934; Westminster, Md.: Newman Bookshop, 1946), Vol. II, pp. 134–156.

Salmon, E. G., "Philosophy and Science," *The New Scholasticism,* XVI (Apr., 1942), 130–149.

Schneider, J., and Sperti, G., "Efficient Cause and Current Physical Theory," *Proc. Am. Cath. Phil. Assn.* (1938), 12–23.

Simon, Y., "Maritain's Philosophy of the Sciences," *The Thomist,* V (Jan., 1943), 85–102.

Taylor, A. E., *Does God Exist?* (New York: Macmillan, 1947), pp. 1–113.

Urban, W. M., *Language and Reality* (New York: Macmillan. 1939), Chap. XI, "Science and Symbolism: Symbolism: Symbolism as a Scientific Principle," pp. 503–570.

Veatch, H. B., "Some Suggestions on the Respective Spheres of Science and Philosophy," *The Thomist,* III (Apr., 1947), 177–216.

Watkin, E. I., *A Philosophy of Form* (New York: Sheed and Ward, 1935), pp. 252–312.

CHAPTER XX

Bruni, G., *Progressive Scholasticism* (St. Louis: Herder, 1929), pp. 15–92.

Forest, I., "The Meaning of Faith," *The Thomist,* VI (July, 1942), 230–250. Includes a criticism of Taylor, below.

Garrigou-Lagrange, R., O.P., *The One God* (St. Louis: Herder, 1943), Chap. I.

Gilson, E., *Christianity and Philosophy* (New York: Sheed and Ward, 1939), Chaps. I, III, IV.

—— *The Philosophy of St. Thomas Aquinas* (St. Louis: Herder, 1937), Pref., Chap. II.

—— *Reason and Revelation in the Middle Ages* (New York: Scribners, 1938).

—— *The Spirit of Medieval Philosophy* (New York: Scribners, 1940), Pref., Chap. I.

Maritain, J., *The Degrees of Knowledge* (New York: Scribners, 1938), Chap. IV.

—— *An Introduction to Philosophy* (New York: Sheed and Ward), Part I, Chap. VIII.

Olgiati, F., *Key to the Study of St. Thomas* (St. Louis: Herder, 1924), Chap. VI.

Ring, G. C., "Motive and Freedom in the Act of Faith," *Theological Studies,* VI (June, 1945), 147–162.

Scheeben, M. J., *The Mysteries of Christianity* (St. Louis: Herder, 1946), Chap XXIX, pp. 762–796.

Taylor, A. E., *The Faith of a Moralist* (London: Macmillan, 1937), Vol. II, Chaps. I–V, IX; "The Meaning and Place of Authority," departs from Catholic teaching.

—— "Knowing and Believing," *Philosophical Studies* (London: Macmillan, 1934), Chap. XX.

CHAPTER XXI

Adler, M. J., "The Demonstration of God's Existence," *The Thomist,* V (Jan., 1943), 188–218. A criticism of the Five Ways.

Bryor, W., "Adler and the Existence of God," *The New Scholasticism,* XVIII (July, 1944), 270–283.

Carpenter, H., O.P., "The Historical Aspects of the Quinque Viae," Lattey, C., S.J., *God* (London: Sheed and Ward, 1931), pp. 196–216.

—— "The Philosophical Approach to God in Thomism," *The Thomist,* I (Apr., 1939), 44 ff.

D'Arcy, M. C., S.J., *Thomas Aquinas* (Westminster, Md.: Newman Bookshop, 1944), Part II, Chap. VI.

Donovan, Sr., M. A., C.S., "Limited Perfection as Requiring Subsistent Perfection," *Proc. Am. Cath. Phil. Assn.* (1945), 136–145. On the Fourth Way.

Doran, W. R., "St. Thomas and the Evolution of Man," *Theological Studies,* I (Dec., 1940), 382–395. This does not bear on the proofs of God's existence, but is relevant to the discussion of evolution in the present chapter.

Farrell, W., *Companion to the Summa* (New York: Sheed and Ward, 1941), Vol. I, Chap. II.

Foote, E. T., "Prologue to Evolution," *The Modern Schoolman,* XIX (Nov., 1941), 7–11.

Garrigou-Lagrange, R., O.P., *God — His Existence and Nature* (St. Louis: Herder, 1934), Vol. I, Chaps. II–III, Appendix.

—— *The One God* (St. Louis: Herder. 1943), Chap. II.

—— *Providence* (St. Louis: Herder, 1937), Chaps. I–V.

Gilson, E., *God and Philosophy* (New Haven: Yale University Press, 1944).
—— *The Philosophy of St. Thomas Aquinas* (St. Louis: Herder, 1937), Chaps. III–V.
—— *The Spirit of Medieval Philosophy* (New York: Scribners, 1940), Chaps. III–IV.
Grabmann, M., *Thomas Aquinas* (New York: Longmans Green, 1928), Chap. XX.
Hoper, D. R., O.P., "Proofs of the Existence of God," in C. Lattey, S.J., *God* (London: Sheed and Ward, 1931), pp. 36–52.
Joyce, G. H., *The Principles of Natural Theology* (New York: Longmans, 1934), Chaps. III–VII.
Klubertanz, G. P., "Causality and Evolution," *The Modern Schoolman,* XIX (Nov., 1941), 11–14.
Maritain, J., *The Degrees of Knowledge* (New York: Scribners, 1938), Chap. IV.
McCormick, J. F., *Scholastic Metaphysics* (Chicago: Loyola University Press, 1928), Vol. II, Chaps. I–VI.
Meyer, H., *The Philosophy of St. Thomas Aquinas* (St. Louis: Herder, 1944), Chap. XVIII.
Olgiati, F., *Key to the Study of St. Thomas Aquinas* (St. Louis: Herder, 1924), Chap. III.
Patterson, E. L., "The Argument from Motion in Aristotle and Aquinas," *The New Scholasticism,* X (July, 1936), 245–254.
—— *The Conception of God in the Philosophy of Aquinas* (London: George Allen and Unwin, 1933), pp. 17–98.
Phillips, R. P., *Modern Thomistic Philosophy* (London: Burns, Oates and Washbourne, 1934; Westminster, Md.: Newman Bookshop, 1946). Vol. I, pp. 321–343; Vol. II, pp. 261–302.
Pollock, R. C., "Cause in Modern Philosophy and the Traditional Arguments for the Existence of God," *Proc. Am. Cath. Phil. Assn.* (1934), 13–37.
Schwartz, H. T., "A Reply: The Demonstration of God's Existence," *The Thomist,* VI (Apr., 1943), 19–48.
Sertillanges, A. D., *The Foundations of Thomistic Philosophy* (St. Louis: Herder, 1931), pp. 45–73.
Sheen, F. J., "God in Evolution," *Thought,* I (Mar., 1927), 575–587.
Taylor, A. E., *Does God Exist?* (New York: Macmillan, 1947), pp. 220–312.
Thompson, W. R., "Providence," *The Thomist,* V (Jan., 1943), 229–245.
Watkin, E. I., *A Philosophy of Form* (New York: Sheed and Ward, 1935), pp. 252–312.
Weserling, T. H., "Being, Life and Matter," *The New Scholasticism,* XI (July, 1937), 220–236.

Chapter XXII

D'Arcy, M. C., S.J., *Thomas Aquinas* (Westminster, Md.: Newman Book-shop, 1944), Part II, Chap. VI.

Farrell, W., *Companion to the Summa* (New York: Sheed and Ward, 1941), Vol. I, Chap. III.

Garrigou-Lagrange, R., O.P., *God — His Existence and Nature* (St. Louis: Herder, 1934), Vol. II, pp. 3–59, 59–186.

———— *The One God* (St. Louis: Herder, 1943), Chaps. III–XIII.

———— *Providence* (St. Louis: Herder, 1937), Chaps. VI–XI.

Geddes, L. W., S.J., "God the Fulness of Being, Spiritual and Personal," in C. Lattey, S.J., *God* (London: Sheed and Ward, 1931), pp. 117–135.

Gilson, E., *The Philosophy of St. Thomas Aquinas* (St. Louis: Herder, 1937), pp. 98–113.

Joyce, G. H., *The Principles of Natural Theology* (New York: Longmans, 1934), Chaps. VIII–IX.

Maritain, J., *The Degrees of Knowledge* (New York: Scribners, 1938), Chap. IV.

McCormick, J. F., *Scholastic Metaphysics* (Chicago: Loyola University Press, 1928), Vol. II, Chaps. VII–VIII.

Patterson, R. L., *The Conception of God in the Philosophy of Aquinas* (London: George Allen and Unwin, 1933), pp. 101–183.

Phillips, R. P., *Modern Thomistic Philosophy* (London: Burns, Oates and Washbourne, 1934; Westminster, Md.: Newman Bookshop, 1946), Vol. II, pp. 303–311.

Sertillanges, A. D., *The Foundation of Thomistic Philosophy* (St. Louis: Herder, 1931), pp. 73–90.

Smith, G. D., "God One and Indivisible: The Divine Attributes," in C. Lattey, S.J., *God* (London: Sheed and Ward, 1931), pp. 53–72.

Chapter XXIII

Farrell, W., *Companion to the Summa* (New York: Sheed and Ward, 1941), Vol. I, Chaps. IV–V.

Garrigou-Lagrange, R., O.P., *God — His Existence and Nature* (St. Louis: Herder, 1934), Vol. II, pp. 338–396.

———— *The One God* (St. Louis: Herder, 1943), Chaps. XIV–XX, XXVI.

———— *Providence* (St. Louis: Herder, 1937), Chaps. XII–XIII.

Gilson, E., *The Philosophy of St. Thomas Aquinas* (St. Louis: Herder, 1937), pp. 114–128.

———— *The Spirit of Medieval Philosophy* (New York: Scribners, 1940), Chap. VIII.

Joyce, G. H., *The Principles of Natural Theology* (New York: Longmans, 1934), Chaps. XI–XIII.

Kendall, Dom E., "God's Knowledge and Love: The Problem of Evil," in C. Lattey, S.J., *God* (London: Sheed and Ward, 1931), pp. 167–195.

McCormick, J. F., *Scholastic Metaphysics* (Chicago: Loyola University Press, 1928), Vol. II, Chaps. IX–X.

Patterson, R. L., *The Conception of God in the Philosophy of Aquinas* (London: George Allen and Unwin, 1933), pp. 284–364.

Phillips, R. P., *Modern Thomistic Philosophy* (London: Burns, Oates and Washbourne, 1934; Westminster, Md.: Newman Bookshop, 1946), Vol. II, pp. 312–341.

Sertillanges, A. D., *The Foundation of Thomistic Philosophy* (St. Louis: Herder, 1931), pp. 135–144.

Taylor, A. E., *The Faith of a Moralist* (London: Macmillan, 1937), Vol. II, Appendix, pp. 417–425.

Chapter XXIV

D'Arcy, M. C., S.J., *Thomas Aquinas* (Westminster, Md.: Newman Bookshop, 1944), Part II, Chap. VII.

Donnelly, P. J., "St. Thomas and the Ultimate Purpose of Creation," *Theological Studies*, II (Feb., 1941), 53–83.

Eslick, L. J., "The Reality of Matter in Creation," *The New Scholasticism*, XVI (Jan., 1942), 46–58.

—— "The Thomistic Doctrine of the Unity of Creation," *The New Scholasticism*, XIII (Jan., 1937), 49–70.

Farrell, W., *Companion to the Summa* (New York: Sheed and Ward, 1941), Vol. I, Chap. VIII.

Gilson, E., *The Philosophy of St. Thomas Aquinas* (St. Louis: Herder, 1937), Chap. VIII.

—— *The Spirit of Medieval Philosophy* (New York: Scribners, 1940), Chap. V.

Joyce, G. H., *The Principles of Natural Theology* (New York: Longmans, 1934), Chaps. XIV–XV.

McCormick, J. F., *Scholastic Metaphysics* (Chicago: Loyola University Press, 1928), Vol. II, Chaps. XI–XII.

Meyer, H., *The Philosophy of St. Thomas Aquinas* (St. Louis: Herder, 1944), Chaps. XXI–XXII.

Patterson, R. L., *The Conception of God in the Philosophy of Aquinas* (London: George Allen and Unwin, 1933), pp. 367–445.

Pegis, A. C., "Necessity and Liberty: An Historical Note on St. Thomas," *Proc. Am. Cath. Phil. Assn.* (1940), 1–27.

———— *St. Thomas and the Greeks* (Milwaukee: Marquette University Press, 1939).

Phillips, R. P., *Modern Thomistic Philosophy* (London: Burns, Oates and Washbourne, 1934; Westminster, Md.: Newman Bookshop, 1946), Vol. II, pp. 329–341.

Pope, H., "The Meaning of Creation," in G. J. MacGillivray, *Man* (London: Burns, Oates and Washbourne, 1938), pp. 89–119.

Roeser, T. P., "Emanation and Creation," *The New Scholasticism*, XIX (Apr., 1945), 85–116.

Sertillanges, A. D., *The Foundations of Thomistic Philosophy* (St. Louis: Herder, 1931), pp. 91–134.

Williams, Dom R., "God Distinct From the Universe," Lattey, C., S.J., *God* (London: Sheed and Ward, 1931), pp. 74–90.

Chapter XXV

Farrell, W., *Companion to the Summa* (New York: Sheed and Ward, 1941), Vol. I, Chaps. VI, XVII.

Garrigou-Lagrange, R., O.P., *God—His Existence and Nature* (St. Louis: Herder, 1934), Vol. II, pp. 354–396, and Epilogue.

———— *The One God* (St. Louis: Herder, 1943), Chap. XXII.

Gilson, E., *The Philosophy of St. Thomas Aquinas* (St. Louis: Herder, 1937), Chap. IX.

———— *The Spirit of Medieval Philosophy* (New York: Scribners, 1940), Chap. VII.

Joyce, G. H., *The Principles of Natural Theology* (New York: Longmans, 1934), Chap. XVI.

McCormick, F., *Scholastic Metaphysics* (Chicago: Loyola University Press, 1928), Vol. II, Chaps. XIII–XV.

Patterson, R. L., *The Conception of God in the Philosophy of Aquinas* (London: George Allen and Unwin, 1933), pp. 446–482.

Phillips, R. P., *Modern Thomistic Philosophy* (London: Burns, Oates and Washbourne, 1934), Westminster, Md.: Newman Bookshop, 1946), Vol. II, pp. 342–351.

Sertillanges, A. D., *The Foundations of Thomistic Philosophy* (St. Louis: Herder, 1931), pp. 144–158.

Sheen, F. J., "The Immanence of God," in C. Lattey, S.J., *God* (London: Sheed and Ward, 1931), pp. 91–116.

Taylor, A. E., *The Faith of a Moralist* (London: Macmillan, 1937), Vol. II, pp. 417–425.

Chapter XXVI

Farrell, W., *Companion to the Summa* (New York: Sheed and Ward, 1941), Vol. I, pp. 129–132, 168–170.

Gilson, E., *The Spirit of Medieval Philosophy* (New York: Scribners, 1940), Chap. VI.

Joyce, G. H., *The Principles of Natural Theology* (New York: Longmans, 1934), Chap. XVII.

Maritain, J., *St. Thomas and the Problem of Evil* (Milwaukee: Marquette University Press, 1942).

McCormick, F., *Scholastic Metaphysics* (Chicago: Loyola University Press, 1928), Vol. II, Chap. XIII.

Phillips, R. P., *Modern Thomistic Philosophy* (London: Burns, Oates and Washbourne, 1934; Westminster, Md.: Newman Bookshop, 1946), Vol. II, pp. 364–375.

Renard, H., S.J., *The Philosophy of Being,* 2 ed. (Milwaukee: Bruce, 1946), pp. 181–187.

INDEX

Absolute good: and freedom, 272 f.; happiness the, 244; will necessarily wills, 243 f.

Absolute reason, doctrine of, 184 f.

Absolutism, 13 f.

Abstraction: degrees of, 410 f.; and formal objects of the sciences, 409 ff.; nature of, 395, 409; of species from phantasm, 229 ff.; three degrees of, 358 f.

Accident: Garrigou-Lagrange on, 389; Kant on, 343, 345; nature of, 363, 388; our knowledge of, 388 f.; and substance, 69, 368 f.

Accidental change, 69, 106, 115

Accidental form: of elements and compounds in the body, 108; nature of, 106; and substantial form, 106

Actio, and *passio*, 72 ff.

Action: and being, 488; a predicament, 363 f.; and process, *see* Process and action; vital, 162

Activity: immanent, 146; and immutability of God, 520 f.; transeunt, 146, 148

Actuality: and intelligibility, and intelligence, 223; and knowledge, 223, 387 f.; nature of, 387 f.

Adam, trial of, 614 f.

Agent, principle and subject, 176 f.

Agent intellect: Aristotle on, 189 f.; function of the, 229 f.

Alteration: natural, 226; spiritual, in sensation, 226 f.

Alternatives: and freedom, 272 f.; in willing, 269 ff.

Anabolism, meaning of, 153

Analogical concepts, 366 f.

Analogical knowledge of God, 505 ff.

Analogical predications about God, 505 ff.

Analogical unity, 366 f.

Analogy: of attribution, 370; of God and creatures, 513 f.; and predication, 527 f.; of proportionality, 370

Analogy of being, 365 ff.

Analysis: empirological, 415 f.; ontological, 415 f.; philosophical, 415 f.; scientific, 415 f.

Anaxagoras: doctrine of the *Nous*, 28 f.; doctrine of seeds, 27 f.; and dualism, 29; on knowledge, 28 f.; and monotheism, 29; philosophy of, 27 ff.; and teleology, 29

Anaximander, philosophy of, 21

Anaximenes, philosophy of, 21 f.

Angelic intelligence, and human intelligence compared, 224 f.

Angels: nature of, 207 ff.; trial of, 614 f.

Animal life, a grade of life, 147

Animals: suffering of, and the problem of evil, 620 f.; thought in, 200 ff.

Anselm, St., ontological argument, 464

Antecedent will, 549 f.

A posteriori demonstration, 465, 491 f.

Appearance, and reality, 13

Appetite: and cogitative sense, 241; concupiscible, 239 f.; defined, 237; distinct from cognition, 238; follows knowledge, 237 f.; and form, 237 f.; human, and will, Chap. XII; intellectual, 238 f.; irascible, 239 f.; kinds distinguished by their objects, 238 f.; natural, 237; notion of, 237; rational, 237; sensitive, *see* Sensitive appetite; will as, 236

Apprehension, simple, 215

A priori demonstration, 465, 491 f.

A priori forms, of Kant, 343; 345 ff.

Aquinas, St. Thomas: accidental forms of elements and compounds in the body, 108; the act of conception, 231 f.; active intellect, 230; all things derived from God's goodness, 516; appetite distinct from cognition, 238; appetitive power of the soul, 238; argument from contingency of world, 474 f.; argument for free will, 249 f.; and Aristotle, 50 ff.; and Aristotle on matter, 206 f.; and Aristotle on soul and body, 206 f.; being defined, 370; being and one, 522; causality, 477; certainty of faith, 455 f.; cogitative sense, 213 f.; conception of truth, 379 f.; concupiscible appetite, 239 f.; contingency, necessity, and divine providence, 592 f.; creation, 567 ff.; definition of philosophy, 4; divine causality, 587; divine concurrence, 585, 587; divine conservation, 583 f.; "double truth," 457; estimative sense, 213 f.; eternity of the world, 570 f., 573; evil, 607; existence of God can be demonstrated, 465 f.; faith and will, 447; falsity in mind, 378; finality and chance, 87; finite beings, 558 f.; five proofs of existence of God, 467 ff.; form and intelligibility, 222 f.; four causes, 71; on free choice, 280 ff.; on free will, 246 f.,

ena, 130 f., 411 ff.; and *quiddity*, 432
Essence and existence: identical in God,
509, 518; our knowledge of, 386 f.;
science presupposes real distinction of,
427
Essences, knowledge of real, 431 ff.; phil-
osophical knowledge attains real, 428 f.
Essential causes, impossibility of an infinite
series of, 488 f.
Essential principles, and physical parts, 103,
130 f.
Estimative sense: Aquinas on, 213 f.;
Aristotle on, 213 f.
Eternal and temporal being, 521 f.
Eternity: of God, 521 f.; meaning of,
521 f.; and time, 571 ff.
Eternity of the world: arguments for,
571 ff.; St. Bonaventure on, 570 ff.; St.
Thomas on, 570 f., 573
Ethics: branch of practical philosophy, 59;
individual, 59
Eve, A. S., on life, 156
"Every agent acts for an end," 85 f.
Evidence, the starting point of knowledge,
298 f.
Evil: and animal suffering, 620 f.; caused
by sin, 613 f.; causes of, 606 ff.; and
divine love, Chap. XXVI, 621 ff.; and
divine providence, 578; efficient cause
per accidens, 609 f.; and the end of
creation, 605; essentially a privation,
607 ff.; explanation of, 601 ff.; and the
freedom of God, 602 f.; God does not
will, 605 f.; God in no way the cause
of, 611 f.; God permits evil, 605 f.; and
God's freedom, 605; material cause *per
accidens*, 609 f.; moral, 610 f.; and the
multiplicity of creatures, 602; the mystery of, 604 f., 612; mystery of, and
Christ, 621 ff.; and the Mystical Body of
Christ, 622 f.; nature of, 606 ff.; necessity of, 615; in Neoplatonism, 53 f.; no
final cause, 609; no formal cause, 609;
and non-being, 607; objections to the
Christian account answered, 615 ff.; permitted for a greater good, 606; and
philosophy, 601 f.; the problem of, 601 f.;
604; and the Resurrection, 622 f.; St.
Thomas on, 607; solution of the problem
of, 611 f.; summary, 609; and Theism,
601 f.
Evolution: creative, 560 f.; and denial of
design in nature, 497 ff.; emergent,
560 f.; and teleology, 96 f., 498 ff.; and
Thomistic theory, 500 ff.; and thought,
203 f.
Exaggerated dualism, of Descartes, 14
Exemplary cause, 76

Exercise of will, 251 ff.
Existence: definition of, 386 f.; and essence,
see Essence and existence; of God, see
God, existence; meaning of, 488; self-
subsisting, 474
Existence of world: proof of existence of
God, Kant on, 480 ff.
Experience: Kant on, 345; Kant's failure
to explain some features of, 348 ff.;
Kant's lack of account of matter of,
351; and understanding, 338 f.
Experience and knowledge: Aristotle on,
45 f.; Plato on, 45 f.
Experimental verification, and metaphysics,
427 f.
Explicit universal, explained, 396
Extension, physical, and hylemorphism,
119 f.
External senses: described, 211 f.; nature
of the operation of, 225 f.; and thought,
199, 216
Extramental being, our knowledge of,
382 ff.
Extramental and intramental objects: confusion of, 305; distinction of, 305
Extrinsic cause, nature of, 71 f.
Extrinsic finality: explained, 89, 95 ff.; in
nature, 116

Facts, in science and philosophy, 414 f.
Faith: act of, 448; adequate grounds for,
453 ff.; answers to objections, 451 ff.;
and belief in human beings, 447 ff.;
certainty of, 454 f.; God the formal
object of, 456; Kant on, 330 f.; and
knowledge, 446 f.; a naturalist view,
451 f.; nature of, 446 f.; necessity of,
449 ff.; not blind, 447 f.; objections to,
450 f.; and opinion, 446 f.; rationality
of, 451 f.; and reason, see Faith and
reason, Reason; supernatural nature of,
448; what is requisite for, 455 f.; and
will, 446 f.
Faith and reason, Chap. XX; agreement,
necessary, 456 f.; anti-philosophical view,
436; Aquinas on, 451 f.; Augustinian
view, 436 f.; and Averroes, 436 f.; basis
of a solution, 443 ff.; "conflicts" between,
456 f.; contemporary views, 437 ff.; doctrine of "double truth," 436 f., 456 f.;
doctrine of entire independence of each,
436 f., 456 f.; faith perfects reason, 454;
medieval views, 436 f.; and modernism,
438 ff.; and naturalism, 437 f.; "rationa-
list" view of, 436; reason aids faith,
458 ff.; reason serves faith, 457 f.; and
St. Bonaventure, 437; and secularism,
437 f.; Thomistic solution, 449 ff.; Tho-

Printed in the United States
116776LV00002B/106-123/A